HISTORICAL DICTIONARIES OF EUROPE
Jon Woronoff, Series Editor

1. *Portugal,* by Douglas L. Wheeler. 1993. *Out of print. See No. 40.*
2. *Turkey,* by Metin Heper. 1994. *Out of print. See No. 38.*
3. *Poland,* by George Sanford and Adriana Gozdecka-Sanford. 1994. *Out of print. See No. 41.*
4. *Germany,* by Wayne C. Thompson, Susan L. Thompson, and Juliet S. Thompson. 1994
5. *Greece,* by Thanos M. Veremis and Mark Dragoumis. 1995
6. *Cyprus,* by Stavros Panteli. 1995
7. *Sweden,* by Irene Scobbie. 1995. *Out of print. See No. 48.*
8. *Finland,* by George Maude. 1995. *Out of print. See No. 49.*
9. *Croatia,* by Robert Stallaerts and Jeannine Laurens. 1995. *Out of print. See No. 39.*
10. *Malta,* by Warren G. Berg. 1995
11. *Spain,* by Angel Smith. 1996
12. *Albania,* by Raymond Hutchings. 1996. *Out of print. See No. 42.*
13. *Slovenia,* by Leopoldina Plut-Pregelj and Carole Rogel. 1996. *Out of print, See No. 56.*
14. *Luxembourg,* by Harry C. Barteau. 1996
15. *Romania,* by Kurt W. Treptow and Marcel Popa. 1996
16. *Bulgaria,* by Raymond Detrez. 1997. *Out of print. See No. 46.*
17. *United Kingdom: Volume 1, England and the United Kingdom; Volume 2, Scotland, Wales, and Northern Ireland,* by Kenneth J. Panton and Keith A. Cowlard. 1997; 1998
18. *Hungary,* by Steven Béla Várdy. 1997
19. *Latvia,* by Andrejs Plakans. 1997
20. *Ireland,* by Colin Thomas and Avril Thomas. 1997
21. *Lithuania,* by Saulius Suziedelis. 1997
22. *Macedonia,* by Valentina Georgieva and Sasha Konechni. 1998
23. *The Czech State,* by Jiri Hochman. 1998
24. *Iceland,* by Guðmundur Hálfdanarson. 1997
25. *Bosnia and Herzegovina,* by Ante Cuvalo. 1997
26. *Russia,* by Boris Raymond and Paul Duffy. 1998
27. *Gypsies (Romanies),* by Donald Kenrick. 1998
28. *Belarus,* by Jan Zaprudnik. 1998
29. *Federal Republic of Yugoslavia,* by Zeljan Suster. 1999
30. *France,* by Gino Raymond. 1998

Historical Dictionary of Slovenia

Second Edition

Leopoldina Plut-Pregelj
Carole Rogel

Historical Dictionaries of Europe, No. 56

The Scarecrow Press, Inc.
Lanham, Maryland • Toronto • Plymouth, UK
2007

SCARECROW PRESS, INC.

Published in the United States of America
by Scarecrow Press, Inc.
A wholly owned subsidary of
The Rowman & Littlefield Publishing Group, Inc.
4501 Forbes Boulevard, Suite 200, Lanham, Maryland 20706
www.scarecrowpress.com

Estover Road
Plymouth PL6 7PY
United Kingdom

British Library Cataloguing in Publication Information Available

Library of Congress Cataloging-in-Publication Data

Plut-Pregelj, Leopoldina.
    Historical dictionary of Slovenia / Leopoldina Plut-Pregelj, Carole Rogel.
— 2nd ed.
        p. cm. — (Historical dictionaries of Europe ; no. 56)
    Includes bibliographical references.
    ISBN-13: 978-0-8108-4717-0 (hardcover : alk. paper)
    ISBN-10: 0-8108-4717-5 (hardcover : alk. paper)
    1. Slovenia—History—Dictionaries. I. Rogel, Carole. II. Title.
DR1375.5.P58 2007
949.73003—dc22   2007006392

Contents

Editor's Foreword

Of all the successor states of Yugoslavia, Slovenia clearly had the most potential. It obtained its independence with relatively little bloodshed, was ethnically homogeneous, was fairly stable politically, and had an economy in reasonable condition. Moreover, it was close to the rest of Europe, with new trade partners at hand, and was eager to make progress. But Slovenia did not have an easy entry into statehood—far from it. It took considerable effort to create a working democracy, convert from a socialist to a market economy, restructure the administration, and refurbish the infrastructure. But the situation is improving in all fields—political, social, and economic—and the country has proven itself enough to become a member of the European Union and the North Atlantic Treaty Organization.

For a young state like Slovenia, which is poorly known and often misunderstood abroad, a reference work such as this is particularly important. It not only provides basic information on the population, geography, history, politics, economy, society, and culture but also covers the emerging leadership and political parties, many of which are new and some of which are a holdover from the previous regime. In fact, it is impossible to understand modern Slovenia without looking back to when it was a part of Yugoslavia or a dependency of the Habsburg Empire. Without knowing where it comes from, we would find it impossible to predict where the country is going.

This second edition of the *Historical Dictionary of Slovenia* was written by the same authors who created the first. Both show an exceptionally good grasp of Slovenia's present and past. Leopoldina Plut-Pregelj was born in Ljubljana, studied education at the University of Ljubljana, and taught in its Department of Pedagogy from 1975 to 1982 before moving to the United States, where she is presently a research scholar at the University of Maryland. Dr. Rogel taught history at Ohio State University from 1964 to 1990. Both have lectured extensively and, between them, written five major books about Slovenia in order to help others learn more about this new and promising state—an effort that will be further aided by this extensively updated and expanded edition.

Jon Woronoff
Series Editor

Acknowledgments

As the second edition of the *Historical Dictionary of Slovenia* is an updated, if much extended, version of the first edition, our thanks, again, go to all the people who in any way helped with the first edition. In alphabetical order we would like to acknowledge France Bernik, Janez Bogataj, Pavle Borštnik, Franc Dolinar, Tone Ferenc, Helga Glušič, Niko Grafenauer, Marina Gržinić, Drago Jančar, Arthur Keys, Dušan Kidrič, Alenka Klemenc, Boris Košorok, Rado Lenček, Marjana Lipoglavšek, Tomo Martelanc, Jože Mencinger, Boris Pleskovič, Rado Pohar, Marjetica Potrč, Damjan Prelovšek, Alenka Puhar, Meta von Rabenau, Božo Repe, Miha Ribarič, Gregor Tomc, Tine Velikonja, Peter Vodopivec, Andrej Vovko, and Igor Zabel.

For their assistance in our work on the second edition we are indebted to the following professionals and friends who took the time to read individual entries relating to their expertise and offered suggestions and information for their improvement: Ana Barbič, Pavle Borštnik, Marjeta Domicelj, Marjan Drnovšek, Jana Ferjan, Tadej Furlan, Milan Hodošček, Maca Jogan, Mojca Keržan, Roman Kuhar, Senka Maver, Bogomir Mihevc, Bojana Piškur, Rudi Podgornik, Amy Schmidt, Nada Šabec, Zdenka Šmid, and Andrej Udovč. We are especially grateful to Vladimir N. Pregelj, who not only proofread the entire manuscripts of both editions but also offered suggestions for their improvement.

We, of course, assume responsibility for all errors and omissions. Readers are encouraged to bring corrections and additional bibliographical items to our attention.

Guide to Slovene Pronunciation

The Slovene alphabet has twenty-five letters: a, b, c, č, d, e, f, g, h, i, j, k, l, m, n, o, p, r, s, š, t, u, v, z, ž. While it lacks the letters q, w, x, and y—but uses them in foreign names—it contains three letters not in the English alphabet: č, š, and ž (see below). The alphabet is phonetic, and letters are generally pronounced uniformly. However, there are many rules and exceptions.

There are significant differences between English and Slovene alphabets in the pronunciation of vowels and certain consonants. Vowels, stressed or unstressed, short or long, are usually pronounced as follows:

a as in father
e as in pen
i as in machine
o as aw in raw
u as in rule

Consonants are pronounced as shown here:

c as ts in pets; never as in cat or certain
č as ch in chair
g as in get, never as in general
j as y in yes, never as in jet
s as in pass, never as z
š as sh in shoe
ž as s in measure

The Serbo-Croatian letter ć that appears in a few entries in this book is pronounced as the tch in batch.

Finally, j following an l or n (Kardelj, Kranj, Ljubljana) is not pronounced fully but softens the preceding consonant, as in million or new.

Acronyms and Abbreviations

In general, Slovene acronyms are used in the entries except when an English one is commonly used in English-language publications. For example, CPY (Communist Party of Yugoslavia) is used rather than KPJ (Komunistična partija Jugoslavije).

AFŽ	Antifašistična fronta žensk Jugoslavije (Antifascist Women's Front)
AVNOJ	Antifašističko veće narodnog oslobodjenja Jugoslavije (Antifascist Council of National Liberation of Yugoslavia)
BBC	British Broadcasting Corporation
BS	Banka Slovenije (Bank of Slovenia)
CAP	Common Agricultural Policy
CC CPS	Central Committee of the CPS
CC CPY	Central Committee of the CPY
CEI	Central European Initiative
CME	Central-European Media Enterprise Ltd.
COBBIS	Cooperative Online Bibliographic System
CP	Communist Party
CPHR	Committee for the Protection of Human Rights
CPS	Communist Party of Slovenia
CPY	Communist Party of Yugoslavia
CSCE	Conference on Security and Cooperation in Europe
CSS	Contemporary Standard Slovene
Demos	Demokratska opozicija Slovenje (Democratic Opposition of Slovenia)
DeSUS	Demoratična stranka upokojencev Slovenije (Democratic Party of Retired Persons of Slovenia)
DO	delovna organizacija (work organization)
DSM	Družba sv. Mohorja (Society of St. Hermagoras)
DSS	Demokratska stranka Slovenije (Democratic Party of Slovenia)
EC	European Community

EEC	European Economic Community
EEZ	Exclusive Economic Zone
EFTA	European Free Trade Association
EIAR	Ente italiana audizione radiofoniche
ERM II	European Exchange Rate Mechanism II
ESCB	European System of Central Banks
EU	European Union
EUFOR	European Union Force
FEC	Federal Executive Council
FESE	Federation of European Stock Exchanges
FLRJ	Federativna ljudska republika Jugoslavija (Federal People's Republic of Yugoslavia)
FPA	Federal People's Assembly
FPRY	Federal People's Republic of Yugoslavia
FRY	Federal Republic of Yugoslavia
GATT	General Agreement on Tariffs and Trade
GDP	Gross Domestic Product
GM	Glasbena matica (Music Society)
GPD	General People's Defense
IADB	Inter-American Development Bank
IMF	International Monetary Fund
ISAFOR	International Security Assistance Force
JLA	Jugoslovanska ljudska armada (Yugoslav People's Army)
JNA	Jugoslovenska narodna armija (Yugoslav People's Army)
JNS	Jugoslovanska nacionalna stranka (Yugoslav National Party)
JRKD	Jugoslovanska radikalna kmečka demokracija (Yugoslav Radical Peasant Democracy)
JRZ	Jugoslovenska radikalna zajednica (Yugoslav Radical Union)
JSDS	Jugoslovanska socialnodemokratska stranka (Yugoslav Social Democratic Party)
KA	Katoliška akcija (Catholic Action)
KBM	Kreditna banka Maribor (Credit Bank of Maribor)
KDZ	kmečka delovna zadruga (farm working cooperative)
KFOR	Kosovo Force
KNSS	Konfederacija novih sindikatov Slovenije (Confederation of New Trade Unions of Slovenia)

KPJ	Komunistična partija Jugoslavije (Communist Party of Yugoslavia)
KPS	Komunistična partija Slovenije (Communist Party of Slovenia)
KSKJ	Kranjsko slovenska katoliška jednota (Carniolan Slovenian Catholic Union; current English name: KSKJ American Slovenian Catholic Union)
KZ	kmetijska zadruga (farmers' cooperative)
LB	Ljubljanska banka (Bank of Ljubljana)
LCS	League of Communists of Slovenia
LCY	League of Communists of Yugoslavia
LDS	Liberalno demokratska stranka (Liberal Democratic Party); Liberal Democracy of Slovenia
LF	Liberation Front
LFJ	Ljudska fronta Jugoslavije (People's Front of Yugoslavia)
LMS	Ljudska mladina Slovenije (People's Youth of Slovenia)
LO	ljudski odbor (people's committee)
LRS	Ljudska republika Slovenija (People's Republic of Slovenia)
LS	Liberalna stranka (Liberal Party)
MVAC	Milizia Volontaria Anticomunista (Volunteer Anti-Communist Militia)
NACC	North Atlantic Cooperation Council
NATO	North Atlantic Treaty Organization
NGO	nongovernmental organization
NLB	Nova ljubljanska banka (New Bank of Ljubljana)
NKBM	Nova kreditna banka Maribor (New Credit Bank of Maribor)
NKOJ	Narodni komite osvoboditve Jugoslavije (People's Committee of Liberation of Yugoslavia)
NNS	Narodna napredna stranka (National Progressive Party)
NOB	Narodnoosvobodilni boj (National Liberation Struggle)
NOO	Narodnoosvobodilni odbor (National Liberation Committee)
NOV	Narodnoosvobodilna vojska (National Liberation Army)
NR	Nova revija (New Review)
NSi	Nova Slovenija–krščanska ljudska stranka (New Slovenia–Christian People's Party)

NSK	Neue Slowenische Kunst (New Slovene Art)
NSM	New Social Movement
NSS	Narodni svet za Slovenijo (National Council for Slovenia)
NSZ	Nova slovenska zaveza (New Slovene Covenant)
NUK	Narodna in univerzitetna knjižnica (National and University Library)
OF	Osvobodilna fronta (Liberation Front)
OSCE	Organization for Security and Cooperation in Europe
OZD	Organizacija združenega dela (Organization of Associated Labor)
PDIA	Pension and Disability Insurance Act
PES	Party of European Socialists
PF	People's Front
PfP	Partnership for Peace
PFY	People's Front of Yugoslavia
PIF	Proti-imperialistična fronta (Anti-Imperialist Front)
PIX	Indeks investicijskih skladov (index of investment funds)
PRS	People's Republic of Slovenia
RS	Republika Slovenija (Republic of Slovenia)
RTV	Radio-televizija (Radio-television)
SAWP	Socialist Alliance of Working People
SAWPY	Socialist Alliance of Working People of Yugoslavia
SAZU	Slovenska akademija znanosti in umetnosti (Slovenian Academy of Sciences and Arts)
SBI	Slovenski borzni indeks (Slovenian stock market index)
SD	Socialni demokrati (Social Democrats)
SDP	Stranka demokratične prenove (Party of Democratic Renewal)
SDS	Socialno demokratska stranka (Social Democratic Party)
SDSS	Socialdemokratska stranka Slovenije (Social Democratic Party of Slovenia)
SDZ	Slovenska demokratska zveza (Slovene Democratic Alliance)
SDZ-NDS	Slovenska demokratična zveza–Narodna demokratska stranka (Slovene Democratic Alliance–National Democratic Party)
SDZS	Socialdemokratska zveza Slovenije (Social Democratic Alliance of Slovenia)

SECI	Southeast Cooperative Initiative
SFOR	Stabilization Force
SFRJ	Socialistična federativna republika Jugoslavija (Socialist Federal Republic of Yugoslavia)
SFRY	Socialist Federal Republic of Yugoslavia
SIM	Slovenska izeljenska matica (Slovene Emigrant Association)
SIT	tolar (Slovene monetary unit)
SKD	Slovenski krščanski demokrati (Slovene Christian Democrats)
SKOJ	Savez komunističke omladine Jugoslavije (League of Communist Youth of Yugoslavia)
SKZ	Slovenska kmečka zveza (Slovene Farmers' Alliance)
SKZ-LS	Slovenska kmečka zveza–Ljudska stranka (Slovene Farmers' Alliance–People's Party)
SLO	Splošna ljudska obramba (General People's Defense)
SLS	Slovenska ljudska stranka (Slovene People's Party)
SLS-SKD	Slovenska ljudska stranka–Slovenski krščanski demokrati (Slovene People Party–Slovene Christian Democrats)
SMS	Stranka mladih Slovenije (Party of Young People of Slovenia)
SND	Slovenska nacionalna desnica (Slovene National Right)
SNOO	Slovenski narodnoosvobodilni odbor (Slovene National Liberation Committee)
SNOS	Slovenski narodnoosvobodilni svet (Slovene National Liberation Council)
SNPJ	Slovenska narodna podporna jednota (Slovene National Benefit Society)
SNS	Slovenska nacionalna stranka (Slovene National Party)
SOZD	Sestavljena organizacija združenega dela (Composite Organization of Associated Labor)
SRS	Socialistična republika Slovenia (Socialist Republic of Slovenia)
SSS	Socialistična stranka Slovenije (Socialist Party of Slovenia)
STO	Svobodno tržaško ozemlje (Free Territory of Trieste)
SV	Slovenska vojska (Slovene Army)
SZ	Slovenska zaveza (Slovene Covenant)

SZDL	Socialistična zveza delovnega ljudstva (Socialist Alliance of Working People)
ŠKUC	Študentski kulturno-umetniški center (Student Cultural and Art Center)
TD	Territorial Defense
TDRS	Territorial Defense of the Republic of Slovenia
TIRG	Trst-Istra-Reka-Gorica (Trieste-Istria-Fiume-Gorizia)
TO	Teritorialna obramba (Territorial Defense)
TORS	Teritorialna obramba Republike Slovenije (Territorial Defense of the Republic of Slovenia)
TOZD	Temeljna organizacija združenega dela (Basic Organization of Associated Labor)
UDBA	Uprava državne bezbednosti (State Security Administration)
UN	United Nations
USSR	Union of Soviet Socialist Republics
VAT	value-added tax
VOA	Voice of America
VOS	Varnostnoobveščevalna služba (Security and Intelligence Service)
WC	workers' council
WO	work organization
WSM	workers' self-management
WTO	World Trade Organization
ZKJ	Zveza komunistov Jugoslavije (League of Communists of Yugoslavia)
ZKS	Zveza komunistov Slovenije (League of Communists of Slovenia)
ZL	Združena lista (United List)
ZLS	Zvezna ljudska skupščina (Federal People's Assembly)
ZLSD	Združena lista socialnih demokratov (United List of Social Democrats)
ZMS	Zveza mladine Slovenije (League of Youth of Slovenia)
ZRJ	Zvezna republika Jugoslavija (Federal Republic of Yugoslavia)
ZS	Zeleni Slovenije (Greens of Slovenia)
ZSJ	Zveza sindikatov Jugoslavije (Federation of Trade Unions of Yugoslavia)

ZSMJ	Zveza socialistične mladine Jugoslavije (League of Socialist Youth of Yugoslavia)
ZSMS	Zveza socialistične mladine Slovenije (League of Socialist Youth of Slovenia)
ZSMS-LS	Zveza socialistične mladine Slovenije–Liberalna Stranka (League of Socialist Youth of Slovenia–Liberal Party)
ZSS	Zveza sindikatov Slovenije (Union of Trade Unions of Slovenia)
ZSSS	Zveza svobodnih sindikatov Slovenije (Union of Independent Trade Unions of Slovenia)
ZŠ	Zveza študentov (Student Union)
ZZB NOV	Zveza združenj borcev narodnoosvobodilne vojne (League of Associations of Veterans of the National Liberation War)
ZZBU NOBS	Zveza združenj borcev in udeležencev narodnoosvobodilne borbe Slovenije (League of Associations of Veterans and Participants in the National Liberation Struggle Slovenija)

Chronology

Early History: Karantania

c. 550   Slovenes begin settling in eastern Alps.

620s   Karantania becomes a Slavic state.

745–800   Karantanians come under semifeudal Bavarian and Frankish domination; Slovenes Christianized; Gospa Sveta church, later seat of the bishop of Karantania, dedicated.

820s   Karantania becomes a Frankish duchy; feudalism strengthened.

962   Holy Roman Empire established; many Slovene lands included; empire abolished in 1806.

c. 1000   Freising Fragments written—oldest examples of written Slovene.

1000–1050   Carinthia, Styria, and Carniola provinces begin emerging on territory of Karantania.

1200s   Kamnik, Kranj, Ljubljana, Maribor, Piran, Ptuj, Škofja Loka become chartered towns.

12th–15th centuries   Counts of Celje rule some Slovene lands.

Habsburg Rule 1282–1918

1282   Habsburg rule over most Slovene lands begins; lasts until 1918.

mid-15th–mid-16th centuries   Humanism flourishes in Slovene lands.

1461   Catholic diocese of Ljubljana established.

1469–1483   Turkish Wars in Slovene lands intensify; frequency diminishes after 1570.

1515   Major peasant revolt, one of many throughout 16th, early 17th centuries.

1520s   Protestant Reformation beginnings in Slovene lands.

1550–1584 Primož Trubar publishes first Slovene books, a primer entitled *Abecedarium* and a catechism (1550); Jurij Dalmatin publishes Slovene translation of the Bible (1584); Adam Bohorič publishes *Arcticae horulae*, the first Slovene grammar (1584).

1580–1600 Counter Reformation stepped up in Slovene lands; Society of Jesus (Jesuits) established in Ljubljana (1597); Protestants required to re-Catholicize or be expelled (1599).

late 1600s–late 1700s Baroque period in Slovene lands.

1689 Valvasor publishes *The Glory of the Duchy of Carniola.*

1693–1725 Academia Operosorum Labacensium (intellectuals' society) active in Ljubljana.

1701–1769 Academia Philharmonicorum active in Ljubljana.

1740–1780 Maria Theresa's reign.

1754 First census of Slovene lands: 750,000 people.

1764–1790 Joseph II's reign; education law of 1774 requires elementary schooling; lower grades taught in Slovene.

1760s–1820s Slovene Enlightenment: Marko Pohlin publishes *A Carniolan Grammar* (1768); Anton Tomaž Linhart publishes history of Slovene lands (1788/1791); Valentin Vodnik begins *Lublanske novice*, first Slovene newspaper (1797–1800); Jernej Kopitar publishes Slovene grammar (1808).

1804 Austrian Empire established.

1809–1813 Illyrian Provinces under Napoleonic rule; many Slovene lands included.

1810s–1850s Age of Slovene romanticism; Illyrian movement.

1815–1848 Age of Absolutism in Austrian Empire.

1820 Carniolan Savings and Loan Bank established.

1831–1833 Alphabet war ending with acceptance of "*gajica*" as official Slovene alphabet in 1848.

1842 Bishop Anton Martin Slomšek publishes *Blaže and Nežica in Sunday School.*

1846 France Prešeren's *Poems* published.

1848 Revolution in Austrian Empire; first Slovene political program adopted: United Slovenia. **December:** Francis Joseph becomes emperor; rule ends 1916.

1849 Railroad from Vienna reaches Ljubljana; extends to Trieste by 1857.

1850–1900 Age of Slovene Realism.

1851 Society of St. Hermagoras (*Mohorjeva družba*) established; first Slovene cooperative established.

1851–1860 Neoabsolutism in Austrian Empire.

1860s–1900 Spread of Slovene reading societies (*čitalnice*).

1863 Sokol/the Falcon (Liberal gymnastic society) founded.

1864 Slovenska Matica (literary society) established.

1866–1867 Venetian Slovene lands become part of Italy after Austrian war with Italy (1866); eastern Slovene lands go to Hungary after Compromise of 1867 creates dual monarchy: Austria-Hungary.

1868–1870 Tabor movement.

1872 Society of Slovene Writers established.

late 19th–early 20th centuries Age of Slovene impressionism; Moderna period in literature.

1890s Slovene political parties established: Slovene People's Party (Clericals); National Progressive Party (Liberals) (1891); Yugoslav Social Democratic Party (a Slovene socialist party) (1896).

1896–1910 Ivan Hribar, Slovene Liberal, serves as Ljubljana's mayor.

1906 Orel/the Eagle (Catholic gymnastic society) begins; universal manhood suffrage begins in Austria.

1911–1921 Ivan Tavčar, Slovene Liberal, serves as Ljubljana's mayor.

1912 Preporod movement established: radical students favor independent Yugoslav state.

1913 **April:** Ivan Cankar talks on "Slovenes and Yugoslavism."

1910–1930 Slovene expressionism in the arts.

World War I

1914 **28 June:** Francis Ferdinand assassinated in Sarajevo. **28 July:** War begins one month later.

1917 **May:** Austrian Yugoslavs' National Program (May Declaration) announced.

1918   5 October–1 December: National Council of Slovenes, Croats, and Serbs. **29 October–1 December:** State of Slovenes, Croats, and Serbs. **31 October:** Ljubljana National Council names first National Government for Slovenia.

Royal Yugoslavia

1918   1 December: Kingdom of Serbs, Croats, and Slovenes established under Karadjordjević rule.

1918   National Gallery established. **23 December:** National Government for Slovenia (est. 31 October 1918) resigns.

1919   20 January: King Alexander names new regional government for Ljubljana; abolished on 12 July 1921 and replaced by regional administration. University of Ljubljana established. Communist Party of Yugoslavia established (banned in 1920); SKOJ, League of Communist Youth, established.

1920   10 October: Carinthian plebiscite results in loss of Slovene territory to Austrian republic. **12 November:** Treaty of Rapallo results in loss of Slovene territory to Italian kingdom.

1920s   Little Entente established—allies Yugoslavia with France and two other new states in the area: Czechoslovakia and Romania.

1921   12 February: SLS presents "constitutional autonomy" plan to national assembly in Belgrade: calls for six autonomous provinces, Slovenia being one of them. In Slovenia, 43 cultural figures across party lines sign declaration supporting autonomy as being of national importance. **28 June:** St. Vitus Day Constitution adopted by Kingdom of Serbs, Croats, and Slovenes. Abolished Slovene as an official language in Slovenia.

1926   Slovene PEN Center established.

1928   Catholic Action organized by Slovene Church leaders. **14 July:** Anton Korošec, SLS leader, prime minister, becomes first and only non-Serb premier in the royal Yugoslavia (resigns September 1930). **28 October:** Radio Ljubljana begins broadcasting.

1929   January 6th Dictatorship established by King Alexander of Yugoslavia; Kingdom of Serbs, Croats, and Slovenes renamed Kingdom of Yugoslavia; Drava *banovina* is "Slovene" administrative unit in restructured Kingdom of Yugoslavia (1929–1941).

1930s–1950s   Slovene Social and Socialist Realism.

1931 Census: 1,144,298 inhabitants in Drava banovina.

1933 Tallest building in Yugoslavia, 70-meter-high nebotičnik (skyscraper), erected in Ljubljana.

1934 King Alexander assassinated in Marseille; Regency Council acts as regent for Peter.

1937 Tito becomes head of Yugoslav Communist Party; Communist Party of Slovenia established at Čebinje.

1938 Academy of Sciences and Arts founded; renamed Slovenska akademija znanosti in umetnosti (SAZU) in 1948.

1939 Sperans (Edvard Kardelj) publishes *The Development of the Slovene National Question*.

World War II

1941 **6 April:** Early Slovene wartime activities; National Council for Slovenia established. **26 April:** Slovenes establish PIF (Anti-Imperialist Front), later renamed Liberation Front.

1942 **Spring:** Slovene Partisans begin establishing control over liberated and nonoccupied Slovene lands; Village Guard established. Slovene Covenant established. **26–27 November:** AVNOJ (Anti-Fascist Council of National Liberation of Yugoslavia) founded.

1943 **1 March:** Dolomite Declaration unites Slovene resistance groups under Communist leadership. **September:** Surrender of Italian army; Partisan force strength is increased. Home Guard (Slovene anti-Communist force) established. **29–30 November:** Provisional Yugoslav government established by AVNOJ.

1944 **November:** Slovene National Liberation Council established in Crnomelj.

1945 **March–May:** Last stages of war. **7 March:** Yugoslav Provisional Government established. **1 May:** Yugoslav army liberates Trieste; establishes provisional regime; forced to leave six weeks later by Allies (12 June). **early May:** Mass exodus of Home Guard and anti-Communist civilians to southern Austria. **5 May:** SNOS names Slovene national government in Ajdovščina. **9 May:** War ends. **late May–early June:** Mass executions by Partisans of Home Guards returned to Slovenia by British forces occupying southern Austria. **7–8 August:** People's Front established in Belgrade; prewar government elements included in government with AVNOJ. **11 November 1945:** Elections affirm Communist rule in Yugoslavia; monarchy abolished.

Communist Yugoslavia

1945 **29 November:** Federal People's Republic of Yugoslavia established.

1946 First Yugoslav Communist Constitution adopted.

1947 First Slovene Communist Constitution adopted; People's Republic of Slovenia established. **15 September:** Free Territory of Trieste under United Nations protection until October 1953.

1947 First Five-Year Plan (1947–1952); Nagode trial.

1948 Dachau trials (April 1948–October 1949). Cominform crisis begins; CPY expelled from Communist bloc. Museum of Modern Art opens.

1950s–1980s Slovene modernism in the arts.

1950 Workers' Councils and Workers' Self-Management introduced in Slovenia.

1952 Communist Party of Slovenia renamed League of Communists of Slovenia; Communist Party of Yugoslavia renamed League of Communists of Yugoslavia.

1953 **25 February:** People's Front of Yugoslavia reorganized and renamed Socialist Alliance of Working People (SAWP). **27 April:** Liberation Front (Osvobodilna Fronta) (LF) becomes Socialist Alliance of Working People (SAWP) of Slovenia. Constitutional Law adopted to reflect structural systemic changes in Yugoslavia since the 1946 Constitution.

1954 London Agreement resolves border issues between Italy and Yugoslavia.

1955 Austrian State Treaty: Article 7 outlines Slovene minority rights in Austria.

1958 International Biennial of Graphic Art opens in Ljubljana.

1961 Nonaligned movement established in Belgrade.

1963 New constitution establishes Federal "Socialist" Republic of Yugoslavia; socialist self-management introduced. Brnik Airport (Ljubljana) opens.

1967–1972 "Liberal" Communist rule in Slovenia: Stane Kavčič government; the "Road Affair" (1969).

1968 Ljubljana archdiocese established, with two dioceses: Ljubljana and Maribor; Koper diocese added in 1977.

1969 Beginnings of Territorial Defense (TD) in Slovenia.

1974 New constitution: concept of "associated labor," self-management vehicles, and the "delegate system" introduced.

1975 University of Maribor established. **11 November:** Treaty of Osimo reaffirms and clarifies the Italian–Yugoslav border.

1978 Alps–Adriatic Working Community established.

1980 **4 May:** Tito dies.

1987 *Nova revija*, No. 57, publishes "Contributions to a Slovene National Program."

1987 Slobodan Milošević comes to power in Serbia.

1988 **July:** Ljubljana Four trial; sparks Slovene national demonstrations against Belgrade.

1989 Pentagonal established. **March:** Serbian economic war against Slovenia. **May:** May Declaration (Slovene national program): Slovene sovereignty within Yugoslavia. **27 December:** Constitutional amendments allow organizations, including political parties, outside Socialist Alliance; Demos coalition established (December).

1990 **January:** Slovene Assembly announces multiparty elections. **22 January:** Slovene Communists walk out of LCY 14th Congress; LCY collapses. **7 March:** "Socialist" Republic of Slovenia changes name to Republic of Slovenia (RS). **8–22 April:** Multiparty elections in Slovenia; center-right coalition wins. **May:** Non-Communist government formed: Lojze Peterle (SKD and Demos), prime minister. **4 October:** Slovene Assembly nullifies 27 federal laws. **23 December:** Slovenia holds plebiscite for independence; 88.2 percent of electorate in favor.

Independent Slovenia

1991 **25 June:** Slovenia declares "disassociation" from Yugoslavia. **25 June:** Bank of Slovenia (BS) established. **27 June–6 July:** Ten-Day War between Slovene territorial defense units and Yugoslav National Army (JNA). **7 July:** Brioni Agreement brings three-month truce for Slovenia. **8 October:** Slovenia implements independence. New currency (the *tolar*) introduced. **25 October:** Last Yugoslav Army troops leave Slovenia. **23 December:** New Slovene constitution affirms independent democratic republic. Central European Initiative succeeds Pentagonal.

1992 January–May: International recognition: Slovenia recognized by European Community (15 January) and United States (7 April); becomes member of United Nations (22 May). **November:** Privatization Law enacted, favoring gradual, consensual approach. **December:** National election, first after new Slovene constitution; Liberal Democratic Party (LDS) receives most votes for national assembly; Milan Kučan elected president.

1993 January: New government formed: Janez Drnovšek (LDS), prime minister. Bailout of major Slovene banks by government begins; rehabilitation completed in 1997.

1994 Slovenia joins NATO Partnership for Peace program.

1996 1 January: Slovenia joins Central European Free Trade Association (CEFTA). **November:** National election (November); government in place after three-month deadlock with "Spring parties"; Janez Drnovšek (LDS) prime minister; lasts until April 2000.

1997 Slovenia put on track for European Union (EU) accession.

1998 Plan adopted to professionalize Slovene army.

2000 May–November: Drnovšek government falls on vote of no confidence (April); Andrej Bajuk representing "Spring parties" becomes prime minister; party mergers and realignments follow. **October:** National election: strong LDS showing. **October:** New government: Janez Drnovšek (LDS) prime minister; opposition organizes "Coalition Slovenia"; lasts until December 2002.

2002 Drnovšek elected president of Slovenia; Anton Rop becomes prime minister. **December:** Rop works with national assembly to complete work on joining international organizations; opposition builds strength after June 2004 and takes over in October 2004.

2003 23 March: Referenda on joining EU and North Atlantic Treaty Organization: 90 percent affirmative vote on EU; 66 percent affirmative vote on NATO.

2004 January: Concordat between Vatican and Slovenia (signed December 2001) ratified by Slovene national assembly. **29 March:** Slovenia joins NATO. **1 May:** Slovenia joins EU. **October–December:** National elections (October 2004): Slovene Democratic Party (SDS) receives most votes; Janez Janša (SDS) forms coalition government of center-right ("Spring") parties.

2005   30 June: Slovene population reaches two million (2,001,114).

2006   April: Maribor diocese elevated to archdiocese and metropolitanate with two new dioceses at Celje and Murska Sobota; new diocese at Novo Mesto created within the Ljubljana archdiocese/metropolitanate.

2007   1 January: Slovenia adopts the euro.

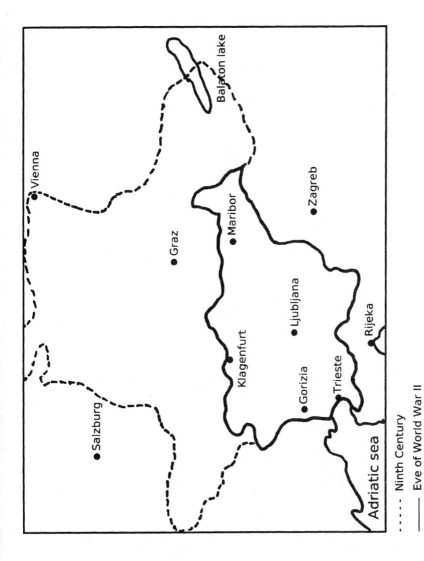

Vienna

Salzburg

Graz

Balaton lake

Maribor

Zagreb

Klagenfurt

Ljubljana

Gorizia

Trieste

Rijeka

Adriatic sea

······ Ninth Century

—— Eve of World War II

1. *Slovene ethnic territory*

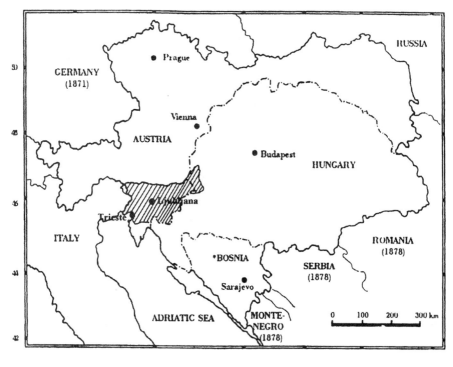

RUSSIA

GERMANY
(1871)

● Prague

Vienna
●

AUSTRIA

● Budapest

HUNGARY

Ljubljana
●

Trieste ●

ITALY

*BOSNIA

SERBIA
(1878)

ROMANIA
(1878)

Sarajevo
●

ADRIATIC SEA

MONTE-
NEGRO
(1878)

0   100   200   300 km

30

45

46

44

42

——— The Habsburg Empire
----- Kingdom of Hungary
▨▨▨ Slovene ethnic territory

*Annexed to Austria-Hungary in 1908

2. *Slovenes in Austria-Hungary*

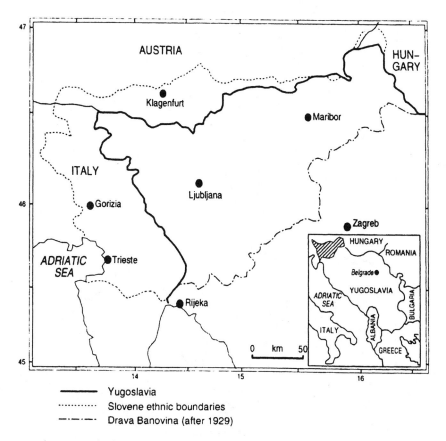

—————— Yugoslavia
·············· Slovene ethnic boundaries
—·—·—·— Drava Banovina (after 1929)

3. Slovenes in the first Yugoslavia (kingdom)

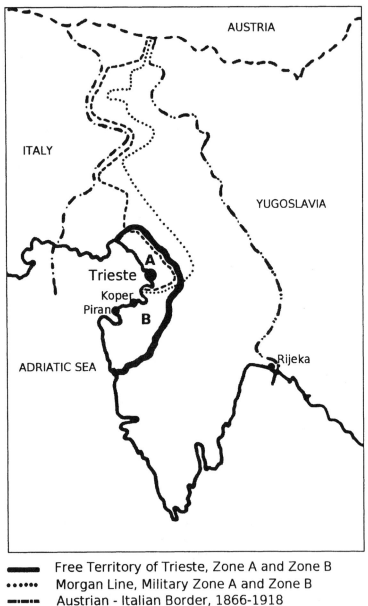

AUSTRIA

ITALY

YUGOSLAVIA

Trieste

Koper

Piran

A

B

ADRIATIC SEA

Rijeka

▬▬▬ Free Territory of Trieste, Zone A and Zone B
•••••• Morgan Line, Military Zone A and Zone B
▬▪▬▪ Austrian - Italian Border, 1866-1918
▬▪▪▬▪▪ Italian - Yugoslav, Border 1924
▬ ▬ ▬ Italian - Yugoslav Border, 1954

4. *Trieste question, 1945–1954*

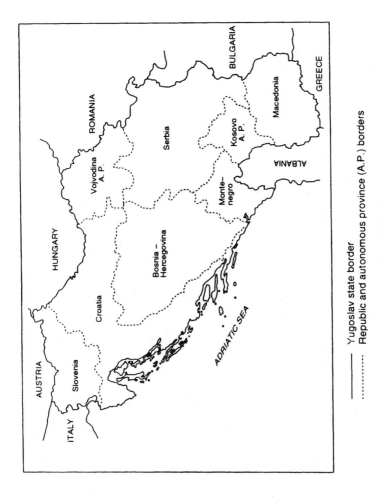

———— Yugoslav state border
············ Republic and autonomous province (A.P.) borders

5. *Slovenia in the second Yugoslavia (post–World War II)*

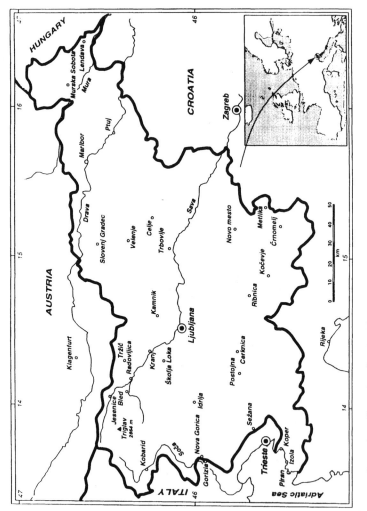

6. Independent Slovenia (after 1991)

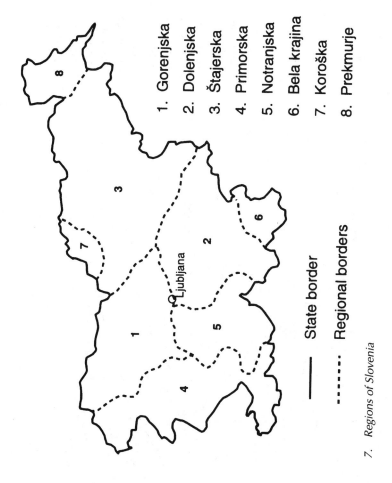

1. Gorenjska
2. Dolenjska
3. Štajerska
4. Primorska
5. Notranjska
6. Bela krajina
7. Koroška
8. Prekmurje

State border

Regional borders

7. *Regions of Slovenia*

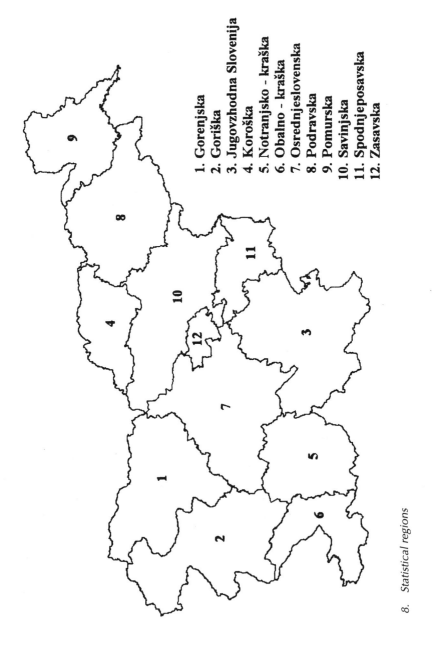

1. Gorenjska
2. Goriška
3. Jugovzhodna Slovenija
4. Koroška
5. Notranjsko - kraška
6. Obalno - kraška
7. Osrednjeslovenska
8. Podravska
9. Pomurska
10. Savinjska
11. Spodnjeposavska
12. Zasavska

8. *Statistical regions*

Introduction

Slovenes have always had a reputation for being hard-working, practical, and cautious. In December 1990, however, they did something completely out of character. They voted for independence, or more appropriately, "disassociation" from Yugoslavia. For more than 1,300 years they had been a part of Europe with no state designation, but by the late 1980s they had had enough. Slovenes resented Belgrade for exploiting them economically and threatening their language and culture, and they fumed in 1988 when they learned that Belgrade had military plans to subdue democratic forces in their republic. Ever cautious, they hesitated until intellectuals and political leaders persuaded them that their nation's small size should not deter them from making their own way. A public relations campaign convinced them that a nation of 2 million hard-working people need not be afraid of an independent future. The December 1990 plebiscite vote was overwhelmingly in favor of separation, and six months later, on 25 June 1991, Slovenia declared independence and prepared for the "new day" promised by their president, Milan Kučan. It was not easy. On the 26th, the Yugoslav army attacked Slovenia. Although the war lasted only 10 days, Slovenia's fate remained uncertain until the end of 1995, when all the wars accompanying Yugoslavia's bloody disintegration were over.

While Slovenes worked diligently to establish a democratic government and institute economic reforms, they struggled to be recognized. Slovenia, though it was never part of the Soviet bloc, was regularly confused with Slovakia, the former Czechoslovak republic that became independent in 1993. The public relations network again went to work, announcing that Slovenia was on the sunny side of the Alps. Slowly, painstakingly, yet reasonably quickly, Slovenia made its mark and is now considered a remarkable success story. In 2004 Slovenia acceded to both NATO and the European Union (EU), the only former Yugoslav republic to do so. By 2004 Slovenia had already served as a nonpermanent member of the United Nations Security Council (1998–1999) and assumed other major international responsibilities. In 2005 it held the presidency of the Organization for Security and Cooperation in Europe, and, in spite of problems restructuring its economy, Slovenia had an annual GDP per capita in 2005 of $17,008 ($18,900 on the basis of purchasing power parity). In this regard it is far ahead of other former communist states with transition economies. As far as the EU is concerned, Slovenia is already a developed country. In January 2007 Slovenia adopted the euro as its currency, and it is scheduled to take over the presidency of the EU in 2008. All in all, as the *Economist* wrote in an October 2005 piece on Estonia and Slovenia, "Small is beautifully successful."

LAND AND PEOPLE

Geography and Climate

The Republic of Slovenia, until 1991 a constituent republic of the Socialist Federal Republic of Yugoslavia, is located in central Europe. Its neighbors are Italy, Austria, Hungary, and Croatia, and it has 46 kilometers of coastline on the Adriatic Sea. It occupies 20,273 square kilometers, which is about half the size of Switzerland. Slovenia has four geographic zones: Alpine (42 percent) in the north; Dinaric with its karst terrain (28 percent) in the south; Mediterranean (9 percent) in the southwest and coastal areas; and Continental (21 percent) in the east where it becomes part of the Pannonian Plain. With 55 percent forestation (beech, birch, cedar, fir, linden, pine, and oak), the country is the third most forested in Europe, behind Sweden and Finland. Slovenia has an abundance of water from underground reservoirs and from rivers, the main ones being the Drava, the Mura, the Sava, and the Soča with their many tributaries. Average annual rainfall is 3,500 millimeters in the northwest and 800 millimeters in the east. Central Slovenia averages 1,400 millimeters of rain each year. Slovenia, divided among three climate zones (Alpine, Continental, and Mediterranean), has average low and high temperatures of 1 and 23 degrees Celsius.

Flora, Fauna, and Natural Resources

With 3,000 plants, both seed-producing and ferns and mosses, the relatively small territory of Slovenia has a large variety of plant species. This is attributable to its varied terrain at the intersection of four major geographic zones, with altitudes ranging from subterranean caves, of which there are thousands, to the upper reaches of Alpine peaks. Seventy of the 3,000 species are found nowhere else. Most of the unique varieties are Alpine and named after a province (Carniola), a mountain range (Kamnik), or a discoverer (e.g., Karel Zois). Much of the flora (and fauna) is considered endangered and therefore protected. Among the special protected areas are Triglav National Park's 83,807 hectares; the Škocjan caves, a United Nations Education, Science, and Cultural Organization (UNESCO) world heritage site; and the Sečovlje salt flats and wetlands.

Slovenia has 50,000 species of fauna. Among the larger animals are brown bear, chamois, deer, lynx, and wild boar. In addition to hundreds of marine animals and subterranean species, there are also varieties of beetles, birds (344 species), dormice, foxes, rabbits, and wolves. Some species are unique to the area: the Carniolan honey bee (*Apis mellifera carnica*); the Lipicanec (Lipizzaner), the white horse once bred by Habsburg royalty; the *Proteus anguinus*, a sightless amphibian found in karst cave waters; and a trout (*Salmo marmorata*) found in the Soča River.

Slovenia has limited natural resources. Its mines (especially brown coal, iron, and mercury) have been depleted or are of poor quality. Many mines have simply closed. The country makes use of crude oil, low-sulfur coal, and natural gas imports for energy. Its abundant forests continue to provide raw material for energy generation as well as manufacturing. Water, too, is an important natural resource. Once used to power forges and mills, it now powers dozens of hydroelectric plants. Water is also a useful tourism resource, drawing not only those interested in fishing and swimming but, in the case of mineral waters, those seeking the health benefits of Slovenia's many spas.

The People

The Republic of Slovenia is divided into *občinas* (communes)—210 of them in 2006—and into 12 statistical regions, but Slovenes more commonly relate to eight historical regions, the boundaries of which are somewhat fluid. The republic's population is just over 2 million. Slovenia's major cities are, in order of size, Ljubljana (the capital), Maribor, Celje, Kranj, Velenje, Koper (a port city), and Novo Mesto. In 2005, life expectancy was 73.5 years for men and 82.08 years for women; the annual population growth was 1.1 per thousand. Although only 4.7 percent of Slovenes are engaged in agriculture (together with forestry and fishing), about 48 percent live in rural areas. It is convenient for Slovenes to be at home in the countryside and commute to urban centers, which are hardly ever more than a half-hour's distance away. The fact that smallish cities of about 1,000 continue to grow indicates that this is a persistent trend. Manufacturing (with mining, energy, and construction) occupies 38.5 percent of those employed, while 57 percent of Slovenes work in the services sector. This sector, which includes tourism and other traditional services, has expanded due to three service areas that have boomed since denationalization: retail, real estate, and especially financial services. In 2005, 61 percent of women and 70 percent of men were employed.

Economic indicators for Slovenia have been very favorable for several years. The unemployment rate in 2005 was 10.2 percent (6.5 percent by International Labor Organization calculations), down 5 percent from a decade earlier. Labor productivity had risen 3.1 percentage points and the GDP 3.9 percent since the previous year. The inflation rate, 117 percent in the last days of life in Yugoslavia, was at a very manageable 2.5 percent.

Ethnically, according to the 2002 census, Slovenia is 83.06 percent Slovene. Nearly 6.5 percent of the population is South Slavic (with co-nationals in areas of the former Yugoslavia), while 0.32 percent and 0.11 percent are Hungarian and Italian, respectively. The official language is Slovene and in ethnically mixed border areas also Hungarian or Italian. In the census, most Slovenes identified themselves as Roman Catholic (57.8 percent), but there were also small Protestant (Evangelical Lutheran) (0.8 percent), Eastern Orthodox (2.3 percent), Jewish (about 100 individuals), and Muslim (2.4 percent) communities. The 2002 percentage for Roman Catholicism, which was down from 71.6 percent in 1991, can probably be accounted for by the large percentage of respondents who preferred not to answer the religion question (15.7 percent) and those whose religion was listed as unknown (7.1 percent).

HISTORY

Karantania

Ancestors of today's Slovenes settled in the eastern Alps in the mid-sixth century, occupying an area more than twice the size of Slovenia today. By the 620s Karantania, a state to which Slovenes trace their political tradition, was Slavic; in the mid-700s it came under feudal Bavarian and Frankish domination. Slovenes were Christianized in the second half of the eighth century. In the age of Charlemagne, therefore, Western European political, religious, and cultural institutions began shaping the future for the Slovenes. Their history in the premodern period is a part of the history of central Europe, for Slovene lands fell within the Holy Roman Empire from its inception in 962 AD. In feudal Europe most Slovenes were peasants, subject to a non-Slovene feudal nobility, and towns in the Slovene lands, many incorporated in the 1200s, existed at the will of the nobility or the emperor. The earliest known examples of written Slovene are from around 1000 AD.

Habsburg Rule

All Slovene lands (duchies, counties) eventually became a part of the Habsburg feudal domain. After the mid-1400s the Habsburgs were also Holy Roman emperors, which gave them a double jurisdiction. For two centuries from the mid-1400s, this part of Europe experienced ongoing crises: Turkish wars, peasant revolts (Slovenes were prominent among the rebels), political struggles between emperor and nobility, and religious revolution, with the Habsburgs defending the Catholic Church against Protestant reformers. The general upheaval of the period resulted in economic, social, and political regression, and development in this part of Europe was retarded for two centuries.

The Slovenes' depiction of the period, however, had a silver lining. The mid-15th to the mid-16th century was an age of intellectual awakening, when humanism encouraged learning and literacy in the vernacular, generally for religious reasons. Slovene Protestant reformers (Primož Trubar, Adam Bohorič, and Jurij Dalmatin) thus produced Slovene language books, including a primer, a grammar, numerous religious texts, and, in 1584, a translation of the Bible. In 1597 the Society of Jesus (Jesuits), as elsewhere in Austria, established a center in Ljubljana as a bastion of Counter Reformation learning. They introduced secondary schools that featured church law, philosophy, theology, and scientific learning—all in Latin. But the Jesuits, too, often employed the vernacular language in music, religious plays, and sermons. By the late 18th century, the Slovene literary foundation established by the mid-16th-century Protestant reformers was revived. Slovene enlighteners would build on it a "national" awakening, in the Slovene language.

That Slovene awakening, in the second half of the 18th century and the first half of the 19th, took place in the context of a state-directed modernization in the Habsburg Empire. In stages, the state emancipated the peasants (completed in 1848) and required them to be literate. Slovenes thereby acquired greater social mobility, and in schools, where the state's aim was to Germanize, they promoted the use of their own mother tongue. The Slovene Enlightenment (1760s–1820s) produced Marko Pohlin's Slovene grammar (1768) and Anton Linhart's history of the Slovenes (1788–1791). In the same period, Valentin Vodnik published the first Slovene newspaper (1797–1800). The work of these intellectuals, many of whom were clergy, was given unexpected endorsement by the French, who ruled in the western Slovene lands, then part of the Illyrian Provinces, between 1809 and 1813. With Ljubljana as the provinces' administrative capital, the use of Slovene was encouraged, and Slovenes were appointed to important positions. Jernej Kopitar published a definitive Slovene grammar in 1808. Then as the Enlightenment flowed into romanticism (1815–1848), idealism helped Slovene intellectuals forge a distinct national language and cultural identity. It is significant that in this formative period Slovene cultural leaders chose not to merge with the Illyrian movement, an intellectual action among other South Slavs, or Yugoslavs (mostly Croats), in the Habsburg Empire, who favored the adoption of a common South Slavic language. France Prešeren, the Slovenes' most cherished romantic poet, was prominent in urging the development of a separate Slovene language and literature, one suitable for a modern age.

Slovene leaders put forward their first political program in 1848 calling for a United Slovenia, while the Austrian state was in the throes of revolution. Based on ethnic principles, it proposed the administrative union of Slovene lands in Austria and the use of the national language in administration and schools. When the revolutions in Austria were extinguished, Slovene political life flickered, but by the late 1860s it began reasserting itself cautiously, deferentially. In 1867 the Habsburg Empire became a dual monarchy, Austria-Hungary, and most of the Slovenes fell within the Austrian part. Here, although not in Hungary, political life evolved in a democratic direction (by 1906 there was universal manhood suffrage for parliamentary elections), and a broadening franchise brought more Slovenes into the political process. Traditional parties were established in the 1890s (Clerical/Conservative, Liberal, Socialist), and Slovenes began to assume real political power in Carniola, the Austrian land where they were most numerous.

By the 1860s there were about 1.1 million Slovenes, who, because of economic pressures in rural areas, were forced to seek a livelihood in towns. Many emigrated, a good number to the United States, especially after 1880. Those same pressures also produced new ways of dealing with economic realities at home. One way was to establish cooperatives, which were widespread and highly successful before World War I. Literacy was high (80–90 percent), partly due to state educational requirements but also because the Slovenes established institutions such as the Society of St. Hermagoras, Slovenska Matica, and the *čitalnice* (reading societies) to promote literacy in the national language. The Catholic Church, and in particular Bishop Anton Slomšek, was especially instrumental in spreading literacy among the rural population.

In the last two decades before World War I, Slovene political life was, for the first time, strongly influenced by Yugoslavism. Although remaining committed to Austria, all Slovene parties sought cooperation with other southern Slavs (primarily those in the dual monarchy) in order to have collective clout in Vienna. (Slovenes were conscious of their small numbers.) Most hoped to achieve an autonomous Yugoslav state within the Habsburg Empire. This was not achieved, however, for Vienna was not enthusiastic about the idea—nor were the Croats if it meant working with the Slovenes. The 1914 assassination of Archduke Francis Ferdinand and the ensuing European war would have dramatic consequences for the Slovenes.

Slovenes in Royal Yugoslavia

World War I (1914–1918) led to the collapse of Austria-Hungary. During the last months of the conflict Slovene leaders tried asserting the principle of national self-determination (United Slovenia), but attempts to establish a state for the South Slavs of Austria-Hungary with a separate government for the Slovenes (established by the National Council of Slovenes, Croats, and Serbs on 31 October 1918) were ignored by the Entente powers. The postwar settlements, confirmed by the Paris Peace Conference and subsequent international actions, brought a dismemberment of ethnic Slovene territory. In December 1918 the bulk of "Slovenia" became a part of the Kingdom of Serbs, Croats, and Slovenes, a Balkan state, which came to be called Yugoslavia (1929). In 1920 southern Carinthia went to Austria and western Slovene lands (one-third of the Slovene population) to Italy. For the Slovenes who became part of the first Yugoslavia (1918–1945), there were decided benefits to being in that state. Some would argue that it was crucial to the Slovenes' later state-building efforts. The Slovene National Gallery (1918), the University of Ljubljana (1919), and an Academy of Sciences and Arts (1938), all Slovene national institutions, were established in this period. With the founding of these institutions and the spread of Slovene language use in schools, the intelligentsia grew in number and became an important and confident Slovene leadership element. The Slovene business community grew as well, and although in general conditions were not favorable in the interwar years for major economic advances, Slovene entrepreneurs moved forward, developing new markets in Yugoslavia for their industrial products. The textile industry made particular strides with the aid of electrification and competitive markets. At least 40 percent of Yugoslavia's Slovenes worked in industry on the eve of World War II, making it a semi-industrialized region in a predominantly agricultural state. The agricultural economy, however, was in a shambles and the rural population suffered. Many emigrated in search of jobs. Slovenes blamed Belgrade for exploiting them for the benefit of the rest of the country.

Slovene political developments took some interesting turns in the 1920s and 1930s. The key issue for all parties was the country's Vidovdan constitution (28 June 1921), a slightly disguised version of Serbia's prewar one. Although Anton Korošec, head of the Slovene People's Party, together with some from the Yugoslav Social Democratic Party (JSDS) pushed hard for six autonomous provinces (one to be Slovenia) for the new state, the constituent assembly in Belgrade rejected their February 1921 proposal. Instead the new constitution established a centralized, Serb-dominated monarchy and buried any hope of non-Serbs for equal rights and political autonomy. It even excluded Slovene from becoming an official language of the new state. Federalists, non-Serbs, and republicans voted against the constitution (Croats were prominent opponents). Of the Slovene parties, only the Liberals (JDS) favored the unitary state and joined a Yugoslavia-based political camp. They worked with the regime from 1921 through 1928 and again from 1933 to 1935, only to be pushed aside then by the new royal leadership. Slovene liberalism fragmented thereafter. The Socialists (JSDS) had splintered already in 1919, and did so several times more in the early 1920s; many would oppose the 1921 constitution as an impediment to the development of a multinational state. Caught in the postwar upheaval and excitement of an as yet unfinished revolution in Russia, some of the Socialists (JSDS) merged with the centralized Yugoslav Communist Party in 1919/1920. The party was soon outlawed and its members, especially after the 1929 dictatorship was established, spent the interwar years in exile (often in Moscow) or in prison. They emerged slowly in the mid-1930s, and after the CPY federalized, the Slovene communists formed their own national party (1937).

Slovene Clericals had the largest and strongest party (SLS) and joined the royal government only in late 1927. They had rejected centralism in 1921 and held firm to their goal of cultural, economic, and political autonomy for Slovenes. In 1928 Anton Korošec, the Clericals' leader, was briefly prime minister (the king had hoped in vain to quell internal problems with his appointment), but the party was again outside governing circles between 1929 and 1935. Between 1935 and 1938 Korošec headed the Ministry of Internal Affairs, having accepted the position with the hope of achieving autonomy for the Slovenes. After 1929 most Yugoslav Slovenes lived in the newly created Drava *banovina*, headed by an appointed *ban*. It was virtually a "Slovenia," which Korošec and the Clericals pressed Belgrade to acknowledge, but to no avail. It should be noted that the Christian Socialists, who had been a strong force among the Clericals since the prewar days, moved away from the party in the 1930s. Inspired by a papal encyclical of 1931, Christian Socialists moved toward the left, stressing democracy as the Clericals became increasingly conservative. Christian Socialists, whose leader was Edvard Kocbek, would become important politically after 1941, when they joined the Liberation Front against Slovenia's occupiers.

The Yugoslav kingdom was for the most part a Serb-dominated, centrally run dictatorship after 1929. The regime was in endless deadlock with Croats, less so with Slovenes and Muslims, though all wanted federalism and cultural autonomy for their respective groups. Serious economic strains from postwar reconstruction and international depression weakened the state further. It was faced, too, with external enemies, particularly neighboring states with revisionist aspirations toward Yugoslav territory. Revisionist radicals from abroad even collaborated with Croat extremists to assassinate the Yugoslav king in 1934. In the late 1930s, as Axis powers began annexing central European states, it seemed that Yugoslavia might escape their imperialist ambitions. Then in April 1941 the kingdom was invaded, occupied, and dismembered by its neighbors. Yugoslavia's Slovene lands were divided among Italy, Germany, and Hungary. Many Slovenes, as well as Jews and Roma, of various political persuasions were put into concentration camps, mostly in Axis-ruled countries. The remaining Slovenes were subjected to denationalization policies and the severe hardships of wartime occupation.

Bleak as prospects looked at the beginning of World War II, "Slovenia" was to reemerge in 1945, and was considerably larger, acquiring most Italian Slovene lands (although not Trieste) as the result of wartime developments. In late April 1941, cut off from the rest of Yugoslavia,

Slovenes had organized an anti-imperialist front. A few months later, after Germany's invasion of the USSR, those Slovenes—Communists (CPS), Christian Socialists, liberal Sokols, and progressive intellectuals among others—established a Liberation Front (LF) of the Slovene nation. The LF, a resistance movement whose army came to be known as Partisans, fought the Italian and German occupiers; they were joined by Slovenes from Austria and Italy. From the outset the CPS assumed leadership, a fact that was sealed with the Dolomite Declaration (March 1943), which required that noncommunists cede authority to the CPS. A noncommunist resistance also developed; the Village Guards (1942) and Home Guards (1943) were anticommunist and soon became embroiled in civil war with the Partisans. Late in 1943, the Slovene LF joined like forces in the rest of Yugoslavia, headed by Tito, a Moscow-trained Communist. In September 1943 the Home Guard established its headquarters in Ljubljana with German approval. The Guard, pro-Catholic and a supporter of the royal government in exile, continued to fight the Partisans. On 20 April 1944 the Guard, at the occupiers' insistence, took a public oath of loyalty to the Germans, leaving the Guard open to charges of collaborating with the occupier. The act damaged the Guard's reputation among Slovenes and angered the Allies.

The Partisans eventually came out the winner, and having gradually established authority over Partisan-occupied Slovene territories, particularly after Italian capitulation in fall 1943, they installed a provisional government, headquartered in Bela Krajina. At war's end, Slovene Communists took power, establishing a national government in May 1945. Communists came to power throughout Yugoslavia in November 1945. Slovene Guardists were exiled or executed. The wartime civil confrontation between Partisans and Home Guard left a residue of animosity that is still palpable today.

Slovenes in Socialist Yugoslavia

The second Yugoslavia (1945–1991), in which Slovenia was one of six constituent federal republics, was a satellite of the Soviet Union until 1948. The association brought with it all the components of the Stalinist system: central planning, collectivization of agriculture, Communist Party rule, ideological conformity, and purges of class enemies and party dissidents. Concerning the latter, pursuit of political enemies in Slovenia was intense immediately after the war. Many thousands of Home Guard, who had fled in 1945 to the British-occupation zone of Austria, were returned to Slovenia by the British and brutally executed at Kočevski Rog. In 1947 in the Nagode trial, the regime targeted Slovene intellectuals accused of treason; in the Dachau trials of April 1948–October 1949, it pursued Slovene Communists who had allegedly collaborated while they were interned in German wartime concentration camps. Many in the 1940s were sent to detention camps (Teharje, Šentvid, and the most feared, the barren Adriatic island of Goli Otok). Decades later, the subjects of both trials were exonerated, but in the 1940s and 1950s the threat of political persecution remained ever present.

In 1950, no longer in the Soviet bloc, Yugoslavia began implementing what came to be known as Titoism, a novel system featuring workers' councils and workers' self-management, and in the international arena, nonalignment. The leading architect of Titoism was the Slovene Edvard Kardelj, who also devised a solution to the nationality problem: federalism and national self-determination, with a right to secession, for Yugoslavia's nations. While Titoism was being launched, times were still hard for average Slovenes. They were hungry, frightened, tired, and disillusioned. Intellectuals continued to be imprisoned for discussing sensitive topics or criticizing the regime. For Slovenia the postwar situation might have been far from ideal, but given the realities of the Cold War, things could have been worse: They could have still been a part of the Soviet bloc.

Slowly, in the late 1950s and early 1960s, things began to change. Within the CPS, and elsewhere in Yugoslavia, conservative and liberal party wings were already discernable. In Slovenia the more liberal, usually younger communists promoted greater decentralization within the federation, economic reforms, and language and cultural rights guarantees. In 1962 Slovenes walked out of the federal assembly in protest of a proposal to tax profits (the fruits of hard work); in 1965 they ardently promoted market reforms. The fight over these issues on the federal level in Belgrade led to the removal of some party hard-liners, mostly notably in 1966 Aleksandar Ranković, the ultra-centralist head of Internal Affairs. With that, liberalization became possible. Frontiers opened up; Yugoslavs (particularly Slovenes who had nearby borders with Italy and Austria) shopped, traveled, and worked abroad. Relations with the Vatican were regularized; a protocol between Belgrade and the Vatican was signed in 1966, and by 1970 full diplomatic relations were established. With things loosening up, liberalization in the political arena was also made possible, particularly in Slovenia and Croatia. In Slovenia the Stane Kavčič government (1967–1972) provided an opportunity for major changes.

Liberal communist in character, it promoted sovereignty for the Slovene republic, pushed for a new, more equitable system for financing the federal state, and urged reforms within the military. Some within the federal government went along with certain liberal reforms, but the conservatives who opposed them ultimately prevailed. (This was the time of "socialism with a human face" in Czechoslovakia, where a short euphoric period of liberal rule ended in Soviet military repression.)

In Yugoslavia, the party began purging liberals in 1971; federal centralism was strengthened, while talk of autonomy for republics ended, and LCY supremacy was reconfirmed. The conservative resurgence was capped with a new constitution (1974) and the introduction of contractual socialism in the economic sphere. Both reinforced LCY strength. Hard-liners were reinstated and heaviness loomed over intellectual life throughout the 1970s. Belgrade's dominance, however, would be challenged again soon, for the issue of centralism versus federalism would not go away. Tito's death in 1980 (and Kardelj's in 1979) brought an end to an era in Yugoslavia. Although the state did not break apart immediately, latent weaknesses in the system were magnified by the developments of the 1980s.

The economy was the first to go; rampant inflation, due mostly to an out-of-control foreign debt, was of great concern to all parties, but there were serious disagreements on how to manage it. The Serbs, who had been tightening controls over the Albanians in Kosovo (part of the Serbian republic) after 1981, favored greater central control (from Belgrade), while the other republics, Slovenia leading them, promoted more autonomy for the republics as well as a market economy. Tensions grew throughout the decade as nationalisms were nurtured by elements that stood to gain in the struggle for power in Yugoslavia. The Slovenes' battle with the two Belgrades (the federal capital and the Serbian capital) generated widespread liberalization—among intellectuals, fringe groups, political movements, and also in the party—after the mid-1980s. The urgency of the situation was brought home by two external developments: the collapse of communism in the USSR and its bloc, and the imminence of European unity in 1992. Slovenes concluded that they did not want to be the last to get rid of a failed system, and they wished to become a part of Europe as soon as possible. Belgrade seemed intent on preventing both.

Slovene intellectuals began writing about Slovene sovereignty and independence (such as in the journal *Nova revija* in 1987, no. 57, and in the May Declaration in 1989). Slovenes rallied behind the "Ljubljana

Four" accused in 1988 of betraying military secrets and tried by a court-martial (conducted in Serbo-Croatian rather than Slovene). The Slovene Assembly passed constitutional amendments increasing the republic's autonomy and nullifying federal laws in 1989 and 1990. Political pluralism came next. Parties were organized in late 1989 and early 1990, the Slovene communists left the Yugoslav League of Communists, and multiparty elections—which ousted the former communists—were held in Slovenia in April 1990. The new government headed by Demos, a center-right coalition, continued the struggle with Belgrade and in December 1990 enabled an overwhelmingly successful plebiscite on Slovene independence. As conditions in Yugoslavia continued to deteriorate, with little chance of a rejuvenated federalism or even the implementation of the confederalism proposed by the Slovenes and the Croats, the Republic of Slovenia declared independence on 25 June 1991.

The following day the Yugoslav People's Army (JNA) began a war in Slovenia, which soon spread to Croatia and later to Bosnia-Hercegovina. For Slovenia it is known descriptively as the Ten-Day War. A truce—the Brioni Agreement—was brokered by the European Community (EC), and by October the JNA had withdrawn its troops and Slovenia embarked on an independent existence. Slovene independence was recognized by the EC on 15 January 1992 and by the United States on 7 April, and membership in the United Nations came on 22 May. War would continue to rage to Slovenia's south, however, until late 1995.

Independent Slovenia

After the Slovenes ousted the communists and severed ties with Belgrade, it was time to dismantle the communist system. Preparing a new constitution was a necessary first step. Voters in the 1990 multiparty election had chosen representatives to governmental bodies outlined in the 1974 constitution, which had to be replaced as soon as possible. By the end of 1991 Slovenia had a new constitution. Like Western counterparts, it established a governmental structure that had executive, judicial, and legislative components. The legislative branch had two bodies, a national assembly or parliament and a national council (a consultative chamber). The former would be the chief law-making body, consisting of 90 elected representatives. In 1992 Slovenia held its first multiparty election based on the new constitution, and it would hold parliamentary elections every four years thereafter. Elections to the council and presidency are on a five-year rotation. Given Slovenia's multiparty system, all elections result in the need to form coalition governments (there were six different governments between 1992 and 2004, although Slovenia had only four elections).

The next step in moving away from the communist system was to rebuild and restructure Slovenia's economy. On the day independence was declared, the government established the Bank of Slovenia (BS) and adopted the *tolar* as its new currency. By 1996 the Bank had proven its effectiveness: It had lowered Slovenia's inflation rate from 117 percent to 9.7 percent, had stabilized the currency, and had begun a course of paying off Slovenia's external debt from the communist era. Another vital step for Slovenia was finishing off the old socioeconomic system (begun in 1990), converting socially owned property into private property. This was a more daunting task and provoked heated political debates between those who supported gradual privatization and those who favored "shock therapy," a rapid, government-directed method advocated by the American economist Jeffrey Sacks. Ultimately, the Slovenes chose a compromise course that combined gradualism with political pragmatism. Moving slowly toward privatization may have cost Slovenia in the short term, but ultimately it avoided social and political instability.

Political stability was established between 1991 and 1996; between 1996 and 2004 Slovenia then worked on the structural reforms: privatization and denationalization of property confiscated, or nationalized, by the communist regime. By 1999, 95 percent of properties, including businesses, had been privatized according to a formula adopted in 1992. The remaining 5 percent was liquidated, with proceeds going to a development fund. With the restructuring of the economy, Slovenia became interesting for foreign investors such as Novartis (the Swiss pharmaceuticals company), Goodyear (the American tire company), and KBS (the Belgian banking establishment). Denationalization was also undertaken, with 35,000 of 40,000 claims for return of property being processed by 2005. The remaining claims, often coming from cultural institutions, are still pending. One notable example is the Catholic Church's claim to land currently a part of Triglav National Park.

In 1991 Slovenia's first official document on foreign policy objectives announced that the country would seek to join Europe and North Atlantic Treaty Organization (NATO). In 1993 a cooperation agreement was signed with the European Union (EU), and in 1996 Slovenia formally applied for membership. The following year the EU put Slovenia on track for admission, providing that it met EU qualifications. That began years of intense work and coordination with the EU and required that Slovenia "harmonize" its laws with those of the EU. Significantly, Slovenia's new constitution needed to be amended and its sovereignty limited in preparation for EU accession. Although initially some had reservations about joining, by March 2003, 90 percent of Slovenes voted to accept membership. On 1 May 2004, Slovenia became an EU member; on 13 June it elected seven representatives to the European Parliament.

Belonging to NATO was less attractive to many Slovenes, including prominent politicians. In 1994, however, Slovenia joined NATO's Partnership for Peace program and in 1996 became a member of the North Atlantic Cooperation Council, hoping that it would be invited to join NATO the next year. Although not on NATO's expansion list in 1997, Slovenia redoubled its efforts, receiving the invitation in late 2003. (In March 2003, 66 percent of Slovenes had voted for NATO accession, considerably less on the EU issue.) On 29 March 2004 Slovenia became a member of NATO. By that time, the Slovene military had undergone considerable changes since independence. Its territorial defense (TD) had excelled in the Ten-Day War (1991), and it was expected that the TD would continue to serve the country. By the mid-1990s, however, the institution of conscription for all 18-year-old males was giving way to the idea of a professional army. A plan to eliminate traditional forces and train flexible mobile units also suited NATO's needs for specialized trainees. Thus Slovenia created a professional army trained in specific tasks, with one unit reserved for peacekeeping operations. In October 2003 Slovenia abolished conscription. Women make up 13 percent of this new professional army.

As Slovenia transformed itself from a Yugoslav socialist republic to an independent democratic state with a functioning market economy and membership in the EU and NATO, Slovene political life matured and found its footing. The political parties that emerged in 1990 ranged from leftist former communists (reformed and renamed) to centrist liberals to rightists with strong aversions to the Titoist era. In the early 1990s, in spite of underlying tensions, there was remarkable agreement on common objectives: independence, a new constitution, and privatization. From 1992 until 2004, with a brief interlude in mid-2000, the Liberal Democracy of Slovenia (LDS) dominated the national assembly. Its party head, Janez Drnovšek, served as prime minister (replaced by LDS's Anton Rop in 2002 when Drnovšek was elected Slovenia's president). LDS ran coalition governments often with leftist United List (ZL) support and always with at least one center or right political party:

Slovene Christian Democrats (SKD), Slovene People's Party (SLS), or Janez Janša's recently renamed Slovene Democratic Party (SDS). Some in LDS had had political experience before independence, knew the political ropes, and remained quite popular with voters who trusted their competency.

Throughout the 1990s, however, there was a persistent undercurrent of opposition from the center right or "Spring" parties (SKD, SLS, and SDS). Their agenda and that of New Slovenia (NSi), which emerged in 2000 (its head Andrej Bajuk was prime minister for several months that year), stressed faster privatization, reform of government spending, and traditional values and goals. Slovene Catholicism was important to many in the opposition parties, who wanted a larger role in public life for the Catholic Church, a favorable agreement with the Vatican, and religious education in public schools. The traditional family was important, and many felt it needed to be nurtured.

Ideological issues were on the agenda, too, which demanded a repudiation of the communist past, a restitution of nationalized property, and a reevaluation of wartime events, especially the role of the Home Guard. Particular hatred was reserved for the communist secret police, whose excesses required exposure and punishment. Many items on this agenda, however, were postponed for more than a decade as more urgent matters, like accession to the EU and NATO, demanded undivided attention. With those goals accomplished in 2004, LDS's hold quickly began to weaken, particularly under Rop's arrogant and inept leadership. In June 2004 only two of the seven elected to the EU parliament were from LDS. Four were from "Spring" parties. LDS's control crumbled, with the party losing to SDS in the national assembly election later that year. SDS's party president, Janez Janša, became prime minister and put together a coalition of almost exclusively center-right parties. The larger issues of independence, privatization, and EU and NATO membership were squared away and the euro was adopted on 1 January 2007. Thus the new government turned to completing economic reforms and dealing with more sensitive issues regarding the social safety net, such as health care and pensions.

The Dictionary

– A –

ACADEMIA OPEROSORUM (1693–1725). Founded in 1693 by the provost of Ljubljana Cathedral, Janez Krstnik Prešeren, Academia Operosorum was the first **society** of intellectuals in **Ljubljana**. Marko Gerbec, a physician with an international reputation, was one of its most active members and also president in its most productive years. The academy sought to bring together scientists, creative thinkers, and artists and was in operation until 1725. Its most important act was the establishment of the first public-study **library** in Ljubljana, today the Seminary Library. The academy, whose languages were Latin and German, had an important role in developing **baroque** arts. In 1781 the academy was revived as a literary and linguistic society. *See also* ARTS; ENLIGHTENMENT; SCIENCE.

ACADEMIA PHILHARMONICORUM (1701–1769). Established in 1701 by Janez Berthold Höffer, a member of **Academia Operosorum**, Academia Philharmonicorum was the first **music** society in the Slovene lands and was in operation until 1769. Besides performing **baroque** music (religious and secular) on various occasions, it also encouraged native musicians to compose. Indirectly, it also influenced Slovene **folk music** and church song books. The academy was an important institution for the later development of musical life in the Slovene lands. *See also* SOCIETIES.

ACADEMY OF SCIENCES AND ARTS, SLOVENIAN / SLOVENSKA AKADEMIJA ZNANOSTI IN UMETNOSTI (SAZU). *See* SLOVENE ACADEMY OF SCIENCES AND ARTS.

ADAMIC, LOUIS (1898–1951). Louis Adamic was an American Slovene writer who emigrated to the United States in 1913. After a stint in the U.S. Army during **World War I**, Adamic explored his adopted country (he became a citizen in 1917), depicting it with idealistic

1

enthusiasm. Much of what he wrote was journalistic and autobio-graphical, and it tended toward social criticism. By the 1930s he was well known; he wrote for the *American Mercury* and was acquainted with writers of the Lost Generation. *Dynamite* (1931), *Laughing in the Jungle* (1932), and *From Many Lands* (1939) are some typical Adamic tributes to his America.

In 1932, after winning a Guggenheim fellowship, Adamic turned his writing attention to the Slovenes and Yugoslavia. Aside from translating **Ivan Cankar**'s *Yerney's Justice* (1926), he had been almost entirely immersed in his new country. *The Native's Return* (1934), a Book-of-the-Month Club selection, *My Native Land* (1943), and *The Eagle and the Roots* (1952) all reflected Adamic's renewed interest in the old country. The latter book, published posthumously (the circumstances of Adamic's death have never been made clear), related the beginnings of the **Tito**–Stalin split following **World War II**. During the war Adamic worked with the U.S. Office of Strategic Services as a Yugoslavia specialist. He became a supporter of Tito and the **Partisan** resistance, a commitment which later contributed to his being investigated by the House Un-American Activities Com-mittee. Post–World War II Slovenia has held Adamic, as a writer and a Slovene, in high esteem. *See also* LITERATURE.

ADMINISTRATIVE SOCIALISM (1945–1952). Administrative socialism was a management system associated with economic cen-tral planning introduced in Yugoslavia following **World War II**. It was based on state capitalism, or state ownership of property, and direction from the federal government in **Belgrade**. State ownership was achieved in the **People's Republic of Slovenia** (PRS) and the **Federal People's Republic of Yugoslavia** (FPRY), primarily in the late 1940s, through **nationalization** of private property. Acceptance of the new system was based on a wartime agreement between the **Communist Party of Yugoslavia** (CPY) and the **People's Front**; it was initiated and legalized by the **Constitution of 1946** and **Consti-tution of 1947**. The Soviet model for economic development, which this system emulated, was believed to be appropriate for economi-cally backward areas where the working class was small and lacking in "socialist" consciousness. The First **Five-Year Plan** (1947–1951) was introduced under this system.

Due to the **Cominform Crisis**—a political and ideological conflict that developed between the USSR and the FPRY, between Stalin and

Tito—administrative socialism was never fully implemented. After Yugoslavia was ousted from the Cominform, its Marxist theoreticians found the Soviet economic model faulty. A process of decentralization was begun in the FPRY already in 1950 with the introduction of **workers' self-management** and with the abolishment of most federal planning agencies in 1951. It culminated in a revision of the **Constitution of 1946** with the **Constitutional Law of 1953**, which modified the Soviet model both politically and economically and officially ended administrative socialism. *See also* MARKET SOCIALISM.

AGITPROP (1945–1952). Agitprop was the **Communist Party** (CP) institution that controlled **education, publishing, libraries,** mass **media, science, art,** and voluntary cultural and **sports** societies from the end of **World War II** until 1952. Agitprop's goal of educating "workers and peasants to become loyal socialist citizens" remained operative throughout the period—and even beyond—although after the 1948 break with the Cominform, Agitprop's reliance on the Soviet model declined, while the Yugoslav dimension in culture was stressed and more influences from the West were tolerated. *See also* ADMINISTRATIVE SOCIALISM; COMINFORM CRISIS.

Responsibility for Agitprop activities fell initially to the Ministry of Education; after 1949 it was shared with the Ministry of Science and Culture. In 1951 the two ministries were combined in the Council for Education, Science, and Art. General educational and cultural activities were carried out by mass organizations but coordinated by *Ljudska prosveta* (the People's Education and Culture Society) with its monthly publication *Obzornik* (Review). Prewar cultural and educational organizations and societies were banned after the war, and new ones could be established only with the CP's approval. Publishing houses and libraries were purged of literary works not only by political opponents but also by "unreliable" people. Agitprop, whose members held key positions in the government structure and in cultural and scientific institutions and mass organizations, directed these organizations. Not choosy in its means, the CP tried either to direct or block activities of artists and intellectuals who did not support its ideology and **socialist realism**.

During the First **Five-Year Plan**, a basic educational goal was to create a workforce and a technical intelligentsia able to carry out industrialization. All decisions regarding investments, curriculum, textbooks, teachers' employment, financial aid to students, and the like were closely monitored by Agitprop. In schools, which were not adequately staffed, there was heavy reliance on Soviet textbooks. Russian was the primary foreign language, and curricula were cleansed of all content not in line with communist ideology. Adult education, general and professional, was carried out by the newly established *Ljudska univerza* (People's University), which organized hundreds of evening minicourses, heavily loaded with ideology.

After the break with the Cominform, followed by the decentralization of Yugoslav society and introduction of **workers' self-management**, changes took place in art, culture, and education. In the school year 1950–1951, there were important reforms in the educational system: The seven-year elementary school was replaced with an eight-year one, Russian was no longer the primary foreign language, and Soviet history textbooks were recalled. Publishing of original Slovene literary works increased, as did translations of works from the West. In 1952 a chain of new cultural and sports **societies**, *Svoboda* (Liberty), was organized on a regional basis, replacing similar ones based in factories. Josip Vidmar and Juš Kozak, opponents of Agitprop control of **literature**, were able effectively to reject **socialist realism**. They introduced contemporary American and European literature in the literary journal *Novi svet* (The New World). In the early 1950s, writers organized a society of their own, *Društvo slovenskih pisatejev* (Society of Slovene Writers), independent of the Yugoslav Alliance of Writers, and the **Museum of Modern Art** organized an exhibition of French modern art. Agitprop was abolished as a separate control structure during the political thaw of the early 1950s. However, this signified only a change of mechanism in League of Communist of Slovenia (LCS) control. In 1956 special committees for ideological questions were formed but had fewer powers than their predecessors. The LCS did not concede its role in these areas until the late 1980s. *See also* COMMUNIST PARTY, OPPOSITION TO; WRITERS, SOCIETY OF SLOVENE.

AGRICULTURAL REFORMS, POST–WORLD WAR II. Yugoslav agricultural reforms were undertaken by implementing three laws: the Law on Agricultural Reform and Settlements (1945), the Law on Farm Cooperatives (1949), and the Law on Farmland Holdings (1953). With these three measures, the Yugoslav government embarked on a devastating agricultural policy more attuned to ideology than to economics of production. A few months after the enactment of the 1945 federal law, the **Slovene National Liberation Council** (*Slovenski narodnoosvobodilni svet*, SNOS) passed the republic law on agricultural reform. Under the slogan "Land to those who work it!" the reform was completed in 1946 through land expropriation. All individual and large institutional landholdings (more than 35 hectares of arable land or more than 45 hectares of all land) were expropriated without compensation. **Catholic Church** organizations were allowed to retain no more than 10 hectares of any land, unless they were exempt due to special historical significance, and were allowed to keep 30 hectares of arable land and 30 hectares of forest. Nonfarmers with more than three to five hectares of land had the excess expropriated, but with compensation. With land confiscated from the German minority and Slovenes who either had left Slovenia or were accused of collaborating with the occupiers, the Land Fund of Slovenia (*Zemljiški sklad Slovenije*) held 266,478 hectares of land, of which over 60 percent was forests. The state retained 85 percent of this land; the rest was given to poor peasants and to those who settled in Apaško Polje and Kočevsko. Although the number of small farms (less than five hectares) decreased, while the number of large farms (between five and 10 hectares) increased, farms were not large enough for efficient and profitable farming. They also were poorly equipped.

The 1949 Law on Farm Cooperatives provided for two types of farmers' organizations. One was the farmers' cooperative (*kmetijska zadruga*, KZ), with roots in 19th-century Slovenia, which assisted private farmers with loans, purchase of seeds, and equipment but involved no pooling of land. KZs were organized anew immediately after the war and served also as buyers, sellers, and processors of agricultural products. In the late 1940s, they became centers of economic, educational, and cultural life in villages. The emphasis of the 1949 law, however, was on collectivization, that is, on the type of farm working **cooperative** called *kmečka delovna zadruga* (KDZ), actually a state farm, in which either state-owned or state-leased private land was worked by worker-farmers who kept enough of their own land to provide for their personal needs. The law provided for four types of KDZ; in the prevalent one in Slovenia, farmers leased their land to the KDZ but remained its formal owners. Although joining a state farm was in principle voluntary, farmers were often coerced into joining. The short and unsuccessful collectivization effort in **agriculture** began in 1949 and reached its peak in 1950–1951, when there were 381 state farms; however, this included less than 5 percent (8,600) of private farms and 3.5 percent (69,300 hectares) of all agricultural land. Since private farms were much more productive than KDZs, farmers were allowed after 1953 to withdraw from them, and KDZs were transformed into KZs or simply abolished.

As farmers were leaving KDZs and acquiring more land, social differentiation in villages became more distinct. The 1953 Law on Land Holdings, which limited private ownership to 10 hectares of arable land, however, was successful in preventing concentration of agricultural land in private hands. The measure remained in effect until 1990. As a consequence of the 1953 law, the average size of individual farms decreased from 8.3 hectares in 1939 to 5.5 hectares in 1981. These agricultural policies caused substantial occupational restructuring, and the share of population engaged in agriculture, which in 1948 had been 49 percent, dropped to 9 percent by 1981.

More farmers joined general farmers' cooperatives, and 70 percent of all farmers were members by 1954. There were 581 general cooperatives in 1958, some with specialized units such as *Agrotehnika* (manufacturing and leasing farm equipment and machinery), *Semenarna* (acquisition of seeds, fertilizers), and *Slovenija-Sadje* (merchandizing of fruits). Eventually, general cooperatives were transformed into independent economic enterprises, and in 1965 they legally acquired the same status as other economic enterprises. The number of cooperatives fell to 65 by 1968. Although agricultural production increased after 1953 and reached the 1939 level in 1956, very little investment was channeled into agriculture. The situation changed, however, after 1968. The cooperative movement was given additional impetus with the establishment of the Association of Cooperatives of Slovenia (*Zadružna zveza Slovenije*) in 1972, and the enactment in 1979 of two laws: one on cooperative self-management, and the other on associations of peasants, both of which pressured society into paying more attention to agricultural policies and development. In the 1980s the number of general cooperatives increased; by 1987 there were 158 with over 100,000 members. *See also* FIVE-YEAR PLAN, FIRST.

AGRICULTURE. Once predominantly agricultural, Slovenia industrialized quickly after **World War II**. In 1931, 58 percent of the population was engaged in agriculture; in 1991, 7.6 percent. The share of agriculture in the gross domestic product (GDP) declined from 20 percent in 1952 to about 5 percent in 1991. The decline was in part due to an economic policy that treated agriculture less favorably than other branches of the economy, and the private sector less favorably than the social one. Since the majority (85 percent) of arable land was owned by individual farmers after World War II, agricultural development was under a double handicap. Agricultural investments were minimal (3.8 percent of total investments in 1952, and 5.6 percent in 1987). On the other hand, agriculture's declining share in the economy is a normal characteristic of a developing, industrialized economy. After Slovenia's **independence** (1991), the GDP share of agriculture with forestry and fishing declined further, reaching 2.4 percent in 2004, slightly up from 2003 (2.2 percent).

Natural conditions for agriculture are poor. Over one-half of Slovenia (56 percent) is covered with forests (similar to Norway), while pastures and meadows take up more than one-half of the remaining land (similar to Ireland). Wooded areas enlarged in the 1990s by about 3 percent annually, and agricultural land decreased from approximately 866,000 hectares in 1990 to 510,000 hectares in 2003. Since 1990, private ownership of agricultural land increased (to 93 percent in 2003), as did the size of individual holdings, the majority of which are still small (on average 10.6 hectares in 2000). The number of individual holdings declined from approximately 112,000 in 1991 to approximately 77,000 in 2003. It is projected that in 2010 there will be about 60,000 holdings. Accounting for about 5 percent of the labor force in 2004, the number employed in agriculture, forestry, and hunting has been falling. However, the percentage of people involved in agriculture part-time is significant: 23.8 percent of total rural population in 2000. Family farms deriving their income also from nonagricultural sources account for 73.8 percent of family farms. Thus, it is safe to conclude that agriculture as an economic branch is more important in the national economy than indicated by official data.

Although both farming the land and animal husbandry are important agricultural branches, the latter is more prevalent in Slovenia than land cultivation because of natural conditions (mountainous terrain). In 2003 agricultural production broke down as follows: animal husbandry, 53 percent; farming, 32 percent; viticulture, 10 percent; and horticulture, 5 percent. Until the mid-1990s, there was a trend toward increased cattle, pig, and poultry production, while the numbers of sheep and horses were declining. Over 50 percent of cultivated land is taken up by fodder (corn), followed by cereals (19 percent), potatoes (10 percent), industrial plants (5 percent), and vegetables (4 percent).

While total livestock production increased in the 1990s and the beginning of the 2000s, the production of poultry, milk, and dairy products decreased in the latter part of the 1990s. Trends show an increase in the production of animal fodder (corn) and industrial crops (sugar beets, rapeseed) and a decrease in cereals and vegetables. Slovenia is self-sufficient in potato production, and it produces large surpluses of hops. Besides farming and animal husbandry, **beekeeping** and **viticulture**, both with long traditions and high-quality products, play an important role in Slovene agriculture.

While Slovenia's possibilities for agriculture are limited (the **European Union** classified 70–75 percent of its farmland as unfavorable), capacities for additional food production lie in organic farming. With new investments in rural development in the 1990s, several organic farms have been established. In 2004 there were close to 400 such farms across Slovenia, except in the northeast region (**Prekmurje**). Most farms are not specialized as to their crop, but some are involved in ecological **tourism**.

Overall food production is far from sufficient for domestic needs; shortages are covered by imports. Slovenia is a large importer of foodstuffs (in order of magnitude: wheat, cooking oil, sugar, beef, and vegetables), and 20 percent of Slovenia's negative foreign trade balance is due to agricultural products and processed foods. Productivity of individual—mostly small—holdings, often run by older farmers or by farm laborers, is lower than their potential. However, despite shrinking farmland totals, agricultural production has been on the rise due to increased yield per hectare. Yet, due to strong protectionist policies, food has been relatively expensive. Since Slovenia's accession to the European Union, Slovenia has had to abolish preferential treatment of farmers and domestic food producers, which face strong competitors from **Austria**, **Italy**, and other EU members. Even before Slovenia's actual accession into the EU, food prices began declining, which contributed to deflation during 2004 and 2005. Although of good quality, Slovenian agricultural products and processed foods remain largely noncompetitive in the European market. Meat and dairy products account for 80 percent of all processed foods, which are exported mainly to the states of former Yugoslavia.

Slovenia's agriculture will be affected by the EU Common Agricultural Policy (CAP) and strategies for gradual inclusion of new economies in the EU. Substantial direct EU subsidies provided to individual farmers will help them adjust to new economic conditions. *See also* AGRICULTURAL REFORMS, POST–WORLD WAR II; COOPERATIVE MOVEMENT; DENATIONALIZATION AFTER 1991; ECONOMY, 1945–1990; ECONOMY SINCE 1991; ENVIRONMENT; FIVE-YEAR PLAN, FIRST; MANUFACTURING; PRIVATIZATION.

ALPHABET WAR / ABECEDNA VOJNA (1831–1833). In the mid-1820s, attempts were made at reforming the Slovene alphabet (*bohoričica*), in use since the mid-16th century. Franc S. Metelko, a grammarian and linguist, in 1825 devised and put into use his revised version of the alphabet (*metelčica*), which was supported by the grammarian **Jernej Kopitar** but opposed by leading members of the literary circle of *Kranjska čbelica* (**Matija Čop, France Prešeren,** Jakob Zupan) as well as by Bishop **Anton Martin Slomšek** and the hierarchy of the **Catholic Church.** In 1831 the controversy turned into a heated polemic, known as the *abecedna vojna* (alphabet war), in which a decisive role was played by Čop with a series of persuasive articles in *Illyrisches Blatt* (Illyrian Bulletin). The alphabet war came to an end when Metelko's alphabet was banned from school use in 1833. In 1824 Peter Dajnko had devised a similar alphabet, *dajnčica*, which remained in use in the eastern parts of Slovenia without much controversy until 1839. Initially a linguistic controversy, the alphabet war later turned into a cultural-political dispute between literary conservatives and progressives.

The alphabet problem ended in 1843 when **Janez Bleiweis** began to use *gajica*, an alphabet devised by Ljudevit Gaj, a Croatian writer and promoter of **Illyrism**, in his newspaper *Novice* (News). Gajica, officially recognized as the Slovene alphabet in 1848, is still in use today. *See also* BOHORIČ, ADAM; DALMATIN, JURIJ; ROMANTICISM.

ALPINE RESORTS. Slovenia's Alpine resorts, located primarily in the country's northwest on the immediate periphery of **Triglav National Park,** are important to the country's **tourism.** Hiking, mountaineering, camping, hunting, and fishing (trout) draw visitors to the **Alps** much of the year, while skiers and skaters come to the **winter sports** centers. Throughout the region there is a wide choice of accommodations, ranging from relatively plush hotels (such as in Bled) to pensions and housing in private homes, or even boarding with farm families (part of ecological tourism).

The three oldest and best-known Alpine resorts are Bled, Bohinj, and Kranjska Gora. Bled, nestled along a lake two kilometers long, was already a fashionable resort in the days of the **Habsburg** Empire; after 1906, vacationers often arrived by train from **Vienna** or **Trieste**. From Bled's castle, which once belonged to the bishops of Brixen, there is a spectacular view of nearby mountains, and on Lake Bled's small island (reached by rowboat) a visit to the church provides a pleasant excursion and an archeology lesson. With its warmish lake, Bled has a long swimming season; it also has thermal baths. Bled is the site of regular rowing competitions and has a popular conference center for both domestic and foreign visitors. Bohinj, also a lake resort, is remote and has a wild, natural beauty. The towering, steep limestone walls of the Julian Alps reach up from the lake's edge to Alpine pastures; the Sava River, which falls spectacularly from its Julian heights near Bohinj, flows through the cold lake, which is four kilometers long. A lift takes tourists and skiers to Vogel, a popular ski center above Lake Bohinj. Kranjska Gora is also a winter sports center, with facilities for international ski meets. Located near Italian and Austrian border crossings, it has many ski trails and can accommodate thousands of visitors. Kranjska Gora is a few kilometers from Planica, where annual international ski-jumping competitions are held.

Two other popular resort areas, whose facilities are newer and growing, are Bovec and Pohorje. Bovec, located in the upper Soča River valley near Triglav National Park, beckons campers, hikers, and rafting enthusiasts in the spring and summer, and in the winter season offers high-altitude (2,300 meters) alpine and cross-country skiing. The highest peak at Bovec is Mount Kanin (2,587 meters), where the skiing season is especially long. Mid-altitude (1,300 meters) skiing is most popular in the Pohorje area, near **Maribor** in Štajerska. Its highest peak is Rogla (1,517 meters), and in its vicinity Slovenia has developed a large major sports training center. Both Slovene and Croatian Olympic ski teams train here. The Pohorje area is also a popular hiking venue year round, where mountain walks are less demanding than in the higher Alps in Slovenia's northwest.

ALPS. Forty percent of the **Republic of Slovenia** (RS) has mountainous terrain, although only a quarter of that, or 11 percent of all Slovenia, has true Alps with characteristic high, steep, rocky limestone peaks. Located in the northwest (the easternmost of Europe's Alpine chain) and reaching altitudes of over 2,200 meters, the three major groupings are the Julian, Kamnik-Savinja, and Karavanke Alps.

The highest peak is **Triglav** (2,864 meters) in the Julian Alps, the republic's best-known geographic feature. The **major rivers** of the RS, especially the Soča and the Sava, are filled by Alpine snow and glacial melting, as are the lakes Bled and Bohinj, which are centerpieces of many **Alpine resorts**. Triglav National Park has some glacial ponds in the higher elevations. The Julian Alps form part of the watershed between two major European water systems: The Soča flows south to Monfalcone into the Bay of **Trieste** in the Adriatic Sea, while the Sava flows eastward to the Danube and the Black Sea. Major passes through the Alps are at Jezersko (Kamnik-Savinja), Ljubelj and Koren (Karavanke), and Vršič and Predel (Julian); the first three connect the RS with **Austria**, the other two with **Italy**. In 1963 the Ljubelj/Loibl tunnel was opened to vehicular traffic; the Karavanke tunnel (a 7,864-meter tunnel through the Alps), opened in June 1991, also links Slovenia with Austria.

Settlements in the Alps are generally small and scattered, although joined by a common Alpine culture and lifestyle. Until the last few decades villagers made their livelihood primarily from farming, herding (dairy), **forestry**, **mining**, and metal forging. Since the 1950s **tourism** has become a major Alpine industry, and to some extent the mountain villages have become bedroom communities for those employed in nearby urban centers. *See also* WROUGHT IRON.

ALPS–ADRIATIC WORKING COMMUNITY. The Alps–Adriatic organization, an association of provinces, regions, and republics of the eastern **Alps** region of Europe, was founded in Venice on 20 November 1978. Parts of **Austria** (Burgenland, **Carinthia**, Salzburg, Styria, Upper Austria), Germany (Bavaria), **Hungary** (the counties Baranya, Győr-Moson-Sopron, Somogy, Vas, Zala), **Italy** (Emilia-Romagna, Friuli-Venezia-Giulia, Lombardy, Trentino-Alto Adige / South Tyrol, Veneto), Switzerland (Ticino), and two republics of former Yugoslavia (**Croatia**, Slovenia) became regular or observing members. The territorial grouping covers about 300,000 square kilometers and has more than 40 million inhabitants. The languages of all the territories are regarded as official languages of the organization. It operates on a modest budget made up of contributions from members.

The community was established to address long-ignored regional interests. After **World War II**, when Europe was still divided into opposing camps, the Alps–Adriatic region, which straddled the postwar East–West border (the Iron Curtain), was artificially divided and the region's concerns became peripheral. Its economic affairs, for example, were not of primary concern to either the East's Comecon or the West's European Economic Community (EEC). In establishing the Alps–Adriatic Working Community, common economic matters could be dealt with regionally. Significantly, when the organization was founded in 1978, an important economic barrier between East and West was breached a full decade before the Berlin Wall came down. Its founding also restored historic political, social, and cultural ties that predated the creation of the area's national states in the late 19th and early 20th centuries. Some have even credited the Alps–Adriatic organization with paving the way toward a united Europe.

The five commissions of the Alps–Adriatic Working Community are: Regional Development and Environmental Protection; Economic Affairs, Traffic, and **Tourism**; Culture and Society; Health and Social Affairs; and Agriculture and Forestry. Over the years the commissions have done much to promote regional dialogue, support research and publications on regional concerns, and realize cooperation on various levels, such as tourism, cultural events, and economic projects. The organization also promotes cooperation in science and learning, and it helped with the establishment of an Alps–Adriatic University in **Klagenfurt** in Austria's province of Carinthia in 2004. Since 2004 most of the community's member units belong to states that have joined the **European Union** (EU) (exceptions are Croatia and Ticino, Switzerland); consequently, Alps–Adriatic has a commission that links it with the EU. Some of its activities and projects overlap with those of the EU.

Slovenia, in the geographic heart of the Alps–Adriatic region, was one of its founding members and continues to be an active participant in the community's various projects. Slovenia's Ministry of Foreign Affairs coordinates work relating to the regional organization. *See also* CENTRAL EUROPEAN INITIATIVE.

ALTERNATIVE MOVEMENTS (1980s). Independent social and cultural groups, otherwise known as New Social Movements (NSMs), emerged in the 1980s, participated in public life, and challenged the existing system in symbolic ways. Calling themselves the Alternative Scene or simply the Alternative, NSMs in 1983 organized a seminar entitled "What Is the Alternative?" and introduced the concept of civil society, which advocated transforming society from totalitarianism to democracy, just as in other European countries.

Punk emerged in 1977 as the first social movement and subculture. Members of several punk music groups (Pankerti was the first, while Laibach was the best known) were harassed by the **police**; their concerts and gatherings were monitored and often prohibited. False charges against punks were spread by the mass **media**, but police persecution failed. Punks not only proved that independent social life was possible but also created a new social and political language, and they initiated a public debate about their persecution by mobilizing the intellectuals and the public at large. The League of Socialist Youth of Slovenia (*Zveza socialistične mladine Slovenije*, ZSMS) legitimized the groups by accepting them into its fold as a legitimate form of youth expression.

Eventually decimated by police repression in the early 1980s, the punk scene was replaced by other special-interest NSMs relating to the **environment, homosexual rights**, peace, the **women's rights movements**, and the **art** groups in **Neue Slowenische Kunst (NSK)**. As these groups were not able to exist independently, the ZSMS became their umbrella organization, providing legitimacy, media for disseminating their ideas, and financial support. The League of Communists of Slovenia (LCS; formerly the **Communist Party of Slovenia**), trying to adjust to new social conditions, tolerated the NSMs, hoping they would fade away. Segments of the public at large were less tolerant, however, fighting the NSMs not for ideological reasons but simply because they were different. Some sociologists described this phenomenon as the "civil society" turning against its own democratic potential with totalitarianism from below. As these attacks on "otherness" intensified, the NSMs worked harder for public support by organizing public events and a stronger presence in the media.

The turning point for the NSMs was the ZSMS congress in 1986, when the ZSMS ceased to be an LCS adjunct and became its own independent political force. The ZSMS adopted the issues of the NSMs as its own political program, declared itself a part of civil society, and began to challenge the LCS openly. By creating a new political force from independent social movements, the Alternative movements ceased to exist as independent political forces. They lost their identity and were marginalized, especially after the **Ljubljana Four trial** and the establishment of the **Committee for the Protection of Human Rights** (CPHR) in 1988. However, alternative culture has been thriving, and after 1992 several groups (gays, lesbians, independent artists) organized their activities in the emerging Metelkova Cultural Center in Ljubljana, the former Yugoslav Army barracks. *See also* HUMAN RIGHTS; LEAGUE OF COMMUNIST YOUTH OF YUGOSLAVIA.

ANTHEM OF THE REPUBLIC OF SLOVENIA. In 1991 the seventh stanza of the **France Prešeren** poem "A Toast to Freedom," set to music by composer Stanko Premrl, was chosen as the anthem of the Republic of Slovenia. It reads (as translated by Janko Lavrin):

God's blessing on all nations,
who long and work for that bright day,
when o'er earth's habitations
no war, no strife shall hold its sway:
who long to see
that all men free
no more shall foes, but neighbors be.

ANTIFASCIST COUNCIL OF NATIONAL LIBERATION OF YUGOSLAVIA / ANTIFAŠISTIČKO VEĆE NARODNOG OSLOBODJENJA JUGOSLAVIJE (AVNOJ). The Antifascist Council of National Liberation of Yugoslavia (AVNOJ) was the central political and representative body of the **National Liberation Struggle** (*Narodnoosvobodilni boj*, NOB) of Yugoslavia. At its founding meeting in Bihać (Bosnia) on 26–27 November 1942, which the Slovene delegation did not attend due to war circumstances, AVNOJ proclaimed itself the supreme political body of the NOB and announced its goal: a reunited Yugoslavia on the basis of democratic federalism. The AVNOJ resolution, whereby Slovenia would join the new Yugoslavia as a free and united nation (including **Trieste**/Trst and **Klagenfurt**/Celovec) with equal rights in a democratic state, was welcomed by the **Liberation Front of the Slovene Nation** / *Osvobodilna fronta* (OF).

The second, historic meeting of AVNOJ, held in Jajce (Bosnia) on 29–30 November 1943, was attended by the Slovene delegation, led by **Boris Kidrič**. AVNOJ elected a state presidency and a government, the National Committee of Liberation of Yugoslavia (*Narodni komite osvoboditve Jugoslavije*, NKOJ) under **Tito**'s leadership. AVNOJ proclaimed itself the supreme legislative and executive body. In 1944 Ivan Šubašić, prime minister of the Yugoslav government-in-exile, met with NKOJ and Tito and accepted the Jajce provisions. The government-in-exile would function as its ministry of foreign affairs. In 1945 the participants of the Yalta Conference requested that AVNOJ include also representatives of other political parties outside the OF who had not collaborated with the Axis powers. At its third meeting, held in Belgrade on 7–8 August 1945, AVNOJ officially became a provisional parliament. *See also* PARTISANS; WORLD WAR II.

ARCHITECTURE, VERNACULAR. There is little evidence of vernacular architecture from before the 15th century. The oldest example still in existence is the *dimnica*, a wooden, one-room, open-hearth dwelling, of which only a few remain. The *dimnica* evolved into a larger building with a "black kitchen," separated from living quarters, to which spaces for storage were added or else built as separate structures (e.g., granary, hayrack). Regional—Alpine, Mediterranean, and Pannonian—variations of this basic house were built later. The building materials varied: stone in Primorska and Istria, logs in the central Slovene regions, and logs and mud in **Prekmurje** and **Bela Krajina**. Straw was the main roof cover, although other materials (wooden shingles in the Alpine regions, slate and stone tiles in the Mediterranean area) were used. Blacksmiths, wood and stone carvers, carpenters, and other self-taught craftspeople and artists added details to architectural structures, which often reflected the owners' prosperity and the art period of the time. Until the late 19th century, houses of regional design with an open-hearth kitchen dominated Slovenia; in the early 20th century, regional differences began to vanish as houses were rebuilt, following trends in urban architecture. Some beautiful examples of Pannonian, Alpine, and Mediterranean houses were saved and restored, but many others were destroyed due to frequent earthquakes, industrialization, and wars.

The most abundant and characteristic wooden architectural structure of the area is the *kozolec* (hayrack), which has been used for drying and storing hay, maize, and other crops. While its age and origin are not known, the oldest illustrations of the *kozolec* date from the 17th century. There are three basic *kozolec* types: a freestanding roofless type, most often found in Primorska; a single, stretched *kozolec* with a roof; and a double hayrack, linked by a roof, found everywhere in Slovenia. The single stretched type, which can also be found elsewhere in Europe, is built with strong upright posts, connected with horizontal beams, and covered with a roof. The double hayrack, known as a *toplar*, which is unique to Slovenia, consists of two parallel single hayracks under a common roof, providing a covered storage area for farm equipment.

Slovenia has hundreds of wayside shrines, often Alpine in character and built since the 15th century. They are found everywhere: in meadows, mountains, towns, villages, and woods. Integrated into the local environment, they have had various functions: commemorative (e.g., of a fatal accident), informational (signposts, way markers), but mostly devotional and dedicated to saints. According to their function and style, wayside shrines vary from simple gothic pillars to small **baroque** chapels. Often a status symbol, wayside shrines were at first the work of talented masons, carvers, and painters but later were frequently built and decorated by amateurs as well. *See also* ARTS; FOLK ART.

A Slovene architectural rarity is the old herdsmen's village of Velika Planina, which has oval, functionally designed houses covered with shingle roofs that reach down almost to the ground; they often provide shelter for animals. This type of structure is regarded by some as a continuation of the old Celtic and Illyrian dwellings. However, the records of the village do not go back beyond the 18th century, and it is claimed that the design of the houses is of a more recent date, the result of adaptation to the environment and local conditions.

ARHAR, FRANC (1948–). Born in **Ljubljana**, Arhar studied law at the **University of Ljubljana**, where he obtained a B.A. (1971) and a Ph.D. (1983). A **banking** specialist, Arhar worked at the National Bank of Slovenia from 1971 to 1988; in the 1980s he was director of its foreign currency section. He continued his career as director of the LHB (International Handelsbank, a member of Nova Ljubljanska Banka) in Frankfurt am Main. Arhar returned to Slovenia in March 1991 and took over the leadership of the National Bank of Slovenia. He was instrumental in establishing the central bank of newly independent Slovenia (Bank of Slovenia) in June 1991, and Prime Minister **Lojze Peterle** suggested him as its first governor; Arhar was confirmed by the parliament to a five-year appointment and reconfirmed in 1996. Although he was not tied to any political party when he returned to Slovenia, he was philosophically close to the **Slovene People's Party**. Since 2001 Arhar has been a director of *Vzajemna*, (The Mutual), an insurance company. In 2002, running as an independent, he was one of the eight candidates for president of the **Republic of Slovenia**. Arhar has lectured on international finance law at the University of Ljubljana and is the author of articles on finance and international business law. *See also* ECONOMY SINCE 1991.

ARMY, SLOVENE / SLOVENSKA VOJSKA. The Slovene Army (SV) has its roots in the territorial defense system established in the late 1960s and early 1970s, when Yugoslavia was rethinking its military organization and strategy. Called the General People's Defense (*Splošna ljudska obramba*, SLO), the new security component was authorized by law and implemented by 1974. It was envisioned as an auxiliary to the **Yugoslav People's Army** (JNA) and intended to focus on regional matters. In Slovenia, where the republic's authorities supervised its operations, the Territorial Defense of the Republic of Slovenia (*Territorialna obramba republike Slovenija*, TORS) evolved into a virtual republican army, backed by a growing "nation-in-arms" mentality. This was increasingly evident after the spring of 1988, when four Slovenes were tried and sentenced to prison terms for betraying military secrets—the charge involved classified military documents that implicated the JNA with planning military operations against Slovenia. In the fall of 1990 the Slovene assembly took control of the TORS, after removing the TO from JNA jurisdiction by constitutional amendment. (Slovenia's future minister of defense, **Janez Janša**, had been one of those imprisoned in 1988.) The amendment was a step toward Slovene **independence**. *See also* LJUBLJANA FOUR TRIAL.

When the **Ten-Day War** broke out in Slovenia in late June 1991, the TO together with the **police** defended the republic against JNA forces. Major General Janez Slapar, trained in territorial defense, headed the republic's successful TO encounter with the JNA. After the **Brioni Agreement** in July 1991, the JNA began its withdrawal from Slovenia, a task completed by the end of October. The TO thus became Slovenia's army, and Slovenia's president its commander-in-chief. But for the next four years—while the wars in former Yugoslavia continued—Slovenia's thinking about security and defense remained in flux, and the traditional TO system stayed in place. It had after all been successful, and it had strong backers, particularly in the person of Janez Janša, who as defense minister hoped to keep control over the military. The TO operation was formalized in April 1992 and required all men at age 18 to perform seven months of military service, followed by a reserve obligation. The goal was to have 15,000 on active duty, with only 7,000 to 8,000 in uniform at any one time. Most of the 2,300 conscripts called up in 1992 served close to home, in one of Slovenia's seven TO regions. Independent Slovenia's TO was to remain solely a territorial defense, or local defense, organization. Its officers were to be university trained for civilian careers, receiving only auxiliary officer training courses. The emphasis was clearly on part-time soldiering both in the ranks and at the officer level. By the mid-1990s it was evident that Slovenia would be living in a new kind of world. Yugoslavia was no longer. The Cold War had ended, and with it the Warsaw Pact and threats from the east. A unified Europe was emerging and a security system based on the **North Atlantic Treaty Organization** (NATO) was expanding. Regarding its military under such circumstances, Slovenia was "caught between tradition and contemporary existence," according to a noted analyst. Slowly, however, Slovenes began to adjust their views. What emerged by 1998 was a 12-year model for a new military. The ultimate goal, to be accomplished by 2010, was a totally professional army under civilian control. The new military would also be integrated into the NATO system of collective defense. Already in 1994 Slovenia had moved toward such reform when it joined NATO's Partnership for Peace (PfP). The following year it participated with other PfP armies in exercises in the **United States**.

The 1998 plan proposed a reduction of traditional forces and the eventual elimination of conscription as a wholly volunteer army emerged. An army featuring light, flexible, mobile units, suited to cooperation with NATO, was to be developed. At the time NATO was rethinking its operations; ultimately the principle of division of labor among its members and aspiring members was implemented. Slovenia thus developed specializations in mountain fighting, mine detection, and nuclear, biological, and chemical defense. Integrating into the NATO system would allow Slovenia's military to play a role in the world and to work with other nations in doing so. In 1998 the newly emerging professional forces—of which 13 percent were women—began working with international forces. One battalion of its 26 was reserved for international peacekeeping activity (generally **United Nations** supervised). Already in 1998 Slovenia was active in such missions in Bosnia, Kosovo, and Afghanistan, and it also joined a multinational force (together with **Austria** and **Hungary**) in Cyprus. NATO membership has brought Slovenia into an international defense system. Given its small navy and virtually no air force, others are to provide Slovenia with defense in these areas. (Italy protects Slovenia's airspace, for example.) Conscription was abolished in October 2003, nine months ahead of schedule, because volunteers had filled the quota for the year. Draftees were no longer needed. The goal for 2010, as projected by Minister of Defense Anton Grizold, who has choreographed the army's transformation, is to have 8,500 professional soldiers and 4,500 reservists.

ARMY, YUGOSLAV PEOPLE'S / JUGOSLOVENSKA NARODNA ARMIJA (JNA). The JNA grew out of the wartime **Partisan** military organization that was credited with liberating the homeland—a point that became an article of faith under the new regime. The Partisans in 1944 fought mainly against Germans, and they coordinated efforts with the Red Army on the Danube and cooperated with the Western Allies in the Adriatic. By the close of **World War II** the Partisans had 19 corps, 57 divisions, 218 brigades, and 80 separate units, totaling nearly 800,000 enlisted men and officers. In 1945 when a **Tito–Šubašić** coalition government was established, the army was named the Yugoslav Army (*Jugoslovanska armada*); it was renamed the JNA in 1951. Slovene Partisan units were integrated into it, and except for one, its units became ethnically mixed.

Between the war's end and about 1951, army organization conformed to the Soviet model. A classical standing army replaced the wartime people's defense units and helped to unify and centralize a much fragmented country. Postwar demobilization reduced the size of the military to 400,000. Most continued to serve in the army, but some served in the small navy or in the air force. Military service of two to four years (depending on service branch) was obligatory for men, as was a reserve obligation for men between the ages of 40 and 55. Translated Soviet texts were generally used for military education and training. The standing national army was maintained from the late 1940s to the early 1960s. It was appropriate for Yugoslavia's security needs at the time: defending the frontiers in the north (**Trieste**, **Carinthia**) and to the south (Albania, and Bulgarian and Greek Macedonia). Also, there was the perceived possibility of attack from the capitalist West, and by 1948 the very real danger of invasion from **Cominform** forces (neighboring **Hungary**, Romania, and Bulgaria all had relatively large armies).

Between 1952 and 1968 there was frequent debate about security strategy and military doctrine. Yugoslavia remained outside both blocs and, while the Cold War was at its height, needed to be concerned about both **North Atlantic Treaty Organization** (NATO) and Warsaw Pact forces. By 1958 a new military doctrine articulated the concept of General People's Defense (GPD; *Splošna ljudska obramba*, SLO). Because of the overwhelming military superiority (including atomic weapons) of potential aggressors, the regime decreed that all citizens were to be responsible for defense against foreign attack. The concept was incorporated into the 1963 **constitution**. By 1964 the military was reorganized to include the beginnings of a territorial defense component; however, the traditional services, numbering 350,000 (of which the navy and the air force each had 20,000), still predominated. Military service remained obligatory for all men, and in order to instill a Yugoslav loyalty among conscripts, most were assigned to serve outside their home republics. By the 1960s Yugoslavia had also become virtually self-reliant in arms production, purchasing only technologically advanced and sophisticated weaponry abroad.

The major change in military organization and doctrine came in the late 1960s, significantly, after the fall of the Serb head of the secret police, Aleksandar Ranković (1966), who was a leading proponent of a highly centralized JNA. (The territorial defense system was generally favored by the republics, including Slovenia, which were wary of Serbian hegemony over the JNA.) The Soviet invasion of Czechoslovakia in August 1968 was decisive. It shocked Yugoslavia's leadership into implementing the GPD in earnest, for it was believed that the country might realistically now expect invasion from either NATO or Warsaw Pact troops. A National Defense Law, long under discussion, was hurriedly adopted in 1969. The Yugoslav Armed Forces would henceforth consist of two components: the JNA (army, navy, and air force) and the GPD (territorial defense units). The latter's duties would include reconnaissance, alerting and protecting the public, and integration with **police** units. In practice, the GPD would also implement a comprehensive civil defense program. The 1969 law made the federal government responsible for arming the GPD, while the *občinas*, or communes, established its units. The GPD was integrated into the self-management institutional apparatus that had become a part of the Yugoslav system. *See also* WORKERS' SELF-MANAGEMENT.

After the 1970s there were two defense apparatuses: the JNA, headquartered in **Belgrade**, and the territorial defense machinery, coordinated by republic territorial defense staffs. According to a national defense law (1974) the JNA was officially superior, the ultimate coordinator of military operations. However, there was enough ambiguity built into the new arrangement that jurisdiction was not always clear.

In 1989 the Yugoslav military was reorganized into four war zones, with Slovenia and **Croatia** falling into the northwest zone, in order to improve quality while also sparing expense. By that time, however, coordination and cooperation between the JNA and the GPD had become complicated. The latter was run by self-managing sociopolitical communities accustomed to working through the *občina* and republic assemblies—that is, exercising power from below. In June 1991, when war broke out in Slovenia, the republic's territorial defense sided with the republic against the centrally run JNA. *See also* ARMY, SLOVENE.

ARTS. Art objects found in Slovenia attest to a human presence in the area long before the **settlement of Slovenes**. Among the most distinguished prehistoric art objects are a clay anthropomorphic statue, the Idol from Ljubljansko Barje (2000 BC), and a richly decorated bronze situla (vessel) from Vače (sixth century BC), both kept in the National Museum in **Ljubljana**. Various art objects (ceramics, glass, jewelry, mosaics) were found at numerous archeological sites from the Roman period. A gilded bronze statue of a Roman citizen (fourth century AD), found in Ljubljana (1836), is considered the most beautiful art object from that period. It is exhibited in the National Museum and a reproduction is displayed where the original was found at Congress Square (*Kongresni trg*). *See also* MUSEUMS.

As elsewhere in Europe, medieval art (architecture, manuscripts, plastic art, and paintings) in the Slovene territories was mostly created for religious purposes. Although there were over 2,000 churches and many castles across the Slovene ethnic territory, few are preserved in their original state. Remodeled structures often hid art from earlier periods; for example, frescoes were painted over. High-quality plastic arts and frescoes were produced in all periods of the Romanesque and Gothic. However, these appeared later than in Western Europe and often on a smaller scale. Two wooden statues, *Madonna* (c. 1220) from the Velesovo nunnery and *The Crucified* (early 13th century) from Cerknica, are rare Romanesque art treasures, both on display at the **National Gallery**. Characteristic Gothic frescoes cover the entire interior of several churches, such as the church of the Holy Trinity in Hrastovlje (Primorska region), and are well preserved. The Hrastovlje frescoes, painted by Janez of Kastav (1490), depict several biblical themes; the most remarkable is the Dance of Death, where the inevitability of death for all, regardless of social class, is portrayed. Well-preserved gothic frescoes can also be seen in the church of St. John in Bohinj (unknown painter, early 14th century) and elsewhere in the Gorenjska region, as well as in the churches in Turnišče and Martjanci (**Prekmurje**), both painted by Johannes Aquila (late 14th century). Illuminated medieval manuscripts, such as the Stična manuscript, were created in monasteries, the centers of **medieval culture and art**. *See also* CASTLES, MANORS, MANSIONS; PTUJ; STIČNA MONASTERY.

Although religious art still dominated the Renaissance and **Baroque** periods, the **Academia Operosorum** also promoted secular art and brought foreign artists to the Slovene lands. In addition to several baroque churches with exquisite details—gold leaf and ornate carved wooden pulpits, altars, and sculptures—secular buildings were built, and secular art was created. Influenced by the well-known Italian painter Giulio Quaglio, Franc Jelovšek (1700–1764), a versatile painter, created a local variant of illusionist ceiling painting. Besides native sculptors such as Jožef Holzinger and his teacher Jožef Straub, active in **Maribor**, foreign ones, including the Italians Angelo Pozzo and Francesco Robba, also worked in the Slovene lands. The baroque tradition of painting was continued throughout the 19th century, coexisting with classicism, neoclassicism and **romanticism**. In the Baroque period, **folk art** began to flourish (painting on glass, beehive panels, peasant frescoes). The Layer family painting workshop in **Kranj** created many paintings in peasant baroque style. Leopold Layer (1752–1828), the best known of that school, painted *Mary Help of Christians* at the pilgrimage church at Brezje, which has become a symbol for Slovene Catholics. Classicists Jožef Tominc (1790–1866) and Matevž Langus (1792–1855) were known mostly for their portraits of important townspeople. Romanticism was present in landscape paintings by Marko Pernhart (1824–1871) and Anton Karinger (1829–1870). Influenced by the 17th-century Dutch landscape paintings, Pernhart produced many characteristic panoramas of the Slovene **Alps**. Unlike the **literature** of that era, visual arts did not contribute to the building of a Slovene national consciousness.

In the late 19th century Slovene painters began experimenting with the new art movements of **realism** and naturalism, but their work was not well received. To survive, they traveled and worked abroad (Jurij Šubic and Ivana Kobilca in Paris, **Anton Ažbe** and impressionists in Munich). At the turn of the century an important and unique variant of lyric **impressionism** was created by **Rihard Jakopič** and his contemporaries. At the same time, some visual artists influenced by the Vienna Secessionist movement organized the club *Vesna* (Spring). Its most influential artists were **Maksim Gaspari** (1883–1980) and

Hinko Smrekar (1883–1942), who focused on Slovene topics and pursued an anti-German art program. Accepted by the general public and the Slovene liberal and conservative political establishment, *Vesna*'s artists began using media more accessible to masses (book illustrations, cartoons, drawings, and graphics). At the beginning of the 20th century, some Slovene art institutions were established, including the Slovene Art Society (*Slovensko umetniško društvo*) in 1900 and the National Gallery (*Narodna galerija*) in 1918. *See also* MODERNA.

After **World War I**, impressionism in visual arts gave way to **expressionism**, which coexisted with realism in the 1920s. Avgust Černigoj (1889–1985) was considered the founder of Slovene expressionism/constructivism. Despite large differences, other Slovene painters and sculptors (**Božidar Jakac**, the Kralj brothers, Veno Pilon) also worked in the expressionist style. Already in the late 1920s, the "new reality" (*nova stvarnost*) movement was established, and by the 1930s expressionism vanished. Variants of **social realism** dominated the 1930s, bringing back traditional painting motifs—still life, nudes, and portraits, rural landscapes and cityscapes. In 1937 artists formed the Independents, a modernist group. Its members included painters Zoran Didek (1910–1975), Marij Pregelj (1913–1967), Stane Kregar (1905–1973), and Zoran Mušič (1909–2005), and sculptors such as the brothers Kalin and Lojze Dolinar, most of whom continued to work during and after **World War II**. During World War II, some artists joined the **Partisans**, but many were sent to prisons or to concentration camps. A large opus of drawings was created by them. For example, Nikolaj Pirnat and the brothers Drago and Nande Vidmar were in Italian concentration camps, such as Gonars, where a Slovene painting school was organized in 1942. Painters most often used graphics and drawings to document life and human suffering during the war. The artists' war experiences echoed in their work long after the war, as is seen in Marij Pregelj's work.

After World War II a relatively short period of socialist realism was present in painting and sculpture. By the early 1950s, painters and sculptors had already turned to **modernism**. Among the most prominent were Marij Pregelj (1913–1967) and Gabriel Stupica (1913–1990). Having studied painting in Zagreb, Pregelj worked in various media, including drawings, frescoes, graphics, mosaics, oils, and pastels. In the 1950s he was influenced by West European painters. Pregelj imaginatively solved visual problems through perspective, choice of color, and the use of unorthodox material. His paintings and mosaics show human existential distress and destruction as if he had anticipated his own early death. Pregelj received large public commissions in former Yugoslavia, and his mosaics adorn many public buildings (the Slovene parliament in Ljubljana, the building of the former Yugoslav government in **Belgrade**) and public spaces. Pregelj created an important modernist opus, which can be seen in the **Museum of Modern Art** in Ljubljana and also in Belgrade. A contemporary of Pregelj, Gabrijel Stupica (1913–1990), who also studied in Zagreb, received many awards and wide international recognition for his artwork. His most important recognition was the posthumous selection of his paintings for the international exhibition "Europe, Europe" (Bonn, 1994), which featured the most important 20th-century Central and East European art. Stupica relinquished traditional painting techniques, and already in the early 1950s his work exhibited a total deviation from socialist realism. Best known are his large white canvases with a barely visible coordinate system in which Stupica placed detailed images. His art can be seen at the Museum of Modern Art in Ljubljana as well as in Belgrade and other European cities. A special place in visuals arts also belongs to Stane Kregar and Zoran Mušič. Although Mušič lived and worked mostly outside Slovenia and achieved international fame, they both, with their cosmopolitan and sensitive paintings, influenced the development of visual art in Slovenia. *See also* GRAPHIC ART, INTERNATIONAL BIENNIAL OF.

In the 1960s, other younger painters and sculptors established Slovene abstract modernism. Internationally acknowledged, Janez Bernik (1933–) and Andrej Jemec (1934–) were among the leading figures, both founding members of *Grupa* 69 (Group 69), which boasted several modernist painters and sculptors, such as Jože Ciuha, Adriana Maraž, Kiar Meško, Slavko Tihec, and Drago Tršar. It networked and organized exhibitions and conferences about visual art issues. Holding a dominant position in Slovene visual arts, *Grupa* 69 and the Ljubljana Graphic School enjoyed the regime's moral and financial support in the 1970s. Being critical of new concepts and energy of younger visual artists, *Grupa* 69 was considered conservative and was disbanded in 1980. In the 1960s the avant-garde conceptualist group OHO appeared. Its founding members were Milenko Matanovič, David Nez, Marko Pogačnik, and Andraž Šalamun, who with other collaborators began reexploring *art as life*. Visual artists organized interdisciplinary projects and happenings in nature, involving poetry and **theater**. After the exhibition at the Municipal Gallery of Ljubljana in 1970, the OHO group had problems with its own direction. The group members decided to leave the art world and continued life as *Družina* (a form of commune in Šempas) and their art activities stopped. OHO disbanded in 1971, and the last exhibition of neoconstructivists was in 1972. The "new art practices" were carried on by Nuša and Srečo Dragan in the 1970s and 1980s, but their work involved mostly **film** and video. The most visible video artists since the 1990s have been Marina Gržinić and Aina Šmid (*On the Flies of the Marketplace*, 1999) as well as Marko Kovačič, Zemira Alajbegović, Neven Korda, and Miha Vipotnik.

In the 1970s a new generation of artists challenged the modernist tradition but had no place to exhibit. Later, the Student Culture and Art Center (*Študentski kulturni-umetniški center*, ŠKUC), an important alternative center, provided such a venue for them. In 1979 the Museum of Modern Art organized the retrospective exhibition "Slovene Art 1945–1978," including artists of all generations, thus legitimizing the younger artists. Influenced by the American modernist tradition, the younger artists were trying to create a new visual language. Their efforts led to "the new image" (1980), a movement that included representatives of all generations of painters and sculptors. Objects and the human figure again became the focus of art, as seen in the work of painters Emerik Bernard, Tugo Šušnik, and Metka Krašovec, and the sculptors Lujo Vodopivec, Jakov Brdar, and Duba Sambolec.

Following punk in the late 1970s, music, performing arts, and visual arts created in the 1980s an alternative art scene and socially critical **alternative movements**, such as the **Neue Slowenische Kunst** (NSK) with the graphic arts group Irwin and New Collectivism groups of visual artists, the theater group Scipion Nasice Theatre (with the work *Baptism under Triglav*, 1986), and the music group Laibach. As elsewhere in the Western world, visual arts in Slovenia in the late 1980s and 1990s went through profound changes leading to **postmodernism**, which promoted an interdisciplinary approach and international interconnectedness as a consequence of globalization. In this view art, existing only as social phenomena in a social space, calls for interactive relations between art works and their audience. Art forms (objects, performances) were not thought of as permanent but as site specific. While larger social discourse dominated the retro-avant-garde art scene of the 1980s, postmodernist artists turned to the examination of everyday life and events. A new concept of contemporary art emerged that has embraced diverse art forms, combining architecture, film, painting, photography, sculpture, theater, and video. Resting on traditions of earlier art movements (especially expressionism, OHO, conceptualism, and retro-avant-garde of the 1980s), Slovene artists have created important contemporary art works, known internationally. Among them are Marko Peljhan (*Makrolab*, 1997–2007), Tadej Pogačar (*P.A.R.A.S.I.T.E Museum*), **Marjetica Potrč** (*Hybrid House*, 2003), Apolonija Šušteršič (*Light Therapy*, 1999), Vadim Fiškin (*Another Speedy Day*, 2005) and Tobias Putrih (*Quasi Random #2, A Study on Fuller's Cloud Nine Project*, 2003).

The Museum of Modern Art and ŠKUC venues (Galerija ŠKUC and Kapelica) have promoted and developed contemporary art. Slovene artists are active internationally, and important international shows and art events have taken place in the Museum of Modern Art, including *Epicenter Ljubljana* (1997, curated by Harald Szeemann) and in *Manifesta Worthless (Invaluable)* (2000, curated by Carlos Basualdo), among others. An important portrayal of Slovene contemporary art was presented by Austrian curator Peter Weibel at the second triennial of contemporary Slovene art U3 (1997), for which he not only selected Slovene contemporary works but also noted their connection with earlier movements. Some art projects have taken place in the newly developing center for alternative culture, Metelkova Center, a former army barracks, in Ljubljana.

ASSOCIATED LABOR / ZDRUŽENO DELO. *See* CONSTITUTION OF 1963; CONSTITUTION OF 1974; CONTRACTUAL SOCIALISM; WORKERS' SELF-MANAGEMENT.

ASSOCIATED LABOR, ORGANIZATION OF / ORGANIZACIJA ZDRUŽENEGA DELA (OZD). *See* CONTRACTUAL SOCIALISM.

AUSTRIA, RELATIONS WITH. The northern neighbor of the **Republic of Slovenia** (RS) is the Republic of Austria, a country's whose former empire was home to ethnic Slovenes for centuries. After losing its imperial realm at the end **World War I**, Austria was in disbelief, thereafter nurturing revisionist politics that made the country receptive to Nazism and unification (*Anschluss*) with Germany in 1938. Austria also harbored designs on the **Yugoslav Kingdom** and in 1941, as a part of the German empire, helped divide the kingdom with the Axis allies. Much of the eastern portion of

Slovenia (southern Styria), and also northern Carniola, were annexed to the German Reich immediately; most of the rest of Slovene lands fell to the Germans after **Italy**'s surrender in 1943. Many who acted as Germany's administrators in occupied Slovenia were Austrians. Slovenes, in general, felt little warmth for the Germanizing occupiers. After **World War II**, Germany and Austria were put under Allied occupation. Austria's occupation ended in 1955 with the signing of the **Austrian State Treaty**. Later in the year, the **Federal People's Republic of Yugoslavia** (FPRY), in which Slovenia had its own autonomous republic for the first time ever, signed reciprocal agreements with Austria recognizing the pre–**World War II** border with Austria. Both Yugoslavia and Austria agreed to protect the rights of their respective **minorities**. In Yugoslavia, both the border agreement and the assurances of protection for minorities affected primarily the Slovenes.

Even before the 1955 treaty, Austria and Slovenia began interacting on a limited basis, usually because of mutual regional interests. In the 1960s, the two eased border-crossing restrictions, eliminated visa requirements, and in 1964 opened the Ljubelj mountain tunnel—ushering in the shopping **tourism** of the 1970s and 1980s. Slovenes shopped and banked in Austria (primarily in Carinthia), while Austrians vacationed in Slovenia and in Yugoslav lands to the south. The **Alps–Adriatic Working Community**, established in 1978, which included Slovenia and several of Austria's provinces, including Carinthia and Styria, offered more opportunities for regional cooperation on various levels. On the eve of the war that dismembered Yugoslavia in 1991, a major tunnel through the Karavanke mountains opened, bringing Austrians and Slovenes closer yet.

By then Slovenia was well into its move toward **independence**, about which its leadership had kept the Austrians apprised. As a neutral country, Austria was not able to openly support Slovenia, but Austrian conservatives, particularly Alois Mock, offered assurances. (Austrian socialists were less sympathetic.) In any event, on 25 June 1991, the day independence was declared, representatives from Carinthia and Styria attended the ceremony as a gesture of neighborliness. When the **Ten-Day War** began the next day, southern Austrian border crossings experienced some fighting, as the **Yugoslav People's Army** (JNA) attempted to put down the Slovenes, but only minor damage was done. Austrian–Yugoslav relations came to an end formally on 31 December 1991. Two weeks later the European

Community (EC) and Austria recognized the RS. Austrian–Slovene diplomatic relations were quickly established, and by the summer of 1992 ambassadors were in place. The two countries also maintained consular offices: Austria in **Maribor** and Slovenia in **Klagenfurt** (Celovec) in the heart of ethnic Slovene territory in Carinthia. (Slovenia has honorary consuls in several other Austrian cities, including Graz, in Styria.) In late 2004 a Carinthian Slovene and career diplomat, Valentin Inzko, was appointed Austria's ambassador to Slovenia—indicating a respect Slovenes had rarely received from Austria.

The years since independence produced literally hundreds of bilateral and multilateral agreements involving Austria and Slovenia. As expected, many former agreements with Yugoslavia had to be reaffirmed, but many new agreements were undertaken in several areas: border-crossing issues (including international crime, drug and human trafficking, and international terrorism); commercial ties and economic projects; cooperation during catastrophes and major disasters; customs duties; educational agreements (equivalency examinations at various levels and student exchanges); industrial and technological cooperation; promotion of tourism and **winter sports**; transportation regulations and improvements, such as building roads and tunnels (the Karavanke tunnel), river navigation and **transport** on the Drava (Drau) and Mura (Mur) rivers, and issues relating to railroad traffic; and international participation in a **United Nations** effort in Cyprus, which began in the late 1990s. Agreements were also signed between individual ministries of the two countries. An example is the **European Union**'s (EU) PHARE-financed projects undertaken through the respective **agriculture** ministries (promoting fruit production, subsidized ecological farming), revitalizing the eastern **Alps** by developing the countryside, preserving local culture, and advocating village tourism. Accession to the EU by Austria (1995) and Slovenia (2004), while rendering some bilateral agreements obsolete, put Austrian–Slovene relations on a European footing.

Economic relations between Austria and Slovenia are extremely important. Austria ranks fourth (behind Germany, **Croatia**, and Italy) as a trading partner. Nearly 8 percent of Slovene exports go to Austria, while nearly 9 percent of Slovenia's imports come from Austria. Austria is also Slovenia's most important foreign investor, totaling more than 45 percent of all inward investment. *See also* BANKING AND FINANCIAL SECTOR; ECONOMY SINCE 1991; INTERNATIONAL TRADE AND FINANCIAL TRANSACTIONS.

However, a number of national and cultural issues have been contentious. By treaties of 1923 and 1958, Austria promised to turn over documents pertaining to Slovenes who had lived in the **Austrian Empire** before World War I. The treaties were not honored during the time of either of the two Yugoslavias, but since Slovene independence, agreements have been reached to photocopy the archives (in 1999 for Styrian Slovenes; in 2001 for Carinthian Slovenes). The provenance of the Lippizaner horses also remains an issue. Austria has declared them Austrian and also claimed the official documents, but in Slovenia, where **Lipica** continues to breed the famous white horses, there is hope that membership in the EU will afford a venue for airing Slovene claims to this national treasure. A larger problem relates to the Austrian State Treaty and the fact that Austria does not recognize Slovenia as a signatory. As a consequence Austria has been demanding indigenous status for a German minority in Slovenia and also monetary restitution for loss of "German" property during the days of Yugoslavia. Tedious haggling has gone on for more than a decade. (A major instigator of the Austrian intractability on the issue seems to be Georg Haider, the ultranationalist leader of Carinthia.) The well-being of the Slovene minority in Carinthia is also of great concern to the RS. The final big issue dividing the two countries is the nuclear power plant in Krško. Concerned about seismic activity and a possible nuclear accident, Austria has been pressing Slovenia to close the nuclear plant as soon as possible.

AUSTRIAN EMPIRE (1804–1867). The official name of the state ruled by the **Habsburgs** between 1804 and 1867 was the Austrian Empire. Before then, each Habsburg ruler had many titles, one for each of the many lands—kingdoms, duchies, counties—of the feudal domain. Following Napoleon's example of creating a "French" empire in 1804, Francis I announced the establishment of an "Austrian" empire the same year. The Habsburg rulers' imperial title had until then designated their position in the **Holy Roman Empire**, which Napoleon in 1806 would abolish forever. Although the title "Austrian Empire" presumed a unitary state, centralized and administered from **Vienna**, unity was difficult to manage, the chief obstructionists being the Magyars, who insisted on the independent status of the Kingdom of **Hungary**. Habsburg control over Hungary eroded as the century progressed. By the **Compromise of 1867** a constitutional arrangement was worked out with the Hungarians, creating the

dual monarchy Austria-Hungary. *See also* AUSTRIA; CONSTITU-
TION, AUSTRIAN EMPIRE; HABSBURG RESTORATION, PRE-
MARCH ERA; NEOABSOLUTISM IN AUSTRIAN EMPIRE.

AUSTRIAN PARLIAMENT, SLOVENES IN. *See* COMPROMISE
OF 1867; TAAFFE'S IRON RING.

AUSTRIAN STATE TREATY, 1955. The Austrian State Treaty of 15
May 1955 reestablished an independent and democratic **Austria**. The
primary signatories with Austria were France, the United Kingdom,
the Union of Soviet Socialist Republics (USSR), and the **United
States**—the Allied powers that had occupied Austria, as they had
Germany, since the end of **World War II**. Since Austria technically
did not exist when the war began, having been annexed to Germany
in 1938, the treaty was called a "state" rather than a "peace" treaty.
It prohibited Austrian unification with Germany, Austrian alliances
with any political or military bloc (the Warsaw Treaty Organization
had been established one day earlier), and Austrian possession of
certain types of armaments. Thereafter Austria assumed the status
of a neutral power. The treaty also required Austria to de-Nazify, to
maintain Allied (including Yugoslav **Partisan**) cemeteries, and to
pay war indemnities to the Allies (primarily the USSR).

For the Slovenes, Article 7 of the treaty was the most significant:
It guaranteed the rights of **minorities** in southern Austrian territories.
In November 1955 the Yugoslav government supplemented the treaty
with reciprocal agreements. Yugoslavia guaranteed Austrian minority rights in the **Federal People's Republic of Yugoslavia** (FPRY)
and agreed to abandon claims to Austrian territory. The provisions
of the treaty were added to the Austrian Constitution. Since 1955,
however, the rights of the Slovene minority in Austria have often
been violated.

After Slovene **independence**, which was recognized by Austria on
16 January 1991, the Austrian State Treaty became an issue between
the two countries. Austria's position has been that, since Slovenia was
not a signatory to the treaty or its corollary agreements (the FPRY
was), the treaty was no longer valid. Using this argument, Austria has
been pressing Slovenia to agree to provisions absent from the original treaty. As the issue has dragged on, the Slovenes have passed on
issues relating to restitution of the nationalized property of Austrian
nationals and accepted the clauses on minority rights agreed to by
the FPRY. However, as of 2005, the Austrians continue to insist that

Germans also be recognized as an indigenous **minority** by Slovenia's **constitution**. Slovenia believes this demand is unwarranted, since there are few Austrians (181 according to the 2002 census) in Slovenia and these are widely scattered, not settled compactly near the border. The Slovenes are attempting to solve the issue by securing legal recognition as a successor to Yugoslavia (and hence Yugoslav agreements with other states), a difficult task complicated by the fact that the depository state of the treaty was the USSR (now **Russia**) and the successorship appeal must be handled through the depository county.

AUSTRO-HUNGARIAN EMPIRE. *See* COMPROMISE OF 1867; CONSTITUTION, AUSTRIAN EMPIRE.

AUSTROSLAVISM. Among Czechs, Slovenes, and Croats in the 19th century, prominent cultural and political figures were proponents of Austroslavism. They viewed **Habsburg Austria** as essentially a Slavic state, a protector of its numerically small Slavic groups, and they considered Austria the home of a distinct Western Christian civilization, one common to all its peoples. Austroslavism saved the Habsburgs. In countering German Liberal nationalism after 1848, Austroslavs and **Vienna** were generally allies. **Anton Tomaž Linhart**, who in the late 18th century wrote that Austria was a Slavic state, is regarded as the Slovenes' first Austroslav. **Jernej Kopitar**, the distinguished Slovene linguist of the 1820s to 1840s, was enthusiastic about Vienna as the center of Slavism and its institutions. And on the eve of **World War I**, **Ivan Hribar**, **Ljubljana**'s mayor, noted that the Slavs numerically were about to be the decisive political force in Austria.

AŽBE, ANTON (1862–1905). Anton Ažbe, a Slovene naturalist painter, was one of Munich's most important art teachers. His painting was influenced by the city's art scene at the end of the 19th century. His work is naturalistic (portraits), but his conception of color has more in common with Secessionist artists. Some of his paintings (*A Black Woman, In a Harem, A Bavarian*) are in the permanent collection of the **National Gallery** in **Ljubljana**. In Munich, the Ažbe Art School attracted students from Europe and America. Among them were well-known and respected painters. The Slovenes Ivan Grohar, Matija Jama, Matej Sternen, and **Rihard Jakopič** developed an independent movement in Slovene **impressionism**. Vasili Kandinsky and Alexei Jawlensky in Europe and Hans Hofmann in the United States developed symbolism, expressionism, and abstract movements in painting.

Igor Grabar was among those whose work laid the principles of Russian socialist **realism**. *See also* ARTS.

– B –

BAJUK, ANDREJ (1943–). Although born in **Ljubljana**, Bajuk spent most of his life outside Slovenia, but he welcomed an invitation to become involved in Slovene politics in the 1990s and, as an established economist and young retiree, returned to Slovenia in 1999. Like thousands of other Slovenes, Bajuk's family left the country at the end of **World War II**. The Bajuks spent three years in refugee camps in Austria before permanently settling in Mendoza, Argentina, where Andrej Bajuk grew up and studied. He obtained a B.A. in economics (Universidad Nacional de Cuyo) in Mendoza, an M.A. from the University of Chicago, and a Ph.D. from the University of California, Berkeley. After graduate studies, Bajuk returned to Argentina and taught economics at the university in Mendoza. His academic career was cut short due to political turmoil in Argentina. He and his young family moved to Washington, D.C., where he worked for the World Bank and the Inter-American Development Bank (IADB) until 1994. At the IADB, he held a range of positions, from economist in charge of analyzing social projects to advisor to the bank's executive vice president. For his last six years at the IADB, he was in charge of the office of the bank president and a member of its board of executive directors. In 1994 Bajuk became IADB representative for Europe in Paris, a position from which he retired in 1999.

Following a coalition agreement between the **Slovene Christian Democrats** and the **Slovene Democratic Party**, in 1999 Bajuk was instrumental in developing the coalition's alternative government program. He was also elected deputy president of the newly formed, united Slovene Christian Democrats and **Slovene People's Party** but soon left it over a major disagreement on the reform of the electoral system. In 2000 he became prime minister (3 May–16 November), and in summer 2000 he and his supporters formed a new political party, Nova Slovenia (NSi). His government was short lived, as the **elections** of October 2000 brought back to power the Liberal Democratic Party. In 2000 Bajuk was elected to the parliament and headed the Committee on Finances. In 2004 the new prime minister, **Janez Janša**, appointed Bajuk his minister of finance. *See also* EMIGRATION, SLOVENES IN SOUTH AMERICA AND AUSTRALIA; GOVERNMENT, SLOVENE, AFTER 1990.

BALANTIČ, FRANCE (1921–1944). Born in **Kamnik**, France Balantič was a contemplative and metaphysical poet who belonged to the **expressionist** movement and the pre–**World War II** Slovene **Catholic** literary circle. At age 19 he wrote his first *Sonetni venec* (*Sonnet Wreath*), a formally complex and rare sequence of sonnets. Balantič studied Slavic linguistics at the University of Ljubljana, but his studies were interrupted when the Italians sent him to the Gonars **concentration camp** in 1942. After his release, he joined the anticommunist **Village Guard** and, in the fall of 1943, the newly formed **Home Guard**. Only a few months later, he was killed during a **Partisan** attack on the Home Guard unit in Grahovo. His first collection, *V ognju groze plapolam* (In the Fire of Horror I Blaze), was published posthumously in 1944. Despite his talent, Balantič was, for political reasons, not recognized in Slovenia as a great poet until recently. His collection *Muževna steblika* (Sappy Sprig), although ready for publication in 1964, was not printed until 1984, when Slovenia had begun to democratize. Balantič's *Zbrano delo* (Collected Work), however, was published in Buenos Aires in 1976.

Balantič's life in many ways resembles that of his contemporary **Karel Destovnik-Kajuh**. Although belonging to opposite ideological camps, they were both poets of great talent who died young in battle. *See also* LITERATURE.

BANKING AND FINANCIAL SECTOR. In June 1991 Slovenia adopted the Banking Law and the Law on the Bank of Slovenia (BS). The BS, which functions as a central bank, in October 1991 replaced the Yugoslav *dinar* with the Slovene *tolar* (SIT) and has pursued an active, restrictive monetary policy. The BS has maintained the stability of domestic **currency**, ensured the liquidity of payments, supervised the banking system, and participated in the processes that enabled Slovenia to become a full member of the **European Union** (EU) in May 2004. In June 2004 the BS entered the European Exchange Rate Mechanism II (ERM II), became a member of the European System of Central Banks (ESCB), and had to comply with Europe's methodology for reporting on financial institutions and their dealings. In late 2005, long-term interest rates, the fiscal deficit, the public debt ratio, and inflation were within the Maastricht Treaty limits. This, combined with the Slovene *tolar*'s two successful years within the ERM II, set the stage for adoption of the euro in January 2007. In July 2006 the parity between the SIT and euro was fixed at 239,640 SIT for one euro, which is the central rate at which the Slovene *tolar* entered the ERM II.

Slovenia inherited a monopolistic banking sector, which impeded the development of an efficient financial system. Before **independence** the largest bank, Ljubljanska Banka (LB), with its headquarters in **Ljubljana** and with 13 regional branches, had conducted over 90 percent of the entire banking business. Due to the former Yugoslavia's peculiar system governing the foreign exchange deposit, the LB and smaller banks had had serious financial difficulties paying out foreign exchange deposit when **Yugoslavia** dissolved. They also had a large number of nonperforming loans. Devised by the Bank Restructuring Agency established in Slovenia in 1991, a rehabilitation program for banks was put in place. Immediately after independence, many new banks and other financial institutions were established. The banking industry grew quickly, and the banking system became not only well developed but also overextended for a country of 2 million. In early 1990 there were over 30 commercial banks and 14 savings banks. Of 21 operating banks, 14 were fully domestically owned, while 15 were either minority (11) or majority (4) owned by foreigners. In addition to banks, there were numerous savings and loan institutions and over 70 savings cooperatives. Hundreds of currency-exchange offices operated independently or within existing banks. Several banks (A-Banka, Creditanstalt-Nova Banka, Probanka) have been helped by foreign capital. In addition, branches of foreign banks were also established.

While the LB monopoly was broken, consolidation of financial institutions was also needed, for many financial institutions were unprofitable and inefficiently run. Over the years, several banks and other financial institutions have merged or declared bankruptcy. By 2004 there were only 18 domestic banks and two foreign bank branches remaining. The numerous savings and loan institutions merged into the Association of Savings and Loan companies, renamed Deželna Banka Slovenije in 2004. In order to aid the national **economy**, banks have been adapting their role, from merely collecting deposits to developing investment banking and other financial services as well, thus becoming an important branch of the **service industry**.

During the 1990s the Slovene banking industry was sheltered by the government. In 1993 the LB was the first to be bailed out by it, followed by the Kreditna Banka Maribor (KBM) and the Komercialna Banka Nova Gorica, at a cost of 2.2 billion German marks. Rehabilitation of the two major banks—the LB, reorganized as the Nova Ljubljanska Banka (NLB) and the KBM as the Nova Kreditna Banka Maribor (NKBM)—was completed in 1997. Accelerated

privatization of the financial industry began only after 2000 as one of Slovenia's EU accession strategies. Being able to enter the local market under the same conditions as local banks, foreign banks enlarged their market share of total banking assets, pushed down the interest rate, stimulated long-term investments, and increased lending to the nonbanking sector and households. In 2001 a French bank, Société Générale, acquired the majority share of the largest private bank, Stanovanjsko Komunalna Banka (SKB). Whereas NKBM remains 100 percent owned by the government (as of August 2005), the NLB was restructured and privatized in 2002. The Belgian KBC is a 34 percent co-owner of the NLB. In 2004 the NLB was the largest bank, with 32.4 percent market share of all banks' total assets, followed by the NKM (10.7 percent). The market shares of six other large banks (A-Banka Vipa, SKB Banka, Banka Celje, Banka Koper, Bank Austria, and Gorenjska Banka) vary between 5 and 8 percent. The foreign banks' market share of the banking system's total assets reached 22.7 percent in 2005; foreign banks are expected to play an increasing role in the local financial market. Accession into the EU was beneficial for smaller domestic banks, which in the past had difficulties borrowing funds under favorable conditions. With easier access to money, smaller banks have increased their assets and have become more significant players in the Slovenian financial market.

Banking in Slovenia has had a long tradition. The first bank, Ilirska Hranilnica (Illyrian Savings Bank), later called Kranjska Hranilnica (Carniolan Savings Bank), was established in 1820. Savings institutions owned by Slovenes developed more extensively in the latter part of the 19th century, creating Slovene—in addition to mainly German-owned—capital and helping to integrate the Slovene economy of the time. In the early 20th century, commercial banks, such as Ljubljanska Kreditna Banka (Ljubljana Credit Banka) in Ljubljana, and Jadranska Banka (Adriatic Bank) in **Trieste** (1905) with its branches in Ljubljana and **Maribor** were established. The banking system in the first Yugoslavia, of which Slovene banks were an integral part, consisted of state, semiprivate, and private banks and savings and loan institutions. After **World War II**, a centralist, one-bank system (National Bank of Yugoslavia) was established, but it was decentralized (through opening of local banks) in 1955 and became specialized (through establishment of the Yugoslav Investment Bank, the Yugoslav Export Bank, and the Yugoslav Agricultural Bank) in 1961. In 1971 the Yugoslav monobank system was broken up, with national banks established in individual republics, serving as an example for other communist countries. In the 1980s Slovenia had 16 banks, 14 of which were branches of the LB.

BANOVINA. Shortly after establishing a royal dictatorship and officially renaming his country the **Kingdom of Yugoslavia**, King Alexander reorganized his state administratively from 33 regions (*oblasti*) into nine new administrative units, *banovinas*. The monarch, upon the advice of the prime minister, appointed the *ban*, or *banovina* head. An advisory council, chosen by the minister of internal affairs, advised the *ban*. The 1931 constitution provided for elected *bans* and council members, but those provisions were never implemented. The *banovinas*, named after **major rivers** and the sea coast, were intended to deemphasize national identities. *See also* DRAVA BANOVINA.

BARAGA, FRIDERIK IRENEJ (1797–1868). Friderik Baraga was a missionary, ethnologist, and linguist. After studying law in **Vienna**, he entered the **Ljubljana** Seminary and was ordained as a priest in 1823. Baraga went to the **United States** in 1830 and worked as a missionary among North American Indians of the Great Lakes region. In 1853 he was consecrated the first bishop of the Upper Michigan diocese with its seat in Sault Sainte Marie. Later the seat of the diocese was moved to Marquette, Michigan, where he spent the last two years of his life. Baraga, known as "the Snowshoe Priest," had deep respect for the Native Americans and their culture; he protected their interests and was much liked by them. He was declared a servant of God by the **Catholic Church** and is being considered for canonization.

Baraga wrote several religious books for the Native Americans in their own languages. Most important, he compiled a Chippewa–English dictionary and a grammar of the Chippewa language, which are still in use today. He wrote a book about North American Indians, *Geschichte, Charakter, Sitte, und Gebräuche der nordamerikanischen Indier* (1837), published in Ljubljana in German, in an abbreviated Slovene adaptation, and in a French translation; a complete Slovene translation was published in 1970. A Shrine of the Snowshoe Priest and Baraga's statue were erected in L'Anse, Baraga County, Michigan, in his memory. In 1984 the U.S. Postal Service issued a postcard in his honor. *See also* EMIGRATION, SLOVENES IN NORTH AMERICA; MISSIONARIES.

BAROQUE. The Baroque period in the Slovene lands, beginning in the late 1600s, was dominated by the **Catholic Church** and the **Counter**

Reformation. At the time, intellectuals, including Slovenes, who were organized in **societies** such as the **Academia Operosorum**, wrote in Latin and German. The first natural science, geography, and historical studies of the Slovene lands were produced at this time. Janez Ludvik Schönleben's *Aemona vindicata* (1672) and *Carniola antiqua et nova* (1681) were followed by **Janez Vajkard Valvasor**'s encyclopedic *Die Ehre des Herzogtums Krain* (The Glory of the Duchy of Carniola, 1689).

Until 1768 **literature** was mostly religious; an exception was the *Kranjska pratika* (*Carniolan Almanac*), first published in 1725. Among religious writers, the Capuchin Janez Svetokriški (1647–1714) had five books of his sermons published in the **Slovene language** under the Latin title *Sacrum promptuarium*. Although there was almost no Slovene secular literature at the time, there were folk poems dealing with topics such as **Turkish** invasions, the Thirty Years War, soldiers' life, love, and the cruelty of the feudal lords. *See also* POHLIN, MARKO.

Baroque architecture, painting, and sculpture in Slovenia were influenced either by the Italian baroque or by the style of Graz and **Vienna**. The Academia Operosorum favored Italian baroque, which left Slovenia with numerous works of a high quality in every field—architecture, **crafts**, **music**, painting, and sculpture. The plans for **Ljubljana**'s cathedral (St. Nicholas) were prepared on the ideas of Andrea Pozzo, one of the most important Italian architects and painters of that time. Besides the cathedral, Ljubljana acquired several beautiful baroque churches (the Annunciation, St. Peter's, Holy Trinity-Ursuline) and the town hall. **Maribor**'s **castle** was rebuilt in the baroque style, and Dol, Dornava, and Planina acquired baroque manor houses with landscaped parks. Francesco Robba, an Italian sculptor of the Bernini school, and his contemporaries decorated churches, castles, and town squares. Robba's most famous work, the Fountain of Three Carniolan Rivers, stands in Ljubljana's town-hall square. Many exquisite baroque altars and statues can be found in churches throughout Slovenia (e.g., parish churches in Solkan and Mekinje).

In the Ljubljana region, besides Valentin Metzinger from Lorraine (1699–1759), Slovene baroque painters Franc Jelovšek (1700–1764), Fortunat Bergant (1721–1769), and Anton Cebej (1722–1774) worked in the baroque style, which continued in the Slovene lands until the mid-19th century. Some of their paintings can be seen in Ljubljana's **National Gallery**. Wall paintings and frescoes also were important baroque art forms. Besides many native baroque painters,

Dutch, Italian, and German painters also were active in the Slovene lands, a characteristic of all of Central European arts of that time. Among them, most known was Giulio Quaglio from Lombardy, who painted the ceiling of Ljubljana Cathedral and the Seminary Library. *See also* FOLK ART.

BAVČAR, IGOR (1955–). Born in Postojna, Igor Bavčar was trained at Slovenia's police academy in Tacen and worked briefly as a policeman before completing a master's degree in political science at the **University of Ljubljana** in 1983. While at the university he edited the student paper *Tribuna* and soon became involved in professional politics, first in the League of Socialist Youth of Slovenia (ZSMS) and then in the **Socialist Alliance of Working People** (SAWP). He is best known as a founder and the informal leader of the Committee for the Protection of Human Rights, established in the spring of 1988 in response to the **Ljubljana Four** arrests. The committee mobilized Slovene public support for those (including **Janez Janša**) who were about to be tried for betraying military secrets.

Bavčar, a founding member of the **Slovene Democratic Alliance** (SDZ), was an active and sometimes combative player in Slovene politics. When the SDZ, as part of the **Demos** coalition, was victorious in the **election** of 1990, Bavčar was made minister of internal affairs, a position he held until 1993. The following year, during the **Ten-Day War**, Bavčar as head of the police cooperated closely and successfully with Janša, who then headed the Ministry of Defense. In the spring of 1992, in an attempt to unseat Prime Minister **Lojze Peterle**, Bavčar was put forward unsuccessfully as his replacement. He remained minister of internal affairs until the election of 1992, after which as a member of parliament he represented the **Democratic Party of Slovenia** (DSS), an offshoot of the SDZ split of October 1991. Elected to a second term in 1996, Bavčar soon moved on to a new position. Between 1997 and 2000, and again in the years 2001–2002, he was Slovenia's minister for European affairs. Since 2002, Bavčar has been president of the management board of Istrabenz, a major petroleum products company located in the expanding port city of **Koper**.

BEEKEEPING. Beekeeping, or apiculture, is an old and well-developed activity in Slovenia, introduced when the Slavs settled the region. In 1687 **Janez Vajkard Valvasor** wrote about beekeeping technology in the Carniola **region**, and in 1769 the Slovene Anton Janša was the first to teach apiculture in **Vienna** (beekeeping had been brought under state regulation during **Maria Theresa**'s reign). The products of beekeeping are wax, pollen, royal jelly (used for medicinal purposes), and honey, which until the 18th century was the only available sweetener. Bees thrived in Slovenia, where buckwheat fields and lindens, pines, and firs were plentiful (all of which are being depleted). Bee products are consumed domestically and shipped abroad, the largest producer and exporter being Medex, in **Ljubljana**. The Association of Beekeepers' Societies represents about 206 societies with 7,000 members. Slovenia currently has about 160,000 bee swarms, and Slovenes have an indigenous bee, *Apis mellifera carnica*, which is described as "industrious, tame, frugal, adaptable to various climates, and resistant to illnesses" and has been exported to all continents because of these favorable characteristics.

Beekeeping among the Slovenes is also associated with a unique **folk art** form: paintings on the end-boards of wooden hives. Hive ends (*panjske končnice*) were first decorated in the late 18th century in the Gorenjska region, the art achieving its golden age between 1820 and 1860. The paintings—their varied colors probably helped bees locate their hives—depicted biblical scenes, moral tales, and, later, humorous peasant wisdom. The Museum of Apiculture in **Radovljica** has a large collection of hive ends.

BELA GARDA / WHITE GUARD. The name Bela Garda, or White Guard, was used for counterrevolutionaries during Russia's Bolshevik revolution. During **World War II** it was applied by the Slovene **Partisans** to the **Village Guard** and the Legion of Death. Later, the general term *belogardizem* (White Guardism) was used for the entire anticommunist movement organized by the conservative forces in Slovenia during the war. Slovene anticommunists regard it as a derogatory term. *See also* HOME GUARD; COVENANT, SLOVENE.

BELA KRAJINA. A unique, generally forgotten Slovene **region**, Bela Krajina is located along the Croatian border in the southernmost area of the **Republic of Slovenia** (RS) between the Kolpa River, the slopes of Kočevski Rog, and the western Gorjanci mountain range. It is part of the Slovene **karst** area, open to the south and east, closed to the north and west. Its mountains are wooded, while hilly slopes descend to flatlands covered with vineyards. The region has few surface rivers, the most important of which are the Kolpa, which forms the border with Croatia, and the Lahinja (both of which flow through protected local parks), and the Dobličica, which provides drinking water for the region. With little rainfall, Bela Krajina has a mild **climate** (with Pannonian and Mediterranean influences), a favorable condition for wine production and fruit growing.

About 600 square kilometers in size, Bela Krajina is sparsely populated. In 1991 the region had 25,000 inhabitants in two main subregions: the lowlands with the municipal ties (*občinas*) of Črnomelj (5,854 inhabitants) and **Metlika** (3,225 inhabitants). The third administrative district, the Semič *občina*, with its seat in the small town of Semič (1,905 inhabitants), was established in 1995. By 2002 the population increased to 27,000 inhabitants, including a few hundred Roma (*Romi* in Slovene). Bela Krajina and a large part of the traditional Dolenjska region constitute Southeastern Slovenia (2,675 square kilometers), the largest of the twelve statistical regions in Slovenia, with its center **Novo Mesto**. *See also* MINORITIES IN SLOVENIA.

Settled since the late Stone Age, Bela Krajina was called Pannonia Superior in Roman times; later it was a part of the Kingdom of **Hungary**. In the 12th century, Albert of Višnja Gora, who conquered the land, annexed it to the **Holy Roman Empire**. An important military border province (Möttlinger Mark) with its own governor, Bela Krajina had a great deal of autonomy until the 16th century. During the period of Turkish raids, the region acquired its name Bela Krajina (*Weisskrain* or White Carniola) and also acquired Serb and Croat refugees (Uskoks), who had fled the Turks. At the end of the 16th century, the Serbs settled permanently; some villages, such as Adlešiči and Bojanci, have a Serbian minority. Metlika and the larger Črnomelj flourished as medieval towns, leaving a spiritual imprint on Bela Krajina's architecture and **art**, which was mostly sacral. The pilgrimage site Tri Fare (Three Parishes), at Rosalnice near Metlika, comprises three churches built in the Gothic style with baroque decor added later. These churches are among the area's most beautiful historical monuments.

Overpopulation and natural disasters (droughts, hail, and phylloxera, which destroyed most of the vineyards at the end of the 19th century) forced economic **emigration**. Between 1896 and 1911, almost one-fourth of the population left the region, most for North America. Bela Krajina, with its meager karst land, was a poor agrarian region with almost no industry; over 85 percent of the population were farmers. Long secluded, the region had a meager **transportation** network. Its first link with Dolenjska was the railway Metlika–Novo Mesto, built in 1914. Two roads—one crossing the Gorjanci at Na Vahti pass, the other via Roško Polje near Semič—are the only connectors to the rest of Slovenia. During **World War II**, Bela Krajina was a **Partisan** stronghold, and the first Slovene Communist government was established here. *See also* PARTISAN-CONTROLLED TERRITORIES.

Industrialization of Bela Krajina, which began in the 1950s, has changed the social structure of the region (most are worker-farmers). Various industries have developed: in Črnomelj, food, wood, and metal processing; in Metlika, textile **manufacturing**; and in Semič, household appliance production. Modest development of industry, however, has polluted the fragile karst, especially near Semič. Polychlorinated biphenyls (PCB), the waste from condenser production, have affected the groundwater and the Krupa River. Due to social changes after 1990 and world market conditions, the region's industry had to restructure and downsize. The clothing manufacturer Beti in Metlika, for example, went from over 2,000 employees (1995) to approximately 450 (2005). Some manufacturers were forced to close; one of these was Belsad, a food processing firm and sister company of Beti in Črnomelj. Registered unemployment in Bela Krajina has been above the national average, higher in *občina* Črnomelj than in Metlika. Besides fruit growing and cattle breeding, wine production has remained Bela Krajina's most important agricultural activity; 20 percent of all Slovene vineyards are in this region, and they have recently become renowned for their excellent wines. With its white birches and vineyards, **folk traditions**, and cultural and historical monuments, the idyllic Bela Krajina and the Kolpa River (the warmest river in Slovenia, also a relatively clean one, suitable for swimming) offer favorable conditions for development of **tourism**. *See also* VITICULTURE.

BELGRADE. After **World War I**, Belgrade was the capital of royal Yugoslavia: the **Kingdom of Serbs, Croats, and Slovenes** (1918–1929), renamed the **Kingdom of Yugoslavia** (1929–1941). It was also the capital of communist Yugoslavia after 29 November 1945: officially the **Federal People's Republic of Yugoslavia** (1946–1963), renamed the **Socialist Federal Republic of Yugoslavia** (1963–1992). As such, it was the political capital of the Slovenes who lived in Yugoslavia. Slovenes who began to work and study in Belgrade after 1918 initially constituted a small community of about 1,000. After **World War II**, particularly in the 1950s and 1960s, that community grew to as many as 10,000, who engaged in a lively cultural life in the Yugoslav capital.

Unlike **Vienna**, which had been the Slovenes' capital before 1918, Belgrade was not a major European city. In the early 19th century, it was still a frontier Turkish fortress town, having come under Ottoman rule in 1521. The city and its surrounding region, the pashalik of Belgrade, was ruled by an Ottoman administrator. During the course of the century, **Austrians** and **Russians** meddled and fought in the area, Turks were slowly driven out, and Serbs who lived in the outskirts of Belgrade displaced Ottoman administrators in the city. Slowly, too, Serbian tribal leaders came to power, and by 1878 Serbia was recognized at the Congress of Berlin as a new European state, with Belgrade as a capital. Initially Serbia was a small state, but by 1918, with the wartime defeat of its neighbors—Austria-Hungary, the Ottoman Empire, and Bulgaria—Serbia fortuitously found itself at the core of the newly created "Yugoslav" state. *See also* KARADJORDJEVIĆ.

In 1991 the territory over which Belgrade was a capital began to disintegrate. First Slovenia and **Croatia** and then Bosnia-Hercegovina and Macedonia seceded from Yugoslavia. In 1992 the remaining parts of the country were called the Federal Republic of Yugoslavia. In April 2002 the country's name was changed to Serbia and Montenegro, reflecting the growing wish of Montenegrins for greater autonomy. In May 2006 Montenegro went its own way, and Belgrade once again was capital of Serbia alone.

BLED. *See* ALPINE RESORTS.

BLEIWEIS, JANEZ (1808–1881). A journalist, politician, and veterinarian, Janez Bleiweis was a pillar of the Old Slovenes political grouping and was considered the first political leader of Slovene peasants and craftspeople. He was a moderate and practical politician who advocated autonomy in the Slovene lands of the **Austrian Empire**. Bleiweis encouraged the development of **agriculture**, animal husbandry, and **crafts**. He was also an important agent for vocational education **publishing**, in 1843 beginning the journal *Kmetijske in rokodelske novice* (*Agricultural and Craftsmen's News*). Under his leadership, *Novice*, where Slovene literati published their work, played an important role in reforming and standardizing the orthography of the Slovene **language**. Bleiweis wrote several books but had little artistic talent or appreciation for **literature**, which was evident from his enthusiastic support of **Jovan Koseski** and lukewarm relations with **France Prešeren**. *See also* ALPHABET WAR; REALISM; ROMANTICISM.

BOHORIČ, ADAM (c. 1520–1598). Adam Bohorič was a Slovene humanist, linguist, and teacher who studied in Protestant Wittenberg and attended lectures by Philip Melanchthon. His major work, *Arcticae horulae*, was the first Slovene grammar, written in Latin and published in Wittenberg in 1584, the same year and place as **Jurij Dalmatin**'s Bible. Bohorič also compiled a small dictionary (German–Latin–Slovene) and texts for teachers who taught catechism and religion to children in Slovene. Bohorič's Slovene orthography, *bohoričica*—a Latin script adapted to Slovene phonetics—was used by writers of the Slovene **Protestant Reformation** and after, until mid-19th-century linguists revised it. Bohorič's grammar was used exclusively for two centuries, until new grammars were written in the 1700s. *See also* ALPHABET WAR; HUMANISM; POHLIN, MARKO.

BREZIGAR, BARBARA (1953–). Born in **Ljubljana**, Barbara Brezigar completed law studies at the **University of Ljubljana** in 1977. In 1980 she became a district state prosecutor in the Ljubjana Public Prosecutor's Office, a department she came to head in 1995. In 1998 Brezigar assumed the position of state prosecutor and continued also to serve on a special task force of public prosecutors fighting organized crime (1996–1999). Politically active in center-right politics, Brezigar served as minister of justice in the short-lived **government** of May–November 2000 of **Andrej Bajuk**. As an independent (and unsuccessful) candidate in 2002, she ran for the presidency of the **Republic of Slovenia** (RS). In 2005 Brezigar began a six-year term as state prosecutor general, elected by parliament, whose members voted along strict party lines for her confirmation. She was the candidate of the center-right coalition.

BRIONI AGREEMENT, 7 JULY 1991. The **European Community**'s (EC) effort in 1991 to mediate the conflict between **Belgrade** and separatist Slovenia and **Croatia** resulted in a declaration, the Brioni Agreement, concluded at **Tito**'s former Adriatic island retreat, Brioni. Three EC ministers met with representatives from the **Republic of Slovenia** (RS) and from Croatia and Serbia. The agreement provided for a cease-fire and a return of federal and republican territorial defense (TD) units to their respective bases, and it allowed Slovenia to retain control of its border crossings, an issue that had provoked the **Ten-Day War**. In addition, both Slovenia and Croatia agreed to delay the implementation of their declarations of **independence** for three months. It was understood that independence three months hence would be dependent upon a continued cease-fire, and that terms of separation would be negotiated at talks to commence on 1 August. The talks, however, did not take place. Whereas the Brioni Agreement did not work for Croatia, where war continued with mounting intensity, it did mark a new beginning for Slovenia. Here the truce held; the Slovene Parliament, after heated deliberations, accepted the Brioni terms on 10 July, and the **Yugoslav People's Army** (JNA) began removing troops and equipment from the RS (completed by 25 October). On 2 October France's President François Mitterand indicated his approval of Slovenia's independence, and on 4 October the EC, meeting at The Hague, announced it would accept independence for former Yugoslav republics, provided they were committed to human rights for national minorities. Consequently, on 8 October, three months after the Brioni Agreement, Slovenia assumed independent status, took over defense of its borders, and announced the introduction of a new **currency**, the *tolar*. International recognition was accorded in early 1992.

BROZ, JOSIP. *See* TITO.

BUČAR, FRANCE (1923–). Born in Bohinjska Bistrica, France Bučar joined the **Liberation Front** (LF) in 1941, during **World War II**. In 1942 and 1943 he spent time in Italian internment camps at Gonars and Novara. After **Italy**'s capitulation, he escaped to Slovenia, joined the Slovene **Partisans**, and in 1944 became a member of the **Communist Party of Slovenia** (CPS). After the war he studied law and earned a doctorate at the **University of Ljubljana** in 1956. He worked for a time in various government institutions and became secretary to the Republican Chamber in the Assembly of the **People's Republic of Slovenia** (LRS). From 1963 to 1978 Bučar was a member of the Department of Public Administration faculty of the Law School in **Ljubljana**. Due to his increasingly critical views of Yugoslav society, which were reflected in his book *Podjetje in družba* (Enterprise and Society, 1972), and his association with the radical **Marxist** group Praxis, Bučar in 1976 was prohibited from teaching at the university and was forced into an early retirement two years later. Besides writing books—*Resničnost in utvara* (1986; published in English in 1989 as *The Reality and the Myth*) and *Usodne odločitve* (Fatal Decisions, 1988)—he became involved in politics. He joined the newly established opposition in the late 1980s and was one of the leaders of the Slovene Spring. After the **election** of April 1990, as one of the most respected members of **Demos**, Bučar was chosen president, or speaker, of the State Assembly of the **Republic of Slovenia** (RS). In the **election of December 1992**, Bučar was reelected to the assembly. In 1994 he was an unsuccessful candidate for mayor of Ljubljana, but he remained in the assembly until 1996.

In the years since Bučar left parliament, he has been engaged in promoting European unity. He helped establish a nongovernmental organization, the Slovenian Pan-European Movement, which has published *Slovenija—Doma v Evropi* (Slovenia—At Home in Europe). Bučar has also been active on the faculty for postgraduate State and European Studies, established at Brdo in 2000. Because of his pan-European vision, he became a favorite candidate of the **Party of Young People of Slovenia** (SMS) in the presidential election in 2002, where he ran unsuccessfully against **Janez Drnovšek**.

BUDGET. *See* FINANCES AND BUDGET.

– C –

CANKAR CULTURAL CENTER / CANKARJEV DOM. The Cankar Cultural Center, named for **Ivan Cankar**, one of Slovenia's greatest writers, is a multipurpose cultural and conference center located in **Ljubljana**. Built in 1981, the spacious (38,000 square meters), technologically equipped center has five halls, which are adaptable to different needs and can accommodate about 4,000 visitors. It also has seven conference rooms, an **art** gallery, and many smaller spaces designed for special purposes. Over the years, it has become Ljubljana's most important cultural venue, hosting concerts, plays, **films**, and exhibitions, which are attended annually by nearly half a million visitors from across Slovenia. In the regular season, concerts performed by the Slovene Philharmonic and the RTV Ljubljana Symphony are well attended. Cultural activities are subsidized by the Ministry of Culture, and most cultural events are affordable. More than 80 percent of the center's use is devoted to cultural activities and the remainder for convention **tourism**. Many international professional conferences and congresses have taken place in the Cankar Center, which is known for its skill at organizing conferences. The best attended events are usually educational or cultural lectures, roundtable discussions, seminars, and workshops as well as musical events. The center has offered programs with international guest artists and has also sponsored events abroad.

CANKAR, IVAN (1876–1918). A poet, short-story writer, novelist, dramatist, and polemicist, Ivan Cankar studied in **Ljubljana** and **Vienna**. His poverty-stricken life and the social situation in **Austria** at the end of the 19th century influenced his political views and permeated his writing. A prolific writer (his collected works encompass 30 volumes), Cankar is the key figure in modern Slovene **literature** and **theater**, influencing contemporaries as well as later generations. As the main representative of Slovene **Moderna**, Cankar began his literary career with the publication in 1899 of the collection of poems *Erotika* (Erotics) and short stories *Vinjete* (Vignettes), which marked the beginning of a new literary period.

Cankar was a master short-story writer. His stories were published in several collections; among the best known are *Hlapec Jernej in njegova pravica* (The Farmhand Jernej and His Justice, 1907), *Moje življenje* (My Life, 1913/1914); *Moja njiva* (My Field, 1914), and *Podobe iz sanj* (Dream Images, 1917). In many of the stories, he described his relations with his mother, and his story *Skodelica kave* (The Cup of Coffee) is known to every Slovene child. Cankar's analysis and critique of Slovene cultural, political, and social life stand out in several short stories; in the essays *Krpanova kobila* (Krpan's Mare, 1906) and *Bela krizantema* (White Chrysanthemum, 1910); in the novels *Tujci* (Foreigners, 1901), *Na klancu* (On the Slope, 1902), and *Hiša Marije Pomočnice* (The House of Mary Help of Christians, 1904); and in the plays *Za narodov blagor* (For the People's Welfare, 1901), *Kralj na Betajnovi* (The King of Betajnova, 1902), *Pohujšanje v dolini Šentflorjanski* (Scandal in St. Florian's Valley, 1907), and *Hlapci* (Servants, 1910), which is Cankar's most popular play.

His work was influenced by fin-de-siècle European literary figures such as Paul Verlaine, Charles Baudelaire, Henrik Ibsen, Leo Tolstoy, Fyodor Dostoyevski, and Friederich Nietzsche, giving Cankar a prominent place not only in Slovene but also in European literature. Cankar influenced his contemporaries, but his work has been an inspiration for later generations of prosaists and playwrights, including **expressionists** in the 1920s, **social realists** in the 1930s, and **modernists** after **World War II**. His works have been translated into several European and other languages (including Chinese), and several of his works are available in English. Most international attention has been given to Cankar's story *Hlapec Jernej in njegova pravica*, which has been translated into all major languages. Although embedded in the Slovene/Austro-Hungarian context of the 19th century, the story deals with a universal theme—the struggle of the ordinary person for justice—and as such it has become a canon of workers' literature. Politically, Ivan Cankar was drawn to socialism. Through his friend **Etbin Kristan**, he became briefly involved in the Yugoslav Social Democratic Party. In 1907 he ran for Parliament but was not elected. Cankar's greatest political impact was made in 1913, when he delivered a famous speech, "Slovenes and Yugoslavs," calling for the creation of a Yugoslav federal republic in which each national culture and language would have autonomy. Cankar died at age 42 due to the influenza epidemic in 1918. The largest monument to Ivan Cankar is the **Cankar Cultural Center** in Ljubljana, built in 1982.

CANKAR, IZIDOR (1886–1958). In 1918 Izidor Cankar, an **art** historian, became a member of the National Council in Zagreb. An advocate of South Slav unification, he coauthored the "autonomist" declaration formulated by Slovene intellectuals in 1921. It held that above all the new state should not curtail the independent cultural development of Slovenia. From 1936 to 1947 he devoted his time to diplomacy, serving as Yugoslav ambassador to Argentina, Norway, Canada, and Greece. In 1944 he was also education minister in the Yugoslav government-in-exile in London. Cankar tried to persuade the **Catholic Church**, the **Home Guard**, and the royal government not to collaborate with the occupiers but rather to join the **Partisans**; his efforts were in vain, however, and he resigned. In 1920 Cankar established the Chair of Art History at the **University of Ljubljana** and the Society for Art History. The **National Gallery** in Ljubljana was reorganized under his supervision, and he was the initiator of the Modern Gallery. He was also a co-founder of the **PEN Center**. *See also* JAKOPIČ, RIHARD; SLOVENES, CROATS, AND SERBS, NATIONAL COUNCIL OF.

CARINTHIA/KOROŠKA REGION OF RS. Bordering on **Austria**, Slovene Carinthia is a forested, mountainous area including the Pohorje and Karavanke mountains, in the eastern **Alps**; it is crossed by three river valleys: Drava, Meža, and Mislinja. The region (1,041 square kilometers) encompasses 5 percent of Slovenia, with a population of about 75,000 living mostly in small historical towns such as Dravograd, Radlje ob Dravi, Ravne na Koroškem, and **Slovenj Gradec**, the regional administrative, economic, and cultural center. Slovene Carinthia's principal and long-established economic activity is **manufacturing**, mainly metal, **textiles**, and food processing, which account for one-half of the region's GDP, followed by **agriculture** (animal husbandry and **forestry**) and, in recent decades, **tourism** (skiing, farm tourism). The Meža valley, with hydroelectric plants, **mines**, smelting, ironworks, and other manufacturing plants, is the most industrialized area in the region and is also rather polluted.

Settled since the late Stone Age, Carinthia was populated by the Celts in the Iron Age. The Romans arrived in the late first century BC; Slavs followed in the mid-sixth century AD. The Roman town of Colatio, today's Slovenj Gradec, and Dravograd, Radlje, and Ravne, established in the 12th and 13th centuries, were prosperous settlements enriched with religious architecture and **art**, especially during the **baroque** period. The natural beauty of the land was enhanced in the 16th century by folk **architecture**, still in existence today. In the 17th century, charcoal-making, glass craft (known from Western Europe to Constantinople), ironworks, and mining developed and thrived for centuries. The Drava River was the most important **transportation** route and linked the region with the rest of the world until a railroad was built in the late 19th century. In the 19th century, one of the largest ironworks in the **Austrian Empire** was built in Prevalje. The world economic crisis at the end of the 19th century and the wars in the 20th century hindered the industrial development of the region.

Until the early 20th century, Carinthia was part of the former **Habsburg** duchy of Carinthia, which was divided among Austria, **Italy**, and **Yugoslavia** after the collapse of the **Austro-Hungarian Empire.** Slovene Carinthia began to develop again after **World War II** through rapid industrialization supported by newly constructed hydroelectric plants on the Drava.

CARNIOLA. *See* REGIONS OF SLOVENIA.

CASTLES, MANORS, MANSIONS. In Slovenia, around 800 different sites have at least traces of early **medieval** castles, Romanesque tower castles, elegant Gothic and high Renaissance palaces, and **baroque**-rococo manors and mansions. The oldest castle in Slovenia, Brestanica, now in ruins, dates back to 895. Ascetic, Romanesque castles can be seen at Bled, Hmelnik, **Kamnik**, Podsreda, and **Ptuj**. The style gave way to more comfortable Gothic residences such as those at Jama, Stari Grad, Turjak, Vurberk, Žovnek, and Žužemberk. At the time of the **Turkish** invasions, Renaissance castles became fortified; examples are found at Bogenšperk, Ig, Otočec, Polhov Gradec. The prosperity of the 17th and 18th centuries was reflected in the baroque architecture of castles such as those at Brežice, Dornava, and **Maribor**, which were built on flatland or hills, surrounded by beautiful parks. Baroque castles and mansions were cultural centers, housing the earliest galleries, **museums**, and rich libraries. A number of castles and manors were located in the Dolenjska **region** along the Krka River, which is called the Slovene Loire.

With the abolition of feudalism, castles and manors often deteriorated in the hands of private owners. Many were destroyed or extensively damaged during **World War II**; those remaining were nationalized and became state property. However, several castles were renovated and became city museums and cultural centers, such as the beautiful castle Rottenturn in **Slovenj Gradec** and Gewerkenegg in **Idrija**, which in 1997 was proclaimed the best museum of technical and industrial heritage in the **European Union** (EU). Lack of financial resources coupled with a negative attitude toward feudal history further endangered castles, manors, and mansions.

About 50 castles are still functional, but some are in bad shape and the rest are in ruins. Some serve as cultural (Bled, Brežice, Maribor), educational, or social institutions (Zemono), or hotels (Mokrice, Otočec, Štatenberg), or are **tourist** attractions, such as the picturesque Predjamski Grad near **Postojna**. In the center of **Ljubljana** alone, besides several mansions and palaces, there are Ljubljana castle, Tivoli castle, and Cekinov castle, all of which are currently cultural institutions. With **denationalization**, some castles and manors were returned to their original owners or their heirs, who struggle with the upkeep.

CATHOLIC ACTION / KATOLIŠKA AKCIJA (KA). Catholic Action, an organization for lay cooperation in the apostolic work of the **Catholic Church**, was formed by Pope Pius XI in 1927 for the purpose of fighting liberalism, secularism, and socialism. In the **Ljubljana** diocese, KA was organized in 1928 by Bishop **Anton Bonaventura Jeglič**, and in the **Maribor** diocese by Bishop Anton Karlin. At the outset, Slovene KA was not an independent organization but a vehicle for cooperation among various existing Catholic organizations and societies. It tried to be nonpolitical, but after the 1931 Papal encyclical *Quadragesimo Anno*, some of its groups became politically active. The abolition in 1929 of the **Slovene People's Party** (SLS) and all other ethnically defined organizations, such as **Orel** (Eagle), created a political vacuum for Slovene conservatives. This void was partly filled by KA, which under a new charter (1936) became an independent and elite organization for Catholic renewal. KA consisted of eight units, established for students, workers, peasants, and teachers—with separate units for men and women—and was led by a national committee. Prominent leaders were Joža Basaj and Ernest Tomc and the priests **Lambert Ehrlich** and Anton Odar. After 1936 the KA leadership tried to dominate all Slovene Catholic organizations. This tendency was especially obvious at the university in the Akademska zveza (Academic Union), which united Catholic students. Mladci (the Young Ones), led by Tomc, wanted to organize all student organizations as professional associations and control them from outside. This idea was opposed by other groups of Catholic university students: Straža (Guard), under Ehrlich's influence, and Zarja (Dawn), under **Edvard Kocbek**'s influence, wanted to operate on the principle of pluralism and autonomy. While Mladci and Straža, although very much at odds with each other, were staunch anticommunists, members of Zarja were prepared to cooperate with the **communists**. In the late 1930s, Akademska zveza weakened and split into three opposing groups of Catholic students. This ideological split among Catholics continued during **World War II**: the liberal element joined the **Liberation Front** (LF), while the other two supported the **Slovene Covenant**, the **Village Guard**, and the **Home Guard**.

CATHOLIC CHURCH. Catholics constitute the largest religious denomination in Slovenia. According to the 1991 census, 72 percent of Slovenia's population was Catholic, whereas the 2002 census recorded only 58 percent. The difference in numbers is explained, in part, by the fact that a larger number of respondents did not answer the religious affiliation question, and a larger number identified as atheist than had previously. A separate Slovene ecclesiastical province, the Ljubljana metropolitanate (*Ljubljanska metropolija*), established in 1968, encompassed the entire **Republic of Slovenia** (RS) and initially consisted of the archdioceses of **Ljubljana** and the dioceses of **Maribor** and Koper—altogether 66 deaneries and 796 parishes as of 2003. In April 2006, Pope Benedict XVI announced the reorganization of Slovenia's Catholic Church, creating the new diocese of **Novo Mesto** within the Ljubljana archdiocese and elevating the Maribor diocese to an archdiocese and metropolitanate with two new dioceses at **Celje** and **Murska Sobota**. In 1983 there were about 1,295 Catholic priests in Slovenia, but the number has been declining steadily. Twelve male and 16 female **religious orders** are active in Slovenia. At the time of the 2006 reorganization, there were 827 diocesan priests and 806 members of male and female religious orders.

The spiritual life of the Slovene Church has been directed by the Slovene Bishops' Conference, headed by Franc Kramberger, archbishop of Maribor. The Conference includes the archbishop of Ljubljana, **Alojz Uran**, who succeeded **Franc Rode** in 2004, Msgr. Metod Pirih, bishop of Koper, and five auxiliary bishops from Ljubljana, Koper, and Maribor. Its several committees deal with the church's pastoral, educational, social, and charitable activities. Slovenia's Karitas, a charitable organization established in 1990 by the Slovene Bishops' Conference, and a member of the International and European Karitas, is well known and has worked with the government on social issues. Since 1990 the Catholic Church has also published extensively. The most important Catholic publisher is Družina, with its wide assortment of publications on history, **literature**, philosophy, and **religion**. Since 1952 it has published *Družina (Family)*, a Catholic weekly, which is a very popular and has one of the largest circulations among the Slovene weeklies.

Political changes since multiparty elections in 1990 have provided a freer atmosphere for the church and its activities. In 1990 new legislation allowed the church to organize social services and legalize existing religious schools. The **Constitution of 1991** provided, as in Western Europe, for freedom of religion and guaranteed the church the right to engage in a broad range of religious and secular activities. Negotiations in 1999 between the Vatican and the **Republic of Slovenia** (RS) began regularizing relations between the two entities. In spite of the opposition from various political groups, a concordat between the two was signed in December 2001. It was ratified by the Slovene parliament only in January 2004, after the Constitutional court had ruled that the agreement did not violate constitutional separation of church and state. The agreement provided for independent and autonomous functioning of the Catholic Church within the legal system of Slovenia; it also allowed for further negotiations between the RS and the Vatican on unresolved issues. The Catholic Church continues to seek greater influence in Slovene social life, particularly in public **education**.

The Catholic Church has organized religious education for children, youth, and adults within individual parishes. It runs a dozen kindergartens and four college preparatory high schools, which have been part of the Slovene educational system since 1990 and are mostly financed by the state (80 percent). The Faculty of Theology was one of the original departments of the **University of Ljubljana** (1919); it was excluded from the University in 1952 but reinstated in 1992. Since 1990 a number of Catholic professional **societies** have been established, such as the Association of Catholic Managers, the Society of Catholic Professionals, and the Society of Catholic Educators; all have local branches across Slovenia. *See also* CATHOLIC CHURCH, HISTORY OF; MISSIONARIES; SOCIETY OF ST. HERMAGORAS.

CATHOLIC CHURCH, HISTORY OF. Christianization of the Slovenes began in the eighth century, while administrative organization of the **Catholic Church** in the Slovene lands was established during the Carolingian Renaissance (10th and 11th centuries). As Christianization spread, a network of dioceses and parishes evolved. Two archdioceses, Salzburg and Aquileia, included most of the lands with a Slovene population. Among the dioceses, **Ljubljana**'s, established in 1461, was the first of real importance for the Slovenes. From the 12th century on, important religious, cultural, social, and economic work was done by the **religious orders**, which had ties to the rest of Europe. Various factors, leading to the **Protestant Reformation**, weakened the Catholic Church. The Reformation, however, although important for the Slovenes culturally, was short-lived. Re-Catholicization of the Slovene areas began at the end of the 16th century and was directed by the Lavantine bishop Jurij Stobej and the Ljubljana bishop Tomaž Hren. *See also* COUNTER REFORMATION.

The **Enlightenment** reforms, introduced in the late 18th century, changed the status of the Catholic Church. Vienna asserted controls over it, many religious orders and monasteries were abolished, borders of existing parishes and dioceses were redrawn, and new parishes were established. In the Slovene areas at the time, Slovene clergy were very active in the **arts, sciences**, and culture and helped stimulate a Slovene national awakening. Although the 18th-century reforms of **Maria Theresa** and **Joseph II** weakened the political and economic role of the clergy, the Catholic Church remained a strong factor in Slovene society, especially in its cultural and educational life. In 1805 the Catholic Church tried to regain control over **education**. After the abolition of the **Illyrian Provinces**, the Catholic Church received state support for its activities. The ties between church and state became stronger still after the 1848 revolution, and the Concordat of 1855 gave the church almost complete control over social and cultural life until 1870.

In the 19th century, some changes in church administrative organization took place; the most significant was moving the seat of the Lavantine diocese from St. Andrä im Lavanttal (Št. Andraž) to **Maribor**, where pastoral and cultural activities blossomed under the leadership of Bishop **Anton Martin Slomšek**. By the end of the 19th century, old religious orders had been reestablished, including the **Jesuits**, the Cistercians (1899), and Carthusians (1899), and new ones were established, such as the Salesians (1901). Catholic political, cultural, and educational **societies** were formed, as was the Catholic National Party. Extensive political activities by the Slovene clergy, however, precipitated an ideological split within the Catholic community. After 1848 most bishops in the Slovene lands were Slovenes who played an important role in the nation's cultural and spiritual life. A special place in the development of the Catholic Church in Carniola was held by Bishop **Anton Bonaventura Jeglič**, who headed the Ljubljana diocese from 1898 to 1930. *See also* CHRISTIAN SOCIALISM; CLERICALS; KREK, JANEZ EVANGELIST.

After **World War I**, because of the formation of the **Kingdom of Serbs, Croats, and Slovenes**, administrative reorganization of the Catholic Church was required: the Lavantine diocese lost to **Austria** some parishes in Styria and acquired new ones in **Prekmurje**; the Ljubljana diocese got two parishes in northern Carniola but had to relinquish to **Italy** authority over its entire western part. While the Slovene Catholic clergy led the resistance to Italianization and Germanization, the official Catholic Church in Italy as well as in Austria supported denationalizing processes. In Slovenia the clergy were very much involved in politics, organizing **Catholic Action** (*Katoliška akcija*), which in the 1930s influenced Slovene political life. The political activities of the Ljubljana bishop, **Gregorij Rožman**, precipitated a political polarization of Slovene Catholics during **World War II**. *See also* KOCBEK, EDVARD; MINORITIES, SLOVENES IN AUSTRIA; MINORITIES, SLOVENES IN ITALY.

During World War II, German and Hungarian invaders sought to weaken the Catholic Church. Six hundred priests were deported from German-occupied Slovenia. In the part of Slovenia occupied by Italians, the clergy, who were anticommunist and politically active, were not repressed because Bishop Rožman effectively protected them. Some priests and lay Catholics joined the **Partisans**, especially in the Slovene Littoral, but many, with the support of the official Catholic Church, helped to organize the anticommunist **Village Guard**, which cooperated with the occupiers. Just before the war's end, over 200 clergy, including Bishop Rožman, retreated to Austria with the Slovene **Home Guard** and thousands of other anticommunists. Many priests who stayed in Slovenia were imprisoned or executed after the war by the Partisans. *See also* TOMAŽIČ, IVAN JOŽEF.

Border changes after World War II affected Catholic Church administration. In 1947 the Vatican appointed special administrators for the Slovene Littoral (the Yugoslav part of the former Italian dioceses of **Gorizia** and **Trieste**-Koper), and for the Slovene part of the Rijeka diocese. An independent apostolic administration for the Slovene Littoral was established in 1964. Pope John XXIII elevated the Ljubljana diocese to an archdiocese (1961), and Paul VI established the Slovene metropolitanate (1968). Also, the **Koper** diocese, established in 1177 and later part of the Trieste-Koper diocese, again became separate in 1977. In 1983 the Slovene regional Bishops' Conference was established, encompasing the Ljubljana archdioceses and the Koper and Maribor dioceses.

Church–state relations after World War II went through various stages. The first period (1945–1953) was one of serious conflicts. Although declaring loyalty to the new communist system immediately after the war, clergy were critical of many state actions (agrarian reform, separation of church and state, abolition of Catholic schools). The conflicts grew serious. A 1953 law required an absolute separation of church and state. In 1945 all Catholic schools (except those for educating the clergy) were abolished. In 1952 religious education ended in public schools , and the Faculty of Theology was excluded from the **University of Ljubljana**. Freedom of **religion** was curtailed, priests were persecuted, and Catholics were ridiculed in the **media** and discriminated against in public life. As an attempt to mitigate the conflicts, the Slovene Catholic Clergy's Society of Cyril and Methodius (*Cirilmetodijsko društvo katoliških duhovnikov*) was formed in 1949.

A more civil era (1953–1966) of church–state relations followed. Control of the Catholic Church was loosened by negotiations, which led to the 1966 protocol between the Vatican and Yugoslavia. The normalizing of church–state relations began. A dialogue was established and substantive problems affecting the Catholic Church, such as construction and restoration of churches, and the renewal of religious orders and the religious press, were dealt with. In 1970 diplomatic relations between **Yugoslavia** and the Vatican resumed.

Also, some 1966 concessions, as interpreted by the church, were curtailed, but the church was granted the right to perform limited public services in 1976. In 1987 a new period in church–state relations began—symbolically—with a discussion of the public celebration of Christmas, and the mass media began to deal openly with questions important to the Catholic Church, which reciprocated by supporting the new democratization processes in Slovenia.

Since the 17th century, the Catholic Church, while working with Slovene emigrants, also sent many **missionaries** to Africa, America, and Asia. *Družba sv. Rafaela* (Society of St. Raphael), established in 1927 in Ljubljana, assisted emigrants between the two world wars. Following the wave of economic **emigration** to Western Europe, which began in the late 1950s, the church became more involved in pastoral activities. In 1959 the Union of Slovene Emigrant Priests and in 1968 a special commission for Slovene emigrants were established in order to relate better to Slovene emigrants.

CELJE. In the rapidly developing **region** of southern Štajerska, Celje is the **Republic of Slovenia's** (RS) third largest city, with a population of 37,834 (more than twice its 1948 size). Located at the crossroads of rail systems—**Vienna** to Celje (1846), extended via **Ljubljana** (1849) to **Trieste** (1857)—and highway networks to Ljubljana, **Maribor**, and **Velenje**, Celje has some unfavorable geographic and climatic features. The Savinja River, on whose banks it is situated, is prone to sudden, violent flooding, and in winter frequent windless days contribute to serious air pollution, which adversely affects the health of Celje's inhabitants.

Celje's most important industry has traditionally been metals and metal products, exemplified by Cinkarna Celje, a zinc factory founded in 1873. Over the years the company, like many in Slovenia, has experienced changes brought on by political and economic necessity. Long before **independence**, Cinkarna became the leading Slovene chemical processing business, emphasizing titanium dioxide production. It became a public limited company in the 1990s and had 1,200 workers in 2003. Its products are tailored to a global market; 72 percent of exports were to the **European Union** (EU) in 2003, the year total Cinkarna sales amounted to 110 million euros. The company also turned its attention to improving Celje's **environment**, having in the past often been cited for the town's noxious air quality. Like Cinkarna, EMO (now Orodjarna EMO), founded in 1948, has reinvented itself.

Originally a producer of mining machinery and equipment, it once had 1,700 employees. Since the 1990s it has privatized and turned its attention to machine tools for the automotive industry, employing over 600. Zlatarna Celje, a 150-year-old company known for fine-quality gold jewelry, also survived in another form. The parent company declared bankruptcy in 1997, while Aurodent, a subsidiary that made dental alloys, continued to profit. The jewelry business was soon resurrected and by 2001 had 33 stores, including branches in other former Yugoslav states. Its profits that year totalled nearly 10 million euros. Aero Celje, a company established after **World War I**, once sold typewriter supplies, and it still features paper products (now including wrapping paper, masking tape, and Post-its) but has added computer supplies like ink cartridges. In 2004 Aero employed 700 and sold 75 percent of its products abroad. ETOL, a company that has made flavorings and perfumes since 1952, produces 60 percent for the export market and has joint venture companies in most Central European states. However, **textile** manufacturing, once an important industry, has floundered and left many workers, mostly women, unemployed.

The newest business in Celje, Tuš, may become its greatest powerhouse. Founded in the early 1990s, the supermarket food distributor has opened stores in every corner of Slovenia. Most Tuš markets also sell appliances and toys and may also have delis, restaurants, cybercafés, beauty salons, and gasoline pumps. Holders of the Tuš Klub card can accumulate points toward various prizes and discounts; online shoppers can download store coupons and recipes from its website. Two regional agricultural products and their processing are of particular importance to Celje's economy: hops (golding) and grapes (for white wines). A teacher training college, a branch of Maribor University, is also located here, and since 1946 Celje has hosted the annual international youth singing festival. Celje puts on an international crafts fair and annual international track and field meets. The town also has its own newspaper and radio station (Radio Celje).

The earliest settlements of the Celje area go back to the Stone, Bronze, and Iron Ages. When the Romans took it (then called Celeia) in 15 BC, it was the most important town in Noricum and was inhabited by Celts, who were later displaced by Langobards (until 568 AD). Slavs settled in the area by about 587. **Medieval** Celje, whose status as a market town was mentioned as early as 1323, became a military and administrative center (1341) and had a thriving economy (financed by Jewish bankers after the mid-14th century). The **Counts** of Celje were particularly powerful in the 14th and early 15th centuries (replaced after the family died out by the **Habsburgs** in 1456) and held vast domains in the region, where they introduced **humanism** and European culture. Many of Celje's **castles**, the town's fortifications, and churches were built during this time. As elsewhere in the Slovene lands, Celje fortified against the Turks in the late 15th century, experienced the spread of **Protestantism** (**Primož Trubar** was for a time assistant pastor here), and had a serious **peasant revolt** (1515)—all of which disrupted development, with effects lasting into the 18th century. Only in the late 1700s did Celje regenerate, spreading for the first time outside its medieval walls.

Slovene cultural and political (1848) activities in Celje faced formidable Germanization pressures. Slovene national unity was nurtured through **reading societies**, newspapers, savings and loan associations (1881), **Sokol** (1890), and a trade society (1893). In 1895 the Celje Slovenes achieved, though temporarily, a Slovene gymnasium. After World War I, when Štajerska was divided between **Austria** and **Yugoslavia**, the Slovene cultural and political position improved; however, the German element was reasonably strong, revisionist, and maintained its own societies. With the rest of Štajerska, Celje was occupied by the Germans in **World War II**, and many of its Slovenes were confined in **concentration camps**, deported, or pressured to Germanize, while the town itself was often bombed by Allied planes.

Celje is an archeological and architectural treasure trove, home to a wealth of Roman ruins, Romanesque and Gothic churches with frescoes from the 14th to 17th centuries, stone sculptures (including a 15th-century Pietà) by Celje artists, and a particularly fine example of a wooden Renaissance ceiling (the knights' hall in the count's castle, which now houses a regional museum). It also has numerous 18th-century **baroque** structures—churches (St. Cecilia's, St. Joseph's), monasteries (Capuchin) with their religious art, and the Old Court (*Prothasijev dvorec*), Celje's most important baroque building. Used by the **Yugoslav People's Army** (JNA) until 1991, the Old Court has been restored, and since 2001 it has been used for official wedding ceremonies.

CELJE, COUNTS OF. An important aristocratic dynasty in the Slovene lands from the 12th to 15th century, with its seat in **Celje**, the Counts of Celje wielded powerful influence in European politics—always siding with winners, first with the **Habsburgs**, later with the Luxembourg dynasty. Through fortuitous politics and marriages, the Counts of Celje acquired much land, including a large portion in the Slovene lands. In 1436 they acquired the status of dukes of the **Holy Roman Empire** and the independent principality of Celje, with their own court system and the right to mint money, and they became a serious obstacle to the Habsburgs' drive toward the Adriatic. The history of the Counts of Celje ended with the sudden death of Count Ulrik II in **Belgrade** in 1456 when his rival, the **Hungarian** king, Ladislas Hunyadi, had him assassinated. It is a typical story of aristocratic rivalries and wars, marriages, inheritances, and successions to the throne. After protracted wars for the Celje succession, the Habsburgs took over their lands, ruling them until the end of **World War I**. Due to strong support of the **arts** and culture by the Celje counts, the town of Celje was an important cultural center in the Slovene lands of the time. The Counts of Celje were also an inspiration to Slovene poets, writers, and playwrights. *See also* HUMANISM; MEDIEVAL CULTURE AND ART; PTUJ.

CELOVEC. *See* KLAGENFURT.

CENTRAL EUROPEAN FREE TRADE ASSOCIATION (CEFTA). In early 1991, after the collapse of communism in the Soviet bloc, representatives from Czechoslovakia (later Czech Republic and Slovakia), **Hungary**, and Poland met at Višegrad and expessed their intention to work jointly toward the goal of European integration. To this end, they pledged to consolidate democracy and nurture a market economy. A formal agreement was signed the following year and came into effect 1 March 1993. In 1996 Slovenia joined these former bloc countries, while Romania (1997), Bulgaria (1999), and **Croatia** (2003) joined later. Slovenia took a very active role in the organization and twice held CEFTA's chairmanship (1997, 2003).

By 2001 CEFTA had completed its transitional period. Customs duties on virtually all industrial goods had been eliminated, and tariffs on **agricultural** products had been reduced or done away with for **trade** within the organization. In 2004, five of the members, including Slovenia, were admitted into the **European Union** (EU), thus automatically ending the CEFTA agreement for them.

CENTRAL EUROPEAN INITIATIVE. In November 1989, within days of the collapse of the Berlin Wall, four Central European states— **Austria**, **Hungary**, **Italy**, and **Yugoslavia**—formed an organization to improve relations and address common regional interests. One pressing concern at the time was that of **minorities** in the region. When Czechoslovakia joined the association, it became known as the Pentagonal (1990), and briefly, after Poland joined, the Hexagonal (1991). When Europe's political boundaries were redrawn because of the breakups of Yugoslavia and Czechoslovakia, the group was again renamed to allow for future expansion. In 1993 this new entity, the Central European Initiative (CEI), was made up of 10 states: Austria, Bosnia-Hercegovina, **Croatia**, Czech Republic, Hungary, Italy, Macedonia, Poland, Slovakia, and Slovenia. Through the end of the 20th century, the group expanded to 17 (Belarus, Bulgaria, Ukraine, Romania, and Albania joined in 1994; Moldavia in 1996; and the Federal Republic of Yugoslavia in 2000). As of 2004 the territory covered by CEI states encompassed 2.4 million square kilometers; the combined population was 260 million. The organization cooperates with groups such as the Organization of Security and Cooperation in Europe (OSCE), the Council of Europe, the World Bank, and also regional organizations. It maintains regular contacts with the **European Union** (EU).

When the organization was established, only one of the states, Italy, was a member of the European Community (EC), now the European Union (EU). The chief goal of the others was to join that association. The CEI assumed the task of implementing the transition, while acting as a forum for cultural, economic, political, and scientific cooperation—with economic priorities perhaps being primary. In 1993 the European Bank for Reconstruction and Development (EBRD) in London began supervising CEI projects, and in 1995 **Trieste** became the headquarters for CEI's Executive Secretariat. Until the end of 1995 the war in the former Yugoslavia still preoccupied states in the region, so little attention was paid to development in the Balkans. In the meantime, the CEI was able to project major transportation links for the future, such as a highway from Trieste to Kiev (Slovenia's portion of that road was completed in 2005). In the second half of the 1990s, CEI focused greater attention on drawing in the states of Eastern Europe. As of May 2004, seven CEI states (Austria, Czech Republic, Hungary, Italy, Poland, Slovakia, and Slovenia) had achieved EU membership.

Unlike the older **Alps–Adriatic Working Community**, which began as an association of provinces or regions within some Central European states, the CEI is a union of states. Prime ministers and foreign ministers are likely to be present at CEI meetings, thereby adding weight to decisions taken by the group. They are certain to weigh in heavily at the annual Summit Economic Forum, begun in 1998 and held each autumn. Slovenia, one of the original members, held the CEI presidency in 2004, and the annual conference held in November at its seaside resort of Portorož drew 1,400 participants and 200 journalists. Bankers, business leaders, members of chambers of commerce and industry, educators, and government officials dealing with economic matters flock to these summits, hoping to strike development deals for their respective states.

CERKNICA LAKE / CERKNIŠKO JEZERO. *See* KRAS/KARST PLATEAU.

CHETNIKS (1942–1945). During **World War II** the noncommunist Slovenes organized three underground legions (Slovene, Sokol, and National); all three recognized General Draža Mihailović, defense minister of the Yugoslav government-in-exile and the leader of royalist forces within **Yugoslavia** (Chetniks), as their commander-in-chief. Unlike the **Home Guard**, the Slovene Chetniks were not supported by **Italy**. Chetnik units, which the **Partisans** called *Plava garda* (Blue Guard), were organized in April 1942. Since their commander, Major Karel Novak, did not recognize the **Covenant** as his superior, the movement eventually split. In 1943 Novak tried to enlarge his groups, asking the **Slovene People's Party** (*Slovenska ljudska stranka*) to supply him with recruits, but without much success. Nevertheless, Chetniks grew in number from 50 to 350 members. After the Italian capitulation in September 1943, the Partisans trapped the main Slovene Chetnik group at Grčarice and completely destroyed it. Smaller groups of Chetniks remained scattered throughout Slovenia, and Major Novak resigned. In his place, Mihailović appointed Colonel Ivan Prezelj, who maintained a small number of Chetnik detachments until the end of the war.

CHRISTIAN SOCIALISM. Christian Socialism began in Central Europe in the late 1860s as a response to the extremes of political and especially economic liberalism (capitalism). It was strong in **Austria** among opponents of German liberalism and extended to Slovene areas, where among the **Clericals** it captured the party's democratic wing after the mid-1890s. The encyclical *Rerum novarum* issued in 1891 by Pope Leo XIII attacking both exploitative capitalism and **Marxist** socialism/communism while urging adoption of Christian socialist principles to address the economic and social dislocations of the time, gave Slovene Christian Socialism theological backing. The conservatives of the Clerical camp, who opposed a democratic social policy, found it increasingly difficult to resist one supported by the pope. When Karel Klun, the leading conservative in the party, died in 1896, Christian Socialism spread rapidly among the young and vital elements in the party. Its work brought a boost in the party's popularity, especially in Carniola.

The leading Slovene Christian Socialist was **Janez Evangelist Krek**. From the mid-1890s until the end of **World War I**, he and his followers established a wide network of workers' organizations, which joined the Yugoslav Professional Union (*Jugoslovanska strokovna zveza*) after 1909 and numbered more than 40,000 by 1914. They also established a less developed system of farmers' **cooperatives**. Among the workers, Christian Socialists had at least as many supporters as the Marxist **Socialists**.

After the collapse of Austria-Hungary in World War I, the Christian Socialists, now in a Yugoslav state, strengthened their union movement and became a stronger political force among workers. In 1931 a new encyclical, *Quadragesimo anno* by Pope Pius XI, drove a wedge between Catholicism and socialism (including the Christian variety). Partly as a consequence of this, the Yugoslav Professional Union and the **Slovene People's Party**, which had become more conservative and corporatist in its thinking, split. The Christian Socialists, although still democratic, moved toward the left politically, with **Edvard Kocbek** emerging as a party leader. In 1941 Christian Socialists joined the **Liberation Front** (LF) linked to **Tito** and the **Partisans**. In 1943, under Communist pressure, they signed onto the **Dolomite Declaration**, dissolving their organization in favor of a united resistance.

CHRISTIANIZATION OF SLOVENES. The lands where **settlement of Slovenes** took place had been Christianized in the late second century AD, and dioceses were established in its provincial capitals. However, except for the coastal areas of Istria, little evidence of this early Christianization remained after the fall of the Roman Empire and several centuries of barbarian invasions. Consequently, when the pagan Slavs arrived in the mid-sixth century the area was pagan as well. Christianity was reintroduced after 745, when **Karantania** became an ally of Bavaria and the Franks. The Slavs' Prince Borut then adopted the Christian religion, suppressing paganism and opening the land to Western missionaries. Some came from Aquilea, but most were sent from the diocese of Salzburg, among them many Irish missionaries who centered their activities in the **Gospa Sveta** area. In 811 Charlemagne made the Drava River the boundary between the two dioceses. Salzburg was by far the more important of the two, continuing its hold for centuries through church authority and vast feudal land holdings in the Slovene areas.

During the reign in Pannonia of the independent Slavic (Moravian) Prince **Kocelj** (869–874), which coincided with the activities of missionaries from Byzantium, a start was made at Slavicizing church liturgy and writings. Kocelj learned the "Slavic" alphabet and plans were made, but not carried out, to teach scholars in neighboring Karantania as well. Consequently, Christianity for the Slovenes retained a firm Western imprint, which is reflected in the use of Latin and, more generally, the Western religious culture and art associated with it. *See also* CATHOLIC CHURCH, HISTORY OF; MEDIEVAL CULTURE AND ART; RELIGIOUS ORDERS.

CLERICALS. Conservatism was first expressed politically among the Slovenes toward the end of the 1860s. Commitment to **Catholicism** and to Rome was its distinguishing feature. However, between 1873 and the early 1890s the conservative national program differed little from that of the **Liberals**. The Clericals, a designation acquired in the 1890s (although the accuracy of the attribution is sometimes disputed by historians), emerged from the conservative camp during a period of shuffling of leadership and philosophical positions. Their party was organized in the early 1890s, gradually coming to dominate Carniola (1908), while it also merged with Catholic parties in other Slovene areas. The name it adopted in 1905, **Slovene People's Party** (*Slovenska ljudska stranka*, SLS), is the one by which it is most commonly known.

The SLS from the mid-1890s had two distinct branches. The first, headed by **Ivan Šušteršič**, was the more traditionally conservative; "For Religion, Home, and Emperor" was its slogan. The other, led by the priest **Janez Evangelist Krek**, was more democratic and **Christian Socialist**. The former worked closely with **Vienna** and had broad support in the countryside, while Krek labored among workers organizing **trade unions**. Together they created a broadly based political force and an economic one as well. The banks, **cooperatives**, and unions, which were established under the auspices of the party, generated an impressive collective capital base for the Slovenes, who in turn reinvested in Slovene enterprises.

The national program of the Clericals was tied to a fear of Germanism, especially if its origin was Protestant Germany, which had a recent history of repressing Catholicism. They worried about Germany's growing influence over **Austria**, particularly after the turn of the century, and they tried to persuade **Vienna** not to think of Austria as primarily a German power. Austria's purpose, the Clericals believed, had always been to defend Christian Europe and Western civilization against the infidel in the Balkans. Prominent in the front lines of that defense stood Austria's South Slavs, who, the Clericals insisted, deserved a state of their own within the **Habsburg** Empire. They promoted trialism, a plan to unite the South Slav lands of the empire, including Bosnia and Hercegovina (annexed in 1908), in a separate state. In effect, the Clericals proposed that the dual monarchy become a triple monarchy, the third unit to be a Yugoslav one, and they hoped that Archduke **Francis Ferdinand**, heir apparent to the throne, would support this proposal. Briefly, in 1912, the Clericals merged their party with the Croat Party of Right, in order to strengthen support for **trialism**. The Croats, led by Ante Starčević, soon dropped out, suspecting that a proposal that included the Slovenes was not realistic, or to their advantage.

Before **World War I**, the Clericals split over Vienna's policy toward the Balkans. During the Balkan Wars in 1912 and 1913, Šušteršič supported the monarchy's anti-Serbian policy, while Krek became increasingly pro-Serb. The rift became even greater during the war, with **Anton Korošec**, a **Styrian** who had risen in the party leadership, backing Krek's position. After Krek's death, Korošec would lead the Slovenes to independence from Austria and to union with the Croats and Serbs in late 1918.

In the period between the two world wars when Slovenia was a part of the first Yugoslavia, the SLS was its strongest party. Its national plan was for economic, political, and cultural autonomy for Slovenia, a program it partially modified when it joined the government in 1927. In 1929 **Yugoslavia** (formerly the **Kingdom of Serbs, Croats, and Slovenes**) became a royal dictatorship; the SLS, like other parties, was abolished. In 1931 the **January 6th dictatorship** established the Yugoslav Radical Peasant Democracy (*Jugoslovanska radikalna kmečka demokracija*), an all-Yugoslav state party (*državna stranka*). In

1933 it changed its name to Yugoslav National Party (*Jugoslovanska nacionalna stranka*, JNS). The Clericals were not active in this party, and when elections were held in 1935, the Clericals boycotted them. The JNS collapsed in 1935 when electoral fraud caused such an uproar that Prince Paul dismissed the prime minister (Bogoljub Jevtić). A new all-Yugoslav state party was organized on the initiative of Paul and the newly appointed prime minister Milan Stojadinović. That party, the Yugoslav Radical Union (*Jugoslovenska radikalna zajednica*, JRZ), brought together part of the (Serbian) National Radical Party (*Narodna radikalna stranka*), the SLS, and the Yugoslav Muslim Organization (*Jugoslovanska muslimanska organizacija*). On the initiative of Anton Korošec, who was the SLS representative on JRZ's executive committee, the JRZ had by mid-1936 decentralized by establishing local and district units by *banovinas*. The first to be established was in the **Drava** *banovina* in November 1935, with Korošec as its president. This decentralization meant for Slovenia, in effect, the resurrection—in all but its name—of the SLS. In June 1936 Korošec was also elected first vice president of the national JRZ, and from 1935 to 1938 he was also the kingdom's minister of internal affairs.

CLEVELAND. In 1900 Cleveland, Ohio, had a population of 381,768 and was the sixth largest city in the **United States**. A leader in the nation's iron and steel production—and the largest producer of steel wire, nails, bolts, and nuts in the world—Cleveland was also an oil refining center for Standard Oil, with a favorable location on Lake Erie, midway between the iron ore mines of the upper Great Lakes and the coal and oil lands of Ohio, Pennsylvania, and West Virginia. The railroad network and good harbor made Cleveland a major port and the greatest iron ore market in the world. Slovenes arrived in search of jobs in the quarter-century before **World War I** when Cleveland's industrial expansion was in full swing. By 1914 the city's population was one-third foreign born, and 20,000 of them were Slovene. At the time, Cleveland was the third largest Slovene city in the world, behind **Trieste** and **Ljubljana**. They were but a portion of the 200,000 Slovenes who immigrated to the United States before World War I due to rural overpopulation in the "old country" of Austria-Hungary, which lacked industrial work to accommodate them.

Mostly unskilled laborers (80 percent were men), the wave of Slovene immigrants settled in five Cleveland neighborhoods: St. Clair, Newburgh, Collinwood, Euclid, and Westpark. Euclid was still rural, full of vineyards, and settled primarily after the war. Westpark was on the west side of the city, near an automobile assembly plant. The rest were on Cleveland's east side, where steel and iron and their products were being manufactured. Many immigrants lived in boarding houses, for the stay was to be temporary, just long enough to save money for a better life back home. Quite quickly, however, the settlements became more permanent as women followed and many of the men became entrepreneurs. Soon each neighborhood had its own groceries, meat markets, saloons, funeral parlors, and clothing and furniture stores—where Slovenes could shop without having to know English—all owned and patronized by Slovenes. Each eastside neighborhood established its own Catholic parish church and elementary school: St. Vitus (1893), St. Lawrence (1901), St. Mary's (1905), and St. Christine's (1925). (In all the United States there would be 39 Slovene parishes.) By 1910, the St. Clair neighborhood also had its own Slovene bank.

Like other immigrants before them, Slovenes in the United States organized societies that provided social insurance benefits: There were three large fraternal organizations and two groups organized by women. Every fraternal organization had local lodges in Cleveland and frequently held national conventions there; Cleveland Slovenes were often society officers. Nine national homes, many established before World War I in Cleveland, became the basis for Slovene social and cultural life. They were supported by the fraternal societies and the rapidly growing Slovene entrepreneurial class, and they were the venue for family weddings, dances, plays, and choral performances. Some of the homes, like the churches, had Slovene libraries—70 percent of Slovene immigrants were literate when they arrived in the United States—and promoted Slovene language classes. They also helped immigrants learn English and promoted education as a means toward economic and social advancement.

Quickly upwardly mobile, Slovenes soon became active in Cleveland politics. By the 1930s five of the 32-member city council were Slovene. The 23rd ward, the St. Clair neighborhood that boasted the largest Slovene parish (St. Vitus), the largest Slovene national home, and the largest Slovene community in America, became a Slovene political fiefdom. By the 1940s a St. Clair Slovene, Frank Lausche, was mayor of Cleveland; he went on to be Ohio's governor, then a U.S. senator. George Voinovich, whose mother was a Slovene, followed in Lausche's footsteps a quarter-century later. Presidential candidates eagerly courted Cleveland's Slovene vote.

Slovenes also kept abreast of political events back home. During World War I, with the increasing likelihood of the collapse of Austria-Hungary, most espoused the idea of a Yugoslav state, although some preferred having a republic rather than the monarchy that was established. During **World War II**, after **Yugoslavia**'s occupation by Axis powers, Cleveland Slovenes quickly became involved in organizations to help the homeland. As Slovenes in the home country split into supporters and opponents of **Tito's** communist resistance/revolution, a rift broadened, too, among Cleveland Slovenes. The chasm between the clerical, church-oriented faction and those who were either liberals or socialists widened after the war. The U.S. government, which had severely restricted emigration from Eastern Europe after 1924, opened its borders a bit to displaced persons, mostly postwar refugees from the area, provided a sponsor and financial backing was forthcoming. This brought a second Slovene immigration that was primarily political, staunchly anticommunist, and church oriented. About 2,500 such Slovenes came to Cleveland in the late 1940s and early 1950s, often settling in the St. Clair neighborhood, which was being vacated by the older immigrants and their offspring, who were moving to the suburbs. The new group rejuvenated the old neighborhood but also heightened the volume of acrimonious factional fighting. The tensions continue to the present, but with the collapse of communism in Yugoslavia and the declaration of Slovene **independence** in 1991, American Slovenes from many political camps lobbied Washington together to recognize Slovenia.

The ties Slovene Clevelanders have for the homeland are deep and strong. Nearly every village has kin in America, and Slovenes in Europe know about Cleveland, even the St. Clair neighborhood, where surely the street was paved with gold, since relatives regularly sent money and, during wars and hard times, provided relief packages. Slovenia's independent government has cultivated political connections with American politicians of Slovene ancestry in order to promote their programs in Washington; often support among Cleveland Slovene Americans was rallied first. For many, Cleveland, with nearly 50,000 Slovene Americans (as of 2004) and thousands more in its suburbs, is a vital Slovene city. *See also* EMIGRATION, SLOVENE; EMIGRATION, SLOVENES IN NORTH AMERICA.

CLIMATE. Slovenia's climate is influenced by three geographic factors: the Adriatic Sea, the **Alps**, and the Pannonian Plain. In areas

—

near the sea, such as the Primorska **region**, the climate is Mediterranean with mild winters and moderate temperature changes. The high Alpine areas have cold winters and cool summers. The Pannonian Plain has a Continental climate, with great temperature fluctuations that produce cold winters, hot summers, and little rain. Precipitation is greatest in the Alps (3,500 millimeters yearly), the least in the east (800 millimeters). Much of central Slovenia is prone to thunderstorms (40 per year average), often with hail. In the cooler parts of the year, mornings in low-lying areas are likely to be foggy; in industrial regions—such as **Ljubljana** or **Celje**—fog, for lack of winds, may last for days, even weeks, producing unhealthy smog. Primorska has the notorious *burja*, a fierce, cold wind with gusts of up to 180 kilometers per hour, which can whip up in any season, but more frequently in winter, descending from the **Kras/Karst** plateau.

COMINFORM CRISIS (1948–1953). In September 1947, as the Cold War was descending upon Europe, Joseph Stalin established the Communist Information Bureau, or Cominform, an institution he would dominate. The purpose of the Cominform was to create cohesion among the European Communist Parties (CPs), including those of **Italy**, France, and the East European states. In Eastern Europe, where the CPs were just coming to power, the Cominform required that they follow the development model established by the Soviet Union (USSR), the only state where communists had ruled before 1945. This included adopting Soviet political and administrative structures, such as a constitution fashioned after the Soviet 1936 constitution, and Soviet-style economic reforms—**nationalization of property**, collectivization of **agriculture**, and rapid industrialization, emphasizing heavy industry. Although the **Communist Party of Yugoslavia** (CPY) was initially among the USSR's enthusiastic and loyal emulators, it soon came into conflict with Moscow and on 28 June 1948 was expelled from the Cominform.

The conflict that followed between the USSR and **Yugoslavia** was personal as well as political—a struggle between Stalin and **Tito** for control of Yugoslavia. The CPY was psychologically stunned by the ouster but continued to adhere to the Soviet model. Meanwhile Moscow charged Yugoslav communists with ideological heresy and directed Cominform members to ostracize Yugoslavia and punish it with economic boycotts. By 1949, however, the CPY's **Marxist** theoreticians (among them **Edvard Kardelj** and **Boris Kidrič**), still professing ideological purity, announced that the USSR, not Yugoslavia, had deviated seriously from the true path to communism. The Communist government of the Soviet Union had become imperialistic, treating the new (post-1945) communist states as colonies because, as the Yugoslav Marxists maintained, the state in the USSR was not "withering away," as Karl Marx had foreseen. The root of the problem was an entrenched party bureaucracy that ruled the state centrally and from above. This was not democratic; rule from below, from the grassroots level, was more what Marx had had in mind.

The Yugoslavs thus proposed to follow the true Marxist road to social democracy by decentralizing party, governmental, and economic institutions. Between 1949 and 1953 the Soviet model was discarded piece by piece. **Administrative socialism** was abandoned in favor of **market socialism**. Decentralization, with the introduction of **workers' councils** and communal political input on the local level, modified central planning. The party, too, was democratized, changing its name to the League of Communists of Yugoslavia (LCY; in Slovenia the LCS), and in February 1953 the Popular Front became the **Socialist Alliance of Working People (SAWP)**. The **Constitutional Law of 1953** formalized the piecemeal changes.

In the end Tito remained in power, for among other things he had support at home and the beginnings of financial support from the West. Stalin died in March 1953, and the new leadership of the USSR would soon reestablish relations with Yugoslavia on a more egalitarian basis. The Cominform, as a goodwill gesture from Moscow, was disbanded in 1956. Meanwhile the Yugoslavs had devised an alternative socioeconomic and political system falling somewhere between Stalinism and capitalist democracy. Yugoslavia's road to socialism would come to be known as **Titoism**. *See also* COMMUNIST PARTY OF YUGOSLAVIA; PURGES, ANTI-COMINFORMIST.

COMMUNIST PARTY OF SLOVENIA (CPS) / KOMUNISTIČNA PARTIJA SLOVENIJE (KPS) (1937–1952); LEAGUE OF COMMUNISTS OF SLOVENIA (LCS) / ZVEZA KOMUNISTOV SLOVENIJE (ZKS) (1952–1990). In Slovenia, the communist movement dates back to 1919 when leftist Social Democrats (part of the *Jugoslovanska socialdemokratska stranka*, JSDS) organized a Workers' Socialist Party of Slovenia, joining the Yugoslav party of a similar name later that year. In 1920 they were united officially in the **Communist Party of Yugoslavia** (CPY). In 1921 there were about 12,000 Slovene party members, a number that dropped to 10 after the CPY was banned later that year. The numbers increased to several hundred in the interwar years, but the Slovene Communists barely survived, particularly after the **January 6, 1929, dictatorship** began. Most Slovene party members served prison terms or lingered outside the country to avoid arrest.

During the interwar years the Slovene Communists were greatly concerned with CPY organization. In 1923 they had already expressed their displeasure with CPY centralism, pressing for national self-determination and a free and united Slovenia within a federation of equal nations (a federated party was, in their view, a necessary preliminary). Although Communists should have been primarily concerned with economic issues, the national question was generally foremost in the Slovenes' speeches and in publications such as *Rdeči prapor* (*Red Banner*) and *Književnost* (*Literature*). In 1934, with **Tito** at a CPY gathering in Slovenia at Goričane, there was talk about national parties within a larger Yugoslav federation, which encouraged the Slovenes. In 1937 at Čebine the promise was realized. The Communist Party of Slovenia (CPS) was established and **Edvard Kardelj** was prominent among its organizers.

Another matter for concern was the growth of Italian and German fascism, for both **Italy** and Germany had territorial designs on Slovene lands. Yet Slovene Communists (and the CPY) were bound to follow the Moscow line, while Germany and the USSR were united by the Nazi–Soviet Pact of August 1939 (which preceded the beginning of **World War II** by one week). The CPY stood by Moscow even after Yugoslavia was invaded on 6 April 1941. The CPS, however, organized an anti-imperialist resistance on 27 April and welcomed all who wished to participate. In 1943 the **Dolomite Declaration** subordinated all elements of the **Partisan** resistance to CPS control.

The CPS, which came to control the Partisan resistance, soon openly instilled it with revolutionary goals and established provisional governing bodies in liberated areas. When the war ended, the Communists took over easily in Yugoslavia. In Slovenia as elsewhere, they instituted one-party rule, abolition of private property, collectivization of **agriculture**, and other measures that conformed to the Soviet model of modernization. That model was modified in the early 1950s (Yugoslavia had been outside the Communist bloc since 1948), when **self-management** and **nonalignment** became cornerstones of

Yugoslav socialism. The party, too, was remodeled in 1952; in Slovenia, it was renamed the League of Communists of Slovenia (LCS; *Zveza komunistov Slovenije*, ZKS).

In the 1960s the LCS, whose members by 1965 numbered 70,000 (the proportion of workers was down, while that of managers and administrators increased), generally moved to liberalize the system. Even Kardelj, in the CPY at the time, was proposing economic and political autonomy for the republics, as well as market economic reforms. Between 1967 and 1972 the liberal reformers in the CPS came to power, led by **Stane Kavčič**. He was ousted by **Belgrade** in 1972, accused of liberalism and Slovene separatism. It was part of a general crackdown by Belgrade against centrifugal forces in the party and the country (especially in **Croatia**), yet the new **Constitution of 1974** affirmed many of the decentralizing principles that had influenced the more liberal Communist Parties, including the CPS, after the early 1960s. *See also* LIBERALIZATION OF THE 1960s.

The 1970s were a less troublesome decade for the LCS, now that it had reasserted party dominance. Party membership grew, reaching a high of 126,437 in 1982, after which it declined slightly due to that decade's economic woes. In the mid-1980s the CPS leadership was rejuvenated. The old guard that had shared the Partisan wartime experience was replaced by a new, considerably more liberal generation. The new leaders, among them **Milan Kučan**, who was elected LCS president in 1986, were less resistant to the dynamic democratization processes that were at work in Slovene society. *See also* CONTRACTUAL SOCIALISM.

In 1988 the LCS became the focus of attention in the Yugoslav political arena. Challenging Belgrade to come to grips with the economic crisis, it also moved toward political pluralism, and the party accepted a multiparty system in late 1989. In January 1990 the Slovene Communist delegation, led by its former president Milan Kučan, walked out of the Fourteenth Congress of the League of Communists of Yugoslavia (LCY), precipitating the fall of that organization. In February 1990 **Ciril Ribičič**, the LCS president, confirmed the independence of the Slovene party. The members adopted a new name—Party of Democratic Renewal (*Stranka demokratične prenove*, SDP)—and prepared for multiparty elections in April 1990. Ribičič's party, unable to form a leftist coalition, lost to the **Demos** coalition, thus marking the end of Communist rule in Slovenia. At a subsequent congress the SDP renounced past party actions and abandoned its bolshevik-revolutionary tradition. *See also* COMMUNIST RULERS; POLITICAL PARTIES.

COMMUNIST PARTY OF YUGOSLAVIA (CPY) / KOMUNI-STIČNA PARTIJA JUGOSLAVIJE (KPJ) (1919–1952); LEAGUE OF COMMUNISTS OF YUGOSLAVIA (LCY) / ZVEZA KOMU-NISTOV JUGOSLAVIJE (ZKJ) (1952–1990).

The Communist Party of Yugoslavia (CPY) was established in **Belgrade**, initially as the Socialist Workers' Party of Yugoslavia, in April 1919. The centrally organized party adopted its new name and joined the Second International the following year. In the 1920 elections it polled the third largest vote (over 12 percent) and soon after was declared illegal.

In the 1920s, the underground party largely restricted itself to intellectual debates. The nationality question (an issue that would divide the party until its collapse in 1990) was a concern throughout the interwar period. In 1923 the party had a major debate on the issue and adopted a resolution allowing nations the right to self-determination and secession; nevertheless, it should be noted that the centralist position, in lively debate, had also been strongly supported by important party elements. When the **January 6, 1929, dictatorship** was proclaimed, the CPY opted for action and embarked on an ill-planned, ill-advised uprising, which was put down by force. The period of state terror and imprisonment that followed resulted in a much weakened party, which did not rally until the mid-1930s. For most of the interwar years, CPY congresses were generally held abroad, and much of the party's activity was supervised by Moscow.

By the mid-1930s, with fascism menacing Europe, the CPY accepted the idea of a Popular Front (1935), and the party began reorganizing into a federation of national units—a development that was sanctioned by Moscow and completed in 1937. A separate **Communist Party of Slovenia** (CPS) emerged during this time. The newly federated CPY moved its headquarters to Zagreb, and **Tito** became its general secretary. Although the Axis invasion of **Yugoslavia** began on 6 April 1941, the CPY declared opposition to it only after the German Reich invaded the Soviet Union (22 June). The CPY, with Tito as military commander, then organized a Yugoslav **Partisan** resistance (**National Liberation Struggle**, NOB) and a revolution. By November 1942 a provisional government—the **Antifascist Council of National Liberation of Yugoslavia** (AVNOJ)—had been established in areas controlled by the Partisans. The party, which in the late

1930s had about 4,500 members, grew with the resistance successes, drawing support from various parts of the country. By the end of the war there were 141,000 regular CPY members, and another 150,000 belonged to the youth organization **League of Communist Youth of Yugoslavia** (SKOJ). An estimated 155,000 Yugoslav Communists had died during the war.

Yugoslavia was declared a republic in November 1945, and after a brief period of coalition government, the Communists, now in charge, initiated a series of revolutionary measures, including agrarian reforms and nationalization of industry. Political parties other than the CPY were outlawed, and the country, although organized and run centrally, was divided into six socialist federal republics, one of which was Slovenia. In foreign relations the CPY relied on guidance from Moscow and the **Cominform** (a reincarnation of the Comintern), established in 1947, until Joseph Stalin expelled the Yugoslavs from the organization in 1948. Some Yugoslav internationalists sided with Moscow, and many were imprisoned.

In 1952 the CPY embarked on a new course. Acknowledging the break with Moscow, and armed with an allegedly clearer understanding of **Marxism**, the Yugoslav Communists set out to build socialism the right way—in the USSR, they asserted, the "new class" of managers and bureaucrats had undermined socialism's progress. The CPY, in the spirit of renewed effort, renamed the party the League of Communists of Yugoslavia (LCY; *Zveza komunistov Jugoslavije*, ZKJ). **Edvard Kardelj**'s socialist self-management and international **nonalignment** were endorsed at this time and became special features of Yugoslav socialism. After Stalin's death in 1953, there was a gradual reconciliation between Belgrade and Moscow, and although Yugoslavia drew nearer to the Eastern bloc, it never rejoined it.

Yugoslav communism's survival ultimately depended on the willingness of its national groups to cooperate. Nationalism, which had been proclaimed extinct by the party, reappeared openly in the 1960s, along with pressure for economic and political liberalization. By the end of the decade, Slovene and especially Croat Communists pushed for greater autonomy in governing their respective republics. Tito alternated between applying federalistic and centralistic policies to balance forces within the state. The **Constitution of 1974**, enacted shortly after the revolutionary years of the late-1960s, strengthened federalism in the party and in the state, yet it also strengthened party authority (the Communists were intent on remaining in control).

The stage was set, however, for the disintegration of both the party and the state. After Tito's death in 1980 (and Kardelj's in 1979), the integrating forces that had balanced nationalism with Yugoslav state interests disappeared. By 1986 the Great Serbism movement, attempting to gain control of both the LCY and the state, met with opposition from Slovenes, and eventually from Croats. In January 1990 the LCY collapsed shortly after Slovene Communists walked out of its final meeting in Belgrade. Multiparty elections were held throughout Yugoslavia that year, and the party lost in all republics but Serbia and Montenegro. The disintegration of the Yugoslav state began the following year. *See also* LIBERALIZATION OF THE 1960s.

COMMUNIST PARTY, OPPOSITION TO (1940s–1950s). Legally, the multiparty system in **Yugoslavia** was restored in 1945 with the Law on Associations, Meetings, and Public Gatherings (*Zakon o združenjih, zborih in javnih zborovanjih*) and later the **Constitution of 1946**. Both allowed political associations, though subject to some restrictions. In reality, however, the Communists were able to assert hegemony. Immediately after **World War II**, the opposition parties, weak and disorganized, were allowed to join the **Liberation Front** (LF), which was renamed **People's Front of Yugoslavia** (*Ljudska fronta Jugoslavije*, LFJ) in late 1945. Because of repression by **Communist Party of Yugoslavia** (CPY), the opposition parties could not follow their political agendas or participate in the 1945 elections. Thereafter, individuals who advocated political pluralism within the LFJ were silenced through purges, treason trials, and executions, which began as early as late 1946. At its Third Congress (1949), the Front also officially adopted the CPY program, thus rendering obsolete all other groups and effectively abolishing political opposition.

Despite the elimination of the CPY's opposition, the criticism of its policies never completely ceased in Slovenia. In the 1940s **Edvard Kocbek**, who called for the participation of Catholics in societal affairs, was the most eloquent critic of the **Communist Party of Slovenia** (CPS) and its role. He was forced to retire and withdraw from public life in 1952. After World War II the only vocal political opposition in Slovenia was the **Nagode** group, which had contacts with opposition leaders in other parts of Yugoslavia, such as Dragoljub Jovanović in Serbia, as well as with former **Slovene People's Party** (*Slovenska ljudska stranka*, SLS) politicians and foreign diplomats.

Members of the Nagode group were charged with treason and prosecuted in August 1947. The **Catholic Church** was considered the most dangerous opposition force, and various measures were taken against it, severely straining relations between the church and the state in the late 1940s and 1950s.

After the purging of liberal elements from the CPY in the early 1950s, opposition views in Slovenia were expressed through cultural institutions such as the **Society of Slovene Writers** and some journals, such as *Beseda* (*Word*) and *Revija 57* (*Review 57*). *Beseda* (1950–1956), whose collaborators were young Slovene poets and writers, was a journal that opened the door to literary and esthetic pluralism by publishing works of contemporary foreign writers (Camus, Joyce, Kafka). The CPS abolished the journal. A nascent informal opposition of intellectuals, many of whom were CPS members, gathered around *Revija 57* (Beseda's successor), which began to deal also with social issues. **Jože Pučnik**, whose critical articles on social issues appeared in *Revija 57*, was sentenced in 1958 to a nine-year prison term; the journal was abolished the same year. The liberalization efforts begun by *Revija 57* were resumed in ***Perspektive*** (*Perspectives*) in the 1960s.

COMMUNIST RULERS (1945–1990). The Communists who came to power in Slovenia (and **Yugoslavia**) in 1945 had been leaders of the **Partisan** resistance and early in the struggle had established their authority in **Partisan-controlled territories**. The party was unlike Communist Parties elsewhere in Eastern Europe whose members had sat out the war in Moscow, only to be brought in at the war's end and empowered by the Soviets. Some Slovene Communists had been trained in Moscow in the 1930s and during the war professed allegiance to Joseph Stalin and the Russian Revolution, but the fact that they had come to power on their own made them a special breed and made a great difference in 1948 in the political fight between Stalin and **Tito** for control of Yugoslavia. Two points are important here: The wartime resistance successes of the Slovene (and Yugoslav) Communists rallied their constituents and gave them an edge over Stalin and the **Cominform**; yet the fact that the Slovenes (and Yugoslavs) had come under communism on their own gave the nation great pause later when considering its predicament under Communist rule.

Although Slovene (and Yugoslav) Communists were considerably less orthodox (i.e., Stalinist) than those elsewhere in Eastern Europe, there were varying degrees of orthodoxy. Among the Slovene party members there were always those who were more rigid, centralist, and **Belgrade** oriented, while other CPS leaders were more liberal and nation or republic oriented. The latter disposition was strongest in the late 1960s (**Stane Kavčič** government) and again in the late 1980s. Many Slovene Communists played important roles in Yugoslavia's federal government, among them **Edvard Kardelj**, **Boris Kidrič**, and Boris Ziherl, who along with Franc Leskošek (minister of heavy industry, 1945–1948) helped to establish postwar Communist rule in the **Federal People's Republic of Yugoslavia** (FPRY). In the late 1960s and early 1970s it was Mitja Ribičič (president of the **Federal Executive Council**, 1969–1971), Sergej Kraigher (president of the SRS Assembly, 1967–1974), and Stane Dolanc, as a CPY functionary, who helped to stanch liberalizing forces in Slovenia (as well as in Yugoslavia). The hard-liner Kraigher reappeared on the federal level as a member (1979–1984) and president (1981–1982) of the collective presidency. Franc Popit, who was head of the LCS Central Committee from 1968 to 1982 and SRS president in the mid-1980s, is also considered a hard-liner. Refer to appendix 1.

COMPROMISE OF 1867. Constitutional experiments in the **Austrian Empire** in 1860–1867 ended with the Compromise of 1867, which created a dual monarchy. **Austria** and **Hungary** became constitutionally separate entities but shared the same **Habsburg** ruler, **Francis Joseph**. He was emperor in Austria and king in Hungary. The two states also shared a common foreign policy, a common defense, and a joint Ministry of Finance. Internally, each was governed by its own constitution. The constitution of Austria provided for a parliament, or *Reichsrat*. Nearly each decade after 1867, the electoral base for the Austrian Parliament was broadened so that by 1906 universal manhood suffrage was achieved. Slovenes, who had initially opposed dualism, voted for it on the promise of greater language rights in schools and administration. By 1873 Slovenes began to organize into political groups (liberals and conservatives), and they traveled to **Vienna** as representatives of their nation. At home, in the provinces, especially in Carniola, they made considerable advances politically. By 1883 Slovenes controlled the Carniolan provincial assembly, and after 1882 the mayors of **Ljubljana** were Slovenes.

CONCENTRATION CAMPS (1941–1945). During **World War II** Slovenes were among those Europeans who experienced the various repressive policies implemented by the Axis powers. Most subjected to such policies were political opponents (Communists, Liberals, and Slovene nationalists of various political persuasions), those considered undesirable social elements (**Jews**, Gypsies/Roma), intellectuals, and members of the resistance. The occupiers applied policies of denationalization (e.g., Germanization in the areas occupied by the Reich), and in the early stages of the war many Slovenes in German-occupied areas, particularly those from Lower Styria (Štajerska), were deported to areas in Nazi-administered Serbia.

The Italians began sending Slovenes to camps in 1942, at first to the Littoral (ethnically Slovene), then to Friuli, where the most notorious camp was Gonars, and to the Adriatic island of Rab, where the high incidence of death was attributed to inadequate diet and particularly harsh climate. After **Italy**'s capitulation, Italian prisoners were transferred to German camps. There were two German camps in Slovene areas, one near **Trieste** for Jews after 1943, and a hard-labor camp, established near the war's end, in Lower Styria (Strnišče). Otherwise Slovenes and other prisoners (mostly Serbs) who wore the letter "J" (for Yugoslavia) were sent to Buchenwald, Dachau, Mauthausen, Ravensbrück, and Auschwitz. The first deportees to these camps were sent as early as 1941. They were forced to perform hard labor or to submit to medical experimentation. Thousands died from overwork, by deliberate extermination, or from disease, which, particularly near the war's end, reached epidemic proportions.

CONSTITUTION, AUSTRIAN EMPIRE (1860–1867). The **neo-absolutism** of the **Austrian Empire** in the 1850s that had been intended to avert revolutionary activity among the most threatening groups from 1848—the Italians, Germans, and Hungarians—came to an end in 1860. Events related to **Austria**'s war with Piedmont-Sardinia (which created a modern Kingdom of **Italy** in 1860) were the immediate cause. Austrian military defeat cost it Lombardy, one of its richest provinces. If repression had failed to preserve the Austrian Empire, perhaps constitutions could. Several proposals in succession were put forward at the request of the Emperor **Francis Joseph**—including first a federalist constitution (October Diploma, 1860), and then a (German Liberal) centralist one (February Patent, 1861), each of which had different supporters. The Slovenes, not yet politically organized, preferred the federalist approach, and though elections were actually held for a parliament based on the centralist constitution, the Slovenes Matija Majar and Andrej Einspieler drafted a state rights (rather than an ethnic) plan for Slovene autonomy—the Maribor Program (1865)—and proposed including Slovene areas as part of Inner Austria, in order to advance Slovene authority in that "historic" unit of the empire. Military defeat rendered the constitutions of the early 1860s obsolete. Austria was defeated by Prussia and Italy in 1866, thus losing her preeminence in the German Confederation (formerly **Holy Roman Empire**) to Prussia and ceding Venetia, another valuable province, to Italy. **Vienna** chose to consolidate power over the remainder of the empire by making a pact with moderates in **Hungary**, where radical nationalists also tended to be separatist. The **Compromise of 1867** divided the **Habsburg** domain in two, creating a dual monarchy, Austria-Hungary. It allowed Hungary to manage its own affairs, including the non-Magyars living within its boundaries.

The developments of the 1860s had profound effect on the program for a **United Slovenia**. In 1866, 27,000 Slovenes remained in Venetia when it was lost to Italy, and 45,000 went to Hungary when the dual monarchy was created the following year. Moreover, in 1866 Prussia exerted its military prowess, took over leadership of Central Europe, and retained the option of incorporating all former Holy Roman imperial lands into a German empire. Slovene lands were thus genuinely threatened by German domination, both political and cultural.

CONSTITUTION, KINGDOM OF SERBS, CROATS, AND SLOVENES. *See* VIDOVDAN CONSTITUTION.

CONSTITUTION OF 1947, SLOVENE. Slovenia adopted its first post–**World War II** constitution in January 1947. Modeled after the **Constitution of 1946** of the **Federal People's Republic of Yugoslavia** (FPRY), it affirmed the establishment of the **People's Republic of Slovenia** (PRS) and institutionalized the principles of "people's democracy" and state ownership and management of the means of production. The chief political organ of the PRS, as stipulated by the constitution, was the People's Assembly (PA). Slovenia's 1947 constitution was superseded by the **Constitutional Law of 1953**. An entirely new constitution was implemented in 1963. *See also* CONSTITUTION OF 1963, YUGOSLAV.

The 1947 constitution, although it was virtually the same as the **Yugoslav Constitution of 1946**, was intentionally adopted separately. This was meant to emphasize that the Slovenes had created their own "people's democracy" during the war of liberation. The act also stressed that Slovenia had joined the Yugoslav federation freely, while reserving the right of national secession. *See also* GOVERNMENT OF SLOVENIA, NATIONAL.

CONSTITUTION OF 1991, SLOVENE. The Constitution of 1991 was written for the newly independent **Republic of Slovenia** (RS), which had disassociated itself from (rather than seceded from) the **Socialist Federal Republic of Yugoslavia** (SFRY). The constitution was approved and became effective on 23 December 1991. The disassociation had been preceded by 1988 Slovene amendments to the **Yugoslav Constitution of 1974** that initiated an economic restructuring process toward capitalism while social property was still in effect. Constitutional amendments in 1989–1990 then strengthened Slovenia vis-à-vis the federal government, enabling the implementation of a multiparty system, the **plebiscite for independence**, and the removal of Slovenia's territorial defense organization from **Belgrade**'s jurisdiction.

The 1991 constitution declared the RS to be a parliamentary democratic republic and a legal (*Rechtstaat*) and social state. Sixty-five articles addressed individual rights, including those traditionally incorporated into Western constitutions (among them public trial and writ of habeas corpus). Among the individual or human rights guarantees were those of indigenous **minorities** (Hungarian and Italian as well as Roma) to cultural and political expression, and all citizens of the republic were entitled to **social security** (**health**, retirement, and disability benefits). Also incorporated into the constitution was the principle of a market economy and the right to live in a healthy **environment**. Regarding the economy and social relations, the constitution provided for joint worker–management decision-making, the freedom of **trade unions**, and the right of workers to strike, which had also been features of Slovenia's previous postwar constitutions.

What is unique about the RS's 1991 constitution is its attention to the separation of powers and the ways in which the three branches of government—legislative, executive, and judicial—check and balance each other. The legislative branch consists of two bodies: a State Assembly (*državni zbor*) of 90 representatives elected for four-year terms has primary responsibility for lawmaking; and a consultative State Council (*državni svet*) of 40 members (representing regional and occupational interests) serving five-year terms has the power to initiate or delay legislation. The president of the republic is directly elected and serves no more than two consecutive five-year terms.

The president nominates the prime minister, who, with the cabinet, is responsible to the State Assembly, or parliament. Parliament can oust the government (the prime minister and cabinet) with a vote of no confidence. The constitution also provides for an independent judiciary, including special constitutional courts. The executive and legislative branches cooperate in confirming judicial appointees and in dismissing them when necessary. The constitution's incorporation of a separation of powers is significant because it enables the workings of the legal and social state as well as the functioning of a multiparty system.

The constitution has been amended three times. The first amendment, in 1997, changed Article 68 to allow foreigners to own property in Slovenia. In 2000 Article 80 was amended to conform with recent changes in the electoral system. And in 2003 a package of amendments was passed to fulfill **European Union** (EU) requirements that the laws of its members harmonize with those of the EU. (Slovenia was then in the last stages of preparation for accession into the EU.) At that time, Article 3A was added to Article 3 to allow Slovenia to transfer a portion of its sovereignty to international organizations and alliances, such as the EU and the **North Atlantic Treaty Organization** (NATO). Article 8 defined relationships between Slovene legislation and supranational organizations. Article 47 permitted extradition of Slovene citizens in accordance with international agreements. And Article 68 was amended again to allow all EU citizens to own property in Slovenia regardless of whether Slovenes could own land in various other EU countries.

CONSTITUTION OF 1946, YUGOSLAV. The second **Yugoslavia,** which emerged as a federation of six republics and two autonomous provinces after **World War II**, changed constitutions once each decade (1946, 1953, 1963, and 1974), and amendments to existing ones were made regularly. The justification for the unending constitutional adjustments, at least while **Tito** and **Edvard Kardelj** were alive, was a perceived ideological need to legalize the rapidly changing socioeconomic and social-political developments in socialist Yugoslavia. All Yugoslav and Slovene constitutions of this period guaranteed the federation's nations both the right of national self-determination and the right to secede from the federation. They also stipulated that republic boundaries could not be changed without the republic's consent.

The 1946 constitution of the **Federal People's Republic of Yugoslavia** (FPRY), modeled after the Soviet Constitution of 1936, was adopted by a constituent assembly on 31 January 1946. The FPRY's constitution provided for a federation of six sovereign and equal republics: Bosnia-Hercegovina, Croatia, Macedonia, Montenegro, Serbia, and Slovenia. Within Serbia (although not to its liking) the constitution recognized an autonomous province of the Vojvodina and an autonomous region of Kosovo-Metohija (Kosmet). The interwar monarchy was thus replaced with a federal republic, governed as a "people's democracy," a form of government designed to implement the transition from bourgeois to popular rule according to the model of the Soviet Union. It was also designed to balance the national forces within the FPRY in order to offset potential nationalistic animosities. The chief ruling body of the FPRY was the **Federal People's Assembly** (FPA). The 1946 constitution was significantly altered by the **Constitutional Law of 1953**. Although the 1946 document was virtually obsolete by that time, it was not discarded until a decade later, when it was replaced by the **Constitution of 1963**. *See also* ADMINISTRATIVE SOCIALISM; GOVERNMENT, YUGOSLAV, 1945.

CONSTITUTION OF 1953, YUGOSLAV. *See* CONSTITUTIONAL LAW OF 1953, YUGOSLAV.

CONSTITUTION OF 1963, YUGOSLAV. In 1963 in the **Federal People's Republic of Yugoslavia** (FPRY), the **Constitution of 1946** was still officially operative. However, the **Constitutional Law of 1953**, intended as a temporary adjustment to the 1946 document, had significantly redirected the course of Yugoslav socialism, or **Titoism**. By 1963 developments had proceeded at what was considered by **Edvard Kardelj**, the theoretical prestidigitator of the system, a rapid pace, and it was concluded that a new constitution was necessary to codify or legalize developments of the previous decade and a half. A committee headed by Kardelj worked more than two years on a draft constitution. The constitution was debated, amended, and finally adopted by the federal government on 7 April 1963, and the Slovene assembly passed it two days later. It officially inaugurated an era of **market socialism**.

The only part of the constitution that resembled a Western-like document was the section that discussed the organization of the federation, now consisting of "Socialist" republics. The rest addressed the complex issue of how **Yugoslavia** was proceeding with the "withering away" of the state. Refining the self-management system further was deemed to be the answer to Karl Marx's goal. The 1963 constitution therefore introduced the concept of free association of labor and merged the ideas of **workers' self-management** in production with self-mangement in the division and allocation of the social product: that is, workers could decide how and what to produce, and they could also now constitutionally decide what to do with the income. Amendments to the constitution in 1968 made Yugoslavia's working people the sole possessors of power with exclusive right to the management of social matters. Those engaged in private production, however, were excluded from representation. (In Slovenia in the late 1960s, where the peasantry constituted 30 percent of the population, there was only one peasant representative in the assembly, because most peasants farmed private land.)

The new constitution made the representative assemblies on all levels organs not of power but of self-management. (The right of self-management had been appended to the classic rights and freedoms of traditional constitutions.) The Federal Assembly (FA) thereafter consisted of five chambers, each with 120 members. The former federal chamber with traditional territorial constituencies remained, but appended to it was a 70-member nationalities body (10 from each of the six republics, five from each of the two autonomous provinces). The remaining four chambers were an elaboration on the Chamber of Producers, which had made its debut in 1953. The chambers, which represented work communities, were grouped by economic or social function: economic; **education** and culture; social welfare and **health**; and political-organizational. In Slovenia, besides the Republican Chamber, there were four chambers representing the following: economic interests; education and culture; organization and political interests; and social welfare and health. The district (*okraj*), which had been declining as an administrative unit, was eliminated, while the *občina* was made central to the system and its role enhanced.

The nature of the new assemblies enlivened parliamentary life in Yugoslavia. (In theory, one could be represented in three different bodies—in the FA, in the FA's nationalities' grouping, and in one of the four occupational chambers). Real debate among different interest groups began, often manifesting itself in sharp criticism of government ministers and resulting in substantive amendments of proposed legislation. After 1963 parliamentary debates often focused on economic matters, a topic that Slovene and Croat leaders savored. They had supported the new constitution precisely because the new document broadened interest group and republic participation, and they used it to promote economic reforms. Kardelj, who chaired the committee that drafted the 1963 document, also favored the "liberal" economic reforms. In 1963 he became president of the FA of Yugoslavia. The Serb leaders, Aleksandar Ranković and Petar Stambolić, who generally opposed **liberalization**, were compensated with the posts of vice president (of Yugoslavia) and president of the **Federal Executive Council** (prime minister of Yugoslavia), respectively.

CONSTITUTION OF 1974, YUGOSLAV. The Constitution of 1974, adopted on 21 February (in Slovenia on 28 February), was perhaps the most unusual of **Yugoslavia**'s constitutions. It was also the most difficult to understand, especially for non-Yugoslavs, for it used terminology invented to describe new concepts in social relations as they had developed and were to continue evolving. The concept of associated labor was basic. All producers—workers, farmers, professionals, and state and party officials—belonged to organizations of associated labor (OALs). The new constitution empowered the OALs, through the delegate system, giving them exclusive representation in the *općina* and indirectly in the republic Chambers of Associated Labor, as well as on the federal level of government. On the *općina* and republic levels the assemblies had three chambers: the Chamber of Associated Labor; the Chamber of Local Communities (territorial constituencies); and the Socio-Political Chamber, including members of the League of Communists of Yugoslavia (LCY; formerly the **Communist Party of Yugoslavia**), **Socialist Alliance of Working People** of Yugoslavia (SAWPY), **trade unions**, and **veterans'** and youth organizations. On the federal level there were two chambers: the **Socialist Federal Republic of Yugoslavia** (SFRY) Chamber of Republics and Provinces, with 88 representatives—12 each from the republics, eight each from the provinces—chosen by the republic and provincial assemblies; and the Federal Chamber, with 220 delegates—30 each from the republics, 20 each from the provinces—chosen by the *općina* assemblies. Delegates were under strict obligation to their constituents, and they could be recalled and replaced for acting against their delegation's wishes.

The presidency of the SFRY consisted of eight individuals, one from each of the republics and provinces, and the president of the LCY (ex officio). The president of the presidency served a one-year term, which rotated according to a specified rotation among the eight members of the federation. Until his death in 1980, **Tito**, by special election (1974), held the post of president of the republic, an office authorized for him personally by the constitution and that outranked the president of the presidency. The eight-person presidency acquired considerable power by the 1974 constitution. It appointed senior judicial and military officials and made senior diplomatic appointments. It regulated relations among Yugoslavia's nationalities, oversaw state security, and nominated the head of the Federal Assembly—the prime minister, or president of the **Federal Executive Council** (FEC).

The Constitution of 1974 specified important roles for the LCY and the army, as no previous constitution had. Both institutions were represented in the *občina* and republic Socio-Political Chambers and had a voice on the federal level. In addition, the president of the LCY was an ex officio member of the presidency. The LCY and the army both could be counted on to exert centripetal influences in a federation where loosening forces were at work. In the late 1980s, when Yugoslavia began to disintegrate, constitutional revisions were again being considered. *See also* ARMY, YUGOSLAV PEOPLE'S.

CONSTITUTIONAL LAW OF 1953, YUGOSLAV. The Constitutional Law of 1953, passed on 13 January (30 January in Slovenia), dramatically altered much of the **Constitution of 1946** but did not officially replace it. Essentially, it pulled together the many laws passed in the previous three to four years, which had incrementally dismantled central planning or **administrative socialism** and established institutions like **workers' councils** and *občinas*, which were intended to facilitate decentralization in economic planning and to strengthen social democracy. In these steps, the foundations of **workers' self-management**, a uniquely Yugoslav system, were being established. Property, most of which had already been nationalized and considered state property, was legally made **social property**. The changes were motivated by a need to bolster a failing economy, ruined by war and by the **Cominform** blockade against the **Federal People's Republic of Yugoslavia** (FPRY) after 1948. The changes were ideologically justified as the true way (unlike Moscow's flawed way) to socialism, and they ushered in the period of **market socialism** (1953–1974). In 1953 the Constitutional Law, in other words, affirmed the de-Stalinization process in the FPRY.

Although the federal structure of the FPRY was not changed in 1953, assemblies on all levels, including the **Federal People's Assembly** (FPA) in the federal capital **Belgrade**, underwent remodeling. The FPA remained bicameral: The Federal Chamber absorbed the Chamber of Nationalities to constitute one house (resulting in a body with a split personality), and the Chamber of Producers (workers) formed the second. (The People's Assembly in Slovenia became bicameral at this time, with the second chamber for producers' representatives.) The Chamber of Producers was designed to reflect institutionally the decentralization that had begun in the early 1950s. The FPA's presidium was replaced with a presidency, and the Council of Ministers was replaced by a **Federal Executive Council** (FEC).

By 1953 the functions of the state and the **Communist Party of Yugoslavia** (CPY), or League of Communists of Yugoslavia (LCY), as it was renamed in 1952, were nominally separated in order to avoid the errors of Soviet development. However, LCY members continued to dominate in government offices. *See also* CONSTITUTION OF 1974, YUGOSLAV.

CONTRACTUAL SOCIALISM (1974–1990). Contractual socialism was a complicated sociopolitical and economic system devised for **Yugoslavia** by **Edvard Kardelj**, implemented by the **Constitution of 1974**, and refined by the federal Law on Associated Labor of 1976. New institutions and new terminology were created for this system, which aimed at two incompatible goals: decentralizing decision-making and strengthening **workers' self-management**, and strengthening the leadership of the League of Communists of Yugoslavia (LCY), formerly the **Communist Party of Yugoslavia**, which provided direction to and liaison among sociopolitical communities.

The first basic concept of the new system, that of associated labor, applied to workers in economic enterprises and public institutions that managed **social property**; it did not apply to the self-employed or workers in privately owned enterprises. This concept, first introduced by the Constitutional Amendments of 1971, also called "workers" amendments, was the basis for a system of organizations of associated labor (*organizacije združenega dela*, OZD), which denoted enterprises or organizations functioning on the basis of workers' self-management. There were three forms of OZDs, also referred to as work organizations (*delovne organizacije*, DO). In factories and enterprises that produced goods and created tangible income, one would generally find basic organizations of associated labor (*temeljne organizacije združenega dela*, TOZD) or composite organizations of associated labor (*sestavljene organizacije združenega dela*, SOZD); the latter consisted of two or more TOZDs. The term *work organization* was generally used for groups such as sociopolitical organizations and communities, self-managing communities of interest, and other legal entities that did not deal in production and tangible income—for example, schools or hospitals. In the self-managing structure, DOs had the same characteristics as TOZDs. The 1976 Law on Associated Labor further described and regulated all forms of associated labor and their relationships in the society. The status of individuals in associated labor, who had a constitutionally guaranteed right to work, was determined by their participation in the work and management of social property. Not an easily comprehensible concept, associated labor was an ideological construct that does not have an equivalent in Western economic or social theory.

The second basic concept of the system was free exchange of labor, an innovation in financing to provide for collective needs that could not be met through market mechanisms. Financing of collective needs was to be assured through contracts: self-management agreements (*samoupravni sporazumi*) and social compact agreements (*družbeni dogovori*) and organizational entities, called self-managing communities of interest (*samoupravne interesne skupnosti*, SIS), in which delegates coordinated the interests of producers and users of services.

There were two major changes in societal functioning. The first change concerned planning. Indicative planning was replaced by what was called social planning, at two levels: micro-planning at the level of individual OZDs, and macro-planning at commune and republic levels, on the basis of an obligatory exchange of information by all organizations collaborating in the planning process. The plans were summarized in contracts: self-management agreements and social compact agreements, which constituted the guidelines for their social activities. Self-management agreements were concluded between OZDs and were legally binding; violations were dealt with by courts of associated labor and the Social Legal Defender of Self-management. Social compact agreements were concluded on a broader scale: for example, between local administrative entities, called **občinas**, and agents of the economy, such as OZDs, **trade unions**, and chambers of commerce. Although the purpose of social compact agreements was to guide economic activities, they existed not only in the economic sphere but also in areas of public and social services. As vehicles for Yugoslav inter-republican cooperation, the social compact agreements were statements of policy objectives in the areas of social interest such as planning, employment, prices, and **international trade**. Although not legally binding, they were used as state laws to regulate activity, and the parties to a compact were expected to undertake such measures as would ensure the realization of the stated policy objectives. The other major change was the abolition of direct election of representatives to legislative bodies. Instead, a complicated delegate system of decision-making was introduced at all governmental levels. This change was supposed to decentralize the decision-making process and bring it closer to the working people, to correct anomalies of market forces, and to develop a kind of controlled political pluralism: In other words, a reorganization of all economic, social, and political institutions was required. According to the new delegate system, workers in every work organization and the residents of local communities elected many delegates to constitute delegations at the communal level; these delegations in turn chose delegates according to their professional occupation, to represent their interests in communal, republic, and federal assemblies. Before voting on any important issue, the delegates were required to consult with their delegation and then to vote as instructed, or be recalled. Every organization with more than 30 employees elected a delegation; in smaller organizations, all workers (except managers) were members of the delegation. Elections were to be held every four years, beginning in 1974. In 1978, there were in Slovenia 5,767 delegations, with 46,178 delegates representing workers employed in social and private (handicrafts, **agriculture**, **tourism**) sectors of the **economy**. Elections of delegations and delegates were coordinated and supervised by the **Socialist Alliance of Working People** (SAWP).

The new delegate system proved to be a wasteful ideological construct that depleted human and financial resources. Delegates were generally not prepared to act capably, for they lacked professional or political expertise, and thus were easily manipulated. Also, in the process of time-consuming and ineffective social negotiating and decision-making, the delegates represented too many conflicting interests, especially at the federal level. The ensuing procedural paralysis resulted in the empowerment of a strong self-management bureaucracy at communal and republic levels. In the end, managerial decisions were usually rubber-stamped by delegates regardless of the electorates' instructions. With the Constitution of 1974, the LCY acquired an important place in social negotiating, playing a major role within the delegate system despite strong opposition by professionals or the general public.

Thus contractual socialism, as designed in legal documents, was an intricate ideological and self-contradictory construct that did not work in practice. It either was inoperable or produced undesirable results. Contractual socialism as an economic and political system was criticized openly in Slovenia after 1980, but despite changes in the economy in the 1980s, the system was legally in place until Slovenia's first multiparty elections in 1990. *See also* CONSTITUTION OF 1963; COURTS AND JUSTICE.

COOPERATIVE MOVEMENT. Cooperatives emerged in Europe in the second half of the 19th century as a response to a modernization driven by competitive (often ruthlessly materialistic), liberal-based ideology and practices. In Central Europe their leading proponents were the Germans Bishop Wilhelm Emmanuel von Ketteler and Karl Vogelsang, who soon influenced the development of cooperatives in the **Austrian Empire**. In **Austria** the Slavic nations took up cooperativism with even greater enthusiasm than did Austrian Germans, who accounted for less than 35 percent of membership in these organizations on the eve of **World War I**. For a less developed society, such as the Slovene, which was primarily agrarian, cooperation was an effective way to be rid of the foreign (primarily Austrian-German) capital that exploited it.

The first Slovene cooperative was established in **Klagenfurt** (Celovec) in 1851 (actually the very first in Austria). The movement, however, achieved momentum only two decades later, after a liberal lawyer-politician, Jože Vošnjak, wrote about the Czech cooperatives he had learned about in 1868 during a visit to Prague. The cooperatives that Slovene **liberals** then sponsored were the Schulze Delitzsch type, which upheld liberal ideals (they opposed government interference in business) and appealed primarily to townspeople. The Slovene **Socialists** eventually established credit cooperatives among miners and town workers, which were therefore strongest in **mining** towns, industrial centers, and larger cities, such as **Trieste** and **Gorizia**. These were controlled by Socialists in **Vienna**, as the party itself was highly centralized. By far the most widespread cooperatives among the Slovenes, however, were of the Raiffeisen, Christian-based, and farmer-oriented type—organized by the **Clericals**—which effected a virtual transformation of the economy in Austria's Slovene-inhabited territories.

The Slovene Clericals became the chief moving force behind the cooperative movement in the 1890s. It was a major subject at **Catholic** congresses and it benefited from the favor that **Christian Socialism** acquired in that decade. Pope Leo XIII's encyclical *Rerum novarum* in 1891 denounced liberalism and materialism and championed the ideals of Christian Socialism, while in Austria the movement's leading exponent was no less than the popular five-term Vienna mayor Karl Lueger. Among the Clericals it was **Ivan Šušteršič**, and even more important the priest **Janez Evangelist Krek**, who promoted cooperativism. The Clericals registered their first credit cooperative in 1893, and in the next two decades hundreds more were established. Their credit cooperatives were united in one union, while the noncredit cooperatives (consumers, craftspeople, farmers) had their own unified organization. Although there were quarrels among the cooperative organizations, as well as regional misunderstandings, cooperativism thrived and truly characterized the Slovene experience in the quarter-century before World War I. In 1910, according to Austrian statistics, there were 902 Slovene cooperatives; the 783 that reported data to the census commission that year listed 195,268 members. (The total Slovene population in 1910 was 1,359,023.) At that time the investment capital amassed by the credit cooperatives was equal to that of all companies based on Slovene territory, including Trieste.

The pre-1914 cooperatives were of major significance for the Slovenes. They helped to mobilize personal savings for investment in **agriculture** and business; they helped to prevent the breakup of agricultural holdings by lending heirs money to buy off secondary inheritors; they promoted the habit of saving and therefore provided useful economic education; and they trained Slovenes in organizational and managerial skills. In addition, because the larger unions that united the credit and noncredit cooperatives were Slovene, transcending Austria's provincial boundaries, the cooperatives served to foster a Slovene national consciousness—one whose purpose was to make Slovenes economically strong and thereby politically independent from Austrian-German domination.

After 1914 the cooperatives declined. Their savings were often co-opted by Vienna for the war effort; what remained after 1918 was used to help support the new government—**Kingdom of Serbs, Croats, and Slovenes**—although the amount shrank due to an unfavorable exchange of pre- and postwar currencies. Cooperativism also suffered because of the division of Slovene ethnic territory. In **Italy**, Slovene cooperatives were destroyed by the Fascists, and in Austria they were co-opted into Austrian-German ones. In 1949 the

Communist regime, hoping to replace cooperatives, introduced state farms, which were to be a stepping-stone to socialism; farmers were reluctant to join these, however. Because state farms were far from a success, cooperatives, which had continued to exist, gradually exacted official approval. *See also* AGRICULTURAL REFORMS, POST–WORLD WAR II.

COUNTER REFORMATION. The **Protestant Reformation** in the Slovene lands was strongest among the feudal nobility and among townspeople, and occasionally among peasants on **Catholic Church** lands. However, the Catholic **Habsburg** rulers, who were also **Holy Roman Emperors**, dealt firmly with religious revolt in this area only after the 1570s. (They had been occupied in the first half of the century with their Spanish domains, including overseas acquisitions, and throughout the century with **Turkish** attacks from the southeast, which threatened their eastern realm, including **Hungary**, Bohemia, and the Hereditary Lands of **Austria**.)

In 1579, with a defense system in place against the Turks and armed with the work of the Council of Trent (1545–1563), which clarified Catholic Church dogma and practices, the Habsburg rulers began to rid their towns and then their feudal noble retinue of Protestants. Decrees were issued requiring Protestants to convert or leave the land. Religious commissions administered imperial decrees, which banished Protestant preachers and destroyed Protestant places of worship, books, and cemeteries. The **Jesuits**, a new religious order, was particularly effective in education as a Counter Reformation force, beginning in the second half of the 16th century. The political-religious war spilled regularly onto the battlefield, ending for the most part in the mid-17th century (Thirty Years War, 1618–1648). When it was over, the Slovene lands, with the exception of the eastern areas (**Prekmurje**), had been re-Catholicized and were firmly under Habsburg control. *See also* BAROQUE; PEASANT REVOLTS.

COURTS AND JUSTICE. Yugoslavia's system of justice, like its **constitutions** and its brand of socialism, was constantly evolving. Constitutional changes (1953, 1963, 1974) generally required adjustments in judicial organization and procedure, yet changes in the courts and the operation of justice sometimes preceded constitutional reform. The **Communist Party**—known after 1952 as the League of Communists—controlled the courts, and Yugoslav **Marxist** theoreticians micromanaged the changes. Their chief concern was developing a socialist justice system that focused on "distributive" justice (building an egalitarian society) rather than on "retributive" or legal justice (punishing crimes).

Yugoslavia's justice system grew out of wartime courts, which after 1942 operated in **Partisan-controlled territories** and dealt primarily with civil and criminal cases. In 1946 a court system was established, affirmed by the **Constitution of 1946**, that provided for centralized judicial uniformity throughout Yugoslavia. It stipulated three kinds of courts: a hierarchy of regular courts, dealing with civil and criminal matters; military courts; and special (generally economic) courts. The latter two could be appointed only by the federal government. The regular court hierarchy consisted of *občina*, district (*okraj*), republic (or autonomous region), and federal courts, with the Supreme Court of Yugoslavia as the highest court of the country. This system remained in place until 1974, with some minor but significant refinements. In 1963 two new types of courts were introduced: the constitutional courts for the federation and for each of the republics and autonomous regions; and the courts of arbitration and conciliation, which were informal and voluntary, and proved to be the antecedents of the self-management courts inaugurated in 1974.

The regular court system continued after 1974 with jurisdiction in cases involving personal relationships, the rights and obligations of citizens, and the rights and obligations of sociopolitical communities. The regular courts also had oversight of matters relating to criminal and administrative disputes and disputes regarding property and labor relations, unless the latter had been assigned to self-management court. The self-management court, or court of associated labor (CAL), was an innovation of the **Constitution of 1974**. It was an outgrowth of the voluntary conciliation court of the 1960s, which seemed increasingly appropriate as the organizations of associated labor (OALs) took shape in the late 1960s and early 1970s. The self-management courts handled cases involving the right of self-government and other self-management rights, and developed autonomously from the regular court system. A new judicial officer, the social legal defender of self-management, was introduced at this time.

Significantly, the court system after 1974 was greatly decentralized. The republics and autonomous provinces were now allowed to create courts and pass legislation. In Slovenia, for example, economic or commercial courts were eliminated and their cases turned over to regular courts. Also, the self-management courts, by their very nature, dealing as they were with cases involving disputes between associated labor groupings, hardly fell under federal jurisdiction. Thus the federal constitutional court virtually ceased to be a high court of the land and became primarily one attending to disputes involving different federal units (e.g., between Slovenia and Vojvodina). That court, in other words, was now a court of the federation, rather than a supreme court. At the same time, each republic (especially in the case of Slovenia) developed its own system of justice and courts, becoming increasingly autonomous—particularly in the 1980s—from **Belgrade**, and engaging more and more in battles with the federal authorities over judicial jurisdiction. Legal experts describe the justice system after 1974 as polycentric centralism.

After Slovenia established its **independence** in 1991 as the **Republic of Slovenia** (RS), its court system resembled ones found in the west. Although it is linked with the Ministry of Justice, the judiciary is one of three independent branches of government (the executive and the legislative being the other two). The role of the judiciary is outlined in Slovenia's **Constitution of 1991**. The court structure is arranged hierarchically. There are 44 local and 11 district courts, as well as four courts of appeal and a supreme court. These courts deal primarily with civil and criminal cases. Judges are independent. Men may serve up to age 65, women to age 62. To assure their independence, judges are not permitted to belong to **political parties**. They are elected by the parliament from nominees provided by the Judicial Council: a body of six sitting judges who have been chosen by their peers, and five presidential nominees elected by the parliament.

The highest court in Slovenia is the constitutional court, provided for by the constitution and governed by a 1994 act of parliament. Its nine members are appointed by the National Assembly from nominees recommended by the president. Members of the constitutional court serve nine-year terms. The primary concern of this court is to safeguard the constitution by monitoring the constitutionality of laws passed by the parliament. The constitutional court was especially active in the years preceding Slovenia's accession to the **European Union** (EU), a move that required Slovenia to "harmonize" its laws with those of the EU. Thus, Slovenia's Criminal Code of 1995 had to be amended in 1997. The constitutional court also deals with cases involving international laws and treaties, and it presides over cases involving possible infringements of individual rights. These are the human, political, and civil rights that are the cornerstone of Slovenia's constitution. In 2004, for example, the court dealt with the issue of "the erased," persons from former Yugoslavia who had been eliminated from official Slovene records because they had not registered for citizenship; the court also weighed in on the debate over the establishment of a Muslim religious center in **Ljubljana**. In monitoring possible rights abuses, the court often acts on cases brought to its attention by Slovenia's ombudsman, a position also mandated by the constitution. *See also* HUMAN RIGHTS; MINORITIES IN SLOVENIA.

COVENANT, NEW SLOVENE / NOVA SLOVENSKA ZAVEZA (NSZ). Founded in **Ljubljana** in 1991, the New Slovene Covenant (NSZ), a successor to the **Slovene Covenant** organized during **World War II**, is an association whose members were wartime anticommunists and **Home Guardists**, and their current supporters. Many are relatives of anti-communists who were brutally murdered immediately after the war. In 1994 it had 700 members. The main goal of NSZ is to explain the true nature of anticommunists who were summarily killed or persecuted as traitors during and immediately after the war. NSZ objects to classifying Home Guardists as collaborators of the Italian and German occupiers and instead sees them as defenders of Slovenia against the outrages committed by the Communist-led **Liberation Front** (LF). Since 1991 the NSZ has been publishing a quarterly bulletin, *Zaveza* (*Covenant*), available online. The organization is also engaged in charitable work, helping old and sick surviving Home Guardists and their relatives. NSZ supports **political parties** of the right. *See also* MASSACRES, POST–WORLD WAR II.

COVENANT, SLOVENE / SLOVENSKA ZAVEZA (SZ) (1942–1943). The Slovene Covenant (SZ), established in spring 1942 as an underground continuation of the **National Council for Slovenia** (*Narodni svet za Slovenijo*), was a loose coalition based on a political agreement among the former Slovene political parties and factions of Slovene patriots that wanted to oversee and direct Slovene public life with the intent to assume power after **World War II**. Opposed to revolutionary action, SZ did not want to challenge the occupiers openly, out of concern for loss of life and property. For this reason, SZ was opposed to the revolutionary **Liberation Front** (LF) and fought its influence with all means, even collaborating with the occupiers. The Covenant favored restoration of the **Kingdom of Yugoslavia** and acknowledged Draža Mihailović as commander-in-chief of the wartime Royal Yugoslav Army. It established contact with the Yugoslav government-in-exile in London, which warned the Covenant not to cooperate with the occupiers and urged it to avoid armed conflicts with either the occupiers or the **Partisans**; rather, the liberation of Slovenia was to await the arrival of the Allies. Despite their common goal of destroying the LF, old frictions between the conservatives and the liberals in the Covenant continued, paralyzing its activities. In October 1944 some members of the Slovene Covenant established the **National Committee for Slovenia** (*Narodni odbor za Slovenijo*), which was supposed to take power in Slovenia after the war. *See also* CHETNIKS; COVENANT, NEW SLOVENE.

CRAFTS, TRADITIONAL. Traditional crafts have thrived in the Slovene lands for centuries. Some craft centers (e.g., shoemaking in Tržič, glassmaking in Rogaška Slatina) developed into industrial **manufacturing** in the 19th and early 20th centuries, while others decreased production (woodenware in Ribnica valley) or almost died out (cooperage in Črni Vrh and **Ljubljana**) after World War II.

Pottery-making is one of the oldest crafts. The earliest written documents about potters near **Kamnik** go back to the 14th century. In the 19th century, more than 400 potters were active in various pottery centers across Slovenia: Filovci (**Prekmurje**), Dolenja Vas near Ribnica (Dolenjska), Komenda near Kamnik, Liboje near **Celje,** and many others. Since then, their number has declined, and only about 30 potters can be found in Slovenia today. Pottery technology and production varied from center to center; glazed and black pottery (baked with smoke), for instance, were characteristic of Prekmurje. Potters produced kitchenware; flower pots; ceramic tiles for stoves, toys, decorative objects; and musical instruments. Modeled and decorated baking dishes for *poticas*, festive breads, and desserts such as *gibanica* are known, for example, in Prekmurje. Toys—decorated whistles in the shape of clay animals—are still produced in Ribnica valley today. Quality pottery from Komenda near Kamnik was sold in **Austria.**

Woodenware (spoons, various kitchen utensils, toothpicks, sieves) was produced in several centers. Ribnica valley was especially known across the Austro-Hungarian Empire, and Ribnica craftspeople even traveled to Africa and Asia to sell woodenware. Slovenes are also known for woven or plaited wicker, straw, and cornhusk articles. Popular straw hats and shopping bags (*cekarji*) were first produced in the 18th century in the vicinity of Kamnik, where merchants from Tyrol established the first straw hat factory. Influenced by Austrians, wickerwork production was well established in Ljubljana, Gorenjska (**Radovljica**), and Štajerska (Haloze and **Ptuj**), where wicker classes and schools were established at the start of the 20th century. The State Wickerwork School in Ptuj (1928–1939) played an important role in disseminating the skills of the craft. Wicker products, primarily all types of baskets, are articles typical of Slovene custom and tradition. Furnituremaking began to develop in the late 18th century. In the 19th century, furniture was often painted. Although painted chests, cribs, and headboards could be found across Slovenia, those from Gorenjska were especially known for their brightly colored flower designs and religious motifs. Cabinetmaking was best developed in two centers: the largest was Vižmarje, today a suburb of Ljubljana, and the other Solkan, near **Nova Gorica**.

Other unique crafts that deserve attention are embroidery (**Bela Krajina**, Gorenjska, Prekmurje), lacemaking (bobbin lace in **Idrija**), **wrought iron** products (Kropa), pipemaking (Gorjuše), clock making, wood carving, and toolmaking of all kinds. *See also* FOLK ART.

CROATIA, RELATIONS WITH. The Republic of Croatia is the only one of Slovenia's four neighbors to have also been a part of the **Socialist Federal Republic of Yugoslavia** (SFRY). Geographical proximity had fated Slovenia and Croatia to live together for much of their history. Before there was an SFRY, both lived in the **Kingdom of Yugoslavia**, and prior to the 20th century, Croats and Slovenes lived for centuries under **Habsburg** rule. Slovenes, however, were in **Austria** and were ruled from **Vienna**, while Croats (except for Dalmatia and Istria) were a part of **Hungary** and thus under Budapest. They shared a common religion—**Catholicism**—and Western culture, and in the 19th century both experienced national awakenings and national political activity. Their respective political programs differed in that the Croats based their claims to nationhood on a **medieval** kingdom, whose legal continuity they traced through a joint monarchy, first with the Hungarian dynasty, then with the Habsburgs. Slovenes, having had no previous state, based their **United Slovenia** program on the "national self-determination" principle. In the quarter-century before **World War I**, Slovenes and Croats made halting steps toward political cooperation, but Croats believed their national program would have better chances for success if they worked alone, rather than tie themselves to the Slovenes, who had no constitutional tradition, and to whom some referred rather demeaningly as "mountain Croats." *See also* CLERICALS; LIBERALS.

World War I ended with the collapse and dismemberment of the Austro-Hungarian Empire. The Slovenes and Croats attempted to achieve a common state from its wreckage, but the winning powers decided otherwise. The self-proclaimed **State of Slovenes, Croats, and Serbs** was simply ignored. In the new Yugoslav state where they found themselves, Croats and Slovenes continued to work for autonomy, yet there was little cooperation to that effect. In the late 1920s, extremists began to set the Croat agenda. They helped assassinate the Yugoslav king in 1934 and then nurtured a native fascist movement, something that did not happen in Slovene lands. During **World War II**, Croatia achieved independence, albeit as a puppet to Nazi Germany and fascist **Italy**. After the war, the federal republics of Slovenia and Croatia emerged as a part of the new communist **Yugoslavia**, each ostensibly with the national autonomy they had wanted in the interwar years. Croatia, however, was not satisfied with its republic's size; Croats would have included the parts of Bosnia and Hercegovina that had been theirs during World War II.

For nearly a quarter-century during the height of the Cold War, life was grim and regimented for both peoples, but in the late 1960s both republics experienced **liberalization** movements, although again there was little cooperation between them. The Croat movement was by far the more visible, and in the eyes of **Belgrade**, the more ominous. Eventually, liberalism was suppressed, and federal Yugoslavia implemented measures to wipe it out and restore central control of the League of Communists of Yugoslavia (LCY), formerly the **Communist Party of Yugoslavia**.

In the late 1980s, as new opportunities for old dreams presented themselves, Slovenes led the way, while Croatia lay low in moving for reform. In June 1991, when both republics declared **independence**, war followed with the **Yugoslav People's Army** (JNA). For independent Slovenia, it was only a **Ten-Day War**, but Croatia suffered economic devastation, massive property destruction, thousands of human casualties, and occupation of one-third of the country until late 1995. When Croatia's situation was finally settled at the Dayton peace talks that year, Slovenia was already standing on its own feet and ready for large strides forward—even daring to hope for **North Atlantic Treaty Organization** (NATO) membership in the very near future. Slovenia, having escaped most of the brutality of the wars in the former Yugoslavia, wished nothing more than to escape the Balkans and all its former neighbors forever. But geography tied Slovenia to Croatia, and the West wanted Slovenia to act as a liaison with the former Yugoslav republics. Croatia, meanwhile, needed to start the hard work of postwar recovery. For the remainder of the 1990s, however, the country was ruled by the Croatian Democratic Union (CDU), more specifically by Franjo Tudjman, the strong CDU president, whose cronies enriched themselves, drove the economy into the ground, and kept the mood of ultranationalism at a high pitch. Only after his death in late 1999, was Croatia able to begin again.

As neighbors with a history, Slovenia and Croatia have not always had the best relations since independence. The border between them has been disputed in several locations, and in spite of a 2001 agreement, there continue to be disagreements and confrontations, particularly in Istria near the coast. In 2004 Croats arrested 12 Slovenes (two of them legislators, who may have been physically roughed up) near Sečovlje. At root was a disagreement over where the border stood. Also not resolved is a dispute regarding Croatian deposits in Ljubljanska Banka's branch bank in Zagreb, Croatia's capital. Depositors, through the government, are demanding access to their money, which the bank says it cannot pay because Croatia during the war did not cover its own debt to the bank. The Slovene government maintains that the bank's debt was included in the Yugoslav succession agreement, therefore the bank is no longer obligated to the depositors. The losers so far are the depositors.

Another point of contention was the Krško nuclear power plant (NEK), which was built with Westinghouse equipment in the late 1970s and started up in 1983. The plant was located in southeastern Slovenia, and ownership and consumption of electricity was shared with Croatia. After Yugoslavia broke apart in 1991, NEK remained in Slovenia, and many questions arose about plant management, cost of electricity to Croatia, and disposal of nuclear waste. The ongoing war prevented resolution, and in 1998 Slovenia cut off electricity to Croatia for payment arrears. An agreement was finally reached in April 2003, and electricity began to flow again to Croatia. The agreement stipulated shared ownership and management and also resolved price issues. NEK, recently refurbished, has been given a clean bill of health, though antinuclear elements at home and abroad (largely Italy and Austria) have over the years demonstrated to shut down the plant. NEK has been declared operational until 2023 and is listed among the **European Union**'s (EU) nuclear energy resources. *See also* ENERGY. Still unresolved is the issue of access to the Adriatic Sea's Bay of Piran, where the coasts of Italy, Slovenia, and Croatia converge. International law allows a country to extend its jurisdiction 200 miles into the sea, but the average width of the Adriatic is not even 200 miles. Croat and Slovene diplomats have been wrangling with the issue of sea access and the international border in coastal waters, while Slovene fishing boats have periodically been denied access to the open sea by vigilant Croat maritime police. In October 2004 Croatia established an Exclusive Economic Zone (EEZ), unilaterally laying claim to one-half of the Adriatic Sea; Slovenia has protested this EEZ, which limits its access to international waters. Croatia seemed less motivated by a concern for fishing rights than by the prospect of finding deposits of oil and natural gas in the sea beds. The issue will likely require international arbitration.

On a multinational level, both Slovenia and Croatia have worked together as members of the **Alps–Adriatic Working Community** (pre-independence), the **Central European Initiative**, the **Central European Free Trade Association** (since 2003), the **Organization for Security and Cooperation in Europe**, and the **United Nations**. Croatia also wants to be a part of the EU and NATO, both of which Slovenia joined in 2004. Memberships in these two are partly dependent on cooperating with the International War Crimes Tribunal in The Hague, which wants to prosecute Croatian war criminals. Unneighborly behavior toward Slovenia on Croatia's part may also delay progress toward EU membership. Croatia's grab for control of the Adriatic has caused Slovenia to threaten withdrawing its support for Croat EU accession.

CURRENCY. The basic monetary unit in the **Republic of Slovenia** (RS) until the end of 2006 was the *tolar*. Divided into 100 *stotinas*, it was introduced on 8 October 1991 when Slovenia stopped using the Yugoslav *dinar*. The *tolar* came in nine bank-note denominations and six coins. The notes, each depicting a prominent Slovene historical figure (**Ivan Cankar, Jacobus Gallus, Rihard Jakopič, Jože Plečnik, France Prešeren, Primož Trubar, Janez Vajkard Valvasor**, and **Jurij Vega**, as well as the painter Ivana Kobilca) and their works, were printed in Great Britain. The coins carried representations of characteristic animals found in the RS (a bull, a goldenhorn, a grasshopper, a stork, a trout, and **Postojna** Cave's *Proteus anguinus*). The international designation for the *tolar* was SIT.

In May 2004 the RS became a member of the **European Union** (EU) and began preparing for the adoption of the euro. Fiscal matters were attended to—especially inflation, which was reined in at 2.3 percent—in order to meet EU qualifications for entry into the euro zone. The government prepared Slovenes for the currency transition well in advance by supplying each household with a brochure explaining forthcoming changes. Also, two years ahead of the transition, all prices on goods were listed in both *tolar* and euro amounts in order to familiarize Slovenes with the change. Thus when the euro was officially adopted on 1 January 2007, only two weeks were allowed for the actual transition, which went relatively smoothly. Entry into the euro monetary zone, which was celebrated with midnight fireworks on New Year's Eve, was no mean achievement for Slovenia. It was the first of the 10 states that joined the EU in 2004 to accomplish this goal and, of course, the first of the post-Communist states to do so. Most Slovenes are quite proud of this achievement.

The euros that Slovenes now use come in bank notes and coins. The coins, minted in Finland, come in seven denominations: the poet France Prešeren appears on the 2 euro coin, and the 16th-century cultural icon Primož Trubar is on the 1 euro coin. There are also coins for 50-, 20-, 10-, 5-, 2-, and 1-cent denominations. In decending order of value, these carry representations of **Triglav**, Lippizaner horses, Jože Plečnik, the artist Ivan Grohar, the **Karantanian** prince's installation stone, and a stork.

– Č –

ČITALNICE. *See* READING SOCIETIES.

ČOP, MATIJA (1797–1835). Matija Čop studied philosophy and theology in **Ljubljana** and **Vienna**. A liberal thinker, Čop was highly educated, a classical philologist, and a literary historian and critic. He was a professor in Rijeka, Lvov, and Ljubljana. From 1828 on, Čop worked in the Ljubljana Lyceum Library. He spoke all classical, Slavic, and major European languages and knew their literatures well. With his broad literary knowledge, he was mentor to Slovene intellectuals who published in *Kranjska Čbelica* (*Carniolan Bee*) and had particular influence on **France Prešeren,** with whom he had a very close relationship. Čop did not write in the Slovene **language**. With his writing on the **alphabet war**, a debate over which orthography was appropriate for Slovenes, he was instrumental in shaping a literary Slovene language for Slovene townspeople. *See also* ROMANTICISM.

– D –

DACHAU TRIALS (APRIL 1948–OCTOBER 1949). Nine trials held in **Ljubljana** involving former Slovene internees of Dachau and Buchenwald are collectively known as the Dachau trials. Thirty-four Communists, former inmates of these **concentration camps**, some of whom had been members of camp committees, were found guilty by military tribunals of cooperating with the German Gestapo. Eleven were sentenced to death, the remainder to prison terms. The trials took place in a particularly charged political atmosphere. The new Communist regime was under threat from the **Cominform**, and the perceived class enemies of the system were treated harshly so that the regime of the **Communist Party of Slovenia** (CPS) could prove its own ideological correctness. Two decades later, in a period of **liberalization** in Slovenia and within the CPS, courts ruled against the accusation of individual guilt in the Dachau cases, citing oppressive camp conditions. On the basis of new documentation, some accusations were dropped in 1971 and in 1976. In 1984 the proceedings, conclusions, and sentences were completely nullified. The 10th Congress of the CPS (1986) politically rehabilitated the accused.

DALMATIN, JURIJ (c. 1547–1589). Dalmatin, who received two degrees from the University of Tübingen, was a prolific writer, translator, theologian, and preacher of the **Protestant Reformation**. In many ways he was heir to the work of **Primož Trubar**. Relying on Martin Luther's German translation of scripture, Dalmatin produced a Slovene Bible, which was published in 1584 in Wittenberg (away from **Catholic** authorities). The printing of 1,500 copies, to be divided among the three Slovene provinces of Carniola, **Carinthia**, and Styria, took five months. The work itself was more than a mere translation. With the collaboration of others, such as **Adam Bohorič** and Sebastijan Krelj, the Bible established a standard Slovene orthography (*bohoričica*) and a common written medium based on the language of **Ljubljana** and Dolenjska. Commissions from various Slovene areas helped to decide the matter of an orthography and a standard written language. The Bible was therefore both a collaborative project and the cornerstone of the Slovene literary language. *See also* HUMANISM.

DECENTRALIZATION (1950–1953). *See* MARKET SOCIALISM; COMINFORM CRISIS; CONSTITUTIONAL LAW OF 1953; OBČINA.

DEFENSE. *See* ARMY, SLOVENE; ARMY, YUGOSLAV PEOPLE'S; EUROPEAN UNION; NORTH ATLANTIC TREATY ORGANIZATION; PARTISANS; TEN-DAY WAR.

DELEGATE SYSTEM / DELEGATSKI SISTEM (1974–1990). *See* CONTRACTUAL SOCIALISM.

DEMOCRATIC PARTY OF RETIRED PERSONS OF SLOVENIA / DEMOKRATIČNA STRANKA UPOKOJENCEV SLOVENIJE (DeSUS). The Democratic Party of Retired Persons of Slovenia was originally named the Alliance of Retired Persons and was founded on 2 February 1990 in **Maribor**. It took its new name in May 1991. It is essentially an interest group that represents retirees, many of whom are also **World War II veterans** or their family members. DeSUS's program, which emphasizes democratic political, economic, social, and ecological goals, also strives to honor the memory of the **National Liberation Struggle** (NOB). It has a broad grassroots organization that stresses cross-generational cooperation and polycentric development in the **Republic of Slovenia** (RS). It has supported the entry of the RS into the **European Union** (EU) and other international organizations. In all elections since 1992, DeSUS has won several seats: 1 in 1992; 5 in 1996; 4 in 2000; and 4 in 2004. In a multiparty state where coalition-building is critical and a governmental majority may hang on a handful of votes, DeSUS has sometimes been able to play a decisive role. It has been a coalition member of **Janez Drnovšek**'s government of November 2000–December 2002, **Anton Rop**'s government of December 2002–December 2004, and **Janez Janša**'s government of December 2004. In 2005 DeSUS had 36,000 members.

DEMOCRATIC PARTY OF SLOVENIA / DEMOKRATSKA STRANKA SLOVENIJE (DEMOCRATS). The Democratic Party of Slovenia was established on 13 October 1991 when the **Slovene Democratic Alliance** (SDZ) split in two. Ideological issues relating to the **Catholic Church**, the **National Liberation Struggle** (NOB), the past regime, and **privatization** divided SDZ members. The liberal wing of the party, which included **Igor Bavčar**, **Dimitrij Rupel**, and the writers **Spomenka Hribar** and Tine Hribar, became the Democrats.

In the **election** of December 1992, the Democrats won only six seats in the parliament and came away with no ministerial positions. Like the **Slovene Democratic Alliance–National Democratic Party**, the right wing of the former SDZ that was also doing poorly after the split, the Democrats looked for a new party affiliation. In 1994 the Democrats joined **Liberal Democracy of Slovenia** (LDS).

DEMOKRATIČNA OPOZICIJA SLOVENIJE (DEMOS). *See* DEMOS.

DEMOKRATIČNA STRANKA UPOKOJENCEV SLOVENIJE (DeSUS). *See* DEMOCRATIC PARTY OF RETIRED PERSONS OF SLOVENIA.

DEMOKRATSKA STRANKA SLOVENIJE (DEMOKRATI). *See* DEMOCRATIC PARTY OF SLOVENIA.

DEMOS. Demos (Democratic Opposition of Slovenia / *Demokratična opozicija Slovenije*) was established on 4 December 1989 in **Ljubljana**, just weeks before the announcement of multiparty elections in Slovenia. The founding groups within Demos were the **Slovene Democratic Alliance** (SDZ); the Social Democratic Alliance of Slovenia (SDZS), later the **Social Democratic Party of Slovenia** (SDSS); and the **Slovene Christian Democrats** (SKD). By early January the coalition also included the Slovene Farmers' Alliance (SKZ), later the **Slovene People's Party**; the **Greens of Slovenia**; the Grey Panthers; and the Slovenian Small Businessmen's Party, later the **Liberal Party** (LS). Since parties were not legal until the end of 1989, most groups initially called themselves alliances.

In the **election** of April 1990, Demos's program stressed multiparty government and sovereignty for Slovenia, goals common to all the coalition members. Internally, the coalition minimized differences in order to achieve its chief objective: defeat of the Communists. **Jože Pučnik** (SDZS) headed Demos and was its candidate for president of the republic. Pučnik lost to recent Communist **Milan Kučan** of the **Party of Democratic Renewal** (SDP) in a run-off election. However, Demos won comfortable majorities in each of the three chambers of the Slovene Assembly, and two of the four positions on the presidency went to Demos candidates **Ivan Oman** (SKZ) and Dušan Plut (Greens). In the forming of a government, the premiership went to Christian Democrat **Lojze Peterle**, whose party had tallied the most votes of any of the Demos partners.

Demos continued as a coalition throughout 1990 and 1991. Differences among its ideologically and politically disparate groups paled in the face of challenges emerging from the federal government, the federal army, and Serb nationalists. Declaring **independence**, surviving the **Ten-Day War**, and achieving international recognition (which came early in 1992) demanded solidarity. But once Slovenia was clearly on its own, party squabbles erupted, and Demos fractured and soon dissolved. It did not participate as a coalition in the election of 1992. Its successor parties thereafter often assumed traditional (pre–**World War II**) liberal and conservative identities. Many former Demos alliance members subsequently split or reorganized. Although short-lived, Demos's significance is enormous, for in ousting the Communists from power, it succeeded in redirecting Slovene political life.

DENATIONALIZATION AFTER 1991. The Denationalization Act, which took effect in December 1991, specified conditions under which citizens could apply for the return of property nationalized between 1945 and 1963. Under this law, one-tenth of **social property**—land, forests, enterprises—was to be returned to former owners. The remaining social property might be **privatized** according to the Privatization Act of December 1992. Although there were approximately 200,000 citizens affected by **nationalization** after **World War II**, the government expected some 60,000 applications for denationalization, the majority involving agricultural land. If the property could not be returned in kind, former owners would receive monetary compensation. (Although the law gave a three-year framework for property restitution, the process had not yet been completed in late 2005.)

Restitution, a complicated and painful process, was slowed by amendments to the 1991 law and by negative public response to restitution itself. The Association of Expropriated Property Owners, a civil society organized to represent expropriated owners living in Slovenia and abroad, appealed to the **European Union** (EU), the **North Atlantic Treaty Organization** (NATO), and foreign governments for fair and speedy restitution; it even asked that restitution be a condition for Slovenia's entry in NATO and the EU. The **Catholic Church**, one of the largest restitution claimants, has pressed for return of the **Triglav** National Park, the island on Lake Bled, vast forest lands, and numerous cultural buildings. Some compromises with the Catholic Church over its property used by the **Slovene Army** have been reached. Others are still pending. More than 40,000 claims for property restitution have been submitted. By mid-2006 more than 93 percent of the claims were resolved. The majority of those still pending involve the restitution of land, forests, and public buildings occupied by cultural institutions. *See also* AGRICULTURAL REFORMS, POST–WORLD WAR II; ALPINE RESORTS.

DESIGN. Graphic and industrial design has a long tradition and a high quality in Slovenia. The *Društvo oblikovalcev Slovenije* (Slovene Association of Designers), established in 1951, is a member of the International Council of National Associations of Industrial Design. Its 17th Congress, held in **Ljubljana** in 1992, was a tribute to Slovene achievements in the field, and a challenge for future development.

Eighteenth-century **crafts** (ceramics, furniture, glass, **wrought iron**) influenced early industrial design in the 19th century. Among the forerunners of modern design who linked crafts, **folk art** tradition, and industrial design was Anton Jamnik (1862–1942), a most diverse personality who painted, carved, photographed professionally, made musical instruments and clocks, and invented and designed all sorts of technical gadgets and machinery. Many of the early designers were engineers, most notable among them Valentin Matija Živic, known best for a thermal generator design (1871), and the younger Stanko Bloudek, known for airplane design (1920s) and the first Slovene automobile (1937). While the architects of European renown such as **Jože Plečnik** and **Maks Fabiani** subordinated design to subjective creative principles, Ivan Vurnik kept it in line with functionalist principles.

After **World War II**, Edvard Ravnikar, who studied with Le Corbusier before the war, enriched the design education of architects at the Faculty of Architecture. He critically evaluated Bauhaus principles, briefly present in Slovenia in the 1920s, and gave a contemporary foundation to industrial design. The field began blossoming during the 1960s and 1970s within development and research units of large state-owned enterprises, including Almira, Elan, Iskra, Mura, Stol, and Tomos. The Academy of Plastic Arts established a department for design in 1984. Slovene industrial design became known worldwide with Niko Kralj's furniture design. Especially successful was his Rex chair, designed in 1956 for the Stol furniture factory in **Kamnik**, which was copied and mass-produced in Slovenia and in several other European countries. Perhaps the finest representatives of contemporary industrial design are Saša Mächtig and Oskar Kogoj. Educated in Slovenia, Mächtig acquired his fame designing modular kiosk systems, waiting rooms, and various containers; his K 67 kiosk was displayed at the Museum of Modern Art in New York. Kogoj, who studied in Venice, became known for his reclining chair, which he developed for the Meblo furniture factory in Nova Gorica. Besides designing an array of everyday objects (bottles, sports equipment, toys), Kogoj has been a craftsman and sculptor. Since the 1950s the design center of Iskra, the largest Slovene manufacturer of home appliances and electric and electronic equipment, has designed many products (especially well known is their design for a telephone) that have received the highest international awards for functional and esthetic excellence.

The development of printing technology was an important factor in graphic design. At the beginning of the 20th century, journals, books, and posters were designed by painters gathered around the club Vesna, such as **Maksim Gaspari**, and their contemporaries. After **World War I**, **expressionism** and **modernism** became evident, especially in posters and commercial advertising of Janez Trpin, educated in Leipzig, and in works of Pavel Kocijančič, educated in Venice. With their work and teaching at the Graphic School, they gave a professional foundation to Slovene graphic design, which was alive even during World War II. **Partisans** and the **Liberation Front** (LF) organized illegal printing of books and political propaganda and, after 1943, also produced the attributes of the newly emerging state (bonds, documents, money) in territories controlled by them.

An internationally educated architect and professor of visual communications, Peter Skalar, and the Studio MSSV, established in 1969, designed representational images for individual enterprises such as Ljubljanska Banka, for which Skalar received the **Prešeren** Prize, the highest distinction for quality artistic work in Slovenia. An important designer, Matjaž Vipotnik, who was working with Skalar, created many posters for theater performances and political events (his poster for the referendum on Slovenia's **independence** is well known) and is considered the first postmodernist in the field. Polish influence is evident in graphic design from the 1970s on. Since there was no formal education for designers in Slovenia before 1984, some painters and visual artists went to Poland to study, among them Tomaž Kržišnik, who designed and illustrated creative posters for theater performances and introduced dynamic, unconventional designs for children's fairy tales. Since the mid-1980s graphic design has been dominated by the studio Znak (Sign), with the prominent designers

Ranko Novak and Miljenko Licul. In 1991–1992 Licul, with collaborators, designed Slovenia's new coins and bank notes.

In the 1980s, with computer technology, graphic design became a mass activity, which sometimes also lowered its quality. The 1980s also brought changes in design orientation from strict functionalism to more playful and fresh approaches of postmodernism, evident in the works of younger designers such as Lara Bohinc, Gregor Markelj, and Tanja Pak. The dramatic social and political changes of the 1990s also had their impact on design. Everyone wanted to exploit its benefits, but there has not been political or economic will to invest in its development. *See also* ARTS.

DESTOVNIK-KAJUH, KAREL (1922–1944). Karel Destovnik-Kajuh was expelled from high school because of his leftist political activity. At the outbreak of **World War II** he was briefly imprisoned by the Germans in **Maribor**. After that he moved to **Ljubljana**, where he worked in the Communist underground. In 1943 he joined the **Partisans** as a cultural worker and acquired the Partisan name Kajuh, by which he is best known. In 1944 he was killed in a battle against the Germans. Kajuh, who began writing early in life, was a prolific and forceful poet. His work is varied thematically and in form, but his main poetic form is the sonnet, with often irregular rhyme patterns and varied meter. Throughout his work, Kajuh exhibits a great sensibility for social injustices and a commitment to a better society. He reached his artistic pinnacle in *Slovenska pesem* (Slovene Poem), the cycle *Ljubezenske* (Love Poems), and poems on women's themes, such as *Kje si, mati?* (Where Are You, Mother?). During the war, Kajuh published in underground newspapers and magazines. He was a talented poet whose life ended early, like that of many other Slovene poets, especially **France Balantič**, whose life bears many parallels to Kajuh's. After the war, Kajuh's poems were published in two collections: *Kajuhove pesmi* (Kajuh's Poems) and *Zbrano delo* (Collected Work). *See also* LITERATURE.

DOLENJSKA. *See* REGIONS OF SLOVENIA.

DOLOMITE DECLARATION / DOLOMITSKA IZJAVA. In early 1943 the Communist leaders **Edvard Kardelj** and **Boris Kidrič** drafted a declaration that required noncommunist co-founding parties of the **Liberation Front** (LF) to forgo the establishment of their own political organizations after the war. Although the LF was a coalition of several resistance groups, it was dominated by the **Communist Party of Slovenia** (CPS). The Communists pressed for this strengthening and consolidation of their power for two reasons: They thought **World War II** would end soon and believed they needed to stress the social revolution aspect of their mission; and they especially needed to restrain LF's **Catholic** elements, which were particularly strong and independent minded. The Dolomite Declaration stated that the Slovene nation should follow the lead of the Russian people. The **Sokol** (Falcon) group agreed to it easily, but the **Christian Socialists** had to be pressured for some time before they would sign. The declaration was finally signed on 1 March 1943 by the Communists Edvard Kardelj, Boris Kidrič, and Franc Leskošek; by the Sokols Jože Rus and France Lubej; and by the Christian Socialists Marijan Brecelj, Tone Fajfar, and **Edvard Kocbek**. With this act, the Communists formally abolished the coalition and destroyed the plural character of the LF. *See also* PARTISANS.

DOMOBRANCI. *See* HOME GUARD.

DRAVA BANOVINA (1929–1941). After establishing a royal dictatorship and officially renaming his country the **Kingdom of Yugoslavia**, King Alexander reorganized his state administratively from 33 regions (*oblasti*) into nine new administrative units, *banovinas*. The Drava *banovina*, with its administrative seat in **Ljubljana**, had jurisdiction over the former Ljubljana and **Maribor** regions (*oblasti*) of Yugoslavia. The *ban*, or *banovina* head, was appointed by the monarch, upon the advice of the prime minister. An advisory council, chosen by the minister of internal affairs, advised the *ban*. Although it had been the intent of Alexander to deemphasize national identities when creating the *banovinas*, the Drava *banovina* included nearly all ethnically Slovene territories of Yugoslavia and was virtually a "Slovenia." When a Croatian *banovina* was created in August 1939 to placate the Croats (*banovina* boundaries were significantly redrawn to accomplish this), the Slovenes began demanding confirmation of a "Slovene" *banovina*. This might have been achieved by simply renaming the Drava *banovina*, but **Belgrade** did not accommodate the Slovenes. *See also* CLERICALS; JANUARY 6, 1929, DICTATORSHIP; KOROŠEC, ANTON.

DRNOVŠEK, JANEZ (1950–). Born in **Celje**, Janez Drnovšek completed an economics diploma in **Ljubljana** (1973) and a doctorate in economics at the Faculty of Economics and Business in **Maribor**

(1986), writing on the International Monetary Fund and Yugoslavia. International economics and finance remained his forte, as he worked briefly as a regional bank manager (Ljubljanska Banka) and as an economic aide in the Yugoslav embassy in Cairo. In 1986 he was elected to the Slovene Assembly, from which he was appointed representative to the Chamber of Republics and Provinces of the Yugoslav Assembly, where his training proved valuable to federal government discussions on debt management.

In 1989, with relatively little experience in politics or government, Drnovšek was elected by Slovenes as their representative to the presidency of the **Socialist Federal Republic of Yugoslavia** (SFRY); as it was Slovenia's turn to preside in that body (in the prescribed annual presidency rotation), Drnovšek at once also became president of Yugoslavia—at the age of 39, its youngest president ever. In that position from May 1989 to May 1990, he promoted political democracy, economic reforms, and unification with the European Community, soon to become the **European Union** (EU). As a member of the presidency, he continued to be privy to much of the heated debate that surrounded the disintegration of the federal state. He remained in **Belgrade** until October 1991, acting as a mediator between the new Slovene leadership and the old Yugoslav government. After the **Ten-Day War** (27 June–6 July 1991), and a successful three-month truce prescribed by the **Brioni Agreement** (7 July 1991), Drnovšek helped arrange the withdrawal of **Yugoslav People's Army** (JNA) troops from Slovenia.

An avid tennis player, quiet and introverted, multilingual, and a modest public speaker, Drnovšek soon became a major political figure in the **Republic of Slovenia** (RS). In spring 1992, Prime Minister **Lojze Peterle** was ousted by a vote of no confidence and replaced by Drnovšek, who had not even participated in the **election** of April 1990. Joining the Liberal Democratic Party (LDS), Drnovšek was its president through 2002. The party, which tallied the greatest number of votes in the election of December 1992, organized a governing coalition headed by Drnovšek, who again became prime minister. Drnovšek and his party also got the most votes (though never a majority) in the elections of 1996 and 2000. From 1992 to 2004, except for the short period during **Andrej Bajuk**'s government of May–November 2000, Drnovšek's party (LDS) controlled Slovenia's government. (In May 2000, his government had fallen on a vote of no confidence.) Drnovšek did not continue his party's mandate for the full four years after the 2000 election. In 2002, as expected, he ran for president of Slovenia; he won in a second run-off election and replaced **Milan Kučan**, who had served two five-year terms in that position. **Anton Rop** replaced Drnovšek as prime minister and head of LDS. Janez Drnovšek's success as a politician in Slovenia has been attributed to his patience and inclination to seek consensus, although some have characterized these tendencies as a sign of indecision and lack of aggressiveness. His governments have been credited with achieving political stability, measured economic advancement, and validation of Slovenia's new position in the international arena. *See also* GOVERNMENT, SLOVENE, AFTER 1990.

– E –

EAGLE. *See* OREL.

ECONOMY, 1945–1990. The Slovene economy went through the same developmental stages as the Yugoslav economy, of which it was an integral part. There were four distinct stages: an administrative, centrally planned economy from 1946 to 1952; a self-management, market economy from 1953 to 1964, when the state still had a strong administrative role; a self-management, market economy from 1965 to 1974, when market forces became stronger; and a contractual economy from 1974 to 1989. *See also* ADMINISTRATIVE SOCIALISM; CONTRACTUAL SOCIALISM; MARKET SOCIALISM.

The key elements of the first stage were state ownership of the means of production, and the first **Five-Year Plan** (1947–1952). The artificially high goals of the plan, however, were not achieved, especially in **agriculture**. While the social product grew annually by 2.3 percent and industrial production by 6.5 percent, agricultural production fell 3.6 percent. Investments, financed mainly (63.5 percent) by foreign capital, were directed mostly toward heavy industry. The economic consequences of the break with the **Cominform** in 1948 and grave economic conditions led to economic reforms and to subsequent legislation that decentralized the economy.

During the 1953–1964 self-management stage, which emphasized a strong administrative role for the state, the economy experienced a high annual growth rate of the social product (8.6 percent), and agricultural (7.3 percent) and industrial (12.7 percent) production, the latter constituting the largest share of the social product (28.4 percent in 1961). The extensive industrial development in the 1950s was due to investments (foreign loans) and newly employed segments of the labor force. In the early 1960s, a three-pronged reform to intensify the economy took place. First, the financial system was modernized, the **bank** system decentralized, and the General Investment Fund, which directed all investments, was abolished. Second, exports and imports became less centrally directed; the *dinar* was devalued, and conventional tariffs were introduced, following **Yugoslavia**'s joining the General Agreement on Tariffs and Trade (GATT). Third, the state stopped controlling personal incomes but kept control over prices. The effect of these reforms, however, was minimal. Personal incomes rose much more quickly than productivity, leading to high inflation and endangering investments and development (accumulation of capital) in enterprises. State control of prices caused an imbalance between the production of raw materials, **energy**, and food on the one hand, and the needs of the rapidly developing processing industry on the other. The growth of the latter resulted in increased imports of raw materials, enlarged the trade deficit, and created a serious debt crisis in 1964. Yugoslavia owed $800 million, which the treasury was unable to service. The International Monetary Fund (IMF) helped to restructure the debt but demanded **liberalization** of foreign trade, giving impetus to the economic reforms of 1965 and the introduction of a self-management economy with emphasis on market characteristics. *See also* WORKERS' SELF-MANAGEMENT.

In the next stage, with the reforms of 1965, banks were further decentralized and empowered to make decisions on investments; several changes in the area of fiscal policy, which weakened the state role in the allocation of resources, were introduced; foreign trade policy was adapted to GATT rules; the *dinar* was devalued again; and the price reform was carried out. These measures caused an immediate substantial decrease in the growth rate of the social product (from 7.8 percent in 1966 to 2.3 percent in 1967), and of industrial (from 4.3 percent in 1966 to minus 0.3 percent in 1967) and agricultural production (from 16 percent in 1966 to minus 1 percent in 1967). Productivity, employment, prices (14.1 percent), and especially personal income (3.5 percent per year in the productive sector and 20.5 percent in the nonproductive sector) steadily increased in the period 1965–1973, when the economy was expanding, but more modestly than in previous years. The economic reforms of 1965 did not halt the negative economic trends. Accumulation of capital continued to decrease, and enterprises financed their development by borrowing. In 1969 over 50 percent of enterprises were unable to service their debts regularly, yet few went bankrupt. In 1971 Yugoslavia again found itself in a deep debt crisis (42 percent of foreign trade earnings went for payments of principal and interest). The crisis was in part resolved with the help of another devaluation, income from tourism, and remittances by workers employed in Western Europe. See also ROAD AFFAIR.

Economic and political power began to concentrate in the economy. The League of Communists of Yugoslavia (LCY), formerly the **Communist Party of Yugoslavia**, fearing loss of its control over society, placed all blame for social problems and economic problems on market mechanisms. These were subsequently abolished by the constitutional amendments of 1971 and the **Constitution of 1974**, whereby the Yugoslav economy came to be based on contractual principles. In the early period of contractual economy (1974–1979), the economic growth (social product, industrial production) was on the rise due to heavy investments in basic industries, financed by foreign loans. However, without a restructuring of the economy, investments did not bring the expected results (e.g., increased exports and efficient use of capital). In addition, the annual growth rate of productivity (2.4 percent in 1974–1979) was lower than in the previous period (3.7 percent in 1965–1973), while personal incomes rose rapidly (20 percent yearly), which further decreased accumulation and caused problems for the foreign trade balance. In the 1970s, economic problems were exacerbated by the international oil crisis.

Yugoslavia did not have in place any economic mechanism by which to adjust to the world crisis, and the Yugoslav external debt rose from $2.5 billion in 1970 to $15.3 billion in 1979. That was also the last year that Yugoslavia registered any growth in the economy. After that, economic indicators (social product, industrial and agricultural production, and productivity) continued to decline, while the growth rates of nominal personal incomes (from 20.5 percent in 1980 to 1,594.6 percent in 1989) and prices (from 30.4 percent in 1980 to 1,255.7 percent in 1989) increased rapidly. The 1980s were haunted by hyperinflation, decreasing economic efficiency, and increasing debts. A comparison of the four main economic indicators (social product, productivity, unemployment, and retail prices) of the Yugoslav and Slovene economies shows the same economic trends, except that the Slovene economy was slightly more efficient. A large difference existed only in unemployment: On the rise in Yugoslavia since the mid-1960s, it remained low in Slovenia until 1989.

After 1964 three trends were obvious in both the Yugoslav and Slovene economies: a decline in the growth of social product; steady decline in the growth rate of productivity after 1973, which turned negative in the late 1980s; and increasing inflation. The reasons were mainly, but not solely, in the underlying socioeconomic systems and economic mechanisms, which were designed to suit political interests rather than economic goals. Although individual economic measures imposed by the so-called contractual economic system were repealed in the 1980s, it was not until early 1990 that the federal government under Premier Ante Marković abolished all the mechanisms of the contractual economy and began the process of **privatization** of **social property**. Its economic program was based on "shock therapy," which tried to curb inflation at once and to stabilize the *dinar* by pegging it to the deutsche mark. The reforms did not succeed and the economic situation did not improve; by the spring of 1991, when Slovenia proclaimed its independence, it had even worsened. *See also* CURRENCY; ECONOMY SINCE 1991; MANUFACTURING; TOURISM.

ECONOMY SINCE 1991. After Slovenia established its **independence** from **Yugoslavia**, its economy badly needed to be rebuilt and restructured. The economy had suffered under Yugoslavia's political and economic system of **workers' self-management**, during that state's disintegration, and due to the civil wars that followed. Slovenia would achieve its economic objective in two somewhat intertwined stages. In the first, from 1991 to 1996, the focus was on macroeconomic stabilization and **liberalization** of the economy; in the second, from 1996 to 2004, structural reforms and **privatization** were pursued with greater intensity, although not completed. In spite of problems in this period, the transitions from regional to national structure and from a socialist to a market economy were successfully completed. Slovenia, with its essentially restructured and viable economy, was able to join the **European Union** (EU) in May 2004.

As a part of Yugoslavia's economy, Slovenia's had been regional. Therefore, the new state needed to establish its own institutions, laying a foundation for national economic development. One of the most crucial was a central **bank**, Bank of Slovenia (BS), which was established on 25 June 1991 on the premises of the National Bank of Slovenia, a former branch of the National Bank of Yugoslavia. A national **currency** (*tolar*) was introduced in October 1991, at a time Slovenia faced serious economic difficulties. In addition to losing the important export market in former Yugoslav republics, there were severe interruptions in industrial production. From Yugoslavia, Slovenia also inherited a large external debt (approximately $1.8 billion of allocated debt and also the republic's share, approximately 16 percent, of nonallocated federal debt). Also, this was a period of hyperinflation (117 percent in 1991).

The government and the BS stabilized the economy with a number of austere monetary and fiscal policies. Slovenia established a new customs system and further liberalized trade. In 1992 Slovenia also began negotiations with foreign creditors: bilateral official creditors (the Paris Club) and commercial banks (the London Club). During this first stage of economic redevelopment (1991–1996), Slovenia became a state with the financial attributes needed to participate in international capital markets. The BS, regarded as a credible institution, was able to reduce inflation to single digits (9.7 percent average in 1996), and to keep the currency stable and strong. It also increased foreign exchange reserves (from zero in 1991 to 1,853 million euros in 1996 and to 6,560 in mid-2006). Slovenia has been regularly repaying its foreign debt to commercial and Paris Club creditors. From June 1991 until June 1996, Slovenia was directing the London Club debt repayments to a special fiduciary account. In June 1996 new bonds were issued, replacing the old ones, and since then the payments have been going directly to the London Club creditors. Slovenia has been admitted to all key international financial institutions and has been able to access new funding for development, while also reducing its costs.

After 1996 attention turned predominantly to structural and institutional reforms. Some reforms had been started already in Yugoslavia. Despite having a legal framework in place, the structural reforms were slow to take off. The main reasons seem to have been the mode chosen for privatization and also protectionism, which hampered both privatization and the inflow of foreign direct capital. In 1997 the government and the BS introduced a structural reform program as a part of Slovenia's EU accession strategy. In the fiscal sector, spending controls and tax reforms were implemented: On the expenditure side there was pension reform; on the revenue side there was introduction of a value added tax (VAT) and an excise tax. Privatization of the major banks also began, and their role in capital investment was strengthened. For public utilities, the program foresaw price liberalization; for the enterprise sector, there were plans to rehabilitate and privatize companies, to reduce subsidies, and to develop mechanisms to stimulate competitiveness. Some reforms were implemented with greater urgency only after 1999, when Slovenia became an EU associate member. These were privatization of the banks and pension reform. Slovenia became an EU member in May 2004 and entered the European Exchange Rate Mechanism II (ERM II) the next month. The 1992 Maastricht Treaty set five conditions (pertaining to budget deficits, public debt, long-term interest rates, the stability of the currency, and inflation) for prospective EU members to fulfill before final accession. Slovenia achieved all five by June 2006. Nearly balanced for a number of years, Slovenia's post-independence government deficit (equivalent to 1.3 percent of GDP in 2003, and 2.3 percent in 2004) and its public debt (29.5 percent of GDP in 2003, and 30.9 percent in 2004) have been low by European standards, and certainly below the Maastricht thresholds (3 percent of GDP for government deficit, 60 percent of GDP for general government debt). The Maastricht criterion regarding currency stability has been met since November 2005, and the Slovene *tolar* remained close to the central parity during the two-year stay in the ERM II. The 2005 inflation rate was down to 2.5 percent (from 3.6 percent in 2004).

Since 1991 macroeconomic indicators, such as growth rate of real GDP per capita, inflation and unemployment rates, international trade indicators, and balance of payments numbers, show that Slovenia's economic development has been favorable and steady despite a gradualist approach to structural reform. Slovenia achieved one of the highest average economic growths among transition economies in Eastern and Central Europe in a relatively stable environment without social or political turmoil. In the early years of independence, the growth rate of real GDP per capita was negative: –8.9 percent in 1991 and –5.5 percent in 1992. The economy, however, began to recover from the initial shock of separation from Yugoslavia (market loss and disruptions due to separation) with relatively rapid reorientation of its trade to Western countries, liberalization of trade, and stimulation of private initiative on one side, and with austere monetary and fiscal policies on the other. The growth rate turned positive in 1993 (2.8 percent), and over the next decade (1995–2003) GDP grew at an average of 4 percent annually. In 2004, at 4.2 percent, it was the highest of the last five years. Growth was due to strong exports and increased domestic consumption.

Given the smallness of Slovenia's domestic market (2 million inhabitants), **international trade** is very important for economic growth. Since trade liberalization and reorientation began already in the former Yugoslavia, Slovenia was able relatively quickly to redirect its exports and open the domestic market to foreign competition. After independence, Slovenia introduced trade policy reforms, such as reduction of customs duties on raw materials and intermediate goods. High protection remained in effect only for consumer goods and agricultural products. Germany, followed by **Italy**, both EU states, became Slovenia's most important trade partners, along with **Croatia** among the countries of the former Yugoslavia. Slovenia also concluded free trade agreements with several states, easing international trading, and joined GATT (30 October 1994). Between 1999 and 2004, the share of trade with the EU countries declined due to renewed trading with the Balkans and the **Central European Free Trade Association** (CEFTA) countries. But since EU accession in May 2004, the volume of trade with EU countries has increased significantly. Changes also have occurred in trading patterns with other states: Trade with the **United States** has stagnated, while it has increased with **Russia** and the Balkan states, with the exception of Macedonia.

The economy has expanded significantly since 1991. Annual GDP per capita in dollars at current exchange rates has more than doubled, increasing from $6,331 in 1991 to $9,431 in 1995, and $16,115 in 2005. The GDP grew at 3.9 percent in 2005, and was projected to expand at 4.2 percent in 2006, and around 4 percent for 2007 and 2008. Even more illustrative are the data for GDP per capita, measured at purchasing power parity (PPP). In 2001, among the economies in transition, the Slovenian GDP per capita in PPP came the nearest (70 percent) to the average of the EU GDP (100 percent), followed by the Czech Republic (58 percent) and **Hungary** (53 percent).

In addition to its real growth since 1993 at an average close to 4 percent annually, the changing structure of the GDP indicates that the Slovene economy has acquired the markers of a developed economy. The **service industry**, especially **tourism**, **transport**, and communications, began to expand, increasing its share in GDP. Accounting for 54.7 percent of GDP in 1996, the services' share grew to 59 percent in 2004. On the other hand, the share of **manufacturing** in GDP dropped from 50 percent in 1987 to 31 percent in 1996, declining further until 2003, when it rose again (36 percent in 2004). The share of **agriculture**, together with hunting and forestry, which had been declining steadily since **World War II**, continued to shrink after Slovenia's independence. Its share fell from 7.0 percent of GDP in

1991 to 5.2 percent in 1996, and further dropped to 2.2 percent in 2003, rebounding slightly (2.7 percent) in 2004.

Slovenia had the lowest unemployment rate among the countries in transition, even lower than some EU countries. Slovene unemployment began rising in 1991 to a peak in 1993 of 15 percent of the labor force, but in 1994 began a gradual decline. According to the Slovene national accounting methodology, unemployment stood at 13.9 percent in 1995 and at 10.3 percent in 2004. Unemployment data as measured by the standards of the International Labor Organization (ILO) have been lower: 7.4 percent in 1995, and 6.3 percent in 2004. The difference between these two sets of data can be explained by different collection methodologies: ILO data exclude all who earn some income but are not formally employed (gray economy, contract workers, etc.), while the Slovene methodology counts all registered unemployed workers. Older and unskilled workers account for the highest percentage of the unemployed. There is also an increasing number of young educated people who cannot find employment. In addition, there are large regional disparities: The highest concentrations of unemployed are in the Pomurska, Podravska, Savinjska, and Posavska **regions**. Although Slovenia's economy increased its real output by 48 percent during 1992–2002, the labor force and its employment have not changed significantly. The increased output was due to higher productivity in manufacturing and by expanded employment in the service sector.

Average yearly inflation declined very rapidly in the early 1990s (from 177.7 percent in 1991 to 12.6 percent in 1995). Single-digit inflation was first achieved in 1996 (9.6 percent) and fluctuated between 7 and 9 percent until 2002; in 2003 it dropped by almost 2 percentage points to 5.8 percent and in 2005 fell to 2.5 percent. In addition to large public consumption and price growth, wages were one of the most significant inflationary factors in the 1990s. Thus the Social Agreement (2003–2005) to keep the growth of wages slower than the productivity of labor did produce results. Average wages rose 2 percentage points, less than productivity, which rose 4.5 percentage points in 2004. Slower depreciation of the *tolar* in 2004 and increased international competitiveness in the domestic market, which reduced consumer prices slightly, especially food, helped the disinflation trend. Aided by the Bank of Slovenia's moderately restrictive monetary policy, and coordination between monetary, fiscal, and other macroeconomic policies, the Maastricht inflation criterion has been met since November 2005.

Gradualism and political pragmatism, the two main characteristics of economic development unique to Slovenia, influenced the speed and the nature of the reforms of the past decade. The slowness of the restructuring affected (weakened) Slovenia's international competitiveness, but the slow, cautious restructuring of the economy and of the public sector contributed positively to the country's political and social stability, although not without costs. The transition index of the European Bank for Reconstruction and Development (EBRD) for the last decade shows Slovenia persistently lagging behind other new EU members. Although the Slovene index remained one of the highest among them, after Poland, the share of exports to European countries by the new EU states (Hungary, Slovakia, and Czech Republic) grew considerably more than Slovenia's during 1995–2001. While Slovenia's share remained constant for this period, the Hungarian share increased by over 130 percent, the Slovakian by about 90 percent, and the Czech by 30 percent. *See also* DENATIONALIZATION AFTER 1991; ECONOMY, 1945–1990; ENERGY; ENVIRONMENT; FINANCES AND BUDGET; INTERNATIONAL ORGANIZATIONS, MEMBERSHIP IN; NATURAL RESOURCES; STOCK EXCHANGE.

EDUCATION. The first schools in Slovene lands were established in the 12th century by the **Catholic Church**, while the first secular schools appeared only a century later, organized in medieval towns for the education of traders and craftspeople. The 16th-century **Protestant Reformation**, as elsewhere in Europe, demanded schools to teach all "boys and girls" to read scripture for themselves in their own language, but very few schools existed at that time. The first printed Slovene books, including the first primer, *Abecedarium* (1550), by **Primož Trubar,** appeared then. In the 17th century, the **Jesuits** began developing **secondary education** and **higher education**. Although there was a short-lived **university** in existence during the period of the **Illyrian Provinces** (1810–1813), the first Slovene national university, the **University of Ljubljana**, was not established until 1919, a year after Slovenes had become part of the **Kingdom of Serbs, Croats, and Slovenes.** Before that time, Slovenes who pursued higher education would attend European universities, most often somewhere in the **Austrian Empire. Enlightenment** thinking, which was basic to many centralizing reforms in Austria in the 18th century, helped justify the development of an educational system. The First School Act (1774) established schools under state control and allocated limited financial resources for them. In the impoverished countryside, where children were used as an agricultural workforce, regular schools were poorly attended, so the law mandated that Sunday schools instill basic literacy among the peasants. *See also* SLOMŠEK, ANTON MARTIN.

More activity in the area of **elementary education** took place after the **Revolution of 1848**. The Austrian Third School Act (1869) introduced compulsory eight-year elementary education and the use of the Slovene **language** for instruction. Slovene was also used in vocational schools, which had been developing since the mid-18th century, while university preparatory high schools continued to use German as the language of instruction until the early 20th century. At the time, there were both public and private schools. After **World War I**, in the **Kingdom of Serbs, Croats, and Slovenes**, the educational system in Slovenia did not change much. Elementary and secondary schools established during the Austro-Hungarian era were more advanced than those in other parts of the new Yugoslav kingdom, where prewar educational laws remained in effect until 1929, the year that the first Yugoslav educational law was enacted. With it education was centralized and directed by the education ministry in **Belgrade**. The number of schools, especially secondary, grew as did the number of students at all levels. The major achievements for the Slovene educational system in the interwar era (1918–1941) were the introduction of Slovene as the language of instruction for all schools and the establishment of a national university.

During the 45 years of socialism (1945–1990), the educational system went through continual reforms. The basic characteristic of the changes was that they were ideology driven and set by the **Communist Party**, which was renamed the League of Communists in 1952. Immediately after **World War II**, all private elementary and secondary schools were abolished, and compulsory elementary schooling was shortened from eight to seven years, to be more in conformity with the rest of **Yugoslavia**. School curricula, especially for history and social sciences, were modeled on the Soviet experience and adapted to the new social ideology. Major changes in the educational system were introduced by the General School Act in 1958, which featured a unified, eight-year elementary school and reduced the eight-year university preparatory high school (*gimnazija*) to a four-year institution. In the 1960s and 1970s, there was extensive growth of **adult education** as well as secondary, vocational, and higher education. In addition to expansion of the University of Ljubljana, a second university was established in **Maribor** (1975). Toward the end of the 1970s and in the early 1980s, major educational reform—toward career-oriented education—was designed for high schools (general and vocational) and for higher education. A practical result was the abolition of university preparatory schools and a lowering of the quality of schooling in both higher and vocational education. Although each republic had autonomy in cultural and educational spheres, this system was strongly promoted by the League of Communists and federal authorities. There was much professional resistance to it in Slovenia, where career-oriented education was nevertheless introduced in the early 1980s, and a general preparatory high school (*gimnazija*) with an external exam (*matura*) was reintroduced. In the 1970s and 1980s, the federal authorities also pressured the republics to follow a unified elementary education curriculum for all Yugoslavia.

After abolishing **workers' self-management** and **contractual socialism** in 1990 and separating from Yugoslavia in 1991, independent Slovenia embarked on educational reforms. The Ministry of Education undertook an extensive three-phase reform of pre-university education, the phases overlapping in time, but each having a distinct focus. The first began with the adoption of the Law on Organization and Financing of Education (1991), which provided the legal foundations for overhauling the entire organizational structure of the educational system and establishing a new centralized one. In addition, private schools were again allowed; the Faculty of Theology, excluded from the University of Ljubljana in 1952, again became its member; and curricula were cleansed of obvious ideological content. The first phase was concluded by the 1995 publication of *White Paper* (*Bela knjiga*), which outlined the framework for the reform. This was followed by the adoption in 1996 of four basic laws regulating pre-university education.

In the second phase (1996–1998), a new curriculum was prepared for every subject taught in elementary and secondary school. The reforms placed major emphasis on individual differences among students, on improving quality of education, and adjusting the educational system to European standards. The third phase, gradual implementation, lasted until the school year 2003–2004, when the new organization and new curricula were adopted by all the elementary schools. Elementary education, which is compulsory, now lasts nine years (instead of eight), beginning at age six (rather than seven).

Secondary education is organized as a dual system—four-year general and technical college preparatory and two- and three-year vocational programs, leading to postsecondary vocational training and higher education. Postsecondary vocational institutions were introduced in 1996. Higher education (college and university level) expanded the most after Slovenia became independent. The number of students in higher education rose threefold in a little more than a decade during which a few private colleges were opened and the third public university, the **University of Primorska** in **Koper**, was established (2003).

The public system consists of: **preschool** institutions (291 kindergartens); nine-year compulsory elementary schools (815); two-, three-, and four-year secondary schools (144); two- to five-year study programs at institutions of higher learning (three universities with 46 academies, schools, or faculties, and four professional colleges); and postsecondary vocational programs. Adult education with varying functions—compensatory, training and retraining, and general continuing education—has been in existence since World War II. In addition, there is parallel **music** education, where students attend a music school along with their elementary or secondary school, for up to 12 years. Private schools have been established at all levels of education, but their number is small, although growing.

The educational system is now considered well developed. The educational level of the adult population rose significantly over the last 30 years, but the country still lags behind developed Western European countries. In 1971 more than two-thirds of the adult population had only an elementary education or less, about 25 percent had secondary schooling, and just over 3 percent had more than a secondary education. Data for 2002 show that about one-third of the population had elementary education or less, more than half had completed secondary education, while 13 percent—four times the 1971 share—had completed higher education. In 1971 only 1.4 percent of the population was illiterate (less than three years of elementary school), and in the 1991 census its share was insignificant (0.4 percent). Therefore, data were not collected in the 2002 census.

The Ministry of Education and Sport formulates school policy and oversees financing and management of the public education system, except for preschools, where responsibility is shared with the Ministry of Health and Social Services, and for higher education, where the Ministry of Science and Technology takes care of finances and research activities. A nationally prescribed core curriculum, approved by the Professional Council at the Ministry of Education and Sport, is in effect for elementary and secondary schools. Curriculum development is carried out by the Institute for Education and Sport. Two new republic organizations, the National Testing Center and a new supervisory agency, were established to monitor the quality of students' knowledge and the legality of school operations. The Institute for Educational Research and the universities also engage in curriculum development and research. The majority of elementary and secondary school teachers are educated at the Pedagogical Faculties at all three universities and at the Faculty of Humanities of the University of Ljubljana. Between 1992 and 2003 the share of GDP expenditure for education increased from 4.7 percent to 6.0 percent. Its largest part was spent for compulsory elementary schools, followed by secondary/high schools, higher education, and preschool institutions. Since independence, 240 schools have been either built or remodeled, a large financial investment in infrastructure.

EDUCATION, ADULT. Over the years, several forms of adult education have existed in ethnic Slovene territory. In the early 19th century, basic skills were taught to children and young adults in Sunday schools, mostly in rural areas. After 1860 **reading societies** played an important role in educating adults. In the mid-19th century there were agricultural schools and in-service training for teachers. Toward the end of the 19th century, **Liberals** and **Clericals** organized educational societies. After **World War I**, people's **universities** appeared. During post–**World War II** reconstruction, professional training was needed, so masses of adults attended evening schools. The Workers' Correspondence University, established in 1958, made home study possible for many. In the 1960s some factories and businesses organized their own courses, centers, and schools for adults. In the 1970s, emphasis on higher education increased, and almost one-half of the students enrolled at universities and other schools of higher learning were also employed. In 1984 "a university for a third life" (for retirees) was established.

Adult education was mapped out in the 1995 *White Paper on Education* in the **Republic of Slovenia** (RS), the official framework for reform of the educational system. The Adult Education Act, which established the aims, principles, organization, and public service in the field of adult education, was enacted in 1996. It recognized adult education as an integral part of the educational system and provided partial financing for it in the budget. Various institutions offered programs, courses, and other activities for students of all ages, professions, and needs. In 2002–2003, there were 342 such providers, who offered 21,700 adult education programs, attended by 269,422 students. Adult education centers have also become involved in job retraining programs in cooperation with the RS's Unemployment Agency.

While illiteracy is not a problem in Slovenia, lack of functional literacy appears to be. In the 1991 census, illiteracy among Slovenes was insignificant (0.4 percent). However, compared with Organization for Economic Cooperation and Development (OECD) countries in a study conducted in 1998, 77 percent of Slovenes age 16 to 65 performed below the international average on a functional literacy test. Also, the differences in literacy performance between the youngest and oldest age groups were the largest for Slovene respondents. A national plan was devised and adopted in 2004 to raise the adult literacy level. The Adult Education Center of Slovenia has been established in **Ljubljana** to further this goal; it is funded by several ministries, including the Ministry of Education and Sport, the Ministry of Labor, Family and Social Services, and the Ministry of Agriculture. Professionals working in adult education are organized in the Society for Adult Education of Slovenia.

EDUCATION, ELEMENTARY. Primož Trubar, in the 16th century, was the first to demand **education** for all Slovene boys and girls in their mother tongue, but public elementary education did not began to develop until the reforms of Empress **Maria Theresa** in the late 18th century. The General School Statute of 1774 established three types of schools: trivial, principal, and at least one normal school in each province. Education became the responsibility of the state. The School Law of 1805, in effect until 1869, reestablished church control over schools, and despite many obstacles, the number of elementary schools, pupils, and Slovene textbooks grew slowly but steadily throughout the 19th century. The Political School Constitution of 1869, which introduced eight-year compulsory education, lay control over schools, and requirements for teacher training, is the most important legislative act in the development of elementary education. This school law regulated elementary education in Slovenia until 1929, when a centralistic Yugoslav law came into force.

After **World War II** the educational system underwent major and frequent reforms. The most far-reaching reform in elementary education was the 1958 introduction of the eight-year, unified compulsory system for children from age seven to 15. The basic characteristics of this reform prevailed until 2003. Organizationally, elementary school was divided into two cycles: The lower one encompassed grades one to four, and the upper one, grades five to eight with subject instruction. The national curricula were ideologically laden and prescribed, and little attention was paid to differences among individual students, especially gifted ones. Although all children in the early 1970s attended elementary school eight or nine years, almost one-third did not finish. In recent years, only 5 percent of students do not finish elementary school.

Extensive elementary education reform was introduced gradually after 1991, and in three stages. The first was marked by the adoption of the Law on Organization and Financing of Education (1991) and by the publication of the 1995 *White Paper* that provided the reform's framework. In the second phase (1996–1998), new curricula were written. In the third and last phase (1998–2003), new curricula and organizational changes were tried out. Finally, in the school year 2003–2004, the major changes were introduced in all elementary schools. Nine-year elementary schooling began at age six, and elementary schools were organized into three cycles: grades 1 to 3, grades 4 to 6, and grades 7 to 9. New national curricula were established for all subjects in all grades, some changes in instructional organization were introduced, and students with special needs were integrated into regular classrooms.

Nine-year elementary education is compulsory for students age six to 15. The school year runs 190 days from 1 September until mid-June. There are about 20 hours of instruction per week through the fourth grade, and around 30 hours in the upper grades. In 2004, 95 percent of students attending elementary school graduated, a great improvement over 1991, when the drop-out rate was 17 percent. The ratios of one teacher to 12 students and 20 students per class create favorable conditions for quality instruction. An intensive in-service teacher training is in place. The language of instruction is Slovene, but in areas with ethnic **minorities** (Italian, Hungarian), the language of the minority is taken into account. Compulsory schooling is free, but parents are required to provide in part for textbooks. A Waldorf elementary school, the only private elementary school in Slovenia, has been in existence since 1991.

In 2004–2005 there were 814 elementary schools, with 172,521 students and 16,000 instructors. Due to a decreasing birth rate, the number of students in elementary schools has been falling since 1990, when 225,640 students were enrolled, 23 percent more than in 2004–2005. *See also* KUMERDEJ, BLAŽ; SLOMŠEK, ANTON MARTIN.

EDUCATION, HIGHER. In the 16th and 17th centuries, the **Jesuits** organized philosophical and theological studies in **Ljubljana**, Graz, and **Klagenfurt**. The French established the short-lived *Ecole Centrale* (1810–1813) in Ljubljana during the **Illyrian Provinces**. **United Slovenia**, the first Slovene political program (1848), called for the establishment of a Slovenian **university**, but one was not realized until after **World War I**. Before that, Slovenes studied at various European universities, most often in **Austria**. At first, theology was the most pursued study. This changed, however, toward the second half of the 19th century. The number of students more than doubled during the four decades before World War I (from 400 in 1875 to 900 in 1913), and many studied natural sciences and engineering. The newly forming Slovene intelligentsia created a political and professional climate (creating a professional Slovene **language** by writing professional literature and textbooks) and a real demand for a national university. When the **University of Ljubljana** was established in 1919, higher education in Slovenia truly began. In the first year of the new university, there were 942 students (28 were women) and 18 professors, many of whom returned to Slovenia from other European universities.

During socialist **Yugoslavia** (1945–1990), higher education was directly or indirectly controlled by the **Communist Party**. The number of students as well as the number of university schools/departments continued to grow. The University of Ljubljana expanded, and independent colleges were established in other Slovenian cities; **Maribor**'s Economic College was established in 1959, and the **University of Maribor** in 1975. In 1945–1946 the University of Ljubljana had 2,565 students. In 1991–1992 there were two Slovene universities and a number of other institutions of higher learning, with 36,504 students (19,489 women). Slovenia's third university, the **University of Primorska** in the coastal city of **Koper**, was established in 2003. The university system included three public universities with 46 departments, schools, faculties, and colleges, and also nine private colleges in 2005. By 2004–2005, the number of university-level students had almost tripled to 91,229 (56,163 women). The total number of students was even larger (112,228), if including students who have completed all requirements but the degree. Part-time study became widespread in the 1960s and the 1970s, dropped considerably in the 1980s, then recovered. In 2004–2005, part-time students accounted for almost 25 percent (21,405) of the total student population.

The number of those completing undergraduate studies has increased in recent years, but the drop-out rate is still extremely high: Only slightly more than 50 percent of the students who enter the institutions of higher learning graduate. Graduate studies have also expanded. There are more programs, and more students are pursuing specialized master's or doctoral degrees. In 2004–2005, there were 8,378 students enrolled in graduate programs; 1,451 were awarded graduate degrees (1,069 masters/specializations and 355 doctorates). The number of citizens with degrees in higher education increased from 8.9 percent in 1991 to 13 percent in 2002.

The first private institution of higher learning, the College of Hotel and Travel Administration, was established in Portorož in 1994. Since then, nine other private colleges (vocational) and one postsecondary vocational school have been established, and there are plans to establish a private university as well. Most institutions of higher learning are financed through the state budget, tuition, and gifts. Education in public institutions is free for full-time students, while part-time students are required to pay partial tuition. As the number of part-time students is on the rise, they represent a significant financial resource for the universities.

The overall spending for education increased from 4.76 percent of GDP in 1992 to 6 percent in 2004, 1.3 percent of it for higher education. The share of state resources for higher education, however, has not been increasing despite a large increase in the number of students. Through partial state tuition and full tuition at private schools, additional private money has been tapped for education.

The institutions of higher education are regulated by the Higher Education Act, passed in December 1993. The law has changed twice. In 1999 universities were granted more autonomy, and greater emphasis was put on research in teaching and promoting university teachers. In 1999 the Bologna declaration signed by the Europan ministers of education introduced unified European standards for higher education that will prepare students better for the general European labor market and also increase their mobility. Slovenia began implementing the Bologna reform in 2004. The major changes in this for Slovene institutions are implementing a credit system of study, and a shift from a four-year to a three-year undergraduate program, on which master's or specialized programs will be built. Implemenation of the reform will be gradual and is to be completed by 2010.

Slovene universities participate in several international exchange and research programs in Europe, Asia, and the **United States**. A small portion of Slovenia's total enrollment in higher education consists of foreign students: in 2004 there were 980 students from 113 different countries, mostly from the states of the former Yugoslavia.

EDUCATION, PRESCHOOL. Through the early 20th century, kindergartens were private institutions, but they were regulated by the state after **Vienna** issued a decree on kindergartens in 1872. After 1880 the German School Society (*Deutscher Schulverein*) and an Italian nationalist organization (*Lega Nazionale*) established German and Italian kindergartens. Wishing to prevent Germanization and Italianization of Slovene children, the Society of St. Cyril and Methodius (*Družba sv. Cirila in Metoda*) organized Slovene kindergartens in industrial towns in Styria and in the Slovene Littoral, areas where the German and Italian organizations were active.

After **World War II** a small number of public kindergartens, which included only a small percentage of children, were established. Preschool education, however, took a new turn in the 1960s, especially after the 1961 resolution on preschool education, which raised the babysitting function of kindergartens to an educational one. As more and more women became part of the workforce, the number of preschool institutions and children in them rose. In 1981 a new preschool education law incorporated preschool institutions into the educational system. Since 1979 the Educational Program for Education and Care of Preschool Children has been the basis for its programs. In 1965 school-preparatory programs, lasting from a few months to one year, were established; in 1981 they were made compulsory for all children, to help with their transition to elementary school. Children who did not attend kindergarten were required to participate in a special preparatory preschool program. The tendency was to include all five- and six-year-olds in the last year of kindergarten, thus lowering the school entry age.

Since the introduction of the compulsory nine-year elementary school in 1998–1999, children enter school at age six, and compulsory kindergarten programs for preschoolers have been abolished. In the school year 1985–1986, the number of children included in organized preschool education reached a peak of 75,669. The number since then has been falling, but the percentage of the cohort attending preschool institutions has increased from 50 to 60 percent. There are two reasons for the decline: a declining birth rate since 1980, and the gradual implementation (1998–2003) of the nine-year elementary school system, which includes six-year-olds. Children age one to six may attend preschool. Those age one to three are grouped together, as are those from four to six. There are also special preschool programs for **minority** children and children with special needs. The physical standards of public kindergartens are very high: Buildings are well designed, new or modernized, spacious, and well equipped; the ratio of teachers to children is about one to eight. Since 1990 the curriculum for public kindergartens has been updated, and there are extensive efforts to train preschool teachers. In the school year 2003–2004, there were 291 preschool institutions with 54,515 children, representing 61 percent of the entire cohort age one to six. In 2003–2004, the number of children attending kindergartens varied greatly, from 9 percent in rural areas to 95 percent in urban ones. Although not free, kindergarten is heavily subsidized. Tuition is based on family income. Since political pluralism was introduced in 1990, private kindergartens have been established by the **Catholic Church** and by private individuals. A Waldorf kindergarten in **Ljubljana**, the first privately run, has been in operation since 1989. In 2003–2004, there were 17 private kindergartens. *See also* EDUCATION.

EDUCATION, SECONDARY. Elementary education was separated from secondary in ethnic Slovene lands in the 16th century. The **Jesuits** adopted the Protestant system and operated secondary schools until 1774, when state control was established over all **education**. Important changes in secondary schooling were introduced by the New School Plan of 1848 and the Political School Constitution of 1869, when eight-year classical and science high schools (*gymnasia*) were introduced. At that time German and Italian replaced Latin as the language of instruction. Slovene was not used as an instructional language in secondary schools until 1905, when the **Catholic Church** opened its first private Slovene classical gymnasium. Vocational schooling began in the 18th century, and **Janez Bleiweis** was one of its most important promoters in the early 19th century. Between the world wars, as part of **Yugoslavia**, Slovenia had three types of secondary schools: eight-year *gymnasia* (classical or science oriented, which were the more numerous), four-year professional and technical schools, and two- and three-year vocational schools.

After **World War II** the General School Law of 1958 brought important changes to secondary education. It abolished the lower four *gymnasium* grades and incorporated them into an eight-year compulsory elementary school; the *gymnasium* thereafter became a four-year university preparatory school for students age 14 to 18. Secondary education also went through major organizational and curricular changes after 1980, when career and work-oriented reform was adopted. *Gymnasia*, technical high schools, and vocational schools were replaced by a multipurpose, comprehensive secondary school with two levels: The first two years were devoted to general education, while vocational education was emphasized in the last two. The reform did not bear the expected results; secondary school graduates were ready neither for a vocation nor for university study. Immediately after the first multiparty election in the fall of 1990, an updated version of the former three-part secondary school system was restored, reinstating: the *gymnasium* as preparatory school for higher education; the four- and five-year professional school; and the two- or three-year vocational school. In 1991 the *matura* (state external testing) was reintroduced for students who had completed secondary school and planned to continue at the university level. The new dual system (general and vocational) of secondary education allowed students to change schools through a system of shorter additional programs and external exams (*matura*).

Over 90 percent of students who finish elementary school go on with their schooling, but the drop-out rate for secondary schools has been high (20 percent in 1991). The number of students has increased in four-year general high schools (*gymnasia*), while their number decreased in all other secondary schools, especially in two- and three-year vocational programs. Enrollment in the general high schools (*gymnasia*) increased from 1999 to 2003 by 20 percent, while the enrollment in two- and three-year vocational school decreased by about 30 percent. In the school year 2003–2004, there were 143 secondary (high) schools with 100,132 students. In addition 21,732 adult students were enrolled in various adult secondary education programs, provided by 138 institutions.

Since 1990 some private secondary schools have been established, mostly by the **Catholic Church** (the university preparatory *gymnasia* in Želimlje, Vipava, **Ljubljana**, and **Maribor**). There has been a Waldorf *gymnasium* in Ljubljana since 2003. The enrollment in these institutions rose from 1,387 students in 1999 to 2,050 in 2003. All in all, secondary schooling has increased since 1971. Then, only 25 percent of the population had a secondary school education, while in 2002 more than half the population (54 percent) did. About 1.5 percent of the GDP has been spent on secondary education annually since 2001.

EHRLICH, LAMBERT (1878–1942). Lambert Ehrlich, a **Catholic** priest, was a member of the Yugoslav delegation at the 1919 Paris Peace Conference as an expert on **Carinthia**. After **World War I** he was a professor of comparative religion and ethnology at the Theological Faculty at the **University of Ljubljana**. Besides his academic work, Ehrlich was also politically active and was a spiritual leader to Catholic students. Staunchly anticommunist, Ehrlich's followers gathered in the academic club Straža (Watch), ideologically midway between the very clerical Mladci (the Young Ones) and the Christian Socialist Zarja (Dawn). Ehrlich advocated the unification of all Slovenes in an independent democratic state in Europe. Considered an enemy of the **Liberation Front** (LF), Ehrlich was shot in May 1942 on a **Ljubljana** street by the Communist **Security and Intelligence Service** (*Varnostno-obveščevalna služba*, VOS). *See also* CATHOLIC ACTION; FOREIGN RELATIONS AND DIPLOMACY; NATIONAL COUNCIL FOR SLOVENIA; ŽEBOT, CIRIL.

ELECTIONS AFTER 1990. *Election of April 1990:* Once a multiparty system had been established in late 1989 and elections announced for April 1990, members of the newly established **political parties** began their electoral campaigns. At stake were seats in the three-chamber Slovene Assembly (80 each in the Socio-Political Chamber and in the Chamber of Municipalities, and 44 in the Chamber of Associated Labor), which was still constituted according to the **Constitution of 1974**, and four seats on the collective presidency, as well as the position of president of the presidency. The election was held on 8 April, with run-off elections on 22 April to decide races in which no candidate had won a majority. Local elections were also held on 22 April. One exception to this schedule was election to the Chamber of Associated Labor, for which votes were to be cast on 12 April at the workplace. *See also* GOVERNMENT, SLOVENE, 1989–1990.

In general, the 15 parties agreed to support **human rights**, representative democracy, and the rule of law. Most backed decentralization of power in **Yugoslavia**, increased marketization of the **economy**, and the preservation of social welfare programs. Regarding the relationship to **Belgrade**, there was general agreement that

Slovenia should have greater autonomy, but the parties differed as to whether and under what conditions Slovenia might separate from Yugoslavia. Most of the campaign debating, which took place over a period of several weeks, focused on this last issue. All parties were "Slovenia" based—as opposed to "Yugoslavia" based—and most had "Slovene" or "Slovenia" in their name. One represented Slovenia's Italian **minority**, one its Hungarian minority, and one was a branch of Kosovo's Democratic Alliance, representing Albanians in Slovenia.

On 8 April, 83.5 percent of Slovenia's 1,480,000 registered voters went to the polls. Final voting took place on 22 April, and the results were known soon after. **Milan Kučan** (League of Communists of Slovenia–Party of Democratic Renewal, ZKS-SDP) won over **Jože Pučnik** (Social Democratic Alliance of Slovenia–**Demos**, SDZS-Demos), 59 to 41 percent in a run-off vote, winning the seat of president of the presidency. Voters on 8 April had divided the presidential vote among four contenders: Kučan 44.4 percent; Pučnik 26.6 percent; Ivan Kramberger (Independent) 18.5 percent; and Marko Demšar (League of Socialist Youth of Slovenia–Liberal Party, ZSMS-LS) 10.5 percent. For the presidency there were 12 candidates; the winners were: Ciril Zlobec (**Socialist Alliance of Working People**, SAWP); **Ivan Oman** (Slovene Farmers' Alliance); Matjaž Kmecl (ZKS-SDP); and Dušan Plut (**Greens of Slovenia**, ZS). The parties of Oman and Plut were in the Demos coalition. For seats in the Assembly, Demos coalition parties were clearly the winners. They won 47 of 80 seats in the Socio-Political Chamber, 50 of 80 seats in the Chamber of Municipalities, and 26 of the 44 seats in the Chamber of Associated Labor. Parties with less than 2.5 percent of the votes were denied seats.

The elections of April 1990 were a clear rejection of the communist system, but not a decisive rejection of the Communists. Kučan, Kmecl, and Zlobec, a former SAWP official, were of the old regime. Also, it should be noted that the ZKS-SDP tallied the greatest percentage (17.3 percent) of the vote for the Socio-Political Chamber, while the ZSMS-LS (former youth organization) came in a close second (14.5 percent). Primarily, it was the coalition strategy of Demos that was responsible for the succession of a noncommunist government in 1990. *See also* GOVERMENT, SLOVENE, AFTER 1990.

Election of December 1992: Slovenia's second multiparty election took place on 6 December 1992. This election was the first to be held after the declaration of **independence** and the ratification of the **Constitution of 1991**. The constitution provided for a new governmental structure, and so voters in December 1992 cast votes for president of the **Republic of Slovenia** (RS) and for representatives to a State Assembly and a State Council. **Milan Kučan** was again elected president. In a field of eight candidates, Kučan received a clear majority in the first round of voting—nearly 64 percent of presidential votes. For the 90 seats in the State Assembly (Parliament), there were 1,505 candidates, most belonging to one of 25 parties that participated in the election. Eight parties won seats in the Assembly: Liberal Democratic Party (LDS) (22), **Slovene Christian Democrats** (SKD) (15), **United List of Social Democrats of Slovenia** (ZL) (14), **Slovene National Party** (SNS) (12), Slovene Farmers' Alliance–People's Party (SKZ-LS) (10), **Democratic Party of Slovenia** (DSS) (6), Greens of Slovenia (Greens) (5), and Social Democratic Party of Slovenia (SDSS) (4); the Italian and Hungarian communities also each elected one representative (as stipulated by the new constitution). Twenty-two of the 40 members of the State Council (a body representing corporate interest groups) were also elected that day. Early the following month, **Janez Drnovšek** (LDS) was elected head of government, or prime minister, by the State Assembly and began forming independent Slovenia's first nonsocialist government based on the new governmental structure. Soon after, the State Assembly elected Herman Rigelnik its president, or speaker, and the State Council elected Ivan Kristan its head.

Before the election Drnovšek (LDS), who had replaced **Lojze Peterle** as prime minister in May 1992, assembled an effective working association with leftist parties. The group included LDS, DSS, SDSS, and the Greens; ZLSD also supported but did not join the group. During the campaign, they promoted an agenda of economic and political modernization. Meanwhile the conservative parties, particularly SKD, clamored for a resolution to issues from the communist period (**privatization**, social policy, and interpretation of **World War II** events). The fact that campaign rhetoric was hotest over these topics proved misleading about what was most important to the voters. When the votes were tallied, it was clear that Slovene voters were most concerned with economic and political stability. After all, the wars in former Yugoslavia were still raging to the south, Slovenia's security was possibly in jeopardy, and its **economy** was struggling due to the war and loss of markets.

Election of November 1996: On 10 November, 21 parties competed for seats in the State Assembly, but given that 2.5 percent of the vote was required to qualify for positions, only seven parties got them: **Liberal Democracy of Slovenia** (LDS), the new name adopted in 1994 by the Liberal Democratic Party after it merged with two branches of the former **Slovene Democratic Alliance** and with the Greens, 25 seats; **Slovene People's Party** (SLS), 19 seats; Social Democratic Party of Slovenia (SDS), 16 seats; Slovene Christian Democrats (SKD), 10 seats; United List of Social Democrats (ZLSD), 9 seats; **Democratic Party of Retired Persons of Slovenia** (DeSUS), 5 seats; and Slovene National Party (SNS), 4 seats. One seat each was reserved for representatives of the Italian and Hungarian communities. Elections for president and also the State Council, where voting was on a five-year cycle, would be held in November 1997.

It was clear already in summer 1996 that the fall election was going to be different. The world had changed for Slovenia. The wars in former Yugoslavia had ended a year before, and the country's breakup was sealed at the Dayton peace conference in November 1995. Security was no longer the grave issue it had been in Slovenia's first two post-communist elections; there was even serious talk that Slovenia was on the short list of states to be asked to join the **North Atlantic Treaty Organization** (NATO) later that year. Also, prospects for the economy were looking up. Parties were therefore less inclined to set aside ideological differences in the name of unity, and those with personal political ambitions seemed bent on achieving power even if it meant making political enemies while also engendering disgust among Slovene voters.

That summer Slovene parties therefore rushed to employ public relations people and election experts. They compiled voter questionnaires and did telephone polling to determine the electorate's opinion. ZLSD set up a candidate training school and, like the other parties, concentrated on creating a positive "image" (they used the English word). That summer the competition was focused on producing advertising with "feel good" themes. SLS party leader Marjan Podobnik was pictured smiling, the caption reading "For Slovenia with Love." The SKD provided handout items carrying the party logo—potholders, neckties, scarves, key chains, chocolates, and other sweets. Party posters used photos of citizens who called for support of the party of their choice. LDS's lethal campaign weapon was Arthur, Janez Drnovšek's dog; when asked whether he was voting LDS, Arthur barked an affirmative "Woof." Issues were hardly discussed, or were lost in the campaign circus. Some voters surely noticed the lack of gravity. Only 74 percent voted—a decline from 86 percent in 1992. Once the vote was tabulated, it would take more than three months to form a government.

Election of October 2000: Sixteen parties participated in the 15 October 2000 election. Because a system of proportional voting had been accepted by amendment to the Constitution of 1991 in July 2000, a minimum of 4 percent of the vote was required for representation in the State Assembly or parliament. The following eight parties qualified for seats: Liberal Democracy of Slovenia (LDS), 34 seats; Social Democratic Party of Slovenia (SDS), 14; United List of Social Democrats (ZLSD), 11; SLS + SKD Slovene People's Party (SLS), 9; **New Slovenia–Christian People's Party** (NSi), 8; Slovene National Party (SNS), 4; Democratic Party of Retired Persons (DeSUS), 4; and **Party of Young People of Slovenia** (SMS), 4. As in previous elections, one seat each was reserved for an Italian and a Hungarian.

The election did not produce any real surprises. The campaign began in mid-September, a month before the balloting. Polls indicated that LDS would win big; some supporters predicted it could capture an absolute majority, which would preclude major coalition-building. In any case, it was expected that the left would return to power easily. Polls also pegged correctly a decline in popularity for the "Spring parties"—SLS, SKD, and SDS. The government of May–November 2000, headed by **Andrej Bajuk**, had tested the abilities of the "Spring parties" at governing and found them wanting. The three turned out to be their own worst enemies: They engaged publicly in bitter infighting, took uncompromising stands, and failed to comprehend that the democratic process required debate and consensus building. It should be noted that the October 2000 election saw two new parties win seats: NSi, a party Bajuk and **Lojze Peterle** (formerly head of the Slovene Christian Democrats) organized the previous summer; and SMS, a party representing young people. The impressive showing of SMS, which had enrolled 6,000 members after it was established in July 2000, was unexpected. Of the 1.6 million eligible voters, 70 percent voted. Twelve new parliament members were women, and only 44 of those elected had held seats in government before. Borut Pahor (ZLSD) was chosen president of the State Assembly. Six weeks after the election, Janez Drnovšek (LDS) completed his coalition government, comprising LDS, ZLSD, SLS, and DeSUS; SMS signed an agreement with the coalition but did not join.

Election of October 2004: The election of 3 October produced a voter turnout of just over 60 percent. The voters had 23 candidate lists from which to choose the State Assembly's 90 new members. With a minimum vote requirement of 4 percent, only seven parties qualified for seats in parliament. The Slovene Democratic Party (SDS) received the most votes, entitling it to 29 seats in parliament and the opportunity to form a government. The other parties winning seats were: Liberal Democracy of Slovenia (LDS), 23; United List of Social Democrats (ZLSD), 10; New Slovenia–Christian People's Party (NSi), 9; Slovene People's Party (SLS), 7; Slovene National Party (SNS), 6; Democratic Party of Retired Persons of Slovenia (DeSUS), 4; and Italian and Hungarian national community representatives, one seat each.

The SDS victory brought an end to 12 years of LDS dominance in Slovenia. This result had not been expected; pre-election polls still showed LDS holding its own in spite of rigorous campaigning by opposition parties in September and the political clashes that characterized the last half year of **Anton Rop**'s government, both among political parties and within LDS itself. No doubt voters had tired of LDS, and by what many perceived as a growing arrogance that was nurtured by LDS's effective monopoly on power. Some viewed LDS's 12-year tenure as an extension of the pre-independence government; now that SDS had won, LDS's reign could be regarded as the long goodbye of communism. Even some with leftist political preferences had been worrying that Slovenia was not developing a real multiparty system. Hence the SDS victory presented an opportunity to see if Slovenia could really produce capable leaders of different political persuasions.

Janez Janša, head of SDS, was asked to form a government. He was confirmed as mandator in early November; his coalition government, which included NSi, SLS, and DeSus, was approved by the assembly on 3 December.

ELECTIONS, PRESIDENTIAL, AFTER 1991. The office of president of the independent **Republic of Slovenia** (RS) was established by the **Constitution of 1991**, adopted on 23 December of that year. **Milan Kučan**, the former communist leader, then an independent, assumed the post as interim president until an official election could be held the next year. The constitution specified that the president be directly elected, that the term of office be five years, and that it be limited to two consecutive terms. The first presidential election was held in December 1992, and Kučan was the winner. He was reelected in December 1997. In December 2002, **Janez Drnovšek**, head of **Liberal Democracy of Slovenia** (LDS) and at the time prime minister, was elected to the post. The RS's next presidential election would be held December 2007. Refer to appendix 1.

EMIGRATION, SLOVENE. According to some estimates, more than 25 percent of all Slovenes live in the diaspora (350,000 permanently and 150,000 temporarily as workers). While there have been different reasons for Slovene emigration in the past, poverty was the most prevalent. Slovene emigration began in the Middle Ages with Slovene peasants and craftspeople moving to **Italy**'s more developed states and cities. During the **Counter Reformation** (17th century), Protestants emigrated to Germany and, later, to the **United States**. The most massive emigration from less developed Slovene **regions** (**Prekmurje** and **Bela Krajina**, Dolenjska, and Notranjska) took place between 1880 and 1914. Slovenes went mostly to the Americas (mainly the United States) and Western Europe (mainly France and Germany), but some also sought work in Bosnia, Serbia, Egypt, **Russia**, and elsewhere. Due to restrictive U.S. immigration laws, emigration to the United States nearly stopped after **World War I** but continued to Western Europe, South America, and Australia. In this period, many Slovenes also emigrated for political reasons, especially from Primorska (Slovene Littoral) to escape fascist denationalization pressures. After **World War II** there was a sizable political exodus of Slovenes (more than 12,000) of every social class (intellectuals, workers, peasants); while some remained in Western Europe, most went to the United States, Canada, Argentina, and Australia. A large number of skilled workers emigrated in the 1960s and 1970s, mostly to Western Europe, to find better working conditions and pay, but a few also left for political reasons. Individual emigration is still taking place in the form of a "brain drain" to technologically more developed countries.

Slovene emigrants have often maintained their ties with their homeland. In 1927 the Society of St. Raphael (*Družba sv. Rafaela*) was founded under the auspices of the **Catholic Church** in **Ljubljana** with branches in **Maribor** and **Murska Sobota**. The society maintained contacts with emigrant organizations abroad and provided them with assistance. The Society of St. Raphael, abolished in 1945, was replaced in 1951 by the Slovene Emigrant Association (*Slovenska izseljenska matica*, SIM), which for many years worked only with the earlier, primarily economic emigrants and their organizations, ignoring the post–World War II political émigrés. Since 1954 SIM has published the monthly *Rodna gruda* (*Native Soil*) and annual *Izseljenski koledar* (*Emigrant Almanac*). Since the 1980s SIM has tried to broaden its activities to include all Slovene emigrants and their descendants, regardless of political orientation, but has had only limited success. The post–World War II political émigrés continue to look upon SIM as a leftist organization. The World Slovene Congress (*Svetovni slovenski kongres*) was established in 1991 in Ljubljana in order to unite all Slovenes—those living in Slovenia and abroad (**minorities** in Italy, **Austria**, and **Hungary**, and emigrants, regardless of their political and ideological beliefs)—to work together for the preservation of their national identity, as well as to promote Slovenia around the world. In 1994 Slovenia in the World (*Slovenija v svetu*) was established, working exclusively among the political right.

Emigrant organizations receive official support from government agencies, such as the Ministry of Foreign Affairs, and there is a state office for Slovenes abroad. In 1987 the Chamber of Commerce and SIM founded a quarterly, *Slovenija*, published in English, which was a well written and beautifully illustrated informative magazine about Slovenia and reached beyond Slovene emigrants abroad. It ceased publication in 2004 due to financial problems. Besides the state agencies and societies, the Catholic Church has always cared for Slovene emigrants. The **Slovenian Academy of Sciences and Arts** established a very active Institute for Slovenian Emigration Studies, which systematically and with a multidisciplinary approach undertakes research on emigration and publishes a scholarly journal *Dve domovini* (*Two Homelands*). *See also* CLEVELAND; EMIGRATION, SLOVENES IN EUROPE; EMIGRATION, SLOVENES IN NORTH AMERICA; EMIGRATION, SLOVENES IN SOUTH AMERICA AND AUSTRALIA; MISSIONARIES, SLOVENE.

EMIGRATION, SLOVENES IN EUROPE. Emigration of Slovenes to non-Slovene ethnic territories in Austria-Hungary and to other European states began in the second part of the 19th century. From poor areas of Gorenjska and Štajerska, Slovenes emigrated to industrial regions of Germany (Westphalia) in the last two decades of the 19th century. At that time, many also went to Bosnia, Romania, and **Russia** as seasonal laborers and forest workers. With severe restrictions on emigration to the **United States** after 1924, Slovenes turned to Western Europe. It is estimated that in the interwar era 50,000 Slovenes (many from **Prekmurje**) went to Germany; 58,000 to France (among them many miners from Zasavje); 8,000 to Belgium; and 6,000 to the Netherlands. Being familiar with the German language, Slovene workers in Germany assimilated rather quickly, but the same was also true for France and other European countries. Early on, Slovene emigrants joined various Austrian and, later, Yugoslav cultural and sport **societies**, often organized along political lines. Catholic societies of St. Barbara (protector of miners) were active among emigrants in Germany and other countries. Slovenes organized many singing societies but, unlike in the United States, released very few publications. During the rise of Nazism in Germany in the 1930s, many Slovenes left Germany for the neighboring countries. Before **World War II**, left-oriented emigrants were active in the People's Front movement in France, and many went to fight in the Spanish civil war. During World War II, they joined the resistance movement in France, and many were supporting the **National Liberation Struggle** (NOB) in Slovenia. After the war, some returned to Slovenia.

In the 1960s and 1970s, there was a new wave of economic emigration to Western Europe, above all to West Germany. Many returned to Slovenia in the 1980s and 1990s, but the rest integrated well, keeping their Slovene cultural societies, such as Sava and Lipa in Paris; Bled in Essen; and a **France Prešeren** club in Brussels. While members of some Slovene societies gather only occasionally, others have developed a rich cultural life. Besides singing societies, Slovene **language** courses for children and adults are popular. An important link for emigrants is the **Catholic Church**.

Due to economic developments in the 1960s, Slovenia became—if only minimally—a country of immigrants, most of whom came from other Yugoslav republics: More people immigrated to than emigrated from Slovenia. Although immigration from the other Yugoslav republics almost stopped in the 1980s because of economic recession, the migration balance remained positive and has increased since Slovenia'a independence. The net inflow increased from 0.1 percent (2,107 persons) of total population in 1990 to 0.3 percent (6,436 persons) in 2005. Immigrants are mostly from the states of the former Yugoslavia. Although Western Europe has drawn predominately economic emigrants from the post-socialist countries, this trend has not applied to Slovenes, who enjoy a relatively high standard of living at home. It was expected that migration would increase after

Slovenia became a member of the **European Union** (EU) in 2004. So far, however, only a small number of highly educated and skilled Slovenes have emigrated, and motives for migration were not economic. Although the brain drain has been numerically small and not significant for the European Union, it is of concern to Slovenia.

EMIGRATION, SLOVENES IN NORTH AMERICA. Slovenes have emigrated to North America since the late 17th century and settled in both the **United States** and Canada. Early Slovene emigration was mainly economic. Emigrants were poor but literate, and peasants who joined the ranks of low-paid labor generally worked their way into the middle class. In the United States, where the heaviest influx of Slovene emigrants took place before **World War I** (1880–1914) and after **World War II** (1946–1956), there are around 300,000 Slovenes and their descendants. Earlier emigrants settled mainly in small mining towns, such as those in Minnesota, but later they populated large urban centers like Chicago, working in factories. The largest Slovene settlement in North America has always been **Cleveland** and its suburbs, where there is a strong Slovene cultural and social life. The **Catholic Church** (over 30 Slovene parishes in 1941) was the main bonding nucleus. Due to restrictive U.S. legislation, emigration to the United States almost ceased after 1924. The thousands of political emigrants after World War II gravitated toward Cleveland and other American cities with significant Slovene populations, because they found immigration sponsors among Slovenes.

Slovenes in the United States organized mutual insurance or fraternal organizations, which have also been engaged in cultural, educational, social, and sports activities. The earliest, established in 1894, is the Carniolan Slovenian Catholic Union (*Kranjsko slovenska katoliška jednota*, KSKJ), renamed American Slovenian Catholic Union in 1964. In 2004 it had 29,000 members with 60 lodges in 31 states. KSKJ has a center in Jolliet, near Chicago. In 1904 the Slovene National Benefit Society (*Slovenska narodna podporna jednota*, SNPJ) was organized. It has drawn its members mainly from nonreligious emigrants and has become the largest institution among Slovenes. In 1994 it had 31,000 members with 229 lodges and 5,700 members in youth branches. Besides serving their members as insurance companies, both fraternal organizations have been dedicated to maintaining and promoting Slovene culture in the United States. In 2001 SNPJ opened a new recreation center in Enon Valley, Pennsylvania, with a Slovene Heritage Center and other amenities; members come together for social, cultural, and sport events, among which the annual celebration of ethnic culture *Slovenefest* is the most prominent. The American Fraternal Union (*Ameriška bratska zveza*) with 27,000 members, the Slovenian Women's Union (*Slovenska ženska zveza*) with 12,000 members, and the Slovenian-American Heritage Foundation, which supports cultural activities, have also played an important role in the Slovene ethnic community.

In the United States, Slovenes founded over a hundred newspapers and other publications; many were short-lived, while others such as *Voice of the People* (*Glas naroda*) lasted for decades. Still published, partially in English, are the weeklies *Prosveta*, organ of the SNPJ; *Voice of Youth* for SNPJ young members; the independent paper *Ameriška domovina* (*American Home*); *Amerikanski Slovenec* (*American Slovene*), the KSKJ organ; and the biweekly *KSKJ Voice*. The Slovenian Women's Union publishes a bilingual monthly, *Zarja* (*Dawn*), and Slovene Franciscans in Lemont, Illinois, publish a religious monthly, *Ave Maria*, in Slovene. Many Slovenes have been prominent in American society, including Bishop **Friderik Baraga** (1797–1868), the writer **Louis Adamic** (1898–1951), Ohio governor and U.S. senator Frank Lausche (1895–1987), and many others.

In Canada, there are about 30,000 Slovenes, who began arriving in large numbers after 1924. Many political emigrants came after World War II and were joined in the late 1950s and 1960s by a sizable number of skilled workers from less-developed Slovene regions. The first Slovene settlements grew in the vicinity of mines (e.g., in Ontario). After World War II, Slovenes settled in industrial centers, mostly in the Toronto area, where five Slovene parishes have been established. The parishes have served also as important Slovene ethnic centers with educational, cultural, and social activities. Branches of KSKJ and SNPJ established in the 1920s ceased to function during World War II. Canada has many Slovene ethnic societies with strong cultural (choral and dance groups), educational (Slovene language courses), and recreational activities. Publishing activity has not been as strong as in the United States. The most important publication has been the monthly *Slovenska država* (*Slovene State*), established in 1950 in Chicago, published in Canada since 1954 by the Slovene National Union in Canada (*Slovenska narodna zveza v Kanadi*), an organization of Slovene anticommunist intellectuals advocating a free and independent Slovene state. In Canada, the eminent Slovene immigrant is Toronto's archbishop, Cardinal Aloysius Ambrožič. *See also* EMIGRATION, SLOVENE.

EMIGRATION, SLOVENES IN SOUTH AMERICA AND AUSTRALIA. Slovene emigration to South America began at the end of the 19th century. Two major periods were the 1920s and the post–**World War II** years. Early on, emigration was mostly economic, but some was motivated by denationalization pressures in **Primorska** (the Slovene Littoral) after its annexation by **Italy** following **World War I**. While Slovenes settled in various countries of South America (e.g., Brazil, Uruguay), the largest group ended up in Argentina. Because of their generally pro-Yugoslav and politically leftist views, many of their activities and organizations were banned during the Perón regime (1946–1955). These Slovenes organized anew after 1957; the Argentina-Slovene society Zarja (Dawn), founded in 1958, and the Slovenian-Yugoslav Society **Triglav**, established in 1974, both in Buenos Aires, have been two main venues for the "old" Slovene immigrants. Both have worked closely with the Slovene Emigrant Society (SIM).

In the late 1940s and 1950s a large (over 6,000) new group of Slovene political emigrants came to Argentina. "Little Slovenias" were organized, with various **societies**, churches, elementary schools, and flourishing publishing activities. While the largest and most active Slovene settlement exists in Buenos Aires, there are others (e.g., in Mendoza). Postwar political émigrés, staunch anticommunists, until very recently had contact neither with the "old" liberal economic emigrants nor with their native land. In 1948 the Društvo Slovencev (Slovene Society), later renamed Zedinjena Slovenija (United Slovenia), was established. The Slovenska kulturna akcija (Slovene Cultural Action) has been very active, organizing cultural events and publishing the quarterly *Meddobje* (since 1956), an informative bulletin *Glas Slovenske kulturne Akcije* (*Voice of Slovene Cultural Action*), and over 200 books in various fields. The Confederation of the United Slovene Anticommunists, with its headquarters in Argentina, has since 1963 published the monthly *Tabor* (*Fort*), earlier called *Vestnik* (*Messenger*). The weekly *Svobodna Slovenija* (*Free Slovenia*), which had underground beginnings in **Ljubljana** during World War II and continued in the postwar refugee camps, is also published in Argentina. *See also* BAJUK, ANDREJ; RODE, FRANC.

Australia also has a large group of Slovene immigrants (25,000), who began arriving after 1924, when emigration to the United States stopped. The influx of immigrants was especially heavy after World War II (1947–1950) and has never completely ceased. The earlier immigrants came mostly from Primorska. Slovenes settled predominantly in industrial centers, especially in Sydney and Melbourne, where Slovene ethnic societies have been the core of all Slovene ethnic activities. Pastoral activities and religious education among the Slovenes have been carried out by the Franciscans, who also built churches in Melbourne, Sydney, and Adelaide. Publishing of literary works written by Australian Slovenes, and periodicals such as the religious monthly *Misli* (*Thoughts*) and *Nova doba* (*New Era*), and other cultural activities are organized by ethnic societies and the **Catholic Church**. Slovenes have been successful in promoting the Slovene **language** in the public educational systems in the states of Victoria and New South Wales. *See also* EMIGRATION, SLOVENE; EMIGRATION, SLOVENES IN NORTH AMERICA; MINORITIES, SLOVENES IN ITALY.

ENERGY. Slovenia has insufficient **natural resources** for generation of energy needed for domestic consumption. More than half of primary energy sources (coal, natural gas, and petroleum) must be imported. In 2003 petroleum and petroleum products accounted for the largest share of energy imports (58 percent), followed by natural gas (20 percent), electricity (12 percent), and coal (7 percent). Due to an expanding national **economy** and a growing standard of living, energy consumption has been increasing: Per capita consumption of electricity went up from 5,413 kilowatt hours in 2000 to 6,455 in 2003. Although industry's share in consumption of energy has declined over the last decade, **manufacturing** (with construction) remains the heaviest energy consumer (46 percent in 1987, 32 percent in 2003), followed by **transport** (21 percent in 1987, 29 percent in 2003); the other users, including households (32 percent in 1987, 39 percent in 2003), account for the rest.

In 1960 over 70 percent of energy was provided by coal and wood, while petroleum accounted for only 7 percent of total energy use. But in 1987 petroleum, with a 38 percent share, led as a source for domestic energy needs, followed by coal and wood (21 percent), electricity (20 percent), and natural gas (16 percent). Since 1992 the demand for gasoline and diesel fuel has been growing; in 2004 it accounted for 46 percent of total energy use. Electric energy is generated by conventional thermal plants (powered by coal, fuel, and natural gas), hydroelectric power plants, and a nuclear plant operated by the Nuklearna Elektrarna Krško (NEK), built in 1981 as a joint Croatian–Slovene project. Starting its operations in 1983, NEK is the single largest electricity generator in Slovenia, producing 4,963 gigawatts net energy in 2003 (38 percent of total annual production of electricity). In the late 1980s and the 1990, because of radioactive waste storage problems, there were attempts—supported by international organizations—to close the plant, but these were unsuccessful. In 2000 the plant was modernized by installing two new generators, increasing its efficiency. In 2003 thermal plants, using mostly coal (lignite, low-sulfur imported coal) generated about the same amount of electricty as the nuclear power plant, while several hydroelectric plants on the Drava, Sava, and Soča rivers produced 24 percent of Slovenia's electricity. Slovene **rivers** have a much higher potential for electricity generation than is being currently exploited (about 43 percent).

Holding Slovenske elektrarne (HSE), the largest producer and distributor of electricity in Slovenia, has six electricity-generating companies: Dravske elektrarne Maribor, Savske elektrarne Ljubljana, Soške elektrarne Nova Gorica, Termoelektrarna Brestanica, Termoelektrarna Šoštanj, and Premogovnik Velenje. In 2003 HSE established a subsidiary in **Italy** (HSE Italia) and also opened offices in **Belgrade**. Employing more than 5,000 people, HSE, an environmentally conscious company, acquired the concession for the construction of five hydropower plants (Boštanj, Blanca, Krško, Brežice, and Mokrice) on the lower reaches of the Sava River. The project, whose completion is planned for 2018, will double the production of clean, water-generated electricity. In 2004 HSE also initiated the project "Modra energija" (Wise Energy) and joined the Renewable Energy Certificate System (RECS). The project has been joined by numerous small and large manufacturing companies and individual households. The largest single Wise Energy user is one of the leading pharmaceutical companies, Krka, in **Novo Mesto**. *See also* CROATIA, RELATIONS WITH.

Historically wood, water, and wind were used as energy resources in the Slovenian lands. Records show that coal became an important energy source in the 17th century, and electricity was introduced in the 1880s. In 1883 the first electric light was switched on in **Maribor**, and in 1884 the first hydropower plant began operating in **Škofja Loka**. A thermal plant was built in **Ljubljana** in 1888, and at the turn of the century, crude oil was introduced as an energy source. Although the electrification of Slovenia began at the turn of the century, it was not completed until the late 1950s. After **World War I**, many large power plants were built on the Drava, Sava, and Soča rivers. By 1941 there were 833 hydropower plants (mostly small), and about one-half of Slovenes had electricity in their homes. With an emphasis on industrialization after **World War II**, increased energy needs required construction of large thermopower plants and a nuclear plant.

Environmental concerns at home and the **European Union**'s (EU) environmental requirements have stimulated more interest—and action—in clean energy production. All stages of energy production affect the environment, which has been polluted in the **Republic of Slovenia** (RS), especially near industrial centers, endangering forests, people's health, and social development. In 1987 a new Slovene energy plan, which called for more rational energy use and an orientation toward cleaner and ecologically safer energy sources (small hydropower plants, and geothermal and solar energy), was adopted by the Assembly. In 1996 the government adopted a new Strategy of Energy Use and Supply, which calls for maintaining a sustainable level of electric power production in the existing thermal plants, constructing new hydropower plants, and increasing the use of renewable energy sources. A 1999 energy law provided for the liberalization and deregulation of the energy market. Thus, an internal energy market, created in 2001, was opened to foreign investors in 2003. Heavily subsidized by the government in the past, energy prices did not reflect real economic costs. The new economic environment allows the market to determine the price of energy, and as a result prices have been increasing. *See also* ECONOMY, 1945–1990; ECONOMY SINCE 1991; FIVE-YEAR PLAN, FIRST; FORESTRY; MINING.

ENLIGHTENMENT. The Enlightenment in the Slovene lands began later than in the rest of Europe and had a different focus. It was primarily cultural. Baron **Žiga Zois** and his group of Slovene intellectuals—**Marko Pohlin**, **Blaž Kumerdej**, **Anton Tomaž Linhart**, and **Valentin Vodnik**—were active promoters of the ideas of the Enlightenment, and especially of the Slovene national awareness. The publication of Pohlin's *Kranjska gramatika* (Carniolan Grammar, 1768) is considered the beginning of the movement, which ended with the death of its two most important figures, Vodnik and Zois, in 1819.

During the Enlightenment period, professional and cultural **societies** and institutions were established. **Academia Operosorum**, which stimulated the development of **baroque** arts, was revived. **Libraries**, public and private, were important centers of cultural life. The Philharmonic Society was established in 1794, **theaters** were built in **Ljubljana** and other larger towns (**Maribor, Klagenfurt, Celje**), and the first Slovene play was performed in 1789. Interest in the natural **sciences** also began to develop. Foreign scientists, such as the physicians Janez Scopoli and Balthasar Hacquet, worked in Slovene lands. Several prominent scientists of Slovene origin went abroad and became known for their scientific discoveries. Among them are the astronomer Avguštin Hallerstein, who worked in Beijing, the oceanographer Žiga Popovič, the physician Anton Marko Plenčič, and the mathematician and ballistics expert **Jurij Vega**. *See also* JOSEPH II.

ENVIRONMENT. Rapid industrialization after **World War II** adversely affected Slovenia's quality of air, water, and natural habitat. Systematic measurements of air quality—sulfur dioxide (SO_2) and carbon dioxide (CO_2) emissions—began in the late 1970s. That decade also saw the passage of Slovenia's first, though not enforced, environmental laws: Air Protection Act and Water Protection Act, 1975; Noise Protection Act, 1976; Waste Management Act, 1978. Environmental policies and legislation changed greatly after 1990. In 1993 an Environmental Protection Act introduced economic incentives to curb environmental pollution. In 1994 an Environmental Protection Fund was established to help finance ecological projects. The Environment Protection Act was amended in 2004 to align Slovene environmental legislation with that of the **European Union** (EU); in 2005 the National Assembly adopted the National Environmental Protection Program, which guides environmental policies in Slovenia.

Data indicate that air pollution has been reduced, but the air still remains critically polluted. From 1977 to 2000 the concentration of SO_2 dropped by about 60 percent. Because of 1995 regulations regarding liquid fuels and the 2001 ban on leaded gasoline, lead emissions have also been reduced. The requirement that thermal power plants use better-quality, lower-sulfur coal has reduced SO_2 emissions, which mostly come from **energy** generation. Since 1989 the largest producer of thermal power, TE Šoštanj, has been systematically introducing new technology to reduce SO_2 and nitrogen oxide (NOx) emissions. In spite of these ecological measures, in

1999 energy production remained the single largest air polluter, 28 percent, while traffic and households followed with 19 and 17 percent, respectively. Since 1992 NOx and greenhouse gas emissions have been increasing because of more traffic and the age of cars (7.3 years in 2002). Traffic not only is an air polluter but contributes to the increasing level of noise in urban areas and along major traffic routes. **Ljubljana**, the capital, is a small city by European standards but has to deal with the same problems as larger cities: air polluted by traffic, energy production, and industry. Air pollution causes damage to people's **health**, natural habitat (trees, animals), cities, and groundwater (affected by acid rain). In order to meet European Union (EU) as well as Kyoto Protocol commitments, Slovenia will have to step up measures to improve its environment.

One of Slovenia advantages has always been its abundance of water (16,000 cubic meters of available water annually per person). Water is concentrated in the central part of the country along the Sava River and its tributaries; the least is available along the Mura River in northeastern Slovenia. The level of groundwater, however, has significantly decreased in the last decade. The most endangered water supply is in the Primorska **region**, particularly when summer **tourism** is at its peak. Although the quality of surface water (**rivers**, lakes) has improved, the quality of groundwater continues to deteriorate. The major water polluter of surface waters is industry. Many **manufacturing** plants still release untreated waste water, containing heavy metal residue and toxic liquids, into water flows. Groundwater across Slovenia continues to be seriously polluted with nitrates, phosphates, and pesticides because of intensive use of chemicals by **agriculture**. The use of mineral fertilizers almost doubled in the period 1990 to 2000, totalling 3.1 kilograms per hectare of arable land, putting Slovenia among the largest consumers of fertilizers in Europe. In 2000 the quantities of pesticides (atrazine is the main culprit) and nitrates significantly surpassed critical levels in seven of Slovenia's 13 aquifers. The northeastern region (Prekmursko, Dravsko, and Ptujsko Polje) is the most polluted. In 2001 an environment-friendly program for farmers, promoting organic farming, was adopted and funded.

Increasing industrial and municipal waste has also become a problem. The increase, which is significant and harmful, is mostly due to industrial waste, which more than doubled between 1999 (30,000 metric tons) and 2001 (80,000 metric tons). Slovenia also produces over 400 kilograms of municipal waste per person annually (418 in 2003). Many unprotected "wild" waste dumps continue to pollute groundwater. As a new EU member, Slovenia is obligated to meet Europe's standards with respect to generation of clean energy, water conservation, and waste treatment.

Air and water pollution have endangered **forest** biodiversity, and in several areas forests (spruce and oak) have been dying off. Although links have been established between polluted environment and health problems in the most polluted regions (**Celje, Velenje**, Mežica, and Zasavje), there has been little systematic research of the issue.

Although there are many environmental problems and concerns in Europe, Slovenia remains one of the countries richest in natural treasures. While its territory accounts for only 0.004 percent of the entire earth, 1 percent of all living creatures (2 percent of land creatures) are represented there. Slovenia's Red List of endangered species contains hundreds of plants and thousands of animals, many of which are endemic and all of which are protected by law. Slovenia is an active participant in the European ecological project Natura 2000, through which many areas and sites covering about 35 percent of the RS territories and many endangered species have been identified. One of the main goals of the project, begun in 2002, is to build public awareness of ecological problems and to stimulate action to protect the environment. In 2004 about 10 percent of the territory was protected by law, but that should be enlarged to 30 percent by 2014. Slovenia adopted the World Conservation Union's (IUCN) classifying system of areas needing protection. IUCN categories range from I, where no human intervention is allowed in protected areas, to V, which permits various degree of human intervention. In 2006, Slovenia had one national park, category II/V (**Triglav** National Park, since 1924), three regional parks, category V (Kozjansko, since 1981; Škocjanske jame, since 1996; and Notranjski regijski, since 2002), and 41 local parks, mostly category V (such as Park Sečoveljske soline and Park Kolpa). In addition, 52 natural reservations and 1,217 registered natural monuments have been identified in these protected areas. Two biosphere reservations, also included in the UNESCO list, are Triglavski narodni park and Škocjanske jame. See also ECONOMY, 1945–1990; ECONOMY SINCE 1991; KARST; KRAS PLATEAU MINING; POSTOJNA; TRANSPORT.

EUROPEAN COMMUNITY (EC). See EUROPEAN UNION (EU).

EUROPEAN UNION (EU), RELATIONS WITH. When Slovenia declared **independence** in June 1991, the nation expressed a strong wish to be accepted back into Europe—the 70 years as part of **Yugoslavia**, the Balkans, were regarded as exile from the homeland. What Slovenes had in mind was joining the European Community (EC), which was scheduled to merge its 12 states into a European Union (EU) in 1992. During the **election** of April 1990 and the **plebiscite for independence** later that year, there was already much talk from all Slovene political quarters about joining a united Europe. After declaring independence, there was a half-year battle to gain the EC's **recognition**; that came on 15 January 1992. Soon after, the **Republic of Slovenia** (RS) associated with various Europe-based organizations, among them the **Organization for Security and Cooperation in Europe** (OSCE) and the **North Atlantic Treaty Organization** (NATO) Partnership for Peace. Slovenia also strengthened participation in European regional associations such as the **Alps–Adriatic Working Community** and **Central European Initiative**, and it joined the **Central European Free Trade Association** (CEFTA). Several of the states belonging to these organizations were EU members, thus Slovenia, by joining them, put a foot in Europe's back door. The real objective, however, was full-fledged membership in the EU.

Slovenia's accession to the EU took more than a decade. In 1993, a year after recognition by the EU, Slovenia signed a cooperation agreement with the union. For several years, however, there was little movement in the relationship. The war in the former Yugoslavia continued until late 1995; the region's future remained a question mark. Meanwhile the EU was going through birth pangs and sorting out its own house. By 1996, however, the time was right for Slovenia to apply for membership, which it did in June of that year. In 1997 the EU Commission Opinion was issued, proposing the names of countries that might be considered for EU accession, and Slovenia's was among them. (The chief criteria were that the state has stable democratic institutions and rule of law, a functioning market economy, the capacity to handle competitive pressures and market forces, and the ability to take on the obligations of union, such as political, economic, and military organizational memberships.) In March 1998 Slovenia's official negotiations toward membership began, with **Janez Potočnik** as chief negotiator. *See also* ECONOMY SINCE 1991.

While the process was underway, the EU, through its various agencies, gave Slovenia 65 million euros in assistance annually through the PHARE program, the Instrument for Structural Policies for Pre-Accession (ISPA), and Special Accession Program for Agricultural and Rural Development (SAPARD). The work undertaken was monumental, for it required coordinating—the EU's word for it was *harmonizing*—Slovene laws and institutions with those of Europe. Literally hundreds of laws and regulations in Slovenia had to be rewritten or amended, which kept the Slovene National Assembly and dozens of ad hoc committees busy for several years. The **Constitution of 1991** was amended, allowing Slovenia's sovereignty to be limited by membership in the EU. Slovenia's negotiating process was completed at the end of 2002, and on 23 March 2003 a referendum on EU membership received a near 90 percent affirmative vote (NATO's referendum that same day tallied only 66 percent approval). The Slovenes, it was clear, were strongly behind union, though they were realistic about its potential costs and sovereignty infringements. A final report was submitted to the EU in November 2003, and on 1 May 2004 Slovenia acceded to the EU, one of 10 new members (the others were Cyprus, Czech Republic, Estonia, **Hungary**, Latvia, Lithuania, Malta, Poland, and Slovakia).

As a member of the EU, Slovenia has 1 percent of the population and 1 percent, or seven, of the seats in the European Parliament (EP). The first Slovenes were elected to the EP in June 2004. **Liberal Democracy of Slovenia** (LDS), **New Slovenia** (NSi), and the **Slovene Democratic Party** (SDS) each got two seats; the seventh seat went to the **United List of Social Democrats** (ZLSD). As spokespersons for one of the smaller states in the EU, Slovenia's representatives, who vote as members of EU political parties, will need to ally with others to promote Slovenia's interests. In 2008 Slovenia will have an opportunity to command attention as it assumes the presidency of the EU for one-half of that year. With the EU membership, some of Slovenia's agreements with multinational organizations, such as CEFTA, have become obsolete; however, bilateral agreements are allowed, and Slovenia has retained them with **Austria** and **Italy**. The 2008 presidency will bring additional jobs for Slovenes, who will be needed to work on the EU's various commissions—this in addition to the 335 high-paying administrative positions in Brussels already available to Slovenes. As a state with external EU (Schengen) borders, Slovenia has acquired important obligations. Its border with **Croatia**, which is not an EU member, requires a security force of 1,900. Its operation is subsidized by the EU, but Slovene personnel are needed to perform the border functions.

Joining the EU has both benefits and drawbacks. The loss of sovereignty and national identity issues seem to concern Slovene intellectuals most; the bulk of the population, however, looks to the EU as an opportunity for economic betterment. **Trade** with the EU members, which in 2004 accounted for 66.5 percent of Slovene exports and 82.4 percent of imports, will probably increase. Once favorable (and traditional) trade relations with southeastern Europe will probably decline because those states are still outside the EU. Also, because Slovenia's gross domestic product (GDP) is high (73 percent of the EU average in 2004 and increasing), it is not likely to benefit long from EU developmental subsidies (75 percent of EU average GDP is the upper cutoff point). Slovenia introduced the euro as its official **currency** in January 2007. The effect that monetary integration will bring is as yet unclear.

There are many other unanswerable questions about what the EU will mean for Slovenia in the future, as there is much about the EU itself that still needs working out, particularly as it acquires new members, and because an EU constitution still needs to be adopted. But Slovenia is now among those who can contribute to the decision-making, and most Slovenes view their return to Europe in a favorable light. *See also* INTERNATIONAL ORGANIZATIONS, MEMBERSHIP IN.

EXPRESSIONISM. Expressionism in Slovene **arts**, which became the dominant but unified movement after **World War I**, can be divided into three periods: from World War I until 1921, when expressionism began to replace symbolism; 1922–1923, when expressionism in painting and sculpture flourished; and 1924–1928, when expressionism was giving way to other art movements—a new reality and, later, color **realism**. There were two geographic centers of expressionism. One was the central Slovene area, whose artists gravitated to **Ljubljana**. This included the Dolenjska **region**, with **Novo Mesto**. **Božidar Jakac** was its central figure. The other area was the Slovene Littoral, centered in **Trieste** (Trst) and **Gorizia**. Avgust Černigoj and Veno Pilon were the most important painters. The founder of expressionism, Avgust Černigoj (1898–1985), organized the first expressionist exhibition in Ljubljana in 1924. His paintings also included elements of Russian constructivism, Dada, and futurism. Expressionism was most distinctive in the sculpture and painting of the brothers Kralj. The work of France Kralj, who was influenced by Gustav

Klimt, was mystical, figurative, full of primitive physiognomies, and laden with religious and peasant motifs. France Kralj organized the Club of the Young (*Klub mladih*), where artists from both centers cooperated in popularizing expressionistic art abroad. Tone Kralj followed his brother but developed his own style. The expressionistic sculpture of the Kralj brothers, France Gorše, Lojze Dolinar, and others had the same characteristics as their expressionistic painting. Human suffering and its contemplative study, symbolic movements, and often religious motifs were reflected in the sculpture of Gorše, Dolinar, and Tine Kos, who were influenced by the Croatian sculptor Ivan Meštrović. Expressionism ended by the 1930s. *See also* LITERATURE; MUSIC.

– F –

FABIANI, MAKS (1865–1962). Maks Fabiani, a contemporary of **Jože Plečnik**, was an architect, urban planner, inventor, and writer. Although he worked as an architect of the Secession style in **Vienna** and in **Ljubljana, Trieste**, and **Gorizia**, he is more important as an urban planner who worked not only in Slovenia but elsewhere in Europe (Vienna, Poland). After the 1895 earthquake in Ljubljana, he drew up the plan to rebuild the city using the principles of Secessionist Vienna's urban planning. He was very much concerned with both esthetic values and functional aspects of city planning. *See also* ARTS.

FALCON. *See* SOKOL.

FEDERAL EXECUTIVE COUNCIL (FEC) / SAVEZNO IZVRŠNO VEĆE (SIV). The Federal Executive Council was a governmental body in socialist **Yugoslavia**. Introduced by the **Constitutional Law of 1953** as a "collegial" cabinet unit to replace the more traditional Council of Ministers, its functions and powers evolved with subsequent **constitutions**. The FEC was elected by the **Federal People's Assembly** (FPA). Its chair, who held the title of president, was essentially the prime minister of Yugoslavia.

FEDERAL PEOPLE'S ASSEMBLY (FPA) / ZVEZNA LJUDSKA SKUPŠČINA (ZLS) (1946–1963). The post–**World War II** government of **Yugoslavia** grew out of wartime political institutions that were established in liberated territories by the Communist-led **Partisan** resistance/revolution in the territories under their control. The program of the **Liberation Front** (LF) was approved in an 11

November 1945 plebiscite, and on 29 November 1945, the third anniversary of the founding of the **Antifascist Council of National Liberation of Yugoslavia** (AVNOJ) and the second of the proclamation of a revolutionary government for Yugoslavia, the **Federal People's Republic of Yugoslavia** (FPRY) was officially proclaimed. The FPRY's government was formalized by the **Constitution of 1946**.

The highest governmental organ of the new state was the Federal People's Assembly (FPA), which had two chambers: a Federal Council, elected on the basis of population, and a Council of Nationalities, in which each republic had an equal number of representatives. Voting for delegates, who served four-year terms, was direct. Although the FPA was constitutionally the highest power in Yugoslavia, in practice the presidium (which was elected by the Assembly and responsible to it) and the government actually wielded the greatest power. The presidium, consisting of a president, six vice presidents (one for each republic), and up to 30 members, had far-reaching powers. It called and dismissed the FPA, called elections, determined the legality of legislation, issued amnesties, ratified international agreements, received foreign diplomats, and named members to the government of Yugoslavia.

The Constitutional Law of 1953 altered the nature of the FPA. It eliminated the Council of Nationalities and substituted a Council of Producers. The law also eliminated the presidium and replaced it with a president of the FPRY. *See also* GOVERNMENT, YUGOSLAV, 1945 (PROVISIONAL).

FEDERAL PEOPLE'S REPUBLIC OF YUGOSLAVIA (FPRY) / FEDERATIVNA LJUDSKA REPUBLIKA JUGOSLAVIJA (FLRJ) (1946–1963). **Yugoslavia** at the end of **World War II** was renamed the Federal People's Republic of Yugoslavia (FPRY), a name it retained for nearly two decades. Rejecting the monarchy of the interwar years, it became a "people's democracy" and focused on developing socialism. Much of the terminology is common to the political-ideological language of Soviet-bloc states after 1945. The **Constitution of 1946** legalized the new state and invested the **Federal People's Assembly** (FPA) with ultimate power. The name of the state was changed in 1963 to **Socialist Federal Republic of Yugoslavia** (SFRY), and the **Constitution of 1963** affirmed the new name and outlined the state's new government.

FEDERATION OF TRADE UNIONS OF YUGOSLAVIA. *See* TRADE UNIONS.

FILM. Slovenes saw their first movies in 1896, only a year after the Lumière brothers' short silent films were shown in Paris. The first Slovene films were made in 1905, when Karol Grossmann shot three short silent films about life in Ljutomer (a town in Pomurje/**Prekmurje**); however, these movies remained unknown until 1948. In the interwar period (1918–1941), only a few Slovenes were involved in feature film production, but several documentaries were made. For example, Metod Badjura, who organized the first film company, Sava, made over 30 silent documentaries. **Božidar Jakac** also shot several short 16 mm films about Slovene emigrants in the United States (1929–1931) and, later, also about different Slovene regions, including **Bela Krajina**. In addition, two full-length silent movies were produced: *V kraljestvu Zlatoroga* (In the Kingdom of the Goldenhorn, 1931) and *Triglavske strmine* (The Triglav Slopes, 1932). Although both films focused on describing the natural beauties of the Julian **Alps**, the latter was already organized around a story and contained a message. A documentary, *Bela Ljubljana* (White Ljubljana, 1932), was the first sound movie. In the late 1930s, the owner of **Ljubljana**'s Union movie theater established the professional filmmaking company Emona (1939–1945), which had its own technical base and permanent collaborators; it specialized in making short films. Before **World War II**, Slovenes were avid moviegoers, supporting 63 movie theaters. However, film was not considered an **art** form in Slovenia at the time, and **liberals** and conservatives alike saw it as a threat to the national culture and **language**.

The professional film industry began to develop more systematically after World War II. Interested in film as a propaganda tool, Slovene **communists** insisted that the film industry, developing in **Belgrade**, should decentralize, and that Ljubljana should get its own film company. They succeeded. Established and financed by the state in 1946, **Triglav** film produced many documentaries and three full-length films yearly. In 1953, after the state stopped financing Triglav, the golden era of Slovene film ended. Domestic production dropped, and Triglav survived mostly by co-producing films with foreign partners. In 1956, Triglav was reorganized into Film-Servis and Viba Film; the latter became the major filmmaking company, producing two to four full-length and some short films yearly, while Film-Servis, which had also been engaged in co-production with foreign filmmakers, closed its operation in 1960s. Since the 1970s, other organizations have been involved in film and video production, such as Studio Ekran and Studio Unikal. In the early 1960s, **Radio and Televison** (RTV) became an important film producer, initially of documentaries, but later also of television plays and full-length films in cooperation with Viba Film. In 2001 Triglav was organized anew as a film production and distribution company. In 1968 the Slovene Film Archive was established as part of the Archive of the Republic of Slovenia, and in 1973 the Slovene film **museum** opened its doors.

The Slovene film repertory consists of around 200 full-length films and more than 1,000 documentaries and short films, which have been shown in Slovenia, at international film festivals, and as retrospectives of individual filmmakers. Filmmakers worked in all film genres: documentary, commercial, and animated short and full-length feature films. Although varying over time, **realism**, based mainly on Slovene literary works, has predominated in full-length films. The films have dealt with war, social and political themes, and the brutality of socialism, the latter especially after the 1980s. After World War II, Franc Štiglic (1919–1993), the most prolific film director, whose work spanned three decades, made the first full-length art film, *Na svoji zemlji* (On One's Own Land, 1948). It marked the beginning of the patriotic, **Partisan** film. His most successful film, *Dolina miru* (The Valley of Peace, 1956), also dealt with the same topic. Another productive director, who began working immediately after the war, was Jože Gale (1913–). He produced the first full-length popular children's film about the child "hero" *Kekec* (1951); its sequel was *Srečno, Kekec* (Good Luck, Kekec, 1963).

After World War II, socialist realism had some impact on film production but it did not last long. In the 1960s Slovene films began emulating European film, especially the French New Wave, with two directors in particular producing a large numbers of high-quality films: Boštjan Hladnik (1929–2006) and Matjaž Klopčič (1934–). One of Hladnik's films, *Ples v dežju / Dance in the Rain* (1961), was proclaimed the best Slovene film ever. In the 1980s and 1990s, film production was revived under younger and middle-aged directors who created socially and politically critical films, which were contemplative as well as poetic. Among these directors is Karpo Godina-Ačimović, who introduced the **postmodernist** film *Splav Meduze* (The Raft of the Medusa, 1980).

Also active in Slovenia was the Czech director František Čap (1913–1972), who made 11 films. His *Vesna* (*Spring*, 1953), the first entertaining Slovene film and certainly a very popular one, the first of a three-film sequence, was followed by *Ne čakaj na maj* (Don't Wait for May, 1957) and *Naš avto* (Our Car, 1962). In *Trenutki odločitve* (Moments of Decision, 1955), Čap was the first to deal publicly with the **National Liberation Struggle** (NOB) and the civil war during **World War II**, and tensions between the **Partisans** and the **Home Guard**. Several important Slovene films were produced by directors from other Yugoslav republics. Dušan Makavejev and especially Živojin Pavlović filmed important Slovene literary works, including **Ivan Cankar**'s *Na Klancu* (On the Slope).

In the early 1990s the Slovene Film Fund was established, which supported the production of three select full-length films per year. Additional films were produced with the support of either national television or independent producers, and thus, in the late 1990s and the early 2000s, a number of young and independent Slovene filmmakers appeared with interesting films. Metod Pevec produced the *Carmen* (1995) and *Pod njenin oknom* (Beneath Her Window, 2004). In the latter, very successful film, shown also internationally, Pevec created an interesting story about a young woman through which he discusses human values (trust, love) and social values (abortion) in Slovenia. Damijan Kozole has directed socially critical films, such as *Rezervni deli* (Spare Parts, 2003), which deals with trafficking in human parts, and *Delo osvobaja* (Labor Liberates, 2005), a film about the "ills" of unemployment. The Slovene film industry co-produced a few international films, such as *Nikogaršnja zemlja* (No Man's Land, 2001), directed by Denis Tanović, which was shown at the film festivals in Cannes and Los Angeles; it received an Oscar for the best foreign language film. Documentary filmmaker Maja Weiss was the first woman to direct a full-length film, *Varuhi meje* (Guardians of the Frontier, 2002), in which she told the story of three women dealing with various social topics, from nationalism and political opportunism to feminism and homosexuality. Hana Slak directed the successful *Slepa pega* (A Blind Spot, 2002), her first film, dealing with drugs and alienation of young people.

Slovenia established a few important film institutions, such as the Slovene Film Library (*Slovenska kinoteka*) in Ljubljana, which functions as a film museum. Since 1990 an International Film Festival (LIFF) in Ljubljana includes a pre-festival program with selected new Slovene films. *See also* ART; LITERATURE; THEATER.

FINANCES AND BUDGET. Under the self-management system, socialist Slovenia had a decentralized budget and an ineffective public expenditure management system. Thus after 1991 the state gave priority to reforming public finances and reducing public spending. Although reform began soon after Slovenia proclaimed **independence**—for example, the centralization of financing the public sector, **privatization**, and restructuring of the social sector—progress was slow at first. The reforms gained momentum after 1996 as part of Slovenia's **European Union** (EU) accession strategy. New budget legislation, the Public Finance Act, was adopted in 1999, enabling tax reforms: introducing a value added tax (VAT) and an excise tax. A new pension system began its first phase of implementation in 1999. Addressing the **health** care system has been central to the reforms. The 1999 finance act detailed procedures for budget preparation and presentation.

In the early 1990s, public expenditure management reforms supported the economic transition by restructuring **banks** and industry, by issuing government bonds to replace nonperforming assets of banks, by bailing out companies with big losses, and by offering technical assistance to the financial sector. The government also funded needed workforce reduction (early retirement programs, unemployment benefits). After 1996 these programs became less generous. Prior to Slovenia's accession to the EU, fiscal policies and public finance reforms, key elements in the transition to a market economy, were also harmonized with the EU legislation and the EU methodologies for gathering, analyzing, and reporting data.

While public finances in most post-communist transition states deteriorated and recorded high deficits, Slovenia's general government budgets remained balanced or had a surplus until 1997, when they reached the equivalent of 1.2 percent of GDP. According to the International Monetary Fund (IMF), government expenditures and revenues relative to GDP fluctuated between 39 to 43 percent for the period 1995 to 2004, and the structure of expenditures was similar to that of the EU members' average. The deficit in 1997 was due to increased public expenditures at a time of lower revenues from **international trade**—there were lower customs duties because of the EU and **Central European Free Trade Association** (CEFTA) trade agreements. Despite plans to reduce the deficit, government spending after 1997 rose more than projected (government growth, higher public sector wages, and pensions, which were the single highest item among the expenditures). The general government deficit rose to its highest level—the equivalent of 2.9 percent of GDP—in 2002. It dropped in 2003 and 2004 (1.4 percent for both years). The Slovene general government deficit was the lowest of all transition states and remained within the EU's Maastricht limits (less than 3 percent of GDP). Slovenia is regarded as a moderately indebted country. Since 1995 the national debt did not exceed the EU criterion for candidate states (equivalent to 60 percent of GDP). It increased from 27.8 percent in 1995 to 59.2 percent in 2004, but as its structure has changed, the increased debt has not been a severe fiscal burden. *See also* CONTRACTUAL SOCIALISM; ECONOMY SINCE 1991; PRIVATIZATION; SOCIAL SECURITY.

FIVE-YEAR PLAN, FIRST / PRVI PETLETNI PLAN (1947–1952). In April 1947 the **Federal People's Assembly (FPA)** enacted a Five-Year Plan for the Development of the National Economy, prepared by the Yugoslav Planning Commission under **Boris Kidrič**. Four months later, Slovenia adopted its own, rather ambitious plan with the same basic goals (elimination of economic and technological backwardness, development of the state sector of the national **economy**, and raising the general welfare of the workers). Although specific projections for particular sectors of the economy varied from republic to republic within **Yugoslavia**, they all featured investment in heavy industry. The year 1939 was used as a base for measuring economic gains. To eliminate disparities in economic development among individual republics, the Five-Year Plan called for a 10-fold (Bosnia and Hercegovina) to 26-fold (Macedonia) increase in industrial production in the underdeveloped parts of Yugoslavia, while relatively small increases were planned for the developed republics, Croatia and Slovenia. Such allocation of resources, particularly in industry, which strongly favored the underdeveloped republics, caused severe economic and political problems, and significantly contributed to the plan's failure. Already in the first year of its implementation, several problems complicated its progress. The expulsion of Yugoslavia from the **Cominform** in 1948 and the ensuing economic blockade against the **Federal People's Republic of Yugoslavia (FPRY)**, the forced collectivization of **agriculture** (1949), and severe droughts in 1950 and 1952 created further difficulties. In 1950 a revised, more limited Key Investment Plan followed the same basic strategy.

None of the four basic or specific objectives of the Five-Year Plan was attained by 1952. Agricultural production was the most problematic: Due to forced collectivization and meager investment (5 percent of total investment), it fell below the 1939 level. There was neither enough food for consumption nor raw materials for industry. The West helped by supplying both, especially food, to prevent widespread hunger. The "political" investments in industry in the underdeveloped republics, which enabled the infrastructure to maintain its operation, increased the cost of industrialization. They also slowed their positive effect on the social product, and prevented the more developed republics, Slovenia among them, from developing and growing. With inept and misguided economic policies, where political goals were more important than economic performance, the Five-Year Plan almost destroyed the already fragile Yugoslav economy.

Slovenia's plan aimed at an increase of 270 percent in heavy industry (chemical and metal), 140 percent in small trade and **crafts**, and 124 percent in agriculture. Almost a half-million square meters of apartment buildings, new schools, kindergartens, and **health** centers were to be built. After Yugoslavia's expulsion from the Cominform, Slovenia faced the same problems as the rest of Yugoslavia. However, Slovenia's plan was not changed but rather expanded, and an additional people's loan was floated to finance it. Youth brigades and voluntary and forced labor were instrumental in the massive construction of that time. Three hydroelectric (Maribor-Otok, Medvode, Moste-Žirovnica) and one thermoelectric (Šoštanj) power plants were built. Several large industrial plants were built in Slovenia, for aluminum (Kidričevo), cement (Anhovo), heavy machinery (**Ljubljana**), textiles (**Novo Mesto**), furniture (**Nova Gorica**), and iron and steel works (Jesenice). Due to this industrialization, Slovenia's social structure changed dramatically; the proportion of peasant population rapidly decreased from 70 percent in 1939 to 40 percent in 1953. *See also* ADMINISTRATIVE SOCIALISM.

FLAG OF THE REPUBLIC OF SLOVENIA (RS). Adopted in 1991, the state flag of the **Republic of Slovenia** is based on the old Slovene national flag. It consists of three equal horizontal stripes: white (top), blue, and red, each occupying one-third of the height of the flag, to which the newly devised coat of arms was added in the top-left corner so that half of it lies in the white and half in the blue stripe. The coat of arms, in the form of a shield, contains the image of **Triglav** in white against a blue background at the center; beneath are two wavy blue lines, depicting sea and **rivers**. Above Triglav are three golden, six-pointed stars arranged in an inverted triangle. The shield is bordered in red. The length and width of the flag are in a 2:1 proportion.

FOLK ART. In late 18th century, with the general improvement of living conditions, folk art became more widespread. Folk artists decorated the farms (houses, hayracks, granaries) of rich peasants and also erected wayside shrines, in a style variant of peasant **baroque**. Paintings and frescoes were schematic, without much detail, and they were generally instructive; usually bright colors were used, and religious and floral motifs dominated. Other Slovene folk art forms included decorative masonry work, **wrought iron**, and wood carvings. Typical folk art products were religious paintings on glass and painted beehive panels, which first appeared in the 18th century and remained popular throughout the 19th century. Painted in oil, beehive panels were decorated with religious and secular motifs (everyday life, folk tales, wars), full of folk wisdom, often satirical and socially critical. A large collection of beehive panels can be seen in the apiculture museum in **Radovljica**. Originating elsewhere in Central Europe, but later mass produced locally, paintings on glass became popular wall decorations in the 19th century and are often found in peasants' homes as part of *Bogkov kot* (God's corner) in the main room of a house. Folk artists also made and painted furniture. Carved and painted chests appeared already in the 16th century in **Gorenjska** but became more popular in the late 18th and 19th centuries, when they were usually part of a bride's dowry. Across Slovene lands in the 19th century, rural homes were decorated with painted wooden chests, cradles, and clocks of all sizes (from grandfather to smaller wall clocks). *See also* ARCHITECTURE, VERNACULAR; ARTS; BEEKEEPING; CRAFTS, TRADITIONAL; DESIGN.

FOLK MUSIC AND DANCE. Instrumental and vocal Slovene folk **music** have both ritual and entertainment functions and vary greatly by region. There are songs relating to love, wine, work traditions, changes of season, and religious and family **holidays**. Based on folk **literature**, the form, lyrics, and music of the songs are simple. Their rhythms and measures vary. Songs are mostly in the major key; sometimes in a pentatonic scale, as found in **Prekmurje**. Except in rare instances, folk singing had three- or four-part harmony long before formal choirs were established in the second half of the 19th century. Slovenes like to sing. Indeed, hundreds of choirs have been established in schools, by cultural **societies**, and in city and village churches.

Instrumental music was used in dance, especially at weddings, or to accompany traditional celebrations. In the past, old instruments—

the *drumlja* (Jew's harp), the *oprekelj* (a small, stringed, percussion instrument), the *trstenka* (panpipe), and the *žvegla* (fife)—were popular. Many instruments were made by local craftspeople. The accordion, the major folk instrument of the 20th century, was introduced into the Slovene lands only in the first half of the 19th century; the *frajtonarca* (button-box accordion) has been especially popular. German zithers and simpler, locally made ones have been also favored by folk musicians from the mid-19th century on. Although in great demand, folk musicians were not particularly respected. Instrument playing was not considered a profession; it was perpetuated as a family tradition. Often playing in groups of three or four, folk musicians were exclusively men before **World War II**.

Old Slovene dances were rather simple, made up of rhythmic walking, jumping, and free combination steps. One could dance alone, in pairs, or in groups. Group dances with a "bridge" element were the most frequently danced in the older days in **Bela Krajina** and in the Gorenjska **region**. The *kolo* (a circle dance), brought from Croatia in the 16th century, was popular in Bela Krajina. Various *kolos*—such as *Lepa Anka* (Beautiful Anka) and *Hruške, jabuke, slive* (Pears, Apples, Plums)—evolved later and are still performed today. The oldest dance forms known are the *povštertanc* (pillow dance), in which a dancer chooses his partner by offering a pillow or handkerchief; *Marko skače* (Marko is jumping) in Prekmurje; and *Igraj kolo* (Dance the *Kolo*) in Bela Krajina. Dances from Rezija (now in **Italy**) differ very much from dances of other Slovene regions. Introduced in the 19th century, polkas and waltzes quickly replaced older dances, which today are performed primarily by folkloric groups.

FOLK TRADITIONS AND CUSTOMS. In Slovenia, many folk traditions are associated with the celebration of seasons. Although some originated in pre-Christian times, folk traditions were adopted, modified, and perpetuated by the **Catholic Church**. A part of everyday life in the past, folk traditions today provide entertainment and education or are used as **tourist** attractions. Their traditional setting was the family, village, or town; now the town square, the street, or the stage are artificial backdrops for folk traditions performed as an **art** form.

Preceding Lent is carnival season, rich with many traditional celebrations, which have regional variations. Such celebrations, often modified traditions, observed today include *kurentovanje* in the vicinity of **Ptuj**, *laufarija* in Cerkno, *Selma* in Kostanjevica, and *pustovanje* in Mozirje. Parades, carnivals, and masquerade balls accompany these events. The best-known tourist *kurentovanje* is in Ptuj. The central figure is the *kurent*, who wears fur clothing and an unusual mask with horns, representing human and animal traits, evokes images of another planet. The custom is a mystery: It is not known when and how it began, nor what it means. Considered harbingers of spring, fertility, and new life, *kurents* are happy, always jingling their bells. They are accompanied by a ceremonial plowman, also known elsewhere in Eurasia, as they visit farms, wishing their owners a good, prosperous year. In **Prekmurje**, if no one in the village marries at carnival time, a *borovo gostüvanje* (pine-tree wedding), a custom originally brought from **Austria** and revived after **World War II**, is staged as punishment. The oldest single man or woman is married to a pine tree, and the whole village, of a hundred or more masked guests, takes part in the wedding ceremony and celebration.

Another spring tradition, revived for tourist purposes in **Bela Krajina** and today only a vestige of the former custom, is the celebration of St. George's Day on 24 April. Originally a shepherds' holiday, the tradition has deep roots in pre-Christian times. It was celebrated with bonfires and boisterous processions followed by feasting. In Bela Krajina, the celebration of St. George's Day was called *jurjevanje*. The original purpose of this ancient ritual was to bring fertility to the land and ward off evil spirits that might harm the crops. A young man covered with greenery, *Zeleni Jurij* (Green George), was escorted by young people dressed in traditional white costumes; they also went from house to house, singing, wishing people a good season, and collecting gifts.

Besides customs organized around the fall harvest (especially grape picking and wine making), religious holidays are also steeped in family folk traditions, especially Easter and Christmas. At Easter time, the *butara* and olive branch are associated with Palm Sunday celebration. The most known is **Ljubljana** *butara*, a neatly arranged bundle of greenery, decorated with colored wood shavings, which is taken to the church to be blessed, along with olive branches, and later is kept at home for protection against misfortune until the following year. This custom is observed across Slovenia, although *butaras* differ regionally in appearance (fruit and greenery often replace colored wood shavings) and in name (*prajtelj* in Gorenjska). Also well-known are Ljubno *butaras*, called *potice*, which are very different from the others. They are figural and represent tangible objects, articles for personal use, or a scene with witty characters. Easter is also associated with food preparation. The baking of festive breads (*potica* is most popular) and egg decorating are traditions alive among most Slavic nations, and they are well represented in all regions of Slovenia. The most beautiful Easter eggs (*pisanice*) are from Bela Krajina, where etching and batik techniques using wax are employed. Easter eggs, *potica*, bread, ham, and horseradish are arranged in an Easter basket, which is taken to church for blessing (*žegen*) on Holy Saturday. *See also* FOOD AND DRINK, TRADITIONAL.

At Christmastime, on 6 December, Slovenes celebrate St. Nicholas (*sveti Miklavž*), who mysteriously visits homes, accompanied by devils and angels, and brings presents. The nativity scene—*jaslice* (crèche)—first introduced by **Jesuits** in 1644 and staged in a Ljubljana church, spread among the rural population as late as the 19th century. Many varieties of nativity scenes are created (their figures can be of wood, clay, plaster, or even paper), representing a characteristic form of **folk art**. Among the printed "cut-out" national nativity scenes, one painted by **Maksim Gaspari** in 1921, and reflecting the enthusiasm for the newly established **Kingdom of Serbs, Croats, and Slovenes**, is worth mentioning. At the beginning of the 20th century, a Christmas tree was added to the family crèche. *See also* FOLK MUSIC AND DANCE.

FOOD AND DRINK, TRADITIONAL. Slovene cooking varies by **region**, according to Alpine, Mediterranean, and Pannonian influences. There are about 30 distinct regional cuisines, each with its own local specialties. Over 100 different soups, including **Piran** fish soup and chicken or veal stew, are known among Slovenes and are also served as a main course. Clear beef or chicken broth with thin noodles can be found everywhere. Popular regional soups include Primorska *jota* (beans and sauerkraut), Trenta *šara* (dried mutton and vegetables), and Štajerska *kisla juha* (pigs' knuckles and head with vegetables and sour cream). Traditional meat dishes mainly contain pork, but poultry is also popular, especially for festive occasions. Famous among pork dishes are Slovene *koline* prepared at slaughtering time, *krvavice* (blood sausage), *koženice* (skin sausage), and smoked stuffed pork stomach; there are also several dried specialties, such as *pršut* (prosciutto) from **Kras**, which is especially valued by culinary specialists. Best known among the sausages is *kranjska klobasa* (similar to a Polish sausage). Pork dishes are often served with sauerkraut or turnips and boiled buckwheat, corn, or wheat mush (*žganci*). In all regions, game is prepared as "hunters" specialties and served with lingonberries.

Slovene flour-based dishes are many and popular. *Štruklji* are made of stretched dough filled with sweet or savory fillings—farmers cheese, nuts—and then rolled. *Štruklji* resemble strudel and can be baked or simmered. Slovenes also like to eat *cmoki* (dumplings), made with potato dough filled with fruit (plums and apricots are the most popular). Most characteristic by far is *potica*. Known in many varieties, the bread *potica* is baked for family celebrations and religious holidays. For centuries, *potica* has been part of festive meals in the homes of all Slovenes regardless of social status. *Potica* recipes can also be found in Austrian and German cookbooks with an explanation that it is a Slovene national leavened pastry with filling. Most commonly filled with ground walnuts, *poticas* are also made with other nuts, carob, poppy seeds, raisins, tarragon, and salty cracklings (*ocvirkova potica*). A time-consuming baking project, *potica* is one of the genuine traditional Slovene foods. In **Prekmurje** and East Slovenia, delicious *gibanica*, a layered pastry (phyllo dough) filled with apples, nuts, raisins, and poppy seeds, is served for dessert. Slovene cooking has also been influenced by southern Yugoslav cuisine; specialties such as *ajvar*, grilled meat, and Turkish coffee are very popular, as is pizza, an Italian import.

Slovenes like to drink. A centuries-old traditional drink is *medica* (mead). More popular are wine, beer, and various fruit brandies (especially plum brandy, *slivovka*), all produced in the home and also by commercial producers, such as Slovenijavino and Vinag Maribor. **Viticulture**, an important branch of the local economy in Roman times, was revived in the 12th century by the Cistercians in **Stična**. Among nonalcoholic beverages are fruit juices produced by the large food processing enterprise Fructal. Slovenes also drink a lot of mineral water from Radenci and Rogaška Slatina. Medicinal and herbal teas are also popular, as are beverages with fruit syrups (e.g., *kokta*, a Slovene version of Coca Cola; *malinovec*, a raspberry drink; and *šabesa*, elderberry).

FOOTWEAR MANUFACTURING. See LEATHER AND FOOT-WEAR MANUFACTURING.

FOREIGN POLICY. Since the Slovenes did not have an official foreign policy until the early 1990s when the **Republic of Slovenia** (RS) proclaimed its sovereignty and soon after its **independence**, it may not be appropriate to discuss "Slovene" international relations before that time. Yet, from the time when Napoleon's armies occupied areas of the eastern Adriatic coastland in the late 18th century, Slovenes began formulating positions that reflected their self-interest vis-à-vis other states. Living under French rule in the **Illyrian Provinces** had presented Slovenes with some options, and whenever European crises and wars threatened thereafter, Slovenes evaluated events in their own national terms. Their primary goal, which is the purpose of all foreign policy, became the preservation of the nation and its interests. In the later 19th century and throughout the 20th, there was much cause for alarm. In 1866, when the newly forming kingdom of **Italy** took the province of Venetia from **Austria**, some Slovenes were detached from the national unit. After **World War I** and the dismemberment of Austria-Hungary, a major portion of the Slovene territory went to Italy, while Slovenes in **Carinthia** were destined to be placed in what was left of Austria. For the Slovenes this was highly distressing, and Slovene representatives who were present at the various deliberations in Paris in 1919 argued forcefully, but in vain, for preserving the unity of their nation.

By the time **Yugoslavia** was created in 1918, Slovenes knew what their position was: a **United Slovenia**. The idea's origins go back to the **Revolution of 1848**, but at that time it might have been achieved within Austria. In the 20th century, given Europe's new boundaries, it required implementing foreign policy objectives and measures to change the frontiers of Versailles Yugoslavia. It was the hope of Slovenes that they might exercise influence within the Yugoslav foreign ministry to help advance their goals. But that was not to happen, partly because the Serbs who dominated foreign policy decision-making had more pressing interests in the southern Balkans. **World War II** brought the total dismemberment of the Slovene nation; Slovenes of most political persuasions tried to influence policy abroad to favor their liberation and unification. The United Slovenia idea was still at the heart of it. After 1945 and the creation of a Yugoslav federation, with Slovenes having their very own republic, they expected to play a larger role in communist Yugoslavia's foreign policy formulation. They were, in fact, strongly represented at the postwar Paris talks that discussed the western and northern boundaries of Yugoslavia (Slovenes lived on both sides of the frontiers with Italy and Austria). One of **Tito**'s chief policy makers, the Slovene **Edvard Kardelj**, was himself in Paris. The issues, however, were settled only partially in the Slovenes' favor. *See also* LONDON AGREEMENT; ŽEBOT, CIRIL.

At the height of the Cold War, communist Yugoslavia felt itself under threat from both East and West. Its enemies were Western capitalists and Eastern **Cominformists**. Expelled from the Soviet bloc in 1948, the Yugoslavs—Slovenes among them—fought for survival by organizing a third-world bloc. **Belgrade**'s policy of **nonalignment** reaped successes but also expended enormous energy and money. As Yugoslav diplomats courted the disaffected anticolonialist peoples in the Far East and Africa, there was only marginal activity devoted to particular Slovene interests. These interests had to wait until East–West détente and until the communist regimes—including the government in Slovenia's republic—experienced the **liberalization of the 1960s**. The 1970s then moved Slovenes in the direction of their own foreign policy, one that linked Slovenia more with the West. In 1971 Slovenia and Italy signed a bilateral agreement regulating border traffic between their two jurisdictions. The following year **Stane Kavčič**, the reformer who then headed Slovenia's Executive Council, implemented an agreement between Slovenia and Bavaria. Separate agreements with Bremen, **Hungary**, Catalonia, and Belarus followed. In 1975 the Helsinki Accords and especially the **Osimo Treaty** between Italy and Yugoslavia made closer contacts with the West more possible. The **Alps–Adriatic Working Community**, established in 1978, was an organization made to order for the Slovenes. It brought together regions with a common interest and helped dissolve the Cold War frontiers.

As contacts with the West increased, Slovenia began pressing for more input into Yugoslavia's foreign policy decisions. In the 1980s, Slovenes concluded that contributing 25 percent to the foreign affairs coffers entitled them to more than a 3 percent representation in the diplomatic corps, most of whose Slovene cadre was dispatched to languish in underdeveloped third-world outposts. Slovenes wanted to interact with developed countries where they could pursue their economic interests. This kind of thinking played prominently in the resurrection of the United Slovenia program: the **May Declaration of 1989**, the establishment of sovereignty for the republic, the holding of multiparty **elections** in April 1990, and the ultimate declaration of independence in June 1991. Even before independence was achieved, however, on 24 April 1991, the Slovene government adopted its first Law on Foreign Affairs. Its stated primary foreign policy objective was to link up with

Europe, specifically with the European Community (EC) and with the **North Atlantic Treaty Organization** (NATO). Slovenia also intended to join various multilateral political and economic organizations such as the **United Nations** (UN), the **Organization for Security and Cooperation in Europe** (OSCE), the **Central European Free Trade Association** (CEFTA), and the **Central European Initiative** (CEI). Among other goals were good relations with neighboring states where Slovene **minorities** lived, promotion of international awareness about Slovenes, and care for Slovenes abroad.

After independence was declared, the first order of business was monumental—achieving international **recognition**. This was accomplished within the year, as was UN membership; memberships in many **international organizations** followed in rapid succession. EU and NATO memberships were attained in 2004. A Declaration on Foreign Policy, passed in May 2001, reiterated many of the goals of a decade earlier, but also added others such as commitments to **human rights**, peaceful resolution of conflicts, and overseeing the proliferation of weapons of mass destruction—no doubt intended to put Slovenia in sync with EU and NATO policies. The country has also committed itself to international goals such as monitoring corruption, drug trafficking, global ecological interests (Kyoto agreement, 1997), and terrorism. Slovenia stepped up to new responsibilities toward the states of the former Yugoslavia through the Stability Pact for South Eastern Europe (1999) and by contributing to peacekeeping forces in Kosovo and in Bosnia. With Slovenia now a part of Europe (EU) and of the North Atlantic security system (NATO), these international objectives are viewed as serving Slovene national interests.

As is the case with all states developing a foreign policy, Slovenia needed also to stabilize its relations with bordering countries: Austria, **Croatia**, Hungary, and Italy. Establishing a good footing with Hungary, a former Warsaw Pact country with whom Slovenia (part of nonaligned Yugoslavia) had a history of Cold War tensions in the 1940s and 1950s, went well right from the start. Slovenia and Hungary have continued to work together to improve road and rail transportation between the two states; they moved cooperatively toward EU and NATO accession; and they have adopted reasonable policies toward each other's minorities. With Austria, designated a neutral by the **Austrian State Treaty** (1955), relations have been more complicated. One section of that treaty addressed Austrian–Yugoslav border issues and treatment of the Slovene minority in Austria. In spite of lively commerce and travel between the two, and hundreds of laws regulating and enabling contacts, tensions still remained in 1991. Austria recognized Slovene independence in January 1992, and Slovenia soon opened an embassy in **Vienna** and consular offices in the border provinces, Carinthia and Styria. However, in Carinthia, the Slovene minority is still under Germanizing pressures, stoked from time to time by rightist elements such as Georg Haider. The republic of Austria, although more accommodating toward Slovenia, continues obstructing the implementation of some 1955 treaty provisions. Even the question as to whether Slovenia can properly succeed to a treaty that was signed by Yugoslavia a half-century ago is still unresolved.

With Italians, Slovenes have had a history of conflicting national interests from the moment an Italian state was established in 1860. They fought on opposite sides in two world wars, partly over territory they both claimed. In 1991, alarmed by a war on its eastern border, Italy's foreign minister led the intervention that brought about a truce, the **Brioni Agreement** (7 July 1991), and de facto independence for Slovenia (October 1991). Thereafter, for about five years, Italian–Slovene relations were not the best, mostly because of issues relating to Italians (and their property) who had left Yugoslavia in the 1940s and 1950s. Rome, however, came around, particularly after Silvio Berlusconi's accession to power. Italy, long a NATO power and EU member, now developing financial and commercial interests in Eastern Europe, became Slovenia's sponsor for accession to NATO and the EU. After 2004 Italy's air force assumed protection of Slovene airspace. Minority issues remain a problem, but in 2001 Rome finally passed a law protecting Italy's Slovene minority. Some rightist elements in Italy continue to make life for Slovenes less than ideal.

Perhaps Slovenia's relations have been most tense with Croatia, also a former republic of socialist Yugoslavia, from which both declared independence on 25 June 1991. The issues dividing them are primarily monetary and territorial. The matter of Croatia's access to nuclear power from Krško (in Slovenia) was resolved in 2003, and issues relating to Ljubljanska Banka's Zagreb branch dispute has been tentatively settled by a succession agreement. However, the location of Croatia's northwestern border with Slovenia is an increasingly contentious matter for **Janez Janša**'s government. Also unresolved is the matter of Slovenia's access to the Bay of **Piran**, which is challenged by Croatia's claim to a 200-mile economic zone in the Adriatic Sea.

Some of these matters may require EU mediation, and Croatia's accession to the EU could be delayed until its border disputes are settled. Relations with Serbia, another former republic of socialist Yugoslavia (though not sharing a border with Slovenia), have progressed satisfactorily only since 2001. In the early 1980s, Slovenia and Serbia clashed over how their common country should be governed, with Slovenia urging greater autonomy for the republics and for the region of Kosovo (part of the Serbian republic). The confrontation between the two republics contributed to the breakup of Yugoslavia. As long as Serbia was dominated by Slobodan Milošević, better relations with Slovenia were difficult. With Milošević's ouster in 2000 and his removal to The Hague the following year, normalization of relations proceeded. In 2001 a Succession Agreement that dealt with major asset and debt issues was signed in **Vienna**, and the new Serbian leadership, anxious for economic development, welcomed Slovene businesspeople and bankers. Slovenia has also committed itself to assisting Serbia in its preparation for EU membership.

Slovene relations with both **Russia** and the **United States**, bastions of the Cold War's East–West struggle, are now also on good footing. Russia and the Republic of Slovenia established contacts in 1991, after the two split from their respective federations and assumed new forms of government. Trade agreements were initiated already in the early 1990s, and after 2000 accelerated in pace and volume. The two are now collaborating in investment projects in southeastern Europe. For Russia, even Slovenia's aspiration to NATO membership was never an issue, since Slovenia had not been a member of the Warsaw Pact. With the United States, relations got off to a shaky start. Slovenia was blamed by some in U.S. diplomatic circles for Yugoslavia's collapse. Slowly, after 1995, relations improved. The chief U.S. concern was that Slovenia commit to securing and stabilizing southeastern Europe. Once Slovenia agreed, the United States became a friend, backing its candidacy for a nonpermanent seat on the UN Security Council and also throwing its support behind NATO membership for Slovenia. U.S. presidents have visited Slovenia, and the country was chosen to host the first meeting of the presidents of the United States and Russia in 2001. The United States maintains a sizable embassy contingent in **Ljubljana**, as a base of operations for its southeast European policy.

FOREIGN RELATIONS AND DIPLOMACY. Although Slovenes may not have had a **foreign policy** of their own until 1990, individual

Slovenes have acted as diplomats since the earliest days of European diplomacy. About 20 served as diplomats for **Habsburg** rulers, representing the interests of **Vienna**. Slovenia's current capital, **Ljubljana** (Laibach), made its debut as a diplomatic venue in 1821, when the rulers of the Holy Alliance held a major international congress there. Slovene diplomats also served in the foreign services of both royal and communist **Yugoslavia**. They helped negotiate the terms and boundaries of post–**World War I** and **World War II** Yugoslavia—particularly its northern and western frontiers. In the first Yugoslavia, the **Kingdom of Serbs, Croats, and Slovenes**, Serbian interests predominated. Slovenes, who had until 1918 been a part of **Austria** and fought on the side of the Central Powers during the world war, were not regarded as reliable spokespersons for **Belgrade**'s interests. Nevertheless some 30 Slovenes served in the diplomatic corps, but primarily in minor posts. Several who had important assignments were **Izidor Cankar**, who served as ambassador to Argentina and later Canada; **Ivan Hribar**, who was posted to Prague; and Leonid Pitamic, who served in the **United States**.

In the second Yugoslavia, the **Socialist Federal Republic of Yugoslavia** (SFRJ), about 85 Slovenes had diplomatic assignments. Most, however, held minor posts or were sent to remote areas of Asia and Africa where Yugoslavia's policy of **nonalignment** was being nurtured. In the late 1980s, several Slovenes held important diplomatic posts. One, **Ernest Petrič**, was ambassador to India and Nepal between 1989 and 1991, an important mission that was cut short because of troubles at home. Few went to European capitals, although **Trieste** and **Klagenfurt**, regional capitals that had large Slovene **minorities**, generally had Slovenes heading their Yugoslav consulates. The U.S. cities of Pittsburgh and later **Cleveland** usually had Slovenes heading their consular offices. Slovenes also served fairly prominently in Yugoslav posts at the **United Nations**. Yet Slovenes were underrepresented (3 percent to the Serbs' 54 percent) in SFRY's Foreign Ministry. Yugoslavia's foreign policy was regarded as Serbian foreign policy, a factor that contributed to Slovene dissatisfaction in the 1980s.

A month before the **election** of April 1990, Slovenia's first multiparty election, it was proposed that the republic have a greater say in Yugoslavia's foreign relations and that Slovenia have its own independent Foreign Ministry to address specific Slovene interests. On 16 May 1990, Slovenia established such a ministry, even though it continued contributing financially to Yugoslavia's for another year.

Slovenia also established separate diplomatic missions, unofficially, in Vienna and Brussels in spring 1990, and in Washington, D.C., in 1991. After **independence** was declared in June 1991, other diplomatic posts were soon opened up in major European capitals.

Slovenia's Ministry of Foreign Affairs was set up in traditional fashion, having both a bilateral division for one-on-one exchanges with individual countries, and a multilateral section for work dealing with **international organizations**, such as the United Nations. In the bilateral area, the focus was on maintaining missions and consulates in European countries. Particularly important were the missions to neighboring states, Austria, **Croatia**, **Hungary**, and **Italy**, where border and economic issues could sometimes be all consuming. Of great importance, too, were diplomatic missions to Germany, which had played a large role in sponsoring Slovenia's independence, and to other Central European states (e.g., members of the **Central European Initiative**). The **Vatican** embassy was also considered quite important.

In the Western hemisphere, embassies were established in the United States, Mexico, Canada, and Argentina; those states also had consular offices—some of them honorary—generally near Slovene immigrant communities. Elsewhere Slovene diplomatic representation was sparse. In Asia and the Middle East, embassies were opened up in the People's Republic of China, India, Iran, Israel, and Japan; in Africa there was only one, in Egypt; and in Oceania, also only one, in Australia. Granted, many of these embassies served not only the state where they were located but also other states in the region. In 2006 Slovenia had 37 diplomatic missions and seven consular posts (not including honorary assignments); it also had six permanent diplomatic missions to international organizations. Three hundred people were employed at the Foreign Ministry in Ljubljana, with about the same number working at its embassies and missions abroad. Of those, the **North Atlantic Treaty Organization** and **European Union** (EU) missions had 30 employees each. In 2006, 34 countries had diplomatic legations in Slovenia.

Diplomacy and foreign relations posed a multifaceted challenge for the small, recently independent Central European state. It needed to establish a foreign department in temporary offices, virtually from scratch, with few diplomatic cadres and little experience to boot. It also had meager financial resources to apply to the task and often faced large problems with neighboring countries. A diplomatic academy, which worked with the Faculties of Law and of Social Sciences of the **University of Ljubljana**, began helping train new diplomats. But the need remained overwhelming, particularly after 2004 with Slovenia's accession to the EU and NATO, where Slovenes are needed to serve on a multitude of committees or act as translators. The traditional division of foreign policy work into bilateral and multilateral is under review. Bilateral missions to individual European states, now that Europe is united, may be redundant with the mission to the EU. Also, given the emerging multilateral issues that require attention, some of the international missions may be reconsidered as well.

The Foreign Ministry has daily contact with the National Assembly and works with that body's committees on the EU and on Foreign Policy. As stipulated by law, the Foreign Ministry must prepare a monthly report on its work for the assembly, and the foreign minister must appear before that body each month for a question-and-answer session. An independent Slovene Foreign Ministry has a decade and a half of work behind it. In 2000 it moved into permanent new headquarters on *Prešernova cesta*, Ljubljana's embassy row, in the restored former young women's lyceum, Mladika, the 1907 work of Secessionist architect **Maks Fabiani**, and seems ready for the challenging tasks ahead.

FORESTRY. Slovenia is one of Europe's most wooded countries. More than half of its territory (56 percent, or 1,157,824 hectares, in 2003) is covered with forests (30 percent deciduous, 30 percent conifers, and 40 percent mixed), which have always been an important **natural resource**. Although forested areas have been expanding in Slovenia because of abandonment of cultivated land and pastures, forestation has not been taking place in areas where it is most desirable (**Prekmurje**, urban areas). Forests were cleared indiscriminately in the Middle Ages to provide more arable land, and in the 15th to 19th centuries to provide **energy** for heating, and wood for building and emerging industries. The first forest management plans were in place in the late 18th century (Forest Ordinance of Carniola, 1771), while a policy of systematic reforestation and regulated cutting has been in place since the early 19th century to ensure ecological balance and also to ensure wood supply for future generations. While the Forest Act of 1993 mandated regard for private property rights, it nevertheless restricts use of the private forests, which have to ensure their continuing ecological, societal, and productive functions.

In the last two centuries, forests in the Slovene **regions** have changed in character. In the **Alpine** region, beech trees have been replaced by pines and spruces. The **karst** region, once almost bare, is being forested with black pines and deciduous trees. Although wooded areas have been enlarged since **World War II** and the quality of Slovene forests improved, air pollution has taken its toll in industrial areas; for example, over 70 percent of the forests around **Slovenj Gradec**, where damage was the greatest, have been affected. Harsh weather has also been a major destroyer of forests, especially around **Kranj**. After 1997 defoliation increased over 25 percent in some forests in industrial areas and along major traffic routes. As of 2004 **denationalization** of forests had not been completed, but it is expected that over 80 percent of forests will be privately owned; of the rest, 15 percent will be state owned and 5 percent owned by the **Catholic Church** and various **cooperatives**.

Forestry has been an important branch of the **economy**. It has provided raw material for **manufacturing** (furniture making, paper production, and wood processing), and, at the same time, ecological viability of the forests for other uses has been assured. Ecological functions of forests (air and water purification, conservation of biotic diversity, energy resource, and prevention of erosion) and social functions (**health**, **sports**) are becoming more important than their production function. In 2003 around 3 million cubic meters of wood were harvested, of which 10 percent was sold abroad, mostly as timber and lumber. Forestry together with **agriculture** accounted for 2.2 percent of the GDP in 2003. *See also* ECONOMY SINCE 1991; ENVIRONMENT.

FORUM 21. An association for political, economic, social, and ethical issues, Forum 21 was organized on 31 March 2004 in **Ljubljana** by a group of more than 200 established personalities, professionals from all spheres of Slovene public life. Among the founding members were important managers of large enterprises such as Mercator, Kompas, and Krka, as well as university professors and artists, most of whom had held important positions in the previous socialist regime. **Milan Kučan**, the former two-term president of the **Republic of Slovenia** (RS), was elected president of the organization. The purpose of the association, which would function as an institution within civil society, was to provide a broad professional base from which to influence political decision-making. Forum 21 has organized public discussions of important issues, such as Slovenia's economic competetivness and matters related to international politics, including relations with the

European Union (EU). Forum 21 also voices its position on burning social issues, as it did in support of **human rights** for **minorities** in Slovenia. The organization finances its activities through membership dues and donations. It claims not to be seeking political power for itself; rather, it seems to be acting as a nonregistered lobby for left-leaning **political parties**.

FRANCIS FERDINAND (1863–1914). Francis Ferdinand was archduke of **Austria** and heir to the throne at the time of his assassination on 28 June 1914 in Sarajevo. His killing by a Bosnian Serb radical allowed **Vienna**, which had been pursuing an anti-Serbian foreign policy, to challenge the small Balkan Serb state. The resulting war between Austria and Serbia turned into **World War I** and ended with the collapse of the **Habsburg** Empire.

Francis Ferdinand was associated with trialism, a vague plan to transform Austria-Hungary into a triple monarchy. The third unit would be a South Slavic **Catholic** one, which could bolster the future ruler's power vis-à-vis the Hungarians. The empire's South Slavs, however, especially the Slovene **Clericals**, equated trialism with their idea of Yugoslav national unification (including South Slavs from Austria, **Hungary**, and perhaps Bosnia and Hercegovina). The Clericals (convinced that the archduke favored uniting all of the empire's South Slavs) and Croat Rightists merged their respective political parties in 1912 in preparation for this development. Bosnian Serbs, including the assassin of the archduke, no doubt also believed that Francis Ferdinand's plan would include Bosnia, which would prevent the realization of a greater Serbia (which would include Bosnia). However, it was unlikely that the archduke was planning to unite South Slavs from all parts of the empire, for it would have created a significant political force—potentially as threatening as the one Hungary represented. If he was considering trialism at all, Francis Ferdinand most probably would have carved the new unit out of Hungary and included in it only Hungarian South Slavs (i.e., mostly Croats).

FRANCIS JOSEPH (1830–1916). Becoming emperor of **Austria** in the revolutionary year 1848, Francis Joseph was, according to some historians, the last unifying force in the **Habsburg** state. From the beginning of his reign the empire was threatened by the nationalisms of the Italians, Germans, and Hungarians. In the **revolution of 1848**, **Hungary** was saved for the Habsburgs only with the help of **Russia**'s troops. In the 1860s Lombardy and Venetia were lost to **Italy**, power in Central Europe was lost to Prussia, and the Kingdom of Hungary achieved independent constitutional status (with the **Compromise of 1867**, Francis Joseph became king of Hungary). By 1867 the Slovenes who lived in Francis Joseph's empire were divided: Some now lived in Italy (Venetia), some in Hungary, and the remainder in Austria. In Austria, where Francis Joseph continued as emperor, Slovenes, although growing increasingly nationally conscious, remained loyal to the state. Many, particularly supporters of the **Clericals**, were staunch backers of the emperor and his dynasty, linking the Slovene fate with those of Austria and **Catholicism**.

FREE EXCHANGE OF LABOR / SVOBODNA MENJAVA DELA. *See* CONTRACTUAL SOCIALISM.

FREISING FRAGMENTS / BRIŽINSKI SPOMENIKI. The Freising Fragments, written around 1000 AD, are the earliest written record of Slovene **language**, as well as the earliest record of any Slavic language in the Latin script. The manuscript, which consists of three liturgical and homiletic texts, was discovered in 1803 when the library collection of the Freising bishop was moved from Freising to the Munich state library. The documents are important for linguistic and sociological research of the Slovene language in the 10th century.

– G –

GALLUS, JACOBUS (1550–1591). Jacobus Gallus, also known as Jakob Petelin, Jacobus Gallus Carniolus, and Iacobus Handl, was a talented Slovene Renaissance composer who worked in Prague and was known across Europe in his own lifetime. He brought Italian Renaissance **music** to Central Europe. He composed several masses and was a prolific composer of motets to liturgical and biblical texts—over 400 were published in a four-volume *Opus musicum* (1586–1590). Gallus also composed secular music such as madrigals (collected in *Harmoniae morales moralia*). His music, of high quality, is performed to this day. *See also* HUMANISM.

GASPARI, MAKSIM (1883–1980). Maksim Gaspari, a painter and illustrator, was one of the founders in 1904 of the Slovene art society Vesna (Spring), whose motto was "From the people for the people." Although sometimes rather provincial in its spirit, Vesna sought to preserve the rich Slovene **folk** heritage. It fought against the adverse effects of industrialization on **art** and against a new wave of Germanization. After his studies in **Vienna** and Munich, Gaspari was influenced by the Vienna Secession. Later, permanently settled in **Ljubljana** (1911) and working in the Museum of Ethnology, he sought inspiration for his work in Slovene **folk tradition**, which was in keeping with Vesna's motto. As seen in *A Peasant Couple, By the Cradle, A Slovene Wedding*, and many others, his work became more realistic, with much attention to detail. It was at times naive, but always rich with poetry. Gaspari also illustrated numerous books and devoted much time to caricatures. His art was very popular.

GASPARI, MITJA (1951–). Born in **Ljubljana**, Gaspari studied at the **University of Ljubljana**, where he obtained a B.S. degree in financial and monetary economics (1975). He continued his studies in monetary economics at the University of Belgrade. Gaspari has spent his entire career at various monetary institutions. He worked at the National Bank of Slovenia, first as a research economist (1975–1981) and then as head of its research unit until mid-1987, at which time he was appointed the bank's deputy governor. From 1988 to June 1991 he served as deputy governor of the National Bank of Yugoslavia in **Belgrade**. He returned to Slovenia with the rest of the "Belgrade Slovenes" after Slovenia declared **independence** in June 1991. After that Gaspari was employed for a short time by the World Bank in Washington, D.C., as senior financial economist. In June 1992 he was appointed minister of finance of Slovenia, a position he held until June 2000. That year Gaspari, a member of the **Liberal Democratic Party**, was elected a member of the National Assembly. From April 2001 to March 2007, Gaspari was governor of the Bank of Slovenia. *See also* BANKING AND FINANCIAL SECTOR; ECONOMY, 1945–1990; ECONOMY SINCE 1991.

GERMANIZATION. *See* MINORITIES, SLOVENES IN AUSTRIA.

GORENJSKA. *See* REGIONS OF SLOVENIA.

GORIZIA/GORICA. Capital of **Italy**'s Gorizia province, in the Soča (Isonzo) River valley, 44 kilometers north of **Trieste**, Gorizia had a population of 35,500 in 2004. It is a border town, from the northeastern portion of which grew a new town, **Nova Gorica**, now in the **Republic of Slovenia** (RS), having been assigned to **Yugoslavia** in 1947. The relationship of Gorizia to Nova Gorica was similar to that of West to East Berlin, but with a chain-link fence rather than a wall separating the two. Gorizia produces cement, cotton goods, timber, and textile machinery. It attracts **tourists** with its moderate climate, **World War I** buffs, and pilgrims bound for the Sveta Gora shrine of Our Lady. Gorizia is also the venue for a variety of annual fairs: a spring trade fair (Expo Mego) begun more than three decades ago, a spring gardening and ecology fair, and in the fall, fairs devoted to agricultural products, wine, and an international fashion event (Mittel Moda). It also hosts music competitions, the most noted being the Rodolfo Lipizer prize event, a violin competition held annually since 1981. Gorizia and Nova Gorica are linked to the Gulf of Trieste by the Isonzo River, to Trieste, Jesenice (RS), and Villach (**Austria**) by rail (1906), and to the RS and Italy also by road. Since Slovenia became a member of the **European Union** (EU), the border between the two Goricas has officially vanished. Italy's Gorizia now bills itself as a main access to Eastern Europe.

Gorizia was under the Patriarchate of Aquileia in the third century and is first mentioned in 1001 AD as a village called by that name in the language of the Slavs. Ruled by independent counts (whose castle still dominates the old town) until 1500, the domain was then acquired by the **Habsburgs**, who ruled it, with one brief Napoleonic interlude, until 1918. Under the Austrians the area produced fruits, vegetables, and wines, and its craftspeople made silk. The population was mixed: Italians and Friulians were generally engaged in commerce and handicrafts; Austrian Germans acted as managers and administrators; and Slovenes made up the urban worker segment as they migrated from the largely Slovene countryside. Much of the town, which together with **Kobarid** (Caporetto) was the site of a major battle front, was destroyed during World War I. The **Treaty of Rapallo** awarded it, together with Gorizia's province, to Italy in 1920. After **World War II** much of the province and a bit of the town went to Yugoslavia. Gorizia today remains a regional center for Slovene **minorities** in the Italian province. They have their own economic and political organizations and maintain Slovene educational and cultural institutions, such as the **Society of St. Hermagoras**, a publishing house. The weekly newspaper *Katoliški glas* (*Catholic Voice*) is influential in the community.

GOSPA SVETA. Gospa Sveta (Maria Saal), a church dedicated to Our Lady (St. Mary) in about 760, is where a mass of celebration was held following each installation of **Karantanian dukes** at Gosposvetsko Polje. For most of the ninth century and half of the 10th, it was the episcopal see of **Karantania** and center of Frankish missionary activity among the Slovenes. Gospa Sveta was hence the first Slovene diocese. The church is located eight kilometers north of **Klagenfurt/ Celovec** in Carinthia, **Austria**, and was rebuilt in the mid-15th century, in late Gothic style.

GOVERNMENT, LOCAL. *See* LOCAL COMMUNITY; OBČINA.

GOVERNMENT OF SLOVENIA, NATIONAL / NARODNA VLADA SLOVENIJE (1945). In accordance with instructions from the **Antifascist Council of National Liberation of Yugoslavia** (AVNOJ), the first post–**World War II** Slovene government was named by the presidency of the **Slovene National Liberation Council** (SNOS) in Ajdovščina on 5 May 1945. Its president was **Boris Kidrič**; other cabinet members were Marijan Brecelj (vice president), Marijan Ahčin (health), Aleš Bebler (finance), Tone Fajfar (forestry), Janez Hribar (agriculture), Miha Kambič (construction), Ferdo Kozak (education), Franc Leskošek (industry and mining), Jože Pokorn (justice), Zoran Polič (internal affairs), Franc Snoj (transportation), and Vida Tomšič (social welfare). On 10 May after the Germans and the **Home Guard** left the city, the Slovene National Government moved to **Ljubljana**. It completed the takeover of power and established **Communist Party of Slovenia** (CPS) domination. This was accomplished with the help of the **Yugoslav People's Army**, the secret police, and a provisional judicial system, the Courts of National Honor, which played the essential role of purging potential enemies. Individual ministries abolished some institutions and reorganized others by purging anticommunist elements from the state administration, public institutions, and other organizations.

The new government also prepared the first general elections for all levels of government. Local elections were held in July, and federal elections in November 1945. Local committees of the **Liberation Front** (LF), as well as irregularities such as cheating and intimidation of voters by the secret police, helped to ensure a Communist victory. The National Government was short-lived, able only to initiate economic reforms, which were then carried out by its successor. The justice ministry engaged in sparring with **Belgrade** over federal legal measures that seemed inappropriate for Slovenia. In February 1947, in accordance with the **Constitution of 1946**, the National Government was renamed Government of the **People's Republic of Slovenia** (*Ljudska Republika Slovenija*, LRS).

GOVERNMENT, SLOVENE, 1989–1990. Post–**World War II** Slovenia was ruled by Communists until 1990. The League of Communists of Slovenia (LCS; formerly the **Communist Party of Slovenia**) was the only party allowed by law. Both the League of Socialist Youth of Slovenia (ZSMS) and the Slovene branch of the **Socialist Alliance of Working People** (SAWP), which was an umbrella organization for various public interest groups, were subservient to the LCS. Although legally precluded from engaging in political activity, the ZSMS and SAWP were becoming more active in the mid- to late 1980s. So, too, was the party itself, which was yielding to reformers in its midst. Democratic forces prevailed in late December 1989. The Slovene Assembly passed a law permitting the establishment of public organizations outside SAWP's umbrella framework. Shortly thereafter, on 8 January 1990, the Assembly's president announced Slovenia's first postwar multiparty elections. In preparation for the **election of April 1990**, the Assembly outlined nomination procedures and campaign and funding regulations and worked out a redistricting plan.

Now that they were legal, **political parties**—15 in all before the election—quickly emerged. The major noncommunist parties united in the **Demos** coalition: **Greens of Slovenia** (ZS); **Slovene Christian Democrats** (SKD); **Slovene Democratic Alliance** (SDZ); Slovene Farmers' Alliance (SKZ); Social Democratic Alliance of Slovenia (SDZS), later the Social Democratic Party of Slovenia (SDSS); and its affiliates, the Grey Panthers Party and the Slovene Small Businessmen's Party (later the **Liberal Party**). The legalization of a multiparty system and the announcement of free elections also prompted the LCS to rename itself the LCS-Party of Democratic Renewal (SDP). The youth organization became the League of Socialist Youth of Slovenia-Liberal Party (ZSMS-LS), and ran as a separate party, as did the Alliance of Socialists of Slovenia (later the **Socialist Party of Slovenia**, SSS). The Alliance had been part of the SAWP and had split from the LCS in February. The Italian Community, the Hungarian Community, and several independent candidates also ran separately and would win seats in the new Assembly.

GOVERNMENT, SLOVENE, AFTER 1990. The main legislative body of Slovenia's government since **independence** has been the State Assembly (*državni zbor*), sometimes referred to as the national assembly or as parliament, terms that Slovenes use interchangably with that of State Assembly. *See also* ELECTIONS AFTER 1991; ELECTIONS, PRESIDENTIAL, AFTER 1991.

Government of May 1990–December 1992: **Lojze Peterle, Janez Drnovšek**, prime ministers. After the multiparty election of April 1990, putting together a government proceeded slowly. There were the expected disagreements among the **political parties** over procedure, but lack of experience with both multiparty rule and holding public office also slowed the process. The parliament's three chambers (still constituted according to the **Constitution of 1974**) were dominated by the **Demos** coalition and had Demos chairmen. Collectively the chambers chose **France Bučar** of the **Slovene Democratic Alliance** (SDZ)–Demos as president of the parliament. The two vice presidents also came from Demos ranks. Selecting a prime minister to head the new government proceeded according to a Demos pre-election agreement. The premier would come from the Demos party that had tallied the most votes, which turned out to be the **Slovene Christian Democrats** (SKD). The candidate for premier was SKD's Lojze Peterle, who chose as his three vice premiers Jože Mencinger (SDZ) for economic affairs, Matija Malešič (Independent) for social affairs, and Leo Šešerko (**Greens of Slovenia**) for **environmental** affairs and regional development. Twenty-three other members of the government were announced on 16 May, and all were approved by vote of parliament. Of the 27 members of the government, 18 were Demos members, while nine came from the outside. Peterle denied that his government was based on a coalition, saying that non-Demos ministers would not act as representatives of parties; they had been selected for their individual competencies.

This first Slovene multiparty government lasted until the end of 1992, overseeing a **plebiscite for independence**, the declaration of independence, the **Ten-Day War**, and the adoption of the **Constitution of 1991**. Until the end of 1991 and the beginnings of international **recognition** of Slovene independence, the Peterle government and parliament worked reasonably well together. Early in 1992, however, serious disagreements developed largely over **privatization** and social policy issues (especially abortion, **health**, and pensions), causing parliament to seek a replacement for the prime minister. Attempts to oust Peterle in late February and early April failed, but in late April parliament voted no confidence in Peterle and replaced him with Janez Drnovšek of the **Liberal Democratic Party** (LDS). Drnovšek's premiership was confirmed by a parliamentary secret ballot on 14 May.

His term continued until year-end elections, the first since a new constitution had been adopted for an independent Slovenia.

Government of December 1992–November 1996: Janez Drnovšek, prime minister. Slovenia's second post-socialist government was formed after the election of December 1992. The newly elected State Assembly selected Janez Drnovšek as head of government (prime minister) on 12 January 1993, by secret ballot (48 of 87 votes cast). Two weeks later, after much negotiating and deal-making, Drnovšek announced his government, which the Assembly approved on 25 January.

Drnovšek's government was based on an unusual left-right coalition, featuring the three parties that had tallied the most votes in the December election—the Liberal Democratic Party (LDS), Slovene Christian Democrats (SKD), and the **United List of Social Democrats** (ZLSD), who were former Communists—plus the Social Democratic Party of Slovenia (SDSS), which had gotten only four seats in the new parliament. The pivotal deal worked out by Drnovšek involved bringing in the Christian Democrats, who bargained hard and were rewarded with the vice premiership and four of the 16 ministerial posts, including the Ministry of Internal Affairs and the Ministry of Foreign Affairs—the latter post going to Lojze Peterle, the previous prime minister, who also was named vice premier in Drnovšek's government. The other ministries went to members of the other two coalition parties, with the exception of the health ministry, which went to a Green, and the defense ministry, which went to **Janez Janša**—who would head the SDSS after 1993. The latter had executed Slovenia's defense effectively in the summer of 1991, and with the former Yugoslav states still at war, his expertise was considered vital.

After the establishment of Drnovšek's government, Slovene multiparty political life embarked on its first four-year term of parliamentary rule. The issues that most occupied the country during those years were the **economy**, high unemployment (14 percent), a steady influx of Bosnian refugees who were provided for and housed throughout Slovenia, and students who demonstrated for and won a reinstatement of meal vouchers. The government coalition seemed regularly on the verge of collapsing as various ministers were replaced, often due to irregular activities or shady dealings. That political life continued to evolve and find its bearings was evident as political parties merged, realigned, and changed names.

Perhaps the most volatile person in the government was Defense Minister Janez Janša, who had higher political ambitions and an agenda of his own. Publicly, he carried on a running feud with President **Milan Kučan**, and was regularly at war with the Ministry of Internal Affairs and elements of the security police—all of whom he suspected had been implicated in his arrest and prosecution during the **Ljubljana Four trial** in 1988. He and his party left the coalition government in March 1994, after it had been revealed that Janša had had Defense Ministry employees beat up a civilian who might have been working for the Ministry of Internal Affairs. The head of that ministry, Ivan Bizjak, resigned in May of that year after a number of scandals. These included revelations that the security service was being funded by casino profits, a scandal known as the "HIT Affair," HIT (*hoteli, igralnice, turism*) being the acronym for the hotel industry association with whom the ministry had concluded a deal. In addition, his police were implicated in a number of illegal break-ins, including some in **Austria**. In January 1996 the ZLSD pulled out of Drnovšek's coalition over a government move to cut pensions. By then ZLSD had also been tarnished by its own scandal involving Maks Tajnikar, who was dismissed as economic minister when it was found that he had arranged financial assistance for friends at **Maribor**'s strapped TAM (*Tovarna avtomobilov in motorjev*) factory.

The only coalition partner that stayed in Drnovšek's government until the end was the SKD. It had expected to do better in the 1992 election but interpreted the results as a mandate for modernization and a reaching out toward Western Europe, so it joined LDS in 1992. SKD's Peterle became foreign minister, and therewith hoped to forge ties with like-minded parties in the West. As foreign minister, however, Peterle ran into serious difficulties at home when he made a deal with **Italy** on expropriated property. He had not had government clearance to do so and he created an uproar among Slovenes at home for giving in to Italy. Peterle was replaced in October 1994 by Zoran Thaler in the Foreign Ministry, but he continued as vice premier. Peterle's party meanwhile did quite well in local elections in December 1994, thereby affording the coalition government a boost.

Government of November 1996–May 2000: Janez Drnovšek, prime minister. The election of 10 November 1996 produced an evenly split State Assembly. **Janez Podobnik** of the **Slovene People's Party** (SLS) was chosen president, or speaker, of that body a few days after its initial meeting, but that was about all the members could agree on for the next three months. President Milan Kučan's role after the new Assembly first met on 28 November was to ask someone to form a government. He turned to Janez Drnovšek, whose LDS had tallied the most votes (25). Drnovšek, however, was in a precarious position. Three conservative parties (SLS, SDS, and SKD) together had 45 of the Assembly's 90 votes. They had come to refer to themselves at the "Slovenian Spring" and vowed to stick together against the leftists. Consequently, Drnovšek needed to secure all of the remaining parliamentary votes and also persuade at least one of the 45 "Spring" people to defect. Even if it could be done, it would be a fragile coalition.

It took until 9 January 1997 before Drnovšek, with only 46 votes, was confirmed as prime minister, but after another month of trying he had still to establish a government. Meanwhile the "Spring" parties struggled to parlay their 45 votes into a coalition. Kučan was willing to allow them to do so, but the "Spring-ers" could not resolve issues among themselves. Crucially, both SDS's Janez Janša and SKD's Lojze Peterle had insurmountable ambitions and refused to take a back seat to anyone. Drnovšek at last achieved his goal at the end of February by reaching an argreement with SLS's head, Marjan Podobnik (Janez Podobnik's brother). On 27 February 1997 a government coalition was established and approved by the State Assembly. The central partners were LDS, SLS, and the **Democratic Party of Retired Persons of Slovenia** (DeSUS), a pensioners' interest group that had gotten five seats in parliament. That assured the new government of 49 votes, which, together with the votes of the Hungarian and Italian members and one defector from the SKD, gave the new government a comfortable margin for the work ahead. The Slovene electorate was grateful that the three-month stalemate was over; by mid-January more than half of the citizens who were questioned by pollsters had rated the Assembly's performance as poor.

The 83 men and seven women of the Assembly were mostly political novices: 58 of the 90 seats were filled by newcomers. But 25 were town and city mayors, whose constituents voted for them hoping to bring local issues before the national political body. This statistic surprised the analysts, who wondered about the legality of simultaneously holding two political offices and also drawing two salaries. Once established, however, the Assembly picked up steam, proving to be an effective, successful, and stable parliamentary body. It turned to the issues of the economy and the establishment of democratic institutions, doing much of the new state's needed grunt work. It also oversaw preliminary legislation necessary for Slovenia's integration into the **European Union** (EU). The latter required an amendment to the 1991 constitution to allow foreigners to own property in Slovenia, an issue that was extremely controversial and was approved only after lengthy debate. This was accomplished in July 1997. The coalition sailed through the local elections in 1998, with LDS picking up additional support and thereby strengthening its national position. Additionally, LDS benefitted from the fact the remaining "Spring" parties (SKD and SDS), who constituted an opposition element, split in summer 1998. Also to LDS's advantage was that SDS's Janez Janša, the party's head and perennial loose cannon, was soundly defeated in an Assembly vote when he tried to smear Drnovšek and bring about an early parliamentary election. The Drnovšek government worked relatively smoothly until April 2000, when it was ousted by a vote of no confidence.

Government of May–November 2000: **Andrej Bajuk**, prime minister. In early 2000 things began to fall apart for Janez Drnovšek's government, which had been in power since the election of 1996. Politicians began thinking ahead to the fall elections and started maneuvering for advantage. In April the SLS pulled out of the governing coalition to join with the SKD, hoping to fuse a stronger conservative, rightist association. The new entity was named the SLS-SKD Slovene People's Party, and Franc Zagožen was chosen its head. A parliamentary crisis ensued as Drnovšek attempted to replace SLS ministers who had left the government. His choices were turned down and a vote of no confidence toppled his government. In order to avoid an early election, President Milan Kučan allowed the newly formed party to put forward Andrej Bajuk as its candidate for the prime minister's post. After several failed attempts, Bajuk (an émigré from the Slovene diaspora in Argentina, who had lived and worked in the **United States** and France for 20 years), an unknown political quantity, was approved by a 46 to 44 vote by the same Assembly that had been elected in 1996. A month elapsed before his cabinet was approved, also by the same narrow margin. The ministers were all from the right or, in the case of a few, were independents.

Bajuk's government lasted from May until November. It initiated an intensive removal of liberal or leftist civil servants, which was not widely popular among the voters. Bajuk also dropped the ball where it came to negotiating with the EU; he chose to handle the task himself, though he had little time to devote to it. And as early as late July, Bajuk's government coalition faltered internally over a vote on a new electoral law, which he and SDS supported but SLS-SKD opposed. He chose to risk his political future (and the unity of the rightist parties) by leaving the SLS-SKD coalition to form an entirely new party, **New Slovenia–Christian People's Party** (NSi), in early August. The Bajuk interlude tied up parliament for several months, left a backlog of pending business, splintered the political right, and enraged the electorate, who were frustrated with its political ineptness. An election was called for 15 October 2000.

Government of November 2000–December 2002: Janez Drnovšek, prime minister. The election of October 2000 returned the leftists to power. Janez Drnovšek, whose LDS won 34 of the 90 seats in parliament, was asked to form his fourth government. He concluded agreements with the ZLSD, DeSUS, and the SLS-SKD Slovene People's Party (SLS). The latter broadened the coalition considerably toward the center and right. The **Party of Young People of Slovenia** (SMS) also aligned with LDS but did not join the coalition. By agreement, most of the ministries went to LDS, although a sprinkling was reserved for ZLSD and SLS. Janez Drnovšek, of course, again became prime minister. It was also agreed that the presidency of parliament would go to a ZLSD member, in this case **Borut Pahor**. Because an election for president of Slovenia was to be held in late 2002, and because Drnovšek was a likely candidate, the coalition agreement addressed this contingency. It was agreed that the understanding among the parties would hold in the probable event that the prime minister would have to be replaced before another parliamentary election (fall 2004 at the latest). Altogether the coalition held 58 assembly seats, a very comfortable majority for the new government.

The SDS and NSi, led by Janez Janša and Andrej Bajuk, respectively, became the nucleus of "Coalition Slovenia," the new government's rigorous opposition. Together they boycotted the first parliamentary session (17 November) when the prime minister and his government were officially confirmed. The two were often supported by the **Slovene National Party** (SNS). Coalition Slovenia, which was initially vocal and sometimes obstructive, gradually moderated its tactics and became a more useful and productive opposition. Ultimately, as the election of October 2004 would show, the opposition leaders' new demeanor would gain them the respect of the electorate.

The Drnovšek government, which lasted two years, focused its primary attention on defining and securing Slovenia's position in the international arena. The prime minister, his foreign minister **Dimitrij Rupel**, as well as others who were charged with semi-official diplomatic assignments, worked diligently on bringing Slovenia into the

North Atlantic Treaty Organization (NATO) and the EU. (The invitation to join NATO came in November 2002 during that organization's meeting in Prague.) Although Slovenia's international goals would not be achieved until spring 2004, much of the groundwork was done during this government. NATO and the EU members had to be courted, and Slovenia needed to promote itself and become a better-known entity. When in spring 2001 Slovenia was approached to host the first meeting of U.S. president George W. Bush and Vladimir Putin, the president of **Russia**, the government enthusiastically welcomed the offer because it brought Slovenia much visibility and favorable media coverage. The Slovene electorate, who feared association with NATO and the EU would bring negative economic consequences and loss of sovereignty, also needed to be persuaded of potential benefits. While promotional work was ongoing abroad and at home, parliament dealt with overwhelming preparations for EU membership. It required passing literally hundreds of laws and acts, and even approving several constitutional amendments, in order to bring Slovenia into uniformity with the European Union's laws and regulations.

The focus on international issues often meant that internal matters, particularly those social issues promoted by Coalition Slovenia and the right, were postponed or neglected. The argument was that, because of external deadlines, NATO and the EU membership took priority; the same argument would be used by Drnovšek's successor, but less successfully. As expected, in November 2002, Drnovšek would run for and win (in a run-off contest with **Barbara Brezigar**) the presidency of Slovenia. His successor, **Anton Rop**, would reap the benefits of the push for recognition in the international arena, but he also inherited the growing force of long-pent-up internal discontents.

Government of December 2002–December 2004: Anton Rop, prime minister. This government was essentially a continuation of the one formed by Janez Drnovšek after the election of October 2000. There was no new election, no new president (speaker) of the State Assembly, and no realignment of political parties in the coalition; there was only a change of prime ministers after Drnovšek's election to the presidency of Slovenia. The transition went smoothly, since it had been provided for in the coalition agreement in late 2000. Anton Rop of the LDS, and finance minister in the Drnovšek government, simply slipped into his predecessor's shoes and was easily confirmed by parliament (getting 63 of 90 votes). Within a few months Rop was also elected head of his party.

The work to prepare Slovenia for NATO and EU membership proceeded. Amendments to the Constitution of 1991 were passed allowing Slovenia to transfer part of its sovereignty to **international organizations**, permitting extraditions in keeping with the laws of the EU and the International Criminal Court, and extending to EU citizens the right to own property in Slovenia. In March 2003 Slovene voters, in a 60 percent turnout referendum, opted to join both NATO and the EU, with 66 and 90 percent affirmative votes, respectively. In Athens in April, Slovenes formally signed documents affirming their entry into the EU, and already the following month Slovene observers sat in the European Parliament. The government's hard work was paying off, and it was capped the following spring with induction into NATO in April and entry into the EU in May. On 13 June 2004 Slovenes would elect their own seven representatives to the European Parliament.

Initially things seemed to be running smoothly for the Rop government, yet in spring 2004 serious cracks began to mar the appearance of success. Anticipating the completion of the NATO and EU goals, the parties of the center and right—including the SLS, who were members of the Rop coalition—began pressing for action on matters important to them. There was continued wrangling over an agreement with the Vatican, and over the rights of former Yugoslav citizens living in Slovenia who had not applied in timely fashion for citizenship. (They were called "the erased" because they had been removed from the register of permanent residents.) **Privatization** of state property, the border with **Croatia**, a cultural agreement with **Austria**, the rights of workers, and the pay of public employees—the list could go on—were among their concerns. In March 2004 LDS's polling numbers began to go down, and in April prime minister Rop's sparring with SLS intensified. Rop threatened to throw SLS out of the coalition, but the three SLS ministers moved first by resigning from the cabinet. Rashly, Rop, without apparent concern for political consequences, appointed new ministers. By mid-April Janez Janša, head of the opposition **Slovene Democratic Party** (SDS), had organized a shadow government; his party's name had been changed from "Social" to "Slovene" Democratic Party in 2003. By April some in Rop's own party were rebeling. When Rop appointed State Prosecutor Zdenka Cerar to be minister of justice, a post recently vacated by an SLS minister, Rop's foreign minister, **Dimitrij Rupel** (LDS), wrote members of parliament to vote against her confirmation (because she was allegedly lenient on white-collar crime), putting

Rupel on a collision course with the prime minister. Cerar was eventually confirmed by parliament. Throughout the spring and summer, Rop suffered growing opposition and serious setbacks. In late April former president Milan Kučan organized **Forum 21**. Representing the old left but new "capitalist" political elite, the Forum became a potential force in the upcoming fall election. What it would mean for Rop and LDS was as yet unclear. The "Spring" parties (SDS, SLS, and NSi) were also regrouping. Meanwhile influential intellectuals, resurrected from the days of the **May Declaration** of 1989, established the Assembly for the Republic (*Zbor za Slovenijo*). Announced in early June as a vehicle for reexamining the Slovene national program—now that Slovenia's institutional framework (EU, NATO) had been completed—it would certainly impact the fall election. Among the 26 signatories of the "Assembly" document were leaders of the "Spring" parties, Janez Janša (SDS) and Andrej Bajuk (NSi), as well as Dimitrij Rupel (LDS). Rop was invited to participate in the debate at the "Assembly's" first meeting on 23 June, but he declined, fully aware that his political control was eroding. He took particular offense at Rupel's involvement, regarding it as an LDS defection. On the eve of Slovenia's independence day (25 June), Rop abruptly fired his foreign minister, the last "founding father" of independence still in government.

Clearly Rop was panicking, and for good reason. On June 13 the election to choose seven Slovene representatives to the European Parliament had been an LDS defeat. Of the seven seats, Rop's party got only two, while SDS and NSi won four between them—with the overwhelmingly strong vote-getter Lojze Peterle coming from NSi. The remaining seat went to the popular speaker of parliament **Borut Pahor** (ZLSD). The EU vote result was viewed by many as a harbinger of the 3 October election. By summer, when politics usually cooled down for extended vacations, politicking remained in full swing. As late as 31 August, just four days before fall campaigning was to begin, parliament was in special session with 80 of its 90 members asking for speaking time. The campaign brought rigorous activity and political rallies, with Forum 21 and particularly the Assembly for the Republic shaping the debate. The result was a defeat for Rop and the LDS, the party that had so dominated government since Slovenia became independent in 1991.

Government of December 2004: Janez Janša, prime minister. On 3 December, Janez Janša's government coalition assumed power.

The SDS (29 seats) had won the election and displaced the LDS (23 seats), the party that had won all previous State Assembly elections since independence in 1991. To form a coalition, Janša gathered together the NSi, SLS, and DeSUS. Parliament approved the new government with 51 votes. Janez Janša, if all went well, would have four years to implement his program. Given the center-right bent of his coalition partners, that program would bring a new focus. In May 2005, when he was reelected to a four-year term as president of SDS, he reconfirmed his intention to put Slovenia on a "new path."

There were indications that the new regime would address issues of Slovene history, particularly interpretations of **World War II** events. Many within the coalition had been anxious for this since the early days of independence, but little had been done in this regard. In May, however, Mitja Ribičič, the second most important figure in the secret police during the war and immediately after, was accused of genocide. The police had uncovered a document linking him to at least 234 deaths (of an estimated 12,000 Slovene soldiers and civilians eliminated in 1945–1946). Whether the 86-year-old Ribičič would be charged was left up to the state prosecutor. Historians at the **University of Ljubljana** also felt pressure from the new regime; some who had been appointed to key institutes were replaced with rightists when their terms expired. In 16 April, many signed a proclamation to the effect that the new government was attempting to politicize history, just as the communists had. They asserted that history must remain independent of politics and the state; without autonomy for its discipline, history, they wrote, would soon degenerate into mythology. In spring, too, there were many discussions on how to inscribe the graves of World War II dead (of various political persuasions). The 64th anniversary of the resistance to the occupier (27 April) provided Janez Janša with an opportunity to express his views. He attempted to strike a middle ideological ground for honoring the war dead, but it was clear that erasing generations of political differences was going to be a daunting task.

Some specific changes were accomplished by the new government. More streets bearing the names of communists were renamed—Kardeljeva ploščad, the plaza named for Edvard Kardelj, is no longer—and new **holidays** appeared on the calendar. The management of the media (Radio-TV) was restructured, eliminating political appointees, particularly leftist ones. Government administration, in general, was renovated. Well over 900 positions in the middle-level bureaucracy were affected between March and November 2005. There were also quite a few changes in ministerial ranks. The government also turned to weightier matters: needed economic and social reforms. Though it was promised that the **social security** safety net would not be removed, it was soon clear that pensioners' living standards would be affected and all would be hit by new taxes. The proposed reforms, when presented, rallied opponents. The left and the **trade unions** stood up for their constituents. In early December there were major demonstrations—25,000 participated—against the government's plan. There was opposition from within the government coalition as well; DeSUS, which represents retirees, has resisted implementing the reforms. The Janša government's viability may rest on whether these reforms irreparably divide the coalition.

In terms of **foreign policy**, the Janša government has reaffirmed Slovenia's commitment to the EU and NATO. As a member of both, Slovenia has pledged to maintain an open-door policy regarding expansion of the two organizations into all Balkan states. In early 2006 the Janša government tweaked Slovenia's policy toward Iraq to a degree. Whereas the previous government had declined to send troops to that war-torn country, Janša committed four soldiers for the purpose of training Iraqi police in Iraq (rather than in Jordan as had been the policy).

GOVERNMENT, YUGOSLAV, 1941–1945 (ROYAL IN EXILE). Peter II **Karadjordjević** became king of **Yugoslavia** on 28 March 1941, just days after Prince Paul, royal regent and cousin to Peter's father, fled the country. Paul had allowed Yugoslavia to be drawn into an unpopular pact with the Germans (March 25), which brought an immediate generals' coup against the government and the installation of Peter, not yet of age, as king. "Better war than the pact!" was the response to a pro-German policy, and war was what Yugoslavia got. On 6 April without declaring hostilities, Germany invaded. The royal army surrendered 11 days later and the royal government, along with its new king, went into exile. The exiled government established itself in London, while remnants of its army joined the **Chetnik** resistance led by Col. Draža Mihailović. The London government recognized Mihailović as its official representative in the homeland and in 1942 promoted him to general and made him minister of war. The Slovene **Miha Krek**, a **Clerical**, was a minister and vice president of the London government until August 1943.

The fate of the government in exile would depend on the effectiveness of Mihailović's resistance against the Axis occupiers and how that was perceived by the Western Allies. By late 1943 the Allies concluded from intelligence missions to Yugoslavia that Mihailović had ceased fighting the Germans. They shifted their support and material assistance to **Tito** and the **Partisans**, while the British pressured the exile government to reorganize. After June 1944 Ivan Šubašić headed the exile government, and he soon went to Dalmatia to meet with Tito. In August Tito and Winston Churchill met in **Italy** and agreed that Šubašić should join Tito's provisional government. In a radio broadcast in September, King Peter urged all Yugoslav patriots to support Tito. The provisional government that the British had sponsored was formed in March 1945, in the last months of the war, and it had three noncommunist ministers. Šubašić received the Foreign Ministry portfolio, but he and his exile government colleagues quickly felt isolated and resigned their posts, refusing also to participate in the postwar election in November. That election, actually a one-list plebiscite, brought a Communist victory. The first act of the newly elected assembly was to depose the king and rename the state the **Federal People's Republic of Yugoslavia** (FPRY).

GOVERNMENT, YUGOSLAV, 1945 (PROVISIONAL). On 7 March 1945 a provisional coalition government under **Tito**'s control was recognized internationally. The 28-member body was formed with the mediation of the Western Allies, pursuant to a 1 November 1944 **Belgrade** agreement between Tito and Ivan Šubašić, representative of the exiled royal government. Besides members of the Communist-led People's Committee of Liberation of Yugoslavia (NKOJ), the coalition government included members of the **Yugoslav royal government in exile** (London) and representatives of other **political parties**. There were two Slovenes in that provisional government: **Edvard Kardelj**, a Yugoslav vice president, and **Edvard Kocbek**, minister for Slovenia.

Despite the coalition nature of the provisional government, internal developments in **Yugoslavia** did not change its leftist direction. Debates in the provisional assembly on agrarian reform and on the election law showed that noncommunists had little power. The opposition, which wanted to reestablish a multiparty system, complained to the Allies about their treatment and the direction of political development. The **Communist Party of Yugoslavia** (CPY) compromised and passed the Law on Associations and Public Gatherings (August 1945), which nominally restored the multiparty system and thereby satisfied mainly the Allies. But in practice, the CPY took control of all spheres of life. The Law on Associations was disregarded and all opposition soon eliminated. With the election of a new Assembly on 1 December 1945, the provisional government was dismantled. Meanwhile in Slovenia, where a **National Government of Slovenia** had already been established in May 1945, the Communists were also easing out their opponents. *See also* COMMUNIST PARTY, OPPOSITION TO.

GOVERNMENT, YUGOSLAV, 1945–1990. Yugoslavia and its constituent republics went through frequent administrative restructuring due to the frequent adoption of revised **constitutions** (1946, 1953, 1963, and 1974). According to the **Constitution of 1946**, elected People's Committees (*ljudski odbori*, LOs) were the highest representative bodies in territorially defined administrative units: *kraj* (a village or a small town), city's district, city, district, **region**. The republic's highest state organ was the People's Assembly (*ljudska skupščina*, LS). With the administrative reorganization in the early 1950s, the *kraj* as an administrative unit was abolished and replaced by a larger unit, the ***občina***, also governed by the LO. The *občina*, the base for the new administrative system established in 1955 (a communal system), became, in theory, the most powerful decision-making unit, especially after the adoption of the **Constitution of 1963**. In practice, of course, decisions needed **Communist Party** approval. Between 1963 and 1990, Yugoslavia's territorially defined administrative units, called sociopolitical communities, were: the federation, the republic, the autonomous province, the commune (*občina*), and the **local community**, whose structure, role, and powers were defined by the constitution. Each sociopolitical community (except the local community) had an assembly (parliament), an executive committee (government), and an administration. After the **Constitution of 1974**, the **delegate system** became a key institution of governing. *See also* CONTRACTUAL SOCIALISM.

The 1974 constitution also established the federal and republic collective presidencies. The position of the president of the Central Committee (CC) League of Communists of Yugoslavia (LCY; formerly the **Communist Party of Yugoslavia**) was the most prestigious, followed by those of the president of the Assembly of the **Socialist Federal Republic of Yugoslavia** (SFRY) (*zvezna skupščina*), the president of the **Federal Executive Council** (FEC) (*zvezni isvršni svet*) (prime minister), and the president of the presidency (*predsedstvo*) of SFRY (head of state). However, only the latter two officials were generally known abroad. The same government structure was in effect in each republic. *See also* COMMUNIST RULERS; FEDERAL PEOPLE'S ASSEMBLY.

GRAPHIC ART, INTERNATIONAL BIENNIAL OF. In existence since 1955, the International Biennial of Graphic Art takes place at the International Center of Graphic Arts, headquartered in Tivoli **castle** in **Ljubljana**, which has been its organizer since 1987. Before that, the event was organized by and held at the **Museum of Modern Art**. Because the exhibitions are often large, Biennal works are shown at various city venues. The 2005 Biennal, the 26th, actually began in December 2004 with an international symposium on the state of graphic art in today's world. Eighteen international institutions offered exhibits, and the show was installed in the exhibition space Tobačna Tovarna (a former cigarette factory).

Established in order to exhibit the latest and best graphic art from abroad and also to promote Slovene artists, the International Biennial has become the most prestigious event in world graphics and is a model for similar art shows abroad (e.g., Fredrikstad, Cracow, Tokyo). The Ljubljana International Biennial has stressed the quality of graphic art over style. Thousands of graphic artists from 80 countries have participated. The event has drawn attention to many unknowns who later became world renowned (e.g., the Americans Robert Rauschenberg and Susan Rothenberg; the Japanese Yozo Hamaguchi and Kosuke Kimura; the French Victor Vasarely; and the Czech Jiři Anderle). The Biennial has also publicized Ljubljana's own Graphic School. In the 1950s this institution was the Slovene artists' only link with the West. *See also* ARTS.

GREENS OF SLOVENIA (THE GREENS) / ZELENI SLOVENIJE (ZELENI). The Green party grew out of a strong 1980s **environmental** movement in Slovenia. As in other states under socialist regimes, Slovenia experienced decades of environmental neglect and mismanagement. Air, water, and forest pollution and irresponsible handling of wastes were readily evident to most Slovenes, arming the Greens with an important campaign issue. Organized as an association on 11 June 1989, the Greens joined the **Demos** coalition in 1990 and campaigned hard for ecological concerns. With Demos's victory in the **election** of April 1990, the Greens not only had seats in parliament and three government ministries, but Dušan Plut, its president, became a member of the republic's presidency. The party, renamed the Greens–Ecological Social Party (*Zeleni– Ekološko socialna stranka*) for the election of December 1992, continued to promote sound ecological practices. As an uncompromising advocate of environmental protection, the party pushed ecology into the forefront of Slovene politics, with the result that most Slovene parties generally acknowledge the need for sounder environmental policies. The Greens promoted ecological vigilance and the monitoring of energy-producing operations (in thermo-electric plants and the Krško nuclear electrical plant), and they urged implementation of environmental regulations based on Western European legislation. In the 1992 election the Greens again made a good showing, winning five seats in the State Assembly. Dušan Plut, who was elected to the State Council, was replaced as party head by Leo Šešerko. In March 1994 the Greens, together with the **Democratic Party of Slovenia** (Democrats) and the **Socialist Party of Slovenia** (SSS), joined with the Liberal Democratic Party to form **Liberal Democracy of Slovenia** (LDS).

– H –

HABSBURG RESTORATION, PRE-MARCH ERA (1815–1848). At the Congress of **Vienna** in 1815, Europe's great powers dealt with the devastation brought on by the French Revolution and the Napoleonic wars during the previous quarter-century. Prince Clemens Metternich, **Austria**'s foreign minister, did much to shape the settlement, which was based on the principles of balance of power and legitimacy. In Europe the conservative powers, or Holy Alliance (Austria, Prussia, and **Russia**), also agreed that peace and order would be maintained through military intervention if necessary. At home, the same strictness would prevail; popular movements, such as liberalism and political nationalism, would be contained. **Constitutions** would not be permitted. Only national cultural activities were allowed. The **Habsburgs** of the restoration era, Francis I and Ferdinand I, ruled over an absolutist **Austrian Empire** (the title their state had acquired in 1804). The police, the army, the church, censorship, and even the bureaucracy served Vienna in preventing revolution, or change of any sort.

Still, change came in the form of an industrial revolution, and Slovene lands were directly affected. Iron, **textile**, glass, and paper **manufacturing** were all revolutionized, usually through the use of steam power. By the 1830s there were two sugar refineries in **Ljubljana**, and the second savings bank in all Austria opened in 1820. **Trieste** grew quickly, particularly after 1836, when the Austrian Lloyd shipping company was established; this development provided employment for excess rural population, which in Trieste's hinterland was largely Slovene. By 1849 a railroad linked Vienna with Ljubljana, pushing its way toward Trieste, which it reached in 1857. The towns still had guilds and the peasants were still burdened with feudal obligations and taxes, but when these last vestiges of feudalism fell in 1848, economic expansion was to have an even freer hand. *See also* ROMANTICISM; TRANSPORT.

HABSBURGS (1282–1918). The Habsburg dynasty, which became the major power in Central Europe beginning in the 1500s, established its first feudal holdings in the area in 1282. The family's original power base was in the territories known as the Hereditary Lands. These included the lands of much of present-day **Austria** as well as **regions** inhabited largely or in part by Slovenes—Carniola (Kranjska), **Carinthia** (Koroška), Styria (Štajerska), **Gorizia** (Gorica), **Trieste** (Trst), and Istria (Istra). Most of these were acquired between the 13th and the 15th centuries through warfare and marriage, and were sometimes known as the Inner Austrian Lands. *See also* MEDIEVAL LANDS.

The Habsburgs' power in the 16th century was greatly increased when the family acquired the kingdoms of Bohemia and **Hungary** (1526). The Habsburgs at the time were also rulers of Spain, the Netherlands, and their respective overseas possessions. In Central Europe they continued to be elected heads of the **Holy Roman Empire**, giving them control over Germanic Central Europe. The Slovene lands, in addition to being Hereditary Lands of "Austria," were also a part of the Holy Roman Empire. Refer to appendix 1. *See also* HABSBURG RESTORATION.

HEALTH. The health of the population in Slovenian lands has been tracked since the mid-19th century. Initially the focus was on causes of mortality, of which tuberculosis was the most frequent, followed by old age and infectious diseases (diphtheria, scarlet fever, and smallpox). At the end of 19th century the mortality rate was highest in cities and among young people under 20; infant mortality was 20 percent. In 1887 **Austria**'s government sought to improve health care by introducing a law on health insurance organizations for factory workers. Before **World War I** there were about 100 of them in the poverty-stricken

Slovene lands (Kranjska and lower Štajerska). As health insurance was being developed, new hospitals were built in **Ljubljana, Maribor,** and some smaller cities such as **Celje** and **Ptuj.** After the war, public health improved dramatically. In the 1920s public health services developed rapidly, and the first preventive local health care institutions, some still in existence today, were established across Slovenia, as was a new Institute for Hygiene in Ljubljana. Hospitals were modernized and new sanatoriums were built to provide additional beds. With the development of a health care network in the **Drava** *banovina*, the number of physicians also increased (in 1932 there was one doctor per about 2,000 inhabitants, whereas in the mid-19th century, there had been only one per about 15,000). The infant mortality rate fell, and tuberculosis ceased to be the leading cause of death. Due to industrialization, death from cardiovascular diseases and tumorous growths increased, surpassing infectious diseases as the main cause of death even before **World War II.** The 1922 Yugoslav Law on **social security** addressed public health care by including aspects of health insurance. A regional office in Ljubljana administered the law, which was fully implemented only in 1937. Also established were private health insurance institutions.

Public health worsened during World War II, and mortality was high as thousands of Slovenes died in battle and **concentration camps.** After the war, there were systematic efforts to eradicate infectious diseases with antibiotics and preventive care (vaccinations). Special services for children and youth were established and much effort was devoted to women's reproductive health. Fewer children died and infant mortality was stabilized in 2000–2005 at 6 deaths per 1,000 live births, lower than the **European Union**'s (EU) rate of 10 per 1,000 births. However, chronic cardiovascular diseases, followed by tumors, became the leading causes of sickness and death (67 percent of all deaths in 1998). Tumorous diseases among those age 45 to 65 have been increasing rapidly, accounting for a death rate one-fifth higher than in the EU. Although links have been established between the polluted **environment** and sickness, there has been little systematic research of the subject. Injuries (traffic accidents, and self-inflicted and work-related injuries) are the third major cause of death; their incidence has been much higher for men than women, and also considerably higher than in the EU. Regarding more recent illnesses, 0.1 percent of adults age 15–49 have been infected with HIV or AIDS

(2001). Life expectancy has increased by 11 years in the last 50 years and in 2000–2001 stood at 72 years for men and 79 for women. Since 1992 health care has been provided by a public health system and by a growing number of private doctors. Under the 1992 Health Care and Health Insurance Act, all employed persons and permanent residents are covered by compulsory health insurance, which provides health services at three levels. The primary level consists of 64 health centers with additional 66 branches, staffed by general practitioners (1,413 in 2000), which also provide specialized services for children and youth, women, dentistry, and first aid. The network of these institutions provides convenient health care to patients within a distance of 20 kilometers. An increasing number of private doctors work through contract with the National Health Insurance Institute. The secondary level, specialized health care, is provided by hospitals and specialized clinics located in the larger cities, primarily Ljubljana. In 2003 there were 28 hospitals (12 specialized), the Institute for Rehabilitation, the Institute for Oncology, and two sanatoriums, with 9,895 beds altogether. The majority of these institutions are state owned, but a few private clinics have been established. Because of insufficient funds, the population is not adequately served by specialists and specialized clinics. There are long waits for specialists' visits and medical treatments; for open-heart surgery, there is a waiting period of several months. The tertiary level of care involves more complex medical problems and takes place at institutions with research capabilities; most of this care is performed at the Clinical Center in Ljubljana. Private practice is not allowed within these institutions. While there has been a decline in the number of beds available, as well as in the length of stay in hospitals, the number employed in the health sector increased from 34,834 in 1998 to 36,019 in 2001. In 2000 there were 3,866 medical doctors, 1,209 dentists, 1,215 pharmacists, 3,339 medical nurses, and 11,796 supporting staff. Although Slovenia has a well-developed network of medical institutions, there are huge regional differences in the doctor–patient ratio (1 to 700 in Ljubljana, and 1 to 2,000 in rural areas).

The present health care system evolved over the 45 years under socialism. After World War II, private and public health care existed briefly side by side, but in 1950 most private care was prohibited and replaced by a socialized system. The new state health insurance, regulated by a 1950 federal law, was generous in employee benefits but did not include farmers and the self-employed until 1969.

Reforms of the 1970s transferred financing of health care to the new self-managing communities of interest. Health services were paid for by contributions from employers and employees rather than from the state budget, but collection of revenues was controlled by the Social Accounting Service. Theoretically, health care was intended for everyone, regardless of cost, and only occasionally were there marginal co-payments. Decentralization, which increased the number of bureaucrats, inefficiency, and deficits, diminished monetary resources; the promise of universal care went unfulfilled. Thus, the late 1970s and the 1980s saw the beginning of private health services (mostly in dentistry), which, although illegal, were tolerated by the state because the demand could not be satisfied by the public sector.

After 1990 the health system went through considerable reform. Health care institutions are now managed by state agencies, through managers appointed by the state. The system ran a large deficit, which was covered by increasing contributions for health care, amounting to 18 percent of the payroll, with employer and employee each paying half. Legislation enacted in 1992 (Health Care and Health Insurance Act, Health Activity Act, Pharmacy Activities Act) provided for the transformation of an exclusively public health system into a combined public/private one. Under the new law, basic health care services are provided within the compulsory insurance scheme, covering not only those employed but all permanent residents. Employers are required to pay added premiums for work-related injuries, while farmers pay for insurance on the basis of the size of their farms and their income. There is a strong belief in Slovenia that equitable access to health services should be fully preserved in the future.

Voluntary insurance has also been introduced, which covers co-payments and many health services not included in the compulsory insurance; 90 percent of the population participates in the voluntary program. Initially payments for voluntary insurance were low, but they have been increasing. Both insurance schemes, compulsory and voluntary, are administered by the Institute of Health Insurance, while licensing and professional development are taken care of by newly formed Medical and Pharmacist Chambers. The voluntary health insurance operation has generated the independent mutual insurance company Vzajemna and the private insurer Adriatic. Licensing and granting concessions to health professionals began in 1992. Despite relative success of the 1992 health reform, the system is burdened with problems that surfaced in 1999. They were the consequence of a huge increase in health care salaries and a new value added tax (VAT) on all health services and drugs. As a consequence, contributions to the voluntary health insurance plan are too low and do not cover the real costs of health services.

The share of the health system in the GDP was rising after World War II until the late 1970s, when it began to decline. With 5 percent of the GDP, the health system was underfinanced; increased expenditures created big losses in health care and a deficit in the health insurance funds. Since 1991 health care's share of GDP has been on the rise again. In 2000 the share of GDP that Slovenia spent for health care was 8.7 percent, more than many EU countries (Italy spent 8.1 percent, and Austria 8 percent). *See also* CONTRACTUAL SOCIALISM, ECONOMY, 1945–1990; ECONOMY SINCE 1991; SERVICE INDUSTRY.

HOLIDAYS, NATIONAL. Official national holidays in the **Republic of Slovenia** (RS) are New Year's, 1 and 2 January; **Prešeren** Day (cultural holiday), 8 February; Day of Uprising against the Occupier **(World War II)**, 27 April; Labor Days, 1 and 2 May; National Day, 25 June; Day of Remembrance for the Dead, 1 November; and Independence Day, 26 December. The RS also recognizes certain religious holy days as work-free days. These are Easter Sunday and Monday; Pentecost Sunday; Assumption Day, 15 August; Reformation Day, 31 October; and Christmas, 25 December. Although Slovenia is primarily a **Catholic** country, Reformation Day, a Protestant holiday, was included to commemorate Slovene participants in the **Protestant Reformation** who established Slovene as a literary **language**.

In 2005 three new holidays that are not work-free days were added. Two of them commemorate the reunification of **Prekmurje** and Primorska with Slovenia, observed on 17 August and 15 September, respectively. The third, 23 November, celebrates **Rudolf Maister**, the Slovene military leader who secured incorporation of southern **Styria** into **Yugoslavia** after **World War I**.

HOLY ROMAN EMPIRE (962–1806). Where Charlemagne's empire, established in 800, failed, the Holy Roman Empire endured for eight centuries. Crowned by the Roman pope, the Holy Roman emperors were ranked at the top of Europe's Christian ruling hierarchy and reigned over much of Central Europe, primarily German lands. The elected position (after 1356, four specific secular and three clerical electors chose the emperor) often went to the **Habsburg** family. After 1477, with one brief hiatus during **Maria Theresa**'s reign, Habsburgs held the emperorship continuously—indeed their imperial title came from this office—until the empire was abolished by Napoleon. Slovene territories had been included in Charlemagne's empire and were a part of the Holy Roman Empire even before Habsburgs had acquired feudal lands in this part of Europe. The peace following the Napoleonic wars (1815) established a German Confederation where the Holy Roman Empire had been, and Slovene lands were again included. Slovenes felt especially pressed in this confederation by German nationalism, and therefore in the **Revolution of 1848**, they voted not to participate in the Frankfurt Parliament, where Germans of the confederation were meeting to create a German national state. War between Prussia and **Austria** ended the confederation in 1866.

HOME GUARD / DOMOBRANCI (1943–1945). The Slovene Home Guard was established in September 1943, in **Ljubljana**, in order to fight against the Communist-led **Liberation Front** (LF) during **World War II**. It was organized, with German approval and assistance, by **Leon Rupnik**, a former Yugoslav army general, who had been appointed president of the former Italian Province of Ljubljana, occupied after 1943 by the Germans. Rupnik acted also as inspector-general of the Home Guard. The Home Guard, whose commander was Lt. Colonel Franc Krener, was formed from remnants of the **Village Guard** and new volunteers. At the end of the war, they numbered between 10,000 and 15,000. In addition to local defense units (village and town garrisons), the Home Guard organized four assault battalions, thus becoming a real threat to the **Partisans**. The Home Guard also established a political police to fight the LF and conducted strong anticommunist propaganda in the media. Similar armed organizations, independent of the Slovene Home Guard but under overall German command, were established in Primorska (*Slovenski narodni varnostni zbor* / Slovene National Security Corps), and in Gorenjska (*Gorenjski domobranci* / Upper Carniolan Home Guard). The two organizations together numbered around 4,000 participants.

Members of the Slovene Home Guard were mostly **Catholic** and anticommunist. In fighting the communists, they believed they were performing valuable service to the Allies. They supported the Yugoslav **government in exile** in London, but operationally and logistically depended on the Germans. They were by and large patriotic

Slovenes who saw collaboration with Germany as the lesser evil, given the LF's outrages. The Germans, who did not trust the Home Guard, demanded that they confirm their loyalty to the anticommunist fight at the side of the German army in a public oath-taking ceremony, which they did on 20 April 1944 and 10 January 1945. Thus, Rupnik and the Home Guard leadership led the movement into open collaboration with Germany. This act damaged the image of the Home Guard in the eyes of many Slovenes at home and abroad; it also angered the British and the Americans.

In the spring of 1945, the **National Committee for Slovenia** demanded Rupnik's resignation as inspector-general. Rupnik refused and instead appointed himself the Home Guard's commander-in-chief. However, at a 3 May meeting of the National Committee, the Home Guard was renamed the Slovene National Army and Rupnik was dismissed. Fearing that they were not strong enough to resist the Yugoslav Partisan army, which was moving toward Slovenia, the Slovene National Army, with family members and many other anticommunists, retreated to **Austria**. There they were met by the British, who disarmed them as German collaborators. In June 1945 the British returned thousands of Home Guardists to Slovenia, where most were brutally murdered at Kočevski Rog, **Škofja Loka**, Teharje, and elsewhere. The number executed was more then 11,000. *See also* COVENANT, SLOVENE; MASSACRES, POST–WORLD WAR II.

HOMOSEXUALS. Homosexuals became socially active in the 1980s as a New Social Movement (NSM). The first gay men's group, Magnus, was founded in 1984 and operated out of **Ljubljana**'s Student Cultural Center (ŠKUC). Magnus, which was also the first gay organization in former **Yugoslavia** and Eastern Europe, worked on various projects that were of interest to its members, such as AIDS awareness. Its principal activity was the Magnus festival—an annual gathering of homosexual culture, since 1988 known as the Gay and Lesbian Film Festival. The feminist group Lilit, organized in 1985, included in its activities lesbians organized in their own group LL, which in 1987 became independent, working under ŠKUC auspices. LL published the newspaper *Pandora*, and the magazine *Lesbo*, which ceased publication when government financial support stopped. In 1990 some members of Magnus and ŠKUC-LL founded the Roza Klub (Pink Club), an independent political organization (now defunct), to fight discrimination against homosexuals. Since the 1990s two new organizations have been established: Legebitra for young gays and lesbians, and the Society for the Integration of Homosexuality (*Društvo za integracijo homoseksualnosti*, DIH). Since 2001 all gay and lesbian organizations have worked together on the Pride Parade. Gay and lesbian groups have a social center at Ljubljana's Metelkova Cultural complex, and they jointly publish *Revolver* magazine. All homosexual organizations have been involved extensively in lobbying activities to assure equal treatment of homosexuals. Slovene **media** reporting on homosexuals has been neutral or sympathetic. Within Slovene society, however, although open hostility has been rare, a 2001 survey showed that half of the homosexual respondents had experienced harassment of some kind—mostly verbal. Complaints about discrimination based on sexual orientation have been filed with the Office of the Ombudsman for Human Rights. As a consequence, the Principles of Equal Treatment Act (2004) specifically prohibits direct and indirect discrimination against, among others, homosexuals and assures legal protection of homosexuals, although such principles are already stated generally in the **Constitution of 1991**, the Penal Code (1995), and labor legislation (2002). It seems that enforcement of basic human rights for gays and lesbians is a problem. Also, parliament has enacted the Registration of Same-Sex Partnership Act (2005), but gay and lesbian organizations are of the opinion that it is discriminatory. *See also* ALTERNATIVE MOVEMENTS; HUMAN RIGHTS; WOMEN'S RIGHTS MOVEMENTS.

HRIBAR, IVAN (1851–1941). A leading **Liberal** politician, Ivan Hribar began his career as a banker, working throughout **Austria** in branches of a Czech national bank. His organizational abilities in directing the rebuilding of **Ljubljana** after a major earthquake in 1895 earned him the post of mayor, a position he held from 1896 to 1910. He also served in the Carniolan assembly and the **Vienna** parliament, and he was president of his party between 1906 and 1910. An ardent nationalist, Hribar was also the Slovenes' leading Pan-Slav. He courted Pan-Slavs among the Serbs and Croats (e.g., Bishop Josip Juraj Strossmayer) and was very close to the Czech Karel Kramař, whose Neoslavism in 1908 attempted to foster Slavic solidarity in the face of growing conflict between Austria and **Russia** over the Balkans. Hribar was convinced that Austria's Slavs were about to assume a leading role in that state. His pro-Serbian leanings grew after 1908, however. When **World War I** began, Hribar was put in a Ljubljana prison (1914–1915) and later confined near Salzburg (1915–1917).

After the **Kingdom of Serbs, Croats, and Slovenes** was established, Hribar became its envoy to Czechoslovakia (1921–1923). As an elder statesman he served the government at home in various capacities, including that of senator (1932–1938). His death in 1941 was a suicide, at the age of 90, caused by despair over the German and Italian invasion and subsequent dismemberment of **Yugoslavia**. *See also* AUSTROSLAVISM.

HRIBAR, SPOMENKA (1941–). The philosopher and sociologist Spomenka Hribar, born in **Belgrade**, received her B.A. (1965) and Ph.D. (1997) at the **University of Ljubljana**. After having worked as a researcher at the Institute of Sociology and Philosophy at the University of Ljubljana (1965–1969), Hribar was on the Faculty of Social Sciences at the same university until 1991, when she was elected to the National Assembly of the **Republic of Slovenia** (RS). Since 1993, she has been a freelance publicist. Hribar is best known for her research on the writer and **Christian Socialist Edvard Kocbek** and her essay *Krivda in greh* (Guilt and Sin), in which she deals with the **massacres** of **Home Guard** members and other anticommunists immediately after **World War II**. She was the first to break the social and political taboo and write openly about this aspect of Slovene history, suggesting that all who died in World War II be treated respectfully; her publication thus began the painful process of national reconciliation. The essay had been written for the Kocbek anthology published in 1987, but it was in part published without her consent in the daily *Delo* in 1984, causing immediate political turmoil.

Hribar was one of the leading members of the **Slovene Democratic Alliance** and the **Demos** coalition, and a collaborator of *Nova revija*, contributing thereby to the democratization and **independence** of Slovenia. She was also the first president of the Slovene branch of *Slovenski svetovni kongres* (Slovene World Congress), established in 1990 with the goal of promoting cooperation among all Slovenes throughout the world. As a left-leaning intellectual, Hribar has been active in **Forum 21**, often creating controversies with her writing and public speaking. She is the author of several books, among them *Edvard Kocbek in križarsko gibanje* (Edvard Kocbek and the Crusade Movement, 1990), *Dolomitska izjava* (The Dolomite Declaration, 1991), and *Svitanja* (Daybreaks, 1994).

HUMAN DEVELOPMENT INDEX (HDI). Established by the **United Nations**, the Human Development Index is a broad, although not comprehensive measure of quality of life. This composite index encompasses three important measurable components of human life: **health** and longevity, **education**, and standard of living (poverty level). Thus, the HDI goes beyond gross domestic product (GDP) and other economic indicators, giving a better picture of life in individual countries. The HDI for Slovenia has been measured since 1992. Despite several methodological changes and problems with calculations, the index for Slovenia for the period 1995–2005 increased steadily, from 0.852 to 0.904, moving Slovenia from 30th to 26th place among 177 countries. For 10 years, Slovenia was rated the best among Central and Eastern European transition countries and was ranked among countries like Greece, Cyprus, Portugal, and South Korea. Relatively high and steadily increasing HDI was due to two indicators: GDP and education—the strongest indicators for Slovenia. In education, Slovenia ranked 23rd in 2000 and moved up to 13th place in 2003. Less favorable have been indicators concerning health and longevity. The 2003 estimate for the latter was 76.4 years, which ranked Slovenia 35th (between Chile and Portugal) but still ahead of all the other transition countries. *See also* ECONOMY SINCE 1991; ENVIRONMENT; SOCIAL SECURITY.

Slovenia's rank in some other measures developed by the United Nations for international comparison has not been as favorable. For example, while still the best performer among the transition countries in the Gender-related Development Index (GDI), which uses the same indicators as the HDI but reflects disparities in achievement between women and men, Slovenia ranked 25th (out of 140 countries). Among the indicators of "gender empowerment" in the GDI are the number of women in parliament (Slovenia, with 12 percent of the seats held by women, ranked 95th, behind Bosnia and Hercegovina), and the overall female-to-male ratio of income earned for identical work (with 62 percent, Slovenia ranks 47th, behind Angola and **Hungary**), although faring much better in regard to professional employment (with 56 percent, ranking 18th, but behind Estonia, Lithuania, Poland, and Romania). *See also* WOMEN'S RIGHTS MOVEMENTS.

HUMAN RIGHTS. Since achieving **independence** in 1991, Slovenia has taken a large step toward affirming a society based on human rights. Slovenia is a signatory to the Universal Declaration of Human Rights as well as many specific international agreements on individual human rights issues, pertaining primarily to children, terrorism, torture, and women's issues. The Slovene **Constitution of 1991** guarantees a wide range of rights, which together with specific legislation, such as the Citizenship Act (1991), the Act on the Legal Status of Religious Communities (1991), the Human-Rights Ombudsman Act (1993–1994), the Political Parties Act (1994), the Law on Asylum (1997), and the Personal Data Protection Act (1999), constitute the legal base for human rights' guarantees. Making human rights one of its priorities, the government has established a number of institutions to ensure they are respected and promoted through public relations and educational activities. These are the Office of the Human Rights Ombudsman (1995), the Office of Nationalities (1991), the Equal Opportunity Office (2001), which replaced the Office of Women's Policies, established in 1992, and the Office of Immigration and Refugees. The Office of Religious Communities, established in 1972, continued its work. While human rights have a firm legal base, enforcement remains a problem.

Although there have been no reports of violation of political freedoms (disappearances, forced repatriation of persons fearing persecution at home, forced exiles, political incarcerations, and torture), violations of other human rights have been part of everyday life. About 3,304 cases of alleged violations of human rights were reported to the Office of the Ombudsman in 2001, and about 2,665 in 2004). Accounting for two-thirds of all cases, the largest number of complaints concerned administrative matters, judicial or police procedures, and **social security**. The judicial system—with its court backlogs and lengthy trials—and use of excessive force by the **police** constitute more than half of all cases. Although the number has declined, the pattern in official data was consistent between the years 1995 and 2004. Less frequent have been cases concerning national **minorities** (ethnic groups from the rest of the former **Yugoslavia** or the Roma); freedom of speech (the **media**); freedom of **religion** and respect for religious values (Muslims); and women and children. Although women and men were treated equally under the law already in socialist times, the general culture has remained discriminatory toward women. Developing awareness of spousal abuse and of violence against women has contributed to the increase in the number of cases reported to the Office of the Ombudsman. A special problem has been trafficking in women. Slovenia has been primarily although not exclusively a country of transit for Eastern European girls and women for prostitution in Western Europe and North Africa. Some have stayed in Slovenia, seeking help there from nongovernmental organizations (NGOs). In 2004 the penal code was amended to criminalize trafficking in persons. *See also* HOMOSEXUAL RIGHTS MOVEMENT; WOMEN'S RIGHTS MOVEMENTS.

A notable violation of human rights in Slovenia was the 1992 removal from the Slovene registry of permanent residents of about 18,000 individuals—mostly Yugoslav citizens residing in Slovenia. Those removed had not applied for Slovene citizenship within the first six months of independence, the deadline set by the Slovene government. Having been "erased" from the registry of permanent residents, they have remained without basic human rights (**education**, housing, travel, and employment) and also without social benefits (**health** care and pensions) afforded to permanent residents. The Slovene Constitutional Court, in 1999 and in 2003, ruled unconstitutional their removal from resident registry, and ordered Slovene authorities to restore retroactively their permanent residency status. In 1999 about 12,000 had permanent residency restored, but not retroactively. After the 2003 ruling, however, the Ministry of Internal Affairs has been approving permanent residency also retroactively, and as of January 2005 about 4,100 such decrees have been issued. As of 2005 the "erased" issue has not been resolved and lawsuits by the "erased" have been dealt with by the European Court of Human Rights in Strasbourg, but dismissed for procedural reasons. In 2005 the Council of Europe Commissioner for Human Rights in Strasbourg addressed this problem and urged the Slovene government to honor the Constitutional Court decisions without delay.

Despite a limited role in enforcing human rights, the Office of the Human Rights Ombudsman has played an important role in building awareness of and educating the public about human rights. It has been involved in public relations and has collaborated with the government and independent organizations in educational projects. Its goal has been to promote preventive measures to avoid systemic human rights violations by drawing attention to them, and by identifying governmental practices that need correction. Slovenia has thus far had three ombudsmen: Ivan Bizjak (1995–2000) and Matjaž Hanžek (2001–2006), who was replaced by Zdenka Čebašek-Travnik in February 2007.

Slovenia has as well been involved in international human rights institutions and projects. It was among the first to support the establishment of the International Criminal Court (ICC) in The Hague in

1998. With a strong interest in children's rights, Slovenia has long been an active member of the Executive Council of UNICEF.

HUMAN RIGHTS, COMMITTEE FOR THE PROTECTION OF (CPHR). The Committee for the Protection of Human Rights (CPHR) was founded in **Ljubljana** in the summer of 1988 by civil society representatives. Initially, its goal was to protect the basic **human rights** of the **Ljubljana Four trial** defendants. Joined by over 100,000 people and sponsored by many organizations, including all the New Social Movement (NSM) groups, CPHR became a mass organization. Its members overcame political differences, since the threat to Slovenia's democratization came from outside forces, specifically the **Yugoslav People's Army** (JNA). The CPHR shifted its focus from independent social activity to independent political activity and became the de facto opposition to the League of Communists of Slovenia (LCS; formerly the **Communist Party of Slovenia**). Among the many activities organized by the CPHR, an early 1989 public meeting of solidarity with the miners of Stari trg (Kosovo), who were protesting the Serbian suspension of Kosovo's autonomy, was very important and had vital consequences for Slovenia. Official political organizations joined the action against the inhumane treatment of the Kosovo miners; it later developed into a common political front against the growing Serbian power in **Yugoslavia**. In the fall of 1988 some political differences within the CPHR had already begun to emerge, resulting eventually in the formation of new **political parties**. *See also* ALTERNATIVE MOVEMENTS.

HUMANISM. Trieste, **Koper**, and **Piran** were the first centers of humanism in the Slovene lands. From Koper, which had a Latin school already in the 12th century, came Peter Pavel Vergerij, or Vergerius (1370–1444), one of the important early European humanists, who wrote the earliest extant humanistic comedy, *Paulus*, as well as educational treatises that influenced humanistic reforms in education. In the early 16th century a poet and bishop of Trieste, Peter Bonomo (1458–1546), associated with humanist circles in **Vienna**, had close ties with Slovene reformers, especially with **Primož Trubar**. In the central Slovene lands, the last three **counts of Celje**, especially Herman II, were distinctly humanist nobles. **Ljubljana**, with Bishop Krištof Ravbar and his circle, also was a humanist center. Ravbar, the head of the Ljubljana diocese in the years 1488–1536, attracted several humanists to work with him, among them Augustinus Tyfernus, known also as Avguštin Prygl. Humanism affected **education**. Latin as a language of instruction was replaced by German or Italian, the languages of the nobility. The curriculum and teaching methods were adapted to new social demands: Mathematics was included, learning by rote was replaced with learning by understanding, and practical use of knowledge was stressed. Around 40 schools operated in the Slovene lands. At the end of the 15th century, about 2,000 Slovenes had been educated at various European **universities**. The Slovene intellectuals, active also in Europe, had an influential role in the development of Slovene cultural life. Matija Hvale, Andrej Prelah, and Bernard Perger, who had studied at German and Italian universities, became professors abroad and later returned home to work as scholars and artists in Slovene lands. The Slovene Tomaž Prelokar was known as a tutor to the future Holy Roman Emperor Maximilian I. Humanism's most important legacy for the Slovenes is the religious and cultural awakening, which produced, among other things, the first Slovene book. *See also* BOHORIČ, ADAM; DALMATIN, JURIJ; PROTESTANT REFORMATION; SCIENCE.

HUNGARY, RELATIONS WITH. The Republic of Hungary is the **Republic of Slovenia**'s (RS) neighbor to the east. Hungary recognized Slovenia's **independence** on 15 January 1992, also the date of European Community (EC) recognition, and the two countries established diplomatic ties the next day. They have ambassadors in each other's capitals, and Slovenia maintains a consulate in Szentgotthárd, a town where there is a Slovene **minority**. Relations with Hungary are the most cordial among all of Slovenia's neighbors. Since 1990 communications and **transportation** links between the former Yugoslav republic and the former Warsaw Pact nation have improved greatly and facilitated better relations. Roads have opened connecting the two, the most important being the link opened in 2001 that is projected as a segment of the trans-European highway linking Barcelona with Kiev. The opening of a railroad connection has enabled **trade** and cross-border contacts in general.

Hungary concluded a variety of bilateral economic agreements with the RS, such as the free trade agreement implemented in July 1994. Other argreements were pursued through multilateral Central European organizations such as the **Alps–Adriatic Working**

Community, the **Central European Initiative**, and the Litomyšl 7 (**Austria**, Czech Republic, Hungary, Germany, Poland, Slovakia, and Slovenia). Both Slovenia and Hungary participated in a number of programs, such as those sponsored by PHARE, in preparation for accession to the **European Union** (EU), and both participated in the Partnership for Peace (PfP) in preparation for **North Atlantic Treaty Organization** (NATO) membership. As members of the EU and NATO, Slovenia and Hungary now also work together within those multilateral organizations. About 4,000 Slovenes live in Hungary, and there are over 6,000 Hungarians in the RS. The well-being of these respective minorities is a concern for both states and continues to command their attention.

– I –

IDRIJA. Located in a narrow mountain valley along the Idrijca River in western Slovenia, Idrija, with 5,878 inhabitants, is the country's oldest **mining** town. The mine, which is no longer operating, was once second only to Spain's Almadén in European mercury (quicksilver) production. Mercury was discovered in Idrija in 1490, and within a century the area had been colonized by German miners and the mine was "nationalized" (1580) by **Vienna**. Idrija was soon accorded town status and autonomous administration, and by the 18th century it had developed a renowned **health** service, concerned especially with the treatment of mercury poisoning. Because of the town's livelihood, geodetic science, metallurgy, mining engineering, and also **forestry** were taught intermittently from the 18th century on. Regarded as a center of rational learning (especially the natural sciences) in the 18th century, Idrija is sometimes known as the "Slovene Athens."

Idrija at the dawn of the 20th century had 5,000 inhabitants and was the second largest town in the Carniola **region**. It thrived economically, politically, and culturally and was at the forefront of Slovene national developments. Workers' parties and **societies** were established in the 1890s, and Idrija elected a Socialist mayor in 1911. The town was awarded to nearby **Italy** after **World War I**, after which Italianization and a fascist regime drove many Slovenes to **emigrate**, mostly to the **Yugoslav Kingdom**. After **World War II**, during the latter part of which Idrija under German occupation was bombed eight times by Allied planes, the town was joined with **Yugoslavia**. Mercury production began to wane in the 1970s, partly because the supply was being depleted but also due to falling demand and prices. Since the last of

Idrija's mines closed in the 1990s, its **economy** has been sustained by **manufacturing** of commutators (Kolektor), components for air conditioning (IMP-Klima), electric motors (Rotomatik), furniture (Iles), and motorcycles. Idrija also supports some **tourism**.

Idrija, which celebrated its 500th anniversary recently, has a unique character shaped by its mining history. Besides its premodern, plain and sturdy, multistory buildings, it has a mining **museum**, a school museum, and even a miners' **theater**, opened in 1769, which now serves as a **film** theater. Idrija is also widely known for its exquisite lace. Because the community was not dependent upon **agriculture** for its livelihood, Idrija's women were free to develop this centuries-old craft. Idrija still has a lacemaking school and every August hosts a lace festival. *See also* CASTLES.

ILLYRIAN PROVINCES (1809–1813). During the Napoleonic wars, about 625,000 Slovenes came briefly under French rule. These Slovenes, along with Croats and a small number of Serbs, Italians, and Germans, were joined in one state, called the Illyrian Provinces—a name Napoleon himself chose because ancient Illyrians had been conquered by Rome and he saw himself as a new Roman emperor. The territories were the spoils of two military campaigns awarded to France by the treaties of Pressburg/Bratislava (1805) and Schönbrunn (1809); they were united, named, and incorporated into the French empire in 1809. The territories included Dalmatia, Venetian Istria, and other former Venetian possessions—all Treaty of Pressburg acquisitions—and the county of **Gorizia**, **Trieste**, western Carinthia, the part of Carniola on the south bank of the Sava River, a part of Civil **Croatia**, six districts of Military Croatia, Rijeka, Austrian Istria, and several islands in the Adriatic. The administrative center, where the French governor-general resided, was **Ljubljana**.

The French wars, which had begun in 1792 under the early revolutionary regimes, had taken their toll on the Slovenes while **Austria** fought the French. Now, under the French, the lot of the ordinary Slovene was still difficult, for conscription, taxes, inflation, and military occupation were all hardships. Nonetheless, the French introduced certain enlightened reforms: The courts became state courts, the Code Napoléon became the basis for civil law (elements of which survive in Slovenia today), and the nobility lost its privileges and tax exemptions. The effect of these reforms was little felt, since French rule had barely begun when Austria reclaimed Illyria after defeating France on the battlefield in 1813.

The Illyrian Provinces, however, play a special role in the history of the Slovene and the Yugoslav national awakenings. The name Illyria itself is of significance, for regardless of Napoleon's reasons for choosing the name, many South Slavs at the time believed that they were descendents of ancient Illyrians. For them Napoleon was merely arousing their nation from centuries of slumber. The inclusion of both Slovenes and Croats in the same state, and their feeling a kinship with one another, gave birth to the notion that their common Illyrian past required a common Illyrian/Yugoslav future. National consciousness among the Slovenes, whether Slovene or more broadly Illyrian, was encouraged by the French, and particularly the governor-general Marshal Auguste Marmont, in several ways. The **language** of the land was designated for use in schools (1810), and **Valentin Vodnik**, superintendent of schools, produced Slovene language textbooks for elementary classes. The local language was also employed in the courts, and an Illyrian edition of the provinces' newspaper was also being planned. Finally, Slovenes (mostly intellectuals and clergy), for whom the idea of nationhood was taking shape and merging with the concept of homeland, soon seized upon the notion of popular sovereignty, an idea that Napoleon's administrators and soldiers, many of them veterans of the French Revolution, had brought with them to the Illyrian Provinces.

The intellectual developments of the Illyrian Provinces left an indelible mark. Even the Austrians, who retook the territory in 1813, sensed the importance of these developments and chose to preserve the name, Kingdom of Illyria (1816–1849). *See also* ILLYRISM; YUGOSLAVISM.

ILLYRISM (1815–1848). Between the retreat of the French and the **Revolution of 1848**, the South Slavs of the **Austrian Empire** experienced a national awakening. It was characterized, as elsewhere in Central Europe during the "Spring of Nations," by study and publication of works on **language**, **literature**, folklore, and history, with the intention of uncovering and defining national identity. At the time Pan-Slavism, which held that all Slavs belonged to one family, encompassed four language groups—Czech, Polish, Russian, and Illyrian. Among the Croats, Ljudevit Gaj seized upon this idea and gave impetus to a movement to create one common language for the Illyrians (South Slavs), or at least those who lived in the **Habsburg** lands and used the Latin alphabet. He convinced the Croats to give up their *kajkavian* dialect in favor of *štokavian*, spoken to the south (in Hercegovina), in order to draw in South Slavs outside the empire as well. In 1835 he named the movement Illyrism and called the language that he and others were codifying Illyrian. Ultimately the language would be renamed Serbo-Croatian, and Gaj and his helpers would be credited with establishing the basis for the Serbo-Croatian literary language. A fellow Croat, Janko Drašković, would invest Illyrism with a political component (1832), first for South Slavs of Austria, later for those of the Ottoman Empire as well. Among the Slovenes, there was little enthusiasm for Illyrism. In **Carinthia** and Styria, where Germanizing pressures were strongest, there were pockets of support for Gaj's movement, with Stanko Vraz most prominent among its proponents. In Carniola, where Slovenes constituted a strong numerical majority and where most of the national cultural work was going on, hardly anyone favored adapting to Gaj's model. Even Vraz's argument that the Slovenes were too small a group for a separate literary language was not persuasive. **France Prešeren** and others from the era of Slovene **romanticism** chose to develop a separate language and literature for the Slovenes.

During the 1848 revolutionary era there was a spurt of Illyrism among Slovenes connected with the newspaper *Slovenija*, but it died out quickly. There would be a third, somewhat more successful surge of Illyrism, or **Neo-Illyrism**, on the eve of **World War I**. *See also* ILLYRIAN PROVINCES.

IMPRESSIONISM. Impressionism was an important **art** movement in Slovenia at the turn of the 20th century, and impressionist painters **Rihard Jakopič**, Matija Jama, Ivan Grohar, and Matej Sternen hold a special place in Slovene history of art. They were educated mostly in Munich, where they came in contact with European impressionism. They first showed their work in 1900 at an exhibit of the Slovene Arts Society (the first organization of Slovene artists), which was established in the same year. The group became better known in 1904 after an exhibit in the gallery Mietke in **Vienna**; as the group Sava, it exhibited in subsequent years (1906–1911) in **Belgrade**, Cracow, London, Rome, Sofia, Warsaw, and Zagreb. Slovene impressionist art, characterized by its poetic nature, strong sensibility for Slovene landscape, and its novel artistic expression, has a unique place in European **modernism**. It became the foundation for modern, 20th-century painting in Slovenia. In **literature**, impressionism is known as the Slovene **Moderna**. In architecture, it was known as the Secession, the best examples of which are the works of Ivan Vurnik and **Jože Plečnik**.

The new arts were firmly established and of high quality before **World War I**, but they were not accepted by the majority of Slovenes. Impressionist painters were ridiculed until they became well known abroad. **Ivan Cankar**'s writings were criticized as immoral, and his poetry collection *Erotika* was burned in 1899 by **Ljubljana** Bishop **Anton Bonaventura Jeglič**. *See also* AŽBE, ANTON; MUSIC.

INDEPENDENCE, DECLARATION OF (25 JUNE 1991). When the parliament of the **Republic of Slovenia** (RS) unanimously passed a constitutional law declaring Slovene independence on 25 June 1991, it was carrying out the will of Slovenes who had voted overwhelmingly for independence in the **plebiscite** six months earlier. Like all such declarations, this one invoked the principles that demanded independence, namely natural law (i.e., the right of the Slovene nation to self-determination), international law, the RS Constitution, and the impressive number of plebiscite votes that favored it. First and foremost, independence meant separation from **Yugoslavia**. But the declaration also spelled out the principles that would govern the newly independent state. The RS would uphold human rights (civil and natural), which included freedom of association and the inviolability of property. Independent Slovenia would be governed as a multiparty democracy, featuring local or regional self-rule and would, in addition, pursue a market **economy**. All in all, the independent RS was adopting Western political and economic institutions.

The Declaration of Independence was celebrated on 26 June, when in front of the Parliament building President **Milan Kučan** reviewed an honor guard and spoke to the crowd. He unfurled the new Slovene **flag** and planted a memorial linden tree. However, **Yugoslav People's Army** (JNA) troops were already moving to prevent Slovenia's separation from the **Socialist Federal Republic of Yugoslavia** (SFRY). The Yugoslav federal government had closed all Slovene airfields and had passed a resolution to activate the JNA. Shortly after midnight on 27 June, with independence festivities still going on, the **Ten-Day War** began.

INDUSTRY. *See* MANUFACTURING; MINING.

INTERNATIONAL ORGANIZATIONS, MEMBERSHIP IN. Since gaining **independence**, the **Republic of Slovenia** (RS) has joined numerous international multilateral and bilateral organizations, institutions, and agreements. The major ones (with effective dates) are noted in this entry. The most important category, from the new country's perspective, are organizations that afforded international political recognition and security: **Organization for Security and Cooperation in Europe** (OSCE) (1992); **United Nations** (UN) (1992), with its many subsidiaries, including the UN Educational, Scientific, and Cultural Organization (UNESCO), UN Children's Fund (UNICEF), International Labor Organization (ILO), UN Conference on Trade and Development (UNCTAD), UN Industrial Development Organization (UNIDO), UN Truce Supervision Organization (UNTSO), World Food Programme (WFP); Food and Agriculture Organization (FAO) (1993); and various United Nations peacekeeping missions (Bosnia, Kosovo).

Slovenia also joined institutions headquartered at The Hague: International Criminal Police Organization (ICPO) (1992), also known as Interpol; Permanent Court of Arbitration (PCA) (1996); and the International Criminal Court (ICC) (1998). It signed agreements that committed the country to restrictions on atomic and chemical warfare abuses: International Atomic Energy Agency (IAEA) (1992) and Organization for Protection against Chemical Weapons (OPCW) (1993). Slovenia joined the **North Atlantic Treaty Organization** (NATO) Partnership for Peace program (1995) and NATO itself in 2004. On the European level, Slovenia became a member of the **Central European Initiative** (CEI) (1992); the Council of Europe (1993); Western European Union (WEU); and the **European Union** (EU) (2004).

Of great importance to Slovenia is participation in organizations and institutions that promote economic development or provide financial assistance: European Bank for Reconstruction and Development (EBRD) (1992); International Monetary Fund (IMF) (1992); International Bank for Reconstruction and Development (IBRD) and World Bank Group (1993); General Agreement on Tariffs and Trade (GATT) (1994); World Trade Organization (WTO) (1995); **Central European Free Trade Association** (CEFTA) (1996–2004); and Bank for International Settlements (1996). Slovenia also has concluded several bilateral free trade agreements.

Slovenia is a member of many organizations that facilitate international communications, among them: World Intellectual Property Organization (WIPO) (1992); International Telecommunication Union (ITU); International Civil Aviation Organization (ICAO) (1992); Universal Postal Union (UPU) (1992); World Health Organization (WHO) (1992); World Tourism Organization (WTO) (1993);

and International Maritime Organization (IMO) (1993). Slovenia has cooperated also with other international organizations, among them the Organization for Economic Development (OECD), and as of 2007 is actively seeking OECD membership.

INTERNATIONAL TRADE AND FINANCIAL TRANSACTIONS. Foreign trade has long been important to Slovenia's national economy. Since 1995 independent Slovenia's combined value of imports and exports of goods and services has been exceeding the equivalent of 100 percent of gross domestic product (GDP). In 2004, for example, it amounted to 120.5 percent. In 2004 the trade deficit was 5 percent of GDP. Although exports of goods grew more slowly than imports, significant surpluses created by **services** (mostly **tourism** and **transport**) had a positive effect on the current account. The merchandise trade balance, the key factor in the balance of payments, was negative for six of the last 10 years but was 1.5 percent of GDP in 2002.

Another important component of international transactions are net financial inflows: foreign direct investments (FDIs), interest, and loans. In the period 1999–2004, net financial inflows were positive but varied substantially from year to year. The net inflow was highest in 2001 (1,724 million euros) due to positive FDI (the Swiss company Novartis bought Lek) and was lowest in 2004 (105 million euros). Foreign exchange reserves, another important measure, grew from 2,703 million euros in 1995 to 7,484 million in 2004, after reaching a peak (7,842 million) in 2002. Slovene external debt also grew from $2,970 million in 1995 to $15,355 million in 2004.

The 1990 Serbian economic blockade and the wars that followed cut Slovenia off from its traditional markets in the former **Yugoslavia**, causing a 38 percent reduction in Slovene exports. Trade with former European communist countries also declined. Independent Slovenia had to adjust to new conditions, reorienting exports westward, and opening its domestic market to foreign competition. With removal of quantitative restrictions (except for **textiles** and **agriculture** products), the foreign trade regimen became relatively liberal. Imported goods were subject to tariffs ranging up to 25 percent, while many nontariff barriers were abolished. Slovenia became a signatory to the General Agreement on Tariffs and Trade (GATT) on 30 October 1994 and was an original member of its successor, the World Trade Organization (WTO), in 1995. Bilateral trade agreements were signed with more than 30 European countries, and in 1996 Slovenia became a member of the **Central European Free Trade Association** (CEFTA). Membership in CEFTA ceased with Slovenia's accession to **European Union** (EU) in 2004. Through such agreements, Slovenia lowered its most-favored-nation (MFN) tariff rates, which fell from an average of 15 percent in 1994 to 11 percent in 2001, and received reciprocal benefits from co-signatories.

With the European Association Agreement in 1996, Slovene foreign trade policies were driven primarily by the strategic goal of joining the EU. Most customs duties and quotas on trade between Slovenia and EU members were lifted in 1997. In 1999 a plan of gradual alignment of Slovenia's MFN tariffs on imports from third countries with the lower EU Common External Tariffs (CET) was adopted; that was followed by numerous negotiations preliminary to Slovenia's EU accession, except for Slovene imports of agricultural products from EU countries, the restrictions on which were removed only after Slovenia joined the EU. The accession offered Slovenia preferential access to the EU market as well as technical assistance under the PHARE program. While Slovenia's foreign trade regime outpaced that of other Central European countries, other economic reforms such as direct foreign investments and **privatization** did not. The slow pace of these reforms adversely affected Slovene foreign trade performance when compared with the other former communist Central European EU candidate states: the Czech Republic, **Hungary**, and Poland.

During the EU candidacy period 1996–2003, Slovenia traded freely and reached a high level of trade with the EU. In 2004, during which—in May—Slovenia became a full EU member, over two-thirds of Slovenia's exports and over four-fifths of its imports were traded with EU members. Since Slovenia declared **independence** in 1991, its most important trading partners have been EU members (57 percent in 1993, 66 percent in 1999, and 65 percent in 2000); Germany was the single most important trading partner, followed by **Italy** and France. Economic recession since 2000, however, has caused trade with Western European countries, especially Germany, to drop off. Except for agricultural products, there were no major changes in the EU trade regimen after May 2004. Overall, 90 percent of Slovenia's trade was with European countries, including former Soviet republics, and 10 percent with the rest of the world.

Initially after independence, trade with the states of the former Yugoslavia was in decline, except for **Croatia**, which remains Slovenia's most important trading partner outside the EU. In 2003 Slovenia's share of exports to Croatia (9 percent) trailed immediately behind those to Germany (23 percent) and Italy (13 percent). Slovenia also reentered the markets of other Balkan countries—Bosnia and Hercegovina, and Macedonia—not only as an exporter but also as a direct foreign investor. In 2004 exports to Serbia and Montenegro—which in 2006 split into separate countries—grew significantly (31 percent). The **United States** is Slovenia's biggest single trade partner outside Europe, but bilateral trade is relatively small. In the years 2000–2004, annual average exports to the United States accounted for about 3 percent of Slovene exports. Goods exports to the United States in 2002–2004 declined by 30 percent. Slovenia's trade balance with the United States, the countries of former Yugoslavia, and the **Russian** Federation is positive, but it is substantially negative with the EU. The latter deficit has doubled in recent years: from 1,244 million euros in 2001 to 2,598 million in 2004. Slovenia's overall trade balance has registered increasing deficits, reaching 1,291 million euros in 2004.

Slovenia has both exported and imported raw materials, semifinished products, and consumer products, with the ratio of exports to imports being similar to when it was part of Yugoslavia. The respective shares of total trade in the GDP did not change much immediately after declaration of independence, and only gradually since then. In 1989 exports accounted for 47 percent and imports 68 percent; in 1992 exports were 45 percent and imports 66 percent; in 2004 the respective shares were 49 and 52 percent, and 53 and 56 percent in 2005. Among industrial products, the most important export items have been vehicles (18 percent), followed by clothing, machinery and mechanical appliances, and electrical machinery and equipment (over 14 percent for each group), while the rest was accounted for by various durable consumer products such as furniture and household appliances, and by pharmaceuticals. The situation changed in the second half of the 1990s. Besides vehicles, machinery and electrical equipment and pharmaceuticals became the most important export goods, while the share of consumer goods (e.g., clothing and footwear) declined significantly. In 2004 the export of intermediate goods increased the most, followed by capital goods, while exports of consumer goods were down. The major imported items were foods, industrial raw materials (cotton, fabrics), and **energy** resources (crude oil, natural gas). *See also* AGRICULTURE; ECONOMY, 1945–1990; ECONOMY SINCE 1991; INTERNATIONAL ORGANIZATIONS, MEMBERSHIP IN; MANUFACTURING; SERVICE INDUSTRY.

ISLAM. Until 1953 few adherents of Islam lived in Slovenia (0.01 percent of the population). After the 1960s many of the migrant workers who came from southern **Yugoslavia** were Muslims, and they organized an Islamic religious community. The community has been officially in existence since 1967, but in 1976 it also registered at the republic level. Its number increased significantly in the last two decades: According to censuses, Islam adherents numbered 29,361 (1.5 percent of the population) in 1991 and 47,488 (2.4 percent) in 2002. The increase was due largely to the inflow of refugees during the war in the Balkans, a large number of whom were accepted by Slovenia. Islamic religious communities have been established in 13 Slovene cities, with the largest concentration in Jesenice (one-third of all Muslims in Slovenia), followed by **Ljubljana** and **Maribor**. Islamic Youth of Slovenia (*Islamska mladina Slovenije*), a youth organization with local chapters, is active in more than a dozen Slovene cities. After the **Catholic Church**, the Islamic community is the second largest religious group in Slovenia. For more than three decades the community has been trying to get permission to build a mosque and a cultural center in Ljubljana. The city has recently allocated land for the project, which will eventually provide Slovenia's Muslims with a permanent place of worship and education, despite some vocal opposition from the local population. *See also* RELIGION; HUMAN RIGHTS.

ITALIANIZATION. *See* MINORITIES, SLOVENES IN ITALY.

ITALY, RELATIONS WITH. For centuries, ethnic Italians and Slovenes lived side by side and intermingled under **medieval**, Renaissance, and early modern period rulers, but neither had a modern national state until Italy came into being in 1860. The major obstacle in uniting Italy's nine states under its only native ruling dynasty, one based in Piedmont, was **Austria**. The **Austrian Empire** controlled the two large northern states, Lombardy and Venetia, and had clients in several of the smaller ones. War expelled Austria from Lombardy in 1859, the Italian Kingdom was proclaimed the next year, and in 1866 Italy captured Venetia in another successful war. When Venetia became Italy's, the Slovene and Italian national ideas came into direct political opposition for the first time. When Venetia changed countries, 27,000 Slovenes were left on the Italian side of the new border. The Slovenes' hope was to prevent more erosion of their national unit, while the goal of Italy became further expansion to the east. Italy hoped to incorporate Italian nationals living in **Gorizia**, Istria, **Trieste**, and points south on the eastern Adriatic coast where Venice's centuries-long empire had deposited Italians over the centuries. In the 20th century, Italy's desire to control the Adriatic became a part of larger imperialistic designs in the eastern Mediterranean and northern Africa.

Italy's ambitions led it to abandon neutrality in **World War I** by signing a pact with the Entente powers in London in May 1915. Its secret provisions promised Italy extensive territorial spoils to be carved out of Austria (where the population was largely Slovene and Croat), should the Austrians lose. In the war, Italians and Slovenes (the latter on Austria's side) faced each other in fierce battles in the Soča Valley in the area of **Kobarid** (Caporetto) in 1917, both fighting esentially for their homeland. When the war ended with Entente victory, Italy began occupying lands stipulated in the London pact, and thus 300,000 Slovenes from Istria, Primorska (including **Gorica**), and Trieste were incorporated into Italy, where they remained throughout the interwar period. The **Treaty of Rapallo**, negotiated bilaterally between Italy and the **Kingdom of Serbs, Croats, and Slovenes**, formalized the new boundary on 12 November 1920. Italy, which early in the 1920s came under fascist rule, immediately introduced anti-Slovene Italianization policies. Some Slovenes fled to the new Yugoslav state, while others emigrated abroad, many to Argentina. *See also* MINORITIES, SLOVENES IN ITALY.

In **World War II** Slovenes and Italians were again on opposite sides. Italy had allied with Germany in 1936 and embarked on an immediate expansionist mission. By 1941 the two Axis powers and their allies had divided up **Yugoslavia**, including Slovenia. Italy annexed **Ljubljana** and areas south of it, attaching them to Slovene lands it had gotten after World War I. Slovenes organized several resistance movements, seeking to liberate territories that had been part of the interwar Yugoslav state, but also hoped to "liberate" Slovenes in Italy and Austria from foreign rule. The Italians capitulated in September 1943, but Italy's north fell to the Germans. Some Italian partisans began cooperating with Slovene **Partisans** to rid the area of Nazis, and they agreed that Slovene lands, including Trieste, should all go to Slovenia after Germany's defeat. They liberated Trieste in 1945, but Slovenes were not allowed to keep it. Instead, because the world war was soon followed by an ideological Cold War, the area that straddles the current Italian–Slovene border was jointly occupied by Allied forces until the **London Agreement** of 1954 (temporarily) disposed of the status of the occupied lands, a settlement finalized in the **Osimo Treaty** (1975). The war years and those under Allied occupation only increased Italian–Slovene tensions, which were to continue during much of the Cold War period. The Slovene minority in Italy, to say the least, did not fare well, particularly in the 1950s and 1960s. *See also* LIBERATION FRONT; RESISTANCE, NON-COMMUNIST; TRIESTE QUESTION.

The easing of Cold War tensions came in the 1970s. The Helsinki Accords of 1975 officially sealed the new direction. But between Italy and Yugoslavia, relations had been improving for about a decade. The border had opened and traffic streamed across it in both directions. In Yugoslavia, Slovenia, because of its location, benefitted most. Italians flocked to Slovenia to buy cheap gas and foodstuffs, and after casinos were built in Slovene border locations, they came to gamble. Slovenes crossed the border in droves to purchase household appliances, ready-made clothing, and other Italian goods. (Over the years, Slovenes must have transported a virtual mountain of laundry detergent from Italy into Slovenia.) Once the **Alps–Adriatic Working Community** was established in 1978, the way was opened to other interaction, such as **tourism**, cultural exchanges, and regional developmental projects. In the late 1980s, as Slovenia was crafting statements about political sovereignty and contemplating a referendum on **independence**, Italy, as one of the European Community (EC) countries, was anticipating the transformation of that organization into a **European Union** (EU) in 1992. When Slovenia delared independence in June 1991 and came under attack by the **Yugoslav People's Army** (JNA), Italy, with a common border to the east, was understandably concerned, and its foreign minister, Gianni deMichelis, was prominent among the EC mediators who negotiated the July **Brioni Agreement** that ended the war in Slovenia. As a member of the EC, Italy officially recognized the independence of Slovenia (also **Croatia**) on 15 January 1992. International agreements between Italy and the former Yugoslavia, it was understood, would devolve to the successor republics.

After independence, Slovene relations with Italy on the international level were strained for many years before they improved. Slovenia, whose goal it was to join the EU and **North Atlantic Treaty Organization** (NATO), considered Italy an obstructor. In 1995 Slovenes hoped to sign the EU's associate agreement, a preliminary to the accession. Italy—the Silvio Berlusconi government had come to power in 1994—raised objections, citing property issues regarding Italians who emigrated or were expelled from Yugoslavia in the late

1940s and early 1950s. Slovenia protested, saying that the Osimo Treaty had provided compensation, while Italy countered that the Slovene laws needed to be "harmonized" with the EU's property rights. This issue dragged on—largely because Slovene rightists were enraged—but Slovenia in 1997 finally agreed to change the **Constitution of 1991** to allow foreigners to buy property in Slovenia, enabling the Italian exiles to repurchase their former property, but not to have it restored outright. In time the Berlusconi regime became a sponsor of Slovenia in its bid for memberships in both the EU and NATO. Slovenia's EU membership, as of spring 2004, provides a land bridge between Italy and **Hungary**—a new EU member—and points east, which opens opportunities for **trade**. Italy has already become one of Slovenia's strongest trade partners, and is also collaborating on projects relating to international **transport** and port facilities in Trieste. And under NATO's policy of collective defense, Italy has become the official defender of Slovene air space.

The issue that continues to occupy Slovenes and Italians is the Slovene minority in Italy. Personal guarantees provided for at Osimo were still unrealized in 2001, when Rome finally passed the Law on Global Protection of the Slovene Minority in Italy. In practice, facing domestic opposition, little has been done in Italy to implement it. (To their credit, the mayor and city council of Trieste strongly supported the law's passage.) Slovene–Italian relations took a turn for the worse in February 2005, when Italian state television aired the film *Heart in the Pit* (*Il cuore nel pozzo*). Its topic was communist atrocities against Italians who had been resettled after World War I. The film raised emotional levels on both sides of the border and could adversely affect personal and official relationships in the two countries.

– J –

JAKAC, BOŽIDAR (1899–1989). Božidar Jakac was one of the most prolific and versatile Slovene artists. His first drawings were realistic, but later watercolors of his native Dolenjska **region** radiated lyric **impressionism**. After **World War I** Jakac turned to **expressionism** and became one of its founders in Slovenia. Jakac's studies in Prague stimulated his interest in graphic **arts**, where he achieved his artistic pinnacle in the early 1920s. In addition, Jakac was one of the pioneers of **film**; in the 1920s and 1930s he produced several ethnological documentaries about Slovenia and Slovene **emigrants** in the **United**

States, where he spent some time (1929–1931). In 1943 Jakac joined the **Partisans** and became their pictorial chronicler. After **World War II** he continued with his **realist** style, which he had begun developing in the late 1920s. Jakac reached yet another artistic peak in the 1950s with his graphic art, expressing new dimensions: youthful creativity, contemplation, and symbolism. The first Slovene graphic artist, Jakac was also a master portraitist, a creative illustrator of many books, and an organizer: He was cofounder of the Academy of Plastic Arts and initiator of the **International Biennial of Graphic Art**, both in **Ljubljana**. A prominent and well-respected artist, he became a member of the **Slovenian Academy of Sciences and Arts** (SAZU). In 1964 Jakac was made an honorary member of the Academy of Painting in Florence, and in 1982 of the European Academy in Paris. Jakac traveled extensively and had over 200 one-man exhibitions. Many of his works, for which he received several prestigious Slovene awards, can be seen in two galleries bearing his name, in Kostanjevica and in **Novo Mesto**. See also FILM.

JAKOPIČ, RIHARD (1869–1943). Rihard Jakopič was the guiding spirit of Slovene **impressionists** and postimpressionists, and the central figure of Slovene plastic **arts** in the first half of the 20th century. He studied painting in **Vienna** and Munich, where he attended the **Ažbe** school and became acquainted with the works of French impressionists. Jakopič, who worked with Slovene impressionists Matija Jama, Ivan Grohar, and Matej Sternen, was a prolific painter. About 1,200 of his paintings and 650 drawings are known to exist, many still in private collections. His paintings reached beyond impressionism into postimpressionism, symbolism, and, after **World War I**, even into **expressionism**. Several of his works are in the National Gallery and the **Museum of Modern Art** in **Ljubljana**. Jakopič also wrote about art. His influential theoretical essays on impressionism deal with the relations between nature, the artist, and impression and expression. His theories, especially on colors and their "musical" interdependence, qualify Jakopič as a postimpressionist.

At the turn of the century, Jakopič argued that a national cultural program required a unification of Slovene creative forces. In addition to establishing an economic base for Slovene society, a lively cultural life with institutions and basic opportunities for artists also needed to be created. Jakopič was thus a tireless organizer and promoter of Slovene plastic arts. He was one of the founders of the Slovene Art Society

(*Slovensko umetniško društvo*) in 1900. In Ljubljana in 1909 he established his own gallery, Jakopič Pavilion (*Jakopičev paviljon*), and he was very active in organizing art exhibitions at home and abroad. With the establishment of **Yugoslavia** after World War I, Jakopič and other cultural leaders were engaged in debates on the nature of the new state and Slovenia's future. Jakopič supported **Izidor Cankar** in the view that the Slovene nation had to preserve its cultural independence and resist Yugoslav ethnic assimilation. As the organizer of a painting school in Ljubljana and a supporter of young artists, he had plans for the establishment of an Academy of Plastic Arts in Ljubljana, but they did not materialize until after **World War II**. *See also* MODERNA.

JANČAR, DRAGO (1948–). Born in **Maribor**, Drago Jančar is one of the best known and most acclaimed contemporary Slovene writers; his literary works have been translated into many languages and published across Europe and in the **United States**. He began publishing in the early 1970s. His first volume of short stories was published in 1972, and his first novel *Petintrideset stopinj* (Thirty-five Degrees Centigrade) in 1974. Since then, he has published several historical novels, including *Galjot* (The Galley Slave, 1978), *Severni sij* (Northern Lights, 1983), and *Katarina, pav in jezuit* (Catherine, the Peacock, and the Jesuit, 2000); plays, including *Veliki briljantni valček* (The Great Brilliant Waltz, 1985) and *Zalezujoč Godota* (Stakeout at Godot's, 1989); and numerous collections of short stories and essays. He has received many awards in Slovenia and Europe, among them the Prešeren Prize for his life work (1993), the European Short-Story Award in Germany (1994), the Herder Award for literature (2003), and the Austrian Cross of Honor for Science and Art (2006). Jančar's literary works, with exceptionally esthetic use of language, well-researched stories and essays, and meaningfulness for contemporary society, have been an important influence on Slovene **literature** in the last two decades.

After completing law studies in Maribor, Jančar worked as a journalist (1971–1974). In 1974 he was sentenced to one year in prison on charges of violating the law against "enemy propaganda" (he had brought a book on **massacres** after **World War II** from **Austria** into Slovenia). In 1979 he moved to **Ljubljana**, where he has been the editor and managing director of the oldest and most prominent publishing house, **Slovenska Matica**. Although Jančar has not held political office, he has been a sensitive observer of Slovene society and a critical voice, thus contributing to the development of a democratic, independent Slovenia. His penetrating essays about contemporary problems regularly appear in intellectual journals as well as in the daily press. He has been president of the Slovene **PEN Center** (1987–1991), a collaborator of *Nova revija* since the early 1980s, and the author and organizer of an important 1998 exhibition *Temna stran meseca: Kratka zgodovina totalitarizma v Sloveniji 1945–1990* (The Dark Side of the Moon: A Short History of Totalitarianism in Slovenia 1945–1990). Jančar is also a member of the **Slovenian Academy of Sciences and Arts**. *See also* THEATER.

JANŠA, JANEZ (1958–). Born in **Ljubljana,** Janez Janša earned a bachelor's degree in military studies at the **University of Ljubljana** in 1982. A member of the League of Communists of Slovenia (LCS; formerly the **Communist Party of Slovenia**), Janša was a high school teacher in the early 1980s and worked as a consultant at the Secretariat of National Defense of the **Socialist Republic of Slovenia** (SRS). As a prominent member of the League of Socialist Youth of Slovenia (ZSMS), he spoke and wrote critically about the **Yugoslav People's Army** (JNA). In 1983 a government committee condemned his views as counterrevolutionary. This led to his expulsion from LCS and continued surveillance by state security police. Unable to find employment after 1985, he started a computer company and began preparing the diary of **Stane Kavčič,** reformist leader of the late 1960s, for publication; he also prepared a draft of a new **constitution** for Slovenia. When in 1987 the ZSMS weekly publication *Mladina* liberalized, Janša wrote again about the JNA. As a result Janša and three others were arrested on suspicion of stealing secret military documents. Janša was kept in solitary confinement for two months before he was tried. The **Ljubljana Four trial** in July 1988, in which Janša was one of the defendants, ended in an 18-month prison sentence (he was released early, in May 1989). It put Janša into the forefront of those who stood for the restructuring of Slovene society, and it activated the Slovene populace in support of reform. This popular involvement in political issues after May 1988 is often referred to as the "Slovene Spring," a development with which Janša regularly identifies.

Released from prison, Janez Janša helped found the **Slovene Democratic Alliance** (SDZ). After the **election** of April 1990, Janša became a member of parliament and was also named minister of defense. When Slovenia declared **independence** and a **Ten-Day War** (27 June—6 July 1991) followed, Janša together with **Igor Bavčar,** head of the police, masterminded Slovenia's defense. In fall 1991, when the SDZ disintegrated, Janša joined the Social Democratic Party (SDS). When in 1993 Jože Pučnik, the party's founder, retired from its presidency, Janša replaced him. He was reelected president of SDS in 1995, 1999, 2001, and again in 2005 (to a four-year term). Janša ran and was elected to parliament (State Assembly) in each of the **Republic of Slovenia's** (RS) elections (1992, 1996, 2000, and 2004). He served as minister of defense from 1990 to 1994, and again during the **government** of May–December 2000. (He was dismissed from the Defense Ministry in 1994 for legal irregularities, an accusation he challenged.)

Throughout, Janša had ambitions to be prime minister. He bore grudges against the former communists, some of whom were now in the **United List of Social Democrats** (ZLSD) and the former League of Socialist Youth (ZSMS), many of whom were now members of **Liberal Democracy of Slovenia** (LDS). He was not reticent about his dislikes and was persistent in challenging his "enemies." During the government of November 1996–May 2000, Janša organized the center-right parties SDS, the **Slovene Christian Democrats** (SKD), and the **Slovene People's Party** (SLS) into a "Slovene Spring" bloc. The intention was to dislodge LDS from power, but the "Spring" parties spent much of their time obstructing parliamentary business and arguing among themselves. The parties eventually had a falling out. In the government of May–December 2000, the "Springers" were briefly in power under the prime ministership of **Andrej Bajuk**, but showed little ability to achieve consensus or to get things accomplished. Only after the election of 2000, which again brought an LDS victory, was Janša able to move forward. The opposition parties formed "Coalition Slovenia" and slowly began to behave in a constructive manner, particularly where **North Atlantic Treaty Organization** (NATO) and **European Union** (EU) membership were at stake. By 2003 polls were showing a decline in popularity for LDS and a corresponding rise in support for SDS. In the election of 2004, SDS got the most votes and Janša was at last able to achieve his goal. His coalition government took power on 3 December 2004 and vowed to put Slovenia on a "new path."

JANUARY 6, 1929, DICTATORSHIP. The **Kingdom of Serbs, Croats, and Slovenes** was established in late 1918 and, with the **Vidovdan Constitution** of 1921, it became a parliamentary constitutional monarchy. By the end of 1928, the year Stjepan Radić, head of the leading Croat party, died after being shot in Parliament, King Alexander concluded that the state could not operate parliamentarily. On 6 January 1929, the king suspended the constitution, disbanded Parliament, outlawed **political parties**, and established a dictatorship. Later that year he renamed the country **Yugoslavia** and restructured it administratively from 33 districts (*oblasts*) into nine administrative units, or *banovinas*, named after **major rivers** and the seacoast, in order to deemphasize the national historical identities that seemed to be undermining the country's unity. Alexander's intent was to foster Yugoslav political unitarism. Yet six of the nine *banovinas* had Serb majorities, raising suspicion among the non-Serbs about the underlying motives for the new arrangement. *See also* DRAVA *BANOVINA*.

Even though Yugoslavia would have a new constitution and a bicameral parliament in 1931, the king, who promulgated the document, retained supreme power. Only one political party, under state sponsorship, was allowed. The Yugoslav Radical Farmers' Democracy (*Jugoslovanska radikalna kmečka demokracija*) was established in 1931 and renamed the Yugoslav National Party (*Jugoslovanska nacionalna stranka*, JNS) in 1933. Elections were no longer free, and many were unhappy with the new system. Some of the opponents even collaborated in the assassination plot that resulted in King Alexander's death in Marseille in 1934. Although the JNS won the election in 1935, it was discredited by electoral fraud, and a new state party, the Yugoslav Radical Union (*Jugoslovenska radikalna zajednica*, JRZ) was established on the initiative of Prince Paul and Milan Stojadinović, the new prime minister. Slovene **Liberals** participated in the JNS until its electoral defeat in 1935; Slovene **Clericals**, resuming political activity after 1935, worked with the JRZ. In the view of many of Yugoslavia's peoples, however, the dictatorial nature of the regime really continued through the 1930s. *See also* KARADJORDJEVIĆ.

JEGLIČ, ANTON BONAVENTURA (1850–1937). Anton Bonaventura Jeglič studied theology in **Vienna**. He was a professor of church history and law, and later also of church doctrine, at the Theology Faculty in **Ljubljana**. In 1898 he was appointed bishop of the Ljubljana diocese of the **Catholic Church**, a position he held until his retirement in 1930. He spent the last years of his life at the **Stična Monastery**. Jeglič was an important political figure with a decisive influence on Slovene politics between 1898 and 1930. As a pillar of the **Slovene People's Party** (SLS), he controlled the political situation in Slovenia, working closely with the **Clerical** leader **Ivan Šušteršič**

until 1916, when he decided to support **Janez Evangelist Krek** and the younger, more liberal group of Clericals. In 1917 he supported the **May Declaration** and organized a Slovene movement, which led to the formation of a new South Slav state. He also fought for the rights of Slovene **minorities** in Italy, particularly after 1920. An enthusiastic supporter of Catholic **education**, Jeglič proposed the establishment of a Slovene secondary school (gymnasium) in Ljubljana, which opened in 1905. He initiated the establishment of the conservative **Orel** (Eagle) as a counterweight to the liberal gymnastic society **Sokol** (Falcon). Jeglič was also convinced of the importance of the peasant **cooperative movement** for the Catholic national movement, and he supported local lending institutions with his own money.

Jeglič's social, moral, and religious thinking was strongly influenced by the Catholic philosopher Aleš Ušeničnik, but within the SLS, Jeglič defended diversity and the right to different opinions. Thus, although a conservative, Jeglič protected Janez Evangelist Krek and his **Christian Socialism**. In the 1930s he tried to reconcile the political schism in Catholic ranks. *See also* CATHOLIC ACTION.

JELINČIČ, ZMAGO (1948–). Born in **Maribor**, Zmago Jelinčič, whose family's noble heritage was bestowed in 1756 by **Maria Theresa**, has been independent Slovenia's most persistently outspoken politician. Trained as a pharmacist at the **University of Ljubljana,** he established a privately owned company for natural medicinal products, and also founded a savings and loan institution (*Kranjska hranilnica in posojilnica*). In 1989 he became active politically and participated in the **Ten-Day War** as part of a special military unit. Only a few months earlier, in March 1991, Jelinčič had founded the **Slovene National Party** (*Slovenska nacionalna stranka*, SNS), of which he has been its only president.

Jelinčič's party was shaped by his philosophy and flamboyant personality. An intensely nationalistic organization, with a fierce loyalty to the militiary tradition of **World War II**'s **Partisan resistance**, it has fought all perceived threats to Slovenia's sovereignty: foreign refugees from the wars in former **Yugoslavia**; foreign ownership of Slovene property; and foreign military controls. As party spokesman Jelinčič railed against Slovene citizenship for refugees, especially those from the south; he opposed joining the **European Union** (EU) because joining meant allowing non-Slovenes to own Slovene property; and he fought against membership in the **North Atlantic Treaty**

Organization (NATO). In most cases Jelinčič swam against the political mainstream; however, in the **election** of 1992 SNS got 12 seats in the national assembly, largely due to backlash against wartime refugees. In all other elections, the SNS has gotten four or six seats (out of 90), with Jelinčič himself heading its delegation and distinguishing himself as the parliamentarian most spectators love to hate. Jelinčič is a lifetime member of the National Rifle Association of America.

JESUITS / SOCIETY OF JESUS. The educational and cultural pillar of the **Counter Reformation**, Jesuits came to **Ljubljana** in 1597. Throughout **Austria** they organized secondary schools, which covered six grades: four grammatical (*studia inferiora*) and two **humanistic** (*studia superiora*). The language of instruction was Latin. The humanistic curriculum included **Catholic Church** law, and philosophy and theology were taught in Graz (1578), Ljubljana (1597), **Klagenfurt** (1605), **Gorizia** (1615), and **Trieste** (1619). The Jesuits were thus the founders of Slovene **higher education**. Although studies at Jesuit institutions were very similar to those in the secular **universities**, the Jesuits were not permitted to award academic titles, except in Graz.

In Ljubljana, Klagenfurt, Gorizia, and Trieste the Jesuits operated **theaters**: school theaters and theaters for the general public, for passion plays and vivid religious processions, combining all performing **arts**. The Jesuits used the Slovene **language** in sermons and sometimes also in theater. The Society of Jesus was abolished in 1773. After being reestablished in Slovenia in 1870, the Jesuits had centers first in Repnje, then at St. Florian's and St. Joseph's Churches in Ljubljana, and also in **Maribor**. After 1945 their premises in Ljubljana, including St. Joseph's Church, were nationalized, and their headquarters have been at the Bogenšperk **castle** near Litija. *See also* JOSEPH II; SCIENCE.

Since 1969 Slovenia has had its own Jesuit province, and 61 members (2005). The Society of Jesus remains a nondiocesan religious organization with operations in Ljubljana and Maribor, engaging in educational, pastoral, and **media** activities. In Ljubljana it administers two parishes, the spiritual center of St. Joseph, and the provincialate; in Maribor it has one parish and a novitiate. The Society is responsible for three other parishes, one in Slovenia and two abroad (**Italy** and Austria). Slovene Jesuits have always been **missionaries**. Today Jesuits, although not members of the Slovenian Jesuit province, work as missionaries in Zambia, Malawi, and Japan.

JEWS. Although numerically small, the Jewish community in the Slovene lands has a long history. Jews were mentioned already in the 12th century in **Maribor** as bankers, traders, and craftspeople. Synagogues in **Ljubljana, Koper,** Maribor, **Piran, Trieste,** and other towns attest to the Jewish presence since **medieval** times. The legal position of the Jews in the **Habsburg** lands was regulated by "Jewish orders," the first one issued in 1244 by Frederick III, the duke of **Austria** and Styria. Animosity toward the Jews began in the time of the plague in the 14th century, and several anti-Semitic riots took place in towns such as **Ptuj** during the 15th century. Emperor Maximillian I expelled the Jews, first from the **Carinthia** and Styria **regions** (1496) and later also from Carniola (1515). However, although they were not allowed residence rights, they could engage in financial services and **trade** during the day. Anti-Semitic laws were repealed during the Napoleonic **Illyrian Provinces.** After the return of Slovene lands to Austria-Hungary, the Jews were again not treated equally under the law until 1861.

In the 19th century, most Jews lived in Trieste and **Gorizia,** in a part of **Italy,** and in **Prekmurje.** Although Italy was most tolerant toward Jews before **World War I,** their treatment changed after the rise of fascism in 1921, when Jews and other **minorities** were persecuted, and many Jews **emigrated.** After World War I, Jews were most numerous in Prekmurje, where there was a large Jewish congregation (**Murska Sobota**). During **World War II,** Hungarians in Prekmurje, Germans in Styria and Carniola, and Italians in the Ljubljana province deported most Jews to **concentration camps.** It is estimated that between 4,000 and 6,000 Slovene Jews perished during the war.

In 1945 a small Jewish community (*Judovska skupnost Slovenije* / Jewish Community of Slovenia) was reestablished in Ljubljana and officially registered in 1972. After World War II, Jews who survived the *Shoa* mostly emigrated to Israel. In the 2002 census, only 99 persons declared Judaism as their faith. It is estimated that their actual number, concentrated mostly in Ljubljana, is somewhat higher: 400–600 Jews of both Ashkenazi and Sephardic origin. The Jewish community has recently been active. The first chief rabbi for Slovenia, visiting from Trieste, was inaugurated in 1999. In 2002 the Maribor synagogue, one of the oldest in Europe, was renovated and now serves as a cultural center. *See also* JOSEPH II; RELIGION.

JOSEPH II (1741–1790). Joseph II was the eldest son and heir of Maria Theresa (a **Habsburg**) and Francis of Lorraine. He ruled the Habsburg lands first as co-ruler with his mother from 1765 to 1780, and on his own until 1790. He was also, after his father's death in 1764, **Holy Roman Emperor**. Joseph, believing in the logic of the centralizing reforms introduced by Maria Theresa, carried them even further. In doing so he often endowed them with a rationalist philosophy, for he was more influenced by **Enlightenment** inclinations than was his mother, having visited or corresponded with leading contemporary thinkers.

During the 1780s Joseph refined the peasant and serf reforms begun by Maria Theresa. In **education**, he took a special interest in higher learning, generally limiting it to the elite. In the towns, he introduced legal changes that conformed with liberal economic theory but fell short of abolishing guilds. Judicial reforms begun under his predecessor were completed and codified by Joseph, bringing the state's jurisdiction to more areas of the law, while the nobles and towns lost autonomy. To strengthen the unity of the monarchy, Joseph made German its official language (1784), a move that was not warmly greeted by non-Germans.

In the matter of **religion** and church–state relations, Joseph was both liberal and pragmatic. He introduced religious toleration, because it was enlightened but also because **Jews** and Protestants were often merchants who brought wealth to the state. The Tolerance Patent (1781) had little impact in the Slovene areas, since there were few non-Catholics there. The test of usefulness was applied to religious institutions: After 1782, monasteries that did not perform beneficial social functions (such as teaching or tending to the sick) were closed. Bistra, Kostanjevica, Velesovo, Vetrinj, and Žiče, all in Slovene lands, were affected. Further, it was Joseph's policy, known as Josephinism, to subordinate the **Catholic Church** to the state. The absolutist state took over the upbringing and appointment of the clergy, supervised education, and introduced civil marriage. (**Jesuits**, who opposed the new developments, had already been excluded, particularly from education, during Maria Theresa's reign.) Joseph's policy in this general area of religion and the church was not opposed in the Slovene lands. The secular clergy there, especially **Ljubljana**'s bishop Karel Janez Herberstein, were strongly Jansenist in their thinking and were inclined toward Josephinism. Understandably, the pope was not pleased by **Austria**'s religious policies during this era.

To enforce his policies, Joseph instituted censorship and a new office of secret police (1782). An enlightened despot, Joseph was determined to modernize his centralized state quickly, by force if necessary. He is sometimes commemorated for freeing the serfs, but for the most part Joseph met with opposition to his reforms and his methods. In **Hungary**, where the new system had not been introduced by Maria Theresa, there was revolt when Joseph imposed it. For this reason Joseph is not listed among the kings of Hungary. Joseph's brother and successor, Leopold II (1790–1792), found that he had to revoke or at least postpone many of Joseph's reforms. Many, however, remained on the books until the mid-19th century.

JUGOSLOVANSKA NACIONALNA STRANKA (JNS) / YUGO-SLAV NATIONAL PARTY. See CLERICALS; JANUARY 6, 1929, DICTATORSHIP; LIBERALS; SERBS, CROATS, AND SLO-VENES, KINGDOM OF; YUGOSLAVIA, KINGDOM OF.

JUGOSLOVANSKA SOCIALDEMOKRATSKA STRANKA / YUGOSLAV SOCIAL DEMOCRATIC PARTY (JSDS). See SOCIALISTS.

JURČIČ, JOSIP (1844–1881). Josip Jurčič was a writer, playwright, and journalist. Politically and literarily he belonged to the Young Slovenes. Among his most important works are several stories, including *Kozlovska sodba v Višnji gori* (A Goat's Trial in Višnja Gora); the first Slovene novel *Deseti brat* (The Tenth Brother); and two tragedies, *Tugomer*, coauthored with **Fran Levstik**, and *Veronika Deseniška*. The motifs for his early literary works were stylistically **romantic**, taken from **folk tradition** and rural life. Later he abandoned romanticism and turned to motifs from Slovene history. *See also* LITERATURE; REALISM.

JUSTICE. See COURTS AND JUSTICE.

– K –

KACIN, JELKO (1955–). Born in **Celje** in southern Styria, Jelko Kacin studied at the **University of Ljubljana** and in 1980 was its first military defense studies graduate. He spent most of the next decade in **Kranj**, where he was adviser to the town *občina* on defense preparedness, and after 1988 was head of its civil defense operation. In the early 1990s, when Slovenia declared **independence** and fought a **Ten-Day War** with Yugoslav army forces, Kacin made an indelible mark on critical events. He was both deputy to Defense Secretary Janez Janša as well as independent Slovenia's first minister for information. As the republic came under military attack in late

June 1991, Kacin quickly organized a press bureau and effectively managed positive **media** promotion of Slovene independence. World public opinion, as a result, was generally favorable to the Slovene cause, and for this Slovenes have remained gratefully to Kacin. Throughout the decade, Kacin continued in **government** in one capacity or another. In spring 1994 he replaced Janez Janša as defense minister. In 1996 and 2000 he was elected to the national assembly on the **Liberal Democracy of Slovenia** (LDS) slate and served on committees related to defense and **foreign relations**, especially European affairs. In 1998 and 2002 he was also elected to the Kranj *občina* government. Since 2003 Kacin has become especially active in LDS politics. Just as LDS's star began flickering, Kacin became head of its regional committee for Gorenjska (2003); at the end of 2004, shortly after LDS went down to electoral defeat, he was elected vice president of the national party; in October 2005 he was chosen its national president. Kacin inherited a badly fragmented party, but one with the distinction of having shaped independent Slovenia and brought the country firmly into the **European Union** (EU) and **North Atlantic Treaty Organization** (NATO). Hoping for rejuvenation, the party turned to Kacin, one of its early heros, for new leadership. That Kacin was one of only two LDS Slovenes (out of a total of seven) elected to the European Parliament in 2004 no doubt influenced the party's decision to make him president.

KAMNIK. Kamnik, a part of the Gorenjska **region**, with a population of 12,197, lies at the foot of the lovely Kamnik-Savinja **Alps**, which border with **Austria**. A half-hour from **Ljubljana** by car or by rail (opened in 1891), Kamnik and its suburbs (population 26,500) are quickly becoming part of an expanding industrial, urban, commuter world. It is home to a variety of industries, many of them with a long tradition—chemical (Kemijska industrija Kamnik, or KIK; Belinka Kemostik), construction, electronics (Zarja Elektronika; Svit), food processing, furniture (Stol), **leather** goods, metal (Titan, recently incorporated into the French Securidev group; and Trival which specializes in antennas), **textiles** (Svilant which specializes in terry cloth, with branches in Zagreb and **Belgrade**), and timber. Nearly half of the town's inhabitants are employed in industry. Kamnik is also a **tourist** center, with a noted health resort, and a stepping-off spot for year around Alpine recreation. Nearby is Slovenia's largest arboretum, Volčji Potok, where in spring 2 million tulips bloom, one each for every Slovene.

Before Kamnik's current incarnation, begun in the late 19th century, the town had an ancient and rich past. It is one of the oldest Slovene towns, formally established in the early 13th century. Located on lands belonging first (11th century) to the Counts of Andechs-Meran (who minted their own coins), and eventually to the **Habsburgs**, Kamnik had a glorious 14th and 15th century. It was situated on the main **trade** route between **Vienna** and **Trieste**. **Crafts**, especially knife and pottery making, and smithing thrived, and Kamnik's townspeople and guilds (the 1478 guild regulations are extant) left an affluent imprint on the town's architecture. Examples of Romanesque, late Gothic, Renaissance (town houses), and later **baroque** (churches) architecture can be found side by side. The most important and oldest structure of Romanesque style in Slovenia is an 11th-century chapel in Kamnik. **Turkish wars** (in the late 15th and early 16th centuries), the **Counter Reformation**, and changing trade routes brought economic decline and masked Kamnik's early glory. *See also* MEDIEVAL TOWNS AND COMMERCE.

KARADJORDJEVIĆ. The Karadjordjevićes were a Serbian dynasty, established when its founder, George Petrović, became prince of an autonomous state, then under Ottoman domination, in 1806. From then until 1918 the Karadjordjevićes alternated with their rivals, the Obrenović dynastic family, as rulers of Serbia (independent after 1878). With the formation in 1918 of the **Kingdom of Serbs, Croats, and Slovenes**, the Karadjordjević dynasty became a Yugoslav one. Alexander I (1888–1934), who helped bring the South Slav kingdom together, succeeded his father, Peter I, as king in 1921. He was active in implementing a unitary Yugoslav policy, which non-Serbs construed as Great Serbism. Authoritarian in temperament, he established the **January 6, 1929, dictatorship** and was assassinated in 1934 by Croat extremists.

Because Alexander's son Peter was still a minor, a three-person regency was named to act for him. Prince Paul (1893–1976), the murdered king's cousin, was the most important of the trio. Although more democratic than his predecessor, Paul was nudged by circumstances into cooperation with Germany and **Italy**. By 1935 **Yugoslavia** was economically dependent upon these two states, and on 25 March 1941 it joined the Tripartite Pact. Two days later, pro-English Yugoslav high military officers rejected the pact, overthrew Paul, and turned him over to the British, who interned him in South Africa. In his place they installed Peter II (1922–1970), having declared him of age. Peter was forced into exile (in Cairo, then in London) only weeks later when the Axis powers invaded Yugoslavia. The **Antifascist Council of National Liberation of Yugoslavia** (AVNOJ), the revolutionary wartime regime, suspended Peter's authority in November 1943. In November 1945 AVNOJ formally designated Yugoslavia a republic, bringing an end to Karadjordjević rule. *See also* LITTLE ENTENTE.

KARANTANIA/KARANTANIJA. Karantania, which is associated with the first **settlement of Slovenes**, was an early **medieval** state centered in the **Klagenfurt** (Celovec) basin of today's **Austria**. The name Karantania, although pre-Slavic in origin, was increasingly used by Slavic settlers, particularly after the 660s AD. From its center, near the plain of **Gospa Sveta**, which had once been the administrative headquarters of the Roman province Noricum, Karantania (the state and its name) expanded greatly from the seventh to the 11th centuries. At first a princedom ruled by an independent *knez* (prince), in 820 it was made a duchy under Frankish domination.

The second half of the eighth century was politically, economically, and culturally definitive for Karantania and its Slavic inhabitants. In 745 Karantanians, allying militarily with the Bavarians in order to fight Avars, acknowledged semifeudal domination of Bavarian and thereby also Frankish lords. This opened the way for the introduction of Frankish feudalism, which was soon imposed in Karantania in fully developed form. **Christianization of the Slovenes** also began at this time with the influx of Western missionaries, soon to be followed by the establishment of a formal church organization. Thus it was that Karantanian Slavs came under foreign, mostly Germanic, domination. The rule of the **Habsburgs**, the last of a line of many medieval Germanic overlords, began in the 13th century and lasted until 1918.

Nevertheless Karantania has special meaning for today's Slovenes. It represents their homeland in this part of Europe, one which knew intermittent independence as a state in the seventh and eighth centuries under an elected ruler. Also, the installation ceremony of the ruler, which in abbreviated form survived until 1414, characterizes the Slovenes as a people with unique political traditions. Some Slovenes maintain that these practices inspired **Enlightenment** political theorists, including Thomas Jefferson, when they wrote 18th-century political tracts about the social contract between rulers and the governed. *See also* KARANTANIAN DUKES, INSTALLATION OF.

KARANTANIAN DUKES, INSTALLATION OF. The ruler of medieval **Karantania** was traditionally (even before 745 AD and Bavarian-Frankish domination) elected by an assembly that represented the land's free men, its nobility. After it became a full-fledged feudal domain, Karantania's dukes were more commonly chosen by higher lords, while the assembly merely confirmed the appointment. Nevertheless, until 1414, when the practice was discontinued, the duke-designate pledged to Karantanians assembled at the prince's stone (the remnants of a Roman Ionic column) in **Gospa Sveta** field to uphold the land's well-being and its Christian religion and to be a just ruler. The ceremony was presided over by a peasant, while the duke, dressed in peasant garb, performed certain rituals, symbolically committing himself to a contract with the Karantanians. The ceremony's language was Slavic, and only after its completion was the duke allowed to assume his seat on the ducal throne, from which he then exercised his feudal prerogatives.

KARDELJ, EDVARD (1910–1979). After **Tito**, Edvard Kardelj, a Slovene, was the most prominent political figure of socialist **Yugoslavia**. From a working-class **Ljubljana** family, Kardelj joined the **League of Communist Youth of Yugoslavia** (SKOJ) at 16, became a member of the **Communist Party of Yugoslavia** (CPY) at 18, and by 19, although he was certified to teach elementary school, became a professional revolutionary. In the 1930s he was often in prison or on the run, pursued by officials of the **January 6, 1929, dictatorhip**, who were intent on suppressing the outlawed CPY. In prison he met future leaders of the party, published extensively, and read widely from the canon of revolutionary literature. Kardelj also spent more than two years in Moscow (1934–1936) studying **Marxism**-Leninism while preparing for revolution in Yugoslavia. He met Tito in 1934, and the two began a close collaboration that would last for the rest of their lives.

When the CPY was reorganized in the late 1930s at Moscow's urging, Tito and Kardelj, along with the Serb Aleksandar Ranković and the Montenegrin Milovan Djilas, emerged as its leadership. In 1938 the party, now federated, moved its headquarters to Zagreb, where Tito presided. The previous year, Kardelj had helped establish the **Communist Party of Slovenia** (CPS; *Komunistična partija Slovenije*, KPS), which then became a part of the new federation. That rejuvenated party, after Yugoslavia was invaded in 1941, organized a resistance movement, the **National Liberation Struggle** (NOB), which it soon transformed into a revolution. Kardelj played a major role in these developments in Slovenia, where he was active in the guerrilla operations, but he also figured prominently in the Yugoslav Communist-led **Partisan** movement. Kardelj (under the war name of Krištof) was a member of the high command, became part of the Yugoslav Communists' revolutionary government, or **Antifascist Council of National Liberation of Yugoslavia** (AVNOJ), in 1943, and also edited the party paper *Borba* for a time.

When the Communists came to power after the war, Kardelj's influence was universal. At one time or another Kardelj held every important post in the country. He survived his political enemies (Djilas and Ranković), and was expected to succeed Tito after the old man's death. In foreign affairs, Kardelj's skills were demonstrated early. At the Paris Peace Conference (1946) he helped negotiate territorial gains for Yugoslavia (the boundary with **Italy** was redrawn in Slovenia's favor), and as foreign minister Kardelj stood firm against Joseph Stalin when he expelled Yugoslavia from the **Cominform** in 1948. Kardelj and Yugoslavia both survived Stalin, who died in 1953.

Most important, Kardelj was chief theoretician of Yugoslav Marxism, or **Titoism**. With Yugoslavia outside the Soviet bloc, its existence needed to be explained ideologically. Kardelj elaborated on the concept of **workers' self-management** to distinguish the Yugoslav path to socialism from that of the Communist bloc. In foreign relations, he developed the idea of international **nonalignment**. Prominent Third World figures (e.g., Jawaharlal Nehru, Gamel Abdul Nasser, and Sukarno), anxious to remain free of East/West bloc commitments, followed Tito's (i.e., Kardelj's) lead, and the movement achieved international presence. Kardelj also played a major role in formulating socialist Yugoslavia's constitutions. His idea of a collective, rotating presidency (which brought Yugoslavia to an impasse in 1991) was incorporated into the **Constitution of 1974**.

Kardelj also wrote extensively on the nationality question. His first major work was book *The Development of the Slovene National Question*, published in 1939 under the pseudonym **Sperans**. National federalism, within a socialist state, was Kardelj's answer to "bourgeois" nationality problems. Kardelj was not popular among the Slovenes, many of whom blamed him for allying with **Belgrade** against the Slovene Republic and for the failed postwar political and economic system.

KARST. A large part of the **Republic of Slovenia**'s (RS) western and southern territory is karst, a term adopted by geographers from the

Karst (**Kras**) plateau, where erosion has formed sinkholes, caverns, and underground streams. Experts do not agree on the precise percentages of karst land (23 to 40 percent), but they do agree that karst phenomena are evident in 40 percent of the territory. Most prevalent is the Dinaric karst in Notranjska and Dolenjska, while alpine karst is less evident. Eight thousand caves have been identified, although there may be as many as 30,000. The karst constitutes a fragile biosphere, where its flora and fauna are protected, such as in the Notranska Regional Park (nearly 23,000 hectares).

KAVČIČ, STANE (1919–1987). Stane Kavčič, a member of the **Communist Party of Yugoslavia** (CPY) since 1941, was active in the **Liberation Front** (LF). After **World War II** he was a professional politician and held many important positions, both in political organizations and in the Slovene **government**. Kavčič served as vice president of the presidium of the People's Assembly of the **People's Republic of Slovenia** (PRS) in 1949–1950, and he was vice president (1951–1956) and later (1967–1972) president of the Executive Council of the **Socialist Republic of Slovenia** (SRS), which was the equivalent of prime minister of Slovenia. After the implementation of economic reform in 1965, Kavčič supported liberal economic policies advocating polycentric regional development in Slovenia, development of tertiary branches of the **economy**, increase of exports, and openness toward the West. His presidency was rocked by the **Žebot** affair in 1968, the **Road Affair** in 1969, and the affair of the 25 delegates in 1971. After party conservatives organized in the fall of 1971 and began purging **liberals** from Slovene institutions, Stane Kavčič was forced to resign in 1972 and was excluded from public life until his death in **Ljubljana** in 1987. His *Dnevnik in spomini* (Diary and Memoirs), published posthumously, is an important document for the study of recent Slovene history. *See also* LIBERALIZATION OF THE 1960s; MARKET SOCIALISM; PETRIČ, ERNEST.

KIDRIČ, BORIS (1912–1953). A publicist and politician, Boris Kidrič joined the **Communist Party of Yugoslavia** (CPY) as a young man and was one of its most active leaders before, during, and after **World War II**, working closely with **Edvard Kardelj**, **Tito**, and Communists internationally. Since the CPY was illegal between the wars, he was imprisoned several times. As a student, he organized underground Communists at the **University of Ljubljana**. He was also involved in publishing the radical, illegal *Rdeči prapor* (*Red*

Banner) and *Rdeči signali* (*Red Signals*) as well as legal publications such as *Književnost* (*Literature*). *See also* PRESS BEFORE 1990.

After the German attack on **Yugoslavia**, Kidrič organized the Slovene Communist resistance, the **Liberation Front** (LF). During World War II, he held leading positions in the LF and wrote numerous reports and documents. With Kardelj he wrote the **Dolomite Declaration** that strengthened Communist political control. In 1943 he was elected a member of the **Antifascist Council of National Liberation of Yugoslavia** (AVNOJ) with the task of leading the liberation war in Slovenia. He is believed to be one of the most ruthless Communists in the fight against anticommunists during and after the war.

On 5 May 1945, Kidrič was elected president of Slovenia's first postwar (Communist) government. In 1946 he became minister of industry in the Yugoslav government in **Belgrade** and president of the Economic Council of Yugoslavia. After the 1948 split between the Soviet Union and Yugoslavia, he tried to introduce a less centralized **economy** and argued for workers' participation in factories. Kidrič was instrumental in formulating the 1950 basic law of the new economic system of **workers' self-management** in Yugoslavia. In 1952 the Communist Party was renamed the League of Communists. Kidrič held leading positions in the League of Communists of Slovenia (LCS) and League of Communists of Yugoslavia (LCY). *See also* GOVERNMENT OF SLOVENIA, NATIONAL; PARTISANS.

KINGDOM OF SERBS, CROATS, AND SLOVENES. *See* SERBS, CROATS, AND SLOVENES, KINGDOM OF.

KLAGENFURT/CELOVEC. Located on the Glan (Glina) River in **Austria**'s Kärnten (Koroška or Carinthia) province, just north of the **Republic of Slovenia** (RS), Klagenfurt/Celovec has a population of about 89,700. As the province's principal city, it is the political, economic, and cultural center of southern Austria. Its oldest structures are from the 16th century: the Cathedral, the Dragon Fountain, and the Landhaus, or Diet building, where the Kärnten assembly still meets today. Nearby Wörther See (Vrbsko Jezero) and the Alps make Klagenfurt a tourist mecca. The overwhelming majority of inhabitants (67 percent) are engaged in **tourism** and services. The city has some machine and metal industry as well as a food and beverage industry developed primarily since **World War II**, and most recently it has been developing in the area of electronics, software, and information technologies. From the mid-1960s through the 1980s it also was a shopping mart for Slovenes, who commuted regularly to Klagenfurt, giving its retail businesses and banks a handsome boost. Since Slovenia's **independence**, however, many fewer Slovenes visit Klagenfurt to shop. The city has its own small airport, a railway that has connected it with **Maribor** since 1863, and a highway that links it with the RS, via the Loibl (Ljubelj) Pass and tunnel through the Kamnik-Savinja **Alps**.

When the **Austrian State Treaty** ended Allied (British) occupation of the area in 1955, **Yugoslavia** opened a consulate in Klagenfurt, and since 1991 the RS has had a consulate there. Klagenfurt has a university, founded in 1970 as a teacher training college. Slovene language and literature courses are taught and there has been an exchange arrangement with the **University of Ljubljana** since the mid-1970s. In 1993 the university added an economics faculty and a computer science component. Beginning in 2004, the institution began promoting itself as the **Alps-Adriatic** University of Klagenfurt, featuring the economic and cultural unity of the tri-state area (Carinthia, Slovenia, and Friuli-Venezia-Giulia in **Italy**). It uses the languages of all three regions. The city of Klagenfurt is the political, economic, and cultural center for Carinthian Slovenes, who have their own grammar school and a Slovene high school. There are also Slovene banks, cooperatives, cultural societies, and weekly newspapers. A branch of the **Society of St. Hermagoras** is located there. *See also* MINORITIES, SLOVENES IN AUSTRIA.

For the Slovenes, Klagenfurt and Kärnten are of special historical importance. It was in this area that Slovenes first settled, organized politically (in **Karantania**), and were **Christianized**. In the early Middle Ages the area was ethnically Slovene, but German settlers thereafter changed the character of the province and of Klagenfurt. The latter became a market town in the 13th century but declined after 1514 due to the fire that destroyed the town, **peasant revolts**, and ongoing religious turmoil. **Protestant** townspeople were resettled by **Counter Reformation Habsburg** rulers, and the town ceased functioning as a commercial center until the late 18th century. By the mid-19th century Klagenfurt was Germanized, and Slovenes were increasingly pressed to assimilate. They countered with a strong Slovene national program after 1848. For the remainder of the century, Slovene cultural and political organizations represented the community's interests. After **World War I**, although the Yugoslav army occupied southern Carinthia, the area, along with Klagenfurt, went to

Austria. Similarly, after World War II, Slovene/Yugoslav claims there were thwarted by the Allied powers and the Austrian State Treaty. *See also* PLEBISCITE, CARINTHIAN.

KOBARID/CAPORETTO. A town of about 1,000 people in the Primorska **region**, Kobarid (Caporetto) has an Alpine-Mediterranean character and a rich history going back to Roman times. From the early modern era on it was under Venetian and later **Habsburg** control. After **World War I** it belonged to **Italy**, after **World War II** to **Yugoslavia**, and since 1991 to the **Republic of Slovenia** (RS).

The Kobarid Museum, opened in October 1990, was named the European Museum of the Year in 1993 by the Council of Europe in Strasbourg, who chose it from among 50 contenders. The museum commemorates a major World War I military engagement between Italian forces and those of the Central Powers (Germany and Austria-Hungary), which Ernest Hemingway wrote about in *A Farewell to Arms*. The battle that took place in the Krn Mountains along the Soča (Isonzo) River during the last week in October 1917 was a major setback for **Italy**'s forces, who lost 300,000 men to **Austria**'s 70,000 (Slovenes fought primarily in the Austrian army) and were forced to retreat westward to the Piave River. The museum displays include 500 rare photographs, original documents and maps, and hundreds of pieces of arms and equipment. Tours of battle sites are arranged by the museum.

KOCBEK, EDVARD (1904–1981). Edvard Kocbek was a writer, poet, editor, translator, and politician. A **Christian Socialist**, Kocbek in the interwar years edited the **Catholic** youth literary journal *Križ* (*The Cross*) and wrote for the journals *Ogenj* (*Fire*) and *Dom in svet* (*Home and the World*). Because of his criticism of the **Clericals** and of the Catholic Church's support of the rightists in the Spanish Civil War, Kocbek came into conflict with the church and triggered a bitter polarization within the Slovene Catholic intelligentsia.

During **World War II** Kocbek and many other Christian Socialists joined the **Liberation Front** (LF). Kocbek's attempts to preserve the independence of Christian Socialists within the LF were in vain, and he signed the **Dolomite Declaration** of 1943, in which the **Communist Party of Slovenia** (CPS) was recognized as the LF's only legitimate political group. After the war, Kocbek held important government positions in **Belgrade** and **Ljubljana**. Because he criticized Communist policies as undemocratic, ideologically narrow, and paranoid, Kocbek was often in conflict with fellow politicians and was forced to retire in 1952. Until the 1960s he lived in isolation, writing and translating German and French literature. In the 1960s he began publishing his diaries, essays, and poems and became a dissident. In 1964 he received the Prešeren Prize for a poetry collection *Groza* (Horror). In a 1975 interview published in **Trieste**, he spoke openly about the **National Liberation Struggle** (NOB), his group's role in it, and his views on the war. In the interview, which earned him much political condemnation, he revealed the **massacres** of anticommunists after World War II. At the same time, however, the interview contributed to more open discussion in Slovenia, which eventually led to the dismembering of the communist system. *See also* HRIBAR, SPOMENKA; PARTISANS.

Kocbek, considered inept as a politician, was an excellent contemporary poet. His first poems were published in 1920 in Slovene Catholic literary magazines. Kocbek's poetry is lyrically reflective, combining **expressionistic** and symbolic elements in a creative fashion, evident in his first poetry collection, *Zemlja* (Earth). His later poetry is sensitive and deals perceptively with the complex social scene, of which he was an ambivalent fellow traveler. His poetry is devoted to transhistorical or metaphysical dimensions of human existence that could only be expressed in the language of poetry. His other poetry collections—*Pentagram*, *Žerjavica* (Embers), *Nevesta v črnem* (A Bride in Black)—were published only in 1977, although many were written during World War II. Most important among his prose writings are his short-story collection *Strah in pogum* (Fear and Courage) and his diaries *Tovarišija* (Comrades) and *Listina* (The Document). Several Kocbek essays, published in the book *Svoboda in nujnost* (Freedom and Necessity), belong to the best Slovene writing of its kind. *See also* LITERATURE.

KOCELJ. From 869 to 874 AD this independent Slavic prince from Moravia ruled Lower Pannonia. His administrative headquarters were in the east at Lake Balaton (now in **Hungary**). Old Church Slavonic, as opposed to Latin, was the language of worship in Kocelj's state, which had negotiated with the Slavic apostles Cyril and Methodius to educate **Karantanian** scholars in writing and reading scripture in Slavic, but the plan was not carried out.

KOPER/CAPODISTRIA. With a population of 23,726 and located in the Primorska **region**, on the northwestern Istrian peninsula not far from **Trieste**, Koper (Capodistria) is Slovenia's largest coastal town.

During the interwar years Koper belonged to **Italy**, which agressively applied Italianization policies toward Slovenes; some preferred to leave rather than live under Italian fascist rule. In 1954 the **London Agreement** put Koper into **Yugoslavia** and all but a few thousand Italians resettled in Italy. The then small town (8,000 inhabitants after **World War II**) slowly grew into the principal Slovene maritime commercial port and an expanding industrial center. The greater Koper area now includes about 48,000 inhabitants. They are primarily Slovenes; some are returnees, while others are newcomers from Istria's interior or from other Slovene (and former Yugoslav) areas.

Koper's greatest economic expansion has occurred since **independence** in 1991, profiting partly from the decline of Rijeka, **Croatia**'s major port in the northeastern Adriatic, because that country remained at war through the mid-1990s, and also from the decline of Trieste, Italy's northern Adriatic shipping center. (In 1991 Trieste and Koper ports had equal capacities; since then, Koper's has far outpaced Trieste's.) Additionally, by the late 1990s Koper's business sector had largely privatized its companies, upgraded and expanded port facilities, and was able to offer potential customers favorable business deals often at lower costs than either Croatia or Italy. The Slovene **government** owns 51 percent of the port itself and is assisting with collaborative efforts with Italy to establish joint Koper–Trieste port operations. One such venture, that of the Trieste International Container Terminal (TICT), a company in which the port of Koper owns a 49 percent share, has taken over Trieste's seventh pier, heralding the beginning of Koper–Trieste cooperation. There is talk as well, with support from Trieste's mayor, of linking his city and Koper by rail.

Favorably located in the northern Adriatic, with rail and new highway links with the rest of Central Europe, Koper is a commercial and **transportion** hub. It services not only Slovenia but also **Austria**, **Hungary**, southern Germany (particularly Bavaria), and the Czech and Slovak states. Of its transit cargo, 60 percent is destined for or originates in these Central European lands. Automobiles, coffee, cotton, metal products, rice, rubber, and sugar come in. Bauxite, fertilizers, fruit, grains, rape seed oil, and timber go out. As if to confirm Koper's economic importance to the Central European region, the **Central European Initiative**'s 1,500 participants held their seventh annual meeting here in late 2004. That same year more than 12 million tons of goods passed through Koper en route to or from Central Europe. The city is also known for its industrial output:

chemicals, metal products, and motorized vehicles—motorcycles made by Tomos, Slovene automobiles made by Cimos (a subsidiary of France's Citroen). It is also home to Istrabenz, a petroleum products company that was privatized in 1991.

Koper has its own publishing house (Lipa), a newspaper (*Primorske novice*) that serves the Primorska province, and its own radio-television station (RTV Koper/Capodistria), which broadcasts in both Slovene and Italian. In 2003 Koper also officially became home to the **University of Primorska**, Slovenia's third university. Establishing such an institution in western Slovenia had been earnestly debated since the 1990s, and some of its components were already in place before the turn of the century. Having a third university was regarded, at least partially, as a bastion against Italianization, both in Primorska, which borders Italy, but also for Slovene **minorities** living in Italy.

Historically Koper has Roman origins. As a **medieval** town, a part of the Venetian state from the 13th century until the late 18th and Austrian thereafter, it flourished as a shipping, fishing, and commercial center. Its golden age was in the 14th and 15th centuries, when it was northwestern Istria's administrative and judicial center. In the late 1400s and early 1500s, it was also a cultural mecca, where **humanism** and religious reformers found hospitable circumstances. Its commerce declined after the early 1700s, when neighboring Trieste, the principal **Habsburg** port, became a free port. Koper's old town architecture proclaims a glorious Venetian past; the newer settlement, which is separate from the old town, is marked by high-rise apartments and industrial buildings that have sprouted since the 1960s.

KOPITAR, JERNEJ (1780–1844). Coming out of the **Enlightenment** and the **Zois** Circle, Jernej Kopitar was a linguist and national awakener. He worked in **Vienna**, where he was a censor for Slavic and Greek works at the imperial court. Kopitar wrote the learned Slovene grammar *Grammatik der slavischen Sprache in Krain, Kärnten und Steyermark* (1808), which was based on the study of everyday **language** and its historical development. Kopitar's work in the field of Slovene linguistics was carried on by the early **romantics Franc Miklošič**, Matevž Ravnikar, and Franc Metelko. As a cofounder of Slavic linguistics, Kopitar had an important impact on Vuk Karadžić, a Serbian language reformer, and his work. Kopitar, an Austroslav, hoped to unite all South Slavs living in **Austria**. He promoted a common orthography and dialect (*kajkavian*) and use of the popular idiom. His goal was thwarted by **Illyrism**, which reached beyond Austria's borders to base the South Slav language on *stokavian*, and by liberal romantics **France Prešeren** and **Matija Čop**. *See also* ALPHABET WAR; AUSTROSLAVISM; HABSBURG RESTORATION.

KOROŠEC, ANTON (1872–1940). Anton Korošec, who held a doctorate in theology from the University of Graz, was influenced in his philosophy and politics by **Janez Evangelist Krek**. Accepting Krek's social program, he helped to organize farmers' unions in Styria, his home province. After winning a seat in the **Vienna** parliament in 1906, he remained involved in politics. In 1914 he was president of the Croat-Slovene Parliamentary Club in Vienna.

Like Krek, Korošec was part of the democratic wing of the Slovene People's Party, one that pushed for a decisive Yugoslav program during **World War I**. In May 1917 Korošec was elected president of the Yugoslav Club, and at the end of the month read the now famous **May Declaration** in parliament. The ensuing declaration movement, urging the unification of all South Slav lands of the empire, led to the establishment of a **National Council of Slovenes, Croats, and Serbs** in October 1918. Korošec (Krek had died in October 1917) led the fight for Yugoslav autonomy, and as head of the National Council called for the independence of the **Habsburg** Yugoslavs on 29 October 1918. He then met with the Serbs, proposing a union based on a confederal arrangement.

In the **Kingdom of Serbs, Croats, and Slovenes (Yugoslavia** after 1929), Korošec was a deft politician. He was vice president until a constitution was adopted in 1921, and thereafter sat in parliament until 1927, when he and his party joined the **government**. Although the **Clericals** stood for Slovene economic, political, and cultural autonomy, they partially abandoned that program once in the government. After King Alexander established a dictatorship in 1929, Korošec stayed on for a while until pressures from Slovenia brought him home. An all-Yugoslav state party (Yugoslav Radical Farmers' Democracy / *Jugoslovanska radikalna kmečka demokracija*), which the Clericals did not support, dominated government until 1935, when it was discredited by electoral irregularities. In that year a new state-sponsored party, the Yugoslav Radical Union (*Jugoslovenska radikalna zajednica*, JRZ) brought the Clericals back into political life. Korošec was soon in the government again, as minister of internal affairs to Prime Minister Milan Stojadinović. He remained in the government until 1938, helping the king's regent Prince Paul to oust Stojadinović, and he assisted in preparing the Cvetković-Maček

Sporazum (a pact that gave the Croats autonomy within Yugoslavia). *See also* JANUARY 6, 1929, DICTATORSHIP; LIBERALS.

KOROŠKA. *See* CARINTHIA/KOROŠKA REGION OF RS.

KOSESKI, JOVAN (1798–1884). A lawyer educated in **Vienna**, Jovan Koseski, whose real name was Janez Vesel, wrote poetry first in German and later in Slovene. His patriotic poems, in which he glorified Slavic history and loyalty to **Austria**, were published in **Janez Bleiweis**'s *Novice* (*News*). His poems, which were politically close to the Old Slovenes, made Koseski the main poet of the movement. As a poet, Koseski introduced into Slovene **literature** the sonnet form; he was very popular during his lifetime, overshadowing **France Prešeren**. The liberal Young Slovene **Josip Stritar**, in his *Critical Letters* of 1868, assessed Koseski's poetry as thematically epigonous and linguistically bombastic and tortured. Since then Koseski has been ranked among minor poets. *See also* ROMANTICISM.

KOSOVEL, SREČKO (1904–1926). Srečko Kosovel is an important personage of Slovene avant-garde **art**. In his short life, he created a large opus, mainly poetry but also prose. His early poetry, published in the collection *Zlati čoln* (The Golden Boat), is **impressionistic** with elements of symbolism. Kosovel continued the traditions of **Moderna**, often using the **Kras/Karst** region of his birth for the motifs of his poems. Kosovel's later poetry is **expressionistic**; it deals with the decline of Western European civilization and with humans' alienation and new beginnings. In 1924 Kosovel came into contact with European avant-garde **literature** (futurism and French surrealism). He was especially interested in constructivism, which is reflected in his collection of poems *Integrali* (Integrals)—poetry of top quality, translated into Italian, German, and English. A poet of world stature, Kosovel was initially considered an impressionist. After all of his work was discovered, however, it was obvious that he went beyond expressionism into constructivism. Since his poetic opus became known in its entirety only after **World War II**, Kosovel had no influence on his generation; his work, however, did leave its mark on Slovene **postmodernist** literature. *See also* ŠALAMUN, TOMAŽ.

KOZOLEC. *See* ARCHITECTURE, VERNACULAR.

KRANJ. The fourth-largest Slovene town (35,587 inhabitants and another 15,000 in its growing suburbs), Kranj is the administrative center of the Gorenjska **region**. It is about a half-hour's drive south of the Ljubelj (Loibel) Pass through the **Kamnik**-Savinja **Alps**, the border crossing with **Austria**. Kranj is located on a rocky promontory at the confluence of the Sava and Kokra Rivers. Slovenia's major north–south highway passes through Kranj, as does the railroad, while Brnik, Slovenia's largest airport, is only seven kilometers away. Kranj is Slovenia's major **manufacturing** center, whose factories have undergone reorganization and restructuring in the years since **independence** in 1991.

For the most part, the largest industries—electronics, rubber tires, shoes and other **leather** products, and **textiles**—have weathered the transition, often acquiring foreign owners or partnerships in the process. Iskra, the electronics powerhouse, which had 30,000 employees in 1990, has broken into smaller components. Most, like Iskraemco, Europe's third largest producer of electric meters, remain in Kranj. Iskratel, also still in Kranj, manufactures telephones; now licensed by the German company Siemens, it focuses on cell phones and other electronic communications innovations (GSM systems, broadband). Other Iskra companies make machine and carpentry tools and low-voltage switching gear. Sava, Kranj's tire factory, was partially rescued by Goodyear in 1998. In 2001 tire production soared to 6 million units (80 percent for export), and in 2005 Goodyear became its sole owner, marketing its products in Europe through Dunlop. Kranj's Planika (hiking boot manufacturer), established in 1951, is also making a comeback after the loss of Yugoslav markets in the 1990s and bankrupcty in 1998. The largest textile manufacturer (the former Tekstilindus), known since 1992 as Aquasava, produces cotton goods and is managed by the Italian Gruppo Bonazzi.

Situated southwest of a fertile agricultural plain, Kranj also has many food processing plants. In addition, it has a printery, a newspaper (*Gorenjski glas*) that serves the region, and its own radio station (Radio Kranj) Since 1952 Kranj has held a large annual agricultural-industrial fair (Gorenjski sejem). Many of Kranj's workers are commuters from nearby mountain villages, while many from Kranj also commute, usually to **Ljubljana**, a half-hour's drive to the southeast.

Kranj has been inhabited since the early Iron Age. It was a part of the Roman Empire, was settled in the early seventh century by proto-Slovenes, and was known as Creina in the early **medieval** period and as Krainburg after it came under German feudal lordship. It acquired town rights in the 13th century and recently celebrated the 700th anniversary of its founding. Its name came to designate the entire Austrian province in which it was located: Kranjska (Krain). After the mid-19th century, Kranj played a major role in developing Slovene national institutions. It was where **France Prešeren**, Slovenia's best-known **romantic** poet lived and is commemorated. Since 1861 Kranj has had a Slovene gymnasium (initially bilingual), and today the **University of Maribor**'s School of Organizational Sciences is located here. The old town's architecture is well preserved and is predominantly late Gothic, although other styles can be seen, including late 19th-century Secession and **Plečnik**'s 20th-century designs. Suburban buildings, constructed in the post–**World War II** period, can generally be described as functional: high-rise worker housing and community structures of little architectural distinction. To the west of the city are the hills of Šmarjetna Gora and Sveti Jošt, popular excursion destinations. Five kilometers northeast of Kranj is Brdo Castle, with 500 hectares of public parkland. The **castle** is used for official governmental functions and entertaining foreign dignitaries—U.S. President George W. Bush and **Russia**'s President Vladimir Putin held their initial meeting there in 2001. *See also* TRANSPORT.

KRANJSKA. *See* REGIONS OF SLOVENIA.

KRAS/KARST PLATEAU. The Kras (or Karst) plateau is located in southwest Slovenia between the Bay of **Trieste** and the Vipava River valley, not far from the seaside resorts of **Piran** and Portorož. About 25 percent of the **Republic of Slovenia**'s (RS) territory can be characterized as having **karst** terrain, a term derived from the particular physical geography of this area. The area's main features are a desolate, rocky, and generally dry landscape of plateaus (altitude 400 to 600 meters), two-thirds forested, and interspersed with shallow depressions (sinkholes or karstholes), which support a meager agriculture; underground streams; and more than 4,000 known caverns, some with magnificent limestone formations (stalactites and stalagmites) produced by the dissolving action of above-ground water upon limestone as it seeps through cracks in the rock.

Kras is sparsely populated. Its only large settlement is Sežana, which borders with **Italy** and has some industry. The peculiarities of Kras's terrain, however, attract numerous **tourists**. Thousands annually visit the breathtaking caverns, especially at **Postojna**, but also Škocjan and Vilenica, where there is an annual literary awards gathering. Cerkniško Jezero (Cerknica Lake; altitude 546 to 552 meters), whose eccentricities were described by **Janez Vajkard Valvasor** in a presentation to the Royal Society in London in 1687, draws visitors in search of the "disappearing lake." Dependent on rainfall and inflow from Kras streams, the lake can be as large as 10.5 kilometers long and 4.7 kilometers wide, or it can dry up entirely. **Lipica** is also located in the Kras region.

KREK, JANEZ EVANGELIST (1865–1917). A professor of Thomist philosophy and theology in **Ljubljana** for two decades (1895–1916), with a doctorate in theology, Janez Evangelist Krek wrote extensively on socialism. He had been much influenced by the **Christian Socialism** movement that had begun in the 1870s in Central Europe and was strengthened by Pope Leo XIII's encyclical *Rerum novarum* (1891), which criticized capitalism for its exploitative nature and suggested that Christian and socialist principles were compatible and might be combined to resolve some of the social and economic problems of the time. Krek accepted the new social theology by organizing his first workers' union in 1894. By 1914, just 20 years later, there were 462 such organizations, representing some 40,000 workers. Moreover, in 1909 the workers' societies had merged into the Yugoslav Professional Union (*Jugoslovanska strokovna zveza*), creating a formidable economic and political force for the Slovenes. Workers needed rights, Krek believed, not charity, and he helped them achieve those rights through organization. He also helped set up buying, selling, and banking cooperatives in some larger rural communities, and he promoted education and self-betterment (including sobriety) for everyone.

Krek was also a politician, along with **Ivan Šušteršič**, a leader of the **Slovene People's Party**. He served in the **Vienna** parliament for a few years in the 1890s but preferred the Carniolan assembly, in order to be closer to his unionizing work. In the assembly he generally spoke on social and economic issues and represented the democratic wing of the party. He and the conservative Šušteršič frequently disagreed, and after 1908 their positions became less and less compatible. Krek was an ardent Yugoslav, promoting Slovene–Croat cooperation and enthusiastically welcoming the annexation of Bosnia and Hercegovina as a step toward the establishment of a South Slav state within **Austria**. Unlike other **Clericals**, including Šušteršič, Krek was not an ultra-**Catholic**. His **Yugoslavism** allowed for equality for Slavs who were Orthodox, and during **World War I**, while Šušteršič stood by Vienna, Krek came to believe that a Slovene–Croat–Serb people could be satisfied only outside Austria in an independent state. He supported the **May Declaration** of 1917. *See also* COOPERATIVE MOVEMENT.

KREK, MIHA (1897–1969). Miha Krek was a lawyer who worked with the Slovene **Clericals** after 1921, was on the national committee of **Catholic Action**, and was an editor of *Slovenec*. In 1935 **Anton Korošec**, Clerical party leader, brought him into the government as a minister without portfolio, later as minister for construction and then **education**. After Korošec's death in 1940, Krek became head of the Yugoslav banking committee's Slovenia division and was in **Belgrade** during Germany's surprise aerial bombing on 6 April 1941. He went into exile with the fleeing **Yugoslav Royal Government**.

Krek remained in London as minister and vice president of the government until August 1943, when an agreement was concluded between **Tito** and Ivan Šubašić. While in London he advised the Allies on **Italy**, spoke frequently on the radio on behalf of the Slovene cause, and warned against allowing a Communist victory in **Yugoslavia**. In Rome in 1944 he established an anticommunist national committee and urged the Allies to bring the war and liberation to Slovenia. In the spring of 1945 he tried to prevent the **Home Guard**, which had fled Slovenia to southern **Austria**, from being handed over by the British to the Yugoslav government (**Partisans**). Later he helped provide for Slovene refugees in Rome and assisted them in **emigrating** abroad. Krek, too, emigrated, resettling in the **United States** in 1947. He continued to be active in Slovene émigré circles, and was a member of the leadership of the Union of Christian Democratic Parties of Central Europe. Krek died in **Cleveland** in 1969.

KRISTAN, ETBIN (1867–1953). The writer Etbin Kristan was a translator of Henrik Ibsen, Friedrich Schiller, and Emile Zola as well as an editor and politician. He joined **Austria**'s Social Democratic Party in **Vienna** in the late 1880s. After the Slovene **Socialists** founded their party in 1896, Kristan became a member of its executive committee, remaining a liaison with the Austrian party. He was committed to Austro-**Marxism**, and proposed solutions to the nationality question in the **Habsburg** Empire for Austrian party consideration. The plan to institute personal autonomy in addition to territorial federalism, attributed to Karl Renner (Austrian Socialist theoretician), was actually Kristan's idea.

The Tivoli Resolution of 1909, which called for cultural and linguistic merging of all South Slavs, was strongly promoted by Kristan. The statement, forcefully **Illyrist**, was drafted in the wake of Austria's annexation of Bosnia and Hercegovina, when many believed Yugoslav political union (within Austria) was imminent. Kristan earned the opposition of his friend **Ivan Cankar** and provoked a wide debate over Illyrism.

Kristan traveled to the **United States** in 1912 to lecture and was present for the Chicago Declaration (1917), which called for the creation of a Yugoslav federal republic. He was elected to the new **Yugoslavia**'s constituent assembly in 1920, and the following year he was sent to the United States as an envoy to Yugoslav immigrants. After he was relieved of that position in 1927, Kristan remained in the United States, returning to Yugoslavia only shortly before his death in 1951. *See also* NEO-ILLYRISM

KUČAN, MILAN (1941–). Born in Križevci, **Prekmurje**, Milan Kučan completed law school at the **University of Ljubljana** in 1964. In 1958, as a high school student, Kučan joined the Leauge of Communists of Slovenia (LCS). His political career began in his student years as a member of the University Committee of the LCS and the Central Committee of the Youth Association of Slovenia (*Zveza mladine Slovenije*, ZMS). After graduation, he became a professional politician working in the Central Committee of ZMS, whose president he was in 1968–1969. Subsequently, he was elected a member of the Central Committee of the LCS, where he worked until 1973, when he became secretary of the Republic Conference of the **Socialist Alliance of Working People** (SAWP) of Slovenia. In 1978 Kučan was elected to his first government post, president of the Republic Assembly, for a four-year term. He became familiar with the broader Yugoslav political scene during his four-year term as the Slovene representative to the presidency of the League of Communists of Yugoslavia (LCY) in **Belgrade**. In 1986 he returned to Slovenia to run the LCS as its president, a post he held until December 1989. In January 1990 Kučan led the LCS delegation when, in protest, it walked out of the LCY's 14th (and last) Congress, an act that endeared him to many anticentralist, anticommunist Slovenes.

In the first free **elections** of 1990, Kučan was elected president of the presidency of the **Republic of Slovenia** (RS), winning 64 percent of the vote, and gave up his LCS membership. He advocated a peaceful resolution of the Yugoslav conflict. As a cautious, patient, and noncombative politician, he was elected RS president twice: in the elections of 1992 and of 1997. In 2001 Kučan was declared the most popular Slovene politician by *Delo*, the leading daily. Kučan's second term ended on 23 December 2002; by constitutional law, he was not allowed a third term. He was succeded by **Janez Drnovšek**. Kučan is a recipient of numerous decorations and awards for his role as a statesman. As a retired, private citizen, Kučan remains active in public life. Subsequent public opinion polls have shown that his popularity among Slovenes remains high. He operates from the office of the former president, a new institution, supported by taxpayers for a period of five years. As a former head of state, Kučan has also been a member of the Club of Madrid. With Michel Rocard, the former French prime minister, Kučan has been serving as co-chair of the International Ethical Collegium. Since March 2004 he has been president of **Forum 21**, a recently formed association for political, economic, social, and ethical questions, an unregistered political lobby of the left.

KUMERDEJ, BLAŽ (1738–1805). Blaž Kumerdej was a Slovene **Enlightenment** figure and philologist. In 1772 he worked out a plan for Slovene elementary schools and sent it to Empress **Maria Theresa**. Although the plan was rejected by ecclesiastical dignitaries and regional administrators, the establishment of elementary schools was mandated by the First Elementary School Law in 1774, and **Vienna** appointed Kumerdej as the principal of **Ljubljana**'s normal school. Kumerdej also wrote the first bilingual German/Slovene primer for elementary schools, and he encouraged the use of the Slovene **language** in schools. He tried to revive the **Academia Operosorum** as a linguistic and literary society. His enormous philological work remained unpublished during his lifetime. Kumerdej's proposal on elementary schooling is considered one of the most important events in the early period of Slovene national awakening. *See also* EDUCATION, ELEMENTARY; ZOIS, ŽIGA.

– L –

LANGUAGE, SLOVENE. Slovene, the official language of the **Republic of Slovenia** (RS), is the common native language of 88 percent of the population of the RS and of the Slovene **minorities** in ethnically contiguous areas of **Austria** (Carinthia), **Hungary** (Porabje/Raba River basin), and **Italy** (Friuli Venezia Giulia). Slovene is also used by the Slovene immigrants in the **United States**, Canada, South America, Australia, and several European countries. Worldwide, Slovene is spoken by well over 2 million people.

In the sixth century AD, the ancestors of Slovenes settled the eastern Alpine and subalpine regions of Central Europe, among peoples speaking Germanic languages (north), Romance languages (west), and other South Slavic languages (southeast); they were joined in the 10th century by Hungarians (northeast). Over the centuries, colonization and denationalizing pressures by the Germans, Italians, and Hungarians greatly reduced Slovene linguistic territory and brought changes to the language itself, especially to the dialects in direct contact with foreign cultures, but also intensified archaizing tendencies in the central Slovene dialects. *See also* SETTLEMENT OF THE SLOVENES.

The earliest written records in Slovene are the **Freising Fragments** (from around 1000 AD). The first printed Slovene books, including a translation of the Bible, were published in the 16th century by **Protestant Reformation** figures such as **Primož Trubar**, **Jurij Dalmatin**, and **Adam Bohorič**. Books in Slovene continued to be published during the **Counter Reformation** and the **Enlightenment**, including grammars by **Jernej Kopitar** (1808) and **Valentin Vodnik** (1811). During the **Romantic** period, **France Prešeren** and **Matija Čop** cultivated and refined the language, creating a modern, urban, written Slovene. *See also* LEVSTIK, FRAN.

Slovene is a Slavic language, a branch of the Indo-European linguistic family, and is geographically the westernmost of the South Slavic languages; it is closely related to Croatian and has similarities with other South Slavic languages. The Slovene linguistic territory is divided into 46 dialects and subdialects falling within seven topographically defined **regions**: **Carinthia** (Koroška), the Littoral (Primorska), the Rovte, Lower Carniola (Dolenjska), Upper Carniola (Gorenjska), Styria (Štajerska), and Eastern Styria (Vzhodna Štajerska) with Pannonia (along the Hungarian border). Slovene, as found in grammar books, taught in schools, and used in the **media** and **literature**, is known as Contemporary Standard Slovene (CSS). It is the language of educated Slovenes. After **World War II** the differences among Slovene dialects diminished, and CSS has spread due to internal migration (a by-product of industrialization and urbanization), **education**, and mass media. Although a composite of several dialects, CSS is based primarily on the central dialects of Dolenjska and Gorenjska.

Slovene is highly inflected and complex. It has three genders (masculine, feminine, neutral), three numbers (singular, dual, plural), and six cases in the declension of nouns, adjective forms, and pronouns. It has retained certain archaic characteristics, such as the dual form and the supine verbal noun, which other Slavic languages have lost.

LEAGUE OF COMMUNIST YOUTH OF SLOVENIA / ZVEZA KOMUNISTIČNE MLADINE SLOVENIJE. *See* LEAGUE OF COMMUNIST YOUTH OF YUGOSLAVIA.

LEAGUE OF COMMUNIST YOUTH OF YUGOSLAVIA / SAVEZ KOMUNISTIČKE OMLADINE JUGOSLAVIJE (SKOJ). The League of Communist Youth of Yugoslavia (SKOJ) was established in October 1919 in Zagreb and accepted the program of the **Communist Party of Yugoslavia** (CPY) in June 1920 at a youth congress in **Belgrade**. Its founding, like that of the CPY, followed many post–**World War I** months of sorting out issues relating to ideology (socialist or communist), procedure (democracy or democratic centralism), and organization (unitary or federal). The latter issue, as with the CPY, would trouble the league throughout its existence. In 1920 SKOJ had 5,500 members, ages 13 to 25, most from urban areas; it promoted Yugoslav unity, worked with international communist youth organizations, and operated according to the principle of democratic centralism. Normal relations with the CPY were not established until 1928, when SKOJ had barely more than 1,500 members.

Between 1941 and 1945, SKOJ's history is similar to that of the CPY. When **World War II** began, it adopted an antifascist platform and recruited support for the antifascist youth movement, United League of Antifascist Youth of Yugoslavia. Its members became units in the **Liberation Front** (LF), and its membership grew. By the war's end SKOJ had 145,000 members, and the antifascist League 827,000.

With the CPY in power after 1946, the two youth organizations expanded, and in 1948 they merged, assuming the name People's Youth of Yugoslavia; in Slovenia, the group was called People's Youth of Slovenia (*Ljudska mladina Slovenije*, LMS). In the late 1940s and 1950s the LMS was a dynamic organization, recruiting members in villages and towns, schools, and enterprises. It engaged actively in postwar reconstruction, particularly in the era of the First **Five-Year Plan**, and was noted for involvement in volunteer work brigades. The brigades helped build the Titan factory in **Kamnik**, and between 1948 and 1960 hundreds of thousands of young people worked on the Brotherhood and Unity Highway that linked first Belgrade and Zagreb, later **Ljubljana** and Zagreb, and finally Belgrade with the Greek border. By the late 1950s, work in the brigades became a spirited summer-camp-like experience, where entertainment and learning accompanied the work.

The LMS maintained its link to the League of Communists of Yugoslavia (LCY)—the name for the Communist Party since 1952—acting as a conduit to party membership. In the 1960s the LMS was renamed the League of Socialist Youth (*Zveza socialistične mladine*, ZSM), more in keeping with constitutional changes, and the organization occupied itself with ideological work. The organization became hierarchical and bureaucratized, however, and lost its dynamism. Closely controlled by the LCY, even reform elements within the ZSM were unable to renew the group's relevance and the élan of the 1950s. At the end of the 1960s, when there were **student** strikes in various Yugoslav cities (as there were in many European and American cities), the ZSM was timid and cautious. Instead, university students belonging to the Student Union (*Zveza študentov*, ZŠ) led the demonstrations for a role in university governance and increased financial aid. The LCY condemned and disbanded the student demonstrators and their organization.

After the **liberalization of the 1960s** was halted, there was a general purging of nonestablishment elements from all institutions. The ZSM therefore remained a junior apprentice to the LCY, exercising particular caution throughout the 1970s in order to avoid official disfavor. Only in the 1980s was the ZSM slowly reinvigorated. In Slovenia the ZSMS presidency of Jožef Školč, which began in 1988, brought a new dynamism to the organization. Thus the ZSMS became an active participant in Slovenia's liberalization at the end of that decade. In November 1989 the league became an independent political organization and in October 1990 renamed itself the **Liberal Democratic Party** (*Liberalno demokratska stranka*, LDS). It has since then become one of independent Slovenia's strongest parties.

LEAGUE OF COMMUNISTS OF SLOVENIA (LCS) / ZVEZA KOMUNISTOV SLOVENIJE (ZKS). *See* COMMUNIST PARTY OF SLOVENIA.

LEAGUE OF COMMUNISTS OF YUGOSLAVIA (LCY) / ZVEZA KOMUNISTOV JUGOSLAVIJE (ZKJ). *See* COMMUNIST PARTY OF YUGOSLAVIA.

LEAGUE OF SOCIALIST YOUTH OF SLOVENIA / ZVEZA SOCIALISTIČNE MLADINE SLOVENIJE (ZSMZ). *See* LEAGUE OF COMMUNIST YOUTH OF YUGOSLAVIA.

LEATHER AND FOOTWEAR MANUFACTURING. Leather and footwear **manufacturing** evolved from the **medieval** shoe craft centers in the towns of Tržič (Peko), **Kranj** (Planika), Žiri (Alpina), **Ljubljana,** and **Maribor.** Shoemaking began to expand during the French occupation (1809–1813) and became industrialized toward the end of the 19th century. In 1903 Peter Kozina established a shoemaking enterprise in Tržič, which soon developed into the first Slovene footwear factory, Peko, marking the beginning of mechanized footwear production. After **World War I** footwear manufacturing was in recession and could not compete with foreign capital, although Peko was an exception. In the communist period, footwear manufacturers struggled with an out-of-date industrial base, which was modernized in the 1980s in order to remain competitive on the international market. At the time, there were eight footwear factories, and several leather accessories makers, such as Toko (Domžale) and Industrija usnja (Vrhnika), who were selling their products to international companies, including Gucci, Ferre, and Trusardi. Most of the footwear and leather accessories were exported (e.g., Peko and Alpina sold over 80 percent of their production abroad). Peko, well known for casual shoes, collaborated with the German firm AFIS, America's Rockport, and **Italy's** Benetton. Alpina was known for its quality cross-country and downhill ski boots.

Like **textile and clothing manufacturing,** two traditional industries in the past that were also basic pillars of **international trade,** leather and footwear manufacturing has been in decline, partly due to strong world market competition. In 1991 the leather and footwear industry employed over 14,000 workers and accounted for 1 percent of GDP. The volume of both declined, as did the number of workers employed. In 2004 only 5,558 (about 60 percent less than in 1991) were still employed by the industry, which has been recording losses since 2001. While Planika declared bankruptcy in 2004, the other two major shoe factories, Peko and Alpina, restructured, the latter with the help of the European Bank for Reconstruction and Development. Both factories export about 60 percent of their product to various post-socialist countries (e.g., Macedonia, Romania). *See also* ECONOMY SINCE 1991.

LEVSTIK, FRAN (1831–1887). A poet, writer, literary critic, linguist, and journalist, Fran Levstik was the most important of the generation of Young Slovenes, a liberal group that advocated a unified South Slav nation and was strongly influenced by his work. His literary opus was diversified: poems, short stories, dramas, essays, and novels. Levstik's writings belong to the school of **realism**, although elements of **romanticism** are present. As a disciple of **Jernej Kopitar** and **Franc Miklošič**, he was also a master of the **language** and its use (though as a linguist he lacked formal training and misinterpreted Miklošič's work).

Levstik formulated a comprehensive Slovene literary program in three works, all written in 1858. First, in a travel essay *Popotovanje od Litije do Čateža* (A Journey from Litija to Čatež), he offered a literary program for the Slovene literati. For him, **literature**'s purpose was to educate and sharpen national identity. Second, in a paper titled *Napake slovenskega pisanja* (Mistakes in Slovene Writing), he advocated correct language use. He was especially critical of those who wrote Slovene using German syntax. Third, in a provocative story, *Martin Krpan z Vrha* (Martin Krpan from Vrh), he laid foundations for Slovene storytelling. Under the influence of the German critic Gotthold E. Lessing, Levstik also established the foundations of Slovene literary criticism. He also expressed his literary esthetic and critical views in the article *Objective Criticism*, published in the daily *Slovenski narod* (*Slovene Nation*) in 1868. Levstik's most important positions were as editor of *Naprej* (*Forward*), a political and economic semiweekly, and as the first secretary of **Slovenska Matica**. *See also* PRESS BEFORE 1914.

LIBERAL DEMOCRATIC PARTY. *See* LIBERAL DEMOCRACY OF SLOVENIA.

LIBERAL DEMOCRACY OF SLOVENIA / LIBERALNA DEMO-KRACIJA SLOVENIJE (LDS). On 3 December 1994, four existing parties merged to form Liberal Democracy of Slovenia. They were the **Democratic Party of Slovenia** (Democrats), the **Greens of Slovenia** (Greens), and the **Socialist Party of Slovenia** (SSS), and the larger and more politically successful Liberal Democratic Party (LDS), whose acronym survived the merger and came to represent all four. The original LDS grew out of the League of Socialist Youth of Slovenia (ZSMS) at the time when a multiparty system was developing in the first months of 1990. Initially it was called the League of Socialist Youth of Slovenia–Liberal Party, and its president was Jožef

Školč. In the **election** of April 1990 it got the second largest number of votes, winning 37 seats in parliament and placing one government minister. The party was officially renamed the Liberal Democratic Party on 30 October 1990.

In the election of December 1992, the LDS won 22 of the 90 seats in the National Assembly, the largest number of any party. Its member **Janez Drnovšek** became prime minister, and four additional ministerial posts (economy and development; education; environment; and justice) went to LDS members. Jožef Školč turned over the party presidency to Drnovšek in spring 1993 in order to lead LDS's parliamentary delegation; in September 1994 Školč became president, or speaker of the National Assembly. With the December 1994 merger that brought the Democrats, Greens, and SSS into the party, LDS became yet larger and more clearly the strongest party in the **Republic of Slovenia** (RS). Between 1992 and 2004, with one brief interregnum (June–November 2000), LDS coalition governments ruled the country. (Janez Drnovšek was prime minister between 1992 and 2002; **Anton Rop** between 2002 and 2004.) LDS assumed a center political position, offering coalition agreements to center-right or center-left parties. Its program was politically liberal, while retaining the previous regime's **social security** net; in **foreign policy** it was the leading proponent of accession to the **European Union** (EU) and **North Atlantic Treaty Organization** (NATO). *See also* GOVERNMENTS AFTER 1990.

That LDS would be defeated at the polls in 2004 was not a foregone conclusion. However, in the 18 months before the December 2004 election, there were many signs that the voters might turn away from the party that had dominated Slovenia's political life since **independence**. In March 2003 referenda were passed in support of joining the EU and NATO, matters that had been foremost on the national security agenda since the mid-1990s. With only formal accession to these organizations left and scheduled for the following spring, many Slovenes began to return to issues that had long been put off. The center-right parties, who were getting better organized, started to press for action on matters vital to their constituents. By spring 2004 Rop, LDS's prime minister, was sparring with the **Slovene People's Party** (SLS), a key component of his ruling coalition. When three SLS ministers resigned, Rop, without consulting members of his own party, appointed a justice minister that key LDS heads opposed. Soon Rop, who was inexperienced and impatient, found that a deluge had been unleashed that would spell LDS defeat. In spring and summer, political figures and intellectuals also began calling for a reassessment of Slovenia's goals; two newly established groups discussed the RS's future (**Forum 21**, organized by former president **Milan Kučan**, and the Assembly for the Republic, organized by **Dimitrij Rupel**, LDS's own foreign minister). The voters sensed it was time for a change. Even many who had supported LDS for a decade justified a vote for center-right parties as a healthy sign of real democracy at work.

LDS as a party had developed a broad-based organization, with country-wide and cross-generational membership. Internationally, it associated with European Liberal Democrats. Two LDS representatives were elected to the European Parliament in June 2004, when Slovenia's first members (seven in all) were elected to that body. After 2004's electoral defeat, LDS's unity and direction faltered, and some members left the party. Somewhat chastened, LDS pulled itself together in the fall of 2005, turning to **Jelko Kacin**, one of its two representatives in the European Parliament, for leadership. Kacin, a hero of the **Ten-Day War** period, was elected LDS president, replacing Anton Rop in October 2005. In late 2005 LDS had 8,000 members and was hoping for party renewal.

LIBERAL PARTY / LIBERALNA STRANKA (LS). The Liberal Party (LS) was established as the Slovene Small Businessmen's Party (*Slovenska obrtniškopodjetniška stranka*) on 27 December 1989, the day Slovenia's parliament passed a law permitting the formation of political organizations. Some of its members, already in parliament, had begun functioning as an opposition to the League of Communists of Slovenia (LCS)—the name for the **Communist Party of Slovenia** since 1952. As a party the LS joined the **Demos** coalition, and when four of its members were elected to parliament in the republic's first multiparty **election** of April 1990, the party was officially renamed the Liberal Party. Two LS members got ministerial posts.

After the 1990 elections the LS, a neoconservative party, refined its program. Founded on the belief that private property was the basis for economic independence, from which flowed personal liberty, the LS worked toward achieving **independence** for Slovenia, implementing national reconciliation, and democratizing public life. It focused especially on **privatization**, pressing for **denationalization** of property. The LS won no seats in the **Republic of Slovenia's** (RS) **election** of December 1992 and essentially vanished from the political arena.

LIBERALIZATION OF THE 1960s. In the 1950s the League of Communists of Yugoslavia (LCY; formerly the **Communist Party of Yugoslavia**) had already developed liberal and conservative factions. The liberal wing pushed for liberalization, mostly economic, particularly after the implementation of economic reforms in 1965. These "liberals" were mostly younger Communists who organized in their respective republics and were able by the late 1960s to exert political power, however briefly.

With increasing decentralization of the state and the LCY in the mid-1960s, a strong liberal faction formed within the League of Communists of Slovenia (LCS; formerly the **Communist Party of Slovenia**). The liberals did not have a formal program, but their ideas were expressed in the journal *Teorija in praksa* (*Theory and Practice*) and in public speeches; their ideas were also evident in political and economic decisions and in cultural life. As Communists, they acknowledged the leading role of the LCS, but they advocated political pluralism through reorganization of the **Socialist Alliance of Working People** (SAWP). Slovene liberal Communists advocated economic and political reforms that would change the system's structure from within. They were united in promoting the market principle for the **economy** and favored long-range social planning, where protection of the **environment** would be essential. They advocated a confederate **Yugoslavia** (although they never used that term) with greater republic independence in economic development, finances, and international relations. They also demanded greater equality in the **Yugoslav People's Army** but also believed it was important to develop territorial defense forces. In general, they advocated Slovene national sovereignty and a new method of organizing and financing the Yugoslav federation; it was in the latter issue that their differences with conservatives were most pronounced.

The central political figure of Slovene liberalization was **Stane Kavčič**, president of the Slovene Executive Council from 1967 to 1972. His rule was marked by a series of conflicts between liberal and conservative Communists. In the summer of 1969, the liberal Slovene **government**, with strong public support, protested the unilateral decision of the federal government to disregard a plan for a highway construction project in Slovenia, the financing of which had already been approved by the World Bank. This protest, known as the **Road Affair**, caused serious conflicts between conservatives and liberals in the republic as well as at the federal level. It marked the beginning of a gradual end for "liberal" power in Slovene public life. There were other "affairs," such as the Žebot affair in 1968, which helped to convince the conservatives that the liberals must be removed from public life. The last and most important of these was the "affair of the 25 delegates" in the spring and summer of 1971. At that time, delegates in the republic's assembly offered their own candidate, **Ernest Petrič**, for the newly established Yugoslav presidency without consulting the LCS or even SAWP, which was responsible for nominating the candidates. Fearful of losing control, conservative Communists purged the party, beginning with the most liberal elements: the LCS committee of **Ljubljana** (in the fall 1971) and the republic's government (fall of 1972). This was followed by an expulsion of liberals from the mass **media**, intellectual journals, and the **University of Ljubljana**, especially its Faculty of Sociology, Political Science, and Journalism. Along with the purges, a new political and economic system—**contractual socialism**—was instituted with the **Constitution of 1974**. It legally strengthened the LCY as the final arbiter in all matters in Yugoslav society. *See also* COMMUNIST PARTY, OPPOSITION TO (1940s AND 1950s); MARKET SOCIALISM.

LIBERALNA STRANKA (LS). *See* LIBERAL PARTY.

LIBERALNO DEMOKRATSKA STRANKA (LDS). *See* LIBERAL DEMOCRACY OF SLOVENIA

LIBERALS. Although liberalism was already evident among Slovene nationalists in 1848, it emerged as a clear political position only in 1867. Debates at the time over whether to support an Austrian Concordat with Rome divided Slovene liberals from their conservative colleagues. The two stood separately for elections to the **Vienna** parliament in 1873, but for nearly two decades their national politics differed little.

Slovenes founded an authentic Liberal party in 1891. Named the National Progressive Party (*Narodna napredna stranka*), or NNS, three years later, it was led by writers, urban professionals, and businesspeople, and counted among its leadership two long-term mayors of **Ljubljana, Ivan Hribar** and **Ivan Tavčar**. (Although "Liberal" was never a part of the party name, the word with a capital L is used to identify anyone who belonged to the NNS.) The Liberals were protectionist while promoting industrialization; they favored separation of church and state; and they stood behind secular **education**. Like

Liberals in much of Europe, they were not democratic, in that they opposed universal suffrage, preferring to restrict the vote to dependable, sensible, tax-paying males. They also tended to be anticlerical, firmly opposing Rome's involvement in Austrian politics.

The party was traditionally Pan-Slavist, idealizing **Russia**, urging Austro-Russian accord, yet embarrassed by Russian autocracy. As Pan-Slavists, Liberals formulated a Yugoslav program that stressed the equality of Slavic nations and their religions. They collaborated with other liberal South Slavs, such as the Croat Bishop Josip Juraj Strossmayer, whose ecumenical efforts sought to unite South Slavic **Catholic** and Orthodox communities. Slovene Liberals hoped that **Austria** would become a federal state in which each nation (including the Slovene) would have its own administrative unit and where its **language** and culture would be secure. Slovene Liberals viewed ultramontanist Catholics, German Liberals, and Germanization as the greatest threats to Slovene freedom and self-realization.

In June 1918, on the eve of Austria's collapse during **World War I**, the Liberal party was renamed the Yugoslav Democratic Party (*Jugoslovanska demokratska stranka*). The party's philosophy did not change appreciably, although it now strongly supported a unitary, centralist Yugoslav state. It was an early supporter of the **Vidovdan Constitution** of 1921, and it worked with interwar governments. In 1929, when **Yugoslavia** became a dictatorship, parties were abolished. After a new constitution was adopted in 1931, the regime established the Yugoslav Radical Peasant Democracy (*Jugoslovanska radikalna kmečka demokracija*, JRKD), an all-Yugoslav state party (*državna stranka*). It changed its name to Yugoslav National Party (*Jugoslovanska nacionalna stranka*, JNS) in 1933. Slovene Liberals, along with some of the membership of two independent Slovene parties—Independent Democratic Party (*Samostojna demokratska stranka*) and Independent Farmers' Party (*Samostojna kmetijska stranka*)—worked with the JRKD/JNS. Liberals were pushed aside after 1935, however, when the JNS, although it won the election, was discredited by electoral fraud. After 1935 Prince Paul and the new prime minister, Milan Stojadinović, preferred to work with Slovene **Clericals**. Liberalism fragmented, as did the Slovene gymnastic society **Sokol**, originally a liberal adjunct, which was coopted into a Yugoslav Sokol by the **Yugoslavism** of the dictatorship after 1929. See also JANUARY 6, 1929, DICTATORSHIP; REALISM; TAAFFE'S IRON RING; UNITED SLOVENIA.

LIBERATION FRONT OF THE SLOVENE NATION (LF) / OSVOBODILNA FRONTA SLOVENSKEGA NARODA (OF)

(1941–1945). Shortly after Germany, **Italy**, and **Hungary** occupied Slovenia in April 1941, the **Communist Party of Slovenia** (CPS) organized an Anti-Imperialist Front (*Protiimperialistična fronta*, PIF), whose aim was to liberate Slovenia with "the help and under the leadership of the Soviet Union." This organization did not extend to the rest of **Yugoslavia**. In addition to the CPS, there were three major co-founding groups: **Christian Socialists**, a group consisting of many members of the liberal **Sokol**, and progressive cultural intelligentsia. Over 10 smaller groups also joined the PIF. After Germany's attack on the Soviet Union (22 June 1941), PIF was renamed the *Osvobodilna fronta slovenskega naroda* (OF), or Liberation Front (LF).

In the summer of 1941, the LF issued a proclamation, "To the Slovene Nation," calling Slovenes to armed resistance against the occupiers. Many people of different political persuasions went "into the woods" and joined military units of the LF, the **Partisans**. The highest organ of the LF was the Supreme Plenum, consisting of representatives of all LF's constituent groups. The co-founding groups constituted the Executive Committee of the Plenum; each group had two or three representatives, among them the Communists **Edvard Kardelj** and **Boris Kidrič**, Christian Socialist **Edvard Kocbek**, Sokol Jože Rus, and the progressive essayist and critic Josip Vidmar. In late 1941 the Supreme Plenum proclaimed itself the only legitimate representative of the Slovene nation. The Plenum also drafted a comprehensive Slovene national program, which was—at least on paper—the most far-reaching program to date. Specifically, the program stressed the right of the Slovene nation to self-determination and upheld the goal of a united, democratic Slovenia.

While the LF included political groups of different ideologies, it was not run democratically. Already by September 1941 it was clear that the CPS had taken control. One goal of the CPS was social revolution, which became evident with the systematic assassinations of important anticommunist Slovenes by the **Security and Intelligence Service** (*Varnostno-obveščevalna služba*, VOS), beginning in the fall of 1941. The LF's political goals, but particularly the methods employed to achieve them, repelled many people and drove many into opposition. Among these were conservatives and the **Catholic Church**. In order to consolidate its position, the CPS required the main co-founding groups of the Liberation Front to sign the

Dolomite Declaration on 1 March 1943. In doing so, the Christian Socialists and the Sokol group renounced their independent political identity and recognized the hegemony of the CPS over the LF. This declaration, which was publicly announced and adopted at the first session of the LF activists at Kočevski Rog in the spring of 1943, also formally established the CPS as the exclusive leader of the LF. *See also* EHRLICH, LAMBERT; HOME GUARD; NATLAČEN, MARKO; VILLAGE GUARD.

The LF, well organized, had control over the **National Liberation Struggle** (*Narodnoosvobodilni boj*, NOB) and joined the **Antifascist Council of National Liberation Struggle of Yugoslavia** (AVNOJ), which laid down the basic principles of new Yugoslavia. In October 1943 the LF's congress at Kočevje, attended by delegates from all of Slovenia, elected a 120-member Slovene National Liberation Committee (*Slovenski narodnoosvobodlni odbor*, SNOO) and Executive Committee of the OF (*Izvršni odbor Osvobodilne Fronte*). SNOO was renamed **Slovene National Liberation Council** (*Slovenski narodnoosvobodilni svet*, SNOS) at its first meeting in Črnomelj in February 1944. SNOO, the first Slovene Communist-controlled parliament, formed its presidency—a provisional government—which issued several resolutions and decrees, pertaining not only to the resistance but also to the establishment of future power in the **Partisan-controlled territories** and for postwar Slovenia.

The Slovene LF became a member of the political organization **People's Front of Yugoslavia** (*Ljudska fronta Jugoslavije*, LPJ) established in Belgrade immediately after World War II. In 1953 the People's Front was renamed the **Socialist Alliance of Working People** (SAWP; *Socialistična zveza delovnega ljudstva*, SZDL).

LIBRARIES. The first public libraries began as reading groups in the early 19th century and were usually organized by **Catholic** clergy. Slovene organizations began establishing libraries after 1848, as did **reading societies** after 1860. By the end of the 1860s there were 58 town and city libraries. Their number continued to grow, as many political organizations, liberal and conservative and their affiliates, such as **Sokol** and **Orel**, organized them for their members. In 1912 there were 450 libraries, holding about 122,000 books. Public libraries in larger cities such as **Ljubljana, Maribor, Kranj,** and **Celje** were especially successful. Before **World War II** there were 855 public libraries, run either by societies, city administrations, or schools. With the establishment of the **University of Ljubljana** in 1919, there was a pressing need for a professional and scientific library, and the former Study Library of Carniola assumed the managing of a university institution. In 1941 that library moved into a new building, and it continued to function after the war as the **National and University Library** (NUK).

After World War II public libraries reorganized, eliminating materials that were deemed ideologically inappropriate, and they continued to operate as local cultural institutions. In the 1960s libraries centralized; larger towns and cities developed into regional library centers, and mobile library units (buses) began serving smaller towns and villages. Each public elementary and secondary school had its own library, as did departments within universities, institutes, and other research and cultural institutions. The 1982 Library Law on organization and development of libraries brought library practices into accord with international library standards. Schools account for the most libraries. A large number of the libraries were linked together through the Slovene Cooperative Online Bibliographic System and Service (COBISS), developed by the Institute for Information Sciences at the **University of Maribor**. In 2003 there were 293 libraries using COBISS, of which there were 67 libraries at universities and other **higher education** institutions, 119 specialized and 43 school libraries. COBISS is also used by all 60 central public libraries, which have more than 200 local branches, operating an additional 170 mobile libraries with more than 600 library stops.

Since 1947 Slovenian librarians have had their own professional organization, the Society of Librarians of Slovenia (*Društvo bibliotekarjev Slovenije*). Library science has been taught at the University of Ljubljana since the 1980s.

LINHART, ANTON TOMAŽ (1756–1795). Anton Linhart, educated in **Vienna**, is considered the most important Slovene figure of the **Enlightenment**. His chief contributions were in the fields of history and drama. Although written in German, *Versuch einer Geschichte von Krain und den übrigen Ländern der Südlichen Slaven Oesterreichs* (An Attempt at a History of Carniola and Other South Slav Lands of Austria), which was published in two parts (1788, 1791), is considered the greatest achievement of the Slovene Enlightenment. For the first time, the history of Slovenes was dealt with professionally and conceived of as the history of a nation. Linhart also provided the Slovenes with their first dramatic text, *Županova Micka* (Mayor's

Maid Micka), which was first performed in 1789. Linhart's most important dramatic work was *Matiček se ženi* (Matiček Is Getting Married), a creative adaptation of Beaumarchais's *The Marriage of Figaro*; although Linhart's play was published in 1790, it was first performed, posthumously, 50 years later. Linhart also directed and produced the first Slovene **theater** performances. *See also* AUSTRO-SLAVISM; ZOIS, ŽIGA.

LIPICA. Located in Primorska near the Slovene–Italian border in the **karst** area of limestone caves, Lipica's population is about 100. It is famed for its horse-breeding center and riding school, which attracts thousands of tourists annually. Here the elegant white horses, dark colored at birth, are trained in sport dressage and for classical and harnessed riding. Established in 1580 by a **Habsburg** archduke, Lipica provided **Vienna** with the noble white horses (Lipizzaners) for its Spanish Riding School. During times of war in the 19th and 20th centuries, Lipica's horses were dispersed to various locations in neighboring countries for protection, so they are now bred outside Slovenia as well.

Since Slovenia declared its **independence**, there has been a running feud between the **Republic of Slovenia** (RS) and its neighbors **Italy** and **Austria** about the horses' official domicile and the right to maintain official breeding records. In late 1998 Italy relinquished its claim to Austria in a bilateral agreement. A European commission in 1999 advised Slovenia to settle its claim with Austria as well. Meanwhile Austria declared its Piber as the official Lipizzaner center. As there was no **European Union** (EU) objection, Slovenia hopes to bring its case regarding the horses to the EU now that it has become a member. Slovenia is very proud of its horses and considers them a part of its cultural heritage. *See also* TOURISM.

LITERATURE. Like many other modern European literatures, Slovene literature began developing during the **Protestant Reformation**. It continued with a deepened interest in the Slovene **language** and national identity during the **Enlightenment** and blossomed during the period of **romanticism**, when Slovene literature reached its first peak in the poetry of **France Prešeren** (1800–1849). Slovene literature of the second half of the 19th century was dominated by **realism** and the post-romantic and realistic writings of **Josip Jurčič**, Janko Kersnik, **Fran Levstik**, and **Ivan Tavčar**. The appearance of many new literary journals, some of which—*Zvon* (*Bell*) and *Dom in* *svet* (*Home and the World*)—were important for literary development and continued to play a role until **World War II**. *See also* LINHART, ANTON TOMAŽ; PRESS BEFORE 1990.

A second peak in Slovene literature was reached during the period of **Moderna** with **Ivan Cankar**. The literature of Moderna freed itself from nationalistic, moralistic, and social functions, very much characteristic of literary works of the 19th century. After **World War I**, **expressionism** and **social realism** were two dominant and coexistent literary movements, which produced freethinking **Catholic** literature on the one hand and leftist literature on the other. Expressionism (1918–1930) manifested itself strongly in the prose of Ivan Pregelj; in the poetry of **Edvard Kocbek, Srečko Kosovel**, and Anton Vodnik; and in the plays of Slavko Grum, while social realism produced rich prose texts: the short stories and voluminous novels by Miško Kranjec, Prežihov Voranc, and Ciril Kosmač. In 1938 Vladimir Bartol published the novel *Alamut*, loosely set in 11th-century Iran. Bartol meditates on the nature of fanaticism and emerging European totalitarianism (fascism, Nazism, and Stalinism) in the 1930s. Although initially not well received in Slovenia, the novel has been translated into several foreign languages and is considered the most internationally successful Slovene novel ever. With the rise of militant Islam in the 1990s, the novel gained new attention and became a European bestseller in the early 2000s.

After the break with the **Cominform** (1948) and abolition of **Agitprop** (1952), socialist realism, which characterized the literature of the 1940s and early 1950s, quickly gave way to other pre–World War II literary movements. In the late 1950s Slovene literature was influenced by new Western literary trends—post-symbolism, existentialism, **modernism**, and **postmodernism**. It also remained close to the Central European tradition, characterized by the dominance of lyric poetry over prose and drama. From that time on, literary pluralism was tolerated in esthetics and style, although not in themes and ideas. There were still many taboos—World War II, postwar events, socialism—for poets, playwrights, and other writers. Slovene literature remained opposed to Communist ideology and politics, but opposition varied from passive and indirect to more aggressive and direct, depending on the rigidity of the regime. As Slovene Communism was not as dogmatic as that of Eastern Europe, literary dissidents were few and underground publishing did not exist. Slovene literature established its artistic autonomy in the mid-1980s.

Lyric poets such as Kajetan Kovič, Ivan Minatti, and others who were considered "soft" opposition, thrived until the 1980s. In the 1960s and 1970s the radicalism of Gregor Strniša and Dane Zajc, who covertly dealt in their poetry with the denial of communist "humanism," influenced many other poets. **Tomaž Šalamun**, also known in the **United States**, is the most prominent modern poet, followed by the younger generation of neo-avant-gardists associated with the group OHO and the journal *Katalog*. The poetry of the younger generation (since the early 1980s), often labeled postmodernist, no longer addresses communist ideology and society; poetic and imaginative, it deals with traditional forms and themes. Aleš Debeljak, Milan Jesih, and Boris A. Novak belong to this group.

Prose writing, beginning in the mid-1960s and continuing through the 1980s, produced many critical novels dealing with the taboos of World War II and repressive socialist society. Pavle Zidar published the first such novel, *Sv. Pavel* (St. Paul), in 1965, followed in the 1970s and early 1980s by Vitomil Zupan, who was imprisoned for several years after the war, and others (Vladimir Kavčič, Jože Snoj, Igor Torkar), with their often autobiographical novels. The literary works of Lojze Kovačič, such as the novel *Prišleki* (Newcomers) published in 1985, have a special place in literature; they deal with communist reality in Slovenia. Kovačič's intimate, historical, and psychological writing resembles that of Marcel Proust and James Joyce. Besides the literature dealing with communist ideology and society, works relating to broader existential motifs and problems have also been published. The most distinctive have been works by Peter Božič, Andrej Hieng, **Drago Jančar**, Lojze Kovačič, Dominik Smole, and Rudi Šeligo.

Playwrights dealing with the communist political system, its challenges, and individual destinies within the system produced numerous plays, such as *Antigona* (1960) by Dominik Smole; *Samorog* (Unicorn, 1967) and *Ljudožerci* (Cannibals, 1972) by Gregor Strniša; *Disident Arnož in njegovi* (Dissident Arnož and His Followers, 1982), *Veliki briljantni valček* (The Great Brilliant Waltz, 1984), and *Dedalus* (Daedalus, 1988) by Drago Jančar. The **theater** of the absurd influenced several Slovene playwrights, such as Dušan Jovanović, and reached its peak in the plays of Milan Jesih. Postmodernist plays have returned to ancient myths devaluating historical traditions, as in Ivo Svetina's play *Šeherezada* (Sheherezade, 1988).

Since the last two decades of the 20th century, Slovene literature has been eclectic in its styles and aesthetic approaches, which is one of the characteristics of postmodernism. A new generation of poets and writers have published their works in literary periodicals such as in *Sodobnost* (*Contemporaneity*), the oldest literary journal in Slovenia, and *Nova revija*. Among them are writers Andrej Blatnik, Alojz Ihan, Brina Švigelj Merat, Maja Novak, and Jani Virk, and poets Meta Kušar and Maja Vidmar.

As often in the nation's history, Slovene writers were among the principal carriers of social and political change in the 1980s, working with a group of sociologists and others to write "The Theses for a Slovene Constitution," better known as "the writers' constitution" (1988). However, after **independence** in 1991, writers and literature lost the dominant role in political and social life that they had had in the past.

Literary works of Slovene **minorities** in **Italy** (**Trieste** region) and **Austria** (Carinthia) are an important part of Slovene literature, as are works by Slovene **emigrants** and their descendants in the Americas (especially Argentina) and Australia. Boris Pahor and Alojz Rebula are the most prominent Slovene writers in Italy, Florijan Lipuš in Austria, and Zorko Simčič in Argentina. *See also* MAY DECLARATION, 1989; SOCIETY OF ST. HERMAGORAS; WRITERS, SOCIETY OF SLOVENE.

LITTLE ENTENTE. The Little Entente was actually a number of formal and informal agreements among **Yugoslavia**, Czechoslovakia, Romania, and France in the 1920s and 1930s. When Yugoslavia was created in 1918, it was in many ways a protégé of the Western Entente powers that redrew the map of Europe at committee sessions held in Paris and its suburbs (Neuilly, Sèvres, St. Germain, Trianon, and Versailles) after **World War I** ended. Since the sovereignty and integrity of Yugoslavia depended on preserving the Paris settlements—Yugoslavia had acquired lands claimed by Central Powers **Austria**, Bulgaria, and **Hungary**—it was logical to ally with other states that also stood by the boundaries of the new Europe. Czechoslovakia, Romania, and Yugoslavia concluded a number of agreements during the course of the 1920s, directed primarily against Hungary and a possible **Habsburg** restoration. France, fearing revived German expansionism, allied with each of these states, politically and through trade agreements. The four states formalized their Little Entente association only in 1933, with a pact signed in Geneva. A Balkan Entente (Greece, Romania, Turkey, and Yugoslavia), concluded in 1934, was aimed at preventing Bulgarian expansion.

By the mid-1930s the revisionists—those who rejected the post-war European boundaries and sought to revise them—were gaining ground. **Italy** and Germany were particularly menacing. Yugoslavia tried to remain independent but was under enormous economic pressures (war recovery, state building, and the depression demanded foreign assistance). Primarily Germany was willing and able to extend aid. This pushed Yugoslavia inevitably into the Axis Powers' camp, in 1941 Yugoslavia's Prince Regent Paul signed the Tripartite Pact. Although the pact was rejected and Paul overthrown, the effects of wavering from Little Entente solidarity in favor of economic and political association with revisionist states boded ill for Yugoslavia and its Little Entente partners. Divided, all became objects of revisionist appetites. When Yugoslavia was invaded in April 1941, Italy, Germany (by then the Third Reich, which included Austria), Hungary, Bulgaria, and even tiny Albania (by then occupied by Italy) cooperated in dismembering the country. Slovenia completely disappeared in the process. *See also* KARADJORDJEVIĆ.

LJUBLJANA. The capital of the independent **Republic of Slovenia** (RS) since 26 June 1991, Ljubljana (Laibach in German, and Lubiana in Italian) has long been a cultural, economic, and administrative center for Slovenes. The city has developed at the juncture of the **Alps** and the Dinaric mountain range, which forms a natural tectonic passage, called the Ljubljana Gap, a crossroads of important routes connecting northeast Europe to the Adriatic and west Europe to the Balkans. Ljubljana is situated at the center of the RS in the southern part of the Ljubljana basin, at 298 meters above sea level, astride the Ljubljanica River and reaching to the Sava River in the north. Its climate is continental. Pollution, annual precipitation of 1,350 millimeters (53.1 inches), and temperature inversion are the major reasons for the city's most distinctive weather feature: 120 foggy days per year. **Medieval** Ljubljana, the predecessor of the modern city, grew around a 78-meter-high hill topped by a **castle**; it expanded first across the Ljubljanica River northward into a fertile plain, and later southward when the Gruber canal (1780) and regulation of the Ljubljanica alleviated river flooding and dried the marshes.

Having grown and changed over the years, the city, an urban municipality since 1994, has more than 250,000 inhabitants and extends over 275 square kilometers. As an *občina* (municipality), Ljubljana is run by elected officials (a mayor and a city council) and is divided into

17 wards, or **local communities** (*četrtna skupnost*), which operate in an advisory role. As the capital, Ljubljana is the seat of most national political institutions: the parliament, the President's Office, the Constitutional and Supreme Courts, various independent public institutions such as the **human rights ombudsman**, the Peace Institute, and over 30 foreign embassies. Ljubljana is also the regional center of the most developed and richest Central Slovenia **region**, encompassing 25 municipalities. With more than 488,000 inhabitants, the region has the highest population density (192 inhabitants per square kilometer) in the RS (the national average is 98). Other measures of the living standard, such as employment, wages, **education**, and **health** indicators, are much higher than the national average. In 2004 the region (with Ljubljana) had the highest average wage: 13 percent higher than the next most developed region, Primorska, and 30 percent higher than the poorest region, Pomurje. Moreover, 14 percent of inhabitants of the Central Slovenia region had a university education (11 percent in Primorska, 5 percent in Pomurje), and unemployment stood at 8 percent (6 percent in Primorska, 17 percent in Pomurje; the national average was 10 percent).

Industrialization of Ljubljana, begun in the latter half of the 19th century and continued intensively through the 1970s, developing various industries (metal, chemical, food processing). Located at the outskirts of the city, industrial zones were built in Moste (east), along the railway in Šiška (north), Rudnik (south), and Vič (west). **Denationalization** and **privatization** after 1990 affected many existing **manufacturers**, which have either restructured successfully or closed down. After **World War II** Litostroj, a manufacturer of water turbines and other heavy industrial equipment that employed several thousand, restructured and organized successfully as holding Litostroj F. I. (Ferrous Industries), with subsidiaries in Egypt and Canada. Iskra, maker of electrical and telephone equipment, has organized anew. It encompasses 10 production companies and three service providers, and the food processing concern Kolinska merged with Droga Portorož. Although manufacturing and the food processing industry with 23,931 workers (12 percent of those employed in December 2005, but down from 40 percent in the late 1980s) are still important in the city's **economy**, its structure has changed in favor of **services**, which accounted for 72 percent of the employed. Trade, with 30,189 and real estate services, with 27,217 employed, accounted for 42 percent of all persons in services. Since 1990s new shopping centers have been built; the largest is the BTC (Business and Technological Center) in Nove Jarše (northeast of Ljubljana). Retail business, with foreign retailers entering the market in the early 1990s, became highly competitive. In existence since 1953 and with its headquarters in Ljubljana, Mercator d.d., which restructured and was privatized in the mid-1990s, bought out many small retailers and has grown into the largest retail business in Slovenia. It has also successfully competed with foreign retailers Spar (Austrian) and Leclerc (French) and a more recent domestic retailer Tuš of **Celje**, which came to Ljubljana in 1998. **Banking** and financial services are also gaining importance, as is **tourism**. An attractive modern city with an old core and many important historical and cultural monuments, Ljubljana was visited in 2004 by 264,660 tourists.

Ljubljana has been a lively cultural city dominated by the **University of Ljubljana**, which in 2005 had 23 specialized schools (faculties) and three art academies, with a total enrollment of 57,064 students. The city has numerous cultural institutions: the **Slovenian Academy of Sciences and Arts** (SAZU); major **arts** centers including the **National Gallery**, the **Museum of Modern Art**, and the International Graphic Center, as well as assorted **museums** (Architecture, City, Ethnographic, Geography, National, Natural History, School, Slovene Theater and Film); three philharmonic orchestras as well as many instrumental, small chamber, and vocal groups; the **Cankar Cultural Center**; Festival Ljubljana; several theaters and an opera house; and many **libraries**, including the **National and University Library**. Ljubljana has been known for its international festivals, such as the Summer Festival, the International Jazz Festival, the International Festival of Contemporary Arts–City of Women, and the Festival of Gay and Lesbian Culture. The **media** are strongly represented in Ljubljana. Besides **Radio and Television Slovenia**, there are other national and local radio and TV stations, several publishing houses, which offer three daily newspapers, and many weekly, biweekly, and monthly publications. Various publications and short radio and TV programs are also available in English.

A lake-dwelling culture (c. 2000 BC) in the Ljubljana marshes (drained in the late 18th century) is the earliest known settlement in the area. The first permanent settlers (urnfield culture) date from the Bronze Age around 1000 BC, but a Roman settlement, Emona, is Ljubljana's historical predecessor, mentioned in the first century AD. It was destroyed by various incursions, including by Slavs in the sixth century. Rich archeological sites attest to its existence, and archeological artifacts can be seen in the City Museum and two open-air museums: an early Christian center and foundations of a Roman house. Still standing are the remains of the Roman south city wall. Today's city has developed from the medieval town first mentioned in 1144 as Laybach. Under a castle on a hill, the city grew around the Old Market (*Stari trg*) and the New Market (*Novi trg*), and evolved into the provincial capital of the Duchy of Carniola. City rights were granted to it by the Spanheims in the 13th century. The Ljubljana castle, mostly renovated, with a great virtual museum of the city and beautiful views of the city and vicinity, is one of the most visited attractions in Ljubljana. Between 1335 and 1918 Ljubljana was under **Habsburg** rule, except during the French occupation (1809–1813). In the Middle Ages, as the capital of Carniola, Ljubljana prospered.

The Ljubljana **Catholic** diocese was established in 1461 and ever since has played an important role in shaping the city and the province. In the 16th century Ljubljana was at the center of the short-lived **Protestant Reformation**. Ljubljana prospered in the 17th and 18th centuries and participated in the cultural life of developed European cities. The **Jesuits** revitalized the school system and began organizing **higher education**. **Societies** of intellectuals were established, such as **Academia Operosorum**, which had a leading role in promoting **baroque** art and learning. Ljubljana's Gothic city center was adapted to baroque principles, and many new religious and lay buildings were built.

Baroque influences from the south and the north, creating a distinct new style—the Ljubljana baroque—left the city with many outstanding historical and art monuments: the baroque Cathedral of St. Nicholas, which houses many art treasures (baroque as well as later periods); the Franciscan Church of the Annunciation; the renovated Town Hall with Francesco Robba's *Fountain of the Three Rivers* in the town square; the Gruber palace and other residences of nobility in the city and its suburbs. Ljubljana's most beautiful baroque church is the Palladian-style Ursuline Church of the Holy Trinity, which has several superb baroque altars. In the second half of the 18th century, Ljubljana was affected by the reforms of **Maria Theresa** and her son **Joseph II**, who greatly weakened Ljubljana's administrative autonomy. Physiocrats of the time promoted economic and also cultural reforms. During the **Enlightenment** and **Romantic** periods, Ljubljana became a center for Slovene linguistic studies and the Slovene national awakening. Ljubljana also served as the capital of Napoleon's **Illyrian Provinces**

(1809–1813). The 1821 international Congress of Ljubljana briefly put the city on the European political map. The **Habsburg Restoration** provincialized Ljubljana, which for most of the 19th century remained the German administrative town Laibach. In spite of the Slovene national awakening of the 19th century, Ljubljana was a city under Austrian rule, and German remained the official language, even in high schools, throughout the 19th century. In 1910, 40 percent of its population was still German.

Ljubljana became a Slovene city only in the 20th century with the help of the emerging Slovene middle class, which began gaining political power in the 1880s. After 1882 all Ljubljana mayors were Slovenes. A devastating earthquake in 1895 was a turning point in Ljubljana's development. Badly damaged, the city was rebuilt and took on a greater Slovene character with help from **Vienna**. In Ljubljana's transformation, Mayor **Ivan Hribar** and the architects **Jože Plečnik** and **Maks Fabiani** played a decisive role. Ljubljana's population in 1910 was 41,727, about half Slovene. After 1918, in the new **Kingdom of Serbs, Croats, and Slovenes**, Ljubljana was at first the administrative center of only a part of the Slovenes of that state, but after the 1929 restructuring of **Yugoslavia**, it became the seat of the newly established **Drava** *banovina*, encompassing all of Yugoslavia's Slovenes. In interwar Yugoslavia, Ljubljana acquired important cultural institutions, among them the University of Ljubljana (1919) and the Slovenian Academy of Sciences and Arts (1938).

During **World War II** Ljubljana was first occupied by **Italy** and in 1943 by Germany. Soon after the Italian occupation, a barbed-wire fence was erected around the city to control movements in and out of the city. After the war, the path of the fence was turned into a memorial walkway around the city. In 1945 Ljubljana became the capital of the **People's Republic of Slovenia** (LRS), and later of the Socialist Republic of Slovenia (SRS), one of the six federated republics of socialist Yugoslavia. In 1991 Slovenes proclaimed their **independence** and Ljubljana became the capital of the Republic of Slovenia (RS).

Ljubljana is a charming capital, and there are many good restaurants and hotels in the city and its vicinity. Ljubljana's location is an ideal departure point for wonderful one-day outings to interesting natural settings, including the Alps; the karst area with its many caves, among which **Postojna** cave is the largest; and **spas** with thermal springs. Tourists are also drawn to historical destinations such as **Stična** and **Piran**; recreation areas for horseback riding, golf, and other activities; or sites in neighboring countries such as Italy (Venice) and Austria (Salzburg and Vienna).

LJUBLJANA FOUR TRIAL. The trial of the Ljubljana Four, also known as the *Mladina* trial, was a political show trial that took place in **Ljubljana** in July 1988. Sergeant Major Ivan Borštner of the **Yugoslav People's Army** (JNA), Janez Janša, David Tasič, and Franci Zavrl—the latter two were editors at *Mladina*—made up "the four" who were arrested and charged with betraying military secrets. They were tried in a military court (although three of the four were civilians) conducted in Serbo-Croatian (although it was a foreign language in Slovenia) and according to proceedings that were unconstitutional. The accused were all sentenced to prison terms, although only Borštner and Janša were actually imprisoned. An appeal on behalf of the four in September to the federal Supreme Court in **Belgrade** was rejected, causing Franc Šetinc, a Slovene member of the presidency of the Central Committee (CC) of the League of Communists of Yugoslavia (LCY; formerly the **Communist Party of Yugoslavia**), to resign in protest.

The trial and events that preceded it united Slovene society as it had never been before. It was probably the turning point in relations between Ljubljana and Belgrade. Slovenes rallied behind a newly formed **Committee for the Protection of Human Rights** (CPHR), headed by **Igor Bavčar** and endorsed by liberal intellectuals, the **press**, university circles, and the **Catholic Church**. The CPHR organized protests against the illegal trial (35,000 demonstrated in Ljubljana on one occasion) and gathered 100,000 Slovene signatures in support of rights for the accused. The army and federal authorities' refusal to yield only radicalized the Slovenes, who formed political groupings that would soon become official parties. The military "secrets," it was subsequently revealed, were details of unconstitutional operations that the army was planning against democratic forces in Slovenia.

LOCAL COMMUNITY. The local community (*krajevna skupnost*) was a territorial administrative subunit of the ***občina***. With the **Constitution of 1974**, local communities became obligatory institutions. In 1979 there were 1,040 local communities, averaging 19 square kilometers and 1,743 residents. While the establishment and activity of local communities was regulated by *občina* bylaws, their powers were defined by the republic's constitution. Local communities dealt with issues of direct concern to their residents as well as to local businesses and organizations. The residents of a local community decided on matters such as communal services, consumer protection, **education**, housing, **environmental** protection, social welfare, and territorial defense. These matters were decided at general meetings, by referendums, or by various elected subsidiary bodies of a community. Each local community had an assembly, headed by an executive council with several committees. Prior to the political reorganization of 1990, each community, jointly with its local **Socialist Alliance of Working People** (SAWP) organization was responsible for the election of delegates to *občina* assemblies and self-managing communities of interest. *See also* CONTRACTUAL SOCIALISM; WORKERS' SELF-MANAGEMENT.

By 1994 the government was restructured, and the *občina* (municipality) became the basic local community unit. If citizens chose, they might form smaller local governance units, or wards, called either *krajevna skupnost* or *območna četrt*. **Ljubljana**, for example, is divided into 17 wards (*območne četrti*). Although functions and competencies of these units differ from municipality to municipality, they are not legal or administrative entities but mostly serve as advisory bodies of citizens to their elected representatives. *See also* REGIONS OF SLOVENIA.

LONDON AGREEMENT. After long negotiations, the London Agreement of 25 October 1954, signed by **Italy**, **Yugoslavia**, the United Kingdom, and the **United States**, finally resolved the post–**World War II** territorial boundaries between Italy and Yugoslavia. In the agreement, the Free Territory of **Trieste** (STO) was divided between Italy and Yugoslavia. The Anglo-American forces left Zone A, where Italy established its civilian administration, while Yugoslavia acquired Zone B. A special statute in the agreement assured the protection of the national **minorities** in both states. It was the first official document protecting the Slovene minority in Italy. While the Yugoslav parliament ratified the London Agreement, the Italian parliament did not. The situation was not resolved until the **Osimo Treaty** of 1975. *See also* RAPALLO, TREATY OF; TRIESTE QUESTION.

– M –

MAGYARIZATION. *See* MINORITIES, SLOVENES IN HUNGARY.

MAHNIČ, ANTON (1850–1920). Anton Mahnič, who held a doctorate in theology from **Vienna**, made his reputation as a writer, critic, and controversial editor in 1888–1896 of *Rimski katolik* (*Roman Catholic*). He derived his philosophy from St. Augustine and St. Thomas Aquinas, often using it in a fundamentalist way to criticize Slovene writers, whose works, many of them now considered the nation's literary classics, did not stand up to **Catholic** principles. Mahnič was appointed bishop of Krk in 1896. Politically, he was the Slovenes' leading ultramontanist, demanding that all public life be tested by religious principles and loyalty to Rome. The first Slovene Catholic congress (1892) adopted Mahnič's principles. Nationalism and individual rights as enunciated by the French Revolution were condemned; Catholicism as a fundamental principle of Slovene life was espoused. Mahnič generated a large following, particularly among **Clericals (Slovene People's Party)**, and is considered responsible for the sharp ideological division between clericals and freethinkers (liberals) in Slovene cultural and political life that developed in the 1890s. Its polarizing effects continue to be felt even today. *See also* PRESS BEFORE 1914.

MAISTER, RUDOLF (VOJANOV) (1872–1934). Born in **Kamnik**, Rudolf Maister was the rare Slovene who chose a military career. He was also a poet. At age 18 in 1892, he enrolled in a two-year national guard training program in **Vienna** and as a cadet trainee served in various ethnic Slovene areas, including **Klagenfurt**/Celovec, where he also engaged in local cultural activities. In 1908 he was transferred to Galicia, where he headed a military school. When **World War I** began, Maister was in **Maribor** in southern (Slovene) Styria, where in 1917 he was the commanding officer of his province's unit. As such he established ties to the Slovene political leadership, and as the war was ending he worked with the National Council as a representative from Styria. *See also* SLOVENES, CROATS, AND SERBS, NATIONAL COUNCIL OF.

With Austria-Hungary's demise imminent in late October 1918, the Maribor town council, heavily German in its composition, voted to join a German **Austria**. On 1 November 1918 Maister, sensing that the Slovene parts of Styria would be absorbed into an Austrian state to the north, took over command of Maribor and the southern Styrian region. Taking the initiative, he organized the Slovenes under his command, along with Slovenes returning from the eastern front, into a voluntary force that would secure southern Styria for Slovenia. His "Slovene" **army**, comprising 400 soldiers and 200 officers, disarmed German forces by 23 November and drove them from the area. Southern Styria came fully under Maister's control, and when the final postwar treaties and settlements were completed, the territory Maister had fought for became part of the **Kingdom of Serbs, Croats, and Slovenes**.

Maister attempted to do the same for southern Carinthia. He participated with four other Yugoslav units that staged successful offensives in that area. Maister's military police controlled the territory that was designated Zone A in preparation for the **Carinthian plebiscite** (20 October 1920). He hoped to influence the referendum by rallying Slovene Carinthians for the Yugoslav state to the south, but it was a requirement of the plebiscite commission that all military police leave the area. Maister left, returned to Maribor, and southern Carinthia went to Austria.

Maister, who had been made a Yugoslav army general, was retired from military service in 1923. He lived in Maribor, wrote journal articles, memoirs, and poetry, and was active in Slovene national organizations that resisted Germanizing pressures in that Styrian city. His home town, Kamnik, erected a statue to him in 1987, as did the city of Maribor. His accomplishments, however, have been fully recognized only since Slovenia's **independence** (1991). Crediting Maister with the vision of a **United Slovenia**, politicians in the 1990s commended him for securing present-day Slovenia's northeastern boundary. In the late-1990s two statues were erected to him in **Ljubljana**: One stands opposite the railway station; one in front of Slovenia's very first Ministry of Defense honors him as the very first Slovene military hero. In 2005, 23 November was named a national **holiday** in honor of Rudolf Maister.

MANUFACTURING. Industrial manufacturing has been an important segment of Slovenia's economy, especially since **World War II**. In the decade 1995–2004, industry—**energy** generation, construction, **mining**, and manufacturing—accounted on average for one-third of GDP, with manufacturing alone accounting for an average of 24 percent. In addition to traditional manufacturing branches (ferrous metallurgy, footwear, furniture, paper, and **textiles**), newer branches of manufacturing (chemical and pharmaceutical products, household appliances and electronics, machinery and mechanical appliances, and motor vehicles and transport equipment) developed after World War II. Besides providing the second largest share of GDP (the **service**

industry was first), manufacturers have been the leading Slovene exporters. Some companies export almost their entire production; Revoz, the largest industrial facility in Slovenia, exported 95 percent of its motor vehicles to Western Europe in 2004. In addition to Revoz, the manufacturing sectors that have expanded since 1995 have been electrical appliances (Gorenje), machinery, steel, and tools (Slovenska Industrija Jekla, Impol, Litostroj), and pharmaceuticals (Lek, Krka). Industrial production had fallen 24 percent in the period 1990–1992. The greatest decline was registered in the production of capital goods, followed by consumer and intermediate goods. In the early 1990s political and economic factors demanded industrial restructuring, which resulted in high unemployment (an average of 14 percent from 1992 to 1998), many bankruptcies, and changes in enterprise ownership. Restructuring proceeded slowly, in part due to the nature of **privatization** and to lack of capital. For several companies that were already competitive in Western markets, there was not an immediate need to privatize. Intensive privatization and restructuring began only after 1998 as a part of Slovenia's **European Union** (EU) accession strategy. Due to restructuring and new investments, manufacturing's share of GDP increased nearly 2 percentage points, from 23.6 percent in 1999 to 25.3 percent in 2004.

Traditional manufacturing industries in the Slovene lands had begun developing in the 19th century. Although industrialization was accelerated by the construction of the **Vienna–Ljubljana–Trieste** railway, completed in 1857, Slovene **regions** developed more slowly than the German and Czech areas of Austria. Manufacturing (clothing, ironworks, smelting, **leather** goods, wood products—construction material, furniture, and paper—and textiles) and mining were major industries of the late 19th century, all dominated by Austrian, German, and French capital. After 1918 in the Yugoslav state, Slovene industry developed rapidly. Industrial development was speeded by new competitive markets, but also by electrification. The depression in the late 1920s affected especially mining and wood production, but manufacturing, especially textiles, continued to develop in the 1930s. Before World War II, with almost 1,000 industrial enterprises and over 40 percent of the population employed in industry, Slovenia was considered a semi-industrialized region in a predominantly agricultural **Yugoslavia**.

After World War II and the establishment of a Communist regime, Slovenia industrialized quickly, but the structure of manufacturing also changed because its branches (capital goods, intermediate goods, and consumer goods) grew at disproportional rates. During the First **Five-Year Plan** (1947–1952), chemical, energy, and metallurgical manufacturing were given highest priority. Existing prewar enterprises were expanded and organized anew, and many new ones were founded. In Ljubljana the pharmaceutical company Lek was established in 1946, and the heavy machinery factory Litostroj was built in 1947, taking advantage of a long tradition of iron production in the region. Making water turbines, pumps, and auxiliary parts, Litostroj developed into a large capital goods manufacturer, which restructured in the late 1990s with government assistance and remains a successful manufacturer of turbines today. After 1952, production of consumer goods (automobiles, clothing, furniture, household appliances, and processed food) was emphasized. Revoz, the only car-producing facility in Slovenia, and Krka, the second pharmaceutical company, were founded in **Novo Mesto** in 1954. **Maribor**, with various industries such as TAM (transport vehicles), Zlatorog (chemicals), and Merinka (textiles), became one of Slovenia's largest industrial centers.

Industrial output grew rapidly until the early 1980s, when it experienced a slowdown. Production of domestic raw materials lagged, and imports were needed for consumer goods manufacturing. Rapid industrial growth had been fueled by large investments (mainly foreign loans) and extensive use of manpower. Consequently, production costs were high, leaving manufacturers noncompetitive in world markets. Although Slovene manufacturing was more efficient than elsewhere in Yugoslavia, it had its own serious problems, including heavy dependency on imported raw materials, and an increasingly obsolete industrial base. Until the 1980s traditional textile, footwear, and wood processing were the basic pillars of Slovenian manufacturing and employed approximately 40 percent of Slovenia's workforce. In the early 1990s, with the loss of markets in the former Yugoslavia and declining exports to Western Europe, it was clear that these industries, as well as the food processing industry, were overextended and no longer competitive internationally. *See also* ECONOMY, 1945–1990; ECONOMY SINCE 1991; INTERNATIONAL TRADE AND FINANCIAL TRANSACTIONS.

MARIA THERESA (1717–1780, r. 1740–1780). The **Habsburg** Hereditary Lands and other territories such as Bohemia and **Hungary**, which were acquired later, came to be ruled by Maria Theresa in 1740. Her father, Charles VI, anticipating problems with a female succession, had secured the consent of the various lands of his empire, but Maria Theresa's succession was immediately challenged by acquisitive neighbors (Prussia, Bavaria, Saxony, and France). The war that ensued lasted eight years, displacing the Habsburgs temporarily from the throne of the **Holy Roman Empire** and raising grave questions about the ability of the dynasty to survive in a Europe of emerging modern states. To meet the military challenge, army recruitment and financing had to be modernized (depending on voluntary contributions of troops and funds from individual land estates was feudal, cumbersome, and unreliable). The state had to be unified and centralized, the method for which was devised and implemented by the end of the 1740s. With the exception of the Kingdom of Hungary, the Habsburg feudal domain was reorganized into a centralized state, characterized by a common administration, with military recruitment, justice, and tax collecting uniform throughout.

A modern defense system, above all, required taxable wealth. Commercial activity was promoted, and the port of **Trieste** was expanded. But the economic heads looked primarily to **agriculture** for solutions. The Physiocratic thinking of the time taught that a prosperous, tax-paying peasantry was all-important, for it was land that produced the wealth of nations. For that reason the peasant and serf needed to be free (or at least freer) and literate. Decrees were therefore issued changing the peasants' legal status, allowing them personal freedoms and limiting their work obligation, while laws were passed instituting primary schooling. A peasant who could read agricultural manuals was a natural resource, able to cultivate rationally the new crops such as potatoes, legumes, and clover, which the regime was promoting. So it was that the Slovenes, the bulk of whom were peasants, found their lives transformed by the state. *See also* EDUCATION, ELEMENTARY.

The reforms begun under Maria Theresa's enlightened absolutist reign would be built upon by her son, co-ruler, and successor **Joseph II**. They were successful at least in that the Habsburg state withstood major wars virtually intact. In other respects, the reforms unintentionally sowed seeds of future, mostly nationalistic, problems. Centralization was resisted at first by the feudal estates, but later also by non-Germans who favored federalism for national communities. Germanization, which Maria Theresa introduced for pragmatic reasons (replacing Latin with German in administration and education), soon provoked resistance from emerging national groups who preferred to use their own language. *See also* ENLIGHTENMENT.

MARIBOR. The **Republic of Slovenia**'s (RS) second largest city and regional capital, Maribor has a population of 93,850; nearly 20,000 more live in the Maribor **region**. Maribor straddles the Drava River in Štajerska where the central **Alps** meet the Pannonian plain. Just below the center of Maribor, the Drava was dammed (Melje Dam, 1968) to control late spring flooding; the dam's hydroelectric station produces **energy** for the area. International highway and rail networks pass through this northeastern Slovene center, linking it with **Celje**, **Ljubljana**, Zagreb, and Graz, **Austria** (in Upper Styria). Millions travel through Maribor annually, by train, bus, or private automobile. It is an important commercial and industrial city, which produces automotive products, clothing, electronics (Elektro Maribor), metal goods (Mariborska Livarna), electric power (Dravska Elekrarna), processed foods, and **textiles** (Svila). Industry, which employs half the city's workers, expanded rapidly, as did the city's size in the post-1945 period. (Maribor, which was 47 percent destroyed by Allied bombing in the last year of the war, was rebuilt, becoming a very proletarian city after 1950.) Since 1991 when Slovenia established its **independence**, however, Maribor has experienced some economic decline. Factories like TAM (automobiles and motorcycles) failed, unemployment rose substantially, and like many older industrial cities in Europe, it was badly in need of major **environmental** cleanup. Slovenia's accession to the **European Union** (EU) could challenge Maribor's **economy** further. Maribor will no longer be a border town, receiving income from perks such as duty-free shops. The city continues to benefit economically from being near the Pohorje **winter sports** region (begun in the late 1950s); since 1964 it has been the venue for Europe's annual international women's ski events. The wine trade is also important for Maribor in the heart of Štajerska, which is a prime wine-producing region. *See also* VITICULTURE.

Among Maribor's new enterprises is **education**. The **University of Maribor**, Slovenia's second institution of higher learning, opened in 1975. It has branches in Celje and **Kranj**, and since 1990 has become the European center for ethnic and regional studies. The university also has a new **library**, the first computerized one in the RS. Like other major Slovene urban centers, Maribor also has publishing houses (e.g., Založba Obzorja), daily (*Večer*) and weekly newspapers, and radio (Radio Maribor since 1945) and television stations. *See also* MEDIA.

Maribor's history is characteristically Central European. Archeological evidence confirms small settlements in the late Bronze Age, late Iron Age, and the Roman period, but written records of a town (Marchpurch, later Marburg) on this site date only from the 12th century. Achieving town status (1254) is associated with the Spanheim lord who established his fiefdom's seat (later torn down) on the hill (Piramida) above the city. In the 13th and 14th centuries walls were built (some of which, including three towers, survive), and the settlement was populated with craftspeople (invited by the lord) and merchants, some of whom were Jewish. The latter lived in a ghetto, worshipped in a synagogue (13th century), and established commercial ties with Dubrovnik, Milan, and Prague. After **Jews** were expelled by the **Habsburgs** in 1497, the town suffered economic decline. Hungarian and **Turkish wars**, religious wars (local Protestant nobles against **Catholic** Habsburgs), frequent fires, and, in the 17th century, recurrent plague contributed to the town's troubles. *See also* MEDIEVAL TOWNS AND COMMERCE.

After the mid-1700s the state-building reforms of **Maria Theresa** and **Joseph II** brought new economic life, including commerce with **Trieste** and **Vienna**, which continued into the 19th century. Rail **transport** began in 1846, as did major urban development, financed largely by German capital. Slovene cultural and political life developed after the mid-19th century, in the face of formidable German liberal assimilation pressures. Among institutions that strengthened the Slovene national position were the seat of the Lavantine diocese (moved to Maribor in 1859 under Bishop **Anton Martin Slomšek**), **reading societies**, recreational clubs (singing, theater), gymnastic societies (**Sokol, Orel**), savings and loan associations (1882), Slovene **political parties** and societies, and various newspapers in the Slovene **language**. After **World War I**, although Maribor became a part of the **Kingdom of Yugoslavia**, the ethnic German element (22 percent in 1921) remained influential and economically powerful. (As a counterweight to the Germans, Yugoslavia's policy was to settle Primorska Slovenes in Maribor; these were largely deported by the Germans in 1941.) In the 1930s Maribor's Germans, most of whom were Protestant, leaned toward Nazism and pushed for the reunification of Slovene Štajerska with Austrian Styria. This was accomplished in 1941, which made Štajerska, and with it Maribor, a part of the Third Reich. Many Mariborans were arrested, and nearly 4,500 were deported to **Croatia** and Germany, but mostly to Serbia. Maribor's architecture is a patchwork beginning with Romanesque, late Gothic, and 18th-century **baroque** structures that survived **World War II** destruction. Now there are new bridges over the Drava and a **postmodern** bus station. Comprehensive historic preservation efforts are underway to renovate older structures while providing new infrastructure. Most new development, like Europark with its 63 shops and restaurants, which opened in fall 2000, is taking place in the suburbs.

MARKET SOCIALISM (1953–1974). Market socialism has two distinct periods: administrative market socialism (1953–1963) and market socialism (1963–1974). Although the first market elements were evident in the **economy** already in 1950, it was only after 1952 that the state systematically began reducing administrative constraints by giving enterprises a more independent role in decision-making. With the abolition of state property under the concept of **social property**, and the adoption of the **Constitutional Law of 1953**, **workers' self-management** was extended to the public **services** domain (**education**, culture, **health** and social services), while **workers' councils** in enterprises acquired more decision-making power. In 1955 the newly organized *občinas* took over the economic functions that until then had been performed by the federal **government**. Despite these changes, all major economic decisions (e.g., those pertaining to income distribution and investment) were still made by the federal government in **Belgrade**, while enterprises were free to decide what to produce and how to organize the production process. In the late 1950s the Second **Five-Year Plan** for Economic Development of Yugoslavia (1957–1961) provided primary direction for economic activities. Investments were channeled more toward light industry, consumer goods, **agriculture**, and social services.

While the rate of economic growth was high for all **Yugoslavia**, there were major differences among the republics. Between 1953 and 1964, for example, the growth rate of national income was 8 percent for Yugoslavia, while for Slovenia it was 15 percent. Similarly, in 1958 when Yugoslavia's annual national income per capita was $220, Slovenia's was $400. A sharp decline in productivity in early 1960 was followed by economic reforms in 1961 and 1965, which decentralized the **banking** system, changed federal investment policies, and allowed market forces to play a greater role in the economy.

The rate of economic growth and productivity declined, yet personal income sharply increased. Workers were using self-management powers to increase their earnings rather than to invest in their enterprises. Transition toward market socialism was a gradual process, but with the adoption of the **Constitution of 1963** enough administrative constraints on the economy were removed to put the system in place. The economic reforms of 1965, a watershed in Yugoslav economic development, allowed more market forces to shape the economy and, consequently, also society. Among economic reforms of the late 1960s were monetary policies to curb inflation and devalue the *dinar*, measures for stimulating exports and decreasing imports, attempts to match domestic prices with those in the world market, and abolition of aid to economically unprofitable projects. The reforms and the adoption of the market system failed to live up to expectations: Growth in the period 1965–1970 was smaller than anticipated; inefficient use of capital and labor, as well as foreign trade problems, continued. Inflation continued to increase. Market mechanisms were blamed for increasing inequalities among the **regions** and among individuals and enterprises within a region, and for the concentration of economic power in financial institutions and in the hands of a managerial elite, which went against principles of socialism. Instead of heeding expert professional advice on economic problems, the League of Communists of Yugoslavia (LCY; formerly the **Communist Party of Yugoslavia**), whose power was waning, halted economic and political **liberalization** in the name of workers' self-management and socialism. The LCY also suppressed nationalistic tendencies and introduced new social and economic reforms, which ended the period of market socialism. *See also* CONSTITUTION OF 1974; CONTRACTUAL SOCIALISM.

MARXISM, SLOVENE. Established when Slovenes lived in the Austro-Hungarian Empire, Slovene Marxism is more than a century old. By the 1890s Slovene Marxists (**Socialists**) had organized a political party and were vigorously addressing nationality issues as well as the more ideologically appropriate economic and political ones. Through **World War I**, although the views of party members differed, Slovene Marxists remained loosely associated within the Yugoslav Social Democratic Party (*Jugoslovanska socialdemokratska stranka*, JSDS); party meetings and publications, however, revealed a considerable spectrum of philosophical differences. Besides orthodox Marxism, Bernsteinism (Revision) was especially strong, as it was in the Austrian party with which the Slovene Marxists were affiliated. Otherwise, prewar Slovene Marxism was generally Austro-Marxist.

After World War I the Marxists divided into two groups: Social Democrats, and Communists (Bolsheviks). Although the **Communist Party of Yugoslavia** (CPY) was outlawed in 1921, the Communists, influenced largely by Leninism and the USSR, gained strength in the interwar years. Within Slovene Marxism at the time there were still some Western Marxist influences evident in the journals *Književnost* (*Literature*) and *Sodobnost* (*Modernity*). The growth of fascism in Europe increasingly pushed Marxists toward the more radical communist positions. *See also* PRESS BEFORE 1990.

When the Slovene Communists came to power after **World War II**, Stalinism was dominant, and they applied it to Slovenia. By the end of the 1940s, however, the Slovene Marxist **Edvard Kardelj** was busily writing ideological tracts supporting **Yugoslavia**'s (and Slovenia's) unique socialist institutions (e.g., **workers' self-management**). Kardelj would also write important theoretical "Marxist" pieces on the national question and on **nonalignment**, which became constituent components of Yugoslav socialism. Ideologically justified by Yugoslav Marxist theoreticians, it is also known as **Titoism**.

Besides official Marxism, new trends in post–World War II Marxist thought influenced the Slovene Marxists (both within and outside the party). By the early 1960s Marx's early humanist writings (1840s) were being studied, as were the works of Western Marxist existentialists. Humanist Marxism of the Praxis circle in Zagreb (late 1960s, early 1970s) and of the Czechs (1968) influenced and coincided with the rise of a new left student movement, associated with the paper *Tribuna*. After the 1970s Slovene Marxists became involved in debates then in the forefront of European literary criticism: first with the structuralists, and then with adherents of deconstructionism. In the 1980s some Slovene Marxists promoted the creation of a civil society and helped to organize new social movements. In this way they helped prepare the way for later transformations in Slovene society.

MASARYKITES. Slovene university students who studied in Prague before **World War I** generally came under the influence of Thomas G. Masaryk, later president of Czechoslovakia. The popular philosophy professor who taught at the Czech university attracted those who were secular-minded but found the liberalism of the time wanting. **Clericalism** usually had little appeal for them, and Marxist socialism was rejected because of its materialism. Masaryk focused their attention on social issues, which they then wrote about in *Naši zapiski* (*Our Notes*), a journal that Slovene Masarykites began publishing at home after 1902. Many Masarykites eventually joined the **Socialists**, but only after Revision (Bernsteinism) had made inroads into European Marxism. Eduard Bernstein's assertion that social democracy might evolve, rather than result, from violent revolution and his rejection of strict historical materialism allowed the Masarykites to commit politically to the Yugoslav Social Democratic Party (JSDS). In 1909, when the Socialists issued the Tivoli Resolution, calling for the cultural amalgamation of all Yugoslavs, the Masarykites disapproved. For them the Yugoslav question was economic and political only. Culturally, they believed, nations needed to be autonomous, and they spoke and wrote eloquently on the need for Slovene **language** and cultural individuality. The best-known Masarykites were Anton Dermota (1876–1914), Anton Kristan (1881–1930), and Dragotin Lončar (1876–1954).

MASSACRES, POST–WORLD WAR II (1945). In the last few days of **World War II**, thousands of members of the **Home Guard** and their families and supporters retreated to Carinthia, **Austria**, and surrendered to British forces. Others went to **Italy**. Besides the Slovene Home Guard, a few thousand Serbian **Chetniks** and around 18,000 Croatian Ustashi and regular army members also gathered in Carinthia. The British returned most of them to **Yugoslavia**. At first, the returned Slovene Home Guardists were imprisoned in detention camps in **Celje** (Teharje), **Ljubljana** (Šentvid), **Kranj**, and **Škofja Loka**. Those under age 18 were mostly freed, but the rest, without trial, were brutally executed at various locations. The largest mass graves are at Kočevski Rog, Celje, Crngrob (near Škofja Loka), and Podutik (near Ljubljana). The graves, which were also the killing grounds, had been for the most part concealed, with most Slovenes learning about them only after 1990. In 2002 the Ministry of Culture financed a research project to systematically identify the hidden graves, and by November 2004 close to 400 had been uncovered, twice the number anticipated. However, not all belong to the Slovene victims. As of November 2004, according to research not yet completed, 11,683 anticommunists were murdered after the war.

Although the Slovene émigré **press** in the West wrote at length about the massacres, they were kept secret from the public in Slovenia until 1975, when **Edvard Kocbek** spoke about them in an interview, published in **Trieste**. The Slovene **media** and politicians attacked Kocbek, but eventually the mass killings, the responsibility for them, and their painful consequences for the Slovene nation came to be discussed openly by the younger generation of Slovene intellectuals, who led the efforts in the 1980s to democratize Slovenia. In 1984 **Spomenka Hribar** was the first in Slovenia to write openly about post–World War II massacres in her essay *Krivda in greh* (Guilt and Sin), and thus began the slow process of a national reconciliation that has not yet been reached. The mass murders remain a politically divisive topic. The formal acknowledgment of the murders by **Milan Kučan**, independent Slovenia's first president, at a reconciliatory commemoration in Kočevski Rog (1990) was a beginning. Much still needs to be done (identifying and burying the victims, issuing death certificates) before true national reconciliation is achieved. *See also* COVENANT, NEW SLOVENE.

MAY DECLARATION / MAJNIŠKA DEKLARACIJA, 1917. Before the end of **World War I** the South Slav delegates in the **Vienna** parliament organized into the Yugoslav Club in an attempt to resolve the Yugoslav national question. Slovene delegates played an important role. On behalf of the Yugoslav Club, **Anton Korošec**, a Slovene **Clerical**, presented the *Majniška deklaracija* (May Declaration) in the parliament on 30 May 1917. The declaration, whose author was **Janez Evangelist Krek**, was signed by all 33 Yugoslav delegates. It demanded the formation of an autonomous South Slav state encompassing all South Slavs living in Austria-Hungary. The May Declaration was rejected in Vienna and at the time did not generate much response among the Slovene public. However, in the fall of 1917 it sparked a mass "declaration movement," which not only supported and fought for the goals of the declaration but also demanded peace and an end to the war. *See also* JEGLIČ, ANTON BONAVENTURA; MAY DECLARATION, 1989; SERBS, CROATS, AND SLOVENES, KINGDOM OF.

MAY DECLARATION / MAJNIŠKA DEKLARACIJA, 1989. The May Declaration of 1989 was a political charter of the alternative, democratic movement, published in the Slovene **media** on 8 May 1989. The primary goals of the declaration, which was signed by the Writers' Association, Slovene Democratic Union, Slovene Peasant Association, Christian Democrat Movement, and Social Democratic Party, were Slovene **independence** and a sovereign, democratic Slovene state. *See also* DEMOS; MAY DECLARATION, 1917.

MEDIA. Forty-five years of one-party rule affected all print and broadcast media: All "public" media were ideologically monolithic. The daily **press**, radio programming, and television broadcasting were very closely monitored and controlled by the **Communist Party**. With the introduction of a multiparty system in 1990, the media and their operations underwent important changes. Hundreds of new private print and audiovisual companies were launched, competing for listeners, readers, and viewers. There are no exact data on how many media sources exist in Slovenia; analysts estimate more than 1,000 in print media alone. In 2005 there were five major dailies (*Delo, Dnevnik, Finance, Slovenske novice,* and *Večer*), dozens of weekly magazines, and hundreds of literary and professional journals, some with long historical traditions. Most newspapers and some magazines are available online, at least in digest form, for no fee. A growing number of Slovene e-publications as well as English e-sources on Slovenia are available to Internet users. The Slovene Press Agency (*Slovenska tiskovna agencija,* STA) is important to all print media. Established in 1991 as a governmental press organization, it collects information about Slovenia and the world and distributes it daily in Slovene and English. It exchanges information with numerous press agencies around the world but has only a few of its own correspondents (e.g., in Brussels, Zagreb, and Belgrade). See also AGITPROP.

In 2003 Slovenia had about 80 radio stations; some 20 of these were local, noncommercial stations offering news and cultural and educational programs, which were in part supported by public monies. (Commercial radio stations depend exclusively on advertising for funding.) The major broadcaster is the public Radio Slovenija, whose origins go back to 1928; it is part of **Radio and Television Slovenia** (RTV). Located in **Ljubljana**, it covers the entire state with its substations in **Maribor** and **Koper,** and it operates three national programs. It also broadcasts specific foreign-language programs for indigenous **minorities** in Slovenia and for foreign listeners. In existence since 1969, Radio Študent, a noncommercial station, was the first station before 1990 to challenge national RTV programming by providing alternative news, talk shows, and **music** to a broad listenership. According to its own data, the station in 2005 had about 20,000 regular and up to 100,000 occasional listeners. A private **Catholic** station, Radio Ognjišče (The Hearth), broadcasting from Ljubljana, has been in existence since 1996. With interesting programs, it has acquired a large listenership among Catholics and others throughout

Slovenia. It has also transmitted Slovene **language** Voice of America (VOA) programs. Commercial radio stations broadcast *24 ur* (*24 Hours*), produced by Pro-Plus, a Slovene production company, majority owned by Bermuda-headquartered Central European Media Enterprise Ltd. (CME). Until the end of 2005, noncommercial stations relayed their Slovene programming from the British Broadcasting Corporation (BBC) World Service. Analysis of the audiovisual and print media and their quality can be found in the Slovene edition of *Media Watch*. *See also* STUDENT MOVEMENTS.

In 2005 there were five television programs with national coverage and 35 regional ones, operating on local frequencies. Televizija Slovenija, a part of the national public institution RTV, offers two channels: TV 1 and TV 2. TV Slovenia, in existence since before 1990, now competes with private TV stations: Kanal A, POP TV, and Prva TV (First TV), formerly TV 3. While Prva TV is exclusively Slovene-owned, with the Catholic Church as the largest funder, Kanal A and POP TV are financed by the CME. The commercial POP TV has been the most successful private station. In 1997 it added a second program, *Gajba* (*Crate*), acquired Kanal A from the Swedish Broadcasting System (SBS) in 1999, and established the radio news program *24 ur* (*24 Hours*). Although the Media Act, discussed later, bars the formation of media monopolies, all media—written and audiovisual—in Slovenia are governed by monopolies: Delo Publishing has a monopoly in the press; RTV Slovenija in noncommercial broadcasting, and POP TV in commercial television. Among commercial broadcasters, POP TV not only has the largest audience but also provides news service to other commercial stations and controls local commercial TV broadcasters. Many find POP TV news interesting, but other programs (films, shows) are considered of poor quality, mostly imported from the United States. All three commercial stations, Kanal A, POP TV, and Prva TV, violate the Media Act, especially provisions on advertising and on consistent use of Slovene.

Since **independence** in 1991, Slovenia has enacted two Media Acts (1994, 2001) and two Radio-Television Slovenia (RTV-Slovenia) Acts (1994, 2005). Although rather general, the 1994 Media Act restricted media ownership: No single shareholder (domestic or foreign) was allowed to hold more than one-third of the capital of any media company. The provision was amended in 2001, reducing the limit to 20 percent, but the government is authorized to increase it in the future. The Media Act, with its 168 articles, regulates every aspect of print and audiovisual media operations: from language used, to advertising time allowed on TV and radio, to fines for violating its provisions. Since the 2001 Media Act was not in complete compliance with the **European Union** (EU) media legislation, a new law was in preparation in 2005. Private broadcasters are less regulated than are public radio and television, which are also governed by the specific RTV Slovenia Act. Because of strong disagreements in the parliament among **political parties** over the 2005 RTV Slovenia law—mostly over who should appoint the general manager of RTV and its Program Board—the implementation of the law was decided by a referendum, demanded by the left-leaning parties. The vote decided in favor of the law, which gives parliament the authority to appoint RTV's general manager as well as five of its 29 board members.

Also relevant and welcomed by media operators were the Telecommunication Acts (1998, 2001), which regulate broadcasting and telecommunication service. Two independent government bodies deal with the audiovisual media: the Agency for Postal Service and Electronic Communication of the RS (*Agencija za pošto in elektronske komunikacije Republike Slovenije*) and the Broadcasting Council (*Svet za radiodifuzijo*, SRDF). The former is responsible for the technical aspects of audiovisual media operations and the development of the telecommunications market, frequency allocations, and control. Its primary goal is to protect the users. The latter provides expert supervision of radio and television programs and assesses their legality. Among other responsibilities, its seven-member council also has the power to revoke station licenses. Thus far, it has not used this power in spite of frequent violations of the Media Act, especially by commercial TV stations.

In 2005 about 60 percent of Slovenia's households had personal computers, of which 48 percent also had Internet access, a 50 percent increase over 2001. Several cable operators, such as Ljubljana Cable (*Ljubljanski kabel*) and PIKA, offer cable TV and Internet services, but their services are technologically incompatible. There are monthly fees for cable services. A growing problem, which will need addressing, is video piracy of satellite programs. While broadcasters need operating licenses, cable operators do not. Also, it is believed that there are too many cable providers for all to survive; some mergers are likely.

MEDIEVAL CULTURE AND ART. In the 12th and 13th centuries cultural life in medieval Slovenian lands was centered in monasteries.

The most important were Carthusian (Žiče, Jurklošter, Bistra, and Pleterje) and Cistercian (**Stična**, Vetrinj, and Kostanjevica on the Krka River). Several religious manuscripts are preserved from that time: the Celovec manuscript (1370) and the Stična manuscript (15th century), written in the Dolenjska dialect. Otherwise, intellectuals at the time generally wrote in Latin or German. In the Middle Ages, monasteries also were centers of **education**, primarily schools for the education of the clergy. Among the most important were those at Stična, Breze in **Carinthia**, Gornji Grad, and Velika Nedelja. Some women were educated in convents such as in Velesovo near Kranj and in Krka (Gurk) in Carinthia. An important development was the establishment of a few parish schools for Slovene peasant boys who trained as altar boys or future priests. The first schools that were not organized by the **Catholic Church** were private lay schools serving the needs of the developing middle class.

Monasteries, churches, and their schools were also centers of musical life. Sacral polyphonic **music** (chorales and musical manuscripts) was developed. Social conditions in Slovene lands were less conducive to the development of secular music. Therefore, many talented Slovene composers went abroad, such as the Vienna bishop and musician Jurij Slatkonja, who also directed a court choir in **Vienna** in the late 15th century. Romanesque and Gothic styles dominated **art** and **architecture**. Romanesque architecture (11th to 13th century) can be seen in rebuilt churches and **castles**. Especially beautiful were castle chapels such as Mali Grad near **Kamnik**. Among rare Romanesque sculptures preserved until today are the Madonnas of Krakovo, Velesovo, and Solčava, and *Christ Crucified* (vicinity of Cerknica).

All stages in the development of European Gothic art can be observed in the Slovene lands, although they developed there much later and on a smaller scale. Gothic architecture (13th to 15th century) began developing aggressively only after the earthquake of 1348 with the rebuilding of Romanesque churches (e.g., Suha near Škofja Loka, the Minorite church in **Ptuj**). The most beautiful late-Gothic church (early 15th century) is on Ptujska Gora, built for the **Counts of Celje**. Gothic plastic arts, especially sculptures in wood or stone, are most often connected with sacral architecture, and they include relief images of the nobility at Ptujska Gora and Velika Nedelja, as well as several Pietàs, tombstones (Friderik Ptujski), and late Gothic side altars, especially in Carinthia. Gothic wall painting in Slovene lands is considered a classical example of the Gothic painting of the period. The walls of the rebuilt and redecorated Romanesque churches were covered with such painting. Church ceilings, made of wood, were also painted. Some, as in Martjanci, Hrastovlje, Suha, and Ptujska Gora, can still be admired today. Among the better-known Gothic painters are Johannes Aquila of Radgona, Janez of Ljubljana, and Jernej of Loka. *See also* MEDIEVAL LANDS; MEDIEVAL TOWNS AND COMMERCE.

MEDIEVAL LANDS. The area that had constituted greater **Karantania** in 1000 AD underwent major restructuring between the 12th and 15th centuries. Magyar invasions from the east and German colonization from the north changed its ethnic composition, while new feudal families vied to establish inheritable control over its individual feudal domains. Babenbergs, Spanheims, and the Czech Otokar (Přemysl) were prominent ruling entities up through the 13th century, but the premier family would ultimately be the **Habsburgs**. In the 1270s Rudolf of Habsburg established a firm stronghold in the eastern **Alps**, where he and his descendants would soon rule over all the Slovene lands, except those on the western and eastern peripheries, which were controlled by Venice and **Hungary**, respectively.

The names of the Habsburg lands where Slovenes lived from the 13th century to the 20th were **Carinthia** (Koroška), Carniola (Kranjska), **Gorizia** (Gorica), Istria (Istra), Styria (Štajerska), and **Trieste** (Trst). Each was a feudal unit (Carinthia, Carniola, and Styria were duchies; Gorizia was a county; Istria a margravate; and Trieste a town) constituting part of the larger dynastic feudal domain. Because most came under the family's rule early, they were considered Hereditary Lands of the Habsburg Crown. They were also a part of the **Holy Roman Empire**. *See also* MEDIEVAL CULTURE AND ART; MEDIEVAL TOWNS AND COMMERCE; REGIONS OF SLOVENIA.

MEDIEVAL TOWNS AND COMMERCE. Until the 12th century the economy in areas settled by Slovenes was primarily feudal, with trade and crafts functioning as an adjunct of **agriculture**. After the various invaders of the previous centuries were subdued and Christianized, towns began to emerge, first in **Carinthia** and then, in the 13th and 14th centuries, in other Slovene lands. In the coastal areas (usually under Venetian rule) ancient towns were revived and old laws reinstated; in the interior, new towns were established under clerical or secular feudal lords and their law.

By the 14th century there were some 27 towns and 70 market towns in the Slovene lands, each with its own magistrate. Most towns remained small; **Ljubljana** (Laibach), Slovenia's present capital, had 7,000 inhabitants in the 1600s, while the Adriatic port **Trieste** (Trst) reached 10,000 only in the 1700s. Commercial goods that were exported from Slovene areas included furs, honey and wax, iron, **leather**, livestock, and wood products. Imported goods, usually from Venice, included glass, jewelry, precious metals, and spices. Crafts developed as an adjunct to commerce, and craftspeople eventually organized into guilds beginning in the mid-14th century, starting with the tailors' guild of Villach (Beljak) in 1347. Coins were used as a medium of exchange and were made in the region as early as the mid-13th century. Moneylending, as elsewhere in Christian Europe, was governed by the **Catholic Church**'s law regarding just price. *See also* MEDIEVAL CULTURE AND ARTS; MEDIEVAL LANDS.

MENCINGER, JOŽE (1941–). Born in Jesenice, Jože Mencinger studied economics at the **University of Ljubljana**, where he was awarded a B.A. in 1964. He continued his studies at the University of Pennsylvania (Philadelphia), where in 1975 he obtained his Ph.D. Since 1987 Mencinger has been a professor and collaborator at the Economic Institute of the Law School of the University of Ljubljana and was its director from 1993 to 2001. In 1998 Mencinger became the University of Ljubljana's provost, a position he held until September 2005. As a macroeconomist dealing with economic systems and analysis of the Yugoslav and Slovene **economy**, Mencinger constructed the first econometric model of the Yugoslav economy. He joined **Demos** and, in 1990, was appointed minister of economic affairs and also deputy prime minister (1990–1991) in Slovenia's first post-communist government. In the early 1990s Mencinger was one of the authors of the **privatization** law, favoring a gradual approach to changing the economy and society. He has held other important positions in Slovenia, among them that of a board member of the Bank of Slovenia (1991–1997). He has published in domestic and international economic journals and is the author of the books *Ekonomski sistem in politika* (The Economic System and Politics, 1987), with Franjo Štiblar, and *Ekonomika Jugoslavije* (Economics of Yugoslavia, 1990).

METLIKA. A small old town in **Bela Krajina** with 3,225 inhabitants, Metlika lies at the southern edge of Slovenia on the Kolpa River, bordering **Croatia**. The seat of the *občina* Metlika (8,123 inhabitants), the town has a well-preserved historic district and is one of the three administrative, cultural, and economic centers of the **region**. Metlika has been one of the important Slovene wine growing and producing centers (Merkator Kmetijska Zadruga, Metlika Winery). The clothing factory Beti, a large and successful enterprise in the early 1990s with strong export activities, is no longer competitive on the European market. Suffering big losses, Beti had to restructure and downsize to 450 workers in 2005, while its sister company in Črnomelj, the largest town in Bela Krajina, declared bankruptcy the same year. After 1991 Metlika became a major border-crossing point with Croatia.

Founded in the 13th century (the region was then called the Metlika March), Metlika acquired town rights in the 14th century and was one of **Austria**'s important border strongholds, first against the Kingdom of **Hungary**, later against the Turks. A prosperous **medieval** town, Metlika was destroyed by fire in 1705. Its historic center was rebuilt in the 18th century and features St. Nicholas's Church, mentioned first in the 14th century; a **castle**, renovated in the **baroque** style, which today houses a beautiful Bela Krajina **museum** and is the venue for various cultural events; the Komenda House (prebend), a two-story building formerly belonging to the Order of Teutonic Knights; and a part of a defense tower. Metlika was a cultural center during the **Protestant Reformation** and again in the 19th century, when national **societies** such as the Bela Krajina **Sokol** (Falcon) and the National Literary Society flourished. At the turn of the century, Metlika declined as natural disasters forced many to **emigrate**. During **World War II** Italian occupiers burned parts of Metlika and nearby villages. In the 1950s the town began to revive due to regional industrialization and improved **transportation**, with roads connecting Bela Krajina to Dolenjska and **Ljubljana**.

MIKLOŠIČ, FRANC (1813–1891). Franc Miklošič was not only a well-known professor of Slavic languages and literature at the University of Vienna (1849–1885) but also an important Slovene politician. He was president of **Vienna**'s society Slovenija, a coauthor of the political program **United Slovenia**, and a member of the Austrian parliament. Miklošič was also, for three years, dean of the School of Humanities at the University of Vienna and the university's rector in 1854–1855. Working with **Jernej Kopitar** and other leading Slavic linguists, such as Pavel Šafařik and Josef Dobrovský, he was one of the most important Slavicists of the 19th century. Miklošič founded the discipline of comparative grammatical studies of Slavic languages.

His impressive, often pioneering work on grammar, lexicography, and etymology of Slavic languages consists of 34 volumes. Miklošič also wrote extensively on other languages spoken on the Balkan peninsula (Albanian, Greek, Hungarian, Romanian, Romany, Turkish). The most extensive among Miklošič's numerous publications is *Vergleichende Grammatik der slavischen Sprachen* (A Comparative Grammar of Slavic Languages), in four volumes (1852–1883). His other important books include *Etymologisches Wörterbuch der Slavischen Sprachen* (An Etymological Dictionary of Slavic Languages) (1886), and *Monumenta serbica spectantia historiam Serbiae, Bosnae, Ragusii*, a collection of old Serbian documents from Serbia, Bosnia, and Dubrovnik (1858). Although Miklošič wrote in German, he is one of the most important personages in Slovene history. *See also* LANGUAGE, SLOVENE; ROMANTICISM.

MILIZIA VOLONTARIA ANTICOMUNISTA (MVAC). *See* VILLAGE GUARD.

MINING. Historically, mining was crucial for the economic development of the Slovene lands. In the Middle Ages, the discovery of iron ore in several locations (exhausted by the 19th century) contributed to the development of towns in the Gorenjska **region**, including Jesenice, Železniki, and Kropa, the latter known for production of **wrought iron**. In the 15th century lead and iron mining began in Koroška and Štajerska, and a rich mercury mine was opened in **Idrija** (1493). In the 19th century coal production in the Zasavje region, lead production in Mežica, and mercury in Idrija created conditions favorable for industrial development. By the 1920s and 1930s, mining had already experienced a decline; many miners **emigrated** to Western Europe, eastern France being a common destination for miners in search of jobs. In the 1950s more than 40 coal and five ore mines were in operation. However, by the mid-1990s most mines were closed, among them major ones: Idrija (mercury), Mežica (lead), and the uranium mine at Žiri (built only in 1990). The coal mines still in operation (Kanižarica, Senovo, Trbovlje-Hrastnik, and Zagorje) have been in the process of closing since 1995 with government financial assistance and also **European Union** (EU) funds. The **environmental** impact of more than two centuries of ore and coal mining has been considerable, and therefore mine closings are technically demanding and expensive undertakings. After 1991 the remaining coal mines also have been among Slovenia's major debt producers. Mining accounted for less than 1 percent of GDP in 2003. All mines, except for the lignite mine in **Velenje**, will be closed by 2010. Slovenia now has to import most of the ferrous and nonferrous ores needed for **manufacturing**, as well as the low-sulfur lignite for **energy** production. Velenje, one of the Europe's largest underground lignite coal mines, with its accessible reserves of 177 million metric tons, is the only mine expected to remain active during the next two decades. Its coal (approximately 4 million metric tons in 2003) is almost entirely used by large thermal power plants (e.g., Šoštanj) for energy generation. To remain competitive in the EU, Velenje must restructure, enlarge production of lignite (the plan calls for an annual 4 percent increase), lower its price by 2 percent, reduce the number of employees, and modernize its mining technology.

Slovenia also has reserves of clay, gravel, and stone, raw materials for construction and related industries (brick, glass, and lime production), but their processing has also declined in the last decade. Across Slovenia there are over 200 surface mines and quarries, half of which are considered small. The largest stone quarries are in Verd and Črni Kal, and the largest sandpits are in the **Ljubljana** and **Ptuj** valleys. Production of gravel, sand, and stone (approximately 12.4 million tons in 2005) provides enough materials for domestic consumption as well as for export. *See also* NATURAL RESOURCES.

MINORITIES IN SLOVENIA. Besides the Hungarians and the Italians, who are considered **indigenous minorities** with specified constitutional rights, the **Republic of Slovenia** (RS) has a number of other minority groups. Most are South Slavs or Albanians who are from or have co-nationals in the former republics of **Yugoslavia**. Many had resided in Slovenia as "guest workers" for a number of years before **independence**. In early 1993 about 130,000 of these—who were legal or actual residents as of 26 December 1990, and who submitted applications in the first year of Slovenia's independence—became citizens. According to the 2002 census their numbers were: Albanians 6,186; Bosniaks 21,542; Croats 35,642; Macedonians 3,972: Montenegrins 2,667; Muslims (ethnic) 10,467; Roma 3,246; Serbs 38,964; and Yugoslavs 527. These and other less numerous minority groups have the same rights and liberties accorded to all citizens of Slovenia. In addition they are guaranteed the right to use their own language and script "in fulfilling rights and obligations, and in proceedings before state and other bodies which perform public services."

About 18,000 persons from the former Yugoslav republics who were official residents in Slovenia in 1990 did not apply for citizenship, for one reason or another. The RS therefore removed them from the residency lists, and thereby made them ineligible for benefits of residency, such as pensions and the like. These became known as "the erased," who found political voice by the end of the 1990s. In 1999 and 2003 Slovenia's **Constitutional Court** ruled that the legislation erasing them was unconstitutional. The **Slovene Democratic Party** (SDS) called for a referendum on the issue, and in April 2004, with 31 percent of the voters casting ballots, the vote was 95 percent against the erased's appeal. The court again stepped in, declaring the referendum unconstitutional, and the state is proceeding on a case-by-case basis, reviewing the status of the erased. As of early 2005, only about 4,000 still remained erased. *See also* HUMAN RIGHTS.

Slovenia continues to deal with a number of other issues regarding minorities. Two involve disputes with neighboring states. **Austria** is still insistent that the "Germans" be recognized as an indigenous minority; and **Croatia**, which has listed Slovenes in its Law on Minorities, wants the Slovenes to reciprocate. In both cases Slovenia contends that the groups are too scattered—not concentrated in border regions—to be authentic indigenous peoples. The Roma, whose official numbers have risen from 2,259 in 1991 to 3,246 in 2002 (but may be as high as 7,000) have been advancing educationally in Slovenia. However, pressure has been applied also to guarantee Roma, who are located primarily in **Prekmurje** and **Bela Krajina**, local political representation. The *občina* electoral law was amended to require Roma candidates on the ballot in 20 *občinas*. One Roma now sits on the city council in **Murska Sobota**. No Roma has as yet held a seat in the National Assembly.

MINORITIES, INDIGENOUS. Slovenia's Hungarians and Italians, 6,243 and 2,258, respectively, according to 2002 census figures (down from 8,000 and 2,959 in 1991) are regarded as indigenous **minorities**. They live in border regions contiguous to **Hungary** and **Italy**, and in Slovenia have specifically guaranteed constitutional rights (**Constitution of 1991**, Article 64). These rights include free use of national symbols; the establishment of organizations; the development of economic, cultural, and scientific research activities; and activities in the area of public information and **publishing** that preserve ethnic identity. The indigenous minorities have the right to **education** in their own language or to bilingual education if they so choose. They are also guaranteed the right to cultivate relations with their parent peoples and their states, with the **Republic of Slovenia** (RS) providing financial and moral support toward this end. An illustration of Slovenia's good will toward these minorities was the unveiling of a statue of St. Stephen, Hungary's first king (969–1083), in the Slovene town of Lendava. In attendance on 21 August 2000, a Hungarian national holiday, were a Hungarian Slovene sculptor and Slovene **government** officials.

Hungarians and Italians in the RS also have the constitutional right to establish their own local government units and are directly represented in the 90-seat National Assembly (each group is guaranteed one representative). Laws and regulations relating to ethnic groups may not be adopted without the consent of ethnic representatives. The Hungarian and Italian representatives in the National Assembly have been increasingly alarmed by the declining numbers of their respective minorities, a decrease attributed to assimilation. Robert Battelli, the Italian parliamentarian, resigned in early 2004 from the presidency of the assembly's nationalities commission to protest alleged Slovene assimilation pressures. *See also* HUNGARY, RELATIONS WITH; ITALY, RELATIONS WITH.

MINORITIES, SLOVENES IN AUSTRIA. The first republic of **Austria** came into existence after **World War I**, its boundaries drawn by Entente peacemakers in Paris and formalized by the Treaty of St. Germain (10 September 1919). It ended with annexation to Hitler's German Reich in 1938. The second Austrian republic, established in 1945 after **World War II**, had a difficult rebirth, undergoing—much like Germany—10 years of Allied occupation and administrative division. Although Austria has been overwhelmingly German ethnically since 1919, it has minority enclaves, located primarily along border areas. Among its minorities are Slovenes who inhabit mostly Alpine lands along Austria's southern frontier. Most live in the Austrian province of Carinthia, while a few live in Styria.

Before there was a "national" (German) Austria, there was an imperial one, where **Habsburg** rulers reigned after the 13th century. Slovenes lived in this multiethnic state, where no national group—not even the Germans—ever had a majority. The **settlement of Slovenes** in the area predated the arrival of German tribes and occurred many centuries before the beginning of Habsburg rule. Slovene-inhabited areas (**Karantania**) originally included much of today's central Austria, but after 1000 AD it slowly shrank in size under the pressures of

German feudal rule and German colonization. Germanization was not a conscious policy of the Habsburgs or other feudal rulers before the modern period, yet by the mid-18th century, when **Maria Theresa** and **Joseph II** began to stress German language use as a feature of state modernization, natural assimilation had in fact absorbed many Slovenes. Various institutions of the modern imperial state—the administration, its bureaucracy, the courts, the military, the schools—became state agents of Germanization. Even in Carniola, where Slovenes constituted more than 90 percent of the population, but particularly in Styria and Carinthia, Germanizing forces rallied. By 1848 those forces were joined by the intellectual and economic middle classes, who envisioned a large national Germany, which they hoped would include an Adriatic port (**Trieste**). Emperor **Francis Joseph**, whose reign began in the same year as the **Revolution of 1848**, attempted to shut out the German nationalists (mostly liberals), but after 1900 he found it increasingly more difficult to sustain the idea of a multinational Austria united by a common Western Christian civilization. Popular politics and a nationalistic **press** expanded the number of supporters of Germanization, and Slovenes, who were economically and politically at a disadvantage, found even their cultural identity besieged.

After **World War I** most Slovenes became a part of the **Kingdom of Serbs, Croats, and Slovenes**, but others found themselves in **Hungary, Italy**, and Austria—"national" states in which they were now officially a minority. In the case of Slovenes in Carinthia, the area where most Austrian Slovenes are concentrated, a plebiscite was held in the south to determine whether the area should remain Austrian or become part of the new Yugoslav state. The **Carinthian plebiscite** (10 October 1920) vote favored the former. Since then the Slovene minority in Austria has continuously experienced negative political, economic, and cultural pressures exerted against it by the majority national group.

In interwar Austria there were between 55,000 and 80,000 Slovenes, but due to discrimination, fewer and fewer were willing to identify themselves as such. In the first Austrian republic Slovene clergy were dismissed or relocated, professionals (lawyers and doctors) lost their positions, and those who had voted for **Yugoslavia** in the plebiscite lost their jobs. Slovene schools were closed, and Slovene homes were vandalized or burned. By 1925 the Slovene **language** ceased to be used in official documents, and bilingual public signs were removed. A theory was developed asserting that Slovenes were not in fact Slovene but Windisch—remnants of another people who occupied these lands in the early Middle Ages. (In Hungary, where the term *Vend* was used, a similar theory was developed.) The Windisch theory acquired strong official support when the Nazis, with their racist proclivities, came to power in Austria in 1938. Slovenes were treated accordingly; identifying themselves as Windisch was often necessary for personal safety. The interwar experience of Austrian Slovenes caused many to join the **Partisans** during **World War II**. They helped liberate certain areas of Carinthia from the Germans, but the Allies (Carinthia was in the British occupation zone after May 1945), fearing the spread of communism, forced the Partisans to leave. This prevented the Austrian Slovenes' becoming part of the post–World War II Slovene republic in Yugoslavia.

Austrian Slovenes, numbering about 60,000, again fared badly after World War II, even though Article 7 of the **Austrian State Treaty** of 1955, designed by Allied occupiers who left Austria only a decade after the war's end, contained guarantees for national minorities. Slovenes in Austria had very little participation in political life, except in local government. The Austrian German rightists (Carinthia's *Heimatdienst*) continued their anti-Slovene pressures, particularly against bilingual topographical signs (often removed at night) and bilingual schools. In 1970 the 50th anniversary of the Carinthian plebiscite provoked intense confrontations, which continued at least until the middle of that decade. **Mohorjeva Družba**, a Slovene publishing house that had been closed in 1940, revived after the war and was guaranteed by Article 7, but was again attacked in the 1970s. The pressure to persuade Austrian Slovenes that they are Windisch was also revived.

Since the late 1980s, the honoring of Slovene minority rights in Austria has taken a positive turn. One Slovene, Karl Smolle, served in **Vienna**'s parliament in the 1980s and again in the 1990s, running as an Alternative Greens' List candidate. Slovenes are represented by two organizations: the conservative National Council of Carinthian Slovenes (*Narodni svet koroških Slovencev*) and the left/liberal Union of Slovene Organizations in Carinthia (*Zveza slovenskih organizacij na Koroškem*). Bilingual schools are guaranteed and have opened even in areas outside of those specified by Article 7. In 2004, 3,577 students signed up for bilingual schooling in the 66 schools that offer that option. There are bilingual nursery schools and a bilingual commercial academy (1990), the latter offering financial aid to Slovene students. There is also a Slovene gymnasium, which has produced much of Carinthia's Slovene intelligentsia. Various cultural societies, sports clubs, and student dormitories in Celovec and Vienna now exist, as do Slovene-language newspapers and journals. Austrian Slovenes own **banks** and stores and operate various cooperatives. The banks in the 1980s often attracted money from Yugoslavia's Slovenes seeking a hedge on inflation in their economically unstable socialist state. Yet, despite some improvement in the cultural and economic life of Austrian Slovenes, assimilation continues its relentless pace. The Slovene minority (12,586 in Carinthia according to Austria's 2001 census; between 40,000 and 60,000 according to **Republic of Slovenia** estimates) is more and more marginalized. The Slovene language is used less and less in public—in 2003 Austria discontinued its support for Radio 2, the Slovene-language radio station—and less even in the home. There is little information available about Slovenes in Styria, where the Slovene minority is not even recognized as such. *See also* KLAGENFURT/CELOVEC; MINORITIES, SLOVENES IN HUNGARY; MINORITIES, SLOVENES IN ITALY.

MINORITIES, SLOVENES IN HUNGARY. Slovenes and Magyars (Hungarians) have lived in proximity since the ninth century. In the area of Lower Pannonia, where the **settlements** of the two peoples overlapped, they often were ruled by the same nobility and **Catholic Church** hierarchy. There was frequent cultural cross-fertilization, and during the **Protestant Reformation**, when many Magyar nobles accepted Protestantism, generally their Slovene villagers did as well. Protestantism, unlike elsewhere among the Slovenes, survived in this northeastern corner of Slovene settlement (an area that currently straddles the Slovene–Hungarian border). In 1867 **Austria** and **Hungary**, although still linked by a common monarch, were by constitution separated administratively. The act that divided the **Habsburg** state assigned 45,000 Slovenes to the Kingdom of Hungary. After 1868 Hungary embarked on a policy of Magyarization of its national minorities, and by the end of the 19th century the Slovene **language**, outside the home, was used only in religious services; elsewhere only Hungarian was allowed. Slovene place names were Magyarized, as were family names in some cases.

After **World War I** Hungary, as one of the defeated powers, was required by the Treaty of Trianon (15 November 1920) to cede a large portion of its Slovene populated area, known as **Prekmurje** (formerly Slovenska Krajina), to the new **Kingdom of Serbs, Croats, and**

Slovenes. Those Slovenes who remained in Hungary lived in what came to be called Slovensko Porabje (Slovene Raba Basin). In both areas the population was mixed, Slovene and Hungarian. In Prekmurje there were few roads, no railroad until 1924, and the eastern areas were linked with the rest of Slovenia only by ferries crossing the Mura River. Many Slovene refugees from the Littoral, which had been incorporated into **Italy**, were resettled in Prekmurje at that time. Development of the region and integration of the Magyarized Prekmurje Slovenes into Slovenia began in the 1920s but was interrupted by **World War II**.

Unreconciled to the dismemberment of its kingdom, Hungary in the interwar period pursued a revisionist policy incompatible with the Treaty of Trianon. Hungary ultimately joined the Axis Powers in attacking **Yugoslavia** and reclaimed, among other lands, Prekmurje, where it reinstituted Magyarization under military occupation. Slovene administrators and educators were dismissed; Slovene societies closed; and Slovene signs and library books were confiscated. Magyar orthography replaced the Slovene. Officially, Hungary maintained that the Prekmurje and Porabje Slovenes were really Vends or Vendish, descendants of Celts who had been Slavicized. Since Vends were not Slovenes, the principle of national self-determination, Hungary argued, could not link them to Slovenes in Yugoslavia. (Austria, pursuing a similar policy, used the term *Windisch*.)

Since World War II Prekmurje has been a part of Slovenia, Porabje a part of Hungary. Both regions have mixed populations, and conditions for their respective minorities have depended on the nature of relations between Hungary and Yugoslavia. The Stalinist period, when Yugoslavia was banished from the communist bloc, was difficult for the minorities. The barbed wire, mines, lookout towers, border incidents, and economic pressures of the early 1950s were removed or modified only after the 1956 Hungarian Revolution. Relations between the states experienced thaws and freezes in the following years, less dependent on the nature of East–West relations as the 1990s neared. The **Alps–Adriatic Working Community**, founded in 1978, established a climate more receptive to interregional cooperation. With democratic changes coming to both Hungary and Slovenia in 1990, improved relations between the two states generated various bilateral agreements, including many that pledged the respective states to acknowledge and promote the cultural and political expression of the other's minorities.

Porabje covers 94 square kilometers and has between 4,000 and 5,000 ethnic Slovene inhabitants. The legal rights of its Slovenes are protected by the Hungarian constitution of 1989. Rights and opportunities for them have been enhanced by the Education Act of 1996 and the Radio and Television Act of the same year. Since 1992 there have been Slovene radio and television programs on Hungarian stations, but in 2000 the first Slovene radio station began its own broadcasts. Slovene language education is not fully developed, due primarily to a lack of teachers. The Union of Slovenes in Hungary (*Zveza Slovencev na Madžarskem*), located in Szentgotthárd (Monošter), oversees the preservation of Slovene identity for the Porabje Slovenes, while aid and encouragement come from the **Republic of Slovenia** (RS), as specified by a government act of 1996 to assist Slovene minorities in neighboring countries. (The RS maintains a consular office in Szentgotthárd.)

Improvements in **transportation** have made better interaction with Prekmurje and Slovenes in the RS possible. Direct border crossings opened in 1992 and 2002, and a railway connection between Hungary's Porabje and Slovenia's Prekmurje was celebrated in 2001. The railroad is part of the Fifth Corridor, a trans-European line that will eventually link Barcelona with Kiev. The Porabje region remains underdeveloped and has high unemployment, but prospects for advancement may improve with infrastructural developments and, since 2004, **European Union** (EU) membership for both Slovenia and Hungary. The welfare of the area also benefits from the fact that the governments of Slovenia and Hungary continue to have very cordial relations and are in agreement regarding the protection of indigenous minorities. *See also* MINORITIES, SLOVENES IN AUSTRIA; MINORITIES, SLOVENES IN ITALY.

MINORITIES, SLOVENES IN ITALY. Slovenes have lived alongside Italians since the sixth century AD. Over the centuries, ethnic and political boundaries have changed, with the Italian–Slovene ethnic border being pushed eastward due to assimilation and, later, deliberate Italianization, which began with the movement for **Italy**'s unification in the mid-19th century and has continued, in varying degrees, to this day. There is no official number for the Slovene minorities in Italy, but some other data indicate that the number has been decreasing. In 2002, according to the Slovene Research Institute (SLORI) in **Trieste** and SWG opinion poll data, there were around

95,000 Slovenes in three northeastern Italian provinces: Trieste (Trst), **Gorizia** (Gorica), and Udine (Videm). Since 1963 these provinces together have constituted the Italian autonomous region Friuli-Venezia Giulia (Furlanija-Julijska Krajina) with Trieste as its capital. The Slovene minority lives in 39 of its municipalities. In addition, in areas surveyed by SLORI, about 100,000 inhabitants speak the Slovene **language** while about 183,000 inhabitants understand it. Although Slovenes do live in urban municipalities, their presence is much stronger in rural ones such as Valle/Dolina or Sgonico/Zgonik, in which they account for 50 percent of the population. In the past, Italy acknowledged the Slovene minority in the provinces of Trieste and Gorizia but not Udine. The latest, most comprehensive, and favorable legislative acts are the 1999 Regulations on the Protection of Historical Linguistic Minorities, and the 2001 Regulation on the Protection of the Slovene Linguistic Minority in the Region of Friuli-Venezia Giulia. Both acts address the use of the Slovene language in public, but implementation has been slow.

In 1866 after the Austrian–Prussian war, Venetian Slovenia and Resia became part of the Italian Kingdom. After **World War I** and the **Treaty of Rapallo** (1920), a large portion of Austrian territory (Primorska and Istria), populated by more than 300,000 Slovenes, passed to Italian sovereignty. At the turn of the 20th century, the Slovenes in Italy, mostly engaged in agriculture, were organized in cooperatives, which sustained the base for the Slovene national movement. Slovene schools, **press**, cultural and political associations, and financial and economic institutions, which had functioned in **Austria**, remained in existence after the war. In 1919 various Slovene **political parties** established Edinost (Unity), representing Slovene and Croatian interests in Italy. Although Edinost became divided along ideological lines (a liberal organization in Trieste and a conservative one in Gorizia), it stayed united in the fight for Slovene national interests (1924 elections). The first few years under Italian rule were tolerable for Slovenes, but the situation worsened considerably after Benito Mussolini's ascent to power (1922), when all democratic, political, and cultural institutions and public use of the Slovene language were abolished. Slavic geographic and personal names were Italianized. Only in **Catholic** churches was Slovene still spoken publicly. After the Concordat between Italy and the Vatican in 1929, Slovene parish priests were replaced by Italians, and parishioners were persecuted for using the Slovene language in church. In the 1920s there were seven **publishing** houses and three printers in Trieste and Gorizia, which published numerous Slovene periodicals and books. One of the societies was **Society of St. Hermagoras** with strong and continuous publishing activities. In the 1930s publishing was curtailed but not stopped. There was underground publishing and some Catholic publications were allowed to continue. Between 1918 and 1940, 40 periodicals and 1,000 books were published.

While other Slovene organizations fought for minority rights by legal means, the underground organization Trst, Istra, Gorica, Reka (TIGR) did not. It fought fascism with terrorism, which called attention to the grave situation of the Slovene and Croatian minorities. In 1930 the Italians sentenced to death several TIGR members and shot them in Bazovica. Unemployment and undesirable economic conditions in the late 1920s, especially among minorities, caused many Slovenes to join the workers' socialist movement, led by the **Communist Party**. In 1934 the Communist Parties of Austria, Italy, and **Yugoslavia** issued a declaration proposing a solution to the Slovene question and argued that Slovenes had a right to self-determination. In 1936 the Italian Communists and national revolutionaries accepted a joint program to fight for minority rights.

Fascist terror, reaching its peak in the early 1930s, drove away several thousand Slovenes and Croats, especially the educated, who **emigrated** to Yugoslavia as well as to South America and Australia. The Austrian census of 1910 counted 466,730 Slovenes and Croats living in the Julian region; by 1936 the number had dropped to 382,113. At the same time, a large number of Italian public servants were resettled from the south of Italy to replace the Slavic exiles and emigrants. In the 1930s, despite relentless fascist terror and executions, the Slovenes organized underground political, social, and cultural life. During **World War II** many Slovenes in Italy supported the **Partisans**, who fought against Italian fascists.

At the war's end in May 1945, the Yugoslav army occupied most of the Slovene ethnic territory that had been part of Italy. However, under threat of the Allies, the Yugoslav army retreated eastward behind the Morgan line, which in June 1945 divided Slovene ethnic territory into military zones A (Trieste and Gorizia provinces) and B (Primorska and Istria). Zone A came under Allied control, while Zone B was under the Yugoslavs. Udine province (Canal valley/Kanalska dolina, Resia/Rezija) immediately came under Italian administration, which did not recognize the Slovene minority. The Allies in Zone A established

Slovene schools, which had 12,000 students in the school year 1945–1946, and several cultural institutions, among them radio and a daily newspaper, *Primorski dnevnik*. Despite the repeal of several fascist anti-minority laws and the Italian government's promise that minority rights would be respected, Italianization of the Slovenes living in Zone A continued and was abetted by the pro-Italian stance of the Allies.

After lengthy negotiations between the big powers, Italy, and Yugoslavia, the Italian–Yugoslav border was determined by the 1947 Peace Treaty of Paris, which awarded Zone A to Italy, Zone B to Yugoslavia, and created the Free Territory of Trieste (*Svobodno tržaško ozemlje*, STO) under UN protection. The STO was divided into Zone A and Zone B, the former being under the Allied and the latter under the Yugoslav administration. The 1947 treaty required that minority rights be respected and the Italian and Slovene languages to be the official languages in both zones of the STO, but in 1949 the Allies issued a decree by which Italian was the only official language in Zone A. Italianization of Slovenes continued, which was later accelerated by large-scale industrialization and migration of Italians from the South. Slovenes remained very active in their cultural and sports organizations and societies but were often politically divided. This did little to advance the cause of Slovene minority rights. Refer to map 4. *See also* TRIESTE QUESTION.

In 1954 the **London Agreement** abolished the STO and revised the border between Italy and Yugoslavia but reaffirmed and extended minority rights in Italy and Yugoslavia. However, Italy did not ratify the agreement and did not feel bound to fully comply with its provisions. From 1958 on, several laws and decrees that required implementation of Slovene minority rights were issued but were applied only in part in the Trieste and Gorizia provinces. The Slovene cultural and economic organizations thrived, and cooperation between the Slovene political left and right began in the 1960s, thus providing more support for the minority rights' cause. A few Slovenes were elected to local legislative bodies; Slovene schools were legalized and public financing was provided for them. The Trieste Credit Bank (*Tržaška kreditna banka*, 1958) was established, and a new cultural center was built in Trieste in 1964. However, in the early 1970s, following the suppression of **liberalization** in Yugoslavia, Slovenes in Italy again became politically divided.

In 1975 Italian and Yugoslav diplomatic activity produced the **Osimo Treaty**, which at last resolved the question of the borders and of those who inhabited the border areas. This gave impetus to cultural, economic, and scientific cooperation. The London Agreement of 1954 was revoked, but the Osimo Treaty provided only loosely for minority rights. Both governments promised that the already accepted rights guaranteed by the London treaty would remain in effect. In subsequent years, Italian Slovenes had problems exercising minority rights, especially under right-wing political rule in general, and in Trieste in particular. On the other hand, in the post-Osimo period, collaboration at all levels between regions improved, and new mechanisms for multilateral cooperation were created, such as the **Alps–Adriatic Working Community** (1978) and the **Central European Initiative** (1989), which affected the Slovene minority positively. Many Slovene cultural institutions were active, including a Slovene **theater**, Music Society (*Glasbena matica*), the Slovene Research Institute (SLORI), and publishing ventures such as *Primorski dnevnik* (*Littoral Daily*), *Most* (*Bridge*), and *Zaliv* (*The Bay*); some had financial support from the Slovene **government**. The Slovene Cultural and Economic Union (*Slovenska kulturno-gospodarska zveza*, SKGZ) functioned as an umbrella organization and fought for the rights of the Slovene minority in Italy, and the Slovene Community (*Slovenska skupnost*), organized as a political party, had representatives in the Italian parliament and in regional and provincial councils.

After Slovenia established **independence** in 1991, Slovene minority rights in Italy again came under attack. Italian–Slovene relations became tenser with the 1993 electoral victory of Italian rightist political parties that have tried to annul the Osimo Treaty and with it the already established minority rights. Bilingual geographical signs, already rare, were removed, the use of Slovene in several public institutions was quietly abolished, and the Slovene minority lost its representatives in local government.

The right to use minority languages in public and in education was a crucial element of minority protection advocated by the **European Union** (EU), of which both Italy and Slovenia are members. In 1999 and 2001 Italian legislation finally recognized the Slovene minority in the Udine province and created possibilities for better treatment of the Slovene minority in the entire Friuli-Venezia Giulia region. While Slovene public schools at all levels had been established in the Trieste and Gorizia provinces after World War II and were part of the Italian educational system, such had not been the case in the Udine province, where the Slovene minority in Špeter established the first

Slovene elementary school (private) only in 1984. From 10 students its enrollment grew quickly to 200, and by 2001 it became part of the public school system. Thus in the school year 2002–2003, in the entire Friuli-Venezia Giulia region there were eight preschool institutions with 807 children, 16 elementary schools (ages 6–14) with 1,724 students, and nine secondary schools—including vocational—with 860 students. In the early 1970s the number of Slovene students enrolled in Trieste and Gorizia provinces rose from 4,000 to 5,200 but began to decline after 1987, and only 3,100 students were enrolled in these schools in 1997. Despite the decreasing number of students in Slovene-language schools, there are some encouraging trends. The Slovene language can be studied at six Italian universities. There is an increasing demand for learning the Slovene language, which is probably the result of increased economic and cultural cooperation between the Slovene and Italian regions, stimulated by the EU. An important Slovene organization, Slovene Provincial Economic Union (*Slovensko deželno gospodarsko združenje*), with 750 entrepreneurs from the three provinces—Trieste, Gorizia, and Udine—established an Office for Europe in 2001 and has been systematically pursuing projects for regional economic and cultural cooperation between the Slovene minority in Italy and the Italian minority in Slovenia. The organization is financed in part by the EU. *See also* MINORITIES, INDIGENOUS, IN SLOVENIA; MINORITIES, SLOVENES IN AUSTRIA; MINORITIES, SLOVENES IN HUNGARY.

MISSIONARIES. According to some historians, Slovenes are a nation of missionaries. They went to America, Africa, and Asia as early as the 16th and 17th centuries. Almost all early Slovene missionaries were **Jesuits**, including Marko Anton Kapus (1657–1717), who worked among the American Indians (Opata, Seri, and Pima) of Arizona, California, and Mexico. Among the early Slovene missionaries, Ferdinand Avguštin Hallerstein (1703–1774), who went to China, was an important scientist (astronomy, ethnology) and very influential at the Beijing court. Perhaps the best-known missionary of the 19th century was **Friderik Baraga**, who worked among the Native Americans in the **United States**' Great Lakes region; he was appointed the first bishop of Marquette and was succeeded by two other Slovenes, Ignacij Mrak and Janez Vertin. Among 19th-century missionaries who worked in Africa (Sudan), the best-known was Ignacij Knoblehar (1819–1858), a scientist and student of the White Nile region. Today,

Slovene missionaries work at missionary posts worldwide, primarily in Africa and Asia, but also in Central and South America. In 2005 there were about a hundred active Slovene missionaries (men and women), among them several lay missionaries, members of the Society LAMIS (Lay Missionaries of Slovenia), a Slovenian philanthropic organization. Slovene missionaries in Madagascar have been overseeing the building of an agricultural educational center in the village of Matanga, a project financed by the Slovene **government**. *See also* CATHOLIC CHURCH.

MLADINA. The weekly *Mladina* (*Youth*) is an unaffiliated political magazine. It began in 1943 as the periodical of the League of Slovene Youth and has since appeared in various formats. It was a political and educational newspaper for young people until the late 1950s, when *Mladina* dealt almost exclusively with culture and entertainment. In 1976 *Mladina* changed radically, featuring critical articles on social concerns and on the political system. In the early 1980s its tone sharpened and its editorial boards were regularly pressured by political organizations: League of Socialist Youth of Slovenia (ZSMS), League of Communists of Slovenia (LCS; formerly the **Communist Party of Slovenia**), and the **Socialist Alliance of Working People** (SAWP). Many of its issues were censored or confiscated. In 1982, after the 11th ZSMS Congress, *Mladina* became an independent, avant-garde, opposition weekly, radical in its dealing with social and political taboos (such as the massacres after **World War II**, the **Yugoslav People's Army**, **Tito**'s personality cult, and **homosexual** rights) and problems relating to the **economy** and **education**. Because of its fearless and incisive criticism, *Mladina* was widely read not only in Slovenia but throughout **Yugoslavia** and was one of the country's strongest public-opinion makers in the 1980s. It riled federal authorities, who demanded that local authorities take action, legal if necessary, against the magazine and its journalists. In the late 1980s its circulation reached 60,000, and it played an important role in the democratization of Slovene society. Although in effect already an independent periodical in 1989, *Mladina* formally ended its ties with its publisher, the ZSMS, in 1990, when the latter transformed itself into the Liberal Democratic Party (LDS).

During the **Ten-Day War** (27 June–6 July 1991) that sprang from Slovenia's move for **independence**, *Mladina* performed an incredible job by covering the war from both the Slovene side and that of the Yugoslav army. The final product was the book *Ten Days of War for*

Slovenia. After 1991 *Mladina* lost its unique appeal as other periodicals became freer and more critical. *Mladina*'s circulation dropped (25,000 in 1995), but a left-leaning liberal *Mladina* remains informative and vigilant with respect to politics and broad social issues. It scrutinizes politicians regardless of party, using humor effectively. Since 1992 *Mladina* has been privately owned. *E-mladina* is available online. *See also* LEAGUE OF COMMUNIST YOUTH OF YUGOSLAVIA.

MLADINA TRIAL. *See* LJUBLJANA FOUR TRIAL.

MODERNA. Moderna, named by **Josip Stritar**, refers to Slovene literary trends (decadence, **impressionism**, naturalism, new romanticism, and symbolism) at the turn of the 20th century. The beginning of Moderna is marked by the appearance, in 1899, of two poetry collections: *Erotika* (Erotics) by **Ivan Cankar** and *Čaša opojnosti* (Intoxicating Cup) by **Oton Župančič**. Moderna ended in 1918, the year **Yugoslavia** was created, for that year marked the death of Ivan Cankar, Moderna's most important writer. Despite encompassing elements of radical, esthetic, and ideological movements, Slovene Moderna remained close to the Slovene national tradition and represented a creative period in **literature**, demonstrating deep allegiance to the national and sociohistorical identity of the Slovene nation. The journals *Ljubljanski zvon* (*Ljubljana Bell*) established in 1881 and *Dom in svet* (*Home and the World*) in 1888 were two publishing venues for *literati* of the time. Exponents of Moderna, including the poets Dragotin Kette, Josip Murn-Aleksandrov, and Oton Župančič, and the prosaist Ivan Cankar, had close ties with Slovene impressionist painters and with nature, both of which influenced their literary works. Literary impressionism can also be detected in the second generation of Moderna (after 1920) in the works of the writer Cvetko Golar and the poets Alojz Gradnik and **Srečko Kosovel** (earlier works). *See also* ARTS; EXPRESSIONISM; PRESS BEFORE 1990.

MODERNISM. The term *modernism* was first applied in the early 20th century to Slovene painting and sculpture to denote all unrealistic tendencies (e.g., post-**impressionism**, **expressionism**, constructivism, and cubism) in the visual **arts** before **World War II**. In the 1950s, when **social realism** was in decline, the older generation of painters became very distinct representatives of Slovene modernism; among them were Anton Gojmir Kos, Stane Kregar, Marij Pregelj, Lojze Spacal, and Gabrijel Stupica. Among the postwar generation, the leading modernist painters, also called abstract modernists, were Janez Bernik, Gustav Gnamuš, and Andrej Jemec. Since 1955 the **International Biennial of Graphic Art** held in **Ljubljana** has been an important source of influence for them. Steeped in existential anguish, contemporary modernist painting is sometimes called "dark modernism" (*temni modernizem*). Modernism in sculpture and especially architecture was strong. Among the sculptors were Zdenko Kalin, Karel Putrih, Slavko Tihec, and Drago Tršar. The leading modernist architects **Maks Fabiani**, **Jože Plečnik**, and Ivan Vurnik in the early 20th century were followed by Edo Ravnikar, Marko Mušič, and others. In the late 1960s and 1970s other contemporary trends in visual arts (conceptualism, video art) were also present. *See also* LITERATURE; MUSIC.

MOHORJEVA DRUŽBA. *See* SOCIETY OF ST. HERMAGORAS.

MURSKA SOBOTA. The seat of an urban municipality with 20,080 inhabitants, Murska Sobota is the largest city (14,178 inhabitants) in **Prekmurje**. After **World War II** it also became the economic and cultural center of the Pomurje **region**. Beside municipal and regional organizations, such as the regional Chamber of Commerce and **media** outlets (the weekly *Vestnik*; Radio Murska Sobota; regional TV Idea-Kanal; and TV AS, also a cable provider), Murska Sobota has a regional hospital, educational institutions, including a music school and an **adult education** center, a gallery, and a Regional and Study Library. An old settlement, the city has historic monuments from many periods: the tombstone of Viator, a Roman courier (150 AD); St. Nicholas's Church (13th century); and a Renaissance castle (17th century). There is also a neo-Gothic Lutheran church, built in 1910, and the late 19th and early 20th centuries are reflected in the urban center, with several Secession buildings along Slovenska Cesta (Slovene Road) and a distinct Pannonian character. Since 1956 the region's and city's history has been displayed in the regional **museum** (*Pokrajinski muzej*) inside Sobota's **castle**. The city also has an enormous socialist-realist monument, dedicated to the liberation of Prekmurje by the Soviets, which catches visitors' attention at the city's main square. Built in 1945, the monument is the work of a Russian engineer and the well-known Slovenian sculptors and brothers Boris and Zdenko Kalin. The Jewish cemetery has been turned into a memorial park, commemorating the earlier presence of **Jews** in Prekmurje.

Sobota, as natives call it, has developed along the Ledava River in the plains north of the Mura River. Earliest records, in 1366, note the city's name as Murazumbota (Hungarian). Although a Slavic settlement, Murska Sobota was under Hungarian civil administration (Železno/Zalalövő district) until 1920 and again during **World War II**. At the end of the 15th century, the feudal lords Széchy freed Sobota's people from feudal obligations, and the legendary Hungarian king Matthias Corvinus awarded free, fair rights to the town in 1479. In the late 17th century, the Szápary family became owner of the town and continued to influence it until the end of **World War I**. The Szápary residence, Sobota castle, was sold to the *občina* in 1934. In Železno district, the city began to develop its urban character in the mid-19th century with the establishment of trade, printing companies, a savings **bank**, and **libraries**, of which Szápary's was the most distinguished. Toward the end of 19th century, as the seat of the Vendish region, Murska Sobota became the cultural center and also the object of Magyarization. While there were religious and public elementary schools in Murska Sobota, there was not a single complete Slovene **language** public elementary school (grades 1–6) before World War I. The Slovene school system began developing after the war; the first Slovene secondary school (gymnasium) opened in Sobota in 1919.

During the interwar period two important Slovene weeklies were published in Sobota: the **Catholic** *Novine* (1913–1941) and *Murska krajina* (1932–1941). Ecclesiastically, Murska Sobota was a part of the Zagreb diocese in the 11th and 12th centuries, and then under the Hungarian dioceses Győr until 1777 and Szombathely until 1923, when it became part of the **Maribor** diocese. In the interwar era Murska Sobota was also a religious center for Lutherans (seat of *seniorat* after 1922) and Jews in Slovenia (the seat of the Jewish *občina*). During World War II, Hungarians occupied the city, establishing a military and then civil administration, which promoted Magyarization. Many Slovenes, especially Jews, were deported or killed.

Situated in the fertile Pannonian basin, Murska Sobota has long been a center of food processing industries. The largest enterprises have been Mesna Industrija Pomurje (meat processing, since 1922) and Pomurske Mlekarne (dairy, since 1955). With its main operation in Murska Sobota, the clothing manufacturer Mura, which exported 80 percent of its production, has been the largest regional employer since the 1980s. Despite a crisis in the **textile** industry, Mura continued to employ over 5,000 people in 2004, but financial losses were being covered by the Slovene **government** while the enterprise restructured. Various small industrial enterprises developed in the city and its vicinity, but in the 1990s and 2000s many declared bankruptcy. Among these were Pan-Agra, a producer of agricultural equipment, and Pomurski Tisk, a printing company. Others privatized, restructured, and continued their operation, including Kartonaža, the producer of packing products. At the edge of the town, Murska Sobota has been developing an industrial zone with small companies, in order to alleviate unemployment (14 percent in 2004). While its railway connection with Hungary—severed in 1968—was restored in 1999, Murska Sobota still needs better road connections. The construction of the new Maribor–Pince highway (Hungary) has begun and its completion is planned for 2008. With new railway and road connections Murska Sobota has the potential for developing **service** industries: **transport** and **tourism**. The city's idyllic hinterland with ethnological curiosities, folk traditions, and historical monuments is an attractive tourist destination. There are health **spas** nearby, and hunting and culinary specialties bring many visitors to the area.

MUSEUM OF MODERN ART / MODERNA GALERIJA. Established in 1948, **Ljubljana**'s Museum of Modern Art (*Moderna galerija*) holds a permanent collection of Slovene 20th-century **art**, beginning with the **impressionists** and continuing to most contemporary works. The museum collection also includes important works of 20th-century non-Slovene artists. Striving to establish a dialogue between the East and the West, the museum has created a unique international collection, 2000+Arteast, which has contributed to the formation of a new view of art history in the late 20th century. The museum operates at three venues: the *Moderna galerija* building, whose construction began before **World War II**; the *Mala galerija*, a small exhibition space, used since the 1960s; and a recently obtained space in the Metelkova Complex, which was a Yugoslav army barracks until 1991. In addition to retrospectives of important Slovene visual artists, the museum regularly organizes exhibits of contemporary Slovenes and world-renowned artists. The Foo Bar, a monthly event involving various **media**, from **music** to the Internet, takes place at the museum. An important project in progress is the evaluation of the Slovene alternative art scene in the 1970s and 1980s. Well-known for its quality and artistic sensibility, the museum cooperates with important contemporary art institutions outside Slovenia and also promotes Slovene artists abroad. A rich **library**, a restoration workshop, a photography lab, and an information center enable the museum to preserve and display art works, do research, and educate the general public about contemporary art. Until 1987 the museum had been the venue for the **International Biennial of Graphic Art**.

MUSEUMS. The first Slovene museum, the Carniolian Regional Museum (*Kranjski deželni muzej*), was established in 1821 in **Ljubljana** with the rich mineralogical collection of Baron **Žiga Zois** as its base. Renamed the National Museum (*Narodni muzej*) in the 1920s, it is one of 10 state museums in Slovenia. Among them are the **National Gallery** (*Narodna galerija*), the **Museum of Modern Art** (*Moderna galerija*), the Natural Science Museum (*Prirodoslovni muzej*), the Slovene Ethnographic Museum (*Slovenski etnografski muzej*), and the Museum of Recent History (*Muzej novejše zgodovine*). Except for the Technological Museum of Slovenia in Bistra, all state museums are located in Ljubljana. The National Museum originally collected all relevant materials from the Kranjska **region**, but later, with the establishment of other specialized museums and institutions, it has focused on archeology, cultural history, and numismatics. Smaller regional museums and galleries have been established in all regional centers: **Celje**, **Koper**, **Kranj**, Ljubljana, **Maribor**, **Murska Sobota**, **Nova Gorica**, **Novo Mesto**, and **Slovenj Gradec**.

The several town and specialized museums across Slovenia include the **Kobarid** Museum, dedicated to the Italian front in **World War I**, the Museum of Apiculture in **Radovljica**, and the **Velenje** Coal Mine (*Premogovnik Velenje*). Several open-air museums, preserving historical, ethnological, and cultural features of entire sites, thrive as independent institutions or as part of other established museums. The largest is in Rogatec (Štajerska), portraying life in a 19th-century village. A similar open-air museum in Pleterje (Dolenjska) has been developed since 1990, a collaboration between the local Carthusian monastery and the Institute for the Protection of Nature and Cultural Heritage of Novo Mesto. One of the oldest open-air museums is the **Partisan** wartime Hospital Franja (*Bolnica Franja*). As of 2005 the Association of Museums of Slovenia had 62 institutional members (museums and art galleries). *See also* VALVASOR, JANEZ VAJKARD.

MUSIC. Slovene music has always been part of the wider historical and social context prevailing in Slovene lands; it has been influenced by neighboring German and Italian musical movements. Before the 18th century, the music performed in the Slovene lands was mostly of the **folk** and religious kind, while talented Slovene composers, such as **Jacobus Gallus** (1550–1591), worked in more sophisticated European music centers (Prague and **Vienna**). Active in **Ljubljana** and Vienna, priest and composer Janez Krstnik Dolar (1620–1673) from **Kamnik** composed beautiful vocal and instrumental music in the **baroque** style, performed throughout Europe. He also taught music at the **Jesuit** college. Ljubljana's first music **society, Academia Philharmonicorum** (1701), brought new musical opportunities for the Slovenes. Among Slovene composers of that time, the most prominent place belongs to Jakob Zupan (1734–1810) from Kamnik, who wrote several church compositions and set to music the first Slovene opera, *Belin* (1780). His compositions, already written in early classicist style, were also preformed in churches throughout Central Europe. *See also* MEDIEVAL CULTURE AND ART.

The German-oriented Philharmonic Society (*Philharmonische Gesellschaft*) presided over musical life in the 19th century, performing works of contemporary European composers with whom it had close ties, including Joseph Haydn, Ludwig van Beethoven, Niccolò Paganini, Johannes Brahms, and Antonin Dvořak; the latter four were also elected its honorary members. Gustav Mahler was appointed conductor for the Ljubljana Regional Theater for the season 1880–1881. During the 19th century an institutional base was established for development of Slovene music. The most important among several music institutions was an all-Slovene music society, *Glasbena Matica* (GM), established in 1872 in Ljubljana (later also in **Maribor** and **Trieste**). The GM promoted Slovene music of all kinds: It published works by Slovene composers, established a music school (the later conservatory), and helped organize the Slovene Philharmonic (*Slovenska filharmonija*) (1908–1913), which performed mostly Slovene and other Slavic music. In the 19th century Slovene composers used folk music and songs as inspiration for their work; examples include *Gorenjski slavček* (The Nightingale of Gorenjska), a comic opera by Anton Foerster (1837–1926); numerous vocal compositions by Bejanim Ipavec (1829–1908); and the first Slovene romantic symphony, *Lovska simfonija* (Hunter's Symphony) by Franc Gerbič (1840–1917). *See also* READING SOCIETIES.

After **World War I** the Philharmonic Society joined the GM (1921). In the interwar years the GM had helped establish the Orchestral Society (1919) and the Ljubljana Philharmonic (1934). The first half of the 20th century was a creative period in Slovene music, marked by three consecutive groups of talented composers.

The music of the group associated with Novi Akordi (New Chords), among them Emil Adamič, Anton Lajovic, and Gojmir Krek, was still traditional, with elements of **impressionism** and new **romanticism.** The second group, the late romantic modernists of the 1920s, with Marij Kogoj (1892–1956) as one of the most distinctive Slovene composers ever, unified the late romantic style with **expressionism.** Educated in Prague, Slavko Osterc (1895–1941), a representative of the third wave, Linear Modernism, wrote more than 170 instrumental and vocal compositions. Following contemporary musical trends (atonality), Osterc created musical works that were successfully performed at home and abroad. Kogoj's opera *Črne maske / Black Masks* and Osterc's numerous compositions of all kinds put Slovene music on a par with contemporary music elsewhere in the world.

In the late 1940s and the 1950s under Communist rule, all creative prewar music movements were rejected, and music was mostly subordinated to functional use. In the 1960s Slovene musicians and composers began participating in international festivals and went beyond music traditionalism. For example, the young composer Ivo Petrič (1931–) organized a group of composers, Pro Musica Viva, which revived Kogoj's and Osterc's musical tradition by composing modernist music. In addition, Petrič established an ensemble (1962–1982), named after Slavko Osterc, which performed music promoted by Pro Musica Viva. Petrič was a prolific composer, of neo-impressionist leanings, producing *Lyrical Episodes* for oboe and orchestra (1974), *Grohar's Impressions* (1980), and *Dresden Concerto* for 15 solo strings (1987). Other contemporary composers were Lojze Lebič (1934–) and Alojz Srebotnjak (1931–). Trombonist and composer Vinko Globokar (1934–), who studied and worked in various European music centers (Berlin, Cologne, Paris) and became one of the leading personages in contemporary music, influenced world composers for percussion instruments.

In the 1970s and 1980s a new generation of musicians and composers born after **World War II** became active in Slovenia. They created stylistically diverse works without clear esthetic and compositional guidelines; among them were Maksimilijan Strmčnik (1948–), Bor Turel (1954–), Brina Jež-Brezavšek (1957–), and younger **postmodernists** such as Milko Lazar (1965–), Žiga Stanič (1973–), and Vito Žuraj (1974–). Slovene composers and musicians have been active in the International Society for Contemporary Music, which organized a Slovene section for contemporary music. It organizes Festival Unicum (its forerunner was the festival Musica Danubiana), where Slovene musicians get international exposure. Many musicians gained international acclaim, among them pianists Dubravka Tomšič-Srebotnjak and Bojan Gorišek, and flutist Irena Grafenauer. In the **Republic of Slovenia** there are two professional symphony orchestras: the Slovene Philharmonic (*Slovenska filharmonija*) since 1947, and the Symphonic Orchestra RTV Ljubljana (*Simfonični orkester RTV Ljubljana*) since 1955, both internationally known. There are also two opera houses (in Ljubljana and Maribor), each with its own orchestra. Many instrumental groups (some with a long tradition and of exceptional quality) and music festivals thrive in Slovenia.

Other music genres, such as light entertainment music and jazz, developed after World War II. Although the first jazz groups appeared in the 1920s and 1930s, it was not until the 1950s that jazz became popular. Soon after the war, the composer and musician Bojan Adamič (1912–1995) established the Dance Orchestra of RTV (*Plesni orkester RTV*), which mostly played jazz, while in the 1950s Urban Koder (1928–) organized the Ljubljana Dance Ensemble (*Ljubljanski plesni ansambel*). Since 1960 there has been a jazz festival, first at Bled, but after 1967 in Ljubljana; due to increased participation of foreign jazz musicians, the event changed its name from "Yugoslav" to "International" festival. Rock entered the Slovene musical scene in the 1970s with two groups: Kameleoni (Chameleons) and Mladi Levi (Young Lions). Socially engaged rock singers and smaller rock groups challenged social taboos (sex, politics) and rocked society. Among them, the group Laibach from Trbovlje, a mining town, had a special place within **Neue Slowenische Kunst** in the 1980s and 1990s.

In the late 19th and 20th centuries, ethnic music and dance—polka and waltz—became very popular in the entire Alpine region, including Slovenia. In 1953 the composer Slavko Avsenik, from Begunje near Bled (Gorenjska), organized the band Avseniki (accordion, bass, clarinet, guitar, trumpet), for which he wrote original songs and music. In collaboration with his brother Vilko, Slavko Avsenik produced over 1,000 original songs. The band created original ethnic music, which became very popular not only in Slovenia but elsewhere in Europe and in America. Countless concerts and millions of sold records across Europe and North America brought Avseniki international fame.

Slovenia has a rich tradition of choral singing. The Association of Slovene Choirs was established in 1894. Choral singing has been one of the most widespread leisure activities among Slovenes. There are still hundreds of adult, children's, and youth choirs organized by schools and churches, or by independent choral societies throughout Slovenia.

– N –

NAGODE TRIAL (1947). The Nagode trial took place in the summer of 1947. A disparate group of 15 Slovene intellectuals, led by Črtomir Nagode, was accused of treason and of attempting to destroy the political system in the **Federal People's Republic of Yugoslavia** (FPRY). Group members, who had contacts with Communist Party opponents in other Yugoslav centers, tried to organize legal opposition to the **Communist Party of Slovenia** (CPS). A number of similar but less publicized trials immediately after **World War II** helped the CPS eliminate potential opposition. Several members of the Nagode group belonged to the old royalists, who had advocated a **United Slovenia** and, for a short time at the beginning of the war, had cooperated with the **Liberation Front** (LF). Among the evidence presented at the trial were members' letters, published in England and the **United States**, which described the situation in Slovenia and called for democratic elections and intervention from abroad. Three defendants—Črtomir Nagode, Boris Furlan, and Ljubo Sirc—were sentenced to death; the other 12 were sentenced to long terms in labor camps. Nagode was executed immediately, while the death sentences of Sirc and Furlan were commuted to long-term imprisonment. However, most of the imprisoned were released from prison on probation or were pardoned between 1951 and 1953. In 1991, when the case was reopened in an **independent** Slovenia, the prosecutor withdrew the original indictments and the court vacated the 1947 verdicts. The following year, Ljubo Sirc became a candidate for president of Slovenia. *See also* COMMUNIST PARTY, OPPOSITION TO.

NARODNA NAPREDNA STRANKA / NATIONAL PROGRESSIVE PARTY (NNS). *See* LIBERALS.

NARODNOOSVOBODILNA VOJSKA (NOV) / NATIONAL LIBERATION ARMY. *See* PARTISANS.

NARODNOOSVOBODILNI BOJ (NOB). *See* NATIONAL LIBERATION STRUGGLE.

NATIONAL AND UNIVERSITY LIBRARY / NARODNA IN UNI-VERZITETNA KNJIŽNICA (NUK). Located in **Ljubljana**, the National and University Library is a national cultural institution and the largest **library** in Slovenia. Besides books, the library contains special collections of 505 incunabula, **medieval** manuscripts, newspapers, **music**, **graphic art**, and maps. Its two reading rooms, with about 250 seats, are used mostly by university students. Around 200,000 visitors come to the library yearly. Since 1992 it uses the Slovene Cooperative Online Bibliographic System and Service (COBISS). NUK also collects materials published by Slovenes and about Slovenes from around the world. In 2002 it had more than 2 million books and journals and 12,684 registered users. Since 1945 NUK has published numerous professional publications, among them *Slovenska bibliografija* (Slovene Bibliography), and it is the central cataloging service for Slovenia. The library oversees the education of librarians.

Its beginnings date to 1774, when Empress **Maria Theresa** established by decree a library in Ljubljana with 637 books saved from the fire of the **Jesuit** Collegium. In 1791 it was officially named the Lyceum Library (*Licejska knjižnica*). Over the years, the Lyceum Library received many books or entire library collections as gifts from nobles, intellectuals, and abolished monasteries. The library was opened to the public in 1794. Two decades later, it was granted the right to receive "obligatory" (deposit) copies of books and thus became the library for the Duchy of Carniola, where many leading Slovene intellectuals, such as **Matija Čop** and **Fran Levstik**, worked. When the Lyceum was abolished in 1850, the library was renamed the Study Library of Carniola (*Študijska knjižnica za Kranjsko*). The Franciscan monastery where the library was located was damaged in the Ljubljana earthquake of 1895, and the library had to move to a secondary school building, where it remained, despite bad working conditions (insufficient space and money), until 1941, when a new library was built.

After the **University of Ljubljana** was established in 1919, many thought that the Study Library of Carniola should be renamed the University Library, reflecting its actual function, but the Yugoslav centralist government opposed the suggested name. Instead it was renamed the State Study Library. In the 1930s university students of all political persuasions, organized in Academic Action, pressured the Yugoslav government to build a library, and finally money was allocated for a new building. Construction began in 1936. By 1941 the State

Study Library, which in 1938 was renamed the University Library (*Univerzitetna knjižnica*), moved into its new building, designed by **Jože Plečnik**. During **World War II** the library was damaged by fire and 60,000 books were destroyed. After the war, it assumed the function of a national library. The institution has been in dire need of more space and of modern information technology; a new building is planned for the future. Partial renovation and modernization of the existing structure were undertaken between 1995 and 2000. Preparations for the new library also began in 1995, but property acquisition and bureaucratic formalities have not yet been completed.

NATIONAL COMMITTEE FOR SLOVENIA / NARODNI ODBOR ZA SLOVENIJO (1944–1990). The National Committee, established in December 1944 by a group of people within the **Slovene Covenant**, was the underground, pro-Western, Slovene anticommunist government, which included conservatives, liberals, and socialists. Its president was Joža Basaj. The Committee issued a National Declaration advocating a **United Slovenia** within a Yugoslav federation under **Karadjordjević** rule. In the spring of 1945 the Committee demanded **Leon Rupnik**'s resignation as president of **Ljubljana** Province and inspector-general of the Slovene **Home Guard**. Rupnik refused and, with German support, proclaimed himself commander-in-chief of the Slovene Home Guard.

On 3 May 1945 the National Committee gathered in Ljubljana with some representatives of the prewar **political parties**, proclaimed itself the legitimate Slovene **government**, and issued "A historic proclamation of the formation of the Slovene national state within the Kingdom of Yugoslavia." The Germans learned about the National Committee's actions and tried to arrest its members. Rupnik, who had by then resigned all his positions, was a mediator between the Committee and the Germans, and convinced the latter to hand the province of Ljubljana over to the National Committee. The Home Guard, which the National Committee renamed the Slovene National Army, feared that it could not resist the approaching Yugoslav **Partisan** army. Therefore, on 5 May the National Committee retreated to the British-occupied zone of **Austria**, followed during the next few days by masses of Slovene anticommunist civilians and the army, which was then disarmed by the British. After **World War II** the National Committee for Slovenia operated in exile. In 1990 when Slovenia became a parliamentary democracy, the National Committee, whose headquarters had been in Argentina for decades, was finally dissolved. *See also* EMIGRATION, SLOVENE; MASSACRES, POST–WORLD WAR II; RESISTANCE, NONCOMMUNIST; YUGOSLAVIA, KINGDOM OF.

NATIONAL COUNCIL FOR SLOVENIA / NARODNI SVET ZA SLOVENIJO (NSS) (1941). During **World War II**, immediately after the German attack on **Yugoslavia** on 6 April 1941, Slovenia's governor (*ban*), **Marko Natlačen**, summoned the representatives of Slovene **political parties** and formed the **National Council for Slovenia** (*Narodni svet za Slovenijo*, NSS), patterned after the National Council of Slovenes, Croats, and Serbs of 1918. Natlačen was named its president. The **Communist Party of Slovenia** (CPS) expressed interest in joining the NSS but was rejected as an illegal party.

The NSS formally took over the governing of Slovenia, but the Royal Yugoslav army refused to follow its orders and withdrew from Slovenia. In a public proclamation, the NSS then asked Slovenes to remain calm and to cooperate with the Italians and the Germans to avoid unnecessary sacrifices. By 11 April, without any resistance, the Axis forces—German, Italian, and Hungarian—occupied all of Slovenia. Neither the Italians nor the Germans recognized the NSS or allowed any kind of local rule, which Natlačen tried to negotiate with them. **Lambert Ehrlich** suggested that an underground Slovene government be formed, but Natlačen and the Council rejected the idea. The NSS functioned for about two weeks. Later, some of its members joined the Italian-established *konzulta* (council) of the province of **Ljubljana** as Slovene advisers, hoping to represent Slovene interests, but except in cultural matters (the Italians assured the Slovenes respect for the Slovene **language** and their cultural institutions), they had very little influence. The mission of NSS was carried on by the **Slovene Covenant** established in 1942. *See also* SLOVENES, CROATS, AND SERBS, NATIONAL COUNCIL OF; RESISTANCE, NONCOMMUNIST.

NATIONAL GALLERY / NARODNA GALERIJA. The National Gallery in **Ljubljana** is the central Slovene institution for pre-20th-century **art**. It contains two permanent collections: Slovene works and works of European artists. The gallery owns over 3,000 paintings, 4,500 graphic works, and 800 sculptures. The permanent collection of Slovene art encompasses works from the 13th through early 20th centuries. Especially valuable among its many works are examples of **medieval** sculpture. Newly available space also enabled the gallery to install a permanent exhibit of its European collection. The gallery organizes important special exhibits, such as "The Gothic in Slovenia" (1995) and "The Life and Works of Valentin Metzinger," the Slovene **baroque** painter (2000). Although some initiatives for establishing a gallery had already been taken at the turn of the century by Ljubljana Mayor **Ivan Hribar** and the Slovene post-impressionist **Rihard Jakopič**, the gallery was not established until 1918. Organized as a **society**, it acquired its permanent location in 1928, when it moved into Ljubljana's National Center (*Narodni dom*). After **World War II** the National Gallery stopped operating as a society and, by government decree in 1946, became a state institution. As the gallery was pressed for space, it gave, in 1951, a part of its early 20th-century collection to the newly established **Museum of Modern Art**. In 1988 the gallery obtained space in a nearby building and began construction of new exhibit venues and other facilities. The expansion was completed in 2000.

NATIONAL LIBERATION STRUGGLE / NARODNOOSVOBO-DILNI BOJ (NOB) (1941–1945). During **World War II** a national liberation movement was organized by the **Liberation Front** (LF), which organized the **National Liberation Struggle** and its own **government** with many social and cultural institutions in **Partisan-controlled territories** in Slovenia. *See also* PARTISANS.

NATIONAL PROGRESSIVE PARTY / NARODNA NAPREDNA STRANKA (NNS). *See* LIBERALS.

NATIONAL QUESTION, THE SLOVENE. *See* SPERANS.

NATIONAL SYMBOLS. *See* ANTHEM OF THE REPUBLIC OF SLOVENIA; FLAG OF THE REPUBLIC OF SLOVENIA.

NATIONALIZATION OF PROPERTY (1946–1991). With the establishment of a "people's democracy" in the **People's Republic of Slovenia** (PRS), reforms following the Soviet economic model were introduced. Since nationalization of property was considered a prerequisite to the development of a Soviet-like socialist economy, both the **Constitution of 1946** for the **Federal People's Republic of Yugoslavia** (FPRY) and the **Constitution of 1947** (PRS) stipulated state ownership of the means of production. Nationalized property was a concept not entirely foreign to Slovenia, since the interwar monarchy had nationalized industrial, commercial, and financial institutions owned by foreigners. But in the post–**World War II** era, virtually all real estate and movable property would become state owned. This also included personal property (patents, licenses) related to nationalized enterprises. Nationalization was achieved through appropriation of private property. In December 1946 those sectors of the **economy** deemed to be of vital importance to the PRS were seized; **agriculture, banking** and insurance, commerce, construction, **forestry, manufacturing** and **mining**, and traffic and **transport** were nationalized. In April 1948 a federal law extended nationalization to cultural and **health** institutes, warehouses, wineries, and the property of foreign individuals and institutions. By the end of 1948, 99 percent of all industrial enterprises in Slovenia had been nationalized. Although private property was never entirely eliminated—by the mid-1960s small private enterprises were even encouraged—in 1958 nationalization was expanded to include private dwellings and land that exceeded an allowable maximum. While owners of nationalized property were legally entitled to compensation, reimbursement was generally ignored or was inadequate. Compensation to foreigners, however, was usually paid in accordance with specific international agreements.

In the period from 1945 until 1952, nationalized property came under state economic management, or central planning. This system characterized the period of **administrative socialism**. The eras of **market socialism** (1953–1974) and **contractual socialism** (1974–1990) thereafter modified how nationalized property was managed. Slovenia established **independence** in 1991 and soon after announced the implementation of **denationalization**. *See also* PRIVATIZATION.

NATLAČEN, MARKO (1886–1942). Marko Natlačen was the pre–**World War II** governor (*ban*) of the ***Drava banovina*** and, as leader of the **Slovene People's Party** (SLS), a close collaborator of **Anton Korošec**. Immediately after the German bombing of **Belgrade** on 6 April 1941, and the escape of the Yugoslav **government** abroad, Natlačen established in **Ljubljana** a **National Council for Slovenia** (*Narodni svet za Slovenijo*, NSS). Although Natlačen tried to extract some political concessions for Slovenes under **Italy**'s rule, he was not successful. Fearing Italian reprisals against them, Natlačen gave orders to destroy official lists of members of the **Communist Party of Slovenia** and its supporters. In order to have at least some influence over developments, Natlačen also joined the Italian-established

Consultative Council of Ljubljana Province. This move was criticized by some conservatives. The **Liberation Front** (LF) branded him a national traitor and in 1942 had the **Security and Intelligence Service** (*Varostno-obveščevalna služba*, VOS) assassinate him.

NATURAL RESOURCES. Slovenia's natural resources are insufficient for its needs and have not been efficiently exploited. Forests, which cover more than half of its territory and provide raw material for **energy** generation and **manufacturing**, and a natural habitat for animals (and venues for hunting), are perhaps the most valued resource. With their protection against erosion and as an air purifier, forests also help to maintain ecological balance. Arable land, another valuable resource, which is used for food production, accounts for 15 percent of Slovenia's area. Since **World War II** the amount of arable land has declined. In the 1980s alone, almost 10,000 hectares were lost to urban development.

An extensive water system with **rivers**, lakes, and mineral water springs is also an important natural resource in the **Republic of Slovenia** (RS). In the 19th century, running waters provided energy for forges and sawmills, whereas in the 20th century, they were used for hydroelectric power. Although Slovenia has several hydropower plants, only 40 percent of potential water power has been used for generation of electricity. A project for the construction of five hydropower plants in the lower reaches of the Sava River, which will double the generation of electricity, was begun in 2002 and is to be completed by 2018. Mineral waters, an additional source of drinking water, also have contributed to the development of health **tourism** (**spas**).

Minerals and ore reserves are either exhausted or of poor quality. Iron ore reserves were already depleted by the late 19th century, and several mines were closed because they were not cost-effective. Fossil fuels have been exhausted (crude oil) or are less frequently mined (brown coal), making Slovenia's **economy** dependent on imported fossil fuels (crude oil, low-sulfur coal, natural gas) for energy generation. There are still sufficient reserves of clay, gravel, and stone, important raw materials for construction, industry, and export. *See also* ENVIRONMENT; FORESTRY; MINING.

NEOABSOLUTISM IN AUSTRIAN EMPIRE (1851–1860). Once the **Revolution of 1848** was at last put down, a decade of repression followed in the **Austrian Empire**; it was **Vienna**'s way of dealing with liberals and nationalists. There was military occupation of the rebellious areas, and police surveillance and censorship everywhere. In 1855 a Concordat with Rome gave Vienna a counterrevolutionary ally in Pope Pius IX. An Austrian liberal characterized the regime as having a standing army of soldiers, a sitting army of bureaucrats, a kneeling army of clerics, and a creeping army of informers. It did not matter that some peoples, like the Slovenes, were **Austroslavs** and relatively peaceful in 1848. All were treated repressively in the 1850s. Slovenes, putting aside thoughts of political union, used the time for cultural activities. They wrote Slovene books and established publishing houses (e.g., **Society of St. Hermagoras** in **Klagenfurt**, 1851) and other cultural organizations. Such activity would continue into the 1860s with the establishment of the **Slovenska Matica (Ljubljana**, 1864) and the push to found **reading societies**.

NEO-ILLYRISM. With the incorporation of more South Slavs into the Austro-Hungarian state in 1908 (annexation of Bosnia and Herce-govina), Yugoslav political unity was again foremost on the minds of many Slovenes. **Illyrism**, the movement for South Slav cultural and linguistic unity, also experienced an impressive rejuvenation. In 1909 **Etbin Kristan**, head of the **Socialists**, had Illyrist goals incorporated into the party's program (Tivoli Resolution), and Fran Ilešič, the head of **Slovenska Matica**, urged the Slovenes to accept Serbo-Croatian as a common literary language with other Yugoslavs. Some of the strongest proponents of Illyrism on the eve of **World War I** were members of youth organizations, including **Preporod**.

Neo-Illyrism was such a hot topic among political and cultural leaders at the time that the journal *Veda* (*Science*) printed a question-naire on its various aspects. The responses, published in several num-bers of the journal, indicated that the central issue had not changed much since Illyrism in the days of Stanko Vraz and **France Prešeren**. Many agreed with some goals of Illyrism, such as using common terminology for new technology, but most balked at forced linguis-tic assimilation. Many still agreed with Prešeren that the real point was to preserve one's own national language and culture. Accepting Serbo-Croatian was just as deadly as succumbing to Germanization, a very worrisome fact of life for Slovenes in **Austria**. In either case, Slovene culture was threatened, resulting potentially in national extinction.

NEUE SLOWENISCHE KUNST (NSK) / NEW SLOVENE ART. Established in 1984 in **Ljubljana**, Neue Slowenische Kunst (NSK) is an organization of artists and **art** groups whose core consists of the rock group Laibach; the theater Kabinet Noordung, formerly Sestre Scipion Nasice (Sisters Scipion Nasice) and Rdeči Pilot (The Red Pilot); the group of visual artists Irwin; the graphic design group Novi Kolektivizem (New Collectivism); and others such as Graditelji (Builders/architects), Retrovision (video and film department), and the Department of Pure and Practical Philosophy. NSK has introduced into Slovene art new ideas and modes of work, known as retro-principles, which emphasize eclecticism, reinterpretation of esthetic models of the past, and affirmation of the nation and national culture. The idea of individual artistic expression and originality is replaced by the idea of group work and the "appropriation" of given visual materials, loaded with symbolism and provocative political messages. NSK was constituted as a collective artistic body, based on autonomy and collectivism. Its members are linked together in an "ideological council" and through it with the "general council," the supreme NSK decision-making body. Although NSK individuals or group members perform in public independently, their ambiguous, ironic, and provocative work has been directed toward the same goal: dissolving the borders between ideology, politics, and art.

Perhaps the most controversial NSK member is the rock group Laibach (*Laibach* is the German name for Ljubljana), which shocked Slovenes with its eclectic music and its physical appearance. In their best-known album, the 1987 *Krst pod Triglavom* (Baptism beneath Triglav), Laibach recreates ancient pagan music and includes modified passages from Johann Strauss as well as music sounding like German marches and singing in German. While performing, Laibach members wore Nazi-style uniforms and evoked various totalitarian images. It has been suggested that appropriated symbols were a parody on Slovene society of the 1980s. The paintings of Irwin—a group that, like Laibach, is well-known outside Slovenia—are collages that combine elements and images taken from the history of art with references to imagery of totalitarian politics. Despite its complex nature, NSK without a doubt helped the Slovenes assert their way to a freer society and **independence**. *See also* ALTERNATIVE MOVEMENTS; POSTMODERNISM.

NEW SLOVENIA–CHRISTIAN PEOPLE'S PARTY / NOVA SLOVENIJA–KRŠČANSKA LJUDSKA STRANKA (NSi). The New Slovenia–Christian People's Party was founded during the first

week of August 2000 under truly unusual circumstances. The previous parliamentary **election** had taken place in November 1996, and the next was scheduled for fall 2000. In April of that year, the relatively stable and successful **government** of November 1996–May 2000, headed by **Janez Drnovšek**'s **Liberal Democracy of Slovenia** (LDS), crumbled when the **Slovene People's Party** (SLS) left the coalition, and LDS fell on a vote of no confidence. The SLS had just merged with the **Slovene Christian Democrats** (SKD) to form the SLS-SKD-Slovene People's Party. With LDS in collapse, the new SLS-SKD offered **Andrej Bajuk**, who held no elected office, as its candidate for prime minister. It was a month before he was confirmed and another before his cabinet was approved. On 26 July 2000 the National Assembly passed a new electoral law, a compromise between the majority and proportional systems that were being discussed. The new law established a 4 percent vote threshold for seats in parliament, only a minor change in the existing law. The SLS-SKD voted for the law, but Bajuk and the Social Democratic Party (SDS) opposed it, favoring instead a majority electoral system with a winner-take-all provision. As a consequence, Bajuk decided to leave his party and form a new one.

Thus on 4 August the NSi was established by Andrej Bajuk, the prime minister, who in doing so left the very party whose coalition government he was heading, to the surprise even of the SLS-SKD president, France Zagožen. Bajuk took with him a contingent from the SLS-SKD, nearly 100 members in the first few days alone. The most prominent of those was **Lojze Peterle**, who was foreign minister at the time. In the ensuing months, Bajuk and NSi would have to deal with issues of party identity (how it might claim to represent the **Clericals** heritage of the late 19th century when SLS-SKD already did) and anger from SLS-SKD for having had its membership ranks cannibalized. Much of this was played out in public, while the business of government was left unattended. All the right parties suffered as a result in the election of October 2000. LDS was returned to power.

Not until one year later, in November 2001, did NSi finally adopt an official party program. It stressed the party's century-old **Christian Socialist** heritage, which it admittedly shared with SLS and SKD. It emphasized its commitment to traditional moral and social values, linking Slovenes to both Christian and **Enlightenment** culture. NSi included Slovenes worldwide in its purview and keeps close contact with especially the Slovene diaspora in Europe, North and South

America, and Australia. The party championed love of nation and civic pride, while stressing respect for the family, religious beliefs, and grassroots democracy. NSi did not reject that which was new, but proposed to strive for a balance between tradition and progress to assure a "Slovene" cultural, economic, and political development. It favored free trade and **privatization**, if achieved with proper social considerations. When expressing its principles, NSi often cited as examples those of similar parties in Europe, and it has affiliated with the European People's Party in the **European Union** (EU). In 2004, when Slovenes first elected representatives to the European Parliament, two of the seven were from NSi; in fact, the largest vote-getter in 2004 was Lojze Peterle. Associating with like-minded European parties has given NSi, as well as other Slovene rightist parties, substance and identity. The association very likely helped their victory in the election of October 2004. NSi, which had eight seats after the 2000 election, increased its number to nine. And in 2004, since SDS had the most votes and was called upon to form a government, NSi was included in the ruling coalition. Andrej Bajuk, the former official of several multilateral **banks**, became minister of finance, while three other party members took over the Ministries of Justice, of Social Affairs, and of Higher Education, Science and Technology. In November 2005 Andrej Bajuk was reelected president of his party.

NONALIGNMENT, NONALIGNED MOVEMENT. The central feature of **Yugoslavia**'s **foreign policy** from the 1960s through the 1980s was nonalignment. The policy grew out of Yugoslavia's sense of isolation after it was expelled from the **Cominform** in 1948, combined with security concerns engendered by the onset of the Cold War. **Edvard Kardelj**, the theoretician of nonalignment, understood that Yugoslavia's unique **workers' self-management** institutions could not survive in a hostile bipolar world. The goal of nonalignment therefore was not neutrality but peace. (War, Kardelj maintained, was not inevitable.) Therefore nonalignment aimed at loosening bloc allegiances, reducing international tensions, and restructuring the world's economy, particularly as it applied to developing (formerly colonial) nations.

Participants in the Bandung Conference in 1955 enunciated common anticolonialist concerns and laid the foundations for nonalignment. But the real founding meeting of the nonaligned nations took place in 1961 in **Belgrade**, the first conference where heads of state were present (25 in all). With **Tito** taking the lead, Yugoslavia gave the movement its ideology, direction, and clout. By 1976 the nonaligned movement—the third world—included more than two-thirds of all nations. During the 1980s, however, the movement was in decline. Instead of developing economically, many third-world powers used borrowed money to arm themselves. The result was indebtedness and armed conflicts between nonaligned nations. Also, Yugoslavia began to fall into disarray after Tito's death and the movement was left without its founder and leading advocate.

For Slovenia, involvement in the nonaligned movement brought easier access to third-world markets. Yet it distanced Slovenia from the more demanding markets. In the long term, it diminished Slovenia's competitiveness in relation to the West.

NON-GOVERNMENTAL ORGANIZATIONS (NGOs). *See* SOCIETIES.

NORTH ATLANTIC TREATY ORGANIZATION (NATO), RELATIONS WITH. As Slovenia was moving toward **independence** in the late 1980s, the broad rationale for it was "to return to Europe." In the 1991 Law on Foreign Policy, adopted by the newly sovereign **Republic of Slovenia** (RS), this goal contained two specific objectives: joining the **European Union** (EU) and associating with the **North Atlantic Treaty Organization** (NATO). The NATO goal was not one most Slovenes might have supported; in 1990 only 30 percent of the population even wanted to maintain an **army**. Until independence, Slovenia had been a part of **Yugoslavia**, protected by one of the largest military forces in Europe—the **Yugoslav People's Army** (JNA). But practical issues involving the new country's security prompted rethinking the matter. To assure its independence in the international community, and to protect itself against future enemies and immediate dangers (war in the former Yugoslavia would last until the end of 1995), some sovereignty might need to be sacrificed in the interests of security. In early 1993, therefore, the RS National Assembly approved a resolution on a national security plan. And so began the first round of Slovenia's quest to become a part of the North Atlantic alliance.

In early 1994 Slovenia joined NATO's Partnership for Peace (PfP) program, which involved military training and joint PfP exercises (Slovenes would first engage in PfP exercises in the **United States** the following year). Later in 1994 Slovenia became an associate partner in the North Atlantic Assembly. By early 1996 Slovenia was a full member of the North Atlantic Cooperation Council (NACC), and in spring the Slovene assembly went on record in support of NATO membership and collective defense. In January 1994 NATO had announced it would expand eastward, and Slovenia hoped—even expected—it would be included in the first group selected for membership. The country's governing center-left coalition pushed hard for NATO, and many at home and in the NATO community believed Slovenia would get in, along with the Czech Republic, **Hungary**, and Poland—the other leading candidates. But when the invitations were offered at the Madrid summit in July 1997, Slovenia was not included.

There are several explanations for Slovenia's exclusion in 1997—some involving the changing positions of NATO leadership, some involving Slovenia's own shortcomings. When NATO began drawing up its list of invitees in late 1996, Slovenia was on the short list for a number of reasons: It had not been in the Soviet bloc (as part of Yugoslavia it was **nonaligned**) and had no contiguous border with **Russia**; it was not important militarily; and it could be sold politically as a bridge between **Italy** and Hungary, a country that would be invited. But NATO's position on Slovenia changed, very likely only weeks before Madrid. This was due partly to France's late support of Romania as a candidate for admission. The U.S. opinion began to shift, as the Clinton White House started to worry that Congress could not be persuaded to vote for more than three new NATO members. (Slovenia might have gotten through, given its size and relative unimportance, but Romania could not; but then excluding Romania would have offended France, so Slovenia was probably sacrificed.) Slovenia also contributed to its own rejection, some contend, due to internal political confusion in the early part of 1996. After three months of trying to form a coalition, the **government** of November 1996–May 2000 had barely gotten started in March of 1997. That same month **Ljubljana** hosted a NATO meeting and failed to impress its guests. It was also clear that Slovenia's military was not up to snuff; it needed restructuring in order to qualify for NATO compatibility. It was also clear that there was strong opposition to NATO within Slovenia that came from the **Slovene National Party** (SNS), the Social Democratic Party (SDS), some prominent individuals from **Liberal Democracy of Slovenia** (LDS) and from the **United List of Social Democrats** (ZL), and especially the **Slovene People's Party** (SLS). In addition, Slovenes in general seemed to be pursuing NATO with a certain complacency, as did Slovenes abroad, particularly in the United States, where a strong push for NATO membership from a large ethnic contingent might have influenced congressional votes. But the Slovene American community was neither large nor strong in its support for the alliance.

At Madrid it was announced that there would be a second round of NATO enlargement. Slovenia and Romania were practically assured invitations, and this time Slovenia decided to move proactively on its own behalf. It got better at selling itself and getting known abroad, and it actively courted support in France and Great Britain. It also got strong support from **Italy**, which would become the official protector of Slovenia's airspace in view of Slovenia's non-existent air force. In 1997 Slovenia's parliament restated its determination to join NATO, and the RS diligently submitted annual Membership Action Plans (MAPs) to NATO after 1998. The RS also adopted a 12-year military restructuring plan. In Prague in November 2003, NATO offered memberships to seven former communist states (Bulgaria, Estonia, Latvia, Lithuania, Romania, Slovakia, and Slovenia). On 23 March, Slovenia held a referendum on NATO membership that got 66 percent approval; several days later, NATO members in Brussels signed a protocol approving Slovenia's accession. Only the formalities still remained: The RS National Assembly passed an act ratifying NATO membership on 24 February 2004, and on 29 March Slovenia formally deposited its Instrument of Accession in the depository in Washington, D.C.

As a NATO power, Slovenia has begun integrating into larger NATO military operations, based on NATO's newly adopted practice of division of labor and filling "niches" with needed expertise. Since Slovenia has no air force and virtually no navy, the RS's contributions to NATO are made through the army. Slovenia therefore has assumed responsibilities for specialized operations such as explosives detection, mountain fighting, reconnaissance, surveillance, and also nuclear, biological, and chemical (NBC) tasks. The RS is especially committed to peacekeeping operations and has sent forces into Afghanistan (20 to ISAF), Bosnia (173 to SFOR, now EUFOR), and Kosovo (34 to KFOR). It refused initially to join military operations in Iraq, because they had not been authorized by the **United Nations**. Instead five Slovenes trained Iraqi police in Jordan; however, in 2005 the new government under Prime Minister **Janez Janša** committed four Slovenes to train police in Iraq proper. In return for its participation in NATO, if Slovenia should come under threat, it expects the NATO alliance to come to its defense.

NOTRANJSKA. *See* REGIONS OF SLOVENIA.

NOVA GORICA. In the Primorska **region**'s Soča River valley, on the border with **Italy**, Nova Gorica is a town of 13,500 (with another 35,650 in Gorica *občina*). Nova Gorica has developed since 1947, after post–**World War II** boundaries severed it from Italian **Gorizia** and with it the community's administrative and cultural institutions. Nova Gorica grew adjacent to but separate from Gorizia; the border was closed, and while relations between the two towns were regularized in 1962, it was only after the **Osimo Treaty** in 1975 that they began to interact more normally, in areas such as commerce, communications, and **transportation**. Beginning in the late 1940s, Nova Gorica's growth was supported by the **government**, but it proceeded slowly; often youth work brigades undertook the task of creating an administrative and cultural center for the orphaned community. The town has developed a number of industries: construction; furniture production (Meblo); machinery (Gostol); children's shoes (Ciciban); and trucking transport (Vozila Gorica). Situated near the Vipava Valley and the Brda Hills, it is also a center for fruit processing and wine making. *See also* VITICULTURE.

Since 1986, with the opening of gambling casinos, Nova Gorica has become a center for entertainment **tourism**, aimed particularly at the nearby Italian tourist. On 30 April 2004, on the eve of Slovenia's accession into the **European Union** (EU), the border between Gorizia and Nova Gorica was symbolically erased. **Anton Rop** and Romano Prodi, the prime ministers of Slovenia and Italy, respectively, raised the EU flag, culminating an evening-long celebration that featured symphony orchestras and choruses from **Ljubljana** and **Trieste**.

Nova Gorica is a regional administrative as well as cultural center for western Slovenia. It has a provincial **museum**, **libraries**, and a theater. The Nova Gorica Polytechnic, whose faculty specializes in science and **environmental** issues of the Primorska region, is located here. The town hosts a small business fair each June as well as an annual international theater festival under the auspices of the **Alps–Adriatic Working Community**. Nova Gorica's central hub is distinguished by post–World War II architecture, whose designers were inspired by Le Corbusier's concept of the modern city. Monuments in the town are of recent, contemporary personages. The only noteworthy historic structure that was left on the Slovene side of the postwar border is a Franciscan monastery on Kostanjevica hill.

An early **baroque** building, begun in the 1620s, it is located in the hills above Nova Gorica to the southeast. Today it houses a priceless library collection, and beneath the monastery itself are crypts of the Bourbon family, members of which found refuge in Gorica after being expelled from France in the mid-19th century.

NOVA REVIJA / NEW REVIEW. Established in 1982, *Nova revija* (*New Review*) brought together the middle-aged and younger generations of Slovene writers, poets, and social thinkers who had been unable to publish their works on civil society, **literature**, political pluralism, and spiritual freedom in existing Slovene journals (*Dialogi, Naši razgledi, Problemi, Sodobnost*, or others specializing in specific professional fields). Besides works of Slovene authors, *Nova revija* published translations of contemporary world literature and became a forum for dialogue among intellectuals of the various Yugoslav republics. Its direction was greatly influenced by Heideggerian philosophers. The journal opened Slovenia to broader artistic and intellectual horizons, providing a vehicle for pluralistic expression, both in Slovenia and **Yugoslavia**.

In February 1987 *Nova revija* published a controversial issue, No. 57, which contained a collection of papers on the "Slovene National Program." Although the journal's authors maintained that their goal in No. 57 was to democratize the **Socialist Federal Republic of Yugoslavia** (SFRY), they were accused of advocating Slovene separatism. The federal prosecutor demanded that the journal and the authors of the No. 57 issue be prosecuted. Slovene authorities, among whom there was a growing opposition to Yugoslav centralism, resisted **Belgrade**'s demands. At the time, Slovene and Yugoslav hard-liners were being challenged by younger, reformist Communist leaders.

Nova revija was instrumental in bringing about Slovenia's first democratic **election** (April 1990) and Slovenia's **independence** (1991). In 1990 *Nova revija* became a **publishing** company; besides *Nova revija*, it now publishes the monthly journal *Ampak* (*But*), five other periodicals, and numerous books grouped in several series: *Phainomena* on philosophy, and *Slovenska kronika* (*Slovenian Chronicles*) and *Korenine* (*Roots*) on Slovenian history. Niko Grafenauer, a prominent Slovene poet, has been *Nova revija*'s chief editor for more than a decade.

NOVA SLOVENIJA–KRŠČANSKA LJUDSKA STRANKA (NSi). *See* NEW SLOVENIA–CHRISTIAN PEOPLE'S PARTY.

NOVO MESTO. The picturesque city of Novo Mesto, situated on the Krka River, is located near the **Ljubljana**–Zagreb highway. With 21,354 inhabitants in 2004, the city is the core of an urban municipality (*mestna občina*), Novo Mesto (41,405 inhabitants), and the center of the Southeastern Slovene region/Dolenjska (138,851 inhabitants). Novo Mesto has been a regional economic, cultural, and ecclesiastic center, a role it has played since **medieval** times. After **World War II** Novo Mesto began to develop **manufacturing** industries and has acquired an industrial character; two-thirds of its population is employed by industrial companies. The two largest employers are the pharmaceutical firm Krka with 4,700 employees and the motor vehicle manufacturer Revoz (a subsidiary of Renault) with 2,600 employees. Both companies have been export-oriented: In 2004 Krka exported 83 percent of its production, while Revoz exported 95 percent. Novo Mesto also has developed clothing, construction, and wood processing industries. **Tourism**, especially **health** tourism at the neighboring **spas**, has become an important regional economic activity. While schooling at the elementary and secondary levels has a long tradition, **higher education** had its modest beginnings only in the 1970s when the **University of Ljubljana** and the **University of Maribor** organized extension offerings here. Established in 1999, the Center for Higher Education has an independent School of Business and Management and aspires to become one of the new university centers of Slovenia. The local weekly *Dolenjski list* and monthly *Udarni list* are the most important regional newspapers. In addition to national broadcast **media**, local radio (Krka, Sraka) and TV stations Novo Mesto and Vaš Kanal operate in the city.

Although the area has been populated since the Bronze Age, Novo Mesto, which grew in the Middle Ages beneath the fortification Gradec, was first mentioned in the 11th century. A defense post against the **Turks** and a prosperous trade center, Novo Mesto was granted city rights in 1365 by the **Habsburg** Emperor Rudolf IV. In 1493 the **Holy Roman** Emperor Frederick III granted Novo Mesto a collegiate chapter, which gave the town ecclesiastical prominence. The chapter was abolished in 1810 but restored in 1831. In the mid-18th century, under the rule of **Maria Theresa**, Novo Mesto became the seat of the district (*kreis*), which brought to it a number of important institutions, such as a postal service (1738) and a gymnasium (1746). When the French ruled the **Illyrian Provinces** (1809–1813), a large peasant revolt against them was cruelly suppressed by the French here.

In 1863, on the occasion of the 500th anniversary of the city, a national **reading society** was established and initiated the building of a Slovene national home, the first in Slovenia. In the latter part of the 19th century, Novo Mesto acquired new schools and Slovene cultural institutions (the newspaper *Dolenjske novice*), a hospital, and a railway connection (1894), but there was little economic development. After **World War I** Novo Mesto tried to broaden its economic base by establishing industrial companies (**textiles**, wood processing) and also initiating the beginnings of **tourism**. During **World War II** Novo Mesto was first occupied by the Italians, and in the fall of 1943 by the Germans. The city was bombed by the Allies, many were deported, and **Liberation Front** sympathizers were killed by the occupiers. Politically polarized Novo Mesto, where the **Home Guard** had a stronghold, suffered not only because of foreign occupation but also from civil war. In the 1950s Novo Mesto began to develop industry, which in 1958 was aided by the construction of a highway connecting Novo Mesto with Ljubljana.

The city of Novo Mesto has numerous historical monuments. Among them are Marof, an archeological excavation site from the Bronze Age; the chapter church of St. Nicholas, with a Tintoretto painting gracing its main altar; and the 15th-century church of the Franciscan monastery (rebuilt in the 19th century). The history of Novo Mesto and its vicinity is well presented in the Dolenjska **museum**.

Situated along the beautiful cascading Krka River, also called the Slovene Loire, Novo Mesto has some interesting nearby attractions: several **castles** (Otočec), spas (Čateške Toplice, Dolenjske Toplice), and the lovely medieval town of Kostanjevica na Krki with a 13th-century Cistercian monastery, now the **Božidar Jakac** Gallery. In the last two centuries, many prominent Slovene artists and intellectuals have worked and influenced the life of this Dolenjska capital. With more than two dozen local cultural **societies**, the Cultural home, and the modern Cultural Center Janez Trdina, Novo Mesto is a lively city.

– O –

OBČINA. The post–**World War II** *občina*, or commune, was established in Slovenia (and **Yugoslavia**) in 1952 and confirmed by law in 1955. It was conceived as a "grassroots" political unit, part of a communal system (*komunalni sistem*) whose committees made policy and took decisions relating to the **economy** of the commune.

The postwar *občina* had two chambers in its governing body: One was elected by all adult citizens; in the other, a producers' council, representation was proportional to types of workers in the commune. This mirrored changes on the federal and republic levels established by the **Constitutional Law of 1953**. Private farmers were excluded from the second chamber and were therefore underrepresented. The *občina* had far-reaching powers: It nominated directors of enterprises, decided which new enterprises should be supported, and controlled the distribution of funds.

The *občina* was created at a time when the **Federal People's Republic of Yugoslavia** (FPRY) and **People's Republic of Slovenia** (PRS) were implementing political and economic decentralization. The reasons for this were both ideological and practical. Strides toward complete decentralization, however, were limited. The reformers were wary of the people's motives and abilities; *občinas* and **workers' councils** were essentially participatory, with limited powers. *See also* ADMINISTRATIVE SOCIALISM; MARKET SOCIALISM.

The *občina* system was expanded and redefined by the **Constitution of 1963** and **Constitution of 1974**. It was broadened to represent all producing groups and was ideologically fine-tuned with each new constitution or amendment. As *občinas* grew in size (there were 62 in Slovenia in the early 1990s), smaller units, **local communities** (*krajevne skupnosti*), were formed as constituent units of the *občina*. These were optional after the Constitution of 1963, obligatory after the Constitution of 1974. Local communities after 1974 elected *občina* delegations. The *občina* became the basic political unit of self-management socialism. *See also* WORKERS' SELF-MANAGEMENT.

The *občina* continued to exist in postcommunist Slovenia but lost its sociopolitical function. According to the Law on Local Self-Government passed at the end of 1993, the *občina* is simply the basic unit of local self-government. *Občinas* are legally permitted to merge into larger regions, but as yet none have done so. Consequently, the *občina* is the only subnational governmental entity in the Slovene republic. Free and fair *občina* elections have been held every four years since 1994. *Občina* size varies greatly: The smallest has as few as several hundred persons; the largest, **Ljubljana**, has more than 270,000 inhabitants. Since 1993, amendments to the *občina* law have outlined procedures for obtaining *občina* status, have specified salaries for elected officials (mayors and councilors), and have required 20 *občinas* to assure Roma representation on the ballot. *Občinas* have varied in their fiscal independence, relying often on national **government** support. In 2006 Slovenia had 210 *občinas*. *See also* MINORITIES IN SLOVENIA.

OMAN, IVAN (1929–). Born in Zminec near **Škofja Loka**, Ivan Oman has been a lifelong farmer and landowner. Intelligent and self-educated, Oman was publicly critical in the 1980s of the **government's agriculture** policies and fought for farmers' rights and more rational policies. For his political work in the Community Assembly of Škofja Loka, which was very critical of mainstream politics, he earned respect among farmers across Slovenia. In 1989 he was one of the founders and the first president of the Slovene Farmers' Alliance (SKZ), a professional association, which later became a **political party**. In the **elections** of 1990, Oman was elected a member of the presidency of the **Republic of Slovenia** (RS). After the elections of 1992 he became a member of the parliament. Although the SKZ was reorganized and renamed **Slovene People's Party** (SLS) under his leadership, Oman left its ranks due to an internal disagreement. A devout **Catholic** and an authority on **Janez Evangelist Krek**, Oman joined the **Slovene Christian Democrats** (SKD). Living on his farm, he is no longer actively involved in politics.

OMBUDSMAN FOR HUMAN RIGHTS. *See* HUMAN RIGHTS.

OREL/EAGLE. Orel (Eagle), a gymnastic **society**, was established by the Slovene Conservatives in 1906 as an alternative to the liberal **Sokol** (Falcon). In 1929 Orel, as an exclusively Slovene organization, was banned along with several other ethnically defined organizations, among them the **Slovene People's Party** (*Slovenska ljudska stranka*, SLS), Orel's founder. *See also* CLERICALS; JEGLIČ, ANTON BONAVENTURA; KREK, JANEZ EVANGELIST.

ORGANIZATION FOR SECURITY AND COOPERATION IN EUROPE (OSCE). The Conference for Security and Cooperation in Europe (CSCE) had it origins in the 1970s, when representatives from East and West began talking about normalizing relations. Mainly they discussed reducing the risks of war and establishing standards for democratic development throughought Europe. The Helsinki Accords of 1975, which had 35 signatories, embodied the accomplishments of their work, and any state in the future that joined the CSCE committed itself to Helsinki principles. The CSCE was unique before the collapse of communism in that it was the only organization that included as equal partners members from both blocs as well as the **United States** and Canada. Shortly after the Cold War ended, the CSCE became the Organization for Security and Cooperation in Europe (OSCE), and in the 1990s it assumed important functions in conflict prevention and post-conflict reconstruction, such as training security police, monitoring elections, and the like.

Newly independent Slovenia, a few days before it was recognized by the **European Union** (EU), applied for membership in the OSCE. On 24 March 1992, Slovenia was accepted into the association and in July signed the Helsinki Final Charter of 1975, which obligated it to comply with all instruments of the organization and to participate in its missions in the area of **human rights** protection, democratization, and civil policing duties. Slovenia was very anxious to be included in the OSCE, as it believed in its general purpose, which was conflict prevention. Appealing, too, was the fact that the OSCE was all inclusive with respect to European states, irrespective of previous Cold War orientation. Slovenia, at the time, also approved of dismantling military alliances. In the 1990s the OSCE was prominent in helping resolve crises in the Balkans and in Caucasian and Central Asian trouble spots. In 1998 Slovenia chaired the OSCE Security Cooperation Forum.

In the 21st century, the OSCE faced new problems, including international terrorism and human trafficking across borders. From its headquarters in **Vienna**, it continued to reach out to trouble spots in southeastern Europe and in the former Soviet Union. But the OSCE's role seemed to be undermined by a resurgence of East–West tensions, and the European divide had moved eastward due to the expansion of the **North Atlantic Treaty Organization** (NATO). Also, NATO appeared to be assuming supervision of nonmilitary functions once performed by the OSCE. The OSCE heads of state had not met since 1999, and all states were reluctant to contribute needed funds for important OSCE missions. In 2005 the OSCE had 55 member states and was headed by Slovenia, whose foreign minister, **Dimitrij Rupel**, presided over the financial and political debates.

OSIMO, TREATY OF (1975). On 11 November 1975, after years of intense diplomatic activity, an agreement was signed between **Italy** and **Yugoslavia** at Monte Santopietro, Osimo, Italy. It clarified the Italian–Yugoslav border, in dispute since the signing of the **London Agreement** in 1954. It also refined the legal position of the respective minorities and laid the groundwork for further cooperation between the two countries. The agreement confirmed the existing Italian–Yugoslav border and retained the London Agreement's special statute on **minorities** and their protection. Several agreements on economic cooperation were also signed. The Osimo Treaty went into effect in May 1977 after being ratified by both states. *See also* TRIESTE QUESTION.

OSVOBODILNA FRONTA (OF). *See* LIBERATION FRONT (LF).

– P –

PAHOR, BORUT (1963–). Born in **Postojna**, Borut Pahor studied international relations at the **University of Ljubljana**, and he became active in center-left politics in the late 1980s. In Slovenia's first multiparty election in 1990, Pahor was elected to the national parliament from the Party of Democratic Renewal list. He remained with that party, whose name was changed to **United List of Social Democrats**, and shortened in 2004 to Social Democrats (SD), and he was reelected to the National Assembly in 1992, 1996, and 2000. In 1992 and 2000 Pahor's party was part of the ruling coalition. Given his specialty, Pahor regularly was a member of the body's **foreign relations** committee. Between 1996 and 1997 he was vice president of the National Assembly and from 2000 to 2004 its popular president (speaker).

Early in his political career, Pahor gained valuable experience in the European political arena. From 1993 to 2000 he headed Slovenia's delegation to the Council of Europe. In 1996 he was one of that body's vice presidents. In 2004, when Slovenia joined the **European Union** (EU), he was elected one of Slovenia's seven representatives to the European Parliament; once there, he was grouped with the Party of European Socialists.

Since 1997 Pahor has also been president of his party, the SD. He stresses that the party is not "communist," that it is firmly in the European social-democratic tradition. In mid-2006 Pahor joined with most other Slovene **political parties**—the exception being **Liberal Democracy of Slovenia** (LDS)—endorsing the Partnership for Development, proposed by Prime Minister **Janez Janša**, whose center-right party, the **Slovene Democratic Party** (SDS), came to power in 2004.

PARTISAN-CONTROLLED TERRITORIES (1942–1945). As the National Liberation Army (*Narodna osvobodilna vojska*, NOV) grew during **World War II**, it became better organized. In the spring of 1942, after forcing the Italians to retreat, **Partisans** established their own administration in the territories they controlled. Elected National Liberation Committees (*Narodnoosvobodilni odbori*, NOO) replaced the old municipal councils; these were thereafter controlled by district or regional liberation committees, ultimately under the Slovene National Liberation Committee (*Slovenski narodnoosvobodilni odbor*, SNOO). The first partisan-controlled territory (May 1942) was in the **region** of Kočevje in southern Slovenia. In the spring of 1942 the Partisans also established often short-lived control in some areas of Dolenjska and Notranjska, exclusively in the Italian-occupied part (**Ljubljana** Province) of Slovenia. More permanent Partisan control over large territories came after the Italian capitulation in September 1943. The National Liberation Council for the Slovene Littoral soon almost completely controlled that area (formerly part of **Italy**) and proclaimed its annexation to independent Slovenia within **Yugoslavia**. In 1944 the Partisans also controlled areas in German-occupied Gorenjska and Štajerska.

The center of Partisan-controlled territory was **Bela Krajina**, where the Supreme Command of the NOV and the **Slovene National Liberation Council** (SNOS) were generally headquartered. The presidency of SNOS established governing departments (ministries) for the **economy**, judiciary, internal affairs, **education**, and **health**. One main concern of the new administration was the food supply for the Partisan army and for civilians, and therefore agricultural production was stimulated. The *Denarni zavod Slovenije*, a monetary institution that issued Partisan money (*scrip*) was also established. Civilian health services with hospitals were organized in addition to Partisan underground hospitals directly under the control of NOV's Supreme Command.

In Bela Krajina, the presidency of SNOS also established several cultural institutions: a Slovene National Theater, a Partisan Academy for the Arts, and a Scientific Institute (which functioned as an important document archive, used later in the peace negotiations). Slovene schools, mostly elementary but also a few high schools, and teacher training courses were organized; these were especially numerous in Primorska and Bela Krajina. At the end of the war, there were over a hundred elementary schools in the Partisan-controlled areas of Ljubljana Province alone. Several duplicating and printing shops were established. In the beginning of the war, Ljubljana, with five illegal newspapers, was the center of the Partisan printing "industry." Printing flourished especially after Italian capitulation, when each region developed its own printing and duplicating services. Many newspapers, bulletins, journals, and even books illustrated with high-quality graphic works were published during the war in the Partisan-controlled areas.

PARTISANS (1941–1945). In the summer of 1941, during **World War II**, the **Liberation Front** (LF) called for resistance to the Axis occupiers of Slovenia in the proclamation "To the Slovene Nation." Many nationally conscious Slovenes, regardless of political beliefs, went "into the hills" to fight the enemy. These Partisans formed the National Liberation Army (*Narodnoosvobodilna vojska*, NOV). Its Supreme Command, established after 22 June 1941, was controlled by LF leadership. Already during the summer of 1941, Partisans engaged in several minor military operations and acts of sabotage, especially in Štajerska and Gorenjska. The Germans and Italians retaliated by executing civilians and burning villages.

As more joined the Partisans, military detachments, battalions, brigades, and divisions were organized. During the war 35 Slovene brigades and six Slovene divisions operated on the territory of Slovenia. Italian Partisans cooperated with the NOV as well. Several Partisan units (brigades) were named after Slovene cultural heroes: **Prešeren**, **Cankar**, and **Kosovel**. Initially a small army, the NOV grew, with material support from the Allies, into a sizable, well-organized army by the end of the war. Both the NOV Supreme Command and LF's Executive Committee had headquarters in **Partisan-controlled territory**, mostly in Kočevsko and **Bela Krajina**.

In September 1941 the Supreme Plenum of the LF issued a decree merging Slovene Partisan formations with the Yugoslav NOV. In Slovenia the NOV was better developed in the Italian-occupied areas, especially in Kočevsko, Notranjska, and Dolenjska, although Partisan units were organized also in Štajerska, Gorenjska, and Primorska. In the summer of 1942 the Italians launched a major offensive against the Partisans in **Ljubljana** Province that lasted several months. The Partisans were not destroyed, but civilians suffered a great deal as Italians burned villages, exiled civilians or sent them to internment camps, and randomly shot hostages wherever they found signs of Partisans. Some Slovenes blamed these Italian actions on the Partisans, and as a result **Village Guards** were formed as local defense units. After **Italy** surrendered in September 1943 a **Home Guard** was organized to fight the Partisans and the Communist-led LF. *See also* RESISTANCE, NONCOMMUNIST.

The Partisans fought many battles against Germans and Italians. After the capitulation of Italy, the Partisans acquired Italian heavy weapons and seized a considerable amount of territory. They also fought successfully against some Slovene anticommunist royalist units—**Chetniks**—and the more numerous Village Guards, who were retreating toward Ljubljana. The Partisans also took bloody revenge on those civilians who supported anticommunists.

In December 1943 the Allies recognized the NOV and its military government as an ally, with **Tito** as its commander-in-chief, and put pressure on the **Yugoslav royal government in exile** to cooperate with Tito. The result was a meeting in June 1944 between Ivan Šubašić, president of the government in exile, and Tito. It produced an agreement recognizing the **Antifascist Council of National Liberation of Yugoslavia** (*Antifašističko veće narodnog oslobođenja Jugoslavije*, AVNOJ) as the temporary supreme political and legislative body of the new **Yugoslavia**, which after the war was to include members of other **political parties**. With the help of the Allies, the Slovene Partisans fought the Germans successfully in 1944 and 1945, coming to control considerable territory also in Štajerska and Primorska. In the spring of 1945 the Germans were in retreat from the Yugoslav army, the Allies, and the Slovene Partisans. The Partisans even pushed the Germans beyond western and northern Slovene ethnic borders, occupying **Trieste** and southern Carinthia, and thus for a short time uniting all ethnic Slovene territory with the exception of Venetian Slovenia. At the Allies' insistence, they had to withdraw from most of these areas. One week after German capitulation, the war ended in Slovenia (15 May 1945), and the NOV was incorporated into the **Yugoslav People's Army** (*Jugoslovenska narodna armija*, JNA). According to 2004 data, 27,135 Slovene members of Partisan military units died during the war. *See also* TRIESTE QUESTION; VETERANS.

PARTY OF DEMOCRATIC RENEWAL / STRANKA DEMO-KRATIČNE PRENOVE (SDP). *See* UNITED LIST OF SOCIAL DEMOCRATS.

PARTY OF YOUNG PEOPLE OF SLOVENIA / STRANKA MLA-DIH SLOVENIJE (SMS). The Party of Young People of Slovenia burst onto the political scene in July 2000 in **Ljubljana**. Its program was designed to engage the youth and others with fresh ideas in Slovenia's political life. It proposed to work toward an improved quality of life and a greater respect for the young, by focusing attention on **education**, employment, affordable housing, the **environment**, and local self-government. More specifically, SMS sought to abolish obligatory military service, legalize drugs and prostitution, lower the voting age to 16, and advocate a pro-life position regarding abortion. In **foreign policy** it opposed joining the **North Atlantic Treaty Organization** (NATO), largely because of the **United States'** dominance in the organization. SMS urged, rather, that Slovenia seek its security within the **European Union** (EU). Its organizers were primarily students from the **University of Ljubljana** and the **University of Maribor**. Its first president, Dominik Černjak, was a former president of the student parliament at the University of Ljubljana.

The SMS campaign in the 2000 **elections** was highly successful. Party leaders launched their campaign in a double-decker bus that traveled across Slovenia appealing for votes and new members. On the eve of the election (October 2000), SMS claimed to have 6,000 members, and polls were predicting the party would get a representative in parliament. SMS actually received four seats in parliament—a runaway victory for a party that was only months old. This success was marred somewhat by accusations, during the last stages of the campaign, that party officials had mishandled funds when they were involved in student government organizations.

Between 2000 and 2002 SMS aligned with the governing coalition led by **Liberal Democracy of Slovenia** (LDS); after 2002 it sided with the opposition camp. In 2002 it supported **France Bučar** as its candidate for president because of his pan-European stance. In the election of October 2004 SMS failed to win even one seat, receiving just a bit over 2 percent of the vote. Černjak, taking the blame, resigned from the presidency. SMS's new president, Darko Kranjc, is a former president of Student Organizations of Slovenia. He and SMS continue to work toward the party's goals and hope for electoral victories in the future. They were heartened by the election of an SMS mayor in the town of Podčetrtek in April 2005. The organization, which linked up with a small party of Greens during the 2004 electoral campaign, also has observer status in the European Green Party.

PEASANT REVOLTS. In the Slovene lands, peasant uprisings were common during the late 15th through mid-17th centuries. Developments related to the **Protestant Reformation** and **Counter Reformation**, as well as the **Turkish wars** of the 16th century, caused peasants to rebel against feudal lords who were exacting ever more taxes and servitude. Peasants organized, sometimes tens of thousands strong, in opposition to the new laws, demanding the right to pursue **craft** trades and engage in commerce, and calling for the restoration of the "old rights" (*stara pravda*). Generally, the peasants believed that the emperor, who was also battling the landed nobles, would restore those rights.

In 1478 there was a peasant revolt in **Carinthia**, and in 1515 a revolt involving more lands used Slovene words in slogans and banners. The largest, best-organized peasant uprising took place in 1573 and included both Slovenes and Croats. It was said that Matija Gubec, a rebel leader, wanted to become king of a Slovene-Croat territory free of feudal lords and feudal obligations. Uskok bands, hired by the nobles, put down this revolt and Gubec was tortured and killed. The last large peasant rebellion occurred in 1635. In all, the peasants' lot of economic hardship and increased servitude worsened. Even the Protestant reformers, urging respect for temporal authority, turned against them. It was not until the 18th-century peasant reforms and eventual abolition of serfdom (1848) that the peasants' bond to the feudal lord was broken.

PEN CENTER, SLOVENE (SLOVENSKI CENTER PEN). Slovene writers are active in the Slovene PEN Center, which was founded in 1926, only a few years after the establishment of the first PEN Club in England (1921). Among the founding members were **Oton Župančič** and **Izidor Cankar**. The PEN center did not function during **World War II**, but became active again in the 1960s. In 1965, the Slovene center organized the World PEN Congress in Bled. Since 1968 the PEN Center, in collaboration with the **Society of Slovene Writers**, has organized, among other activities, yearly international conferences on specific themes (e.g., Why We Write, 1971; PEN and Sword, 1992). The Slovene PEN Center's international reputation was enhanced with the establishment of the Writers for Peace Committee (1984), the initiative for which came from Slovene writers; the seat of the committee is in **Ljubljana.** The committee has helped writers in war-torn areas, such as Bosnia. In 2006, the Slovene PEN Center had 120 members.

PENSIONS. See SOCIAL SECURITY.

PEOPLE'S FRONT OF YUGOSLAVIA (PFY) / LJUDSKA FRONTA JUGOSLAVIJE (LFJ). Established in August 1945 in **Belgrade**, the People's Front of Yugoslavia (LFJ) evolved from similar regional organizations, including the **Liberation Front** (*Osvobodilna Fronta*, LF), and it was intended to be a coalition of various smaller parties (Yugoslav Republican, People's Peasant, Socialist, Croatian Republican Peasant, Peasant Union). From the very beginning the LFJ was controlled entirely by the **Communist Party of Yugoslavia** (CPY) and would formally accept the CPY program as its own in 1949. The LFJ won the 1945 **elections** (it was the only party that participated) and became the sole legal political organization in **Yugoslavia** other than the CPY. In 1953 the LFJ was renamed the **Socialist Alliance of Working People of Yugoslavia** (SAWPY). *See also* COMMUNIST PARTY, OPPOSITION TO; GOVERNMENT OF SLOVENIA, NATIONAL; GOVERNMENT, YUGOSLAV, 1945.

PEOPLE'S REPUBLIC OF SLOVENIA (PRS) / LJUDSKA REPUBLIKA SLOVENIJA (LRS) (1947–1963). The **Constitution of 1947** stipulated that the official name of Slovenia was the People's Republic of Slovenia (PRS). The PRS and its **government** had evolved during **World War II**, as Slovene territories were freed of their occupiers and as the resistance led by the **Communist Party of Slovenia** (CPS) set up local administration in **Partisan-controlled territories**. The resistance and revolutionary developments had paralleled and integrated with those in the rest of prewar **Yugoslavia**. Consequently, when the **Federal People's Republic of Yugoslavia** (FPRY) was established in 1946, Slovenia became one of its federative republics, adopting a constitution in 1947. Until the Constitutional Law of 1953, the chief governmental organ was a one-chamber People's Assembly (PA); between 1953 and 1963 the assembly had two chambers. With the **Constitution of 1963**, Slovenia's official name became the **Socialist Republic of Slovenia** (SRS). Following **independence** in 1991, the name became the **Republic of Slovenia** (RS).

PERSPEKTIVE/PERSPECTIVES (1960–1964). *Perspektive* (*Perspectives*) was a journal established by a group of liberal-minded intellectuals, some of them former Communists, who published articles critical of the **Communist Party of Slovenia** (CPS) and its policies, especially its relations with the **Communist Party of Yugoslavia** (CPY). After 1962 *Perspektive* developed a loyal following, and articles by **Jože Pučnik** and Veljko Rus alarmed CPS conservatives. Rus called for establishment of a legal opposition, and Pučnik, among others, was especially critical of the postwar development of Slovene **agriculture**. In early 1964 **Stane Kavčič**, then president of the committee that oversaw ideological correctness, attempted without success to persuade the journal's editorial board to alter the journal's direction. Conservative CPS pressure, especially from **Edvard Kardelj**, forced the State Publishing House to close *Perspektive*. Jože Pučnik, the only real dissident in Slovenia in the 1960s, was imprisoned, and *Perspektive*'s editor, **Tomaž Šalamun**, was arrested and detained for a day. Despite a rare—for **Yugoslavia**—public protest against the abolition of *Perspektive*, opposition views were silenced. The editor of the student newspaper *Tribuna* was replaced, and measures were taken against the editorial boards of journals such as *Problemi* (*Problems*) and *Sodobnost* (*Modernity*), which, although not of the same political views, supported *Perspektive*'s right to publish.

Perspektive played an important role in the democratization and **liberalization** of the mid-1960s. It helped to create a climate favorable for liberal developments. When the Ninth Congress of the CPY (1964) allowed economic reforms and greater economic autonomy for individual republics, it appeared to be fulfilling *Perspektive*'s mission. *See also* COMMUNIST PARTY, OPPOSITION TO.

PETERLE, LOJZE (1948–). Born in Čužnja vas, Lojze Peterle studied economics (1971) and received a B.A. in geography and history (1975) from the **University of Ljubljana**. From 1975 to 1984 he worked at Slovenia's Institute of Urban Planning, and from 1985 to 1989 he was an environmental protection adviser at the Institute of Social Planning. From political obscurity in the late 1980s, Peterle, who belonged to a group of **Catholic** intellectuals gathered around the journal *2000*, rose to become leader of Slovenia's Christian democratic movement. In 1989 he helped organize the **Slovene Christian Democrats** (SKD) and was its president until 2000, when he joined with **Andrej Bajuk** in establishing a new party, the **New Slovenia–Christian People's Party** (NSi). Peterle has been chair of NSi's Council since its founding.

In the **election** of April 1990, SKD was part of the **Demos** coalition. After the Demos victory—and because SKD tallied the most votes of the coalition parties—Peterle became prime minister. He resigned in spring 1992 after a vote of no confidence, ceding the remaining months of his term to **Janez Drnovšek**. From December 1992 through October 1994, Peterle was deputy prime minister and also the **Republic of Slovenia**'s (RS) foreign minister. He was foreign minister again briefly during Andrej Bajuk's **government** of May–November 2000. In the various ministerial positions he held, Peterle, like many of the center-right politicians, was driven primarily by ideological principles. For example, as foreign minister in 1993–1994 his goal (unauthorized by parliament) was to build ties with **Italy** and the Vatican, though it might mean reversing post–**World War II** territorial agreements with Slovenia's western neighbor. This produced an uproar at home. Like many newcomers to politics, Peterle's inexperience was no match for the leftist parties; hence, from an early explosion onto the political scene in 1990, Peterle lost influence and the party's strength waned through the decade. Peterle, however, continued to be interested in contacts across Europe with like-minded politicians. Slovenia's accession into the **European Union** (EU) put a new lease on Peterle's political life. After initial agreements with the EU in 2003, Peterle became an observer in the European Parliament. In June 2004, with Slovenia officially a part of Europe, seven representatives were elected to the European Parliament. Of the seven, Peterle tallied the most votes, an indication that he had grown in popularity and respect among Slovenes.

PETRIČ, ERNEST (1936–). Born in **Ljubljana**, Ernest Petrič studied at the **University of Ljubljana**, obtaining a law degree (1960) and a Ph.D. in international relations (1965). Immediately thereafter, Petrič began working as an assistant professor at the University of Ljubljana, where he, with a few breaks, was employed until 1989. A professor of international law and international relations, he held important administrative positions at the university, including director of the Research Institute and dean of the Faculty of Sociology, Political Sciences, and Journalism. He studied and lectured abroad (in Graz, Heidelberg, and **Vienna**), and from 1983 to 1986 he was professor of international relations and international law at the University of Addis Ababa, Ethiopia. His main professional areas were international law, international relations, **human rights**, and **minority** rights. He also served as an expert in several international organizations. Petrič wrote over a hundred articles on these topics and is the author of three important professional books: *Mednarodno varstvo narodnih manjšin* (International Protection of Ethnic Minorities, 1977), *La posizione giuridica internazionale della minoranza slovena in Italia* (The International Legal Position of the Slovenian Minority in Italy, 1981), and *Pravica do samoodločbe* (The Right to Self-Determination, 1984).

Since his student years, Petrič has been active in Slovene politics. He was a member of the Executive Council of Slovenia (the Slovene **government**) during a liberal political interlude under President **Stane Kavčič**. He was responsible for science and technology (1967–1972) and was also a deputy in the National Assembly of Slovenia (1967–1972). In 1971 the liberal-minded Petrič was involved in "the affair of the 25 delegates." This unofficial group in the National Assembly challenged the Communist hard-liners' control and put Petrič forward as the group's candidate for the **Federal Executive Council** (ZIS) without consulting the republic leadership of the **Socialist Alliance of Working People** (SAWP) or the League of Communists (LC; formerly the **Communist Party**). Although Petrič did not officially accept the candidacy—he was considering it—and consequently, in the early 1970s, he was put on a list of those who were to be excluded from politics. *See also* LIBERALIZATION OF THE 1960s.

In 1989 Petrič began his diplomatic career as the **Socialist Federal Republic of Yugoslavia**'s (SFRY) ambassador to India and Nepal. His service was cut short when **Yugoslavia** broke up in 1991, and in the fall of that year Petrič went to Washington, D.C., as unofficial representative of the **Republic of Slovenia** (RS) to the **United States**. He worked hard for U.S. **recognition** of Slovenia and, in 1992, was appointed Slovenia's ambassador to the United States and to Mexico, a position he held until 1997. After returning to Slovenia, he became state secretary (deputy minister) in the Ministry of Foreign Affairs (1997–2000). Since 2000 Petrič, as a senior Slovene diplomat, has held several key diplomatic positions: permanent representative to the United Nations (New York) and ambassador of Slovenia to Brazil, 2000–2002; permanent representative to the **Organization for Security and Cooperation in Europe** (OSCE), September 2002–August 2003; ambassador to **Austria** and permanent representative to international organizations headquartered in Vienna, since September 2002. *See also* FOREIGN RELATIONS AND DIPLOMACY.

PIRAN. In Istria, Piran (population 4,140) is Slovenia's most lovely coastal town. Unlike **Koper**, a larger commercial center to the north, Piran is primarily a Primorska tourist mecca. Located on a long, narrow peninsula that stretches into the Adriatic, the town, which flourished in the days of Venetian sea power during the 13th to 16th centuries, sustained itself with fishing and the salt trade. With narrow streets; squares and fountains hidden among Romanesque, Venetian Gothic, and Renaissance structures; and a bustling harbor for small fishing and recreational boats, Piran is especially picturesque. The town walls were built in the 16th century to keep out the Turks, who invaded Istria 16 times. Piran's most famous son was the composer-violinist and music teacher Giuseppe Tartini (1692–1770), whose violin, crafted by Amati, was replicated for the 300th anniversary celebration of Tartini's birth. A bronze statue of Tartini stands proudly in Piran's main square, as if posing for the tourist camera. *See also* TURKISH WARS.

Ancestors of modern-day Italians and Slovenes have lived together in the Piran area since the arrival of Slavs in the northern Adriatic **region**. After it became a commercial town, Piran was first Venetian, then under **Austria**'s control after 1815. Between the two world wars it was part of **Italy**, experiencing economic decline and Italianization. After **World War II** it went to **Yugoslavia**, and since 1991 is in the **Republic of Slovenia** (RS). In addition to **tourism**, which also extends to Portorož (Portorose) two kilometers to the southeast—where sandy beaches, luxury hotels, and casinos beckon—Piran is a center for the salt, olive oil, and wine trade. It is also still a fishing center and has a distinguished maritime **museum**. Since **independence**, however, fishing rights in the Bay of Piran have been hotly disputed with **Croatia**, whose land border with Slovenia runs just south of the Piran–Portorož resort strip.

PLANNING (1945–1990). After **World War II** the **Federal People's Republic of Yugoslavia** (FPRY) implemented a system of centralized planning, closely following the Soviet model. Initiated by the First **Five-Year Plan** (1947–1951), it did not bring satisfactory results, and centralized planning was gradually dismantled. In the early 1950s the Yugoslav economy was guided by yearly plans, but after 1957, five-year plans again directed the development of **market socialism**. The 1966–1970 and 1971–1975 five-year plans were characterized by indicative planning. The republics, however, could not agree on the plans' objectives and methods of implementation, and the federal **government** was unable to guide economic activity with ad hoc, often ideological interventions. In the early 1970s persistent economic problems were blamed on the market. The League of Communists of Yugoslavia (LCY), formerly the **Communist Party of Yugoslavia**, hence urged strengthening the role of planning, while reducing the role of market forces.

The social reforms of the early 1970s placed emphasis on social, participatory planning, which involved *občinas* and self-management structures under the guidance of the LCY. The **Constitution of 1974**, and especially the Law on Social Planning, set out in detail the planning processes, the relations among the planning agents, and the implementation of the plans. The new system required that the plans be drawn up by each enterprise, *občina*, and republic Self-managing Communities of Interest under the supervision of the Institute of Planning (*Zavod za planiranje*). Individually developed plans were then coordinated among the various sectors of production at the republic and federal levels. In general, consensus-building (conciliation process) among planning agents was slow and sometimes never realized because of conflicting, often regional interests. Social compacts, not legally binding on the signatories, were the mechanisms for codifying these "social" plans and consequently for giving direction to economic and social policies, which were to be executed by governments, which did not have any legal means to enforce proposed policies. Therefore, local, republic, and federal governments were unable to guide economic activities, while political organizations, the LCY in particular, became more powerful and intrusive. The result was the loss of government power at all levels and collapse of the Yugoslav social and economic system in the 1980s. *See also* CONTRACTUAL SOCIALISM; ECONOMY, 1945–1990.

PLEBISCITE, CARINTHIAN (10 OCTOBER 1920). Austria-Hungary's breakup following its defeat in **World War I** resulted in the creation of new states in Central Europe, which required the establishment of new international borders. The issue was of vital importance to Slovenes, who occupied the northernmost part of the newly created **Kingdom of the Serbs, Croats, and Slovenes**. They also predominated in southern portions of two Austrian border provinces: Carinthia and Styria. The issue was where the border between the Yugoslav kingdom and **Austria** was to be set. The border decisions were incorporated into the Treaty of Saint-Germain (10 September 1919), the postwar document that dealt exclusively with Austria. The border with Styria followed the demarcation line between the territories controlled by Austrian and Yugoslav armed forces. The same would not be the case to the west, with Carinthia, the southern part of which was predominantly Slovene and included its capital, **Klagenfurt**/Celovec. At the time, the area was controlled and administered by Yugoslav forces, although there were still occasional hostile skirmishes there.

A border encompassing the entire Slovene ethnic area of Carinthia was demanded at Saint-Germain by the Yugoslav representatives, who had France's support but were strongly opposed by **Italy** and the **United States**. Due to pressure from the latter, the treaty called for a plebiscite in the area of Yugoslav administration to determine the fate of southern Carinthia. The area was divided into a large Zone A, contiguous in the south to the Karavanke mountains, and north of it, a smaller Zone B, which included Klagenfurt/Celovec. On 10 October 1920 a plebiscite was held in Zone A. Because of strong pro-Austrian and anti-Serbian propaganda, the Zone A vote favored Austria 59 to 41 percent. With that result, the Zone B plebiscite was not held, for St. Germain provided that the latter vote should be taken only if the Zone A vote favored the Yugoslav state. Consequently the entire plebiscite area fell to Austria, leaving a large Slovene ethnic **minority** in Austria.

PLEBISCITE FOR INDEPENDENCE (23 DECEMBER 1990). After Slovenia's multiparty **election** in April 1990, a movement for **independence** grew. Greater Slovene autonomy within **Yugoslavia** had been favored by all **political parties**, but until then few would have backed complete separation. Indeed, for much of 1990 political support was greatest for a Yugoslav confederation (or loose federation), for many within the **Demos** coalition, as well as former Communists, were hesitant about severing ties with **Belgrade**. Yet constitutional amendments had already been made to facilitate independence. The rights of self-determination, secession, and rejection of federal laws had been adopted in Slovenia in late 1989. In the summer of 1990 the Socialists began promoting separation; by December others had come around to their view. *See also* ELECTIONS AFTER 1990.

Slovene parties had broken with the communist past. Representative democracy, rule of law, **human rights**, and market reforms were generally agreed-upon goals. Communism in the late 1980s was collapsing everywhere, the Cold War was ending, and Europe in 1992 was to be united. The Slovenes and their politicians wanted to be a part of these developments. The campaign for a referendum on independence even featured the slogan "Europe Now!" and posters depicted a 13th star, representing Slovenia, along with the 12 that appeared on the European Community (EC) flag. The major obstacle to achieving Slovenia's objectives was Serbia. Serbia effectively blocked the decentralization of Yugoslavia by controlling four (its own and those of Kosovo, Montenegro, and Vojvodina) of the eight votes on the federal presidency. Serbia continued to violate the rights of Albanians in Kosovo and opposed the reforms for Yugoslavia that would allow eventual admission into the EC. On the very day that Slovenia held its independence plebiscite, Serbia in its first multiparty elections reelected a Communist regime—as if to confirm that the Slovenes had been right in holding the referendum. Slovenes did not wish to live in a Serbian-dominated Yugoslavia, or "Serboslavia" as they called it. The independence plebiscite was held on 23 December, after two weeks of vigorous campaigning by all parties, who believed it was necessary to have a large voter turnout with a large affirmative vote. They were not disappointed: 93.2 percent of those registered voted, and 88.2 percent of registered voters voted "Yes." The results, announced on the 26th, were welcomed with statewide celebrations, which coincided with the Christmas holidays being celebrated for the first time since **World War II**. The plebiscite stipulated a six-month waiting period for independence to be declared, for negotiations with Yugoslavia's other republics might yet bring an acceptable solution that could eliminate the need for separation. Independence was declared on 25 June 1991.

PLEČNIK, JOŽE (1872–1957). Slovene architect Jože Plečnik studied in **Vienna** with Secession's great architect Otto Wagner. Plečnik worked on the Vienna railway station, the Sacherl House, and the Holy Spirit Church, and for this work is considered one of the founders of modern European architecture. In Prague, where he was a professor at the Art School, Plečnik is known for his renovation of the Prague Castle and the Church of the Sacred Heart. After 1920 he lived and worked mostly in **Ljubljana**, where he taught at the **University of Ljubljana**. Plečnik established the foundation for a new Slovene architecture, combining classical forms with natural materials that blended with the local environment—a concept that he deeply respected. His main works in Ljubljana are the **National and University Library**, the Market, the City of the Dead at Žale cemetery, and the landscape design of the banks of the river Ljubljanica, including the three bridges. His works also are found in many other parts of Slovenia and also in parts of the former **Yugoslavia** (Sarajevo, Split). Plečnik is the most important Slovene architect—one of world-class magnitude—who taught several generations of Slovene architects. *See also* ARTS; FABIANI, MAKS.

PODOBNIK, JANEZ (1959–). The future **Slovene People's Party** (SLS) leader Janez Podobnik was born in **Ljubljana**. During his student years at the **University of Ljubljana**, he was active in the **Catholic** student movement and wrote for the journals *2000* and

Tretji dan (*The Third Day*). Receiving a medical degree in 1984, he began medical practice at the **Idrija health** center, where he worked from 1985 to 1992. In the early 1990s he became involved in local politics, running on the **Demos** slate for the Idrijan provincial assembly. He was elected and became president of the assembly, a position he held from 1990 to 1995. From 1995 to 1998 Podobnik was mayor of Cerkno *občina*, whose major city was Idrija.

While practicing medicine (he stopped in 1992) and serving in local government, Podobnik also sought national political office. He was elected to the National Assembly in 1992 and has served in that body ever since. In the **election** of 1996, he was one of the popular mayors of Slovenia (25 in all) who were elected to National Assembly positions. Podobnik was popular, too, with opposition party politicians; hence, when the **government** of 1996 was being formed—although **Janez Drnovšek**, leader of **Liberal Democray of Slovenia** (LDS), had difficulties building his coalition—Podobnik was quickly and easily elected president (speaker) of the assembly. Podobnik is respected by colleagues for his level-headedness and ability as a consensus builder, and he and his party have served in all LDS left-of-center governments as well the right-of-center government of May–November 2000 and that elected in 2004. Often SLS and Podobnik played key roles in making a coalition viable.

Both Janez and his brother Marjan have been active in party and government politics, but Janez has by far been the more successful. Since 2000 Janez Podobnik has been SLS's pivotal figure. He has headed his party's parliamentary delegation, sat on its executive committee, and since November 2003 has been SLS president. As an observer in the **European Union** (EU) parliament, Podobnik has worked closely with the European People's Party.

POHLIN, MARKO (1735–1801). An Augustinian monk, Marko Pohlin worked in **Ljubljana** and **Vienna**. Although an opponent of the ideas of the French Revolution, he was an important figure in the Slovene **Enlightenment**. His 1768 grammar of the Slovene **language**, *Kraynska grammatika* (Carniolan Grammar), was of limited scholarly value, but it was extremely important for the Slovenes because it advocated the use of Slovene for both secular and religious purposes, and it prepared the way for the development of a modern literary language. He also authored several popular books and a Slovene–German–Italian dictionary (1781). *See also* ZOIS, ŽIGA.

POLICE. Between 1945 and 1991 the security forces in Slovenia were called "militia." Evolving from people's army elements in the resistance and revolution movement during **World War II**, the militia (an institution with 19th-century intellectual revolutionary roots) was initially modeled after similar forces in the USSR. By a **Federal People's Republic of Yugoslavia** (FPRY) law of 1946 the *ljudska milica* (people's militia) was extended to the entire country and organized militarily. It was divided into several working sectors, but in the end a major purpose of the militia in this people's state was to protect the people from its ideological enemies. Therefore the militia, as supervised by the Ministry of Internal Affairs, was at least partly a surveillance institution. After 1956 the militia's military and militant character began to diminish, and it allowed its operation and organization to be influenced by foreign models. The Slovene militia, which in 1967 became mostly the republic's preserve, absorbed some organizational features from the Swiss. About one-third of Slovenia's militia also functioned as border police. It was these who, together with the Slovene territorial defense units, clashed with **Yugoslav People's Army** (JNA) forces for control of the **Republic of Slovenia's** (RS) borders in June 1991 during the **Ten-Day War**.

Since **independence** (June 1991) and the establishment of a new political system, many institutions in the RS—including policing—have undergone transformation. In 1991 Slovenia's militia was renamed *policija* (police) and issued new uniforms. Between 1990 and 1996 the RS's police structure and its operation were fundamentally reorganized. Its tasks were enumerated as crime control, traffic control, border control, and the maintaining of public order. (From time to time, the police might also be charged with special tasks, such as protection of certain buildings or persons.) Located within the Ministry of Internal Affairs, the general police directorate, with headquarters in **Ljubljana**, topped the new three-tiered structure. Eleven regional directorates made up the second tier, while 39 police stations constituted the base. In addition to the 39, there were also separate units for police offices (51), traffic police (11), border police (16), air police (1), maritime police (1), mounted police (1), and two dog-handling units. In 1998 the Law on Police confirmed this reorganization and brought the operation of policing into line with Western European standards. Since then the police in Slovenia have acquired new equipment, discarding old Yugoslav-produced pistols for 9mm berettas. They also have at their disposal four helicopters and two boats for maritime policing, one of which is equipped with radar and satellite surveillance capabilities. In early 2005 Slovenia had 7,618 police, most of whom had high school educations, while 712 had college training and 56 had either master's or doctoral degrees. In addition to duties at home, Slovenia's police often undertake international responsibilities. This reflects not only Slovenia's new independent status but also the realities of international crime, where terrorism, human trafficking, and the like have become common. Thus since the late 1990s, the RS's police have engaged in joint training exercises with police in neighboring countries, and they have hosted instructional meetings with the U.S. Federal Bureau of Investigation (FBI). Slovenia's forces have participated in policing or police-training operations in Albania, Bosnia-Hercegovina, East Timor, Iraq, Jordan (where Slovenes initially trained Iraqi police in lieu of sending troops to fight in Iraq itself), Kosovo, and Macedonia. In May 2004, when Slovenia became part of the **European Union** (EU), Slovenia also took over monitoring the EU's border with **Croatia**. The EU finances this policing of Slovenia's portion of the Schengen, or external, border of Europe; however, Slovenia was required to provide the personnel to fill the positions. Policing this new border requires nearly 1,400 police and 500 customs officials. In 2003 Slovenia trained 390 new officers—its largest trainee class ever—at its police academy in Tacen, to fulfill its new EU responsibilities.

POLITICAL PARTIES, 1890–1918. In the Slovene lands of **Austria** there were three main political groupings, all of which formed into political parties in the 1890s. The names by which they were generally known in the period through **World War I** are: the National Progressive Party (*Narodna napredna stranka*, NNS), the **Liberals**; the Slovene People's Party (*Slovenska ljudska stranka*, SLS), the **Clericals**; and the Yugoslav Social Democratic Party (*Jugoslovanska socialnodemokratska stranka*, JSDS, the **Socialists**. They espoused political philosophies that were usually typical of corresponding parties elsewhere in Austria and the rest of Europe. Each of the Slovene parties also had a Slovene national program, essentially based on the **United Slovenia** program. Each planned to work with other Southern Slavs, usually those inside Austria-Hungary. In their national and "Yugoslav" programs, all three parties were loyal to "Austria."

In the Austrian (Cisleithanian) part of the dual monarchy, electoral laws changed every decade after the 1870s, broadening the franchise by gradually removing social and economic qualifications for voting until universal manhood suffrage was established in 1906. Extending the vote to include the lower ranks of society meant more Slovene voters. Broadening the franchise also favored the "socialist" elements (the Social Democrats and the **Christian Socialists**, a wing of the Slovene People's Party). In provincial assemblies, where universal suffrage was not introduced before World War I, Liberals had a somewhat better chance of being elected, particularly by town constituencies and especially by **Ljubljana** voters.

POLITICAL PARTIES AFTER 1990. On 27 December 1989, the Slovene parliament passed a law that permitted the establishment of political parties other than the League of Communists of Slovenia (LCS), the name of the **Communist Party of Slovenia** since 1952. Political parties then proliferated (numbering as many as 70 by some counts) and participated in the multiparty **elections** of April 1990, December 1992, November 1996, October 2000, and October 2004. Some parties have disappeared, while others have merged, split, or changed names in their brief lifetimes. (Only those parties that have won seats in elections have been included in this dictionary.) Each of the following parties has its own dictionary entry; an asterisk (*) indicates the party got seats in the State Assembly in the 2004 election:

*Democratic Party of Retired Persons of Slovenia / *Demokratična stranka upokojencev Slovenije* (DeSUS)

Democratic Party of Slovenia / *Demokratska stranka Slovenije* (Democrats)

Greens of Slovenia / *Zeleni Slovenije* (Greens)

*Liberal Democracy of Slovenia / *Liberalna demokracija Slovenije* (LDS)

Liberal Party / *Liberalna stranka* (LS)

*New Slovenia–Christian People's Party / *Nova Slovenija–Krščanska ljudska stranka* (NSi)

Party of Young People of Slovenia / *Stranka mladih Slovenije* (SMS)

Slovene Christian Democrats / *Slovenski krščanski demokrati* (SKD)

Slovene Democratic Alliance / *Slovenska demokratična zveza* (SDZ)

Slovene Democratic Alliance–National Democratic Party / *Slovenska demokratična zveza–Narodno demokratska stranka* (SDZ-NDS)

*Slovene Democratic Party / *Slovenska demokratska stranka* (SDS)
*Slovene National Party / *Slovenska nacionalna stranka* (SNS)
*Slovene People's Party / *Slovenska ljudska stranka* (SLS)
Socialist Party of Slovenia / *Socialistična stranka Slovenije* (SSS)
*United List of Social Democrats / *Združena lista socialnih demokratov* (ZLSD)

POLITICAL SYSTEM IN YUGOSLAVIA, 1945–1990. *See* ADMINISTRATIVE SOCIALISM; CONTRACTUAL SOCIALISM; GOVERNMENT, YUGOSLAV, 1945–1990; MARKET SOCIALISM.

POSTMODERNISM. The beginnings of Slovene postmodernism date to the 1970s. In **literature**, older writers such as Lojze Kovačič and Gregor Strniša, and younger ones such as **Drago Jančar**, Milan Jesih, and Ivo Svetina, follow postmodernist style. Among poets, Aleš Debeljak and Brane Gradišnik, influenced by American metaphysics, are most often labeled as postmodernists. In the early 1980s postmodernists were closely connected to the **alternative movements**. **Ljubljana**'s subcultural scene gave birth also to new **art** organizations such as **Neue Slowenische Kunst** (NSK). New groups and artists gathered around the Student Cultural-Art Center (*Študentski kulturno-umetniški center*, ŠKUC) challenged **modernism**. Painters such as Tugo Sušnik, Andraž Šalamun, and Tomo Podgornik, influenced by the American modernism tradition, tried to create a new visual language: fundamental painting. The movement Nova podoba (New Image) renewed a focus on objects in 1980, but was soon replaced with the introduction of "auto-poetics" in painting and sculpture.

Toward the end of the 1980s and in the 1990s, a new generation of postmodernist artists who did not follow Nova podoba emerged. Innovative Mojca Oblak created a transcendental Mannerism. Artists continued the artistic trends of the 1920s (**expressionism** and constructivism) and the 1960s (conceptualism of the OHO group). In postmodernist fashion, they followed various esthetic approaches, and their artwork is eclectic, as seen in the Irwin group. Dealing with everyday life instead of with big social issues, as was the case in the 1980s, their artworks are not permanent but often interdisciplinary installations and performances, which are locally constructed and invite public interactive participation. By switching to everyday life, postmodernists stressed de-esthetization of the autonomous art and were critical of formalism and institutions. Postmodernists include the group Veš, slikar, svoj dolg? (VSSD), whose name translates as "Painter, do you know your due?" as well as the artists Marko A. Kovačič and Tadej Pogačar; sculptors **Marjetica Potrč** and Jože Barši; video artists Marina Gržinić and Aina Šmid; Tomaž Pandur and Vito Taufer in **theater**; and Milko Lazar and Vito Žuraj in **music**. *See also* ARTS.

POSTOJNA. Notranjska's primary town, Postojna has 8,550 inhabitants. It has a major railway depot on the line between **Ljubljana** and **Trieste** (completed in 1857) and is a crossroads between those two cities as well as **Nova Gorica** and Rijeka. During the interwar years as part of **Italy**, it was a regional administrative center; after 1945, due to its proximity to potentially hostile Italy, Postojna acquired a large **Yugoslav People's Army** (JNA) base. Because of the area's **natural resources**, the town has some lumber and construction industry, and its LIV Postojna Group manufactures tools and hydraulic equipment for export. Postojna, however, is mainly a **tourist** center, best known for its magnificent limestone cave, Postojnska jama (Postojna Cave), a European travel attraction since the early 19th century. Postojnska jama is 20 kilometers long and today has five kilometers of tourist trails. It opened in 1819, professional cave guides were employed by 1825, and 1.5 kilometers of railroad tracks were installed in 1872. For tourist **transport** in the cave, wagons pushed by workers were used until 1924, when gas-powered locomotives were introduced; since 1955 the wagons have been battery-powered. The cave and Slovenia's other **karst** caverns are a center for speleobiology. Thirty-seven of 190 cave species can be found in Postojna, several of them indigenous to this particular cave complex. Unique to the area is the amphibian *Proteus anguinus* (up to 30 centimeters long), which is called the "human fish" because it is flesh-colored. Postojna's first tourist hotel was built in 1874 by a Swiss hotelier. Others have been opened, mostly since 1950, when tourism became an important industry. Today cave tourism has been combined with special events, generally scheduled for holidays: choral concerts, **folk** dance performances, and a crèche display for Christmas.

POTOČNIK, JANEZ (1958–). Born in Kropa, the town long known for **wrought iron** production, Janez Potočnik studied economics at the **University of Ljubljana**, where he received a doctorate in 1993. His dissertation compared Slovene economic development to that of the rest of **Yugoslavia**, a timely topic. From 1984 to 1987 he had worked for **Ljubljana**'s Institute for Macroeconomic Analysis and Development; from 1988 to 1993 he was a senior researcher at the Institute for

Economic Research, but after completing doctoral work, he returned to the former institute as its director, where he remained until 2001.

His political career began officially in 2001, when he was appointed minister councillor to the prime minister's cabinet. He worked with **Janez Drnovšek**, then prime minister and also an economist, as adviser on **European Union** (EU) accession. Potočnik had already assumed major responsibilities in this regard, having headed the negotiating team for Slovenia's EU accession since 1998. When **Igor Bavčar** resigned his position as minister for European affairs, Potočnik replaced him (2002–2004). Once Slovenia became an EU member in May 2004, Prime Minister **Anton Rop** appointed Potočnik as the nation's first representative to the European Commission. The five-year assignment is due to expire in 2009. Potočnik, as one of 25 European commissioners, one for each state in the EU, heads the Department for Science and Research and reports directly to the European Parliament and its Council of Ministers. His current appointment, at least partially a reward for his herculean efforts in preparing Slovenia for EU membership, may lay the groundwork for future political office. There is talk that when the Slovene presidency is next vacant, Potočnik would be an attractive candidate.

POTRČ, MARJETICA (1953–). Born in **Ljubljana**, Marjetica Potrč received degrees in architecture (1978) and sculpture (1986, 1988) from the **University of Ljubljana**. She lives in Ljubljana but has been working mostly abroad. Her work has been exhibited extensively in Slovenia and around the world, including at the Venice Biennial (1993, 2003) and Sao Paulo Biennial (1996, 2006). Beside having participated in numerous group exhibitions, Potrč has had several one-person shows at prestigious venues, among them the Guggenheim Museum (New York, 2001) after receiving the Hugo Boss Award in 2000; the Max Protech Gallery (New York, 2002, 2005); the Nordenhake (Berlin, Germany, 2003); the PBICA (Lake Worth, Florida, 2003); and the De Appel Foundation for Contemporary Art (Amsterdam, 2004). Her on-site installation *Genesis* (2005) is on permanent display at the Nobel Peace Center in Oslo. Potrč was a professor at the University of Ljubljana from 1995 to 2005. Since then she has been a freelance artist, working on various projects as well as teaching at prestigious art schools and universities; in 2005 she was a visiting professor at the Massachusetts Institute of Technology.

Active as an artist since the mid-1980s, Potrč initially produced very complex, beautiful sculptures, in which she examined relations between self, others, space, and objects, as in her sculptures in the Interferenzen VII exhibit at the Museum Moderner Kunst, **Vienna** (1992), and the Theatrum Mundi exhibit at Emerson Gallery, McLean Project for the Arts, Washington, D.C. (1996). Her artistic intuition and systematic research led Potrč organically closer to architecture and cities, urban planning, and human sustenance in today's world. She has created numerous intricate artworks, site-specific projects, and installations embedded in historical context (Magadan, Münster, Germany, 1997), and more recently, in the context of **environmental** and social problems, as in *Power Tools* (2001–); *Dry Toilet* (2003), and *Balcony with Wind Turbine* (2004). In creating personal and poetic stories about the contemporary world, Potrč is a storyteller who displays a deep understanding for basic human needs and, with her work, points to simple and also beautiful solutions to problems of human dwelling. *See also* ARTS; POSTMODERNISM.

PREGL, FRIDERIK (1869–1930). Born in **Ljubljana**, Friderik (Fritz) Pregl studied medicine at the University of Graz in **Austria**, where he received his M.D. degree (1894) and became an associate professor (1904). Specialization and teaching at other European universities (Leipzig, Tübingen, and Berlin) took him away for a year. When he returned to Graz, Pregl began working at the Institute of Medical Chemistry. From 1910 to 1913 he was full professor of applied medical chemistry at Innsbruck University. Returning to Graz in 1913, he worked until his death at the University of Graz, where he was dean of the Institute of Medical Chemistry (1916–1917) and vice chancellor (1920–1921). Besides being a scientist, he was also a devoted teacher. Many renowned European and American scientists studied with him and popularized his knowledge of new, more efficient instruments and methods for studying organic chemistry. In the scientific world, Pregl is known as the father of microanalysis. For his work on the development of microanalytical methods for organic substances, Pregl won the Nobel Prize in chemistry in 1923. He was also awarded the Lieben Prize for chemistry by the Imperial Academy of Science in **Vienna** (1914), received an honorary doctorate in philosophy from the University of Göttingen, and was elected a member of the Academy of Sciences in Vienna (1921). Pregl bequeathed his valuable microanalytical equipment to the University of Ljubljana. *See also* SCIENCE.

PREKMURJE/POMURJE. Located in the **Republic of Slovenia's** (RS) far northeast, on the edge of the Pannonian basin, Prekmurje borders **Austria, Croatia,** and **Hungary.** When the post–**World War I** Trianon Treaty (1920) divided the part of ethnically Slovene territory north of the Mura River between Hungary and the new **Yugoslavia,** Prekmurje was the latter's share. The part that remained in Hungary was known as Porabje. For over a millennium before that, and again during **World War II,** Prekmurje, populated by Hungarians and Slavs, was under Hungarian rule, which left a strong imprint on both Prekmurje and Porabje Slovenes. Prekmurje, a **region** of 950 square kilometers, is divided into two areas: the hilly Goričko and Lendavske Gorice (wine-growing areas) in the north and east, and the plains of Dolinsko and Ravensko (grain-producing areas) in the south. **Murska Sobota** and Lendava (3,395 inhabitants) are its largest towns. *See also* MINORITIES, SLOVENES IN HUNGARY.

After World War II, Prekmurje and the territories on the south bank of the Mura River, Apaško and Mura plains, with two larger towns Gornja Radgona (3,259 inhabitants) and Ljutomer (3,418 inhabitants), were combined into the Pomurje region, covering 1,377 square kilometers. Although the concept of a Pomurje region as a cultural unit first appeared in the mid-19th century, it did not materialize as a political and economic unit until 1955, with establishment of the Murska Sobota district (*okraj*), which included the territories south of the Mura River. The Pomurje region today contains 26 municipalities (*občinas*), with Murska Sobota as its regional center. The Pomurje region has 120,875 inhabitants, including two indigenous **minorities:** 5,445 Hungarians and 989 Roma. Numbers for the latter appear to be officially underreported; data obtained from the region's social services in the 1990s indicate that their number was three to four times higher than in the 2002 census.

There were **settlements** in this area from as early as the late Stone Age, but the region developed significantly only when a part of Roman Pannonia (first–fourth centuries AD). A Roman road connected Rome with Pannonian cities, and Romans built settlements along it; some were in southeastern Prekmurje. In the mid-sixth century AD, the area was settled by Slavic tribes, who became **Christianized** during Frankish rule. Hungarians occupied the region in the late ninth century and ruled it until 1920. In the turbulent times of **Turkish wars** and **peasant uprisings** (16th century), Slovenes in Prekmurje accepted the Lutheran religion under the **Protestant Reformation,** but they mostly returned to the **Catholic Church** in the late-18th century. Since the **Counter Reformation** was late reaching Hungarian-held Prekmurje, Protestant cultural activity lasted longer here than elsewhere in **Austria**'s Slovene lands. Protestants published religious books, among them Štefan Küzmič's notable translation of the New Testament (1711). Establishing the use of the Slovene **language**, albeit in its Prekmurje dialect, using Hungarian orthography, Lutheran churches introduced Slovene language **education**. After 1733, when the Counter Reformation reached the last Lutheran towns and villages, Protestant activities were banned. However, toward the end of the 18th century, Protestant religious schools were again allowed and coexisted with Catholic ones, which had also introduced Slovene language education. State-controlled schools, introduced at the beginning of 19th century, initiated systematic Magyarization pressures on the Slovene population that lasted until 1920.

The 1848 agrarian reforms and the creation of Austria-Hungary (1867) affected Prekmurje Slovenes in two ways. Firstly, large landowners acquired more land, while free peasants were quickly turned into impoverished farm laborers. Extreme poverty led to mass **emigration**; about one-third of Slovenes from Prekmurje immigrated mostly to the **United States**. Second, the Slovene population, which doubled in 1850–1900, was subjected to stronger Magyarization pressures. This was supported by most Lutheran clergy, who were oriented toward Budapest and Hungarian culture. Consequently, Slovenes here lost contact with mainstream Slovene culture. After 1848 on the other hand, Slovene Catholics established closer ties with the Slovenes south of the Mura River. They promoted Slovene books (among them publications of the **Society of St. Hermagoras**), printed in the "gajica" orthography, which Slovenes had adopted after 1848. Although the Slovene language was used as the language of instruction in religious education, it was not permitted in any schools beyond the fourth grade. In the early 20th century, Prekmurje Slovenes unsuccessfully demanded schooling in the Slovene language. *See also* ALPHABET WAR.

From the Middle Ages until 1920, Slovenes in Prekmurje were administratively divided between two Hungarian districts (*županijas*): Železno (northeastern Prekmurje) and Zala (southeastern Prekmurje). As to Catholic Church administration, Prekmurje was part of the Zagreb dioceses in the 11th and 12th centuries, and then of the Hungarian dioceses Győr and later Szombathely until 1923, when it was incorporated into the Lavantine (**Maribor**) diocese. Although the majority of Prekmurians are now Roman Catholic, 14,736 Lutherans still live in the region. Prekmurje also had a strong **Jewish** community, which would be eliminated through deportation and execution by the wartime occupiers during World War II.

In 1920 Prekmurje, with a sizable Hungarian minority, was annexed to the **Kingdom of Serbs, Croats, and Slovenes**. During the interwar era, Slovene language education (elementary and secondary schools) was begun. Although modest beginnings of industrialization in Prekmurje began in the late 19th century and continued between the two world wars, Prekmurje and the Pomurje region remained predominantly agricultural until the 1960s. Slow economic development and persisting poverty were due largely to poor connections with the Hungarian center and virtually no connection with Slovenes south of the Mura River. The first railway connecting Prekmurje with the Hungarian centers was built in the early 20th century, whereas the first rail connection with other Slovenes (Murska Sobota–Ormož) was built in 1924. Despite existence of some **transport** infrastructure after World War II, Prekmurje has been hard to reach, and towns within the region have been poorly connected. Since 1991 a few new routes have been opened; for example, the Puconci–Hodoš railway tracks removed in 1968 were restored in 1999, and the Vučja vas–Beltinci highway (14 km) was built and opened to traffic in 2003. The construction of the highway through Pomurje, connecting Maribor and Pince on the Slovenian–Hungarian border, was begun in 2005 and is to be finished by 2008.

That the predominantly rural Pomurje is the poorest region in Slovenia is reflected in its employment figures: 7 percent in **agriculture**; 8 percent each in food processing and construction; 27 in **services**; and 29 percent in industry, mostly in labor-intensive **manufacturing** branches (**textiles**). Main economic and human development indicators (life expectancy, **health**, number of students in **higher education**) have been below the Slovene average. In 2002 Pomurje's gross domestic product (GDP) per person reached 69 percent of the national average, and registered unemployment was 17 percent (24 percent in Lendava municipality), while the national average was 11 percent. With support from the national **government**, the Pomurje region has developed an industrial zone in Murska Sobota, and a business park in Lendava where several small businesses have been established. Economic growth in the region has also been stimulated by other factors. For example, in the period 2000–2003, the **European Union**'s (EU) cross-border PHARE program financed a dozen small projects intended to stimulate economic cooperation between the Pomurje region and the Hungarian districts Zala and Železno. Agriculture and food processing remain important for the region's **economy**. While the hilly part of Prekmurje is suited for wine production, the plains are ideal for farming; corn, fodder crops, potatoes, soybeans, and wheat are prevalent. Cattle breeding has also developed in the region, as have agricultural industries (meat and dairy processing; production of fertilizers). Pomurka Mesna Industrija, a part of the restructured ABC Pomurka holding (meat processing), and Pomurske Mlekarne (dairy) provide work for over 500 employees. Radenska d.d. is also an important regional company. Since its modest beginnings in the late 1869, it has developed into a quality operation bottling mineral water and nonalcoholic beverages, and it is export oriented. It employed 450 people in 2003. The largest employer in the region has been the clothing manufacturer Mura, with subsidiaries across Pomurje; it provided work for over 6,000 workers in the 1980s and early 1990s. Despite losses, covered by the national government, it still employed 5,350 workers in 2004. Crude oil and natural gas, discovered near Lendava, were important in the past, but reserves have been exhausted. Beginning its operation in 1945, Nafta Lendava expanded in the 1970s into petrochemicals and refining, which replaced crude oil extraction and processing in the 1970s. The company encountered huge financial problems in the 1980s and barely survived. In 1994 the company Petrol and the government became co-owners of Nafta Lendava. In 2002 the RS became the sole owner of a restructured Nafta Lendava enterprise, with its six new sister companies (about 500 employees in 2004).

Services, **tourism**, and transport have become important to the regional economy and have prospects for further development. The abundance of thermal waters in the region offers favorable conditions for expansion of health tourism, which already has a long tradition, and several **spas** (Terme 300–Moravske Toplice, Terme Lendava, Radenci, and Banovci) have already become popular tourist centers. Tourists are also drawn to the idyllic region's natural beauties, colorful **folk traditions**, historical monuments, possibilities for **sports** (hunting, riding, biking), and culinary specialties.

PRE-MARCH ERA. *See* HABSBURG RESTORATION, PRE-MARCH ERA.

PREPOROD. Before the outbreak of war between Austria-Hungary and Serbia (**World War I**), the only Slovene group that opposed **Austria**

and advocated an independent Yugoslav state was the student organization Preporod (Rebirth). The high schoolers, who by 1914 numbered from 700 to 1,000, established the secret society in January 1912. Preporod's center was in **Ljubljana**, but soon most Slovene towns also had branches. Preporod established ties with Slovene university students and with South Slav students throughout the empire, and in Serbia and Bulgaria as well. They even had contacts with the Young Bosnia society, a member of which assassinated Archduke **Francis Ferdinand**. They probably received some funding from Serbia.

The organization's anti-Austrian, pro-Serbian stance was promoted in the newspaper *Preporod*, and later in *Glas juga* (*Voice of the South*), both of which were severely censored. They rejected outright all plans to reform Austria, such as **trialism**, and they denounced their fathers' generation for its opportunism and cowardice in the face of Austrian authority. In March 1914 a Preporod-sponsored pamphlet, *Klic od Gospe svete* (The Call from Gospa Sveta), provoked a six-day student strike in Ljubljana. Although most Preporodovci supported Slovene cultural and linguistic integrity, some among the leadership probably were **Illyrists**.

When Francis Ferdinand was assassinated in Sarajevo, many Preporodovci were arrested and tried for treason, some in Ljubljana, others in Graz; however, evidence was generally too flimsy for convictions. The more committed members immediately fled Austria and fought for Serbia as volunteers. Many others joined in later. Preporodovci were regarded as heroes of Yugoslav political unity.

PRESIDENTS OF SLOVENIA. *See* ELECTIONS, PRESIDENTIAL, AFTER 1991. Refer to appendix 1.

PRESS BEFORE 1990. The first Slovene newspaper was *Lublanske novice* (*Ljubljana News*), inspired by the ideas of the **Zois** Circle. Published from 1797 to 1800, first as a weekly and later as a semiweekly, *Lublanske novice* had a circulation of 130 subscribers. Its editor was **Valentin Vodnik**. Oriented toward other Slavic nations, *Lublanske novice* was devoted mostly to foreign news. In accordance with **Enlightenment** trends, the paper was educational and practical. Because of financial problems and competition from the German-language *Laibacher Zeitung* (*Ljubljana News*), it ceased publication in 1800. In 1843 the Slovene weekly *Kmetijske in rokodelske novice* (*Peasant and Craftsmen's News*) appeared, published by **Janez Bleiweis**. The voice of the Old Slovenes, it was published continuously until 1902. Many literary, political, and professional newspapers and journals were spawned by the Slovene awakening and the development of Slovene political life in the second half of the 19th century. In 1863 the Young Slovenes began to publish *Naprej* (*Forward*) and in 1868 *Slovenski narod* (*Slovene Nation*), which advocated a **United Slovenia**, national equality, and brotherhood with other Slavs. *Slovenski narod*, which became a daily in 1873, was the pillar of Slovene liberalism; it would cease publication in 1943. In 1873 the political newspaper *Slovenec* (*The Slovene*), the pillar of emerging Slovene clericalism, appeared. Its editorial policies came under the influence of **Anton Mahnič** (1880s) and later **Janez Evangelist Krek** and his **Christian Socialism**. The **Clerical** *Slovenec*, joined in 1935 by *Slovenski dom* (*Slovene Home*), challenged the liberal dailies *Slovenski narod* and *Jutro* (*Morning*).

Toward the end of the 19th century, several other specialized weeklies and biweeklies with a **Catholic** orientation began publication in **Ljubljana**: *Dom in svet* (*Home and the World*, (1888–1944), first as a family magazine, then as a literary magazine; *Naša moč* (*Our Strength*); and *Glasnik* (*The Herald*), which spread the ideas of Christian socialism. Mahnič's *Rimski katolik* (*Roman Catholic*, 1889–1896) and Aleš Ušeničnik's *Katoliški obzornik* (*Catholic Review*, 1892–1906) were scholarly Catholic publications. Along with *Slovenski narod* (1868–1943), there were several other liberal publications. A special place was held by the liberal monthly literary magazine *Ljubljanski zvon* (*Ljubljana Bell*, 1881–1941), which published Slovene **literature** of the highest quality. After a split among the **liberals**, two important but short-lived journals appeared: *Slovan* (*The Slav*, 1884–1887) and *Ljubljanski list* (*Ljubljana Bulletin*, 1884–1885). In the early 20th century, several other papers appeared: the Yugoslav-oriented *Dan* (*Day*, 1912–1914), the radical student paper *Preporod* (*Rebirth*, 1912–1913), and the literary and scientific *Veda* (Knowledge, 1911–1915). *See also* FRAN LEVSTIK; MODERNA; REALISM; ROMANTICISM.

The Slovene leftist press between 1918 and 1945 was primarily an underground medium, which issued papers irregularly, had limited circulation, and, until the war broke out in 1941, had a small readership. Since the **Communist Party of Yugoslavia** (CPY) was outlawed in interwar **Yugoslavia**, leftist publications were produced abroad or illegally at home. The most durable was *Delo*, whose title varied during its lifetime from 1920 to 1940. It began as a Communist paper for Slovenes in **Italy**, and was published initially in **Trieste** and later in **Ljubljana**, Paris, **Vienna**, and again Paris—away from Italian fascist controls. *Delo* was read by workers, who were Slovene, Croatian, and Italian, most of whom lived in Trieste and its Italian and Yugoslav environs. In the early 1920s the weekly *Delo* at its peak had 800 subscribers and put out 2,300 issues. Slovene **Marxist** intellectuals wrote for the journals *Književnost* (*Literature*, 1932–1935) and *Sodobnost* (*The Present*, 1933–1941).

Under foreign occupation during **World War II**, publications in the Slovene **language** were mostly banned. The ban was strictly enforced by the Hungarians and Germans but not by the Italians. In the latter stages of the war, Germans permitted publications that were deferential to them or conveyed information that the occupier wanted made public. Labeled collaborationist, the conservative *Slovenec*, staunchly anticommunist *Slovenski dom*, and the liberal *Jutro* and *Slovenski narod* were published in Ljubljana during the war but were banned in 1945 along with the prewar **political parties**.

During the war, the **Partisan** press began underground **publishing** to inform Slovene readers of war developments and especially to rally them to the resistance movement. Sometimes only a page or two appeared—often mimeographed or even handwritten. Two papers that survived the war to become daily newspapers in May 1945 were *Slovenski poročevalec* (*Slovene Reporter*), which was the organ of the **Liberation Front** (LF) after 1941, and *Ljudska pravica* (*People's Justice*), the **Communist Party of Slovenia** (CPS) organ after 1943.

In 1959 *Slovenski poročevalec* and *Ljudska pravica* merged to create the present *Delo*, which became the organ of the **Socialist Alliance of Working People** (SAWP). It was the main paper in Slovenia, with the largest circulation among Slovene dailies (109,000 in 1987). *Dnevnik* (*The Daily*), later named *Ljubljanski dnevnik* (*Ljubljana Daily*), which began publishing in 1951, also had SAWP sponsorship. An afternoon paper, it relates information, events, and political news in abbreviated fashion. It has a limited number of correspondents, located exclusively in Slovenia. Since 1982 *Dnevnik* has produced a very popular Sunday edition, which is informational and entertaining. *Dnevnik* had about half the circulation of *Delo* (60,000 in 1987); its weekly *Nedeljski dnevnik* (*Sunday Daily*), however, had the largest circulation of any Slovene papers (245,000 in 1986).

In **Maribor**, the daily *Večer* (*Evening*), published since 1952, is a successor of *Vestnik*, which began its publication immediately after

World War II, at first as a weekly and then a daily since 1949. *Večer* has been the main newspaper of the Štajerska **region**, which later expanded its content with correspondents in other Slovene cities. It was published by the Večer publishing house in Maribor, which has put out other publications, such as the weekly *Sedem dni* (*Seven Days*) since 1972, and the first hardcore tabloid in Yugoslavia, *Kaj* (*What*), later renamed *Vroči kaj* (*Hot What*), which reached a circulation of 500,000 in 1989.

In addition to the three major dailies *Delo*, *Dnevnik*, and *Večer*, every region and larger city in Slovenia had its own local newspaper. These included *Dolenjski list* (*Dolenjska Gazette*) in **Novo Mesto**, *Primorske novice* (*Littoral News*) in **Koper**, and *Gorenjski glas* (*Voice of Gorenjska*) in **Kranj**. Since 1945 *Primorski dnevnik* (*Littoral Daily*) has been published by the Slovene **minority** in Italy, in **Trieste**.

After World War II, hundreds of magazines and professional journals were begun. Most were supported by public monies, but they, as well as the daily press, were closely monitored by the Communist Party, first by the **Agitprop** (1945–1952), and later by "reliable" editors and "trustworthy" persons chosen for their editorial boards. However, journals such as *Perspektive* (*Perspectives*) in the early 1960s, *Problemi* (*Problems*) in the 1970s, and *Mladina* (*Youth*) and *Nova revija* (*New Review*) in the 1980s published pieces that broke social taboos and caused legal and practical problems for their writers and editors, who were sued and often imprisoned, while individual issues of journals were sometimes censored or confiscated. In the 1980s journals and magazines became more independent and critical of society. Yet many journalists and writers self-censored to avoid problems for themselves. That self-censorship and fear of retribution were often reflected in the writing, which was often unclear and convoluted, or bureaucratic and lacking meaning for a reader.

PRESS SINCE 1990. At the beginning of the 1990s there were three main daily Slovene newspapers: *Delo* (*Work*) and *Dnevnik* (*Daily*) in **Ljubljana**, and *Večer* (*Evening*) in **Maribor**. But with the introduction of political pluralism and **independence**, new dailies, *Slovenec* (*The Slovene*) and *Republika* (*Republic*), were launched to provide alternative points of view. *Slovenec* began in 1991, with substantial **government** support, as the **Slovene Christian Democrats** (SKD) newspaper. Established in the tradition of the conservative *Slovenec* that had been abolished in 1945, the paper was right-leaning and had a circulation of about 32,000 in 1995. The newspaper folded in November 1996 due to poor circulation; soon thereafter, its **publishing** company declared bankruptcy. In 1992 *Republika*, a daily with a leftist political slant, was started in **Trieste**. The intellectuals who founded it were concerned that *Delo*, *Dnevnik*, and *Večer* would change their ideological orientation. Their aim was to sustain a press that would attract leftist readers in Slovenia and speak to Slovene **minorities** in **Italy** and **Austria** as well. But the existing papers remained leftist oriented, while *Republika* struggled to establish an identity and to fight declining readership. It closed in 1996. Trying to fill a void, the daily *Jutranjik* (*Morning Paper*) appeared in June 1998, only to cease publication three weeks later. *See also* PRESS BEFORE 1990.

Since 2000 the circulation of most dailies has declined, with the exception of the tabloid *Slovenske novice*. *Delo*, *Dnevnik*, and *Večer* were able to keep their market share, readership, and especially advertising revenue. Of the new papers, only the tabloid *Slovenske novice* (*Slovene News*), published by *Delo*, has been successful. Because it filled the void in the Slovene market, *Slovenske novice* not only survived but blossomed into the most popular paper in Slovenia, with a circulation around 85,000 in 2000 and approximately 101,000 in 2004. It is read by an estimated 400,000 people of all ages. In 2001 *Finance* (*Finances*), the only newspaper funded by foreign capital, became the leading economic daily and forced a successful weekly, *Gospodarski Vestnik* (*Economic Gazette*), established in 1951, out of business in 2005. The independent *Finance* offers news and analysis of the **economy**. With an investment of 3 million euros, the Swedish corporation Bonnier AG became the largest shareholder of the successful new daily. Most of the major newspapers and some magazines are available in full or in abbreviated form online.

Delo, the former organ of the **Socialist Alliance of Working People (SAWP)**, began to describe itself in 1991 as "an independent paper for an independent Slovenia." It continues to be the main serious daily in Slovenia. The paper's circulation fell from 93,000 in 2000 to 87,000 in 2003 but bounced back to 93,000 in 2004. It has correspondents at home and in major world capitals and has modernized its appearance. It produces numerous supplements, including a Saturday supplement of critical essays, a weekly book review section, a weekly radio and television guide, a Monday sports section, and cultural and scientific supplements. With close to 2 million copies of various newspapers and magazines produced each week, Delo Publishing controls over 70 percent of the Slovene press market. The publishing house was privatized and has over 400 shareholders; Pivovarna Laško (Laško Brewery), with 25 percent, is the largest. *Večer*, published in **Maribor** by Večer Publishing, continues to be the main newspaper in the northeastern part of Slovenia, with a circulation of approximately 57,000 in 2005. The weekly *7 dni* (*Seven Days*), the semimonthly *Naš dom* (*Our Home*), and a profitable porno publication *Vroči kaj* (*Hot What*) are the most popular Večer publications. The publishing company Dnevnik, acquired by Državna Založba, continues to publish the third most-read daily, *Dnevnik*, as well as its popular Sunday edition *Nedeljski dnevnik* and some new magazines.

In 2004 an estimated 1,000 printed **media**—newspapers, magazines, and professional journals of all kinds—were published in Slovenia. Several local newspapers, such as *Primorske novice* in **Koper**, and *Dolenjski list* in **Novo Mesto**, are published several times a week and report mainly local and regional news. There are many weekly magazines, some of a general nature, such as the independent *Mladina*, and *Mag* (since 1994), and numerous specialized ones, such as *Delo in Dom* (*Work and Home*) and *Zdravje* (*Health*). Expanding since the 1980s, the **Catholic** press commands an important market share. The weekly *Družina* (*Family*) and the monthly *Ognjišče* (*Hearth*), with a combined circulation of more than 80,000, certainly have a wide readership.

Very few English-language publications were available before Slovenia became independent in 1991. This has changed, with regular and occasional publications by the government as well as independent publications. Important information on Slovenia in both Slovene and English is provided by the government website. The Government Relations and Media Office puts out a number of publications in English, such as the bimonthly *Slovenia Times* and an informational and promotional monthly, *Sinfo* (since November 2004). It also maintains a number of interesting websites that contain current information about Slovenia, such as Discover Slovenia and Slovenia News. The yearly publication *Facts about Slovenia* is published by the Statistical Office of the RS. These publications can be viewed online without charge. Established in 1991 by the government, the Slovene Press Agency offers daily news in Slovene and English. Business news can be obtained online in *Slovenia Business Week*, provided by the Chamber of Commerce in cooperation with STA.

Since 2003 the biweekly *Slovenia Times*, intended primarily for foreign businesspeople and diplomats living in Slovenia, offers short, analytical articles and current news about various topics to 10 million yearly visitors to Slovenia and to Slovene expatriates worldwide. *Slovenia Times* is distributed free at the Ljubljana airport. Two publications intended primarily for **tourists** are available: the bimonthlies *Ljubljana Life* and *Slovenia Bulletin*. The former is available in print and online and is offered free at travel agencies, hotels, restaurants, and other public places. The latter, also available in both forms, is similar to the first but also highlights top stories as reported in the daily Slovene media.

PREŠEREN, FRANCE (1800–1849). A lawyer by profession, France Prešeren, who was born in Vrba near Bled, was the greatest Slovene **romantic** poet and a celebrated European poet of the time. With Prešeren, Slovene **literature** reached its first peak. For some, he is the greatest Slovene poet of all time. Under **Matija Čop**'s influence, Prešeren introduced new poetic forms. He combined classical, renaissance, and romantic elements with Slovene **folk traditions**. *Poezije doktorja Franceta Prešerna* (Poems of Dr. France Prešeren), first published in 1845, is the first Slovene poetry book of world stature. In his poetry, Prešeren deals with unfulfilled love, the problems of an artist in a backward society, homeland, humanity, friendships, and other existential laments. His most-known epic is *Krst pri Savici* (Baptism at the Savica), which deals with the **Christianization of Slovenes**. Politically, he was a **liberal** with strong anti-German sentiments. Due to his political views Prešeren was in frequent conflict with the **Vienna** government as well as with the **Catholic Church**, which considered his romantic poetry immoral. The poem *Zdravljica* (A Toast), a stanza of which was chosen as the national **anthem** of the **Republic of Slovenia** in 1991, was excluded by Vienna censors from the first edition of his collection because it was allegedly too nationalistic. *See also* ALPHABET WAR; HABSBURG RESTORATION; KOPITAR, JERNEJ; LANGUAGE, SLOVENE; REVOLUTION OF 1848.

PRIMORSKA. *See* REGIONS OF SLOVENIA.

PRIVATIZATION, 1992–2005. Although privatization began even before Slovenia's **independence**, it had not yet been completed by mid-2006. The state continues to control a large portion of the public sector, as well as some enterprises: Nova Kreditna banka Maribor, Slovenia's second largest **bank**, is 100 percent state owned. The right-of-center **government** in office as of December 2004 hopes to achieve a more competitive **economy** and has been pursuing privatization more vigorously.

Two major legislative approaches to privatization were proposed in 1991; the first was the Korže-Mencinger-Simoneti bill, the second the Sachs-Peterle-Umek bill. Opposed to undue systemic shock, the first proposal advocated gradual, decentralized privatization, where companies themselves would determine the pace and method of privatization, albeit within legal limits. The only government role would be to ensure the legality of the privatization. The second proposal, prompted by foreign consultants—among them Jeffrey Sachs, the noted American "shock therapy" advocate—pressed for a centralized, top-down, speedy distributional privatization, used in other post-communist states, that was designed quickly to establish private ownership of companies and corporate governance. Both proposals had their advantages and disadvantages, and the ensuing debates were politically loaded and bitter. After two years and three drafts, the result was a compromise, the Ownership Transformation Act of November 1992, which favored a gradual and consensual approach. It limited foreign investment in privatization. It allowed a variety of privatization methods. But it did not address privatization of institutions providing public **services** (42 percent of social capital) or of companies that had filed for bankruptcy. Privatization would be achieved by distributing social capital in several ways: directly to employees in the form of vouchers (40 percent); through sales to workers, managers, and outside investors (40 percent); and through allocations to the Pension Fund (10 percent) and the Compensation Fund (10 percent). Depending on age, each Slovene citizen was entitled to receive ownership certificates, amounting to from 4,000 to 6,000 German marks, which were then exchanged for shares of the beneficiary's choosing. Shares acquired in this manner could not be resold for two years.

The privatization of 2,600 socially owned enterprises with a book value of approximately $8.8 billion (58 percent of the value of social capital) began in accordance with the 1992 law. Of these enterprises, 150 were considered large (more than 500 employees), 750 were medium-sized (over 125 employees), and the rest were small. Two government agencies were established to supervise the process:

the Agency for Restructuring and Privatization, which advised on methods and monitored procedures, and the Development Fund, which managed the distribution of securities and sales of enterprises (similar to the *Treuhand* in Germany). The Development Fund was responsible for restructuring and privatizing (through sales) of unprofitable companies, while remaining enterprises were to be privatized under the provisions of the Ownership Transformation Act. The task of privatizing large public utilities companies, such as railways and transportation systems, was left to the government.

Privatization decrees, issued in March 1993, required each enterprise to choose a method of privatization and to prepare an implementation program by the end of 1994; for enterprises that failed to do so, this would be done by government agencies. Following a set of rather complicated rules, socially owned enterprises could be privatized by being sold in their entirety or in part, or by investment of fresh capital. If foreign offers of more than 10 million euros were involved, the transactions needed to be approved by the Privatization Agency. Internal buyouts, especially for small enterprises, were the most popular method of privatization. Although several joint ventures were established in Slovenia, there was considerable resistance to foreign purchase of Slovene enterprises and also to foreign direct investment (FDI). Over 20 investment funds were established. According to 1999 data from the Agency for Restructuring and Privatization, over 95 percent of the companies obtained approval for privatization, while the rest were liquidated or transferred to the Development Fund. However, a large percentage of social capital remained state property. The state-created funds, managed either privately or by the state, among them the Pension Fund (*Kapitalska družba*, KAD) and the Restitution Fund (*Slovenska odškodninska družba*, SOD), became the largest shareholders in the enterprise sector; their share, however, is beginning to decrease.

One problem some enterprises faced was multiple owners who had conflicting interests—for example, between workers and managers over strategic, long-term development of companies. The majority of new owners of the privatized enterprise sector are domestic. For several reasons, until recently there has been little interest on the part of foreign capital to invest in Slovenia. Consequently insufficient investment capital has negatively impacted on economic competitiveness. Since 2000 attitudes toward foreign investment (FDI) have been changing, and slowly the foreign investment climate has improved.

Novartis, the Swiss multinational company, has become an owner of Lek, the large, profitable, pharmaceutical manufacturer. KBC, a Belgian bank, has acquired one-third of the shares of Nova Ljubljanska banka. *See also* DENATIONALIZATION AFTER 1991.

PROTESTANT REFORMATION. Although today most Slovenes are professed **Catholics**, some of their ancestors in the 16th century were converts to reformed religion. The underlying reasons, or causes, a part of general European history, include political factors (**Habsburg** lord and emperor vying for power with feudal vassals) and socioeconomic factors (feudal lords holding off townspeople and peasants who were developing a money economy based on trade). In the end, Slovene lands returned under Habsburg, Catholic rule. Consequently socioeconomic development, as in much of the rest of the **Holy Roman Empire**, lagged behind that of Western Europe for nearly two centuries.

Intellectually, the Protestant Reformation had two effects, both related to the **humanism** that characterized the age. The first was a genuine religious renewal, subscribed to by innovators within the church and the emerging townspeople. Leading Reformation centers were **Trieste**, where the humanist Bishop Peter Bonomo influenced young scholars, and **Ljubljana** (Laibach), a diocese seat since 1461, where church reformers like **Primož Trubar** preached. The religious revolution, which began around 1525 and was receptive to various Reformation theologies—Lutheran, Zwinglian, and Calvinist— lasted about a half-century, until it was snuffed out by the **Counter Reformation**. Protestantism survived in eastern Slovenia because the rulers of **Hungary** who were overlords there were tolerant and sometimes themselves Protestant.

The second effect has to do with the shaping of national identity. As humanists, the reformers sought to promote literacy in the vernacular, so that individual Christians might themselves comprehend God's will in their own language. Slovene humanist reformers therefore wrote in the Slovene **language**, refining a standard orthography for the time (*bohoričica*), and they established the foundations of a Slovene literary language. Between 1550, when the first Slovene book appeared, and 1584, when a Slovene translation of the Bible was printed, Slovene Protestant intellectuals effected a virtual national cultural revolution. Fifty Slovene language books were printed in the second half of the 16th century, where there had been none before. Primož Trubar and **Jurij Dalmatin** were the most notable figures of this development. *See also* BOHORIČ, ADAM; PEASANT REVOLTS; TURKISH WARS.

PTUJ. Situated along the banks of the Drava River in northeastern Slovenia, Ptuj is one of the cultural, educational, and economic centers of the Podravje **region**. It had 18,339 inhabitants in 2002. The city's sub-Pannonian territory of 66.7 square kilometers extends over Dravsko and Ptujsko Polje (lowlands) and into the hills of Slovenske Gorice. The Podravje region has excellent conditions for **agriculture**, and Ptuj has been the region's agricultural center. It has the largest poultry farm in Slovenia, Perutnina Ptuj; the dairy Mlekarne Ptuj; and the farm cooperative Kmetijski Kombinat, with its large and well-known winery. Ptuj has also developed less successful industries, such as chemical, metal, and **textile**; some had to restructure, while others closed operations in the 1990s. The Podravje region in general experienced an economic decline and unemployment above the national average after 1990. This was also due to the closing of some major industrial plants in **Maribor** that had employed many workers from Ptuj. *See also* ENVIRONMENT.

Archeological excavations attest that the Ptuj area has been populated since the Neolithic period. During Roman rule it was at first a military post, but in 102 AD Emperor Trajan awarded it city status as *Colonia Ulpia Traiana Poetovia*. A prosperous commercial crossroads, it was destroyed around 450 AD. Upon its ruins the Franks, in the late eighth century, built a city by the same name, Poetovia. Growing as an economic and administrative center, it received formal rights in 977 and was part of the Salzburg archdiocese until the mid-16th century.The city's second prosperous age was the Middle Ages. In the old, mostly **medieval** center of Ptuj are still preserved a **castle**, since 1946 the seat of Ptuj Museum; the Dominican and Minorite monasteries, the former also a museum since 1928 and now part of Ptuj Museum; the Provost's church and the Renaissance city tower; the old City Hall of Renaissance origin; and some patrician houses with much rich detail. Since **World War II** the city has expanded, and the old center has been going through extensive restoration.

In the 17th century, when the Turks occupied a large part of **Hungary**, Ptuj lost its appeal as a strategic post and began to decline economically and culturally. The Vienna–Ljubljana–Trieste railway (1854) bypassed Ptuj, which despite occasional and brief economic upturns remained a sleepy rural town until after World War II. Ptuj had a large politically powerful German population, which in the second half of the 19th century exerted Germanizing pressure on the Slovenes. In 1900 about 60 percent of Ptuj's inhabitants were Slovene, but more than two-thirds listed German as their primary language of communication. In 1908 when the Slovene national school society of Cyril and Methodius held its annual meeting in Ptuj, Germans staged an anti-Slovene demonstration, which ended in fights between the two ethnic groups. These Ptuj events triggered a large anti-German demonstration in **Ljubljana**, which in turn caused anti-Slovene demonstrations in several cities across **Austria**. After **World War I**, Ptuj became part of the **Kingdom of Serbs, Croats, and Slovenes**, and although the German **minority** and Germanized Slovenes lost their political power, they remained numerous in the city. During World War II they supported the German occupiers, who had a stronghold in Ptuj. The Germans deported more than 600 Slovenes and arrested and killed a number of activists and sympathizers of the **National Liberation Struggle** (NOB). *See also* TURKISH WARS.

Ptuj has been a lively city culturally. The city has elementary and high schools (gymnasia, and also agricultural and technical) and a school of **music**. In 2004 a regional center of higher **education** with studies in mechatronics was established in cooperation with the **University of Maribor**. The Ptuj Museum, operating at eight different locations, has several permanent exhibits, the largest at the Ptuj castle; it organizes many shows and other activities for all ages. The City Theater is thriving and has been organizing the Monologue Festival since 2000. Also since 2000, Ptuj has hosted the international music festival, "Youth in the Ancient City." One of the oldest towns in Slovenia, Ptuj has a rich history, documented by many monuments. In addition to its beautiful landscape, the Ptuj **spa** and interesting pre-Lenten **folk traditions** (Kurentovanje) attract many visitors. Near the city are historic and tourist attractions such as Ptujska Gora, with Slovenia's most beautiful Gothic church (built by the **Counts of Celje**), a destination for pilgrims. Ptuj hopes to expand its **tourism** appeal.

PUBLISHING AND PUBLISHING HOUSES. Slovene publishing began during the **Protestant Reformation**, and **Primož Trubar** is considered the first Slovene publisher. While most Slovene texts printed during the 17th and 18th centuries were religious, some important secular tracts were produced, such as the first Slovene secular text, *Nova kranjska pratika* (New Carniolan Almanac, 1726), and the first history of the Slovene lands by **Janez Vajkard Valvasor**

(1689). Although a few publishers and printers operated in the late 17th and 18th centuries, publishing of secular **literature** on a larger scale, also supported by the **Catholic Church**, began developing in the mid-19th century. Mohorjeva Družba, or **Society of St. Hermagoras**, established in 1851, was the major publisher of Slovene books of all kinds (educational, historical, literary, and religious) before **World War II**. **Slovenska Matica**, established in 1864, was also an important 19th-century publisher. In addition to literature, it published textbooks and early scientific texts in Slovene. While Mohorjeva Družba books mostly aimed at a general Slovene public, Slovenska Matica publications were intended for professionals and intellectuals. Publishing and printing was developed not only in **Ljubljana** but also in regional cities such as **Novo Mesto** and **Gorizia**/Gorica. The number of publishers and printing houses increased throughout the century, as did the volume and diversity of publications. Also begun were the first Slovene translations of world literature. At the turn of the 20th century, publishing and printing reached West European standards. Book **design**, supplied by artists and architects, was of high quality.

After the Slovene lands became part of the new Yugoslav state (1918), and with the establishment of the first Slovene university (1919), there was a need to publish more Slovene books, especially scientific literature and textbooks. Twelve new publishers and printers and 10 book **societies**, including Vodnikova Založba and Cankarjeva Družba, operated between **World War I** and World War II. Some were specialized, such as Akademska Založba. In addition, professional societies, such as the Society for Humanistic and Social Sciences and the **Slovenian Academy of Sciences and Arts** (SAZU), became engaged in publishing activities. During the interwar period, publishing was also divided along ideological and political lines. Both the **liberal** Tiskovna Zadruga (Printing Cooperative, 1916) and the **Catholic** Nova Založba (New Publishing House, 1917), later renamed Jugoslovanska Knjigarna (Yugoslav Bookstore), were highly successful publishing companies, which issued over a million copies of books and undertook important publishing projects, including the collected works of **Ivan Cankar**. They existed until the end of World War II. During the war the **Partisans** organized their own publishing and printing operations.

Except for Mohorjeva Družba, Slovenska Matica, and SAZU, most publishing houses ceased operating after 1945, when three large state publishing houses were established: Cankarjeva Založba (Cankar

Publishing House), an arm of **Agitprop** that produced political and **Marxist** literature, often in cooperation with other Yugoslav publishers; Državna Založba Slovenije (State Publishing House of Slovenia), which specialized in school texts and dictionaries, and later expanded its scope to include belles-lettres, popular instruction books, and scientific and art texts; and Mladinska Knjiga (Books for Youth), a printery and graphics shop, which concentrated on children's publications, and also expanded into belles-lettres, popular works, monographs, and the 16-volume *Enciklopedija Slovenije* (Encyclopedia of Slovenia, 1987–2002). The introduction of new offset technology in 1965 allowed Mladinska Knijiga to expand into publications for export. In addition to the big three publishers, about 20 smaller ones were established in regional centers, such as Lipa in **Koper** and Pomurski Tisk in **Murska Sobota**. Officially there was no censorship, but until 1952 book publishing was controlled by Agitprop. With the introduction of self-management, publishing councils in each publishing house had autonomy in deciding what to publish. However, the **Communist Party** controlled matters by influencing allocation of state monies and by selecting the leadership of each publishing enterprise. Until the mid-1980s, publishing was strongly subsidized by the state.

With the introduction of a market economy and a multiparty system (1990), new private publishers mushroomed in number. In 1992 the **Republic of Slovenia** (RS) had 40 publishing houses, which biennially participated in the Ljubljana book fair, established in 1972. However, economic reality forced many to close. State publishing houses were privatized and two of the largest three, Cankarjeva Založba and Državna Založba, merged in 1998. In cooperation with domestic publishers, foreign publishers such as National Geographic have also entered the Slovene market. *See also* PRESS BEFORE 1990; PRESS SINCE 1990.

PUČNIK, JOŽE (1932–2003). Born in Črešnjevec near Slovenska Bistrica, Jože Pučnik earned a degree in philosophy and world literature from the **University of Ljubljana** in 1958. More than a decade later, in 1971, he completed a doctorate in sociology at the University of Hamburg, West Germany, where he had settled after a personally turbulent decade in Slovenia. From the mid-1950s to the mid-1960s while still in Slovenia, Pučnik was twice sentenced to prison for heretical writings (in *Revija 57* and *Perspektive*); he served five years of a nine-year maximum-security sentence (1958–1963); the second sentence in 1964 was suspended. In 1966, when he moved to Germany, he was granted political asylum and worked as a laborer while studying at the university. From 1971 to late 1989, Pučnik was at the University of Luneburg as an academic adviser.

Returning to Slovenia in late 1989, Pučnik at once became involved in political activities, helping found the Social Democratic Alliance (SDZ), which had a worker and **trade union** base and a philosophy similar to that of the German Social Democrats. After late December 1989, when **political parties** became legal, SDZ became the Social Democratic Party of Slovenia (SDSS). The SDSS joined the **Demos** coalition, established in 1989, and Pučnik became Demos's president and its presidential candidate for Slovenia in the **election** of April 1990. His candidacy was unsuccessful, but he did receive 41 percent of the vote in the run-off election against **Milan Kučan**. As president of his party, Pučnik promoted independence for Slovenia, working hard to bring about the **plebiscite for independence** in December 1990, and he continued to push for separation from **Yugoslavia** thereafter. After the election of December 1992, Pučnik became a member of the parliament and head of its SDSS delegation until 1993, when he turned over the the party's presidency to **Janez Janša**. In 1996 Pučnik chose not to run again for the National Assembly. He remained active in SDSS and wrote from time to time for *Nova revija*.

PUPPETRY. Puppetry, well-established and of high artistic quality, thrives in a few professional puppet **theaters** in **Ljubljana** and **Maribor** and in several amateur puppet theaters, as well as among Slovene **minorities** in **Austria** and **Italy**. The professional Ljubljana Puppet Theater (established in 1948) has produced many exquisite shows, attended by thousands of children every season. The Jože Pengov puppet theater, named after the most important personality of Slovene puppetry after **World War II**, has long been the most creative and innovative puppet theater in Slovenia and has received prestigious international awards. Ethnological studies (by Niko Kuret) after World War II have shown that puppetry had long been a widespread element of **folk traditions**. The centers of folk puppetry were Ptujsko Polje in northeastern Slovenia, and the area around **Stična** and in Suha Krajina, both in the Dolenjska **region**. However, folk puppetry had no influence on the beginnings of the artistic puppet theater, founded in 1910 by the painter and theater personality Milan Klemenčič. Performances at Klemenčič's home and his plans to establish a marionette theater were interrupted by **World War I** but materialized in 1920, if only for a short time; the theater closed in 1924. Until 1948, when the first professional puppet theater was founded in Ljubljana, puppet performances continued at Klemenčič's home. In the interwar years, amateur puppet theaters, much under the influence of Czech puppetry, were established by many **Sokol** organizations across Slovenia.

PURGES, ANTI-COMINFORMIST. After 28 June 1948, when the **Cominform** ousted the **Communist Party of Yugoslavia** (CPY) from its organization, it urged all Communist Parties to expel deviants. For the next four years an anti-**Tito** mania contributed to the purging, arrest, and even execution of undesirable party members throughout the Communist bloc. The Cominform urged the CPY to purge its deviants, but to little avail. The bulk of the CPY stood firmly behind Tito, while Yugoslav Cominformists, or *ibeovci* (Inform Bureau-ists), found themselves under attack instead. The Yugoslav Cominformists, however, were a disunited and disparate group, which made them easy prey for the regime.

In early 1949, when Tito denounced Cominformism as counterrevolutionary, the campaign against the *ibeovci* began. Investigators with the secret police—the State Security Administration (*Uprava državne bezbednosti*, UDBA)—generally supervised the action: arrest, expulsion from the party, interrogation, and imprisonment. Very few (about 19 percent) were accorded military or civil trials. The desire to downplay the size of Cominformist support made public trials rare. Those Cominformists who were imprisoned were generally sentenced to perform "socially useful labor." The most notorious prison camp was on Goli Otok (Naked Island), where prisoners regularly beat and spat upon each other and spent their days carrying rocks from one location to another. Of 16,288 imprisoned, fewer than 400 died in these camps (175 from typhus on Goli Otok in 1951). Most were released after "rehabilitation" and were forbidden to speak of the prison experience. The average sentence was 10 years.

In **Yugoslavia** Cominformism was strongest among the Serbs (7,235, or 44 percent), while Slovenia had the fewest (934, or less than 2 percent). Of those arrested and convicted, 556 (3.47 percent) were Slovene party members. The most prominent Slovene among them was Dragotin Gustinčič, a party leader who was active in factional fights in the 1920s and 1930s, and who spent the years 1931–1945 in Moscow, with an interlude abroad fighting in the Spanish Civil War. Other than Gustinčič, no prominent Slovene party leader defected, only an occasional high-level official or an old party cadre. Dušan

Kermavner, the historian, was an *ibeovec*. Boris Ziherl, the **Agitprop** commissar in **Belgrade**, wavered but was talked out of Cominformism by **Boris Kidrič**. All in all, the **Communist Party of Slovenia** (CPS) remained uniquely loyal. The Slovene Communists understood well that supporting a federated Yugoslav republic was their only option. Only such a Yugoslavia would support Slovenia's claims to Slovene ethnic territories in **Austria** and **Italy**; the USSR, meanwhile, had accepted Austria's 1938 frontiers and was backing Italy's claims to **Trieste** and its hinterland because Italian Communists had backed the Cominform. For Slovene Communists, Cominformism conflicted with Slovene patriotism. Slovene Cominformists, few though they were, were therefore meticulously sought out, purged, and punished.

– R –

RADIO AND TELEVISION SLOVENIA / RTV SLOVENIJA. RTV Slovenia, the largest public broadcasting network, is made up of eight independent organizations: Radio Slovenia, TV Slovenia, Radio Maribor, Radio Koper/Capodistria, TV Koper, Music Production, Record and Cassette Publishing, and Transmitters and Communications, which are also used by private broadcasters. RTV has its own symphony orchestra and big band (jazz group) as well as several choirs (chamber, children's, and youth). It is a large operation with more than 2,000 employees, and it produces and broadcasts programs for all target groups, including national **minorities** (Hungarian and Italian). Radio Slovenia provides programs for three channels—news, light entertainment, and cultural and educational. TV Slovenia broadcasts on two channels, TV 1 and TV 2, which have national coverage. In 2004 Radio Slovenia broadcast over 25,000 hours. Covering one-third of the **media** market, TV Slovenia broadcast over 13,000 hours, of which almost 60 percent was locally produced. Both Radio and TV Slovenia have become responsive to foreigner listeners/viewers and to the Slovene diaspora. Televizija Slovenija broadcasts a weekly TV program, *Slovenia Magazine*, in German and English about Slovene culture and history, while RTV Slovenia's Radio Slovenia International (RSI), the first foreign-language station in Slovenia, broadcasts 24 hours daily in English and German. Its programming, heavy on international news, is mainly intended for foreign visitors.

The operation of RTV Slovenia is regulated by the Media Act and by a specific RTV Slovenia Act. Its general manager is appointed by the parliament but is required to execute policies set by its board (*Programski svet RTV*), which consists of 29 members representing its employees and various public institutions such as universities, and five members who are appointed by the parliament. RTV has a network of international correspondents in neighboring countries as well as in major world centers (New York, Brussels, and Moscow). The production of television and radio programming is financed by obligatory subscription from all households owning television sets (600,000 subscribers, accounting for about 60 percent of total revenue). The remaining operational funds are acquired through advertising, the state budget, and other sources. RTV Slovenia is a member of the European Broadcasting Union and contributes to satellite broadcasting through cooperation with foreign stations and by leasing satellite channels. Until 1991 RTV Slovenia was Slovenia's only broadcasting organization. Its monopoly ended with the establishment of new, private radio and television organizations such as Kanal 3 and POP TV.

Radio Ljubljana officially began broadcasting in late 1928. During **World War II**, except for a short initial break, its broadcasts in Slovene continued, run by the Italian company EIAR until the Italian capitulation in late 1943, and thereafter by the German-run broadcasting network for the Adriatic Littoral. In 1941 Kričač (Screamer), an underground mobile radio station of the **Liberation Front** (LF), was established in **Ljubljana** but stopped broadcasting in 1942 and resumed its activities from **Partisan-controlled territory** only in 1944. After World War II, besides Radio Ljubljana, two new radio stations, in **Koper** and **Maribor**, began operation. By insisting on broadcasting only in the Slovene **language**, Radio Ljubljana, renamed Radio Slovenija in 1950, played an important role in fighting federal unitarism in the late 1950s and the 1960s, when there were strong pressures to create a "Yugoslav" culture throughout the **Federal People's Republic of Yugoslavia** (FPRY).

Although TV Ljubljana began broadcasting experimental programs in October 1958, it was not until 1960 that it began transmitting daily programs. In the same year, the first direct television transmission from Slovenia to Eurovision took place. TV Ljubljana completed its major transmitter network in 1964, and it began broadcasting daily news programs in Slovene in 1968. In the most recent decades, TV Ljubljana has broadened its technological base—introducing cable television in 1992—and its program offerings. All of its principal transmitting facilities suffered considerable damage in 1991 during the **Ten-Day War** for **independence**, but these were soon repaired.

RADOVLJICA. With 5,740 inhabitants, Radovljica, situated between the Sava and Suha Rivers in the heart of the Gorenjska **region**, is one of Slovenia's famed "old" towns. Its history was richest in the **medieval** period, when feudal lords (bishops of Brixen, later Ortenburg and **Habsburg** nobles) held vast estates here. Known as Radmannsdorf in the mid-12th century, Radovljica evolved from market town (1340s) to town (1500s). With **agriculture** prospering to the east of the Sava and **wrought iron** foundries (Kropa) to the southwest, Radovljica in the 15th century became a vital trading center. Taxes on toll roads that passed through the area were collected here, and the town became a fortress for the region as the forces of the **Counts of Celje** and soon after the **Turks** (who destroyed Radovljica in 1475) ravaged it.

Rebuilt in the 16th and 17th centuries, the town has a late Gothic and Renaissance character. On its main square are the Ortenburg **castle** (which houses a historical **museum** and a museum of apiculture), the Gothic parish church, and a Protestant church. (Protestantism survived in spite of militant **Counter Reformation** efforts.) The main square is named after **Anton Tomaž Linhart**, the **Enlightenment** writer-historian, who was born in Radovljica. Remnants of the medieval town walls and nine of its 16 towers also survive. That the town has retained its 17th-century character can be attributed to the economic decline that began in that century. The railroad and new highways, along with **tourism**, have revived Radovljica somewhat. Most development has taken place outside the town to the northeast, toward Lesce, a small industrial center, which has two profitable enterprises—Veriga, which produces chains, and Gorenjka, a chocolate factory. Also nearby, in Begunje, is Elan, a major producer of sporting equipment with branches across Europe and over 1,000 employees locally. The company is best known for its skis and yachts. *See also* BEEKEEPING.

RAPALLO, TREATY OF (12 NOVEMBER 1920). In 1919 at the Paris Peace Conference, the border between **Italy** and the **Kingdom of Serbs, Croats, and Slovenes** could not be agreed upon. After long negotiations, it was decided that the border question be resolved by the two states themselves. This was done with the Treaty of Rapallo, in which Italy recognized the new kingdom, but the latter had to accept a border that allowed Italy to annex almost one-fourth of Slovene ethnic territory, which included about 300,000 Slovenes and two important cities, **Trieste** and **Gorizia**. The new border along the Wilson line, established at the Paris Peace Conference, ran from north to south: Peč, Jalovec, Triglav, Možic, Porezen, Blegoš, Črni vrh above Cerkno, Bevki, Hotedršica, Planina, Javorniki above Cerknica, Snežnik, Kastav east of Matulji to the Adriatic Sea (refer to map 3). Italians named the annexed territory Venezia Giulia (Julijska Krajina). The Rapallo border remained in effect until 1947. *See also* MINORITIES, SLOVENES IN ITALY; WORLD WAR I.

READING SOCIETIES / ČITALNICE. Reading societies (*čitalnice*), which were unique Slovene institutions, flourished in the 1860s and lasted until the beginning of the 20th century. Their goal was to develop cultural and social life among Slovene townspeople. Earlier such nationally and politically oriented reading societies had existed among Slovene students in Graz. A few reading societies began to emerge after the **Revolution of 1848**, but *čitalnice* really developed during the period of constitutional experiments. *Slovanska čitalnica* (Slavic Reading Society) in **Trieste**, *Narodna čitalnica* (National Reading Society) in **Maribor**, and *Ljubljanska čitalnica* (**Ljubljana** Reading Society) were established in 1861. The Ljubljana Reading Society, with about 300 members the largest in Slovenia in 1869, was a model for several others established later in smaller towns. There were also many reading societies in the Slovene Littoral and in **Prekmurje**. Although they were most active politically in the 1860s, some 80 reading societies were still functioning at the turn of the century.

The societies organized cultural events—Slovene plays, poetry readings, concerts, and lectures—which often ended with dances and parties. The societies established **libraries** with Slovene books and newspapers. Their cultural activities were often nonprofessional, for their main goal was to stimulate the use of the Slovene **language** and national awareness. However, the societies influenced the development of the professional **theater**, libraries, and other cultural and political organizations before they disappeared in the beginning of the 20th century. Their role was taken over by cultural and educational **societies** associated with **political parties**. *See also* REALISM; TAAFFE'S IRON RING.

REALISM. Within Slovene realism (1850–1900) there were two distinct literary groups: Old Slovenes (*Staroslovenci*) and Young Slovenes (*Mladoslovenci*); both had a literary and political program. Although the Old Slovenes' literary work contained more elements of **romanticism** than that of the Young Slovenes, and the former were prevalent in the first 20 years of the period, both groups were active literarily and politically throughout the period of realism. The leading Old Slovenes, political conservatives, were **Janez Bleiweis**, their literary star, and Lovro Toman, who published in the newspaper *Kmetijske in rokodelske novice* (*Farmers' and Craftsmen's News*). The Old Slovenes' political orientation can be summed up in their slogan: "Everything for religion, homeland, emperor!" (*Vse za vero, dom, cesarja!*). They supported the dynasty, Alexander Bach's absolutism, and the **Catholic Church**, but they fought for the rights of the Slovenes within the existing political structure.

The petty opportunism of the Old Slovenes infuriated the young generation of the *literati*. The Young Slovenes' ideological leader was **Fran Levstik**, editor of *Naprej* (*Forward*), begun in 1863, and later the more radical *Slovenski narod* (*Slovene Nation*), begun in 1868. Their political program stressed a **United Slovenia**, national equality, and association with other South Slav nations. They also wanted to continue the efforts of **France Prešeren** to establish a modern Slovene **literature** while bringing it to the European level. The Young Slovenes, who often based their writings on Slovene **folk traditions**, initiated a comprehensive Slovene literary program and also introduced literary criticism. Anton Aškerc, Simon Gregorčič, Simon Jenko, **Josip Jurčič**, Janko Kersnik, **Josip Stritar**, and **Ivan Tavčar** were prominent Young Slovenes whose works are considered classics of Slovene literature.

After 1848 many literary projects aimed at developing national awareness. **Reading societies** and a number of journals began appearing. Publishing houses such as the **Society of St. Hermagoras** and **Slovenska Matica** were established. Despite differences in political and literary views, the Old and the Young Slovenes joined political forces after 1871 because of strong Germanizing and centralizing pressures. An important milestone in Slovene literary realism is the appearance of the literary magazine *Ljubljanski zvon* (*Ljubljana Bell*) in 1881. *See also* PRESS BEFORE 1990.

Realism in painting began in the 1870s. Slovene painters, many educated in Munich, Paris, Rome, Venice, and **Vienna**, were still dependent on church commissions and had little public support. Among the leading Slovene realist painters were the brothers Janez Šubic (1850–1889) and Jurij Šubic (1855–1890), Ivana Kobilca (1861–1926), and **Anton Ažbe** (1862–1905). The broader movement of realistic painting continued into the 20th century. A group of realist painters organized the society Vesna (Spring) in 1904 and formed a national program through which they hoped to preserve the rich folk heritage of the Slovene nation against Germanization and the effects of industrialization. *See also* ARTS; MUSIC; NEOABSOLUTISM; TABOR MOVEMENT.

RECOGNITION, INTERNATIONAL. The **Brioni Agreement**, concluded on 7 July 1991, prepared the way for international recognition of Slovenia's **independence**. On 8 October, according to the agreement's understanding, the **Republic of Slovenia** (RS) assumed independent status and began conducting its affairs outside the framework of **Yugoslavia**. The international community, at various meetings that fall, verged on recognition, and Slovenia hoped it would come by Christmas. Of the major powers, only Germany recognized Slovenia before the end of 1991 (19 December). The long-awaited recognition by the European Community (EC) came on 15 January 1992 (preceded on the 13th by that of the Vatican). Association with the Council of Europe and the Conference on Security and Cooperation in Europe (CSCE) came that spring. Other major powers also recognized Slovene independence early in 1992: **Russia** (February), People's Republic of China (April), and the **United States** (April). On 22 May the RS was admitted to the **United Nations** as its 176th member. *See also* INTERNATIONAL ORGANIZATIONS, MEMBERSHIP IN; TEN-DAY WAR.

RECONSTRUCTION, POST–WORLD WAR II (1945–1946). Slovenia's infrastructure and **economy** were severely damaged during **World War II**. Yet, despite a general shortage of goods and the dissatisfaction of some groups with the new regime, postwar reconstruction began on an optimistic note. Financial resources came from the confiscated property, war profits, reparations, and cash from defeated enemies, and most of the work was done with volunteer or forced labor. As more than 19,000 families were homeless, the Ministry for Reconstruction began with rebuilding people's homes. Much work was done as "shock work" on Sundays; city dwellers helped to demolish damaged houses and build new ones. By the end of 1945, 4,250 buildings and 78 schools functioned as a result of their efforts. In addition, "work brigades" were organized in Slovenia for local reconstruction. By the end of 1945 almost the entire road and railway network was again operational. The most ambitious Slovene projects were the cultivation of abandoned fields at Brežice and wood cutting in Bohinj, where 150 brigades from all parts of Slovenia worked. Many young Slovenes also worked in other parts of **Yugoslavia** building railways (Brčko–Banovići, Šamac–Sarajevo) and roads. Voluntary labor was encouraged, for it educated the young in the values of a new society. Those who participated received supplementary coupons for rationed food and other scarce goods. *See also* FIVE-YEAR PLAN, FIRST; LEAGUE OF COMMUNIST YOUTH OF YUGOSLAVIA; STUDENT MOVEMENTS.

REFORMS, 18TH CENTURY. *See* ENLIGHTENMENT; JOSEPH II; MARIA THERESA.

REGIONS OF SLOVENIA. Historically, the **Republic of Slovenia** (RS) has had eight fairly distinct geographic regions: Gorenjska, Dolenjska, Štajerska, Primorska, Notranjska, **Bela Krajina**, Koroška/ **Carinthia**, and **Prekmurje** (refer to map 7). Before 1918 Bela Krajina, Dolenjska, Notranjska, Primorska, and Gorenjska were part of the duchy of Kranjska (Krain or Carniola), which together with Koroška (Kärnten or Carinthia) and Štajerska (Steiermark or Styria) was Austrian, while Prekmurje belonged to **Hungary**. Most of Koroška and about half of Štajerska remained in **Austria** after **World War I**. *See also* MEDIEVAL LANDS.

The regional names have survived since **Habsburg** days, although they carried no legal or administrative function in **Yugoslavia**. Since independence, although the names persisted, Slovenia moved toward giving official political and administrative status to 12 new units, "functional regions," that geographers Igor Vrišer and Vladimir Kokole devised in the 1970s for intermunicipal cooperation. These have been used ever since, particularly for urban planning and economic cooperation. Some functional regions, like Pomurje, have been more active in this regard than others. In 1995 the Slovene Bureau of Statistics adopted the 1970s units as the basis for 12 "statistical regions," which it uses for official data collecting. The statistical regions have evolved; their activities expanded as the size and power of the *občinas* shrank. The regions have their own chambers of commerce, employment offices, and other bureaus, and they act in an advisory capacity for *občinas* in their region. Constitutionally, *občinas* still have power legally; the statistical regions do not. However, that is likely to change.

The moving impetus for giving constitutional validity to the 12 regions is to bring Slovenia into conformity with other **European Union** (EU) states, which do have provincial or regional administrative divisions. Creating regions, which might also be grouped into three larger units (western, central, and eastern), might also enable at least part of Slovenia (probably the eastern unit) to qualify for EU funds for less-developed regions. The 12 statistical regions (capitals are noted in parentheses), whose names are beginning to displace the historical designations, are Dolenjska (**Novo Mesto**), Gorenjska (**Kranj**), Goriška (**Nova Gorica**), Koroška (**Slovenj Gradec**), Notranjsko-kraška (**Postojna**), Obalno-kraška (**Koper**), Osrednjeslovenska (**Ljubljana**), Podravska (**Maribor**), Pomurska (**Murska Sobota**), Savinjska (**Celje**), Spodnjeposavska (Krško), and Zasavska (Zagorje ob Savi). Refer to map 8.

RELIGION. Since the **Christianization of Slovenes** (eighth century), Roman Catholicism has been the predominant religion of Slovenes. In addition to Catholics, two other religious communities existed in the Slovene lands before the 20th century: the **Jewish**, first mentioned in connection with **Maribor** in the 12th century, and the Protestant (Lutheran) after the 16th century **Protestant Reformation**. Both religious groups survived in **Prekmurje**, which was under Hungarian rule. In other Slovene lands, those under **Austria**, the fate of non-Catholics was less favorable. Despite the Tolerance Patent issued by **Joseph II** in the late 18th century, there was less religious tolerance of non-Catholic religious groups in Austria than in **Hungary**. The 20th century, however, brought more religious toleration as the **Catholic Church** in the late 1930s and especially after the Second Vatican council in the early 1960s altered its stance toward other religious communities. In the first **Yugoslavia**, the Roman Catholic, Lutheran, Eastern Orthodox, and Muslim religious groups were recognized as "churches," while some religious communities functioned as **societies**, including the Pentecostal Church, Old Catholic Church, Baptist churches, and Jehovah's Witnesses. In the interwar period (1918–1945), Slovenia remained predominantly Roman Catholic. According to the 1921 and 1931 censuses, 96 and 97 percent of the population, respectively, declared themselves Catholic. Lutherans were the second largest group with 2.6 percent, while adherents of other creeds were very few. European trends of laicization among urban intellectuals did not have an important impact on Slovenes after **World War I**, in part due to the large rural population in Slovenia.

After **World War II** the state and church were separated, and religion became a personal matter of each individual. Due to its

Marxist ideology, the socialist state treated religion and the church unfavorably—especially the Catholic Church because of its role during World War II. Until 1953, state-church relations were tense, freedom of religion was seriously curtailed, Catholic priests were persecuted, and people were hesitant even to acknowledge their creed. In the 1953 census all religious communities accounted for a smaller share of the population than in the prewar era, while atheists were the only group whose number increased from virtually zero before the war to 10 percent. In subsequent censuses their number fell to 4.4 percent of the population in 1991, but rose again in 2002 to 10.2 percent. Censuses after World War II show a decline in the Catholics' share of the population (from 83 percent in 1953 to 57.8 percent in 2002) and an increase in the number of, and membership in, other religious groups. The drop in the number of Roman Catholics might be explained in part by a large percentage of people (15.7 percent) who did not want to answer the question of religious affiliation in 2002.

The number of Lutherans has also been steadily declining: In the 1953 census they accounted for 1.5 percent of the population, and for 0.8 percent in 2002. Lutherans, initially numerous, especially among the nobility, were either re-Catholicized or forced to leave during the early 17th-century **Counter Reformation**. Due to local political circumstances, they have survived, mostly in **Prekmurje**, where 11 out of their 13 parishes are located. The other two are in **Ljubljana** and Maribor.

The Law on the Legal Status of Religious Communities enacted in 1972 guaranteed religious freedom and legal equality of all religious organizations, but it required religious communities to be officially registered. Ten religious communities did so immediately, and by 2005 their number had increased to 40. The Serbian Orthodox Church and **Islam** were active before the 1972 law, having been officially recognized in 1967. Their existence in Slovenia is due to population migration—inflow of military personnel and migrant workers from other parts of Yugoslavia. In the 2002 census they had 45,908 and 47,488 adherents (2.3 percent and 2.4 percent of the population, respectively). A small group of Serbian Orthodox, however, has lived in **Bela Krajina** since the 16th century. All other churches and communities (36 in December 2005), most of them registered since the 1980s, are numerically very small, accounting altogether for less than 0.2 percent of the population. Among these are various Western churches, such as the Mormons, as well as Eastern religious groups, such as Hare Rama, Hare Krishna, and the Buddha Dharma. In 2002, 10 percent of the population declared as atheists, the same as in 1953. In the same year, over 15 percent of the census respondents declined to answer the question regarding religion. Slovenia is considered less religious than other post-communist states. In 1992 the 1972 legislation was only slightly changed, and it is considered outdated. Religious communities are not well defined and the **government** (Office of the Religious Communities) allegedly does not treat them equally. Preferential treatment is being accorded to the majority church, the Roman Catholic, as well as to the Lutherans, both of which have special legal status and privileges due to their historical roles in the development of the Slovene nation. In 2000 the state concluded an agreement with the Lutherans of the Augsburg Confession, giving that church a special legal status. Since 2004 a concordat between the state and the Holy See has been in effect, giving the Catholic Church the power to negotiate on unresolved issues and privileges, including the ability to engage in pastoral activity in hospitals, retirement homes, and the army. Some religious communities have challenged the preferential treatment of the Roman Catholic Church and filed antidiscrimination petitions with the Ombudsman for **Human Rights**. Despite these issues, Slovenia has created a relatively friendly environment for minority religious groups. *See also* RELIGIOUS ORDERS.

RELIGIOUS ORDERS. Religious orders have been important among the Slovenes since the eighth century. In the period of **Christianization**, the first to arrive in **Carinthia** were Irish Benedictines (in 755) of the **Catholic Church**. In the 12th century, the Benedictines established an abbey at Gornji Grad, which served as a base for the establishment of the **Ljubljana** diocese (1461). Other orders followed. The Cistercians, who were very much involved in everyday life, established monasteries in **Stična** (1135), Vetrinj in Carinthia (1142), and Kostanjevica in Dolenjska (1234). The contemplative Carthusians established monasteries in Žiče near Slovenske Konjice (1160), Jurklošter near **Celje** (1170), and Bistra near Ljubljana (1255). Pleterje, also run by the Carthusians, was established by the **Counts of Celje** in 1403. Mendicant religious orders (Minorites, Dominicans, and later also Franciscans and Augustinians) arrived in the Middle Ages and cared for the poor, sick, and uneducated. All monasteries, especially the Cistercian and Carthusian, were centers of **medieval** culture and art, and often also important to the **economy** of the area.

During the **Protestant Reformation**, Catholic religious orders and monasteries experienced crisis and decline; some closed, while others survived only with difficulty. During the **Counter Reformation**, new religious orders (**Jesuits** and Franciscans/Capuchins) were established to revitalize the Catholic Church. In 1782, however, 35 monasteries were abolished by Emperor **Joseph II**, and many of their rich archives, **libraries**, and **art** treasures were dispersed or destroyed. Religious orders began to flourish again in the second half of the 19th and the early 20th centuries, marked by the return of the old orders (Cistercians and Carthusians) and the arrival of modern congregations—Lazarists in 1852 and Salesians in 1901, the latter working among poor youth. The Salesians established schools, training centers, and youth homes across Slovenia.

The first women's religious orders in the Slovene lands were the Dominicans (13th century). The Ursulines, devoted to teaching and educating young women, were established in Ljubljana in 1702 and in **Škofja Loka** in 1782. They organized convent schools and church Sunday schools, even in many remote mountain villages. Instruction was in the Slovene **language**, and schooling was free. Among the newer communities, the Sisters of Charity have been the largest and most active; before **World War II** they ran 30 hospitals, 17 kindergartens, and taught in six schools.

After 1945 the **Communist** government made the survival of religious orders difficult. By a 1948 decree, women in religious communities were prohibited from working in hospitals and other institutions and also from wearing habits in public. As of 2000 there were 13 women's and 12 men's religious communities, working together with diocesan priests in over 80 parishes. Religious orders have also sent members to work as **missionaries** and among Slovene **emigrants**. Although some public **services** have been performed by religious orders since the mid-1970s, it was only after the fall of communism and with new legislation (1990) that they became equal partners with secular agencies in delivering social services. They also assumed a greater role in education. The number of members of religious orders has been in decline for many years. In 2000, for example, there were 1,136 women active in religious orders (the most numerous were the Sisters of Charity and school sisters of St. Francis of Christ the King), one-third fewer than in 1978. Of those 1,100, one-third worked abroad. *See also* RELIGION.

REPUBLIC OF SLOVENIA / REPUBLIKA SLOVENIJA (RS). In March 1990, only weeks before Slovenia's first multiparty **elections** since **World War II**, the Slovene parliament voted to eliminate "Socialist" from its official name; thus the **Socialist Republic of Slovenia** was renamed the Republic of Slovenia (RS). The RS remained a part of the Yugoslav federation, hoping to loosen the union and establish a confederation. As hopes for the latter faded, a referendum on **independence** was held. The overwhelmingly favorable result of the **plebiscite** on 23 December 1990 led to a declaration of independence on 25 June 1991. After Slovenia separated from **Yugoslavia**, the name Republic of Slovenia was retained. The **Constitution of 1991**, which went into effect with general elections in December 1992, spells out the character and structure of the RS state and its **government**.

RESISTANCE, NONCOMMUNIST, 1941–1945. During **World War II**, in addition to the resistance organized by the Communist-led **Liberation Front** (LF), there existed also a small noncommunist underground. On 29 May 1941 an underground Slovene Legion (*Slovenska legija*), supported mostly by the **Clericals**, was established. The Slovene Legion operated in small groups, gathering armaments for eventual active resistance to the occupiers at the appropriate time, and providing intelligence for the British and for the Yugoslav **government in exile**. It also published a bulletin, *Svobodna Slovenija* (*Free Slovenia*). As the **Partisan** terror increased, the Slovene Legion played an important role in organizing the **Village Guard** (1942) and in 1943 ordered its members to join the **Home Guard** units. Some **Sokols** not in the LF organized an underground Sokol Legion (*Sokolska legija*) in August 1941. Ideologically **liberal**, the Sokol Legion was mostly active in **Ljubljana** and later in the Primorska **region**, and its members joined **Chetnik** military units. The Sokol Legion was at first tolerant toward the LF and declared that it would not fight against any liberation group, while the Slovene Legion, supported by the rightist Stražarji and the Mladci of the **Catholic Action**, took the opposite position.

The resistance group Pobratim (Oath Brother) was organized in spring 1941; in 1943 it was renamed the National Legion (*Narodna legija*). Politically, most of its members belonged to the Yugoslav National Party. It was numerically small and militarily unimportant. After **Italy**'s capitulation in 1943, some of its members joined the

LF. In mid-1944 the Legion suffered the final blow when most of its leading members were arrested by the German Gestapo.

To counteract LF terrorism, leading conservatives and liberals established the **Slovene Covenant** (*Slovenska zaveza*) in spring of 1942. The Covenant tried to raise an army as requested by the Yugoslav government in exile in London. Thus the Slovene Legion became nominally a part of the Royal Yugoslav Army under the command of Draža Mihailović. In Slovenia the Chetniks, after 1943 referred to as Plava Garda (Blue Guard), were mostly liberals. *See also* NATLAČEN, MARKO; EHRLICH, LAMBERT.

REVOLUTION OF 1848. The Revolution of 1848, which affected all of continental Europe, was precipitated by economic crisis and in some places famine, due to several years of bad harvests. Constitutional government, abolition of guilds, and abolition of feudal taxes and obligations were among the goals of the revolutionaries. In general, however, the groups did not agree on objectives, nor did they cooperate in achieving them. Old regimes were thus able, eventually, to put down the rebellions. In **Austria**, for example, once peasant emancipation was granted (September 1848), the rural population, which in the spring had been in revolt against its landlords, was no longer a revolutionary factor.

In **Vienna** the revolution began on 15 March; it began in **Ljubljana** the next day. Prince Clemens von Metternich, although foreign minister, not interior minister, was blamed for many of the empire's internal woes and was quickly sacrificed by the regime. By the end of the year there were further concessions by Vienna when a new emperor, **Francis Joseph**, just 18, replaced his predecessor, who had been forced to abdicate. A constituent assembly of elected representatives meeting at Kremsier meanwhile was allowed to work on a federal constitution, which it completed in March 1849. By that time the revolution was meeting with fatal military force; only the revolts in Venetia and **Hungary** were still to be subdued by the Austrian field marshals. Consequently Vienna's chief minister, Prince Felix Schwartzenberg, felt comfortable in dismissing the constitution drafted at Kremsier. He replaced it with one of his own, which reasserted **Habsburg** power and made the **Austrian Empire** indivisible—a reply to Italians, Germans, and Hungarians whose nationalistic ambitions had unleashed centrifugal forces in the empire. Schwartzenberg thus ushered in a decade of **Neoabsolutism**.

In the Austrian Empire, more than anywhere else in 1848, the revolution was characterized by nationalism. In that year the Slovenes put together their very first political program. It was the work of a small group of intellectuals from Graz, Ljubljana, and Vienna. The objective was clear and simple: a **United Slovenia**. Its goal, which rested on "ethnic" principles, was to join together all Slovene-inhabited areas of the empire, irrespective of existing provincial boundaries, in one administrative unit within Austria. The program further stipulated that the Slovene **language** be used in **education** and administration in this territory. Finally, it indicated a preference for separating "Austria" from the German Confederation (**Holy Roman Empire** until 1806), where in 1848 a German national state seemed to be emerging. The plan was moderate and definitely not separatist; nevertheless, it had few adherents other than students, intellectuals, and some townspeople.

Slovene nationalists in 1848 also flirted with **Illyrism** or **Yugoslavism**, although there was less enthusiasm for this than for the United Slovenia program. The nationalists, in general, tended to be Pan-Slavic and attended the Prague Slav Congress (June 1848); their Yugoslavism was probably a natural component of this. Ultimately what was important for Austria was that its Slavs, including the Slovenes, pronounced a loyalty to the empire—although they wished to reform it. Their **Austroslavism** would help to keep the state together until 1914.

RIBIČIČ, CIRIL (1947–). Born in **Ljubljana**, Ciril Ribičič completed a doctorate at the Law Faculty of the **University of Ljubljana** in 1977, where subsequently, as a full professor, he taught constitutional law. He is the son of Mitja Ribičič, a Communist hard-liner who was head of internal affairs and a Central Committee member in Slovenia as well as president of the **Federal Executive Council** (FEC) and prime minister of the **Socialist Federal Republic of Yugoslavia** (SFRY) in the 1960s. Ciril became a member of the League of Communists of Slovenia (LCS)—the name for the **Communist Party of Slovenia** since 1952—and was soon active in politics and government work, serving for a time as president of the Socio-Political Chamber of the Slovene Assembly (1982–1984). Ciril took over leadership of the party from **Milan Kučan** in December 1989 and helped transform it into the Party of Democratic Renewal (SDP), hoping the "democratized" party would be victorious in multiparty **elections**. The SDP, however, was beaten by the **Demos** coalition in the election of April 1990. Ciril Ribičič held seats in parliament after the elections in

April 1990 and December 1992. After that second election, Ribičič's party became the mainstay of the **United List of Social Democrats** (ZLSD), and it was often included in coalition **governments** headed by **Liberal Democracy of Slovenia** (LDS).

Ciril Ribičič has written extensively on the law, consitutional issues, and political systems. Before **independence** his writings examined socialist **Yugoslavia**'s legal and political institutions. After independence, he turned to the **Republic of Slovenia**'s (RS) legal system, and he has helped prepare new educational texts for university students. He also served as an expert at the War Crimes Tribunal in The Hague that investigated war crimes in the former Yugoslavia. In 2000 Ribičič was elected to a nine-year term as a judge of the Constitutional **Court** of Slovenia.

RIVERS, MAJOR. Slovenia has four major rivers: Drava, Mura, Sava, and Soča. The Soča (Isonzo) and the Sava originate in the Julian **Alps**. The Soča flows south and west through **Italy** into the Adriatic Sea near Monfalcone in the Bay of **Trieste**, while the Sava, Slovenia's longest river, travels southeast through **Kranj** and **Ljubljana** into **Croatia**, eventually merging with the Danube at **Belgrade**. Before leaving Slovenia, the Sava is enlarged by three major tributaries: the Savinja, which originates in the Kamnik-Savinja mountains and flows through **Celje** on its way south; the Krka, which emerges from underground **Kras** repositories to flow gently through **Novo Mesto** before reaching the Sava; and the Kolpa, which arises in Croatia and forms over 100 kilometers of the Slovene–Croatian border in the south. The Drava (Drau) and the Mura (Mur) flow into Štajerska from **Austria** in the north. The Drava flows through **Maribor**, merges in southeastern Slovenia with the Mura, and eventually flows into the Danube at Osijek. Only the Mura, which flows primarily through marshy lowlands prone to flooding, has no dams or hydroelectric installations. The other three major rivers—Drava, Sava, and Soča—which descend from Alpine heights, have all had their waters diverted through power plants (17 in all). *See also* ENERGY.

ROAD AFFAIR, 1969. In 1968 the World Bank, which assisted **Yugoslavia** financially in rebuilding its highway system, agreed to finance three road projects—one each in Macedonia, **Croatia**, and Slovenia—and to consider financing roads in Serbia at a later date. In June 1969 Yugoslavia signed an agreement with the World Bank for a $30 million loan and allocated funds to the three projects. Under the Yugoslav presidency of a Slovene, Mitja Ribičič, the **Federal Executive Council** unilaterally decided in July 1969 not to apply the loan to the projected sections of the trans-Slovenian highway (Šentilj–Nova Gorica) but rather to use the funds in other republics. The decision triggered public protests throughout Slovenia, supported by the Slovene **government**, other public institutions, and the mass **media**. The Executive Council of Slovenia protested immediately, noting that the Slovene road project was of utmost importance for the Slovene as well as the Yugoslav economy, and demanded that the funds for the project be restored. The secretariat of the League of Communists of Slovenia (LCS) convened and complained that the decision of the Federal Executive Council was unilateral and not in the spirit of policies set in 1964 by the Ninth Congress of the League of Communists of Yugoslavia (LCY). It argued that the decision could have serious consequences for relations between the republics and the federation if it were not reversed. Some delegates of the republic's assembly called for assembly deliberation on the matter, but the conservative wing of the leadership—Franc Popit (then president of the LCS) and Sergej Kraigher (then president of the Assembly)—prevented it.

In August the executive bureau of the LCY joined the conflict. Taking to task the Slovene media for exposing the affair, the bureau characterized the protest as nationalistic and exacerbating existing conflicts among individual republics. This was the first time a republic challenged a federal (Yugoslav) decision. **Croatia** supported the Slovenes in their fight, but Serbia and Macedonia accused them of being selfish and nationalistic. Around the same time, an internal meeting of the Slovene delegates (with **Tito** present) took place. A rift between the conservative faction and the liberal one (**Stane Kavčič**) grew. In the end, the conservative faction exerted power in Slovenia, limited the influence of Kavčič and the liberal faction, and took control of the Slovene media, which generally supported liberal policies.

In the long run, the Road Affair did not significantly hamper the construction of roads in Slovenia: Eventually all those planned were built. However, the crisis had enormous political consequences for Slovenia and all Yugoslavia. It set a precedent for changes in relations between the republics and the federation and, in Slovenia, enabled the conservatives to block further democratization. Therefore, the Road Affair meant also the culmination of **liberalization** in the 1960s. *See also* TRANSPORT.

RODE, FRANC (1934–). Born in Rodica near **Ljubljana**, Franc Rode became a refugee in 1945, when his family fled from the Communists to **Austria**, and he later **emigrated** to Argentina along with many other Slovenes. In 1952 he joined the Missionary Congregation (Lazarists) and later studied theology in Buenos Aires. Rode continued his studies in Rome and Paris, where he was ordained a priest in 1960. Continuing his studies in Paris, he was awarded a doctorate in theology in 1963. Rode returned to Slovenia in 1965 and served at St. Joseph's parish in **Celje**. In 1967 he assumed the role of director of the Lazarist seminary in Ljubljana and later became its visitor. At the same time, he began teaching at the Faculty of Theology in Ljubljana. From 1981 to 1997 Rode served at the Vatican, where he worked in the office for a dialogue with unbelievers. After the establishment of the Pontifical Council for Culture, Rode was its secretary from 1994 to 1997, the year Pope John Paul II appointed him archbishop of Ljubljana and metropolitan of Slovenia, replacing the retiring archbishop, **Alojzij Šuštar**. The Slovene **Catholic Church** under Rode's leadership fought hard for stronger church influence in the public sphere, especially in **education**. Charismatic but outspoken and direct, Archbishop Rode was a controversial figure, not always conciliatory toward the new Slovenian state in transition and its leadership.

In 2004 Rode was summoned to the Vatican, and **Alojz Uran** replaced him as Ljubljana's archbishop. Since April 2004 Archbishop Rode has been serving in the Roman Curia as the prefect of the Congregation for the Institutes of Consecrated Life and Societies of Apostolic Life. In early 2006 Pope Benedict XVI elevated him to the position of cardinal. Rode's publications, issued mostly in Slovenia and France, include *Spomin, zvest načrt Cerkve na Slovenskem* (Memory, Faithful Plan of the Church in Slovenia) and *Za čast dežele* (For Honor of the Country). These latest publications have been popular among Slovene Catholics. Well respected and known both inside and outside Catholic Church circles, Rode was in 1995 awarded the Order of Knight by French President Jacques Chirac.

ROMA. *See* BELA KRAJINA; MINORITIES IN SLOVENIA; PREKMURJE.

ROMANTICISM. Slovene romanticism flourished in the first half of the 19th century. Intellectuals continued with linguistic studies and other cultural activities (collecting **folk** art, history, and **literature**) that had began during the **Enlightenment**. Cultural nationalism, which was tolerated by the **Vienna** government, was promoted by the older group of Slovene romantics: **Jernej Kopitar** and his disciples Franc Metelko, **Franc Miklošič**, and Matevž Ravnikar, who were strong supporters of **Austria**. The younger Slovene romanticists, **France Prešeren, Matija Čop**, and the group around the newspaper *Kranjska čbelica* (Carniolan Bee) were especially committed to the development of a Slovene literary **language**, which would also be used in public life. They did not agree with the older group politically, and were considered liberal and dangerous to the Vienna establishment. With their literary work, they tried to create an independent Slovene culture for townspeople, oriented toward classical Western principles. Their literature sought to stimulate national awareness among the emerging Slovene middle class.

Romanticism also influenced **art**. **Baroque** traditions in church painting were gradually replaced by Nazarene painting. Influenced by Viennese and Italian art, portraits of townspeople and Slovene landscapes were motifs most used. Many of these works—such as those of Josip Tominc, Matevž Langus, Mihael Stroj, Anton Karinger, and Marko Pernhart—are on display in the permanent collection of the **National Gallery** in Ljubljana. *See also* BLEIWEIS, JANEZ; HABSBURG RESTORATION; ILLYRISM; MUSIC; SLOMŠEK, ANTON MARTIN.

ROP, ANTON (1960–). Born in **Ljubljana**, Anton Rop was trained in economics, receiving a master's degree in 1991 from the **University of Ljubljana**, writing on state expenditure and economic growth. Even before getting the degree, beginning in 1985 and continuing through 1992, Rop worked as an intern and then assistant director of the Slovene Institute for Macroeconomic Analysis and Development. He wrote on investment, the market, and housing issues, and in 1992 he also began exploring the area of **privatization** and legislation.

In 1992 he won a seat in parliament as a candidate for **Liberal Democracy of Slovenia** (LDS). The following year Rop was appointed state secretary at the Ministry of Economic Relations and Development, which involved him more deeply in privatization issues. In the LDS **government** of November 1996–May 2000, he was appointed minister of labor, family, and social affairs. After the **election** of 2000 Rop became minister of finance in the government of November 2000–December 2002. With prime minister **Janez Drnovšek**'s election to the presidency of Slovenia, Rop, by prior agreement with members of the government coalition, became prime minister. A few months later he was elected president of LDS. Some viewed it as a meteoric rise for one who was a relatively unknown political factor in the early 1990s.

Rop's government reaped the fruits of hard work done by previous LDS governments. His administration put the finishing touches on Slovenia's entry into the **European Union** (EU) and **North Atlantic Treaty Organization** (NATO), and in spring 2004 celebrated the results. But what had begun auspiciously for Rop ended with LDS's defeat in the election of October 2004. That spring, perhaps in preparation for the fall vote, the opposition parties began urging attention to domestic matters that had been postponed. The **Slovene People's Party** (SLS), members of the government coalition, and **Dimitrij Rupel**, Rop's foreign minister, also began to strain at the bit. Rop lost three SLS ministers to resignation, and some weeks later Rupel was fired for what in Rop's view was insubordination. In June the LDS won only two of the seven seats in the first election to the European Parliament. Political control was unraveling for Rop, whose impatience and inexperience exacerbated the deteriorating situation. An ad hoc Assembly for the Republic, organized in June, evoked national debate on Slovenia's future, captured the electorate's attention during the fall campaign, and helped oust Rop and LDS from power. Rop was elected a member of the parliament in 2004, and he continued as president of his party, a position he inherited from Drnovšek. He was replaced in 2005 by **Jelko Kacin**.

ROŽMAN, GREGORIJ (1883–1959). A Carinthian by birth and professor at the Theological Faculty in **Ljubljana**, Gregorij Rožman was installed as bishop of Ljubljana in 1930. In the 1930s Rožman had an important role in organizing large **Catholic** events in Slovenia, including the commemoration of the 1900th anniversary of Christ's death (1933), the Second Eucharistic Congress for Yugoslavia (1935), and the Sixth International Congress of Christ the King (1939). Supporting the **Clericals** and **Catholic Action**, he advocated integration of Catholicism and politics. Influenced by the conservatives, he strongly opposed **Christian Socialism**, and helped to polarize ideological differences among Catholic intelligentsia. During **World War II** Rožman was engaged in the ideological fight against the **Liberation Front** (LF), giving support to the **Home Guard** and other anticommunists, and cooperating with the occupiers (with support from Rome). At the end of the war, like many thousands of other anticommunist Slovenes, he fled to **Austria**. In 1946 he was tried in absentia for his war activities and sentenced to 18 years imprisonment. Rožman **emigrated** to the **United States** and lived in **Cleveland**, Ohio, until his death in 1959. *See also* KOCBEK, EDVARD; RESISTANCE, NONCOMMUNIST.

RUPEL, DIMITRIJ (1946–). Born in **Ljubljana**, Dimitrij Rupel obtained a degree in sociology and world literature at the **University of Ljubljana** in 1970, and he earned a doctorate in sociology at Brandeis University in Waltham, Massachusetts, in 1976. A full professor on the Faculty of Social Sciences, Rupel has taught at the University of Ljubljana and at several universities in the United States and Canada in the late 1970s and 1980s. A prolific writer (novels, sociological studies, contemporary politics, and autobiographical works), Rupel was among those "dissidents" who worked on the publications that contributed to Slovenia's democratization. At various times he edited *Tribuna*, *Problemi*, and *Nova revija*. For the latter, he was managing editor of the noted issue No. 57, which is credited with setting the stage for the **May Declaration, 1989**.

In January 1989 Rupel helped to organize the **Slovene Democratic Alliance** (SDZ) and in January of the next year the **Demos** coalition, which led the opposition to victory over the Communists in the **election** of April 1990. After that election Rupel became the **Republic of Slovenia**'s (RS) first foreign minister, a position he held until January 1993. As foreign minister he saw the RS through a truly critical period, which included disassociation from the **Socialist Federal Republic of Yugoslavia** (SFRY), the establishment of **independence**, and **recognition** by the international community. Rupel was elected to the National Assembly in December 1992, representing the Liberal Democratic Party (LDS). In December 1994 Rupel, candidate of the LDS, was elected to a four-year term as mayor of Ljubljana, a position he held until fall 1997, when he was appointed ambassador to the **United States**.

Rupel's forte has been foreign affairs, and except for the interlude when he was Ljubljana's mayor and several short interruptions during political skirmishes at home (during **Andrej Bajuk**'s **government** of June–December 2000 and the latter months of **Anton Rop**'s government of December 2002–December 2004), Rupel has been a major force in formulating and implementing his country's **foreign policy**. Slovenia's goal during this period was achieving international validation. While ambassador to Washington, Rupel persuaded President

Bill Clinton to make a state visit to the RS; it took place in June 1999. Rupel also worked hard to attain **North Atlantic Treaty Organization** (NATO) and **European Union** (EU) membership. Although he was disappointed that Slovenia was not among those that received an invitation to join NATO in its first enlargement round in 1997, NATO membership as well as induction into the EU were achieved in spring 2004. Rupel, who had again become foreign minister in December 2000, was on hand for the celebrations. Rupel was also instrumental in arranging the first George W. Bush–Vladimir Putin meeting, which took place in June 2001 in Slovenia. That meeting, with its extensive **media** coverage, put Slovenia in a spotlight it felt it needed.

On the eve of Independence Day in June 2004, Rupel was dismissed from his ministerial post by prime minister Anton Rop because Rupel, while still foreign minister, together with Slovene intellectuals and leaders of center-right political parties, organized an "Assembly for the Republic" to examine and debate issues that Slovenia faced now that its place in the international arena had at last been established. For Rupel, who was first—in John Hancock fashion—to sign the "Assembly" document, it was a return to the late 1980s and *Nova revija* number 57 deliberations on Slovenia's future; for Rop, head of LDS, it was party disloyalty. Over the summer of 2004 Rupel was drawn into the **Slovene Democratic Party** (SDS) and ran on its slate for member of the parliament in the election of October 2004. Both Rupel and his new party were victorious; the new prime minister, **Janez Janša**, reappointed Rupel foreign minister. In early 2005, with the RS as one-year chair of the **Organization for Security and Cooperation in Europe** (OSCE), Foreign Minister Rupel again had his hands full.

RUPNIK, LEON (1880–1946). Leon Rupnik, a professional soldier, began his career in the Austro-Hungarian army and reached the rank of major during **World War I**. After the war Rupnik joined the Yugoslav **army**, where he rose to the rank of major general. After the outbreak of **World War II** in **Yugoslavia**, he returned as a civilian to Slovenia and was mayor of **Ljubljana**, appointed by the Italians. After the Germans occupied Ljubljana in 1943, Rupnik was named president of Ljubljana Province; he founded the **Home Guard** and became its inspector-general. As a staunch anticommunist, he collaborated with the occupiers in fighting the Communist-led **Liberation Front** (LF). In 1944 Rupnik was instrumental in a controversial public Home Guard oath-taking ceremony, which has been interpreted by many as an expression of their allegiance to the Germans. In late April 1945 the

National Committee for Slovenia demanded Rupnik's resignation as president of Ljubljana Province and inspector-general of the Home Guard. Instead, Rupnik assumed Home Guard command. A few days later, because of National Committee pressures to disassociate the Home Guard from the Nazis, Rupnik submitted his resignation. Just before the end of the war, he and his family left Ljubljana for **Austria**. He spent time in Italian refugee camps until January 1946, when the Allies returned him to Yugoslavia. Imprisoned and tried in Ljubljana, he was executed by firing squad as a national traitor.

RUSSIA, RELATIONS WITH. Before **independence** in 1991, Slovenia did not have direct political or diplomatic relations with Russia. For the Slovenes, whether in Austria-Hungary or in royal or socialist **Yugoslavia**, relations with Russia (the USSR during the communist period) were the purview of statesmen in **Vienna** or **Belgrade**. Occasionally, individual Slovenes were a part of diplomatic exchanges, but more than likely not. For the most part, relations between Russia and **Austria** were not the best, particularly after the 1870s. A deepening rivalry between the two countries put them on opposite sides in **World War I**. In the years between the two world wars, there was not much contact between the Yugoslav kingdom and the USSR, other than for Yugoslav **Marxists**, who found refuge in Moscow during the 1930s. After **World War II**, although both Yugoslavia and Russia now had communist regimes, relations between the two countries quickly deteriorated. Yugoslavia, espousing a policy of **nonalignment**, soon pronounced the USSR a threat to its survival. The Yugoslav **army**'s military buildup in the late 1940s was intended as a deterrent not only to the West but to the East (the USSR and its **Cominform** allies) as well.

In the cultural sphere, however, Slovene–Russian relations have a long cordial history, going back to the early 19th century. Ties between writers and intellectuals, primarily linguists and those who idealized Slavic cultural unity, ran deep. By the late 1860s, with German power looming large in Central Europe, Slovene **liberals** even began looking to Russia for political leadership. Until 1914 there were successive waves of Slovene Pan-Slavism—after 1900 Neoslavism—that led some Slovene army deserters in World War I to join the Entente powers (Russia and Serbia). Slovene leftists in the interwar years were often drawn spiritually to Russia and the communist revolution. Cultural and intellectual ties, however minimal, seemed to continue in one form or another despite political differences.

In 1990 and 1991 both the USSR and Yugoslavia were disintegrating. One component of the USSR, the Russian Federation, declared its sovereignty in June 1990. In May 1991 it concluded an agreement on economic, scientific, and cultural cooperation with the newly sovereign **Republic of Slovenia** (RS). On 14 February 1992 the Russian Federation was the 46th to recognize Slovenia as an independent state. The Baltic states, Belarus, and Ukraine—all former republics of the USSR—had extended recognition earlier. Slovene–Russian diplomatic relations were formally established in May 1992, and ambassadors were exchanged later that year. In 1993 economic relations were also initiated. For the RS, securing a long-term agreement for the purchase of natural gas (guaranteed to 2010) was the most important. In 1995 a new agreement on cultural cooperation was signed at the opening of Slovenia's embassy in Moscow.

In 1995 the RS and Russia also signed a bilateral trade agreement, and trade between the two grew slowly for about five years, but since 2001 Slovene–Russian trade has grown at a much faster pace. In 2002 trade between the two reached $500 million, and the following year a goal of reaching $1 billion was announced. In 2006 President Janez Drnovšek reported that trade levels had nearly doubled during the previous five years. About 270 Slovene companies have representatives in Russia (primarily Moscow), where they sell buses, foodstuffs, footwear, furniture, electrical appliances, paints, and pharmaceuticals, among other things. In return, Russians provide the RS with natural gas and oil, and also automobiles, cellulose and paper products, chemical goods, crude rubber, and yarn. Slovene banks are beginning to enter the Russian market, and Slovenes are building an airport in Sochi.

The RS and Russia also have embarked on joint business ventures in southeastern Europe. Russia is particularly interested in trading and investing in Serbia and Montenegro, longtime Slavic and Orthodox protégés in the Balkans, and so is Slovenia. Each year since 1992, Russian–Slovene unity has been sealed at an annual gathering at Vršič, Slovenia's highest Alpine pass and the site of a Russian-style chapel. The shingled wooden structure with an onion dome commemorates the deaths of 300 Russian prisoners of war killed by an avalanche in 1916. The soldiers were among the 10,000 Russians building a road over the **Alps** in 1915–1916 to assist Austria's **World War I** effort on the Italian front. The annual Vršič gathering, attended by political and religious figures from both countries, has served to renew the sense of a common culture and to confirm a newfound friendship. *See also* KOBARID/CAPORETTO.

– S –

SCIENCE. In Slovenia as in most European countries, science is a broad category encompassing not only such disciplines as biology, chemistry, mathematics, and physics, but all fields of knowledge based on empirical investigation and systematic recording of data. Thus for Slovenes what is regarded as the social sciences and even humanities research might be regarded as science. Given that understanding of the term, it can be said that the first notable "scientists" in Slovene lands were the inhabitants of monasteries, such as **Stična monastery**, which in the 10th century were centers of **medieval** culture and art, and instrumental in developing a scientific body of knowledge. Monasteries established **libraries** and undertook study of astronomy, medicine, **music**, pedagogy, and philosophy as well as theology. In the 15th and 16th centuries, **humanism**, flourishing in the coastal towns of **Koper** and **Piran**, and in **Ljubljana** diocese, gave impetus for the acquisition of knowledge. Some early scientists studied and worked abroad, but in late 15th-century **Idrija**, where mercury was mined, the first center of modern technological engineering, natural sciences, and medicine was established. Around 1525 Santorio Santorio from **Koper**, a professor at the University of Padua, constructed a thermometer and was the first to measure body temperature, thus advancing the science of quantitative medicine. Humanism and the **Protestant Reformation** led to the publication of the first Slovene book and **publishing** in general, important tools in the dissemination of knowledge and the development of science. *See also* MUSEUMS.

The 17th century saw further advances in science in Europe. In the Slovene lands, the polymath **Janez Vajkard Valvasor** (1641–1693), a member of London's Royal Society, strongly opposed random speculations regarding nature. As an astute observer of nature, he established important empirical knowledge about the **Kras/Karst** plateau and the Slovene lands in general. In Ljubljana the mathematician and astronomer Marija Kunic von Love, the first Slovene woman scientist, published her books already in 1678. The late 17th century also saw the beginnings of institutional support for scientific work. The **Academia Operosorum**, founded in 1693, was established for that purpose. It was the first **society** that brought together Slovene scientists, supported their work, and invited foreign researchers to the Slovene lands. By organizing **higher education**, the **Jesuits** contributed their part to the development of science, especially in the areas of physics and mathematics. One important Jesuit in this regard was Gabrijel Gruber (1740–1805), who came to Ljubljana in 1769 and taught as the chair for mechanics. Among the Jesuits' students was mathematician **Jurij Vega** (1754–1802). In the 18th century a number of scientists worked at home and abroad. Their pioneering work has remained relevant to this day. One of them was Anton Janša (1734–1773), who wrote *Popolni nauk o čeberlastvu* (Complete Teachings on Apiculture). During the **Enlightenment**, Baron **Žiga Zois** (1747–1819) strongly supported the development of natural sciences, and the members of the Zois circle, especially **Anton Tomaž Linhart** (1756–1795), were instrumental in the development of historical and humanistic studies, providing a base for a national awakening in the 19th century. *See also* BEEKEEPING.

In addition to science, medicine, and technology, great strides were made in linguistics in the 19th century by **Franc Miklošič** (1813–1891), who wrote a comparative grammar of the Slavic languages. Scientific contributions were made also by **missionaries** of that time, such as **Friderik Baraga**, who worked as linguist and anthropologist among Indians of the Great Lakes area in the **United States**, and by the Jesuit Ignacij Knoblehar, a systematic researcher of the ethnology, geography, linguistics, and nature on the Upper White Nile in the Sudan. Among the late 19th- and early 20th-century scientists, the physicist **Jožef Stefan** (1835–1893) and the mathematician Josip Plemelj (1873–1967), both professors at the University of Vienna, occupy a special place. Jožef Stefan educated many important scientists, among them famous Austrian mathematician and physicist Ludwig Boltzmann, known for his entropy law. Boltzmann refined and advanced some of Stefan's initial discoveries.

Efforts in the 19th and 20th centuries to improve the general education of Slovenes, to publish Slovene textbooks and professional literature, and to develop a Slovene professional **language** contributed greatly to the development of science and also to the establishment of the first Slovene university (1919) and the Academy of Sciences and Arts (1938). Several Slovene scientists established themselves abroad. One was Milan Vidmar (1885–1962), an electrical engineer known throughout Europe. Another was the botanist and geneticist

Fran Jesenko (1875–1932), who came to Ljubljana to help establish the **University of Ljubljana**. Besides their own research, they were important as teachers and organizers of research facilities that allowed a large number of Slovenes to advance scientific disciplines. Some Slovene scientists continued their work abroad, such as **Friderik Pregl** (1869–1930), who was in 1923 awarded the Nobel Prize in chemistry, and the rocket engineer Herman Potočnik-Noordung (1882–1929), one of the founders of aerospace science. Potočnik's 1929 book *Das Problem der Befahrung des Weltraums* (The Problems of Space Travel), which has current scientific and ethical significance, was published in the United States in 1995. During **World War II** scientific research slowed, although in 1944 the zoologist Jovan Hadži published one of his most important works, *Turberalijska teorija knidarijev* (Turbellaria Theory of Cnidaria). Correcting Ernest Haechel's famous philogenetic tree, Hadži achieved international fame. The same year, ethnologist Rajko Ložar published his important book *Narodopisje Slovencev* (The Ethnology of the Slovenes), and the **Partisans** established an Institute for Science at the presidency of the **Slovene National Liberation Council** (*Slovenski narodnoosvobodilni svet*, SNOS).

After World War II several research institutes were founded by the state, by the **Slovenian Academy of Sciences and Arts** (SAZU), and also by business enterprises. In 1946 the **government** established a chemical institute and also the Institute for Nuclear Physics, which was renamed for Jožef Stefan in 1949, with the intention of promoting applied research that would advance the country's economic development. The Institute Jožef Stefan developed into the largest interdisciplinary research center in Slovenia. Political controls and central planning affected the university, the institutes, and research activities but eased after 1952, although they continued in the social sciences until the 1980s, maintaining tension between the scientific community and politicians. Some scientists **emigrated**, such as the world-renown physicist Anton Peterlin, one of the founders and early directors of Institute Jožef Stefan. Some were not permitted to teach and were forced into a "domestic exile" in research institutes, which employed those university professors and scientists whose ideas and work were thought to endanger society. The Institute of Sociology in Ljubljana, established in 1958, played such a role especially in the 1970s, when several "liberal" professors were removed from the University of Ljubljana. However, despite problems, research at the university increased, and the number of research institutions grew from 43 in 1954 to 191 in 1987. The number of researchers grew five-fold from 1966 to 1987, while the number of researchers with doctoral degrees rose tenfold. In the mid-1980s several indicators of scientific excellence showed that Slovenia lagged behind developed countries; one of the most problematic indicators showed that researchers were poorly qualified. Research capacity has expanded, in part due to the program "2000 Young Researchers," which has financially and institutionally supported research by young people. Research is supported by private (60 percent) and governmental (40 percent) monies. Although the share of GDP spent for science declined in the first few years after **independence**, its share rose to 1.5 percent in 2004. *See also* AGITPROP; LIBERALIZATION OF THE 1960s.

With the introduction of a multiparty system (1990) and Slovenia's independence, many administrative changes in the organization and financing of science have taken place. In 1991 a new law on science was enacted, and in 1995 the first national program for the advancement of science was prepared. Recognizing the importance of **education** for science, the Ministry of Science and Technology merged with the Ministry of Education and Sport, only to split again five years later into the Ministry of Higher Education, Science, and Technology, and Ministry of Education and Sport.

Because small states like Slovenia have neither the means nor human capacity to advance science on their own, international collaboration is crucial. Since 1991 Slovenia has been an active participant in European development and research projects, and many individual Slovene scientists, universities, and research institutes work with their counterparts abroad, such as the National Institutes of Health in Bethesda, Maryland (U.S.), and Karolinska University in Stockholm (Sweden).

SECURITY AND INTELLIGENCE SERVICE / VARNOSTNO-OBVEŠČEVALNA SLUŽBA (VOS) (1941–1945). In August 1941 the Communists in the **Liberation Front** (LF) established the Security and Intelligence Service (*Varnostno-obveščevalna služba*, VOS) without the knowledge of the LF Executive Council. While ostensibly an arm of the LF, VOS was under exclusive control and in the service of the **Communist Party of Slovenia** (CPS). Its task was to fight the enemies of the LF and CPS, and in the fall of 1941 VOS began executing Slovene civilians. The victims were primarily anticommunist Slovenes but also included those who had collaborated with the Italian occupiers. These actions created opposition and resistance to the LF among Slovenes of different ideologies and discredited it in the eyes of many. *See also* EHRLICH, LAMBERT; NATLAČEN, MARKO.

SELF-MANAGEMENT AGREEMENT, SOCIAL COMPACT / SAMOUPRAVNI SPORAZUM, DRUŽBENI DOGOVOR. *See* CONTRACTUAL SOCIALISM; WORKERS' SELF-MANAGEMENT.

SELF-MANAGEMENT COURT. *See* COURTS AND JUSTICE; TRADE UNIONS.

SELF-MANAGING COMMUNITY OF INTEREST / SAMOU-PRAVNA INTERESNA SKUPNOST (SIS). *See* CONTRACTUAL SOCIALISM; WORKERS' SELF-MANAGEMENT.

SERBS, CROATS, AND SLOVENES, KINGDOM OF (1918–1929). Established on 1 December 1918, the new political entity named the Kingdom of Serbs, Croats, and Slovenes united the Kingdom of Serbia with the **State of Slovenes, Croats, and Serbs**, which had recently proclaimed its independence from the collapsing Austro-Hungarian monarchy. One week later the independent Kingdom of Montenegro and the Vojvodina (a part of the former Kingdom of **Hungary**) joined the new state. Consisting largely of South Slavs, or Yugoslavs, the union of these territories was regarded as a fulfillment of the principle of national self-determination, an idea in vogue among peacemakers in Paris after **World War I**. In 1921, when the new kingdom adopted the **Vidovdan Constitution**, it had about 12.5 million inhabitants. In 1929 the state was renamed the Kingdom of **Yugoslavia**.

For the Slovenes, becoming a part of the Kingdom of Serbs, Croats, and Slovenes, in which they constituted 9 percent of the population, was a traumatic experience. The **Habsburg** state in which they had lived for many centuries had collapsed, and the Slovene community was divided. Some remained in **Austria** (**Carinthian Plebiscite**, 10 October 1920), and nearly one-third of the Slovenes came under **Italy** (**Treaty of Rapallo**, November 1920). In the new kingdom Slovenes generally continued to press for national federalism, as they had done before World War I in the **Habsburg Empire**.

SERVICE INDUSTRY. The service industry has become an important branch of Slovenia's **economy**. Its share in the gross domestic product (GDP) has been growing since the 1960s, and in 2005 it reached 63.2 percent, displacing **manufacturing**, which until the early 1980s held the major share of GDP. For many years two branches of the service industry—**tourism** and **transport**—contributed most to the share of GDP, but retail, real estate, and financial services have expanded most aggressively since Slovenia's **independence** (1991). Financial services, the latest bloomer, surged only after 2000 when **banks** were **privatized** and foreign direct investments began, increasing its share of GDP from 6.4 percent in 2001 to 10.4 percent in 2004. **Health** and social services, another growing service industry, increased its percentage of GDP from 2.6 percent in 2001 to 4.9 percent in 2004. The Slovene **stock exchange** also expanded after 2001, when the Bank of Slovenia (BS) dropped restrictions on securities trading.

The retail sector, which has been transforming rapidly since 1990, is well developed. Its growth has been stimulated by the increasing standard of living. Wholesale and retail stores experienced an expansion boom, perhaps too quickly for a relatively small market; late in the 1990s many stores merged, and some declared bankruptcy. Consolidation of the market was intensified by foreign competitors, such as the Austrian Spar and the French Leclerc, which were allowed to enter the Slovenian market in 1997. Mercator, the largest Slovene retailer, has also been one of the most successful, with 1.7 billion euros of consolidated revenues, and about 15.7 million euros of net profit in 2005. It controls about 40 percent of the local market and also has opened new stores in large cities in **Croatia**, Bosnia-Hercegovina, Serbia, and other post-socialist states. In 2004 the Austrian Spar/Interspar, with 20 percent of the market, was Slovenia's second largest retail chain, and Tuš, a relatively new (1989) and expanding retailer from **Celje**, followed with about 10 percent, while the market share of small private stores continued to drop. *See also* INTERNATIONAL TRADE AND FINANCIAL TRANSACTIONS.

SETTLEMENT OF SLOVENES. The ancestors of present-day Slovenes settled in Central Europe in the second half of the sixth century AD. They arrived in six waves, during the time of Europe's migration of peoples, from the proto-Slavic homeland north of the Carpathians and colonized territory in the eastern Alps vacated by the Lombards after 568 AD. The land these western Slavs came to inhabit extended in the north from Linz along the Danube to **Vienna** and in the south from **Trieste** eastward approximately along Slovenia's current southern boundaries to Lake Balaton in **Hungary**. At its largest expanse, in the ninth century, the territory settled by these proto-Slovenes was 70,000 square kilometers, more than three times the size of Slovenia today.

Numbering about 200,000 in the seventh century, these Slavs were herders and farmers whose social and economic organization and practices can be traced linguistically and archeologically to the original Slavic homeland. Their new home, sparsely and unevenly settled because invasions and migrations of peoples continued, remained an unstable place for centuries. In order to defend themselves against intruders, such as the Avars and the Bavarians, who were their enemies at the outset, these Alpine Slavs concluded a union in 623 AD with the Slavs of the Czech and Moravian lands. Their common ruler until 658 was a merchant called Samo, presumably of Frankish origin. After his death the union ended, and **Karantania**, the name of the proto-Slovenes' new homeland, developed a political history of its own.

It should be noted that certain dissenting scholars dispute the preceding explanation about the origin of the Slovene settlement. *See also* VENETI THEORY.

SLOMŠEK, ANTON MARTIN (1800–1862). A poet, religious writer, and bishop of **Maribor**, Anton Martin Slomšek was most important for the development of Slovene **elementary education** in rural areas, where he actively promoted the establishment of Sunday schools, which helped achieve basic literacy, especially among girls. Slomšek wrote one of the two most important Slovene readers of that period, *Blaže in Nežica v nedelski šoli* (Blaže and Nežica in Sunday School, 1842), which was not merely a school text but also a veritable mini-encyclopedia for Slovene farmers. Slomšek was also instrumental in moving the seat of the **Catholic Church's** Lavantine diocese from Št. Andraž (St. Andrä) in **Austria** to Maribor and in redrawing the borders of the diocese according to the nationality of its people. He also helped found the **publishing** house **Society of St. Hermagoras** and established a Slovene School of Theology in Maribor, which is considered the beginning of **higher education** in that city. Slomšek's work played an important role in developing a national consciousness among Slovene peasants.

SLOVENE CHRISTIAN DEMOCRATS / SLOVENSKI KRŠČANSKI DEMOKRATI (SKD). The Slovene Christian Democrats, organized as an alliance in November 1989 and upgraded to a **political party** after parties were legalized, was one of the organizers of the **Demos** coalition. Demos won the **election** of April 1990 and thus ended one-party Communist rule in Slovenia. The SKD, with about 12,000 members at the time, tallied the largest number of votes for the coalition, and on that basis **Lojze Peterle** of the SKD became prime minister. Five **government** ministers also came from the SKD.

The SKD's program reflected its philosophy, which stressed the importance of the individual in accordance with Christian principles. The SKD traced its ancestry to the Slovene People's Party **(Clericals)** of the late 19th and early 20th centuries, drawing upon the social philosophy of **Janez Evangelist Krek**, and from **Anton Korošec** it got its drive for Slovene autonomy. The party generally promoted the interests of the **Catholic Church**, its philanthropic efforts, and the introduction of the Catholic religion as an elective in schools. The Christian Democrats saw social crises as moral ones, and thus promoted policies aimed at moral regeneration. They were at the forefront of the anti-abortion campaign when the **Constitution of 1991** was being debated. The SKD also urged the rehabilitation of Slovenes (including the **Village Guard** and **Home Guard**) who had been anticommunist during **World War II**. Its program, like that of many other Slovene parties, approved of a market **economy**, but one adjusted by government social policy in order to prevent inequities. It also backed **denationalization** of property and was the strongest supporter of returning to the church the lands it lost after 1945.

In the election of December 1992 the SKD, with 34,000 members, maintained its strength among the electorate, winning 14 (of 90) seats in the State Assembly. (Ignac Polajnar headed its parliamentary delegation.) The SKD also became part of the ruling coalition with **Liberal Democracy of Slovenia** (LDS) and the **United List of Social Democrats** (ZLSD) in Janez Drnovšek's (LDS) government, holding four ministerial posts, including the Foreign Ministry with Lojze Peterle as foreign minister, a position from which he resigned in the fall of 1994. SKD's Perterle was also made vice premier; in January 1995 his successor in that post was Janko Deželak, also a Christian Democrat.

After the mid-1990s, SKD experienced internal rifts, primarily between its right and left wings. In April 2000 the party merged with the **Slovene People's Party** (SLS) and campaigned as the SLS-SKD party. A few months later some in the party, most notably Lojze Peterle, joined the new **New Slovenia–Christian People's Party** (NSi), headed by **Andrej Bajuk**. In 1990 SKD had gotten 13 percent of the vote; in 1992, 14 percent and 14 seats in parliament; in 1996,

SKD's seats were reduced to 10. SKD figured in ruling coalitions in the governments of May 1990–December 1992 and December 1992–November 1996, and the short-lived government of May–November 2000. Later as constituents of the SLS-SKD party, they were in the government of November 2000–December 2002 and the government of December 2002–December 2004. After the election of October 2004 and the victory of **Janez Janša**'s **Slovene Democratic Party** (SDS), both the SLS-SKD and NSi became members of the ruling coalition.

SLOVENE DEMOCRATIC ALLIANCE / SLOVENSKA DEMO-KRATIČNA ZVEZA (SDZ). The Slovene Democratic Alliance was established in January 1989 on the initiative of intellectuals and reformers, some of whom worked with civil society organizations. The sociologist and writer **Dimitrij Rupel** was elected its president. Many members were associated with *Nova revija*, the journal where Slovenia's future was being vigorously debated in the late 1980s. In general SDZ supported **independence**, a market **economy**, parliamentary democracy, and unity with Europe. Tactically SDZ took the lead in promoting cooperation against the Communist regime, hence the creation of the **Demos** coalition in late 1989. In early 1990 SDZ had about 5,000 members; among them, besides Rupel, were **Igor Bavčar** and **France Bučar**, and all of them became leading political figures after the **election** of April 1990. Alliance candidates won 27 seats in the National Assembly and Bučar became its president (speaker). Bavčar became minister of internal affairs and Rupel took over the Foreign Ministry.

After the tense days of spring and summer 1991, punctuated by Slovenia's declaration of independence and the **Ten-Day War**, alliance unity began to wear thin. In mid-October 1991 SDZ split into two new parties: the **Slovene Democratic Alliance–National Democratic Party** (SDZ-NDS) and the **Democratic Party of Slovenia** (Democrats). Neither of the two new parties was long-lived.

SLOVENE DEMOCRATIC ALLIANCE–NATIONAL DEMO-CRATIC PARTY / SLOVENSKA DEMOKRATIČNA ZVEZA–NARODNA DEMOKRATSKA STRANKA (SDZ-NDP). On 13 October 1991 the **Slovene Democratic Alliance** (SDZ), a major force within the **Demos** coalition, split into two components over issues relating to communism, the **National Liberation Struggle** (NOB), the role of the **Catholic Church**, and **privatization** of social property. The more conservative right wing of the party, headed by Rajko Pirnat, took the name Slovene Democratic Alliance–National Democratic Party (SDZ-NDP). The SDZ-NDP did poorly in the election of 1992. In search of a stronger yet appropriate **political party** affiliation, members briefly joined the **Slovene Christian Democrats** (SKD) and finally settled on an association with the **Slovene Democratic Party** (SDS).

SLOVENE DEMOCRATIC PARTY / SLOVENSKA DEMOKRATIČNA STRANKA (SDS). Like other Slovene political organizations that emerged in the late 1980s, the Slovene Democratic Party (SDS) went through several developmental stages and name changes. The inspiration for organizing came out of a workers' strike at the Litostroj factory in **Ljubljana** in 1987. The initiative was formalized in February 1989 with the founding of the Social Democratic Alliance of Slovenia (SDZS) that was headed for several months by the 1987 strike organizer France Tomšič. Once parties were legalized by parliament at the end of 1989, the "alliance" was renamed a "party," the Social Democratic Party of Slovenia (SDSS). Shortly after the first multiparty **election** in 1990, the acronym was shortened to SDS. In 2003 the acronym remained the same, but the party title changed to Slovene Democratic Party.

In 1990 the party joined the **Demos** coalition. The party president, **Jože Pučnik**, was Demos's president, and the coalition was one of the winners in the election of April 1990. Pučnik was Demos's unsuccessful candidate for president of Slovenia that spring. Meanwhile the party made a good showing, getting 19 seats in the National Assembly and placing two ministers in the **government**. In the election of December 1992, SDS won four seats in a much smaller body (90). Its member **Janez Janša** was reappointed defense minister and served in **Janez Drnovšek**'s government of December 1992–November 1996. In 1992 SDS grew larger when the **Slovene Democratic Alliance–National Democratic Party** (SDZ-NDP), a wing of the former **Slovene Democratic Alliance** (SDZ), merged with SDS.

The party saw itself as a descendant of the Yugoslav Social Democratic Party (JSDS) founded by the **Socialists** in the 1890s and outlawed by the Communists after 1945. In its original incarnation the party had a "Yugoslav" orientation; a century later it supported **independence** for Slovenia. The new party's socialist program was modeled after social democracy in Western Europe, particularly Germany. It rejected the militant **Marxist** concepts of class warfare and revolution, embracing instead the principle of evolutionary progress toward socialist goals. The SDS advocated partnership between labor and capital, collective agreements, **trade unionism**, and social legislation. It supported the idea of a market **economy**, as long as capital acted in a socially responsible way. The SDS's goal for the **Republic of Slovenia** (RS) was to match the European Community's (EC) social program of 1989. During the 1990s and early part of the next decade, SDS strove with little effect to implement the domestic economic and social programs that it believed had not been addressed by the leftist governments of the 1990s.

Janez Janša became the driving force of SDS. Jože Pučnik, its first president, served from late 1989 until 1993. Thereafter Janša held the party presidency, with reelection in 1995, 1999, 2001, and again in 2005 (four-year term). Janša not only dominated the party but tried very hard to bring his party and himself to power in Slovenia. The party shared coalition power after the elections of 1990 and 1992 (until March 1994), and between May and November 2000 during the interregnum headed by Prime Minister **Andrej Bajuk**. The party would not achieve power in its own right until after the election of 2004, when it won the most seats in parliament (29) and Janša was at last asked to form a government, thereby ending 12 years of rule by **Liberal Democracy of Slovenia** (LDS).

While in opposition, during much of the time between 1994 and 2004, SDS and Janša used varying tactics and appeals to get the voters' support. In the 1990s they tried to revive the "Slovenian Spring" idea of the late 1980s, evoking the popular movement that supported Slovene sovereignty, and also justice for the **Ljubljana Four** (of whom Janša was one). The "Spring" parties besides SDS were the **Slovene Christian Democrats** (SKD) and the **Slovene People's Party** (SLS). Together these center-right elements strove unsuccessfully to oust the Slovene leftists. They fared somewhat better in the 21st century as "Coalition Slovenia," which included SDS, SLS, and the **New Slovenia–Christian People's Party** (NSi), which had been formed in 2000 and inherited many SKD members. Janša and SDS improved their image after 2003 among the electorate and won in the balloting in 2004, promising to put Slovenia on a new path. In 2005 SDS had 22,000 members.

SLOVENE FARMER'S ALLIANCE–PEOPLE'S PARTY (SKZ). *See* SLOVENE PEOPLE'S PARTY.

SLOVENE NATIONAL LIBERATION COUNCIL / SLOVENSKI NARODNOOSVOBODILNI SVET (SNOS). The Slovene National Liberation Council (SNOS) was a Communist-controlled parliament established in February 1944 in **Bela Krajina** (Črnomelj). At that meeting SNOS stressed that Slovenia was a sovereign nation, a part of the Yugoslav federation, joining it voluntarily and reserving the right to secede or to join with other nations. In addition to adopting the conclusions of the second meeting of the **Antifascist Council of National Liberation of Yugoslavia** (AVNOJ), SNOS elected its presidency, which served as a provisional **government** and issued several important decrees: on local and regional elections; on the establishment of departments (local government and administration, internal affairs, **economy**, **education**, **health**, information); on the presidency; on the establishment of the national treasury; and on the Office of the Public Prosecutor. SNOS's presidency, which operated in the **Partisan-controlled territories**, was to prepare for the establishment of a Communist-controlled administration and takeover of power in Slovenia after the war.

Because of a German and **Home Guard** offensive in Bela Krajina in April 1945, the SNOS presidency moved its seat to Ajdovščina, a small town in Primorska. At the same time, the **Partisans** were advancing toward **Trieste**, occupying it on 1 May 1945. On 1 May the SNOS presidency named the first post–**World War II** national government, with **Boris Kidrič** as its president. On 10 May the government came to **Ljubljana**, where it was generally welcomed. SNOS was dissolved on 10 September 1946, when also a decree on the election to the constitutional assembly was issued. *See also* COMMUNIST PARTY OF SLOVENIA; GOVERNMENT OF SLOVENIA, NATIONAL; TRIESTE QUESTION.

SLOVENE NATIONAL PARTY / SLOVENSKA NACIONALNA STRANKA (SNS). The Slovene National Party (SNS) was established in March 1991, billing itself as a secular and anticlerical organization. In practice, its position has been leftist combined with a large dose of ultra-nationalism, and it has appealed to voters of both extremes. In 1992, with the wars in former **Yugoslavia** raging and Croatian and Bosnian refugees spilling into Slovenia by the thousands, SNS actively urged their expulsion. As a result and to the surprise of many, the SNS tallied nearly 10 percent of the vote and won 12 seats (of 90) in the State Assembly in the **election** of December 1992. In later elections the number of SNS mandates declined, but the party continued to get some seats in all future elections: four in 1996, four in 2000, and six in 2004. The party's founder, **Zmago Jelinčič**, has been its only president.

Many SNS stalwarts share the **Partisan** experience and work to keep the **National Liberation Struggle** sacred, while damning the **Home Guard** as collaborationists. The party, at the same time, has been fiercely nationalistic, demanding strict requirements for Slovene citizenship and restrictions on privileges for foreign workers, especially those from other former Yugoslav republics. It also opposed foreign ownership of Slovene property, a right that was granted by constitutional amendment in 2003 in order to complete Slovenia's eligibility for entry into the **European Union** (EU). SNS has also been very vocal in its opposition to **Croatia** and its claims to Slovene territory and its restrictions on Slovene access to the Adriatic Sea. The party, consistent with its nationalistic bent, also opposed joining the EU and **North Atlantic Treaty Organization** (NATO).

SLOVENE PEOPLE'S PARTY BEFORE 1945. *See* CLERICALS.

SLOVENE PEOPLE'S PARTY / SLOVENSKA LJUDSKA STRANKA (SLS). The Slovene People's Party went through several name changes in its short post-communist existence. It began on 12 May 1988 as the Slovene Farmers' Alliance (*Slovenska kmečka zveza*, SKZ) within the framework of the **Socialist Alliance of Working People** (SAWP)—an umbrella organization for all groups outside the League of Communists of Slovenia (LCS), which was the name of the **Communist Party of Slovenia** after 1952. The founding of the SKZ was, in fact, a first step in the dismantling of the one-party system in Slovenia, and in two years SKZ would achieve one of its long-term goals: its own delegates in parliament. Once founded, the SKZ became a kind of trade union for farmers, who were greatly underrepresented politically in socialist **Yugoslavia**, and it established branches throughout Slovenia. Because of its extensive network, it was able to influence "revolutionary" developments in 1989 and 1990. The SKZ helped to establish a commission to revise the **constitution**, which produced amendments giving Slovenia greater autonomy. The SKZ also had input regarding the law on political organizations (December 1989) and the law on parliamentary elections (January 1990). In early 1990, with about 30,000 members, it joined **Demos** and was therefore a part of the winning coalition in the **election** of April 1990. Two **government** ministers came from the SKZ.

Once it became politically active, the organization revised its name, becoming the SKZ–People's Party (SKZ-LS) in June 1992. Its program, as might be expected, served its rural constituents. The SKZ-LS supported **denationalization** of property and reforms of social benefits, and it urged greater financial aid for underdeveloped regions. In the election of December 1992 the SKZ-LS won 10 (of 90) seats in the State Assembly; the head of its delegation was Franc Zagožen. **Ivan Oman** was president of the party in 1992 and a member of Slovenia's presidency after the first multiparty election (April 1990). He later joined the **Slovene Christian Democrats** (SKD). After December 1992 the party's name was shortened to Slovene People's Party (SLS). This center-right party stressed traditional Slovene values and Christian ethics but maintained a secular profile. It traced its roots to the **Clericals** (also called the Slovene People's Party) of a century earlier, particularly to the **Christian Socialist** movement of **Janez Evangelist Krek**.

After the establishment of parliamentary government in Slovenia, the SLS initially maintained a strong political profile. In 1992 and 1996 it got solid representation in the National Assembly: 10 and 19 seats, respectively. In 2000 and 2004, however, its electoral success diminished to nine seats in 2000 and only seven in 2004. In April 2000 SLS merged with SKD to form the SLS-SKD party. There was hope that the two together, given their electoral strengths in the 1990s, could oust the center-left from power. The new party, however, had difficulties integrating and formulating clear goals. Their lack of direction was chronicled in the **media**, no doubt persuading voters that SLS-SKD could hardly manage the country if it could not get its own house in order. At the end of January 2002 the party readopted its old name and acronym, SLS.

With the exception of the period between 1992 and 1996, SLS played a role in all government coalitions. Although it was more philosophically in tune with the Slovene Christian Democrats (SKD) and to a lesser degree with the **Social Democratic Party** (SDS)—both center-right groups—SLS participated in center-left coalitions led by **Liberal Democracy of Slovenia** (LDS) from 1996 through 2004. Among the dominant political figures in the party were the Podobnik brothers, Marjan and Janez, both of whom have served as party president. **Janez Podobnik**, SLS president after November 2003, served effectively as president (speaker) of the National Assembly in **Janez Drnovšek**'s government of 1996–2000. After 2005 SLS was once again in the government, but this time as part of a center-right coalition headed by **Janez Janša** (SDS). Since Slovenia joined the **European Union** (EU), SLS has been a member of the European People's Party.

SLOVENES, CROATS, AND SERBS, NATIONAL COUNCIL OF (5 OCTOBER–1 DECEMBER 1918). As the **Habsburg Empire** was collapsing under Entente pressures in the final stages of **World War I**, the South Slavs of Austria-Hungary established a National Council to deal with their problems. Its headquarters was in Zagreb (**Croatia**) and its president was the Slovene **Clericals'** leader **Anton Korošec**. When the Habsburg Emperor Charles, in a last effort to save his domain, announced the implementation of national federalism, the National Council declined his offer, announcing instead its intention to declare independence. Independence was declared on 29 October, one day after **Vienna**'s capitulation. The new **State of Slovenes, Croats, and Serbs** was short-lived, however. The Austro-Hungarian South Slavs soon united with the Kingdom of Serbia and with other Yugoslavs from former Ottoman imperial lands to form the **Kingdom of Serbs, Croats, and Slovenes**. *See also* YUGOSLAVIA, KINGDOM OF.

SLOVENES, CROATS, AND SERBS, STATE OF (29 OCTOBER–1 DECEMBER 1918). On 29 October 1918 the South Slavs of the expiring **Habsburg Empire** (excluding those living within the Kingdom of **Hungary**) announced the formation of the independent State of Slovenes, Croats, and Serbs. For the Slovenes, who established their own representative governmental body in **Ljubljana**, separate from and authorized by the **National Council of Slovenes, Croats, and Serbs** headquartered in Zagreb on 31 October, this constituted an important step toward achieving Slovene national sovereignty and a united Slovene state. The new state based its operations on federalistic principles.

Although U.S. President Woodrow Wilson accepted the Yugoslavs' right to independence on 18 October, a principle also accepted by Austria-Hungary when it asked for a truce 10 days later, the State of Slovenes, Croats, and Serbs was not recognized by the international community. **Anton Korošec**, as head of the National Council, had pressed the issue with the Entente in November, but to no avail. On 1 December 1918 the State of Slovenes, Croats, and Serbs thus joined with the Kingdom of Serbia to form the **Kingdom of Serbs, Croats, and Slovenes**.

The Slove "national" government in Ljubljana continued until 23 December 1918, when it resigned. King Alexander replaced it with a regional administration on 20 January 1919, which was abolished after the **Vidovdan Constitution** was put in place on 28 June 1921. Meanwhile Korošec, as head of the Slovene People's Party (SLS), together with some from the Yugoslav Social Democratic Party (JSDS) had campaigned hard for autonomy for Slovenia within the new Yugoslav state. They proposed an "autonomistic" constitutional plan to the constituent assembly in **Belgrade** on 12 February 1921. Not only was their plan for a **Yugoslavia** of six autonomous provinces rejected, but the Vidovdan Constitution also rejected the Slovene **language** as one of the official languages of the new state. The hope of attaining an autonomous Slovenia was kept alive for the next two decades by the SLS and JSDS supporters. *See also* CLERICALS; SOCIALISTS.

SLOVENIAN ACADEMY OF SCIENCES AND ARTS / SLOVENSKA AKADEMIJA ZNANOSTI IN UMETNOSTI (SAZU). Although a 20th-century institution, the Slovenian Academy of Sciences and Arts has its roots in the **baroque Academia Operosorum** and earlier scientific **societies**. In 1919, with the establishment of the **University of Ljubljana**, a need for a modern academy of **sciences** and **arts** arose. It was partly realized in the Scientific Society for Humanistic Sciences established in 1921. After nearly 20 years of effort on the part of various Slovene organizations, the Academy of Sciences and Arts (*Akademija znanosti in umetnosti*, AZU) was finally founded in 1938. AZU was renamed the Slovenian Academy for Sciences and Arts (*Slovenska akademija znanosti in umetnosti*, SAZU) in 1948. After **World War II** a few members were expelled or resigned from AZU for political reasons. The academy was under less **Communist Party** control than the University of Ljubljana, but the institution did not publicly oppose the policies harmful to sciences or arts. *See also* AGITPROP.

SAZU has six departments: history and social sciences; philology and literary sciences; mathematics, physics, and technical sciences; natural sciences; arts; and medical sciences. There is also a Scientific Research Center with 14 institutes: the Fran Ramovš Institute of Slovene language, the Institute of Archeology, the Milko Kos Institute of History, the France Stele Institute of Art History, the Institute of Musicology, the Institute of Slovene Literature and Literary Sciences, the Institute of Slovene Ethnology, the Institute for Slovene Emigration Research, the Institute of Philosophy, the Anton Melik Institute of Geography, the Ivan Rakovec Paleontological Institute, the Jovan Hadži Institute of Biology, the Karst Research Institute, and the Institute of Medical Sciences. SAZU also has two important ongoing research projects: Investigations into the Natural and Cultural Heritage of the Slovene Nation, and the Study and Preservation of the Environment. SAZU publishes various periodicals and books. Since 1938 SAZU, with its research institutes, has published over 600 titles, among them *Slovar slovenskega knjižnega jezika* (Dictionary of the Slovene Literary Language), five volumes (1970–1991); *Slovenski biografski leksikon* (Slovene Biographical Encyclopedia), sixteen volumes (1925–1991); *Literarni leksikon* (Literary Lexicon), thirty-eight volumes (1978–). SAZU's **library**, with over 200,000 volumes, has an exchange program with more than 1,000 addresses worldwide. SAZU also collaborates with several similar institutions, such as the Austrian Academy of Sciences, the Swiss Academy of Natural Sciences, Accademia Nazionale dei Lincei in Rome, the Royal Society in London, the British Academy of Science, and the National Academy of Sciences in Washington, D.C. In 2005 SAZU had 183 members (71 regular, 28 associated, and 84 corresponding); among them were eight women. SAZU has had eight presidents: Rajko Nahtigal, Milan Vidmar, France Kidrič, Fran Ramovš, Josip Vidmar, Janez Milčinski, France Bernik, and Boštjan Žekš, the current president.

SLOVENJ GRADEC. Located near the border with **Austria** in the Mislinja Valley, at the confluence of the Mislinja and Suhodolnica Rivers, with a population of 7,712, Slovenj Gradec is the administrative center of an *občina* of the same name (population 16,774) and of the Koroška (**Carinthia**) region. Quite small until the 1960s, the town more than doubled its size as it developed an industrial complex. Its factories make automobile parts, **leather** goods, and various metal products. It also produces wood and paper products, as is evident from the lumber mills in the old town area. There has been no railway connection through Slovenj Gradec; even commercial traffic uses roads, which link it with Dravograd and Ravne na Koroškem to the northwest, where there is a rail line, or to the south with **Velenje** and **Celje**. With the Pohorje mountain range just to the east, Slovenj Gradec attracts hikers, horseback riders, mountaineers, and skiers. Each summer it holds a music festival.

Earliest recorded **settlements** were in the first to third centuries AD, when, as the Roman town of Colatio, it linked Celeia (Celje) with Virunum (Celovec/**Klagenfurt**) by road. The site of a fortress in the 11th century, the town engaged in commerical activity, and by the 12th century it was minting its own coins. In 1267 its town status was first recorded, and by 1270 walls surrounded it. **Craft** and artisan guilds were established, their number reaching 43 by the mid-16th century. Like many other **medieval** towns in Slovene lands, Slovenj Gradec had noble patrons; the earliest were from the Andechs family, and later the Windischgrätz name was associated with it. Like other towns at the time, it was menaced by Turks and Hungarians: **Turkish** invasions began in the 15th century, and the Hungarian king Matthias Corvinus attacked in 1488. The next two centuries remained troubled with **peasant revolts** and religious wars, so it was only in the latter 17th century that the area was relatively stabilized under **Habsburg** rule, where it remained until **World War I**. After the war it was separated from the rest of its province when the **Carinthian plebiscite** (10 October 1920) determined that the bulk of Carinthia would become part of the new Austrian republic. Slovenj Gradec was in the small corner of Koroška that remained politically linked with the ethnic Slovene community, and as such was part of both **Yugoslavias** (interwar kingdom and socialist republic).

During **World War II** the town fell under German rule. Local Slovenes were expelled, mobilized by the German army, or Germanized. In November 1944 a local resistance movement captured Germans and their sympathizers, many of whom were executed in the aftermath of the war. After 1945 Slovenj Gradec and Slovene Koroška were reintegrated into Yugoslavia and participated in the reformed **economy** initiated by the new order.

Slovenj Gradec is the cultural center of Slovene Koroška. Its regional **museum** holds archeological remnants from Roman times and jewelry from old Slavic burial grounds, as well as more recent materials ranging from farm implements to local **sports** heroes. It has a fine **arts** gallery, which displays local artists, among them Jože Tisnikar (1928–), and it has extensive holdings of African folk art as well. In front of the town hall stands the Venetian Horse, a contemporary equine sculpture by Oskar Kogoj that has become the town's symbol. The Šoklič Museum holds an eclectic assortment of local artifacts, collected by Jacob Šoklič, who was a church pastor in the mid-20th century. Of the town's churches, St. Elizabeth's is the oldest (1251), but having been added to over the centuries, it displays a variety of styles from its original Romanesque nave to later Gothic and **baroque** embellishments. Slovenj Gradec was the birthplace of composer Hugo Wolf (1860–1903), who studied in **Vienna** and directed Salzburg's symphony orchestra for a time; Slovenj Gradec honors Wolf with a musical **society** named for him.

SLOVENSKA DEMOKRATSKA ZVEZA (SDZ). *See* SLOVENE DEMOCRATIC ALLIANCE.

SLOVENSKA DEMOKRATSKA ZVEZA-NARODNA DEMO-KRATIČNA STRANKA (SDZ-NDS). *See* SLOVENE DEMO-CRATIC ALLIANCE-NATIONAL DEMOCRATIC PARTY.

SLOVENSKA KMEČKA ZVEZA-LJUDSKA STRANKA (SKZ-LS). *See* SLOVENE PEOPLE'S PARTY.

SLOVENSKA LJUDSKA STRANKA. *See* SLOVENE PEOPLE'S PARTY (SLS).

SLOVENSKA LJUDSKA STRANKA (SLS) BEFORE 1945. *See* CLERICALS.

SLOVENSKA MATICA. Slovenska Matica, a cultural, literary **society** established in 1864 in **Ljubljana**, was organized for the purpose of **publishing** scientific and general **literature** in the Slovene **language**. Initially, conservatives and **liberals** cooperated in this venture, but as political life grew confrontational, it had an effect on cultural institutions. Thus, conservatives separated from the Slovenska Matica at the end of the century.

At its outset, the society published mostly high school textbooks and translations, but after 1880 original Slovene scientific books began to appear as well. By publishing scientific literature, the society was instrumental in developing a Slovene professional language and, with its activities, created favorable conditions for the establishment of the **University of Ljubljana** after **World War I**. Slovenska Matica prospered at the turn of the 20th century: Its books were printed in large runs, and it had relations with important universities across Europe. In the interwar period it helped establish the **Slovenian Academy of Sciences and Arts**. During **World War II** the German occupiers banned its operation. Although considered a conservative institution after the war, Matica was not banned and received **government** financial support for its publications. Thus, it has had a 140-year history of uninterrupted publishing of original Slovene works and also translations. As a modern publishing house,

Slovenska Matica focuses on philosophy, history, and literature. Since the 1990s it has also published works by Slovenes living abroad, thus creating a link with Slovenes worldwide, and it has organized or co-sponsored conferences, symposia, and exhibits about important Slovene historical events and issues.

SLOVENSKA NACIONALNA STRANKA (SNS). *See* SLOVENE NATIONAL PARTY.

SLOVENSKI KRŠČANSKI DEMOKRATI (SKD). *See* SLOVENE CHRISTIAN DEMOCRATS.

SOCIAL DEMOCRATIC PARTY OF SLOVENIA (SDSS). *See* SLOVENE DEMOCRATIC PARTY.

SOCIAL PROPERTY. Social ownership of property was the basic principle of **workers' self-management** in **Yugoslavia**. It specified that all productive resources were collectively owned, not by the state but by society. Groups of workers joined in work organizations managed the social property. After **World War II** private ownership was abolished through **nationalization of property**, with ownership vested in the state. In the early 1950s state ownership was changed to social ownership. In the **Constitution of 1974**, social property was specifically defined as including means of production (and other assets managed by workers in work organizations), workers' products and income, the means with which public and social services were performed, and **natural resources**. The use of social property was safeguarded not only by regular **courts** but also by special judicial institutions: social legal defenders of self-management and courts of associated labor. With the introduction of a market **economy** and a multiparty political system in 1990, social property was abolished. *See also* CONTRACTUAL SOCIALISM; PRIVATIZATION.

SOCIAL REALISM. Social realism in the **arts** and **literature**, a critical introspection of social and living conditions in Slovenia, began around the 1930s and ended in the 1950s. New forms of **realism** had developed from **expressionism** and were deeply influenced by reality: the world economic crisis of the 1930s; Yugoslav centralism and unitarism; and later also **World War II**, the social revolution, and Soviet socialist realism.

In Slovene fine arts in the 1930s and 1940s, the movement of social realism introduced new styles of expression. It is especially noted for socially radical themes and attempts to popularize the arts. Even those artists who strived for autonomous and spontaneous expression believed that art needed to engage society. These movements were advocated by the so-called fourth generation of artists. Its program was first expressed by the painter and sculptor Nikolaj Pirnat and his socially critical paintings, exhibited in **Ljubljana** in 1928. Socially engaged painters and sculptors who were trying to establish contacts with the European as well as the Yugoslav (Krsto Hegedušić) art scene organized themselves along ideological lines in societies such as Slovenski Lik (Slovene Image), Gruda (The Sod), and Klub Neodvisnih (The Club of Independents), forming a progressive cultural front of the 1930s, which continued into the war years (1941–1945). To bring art closer to the public, painters began using the more democratic **media** of graphic art and drawing. Many artists illustrated books and published socially critical picture novels. They often created whole opuses of artistic works rather than individual monumental works. Among the painters, Tone Kralj, France Mihelič, Nikolaj Pirnat, Maksim Sedej, Hinko Smrekar, and especially the brothers Nande and Drago Vidmar have a special place in the movement of social realism. The Vidmar brothers, who were very active during World War II and the immediate postwar period, created an enormous volume of social realist art. *See also* DESIGN; PUBLISHING AND PUBLISHING HOUSES.

Although there were quite a few talented young sculptors (France Gorše, Zdenko Kalin, Tine Kos, Peter Loboda, Karel Putrih, Frančišek Smerdu), the 1930s were not very productive years for Slovene sculpture. The situation changed after World War II, when many monuments and plastic works with **National Liberation Struggle** themes and post–World War II reconstruction were erected throughout Slovenia. Although the sculptors worked within the overall rigid schemes of socialist realism, they were quite independent in the execution of details, in which they demonstrated their talent.

In the 1920s Slovene architects turned to functionalism and began for the first time to design apartment buildings for workers. Residential buildings and complexes, mostly in Ljubljana and **Maribor**, afforded a high living standard. In design, they were similar to **Vienna**'s, but on a smaller scale. The most prominent buildings from that era were designed by Vladimir Mušič (Rdeča hiša on Poljanska Street), Jože Sivec (Dukič apartment complex), and Vladimir Šubic (Meksika, on Njegoševa street)—all in Ljubljana—and by Ivan Vurnik (the Hutter apartment complex in Maribor). *See also* AGITPROP; MUSIC.

SOCIAL SECURITY. With the development of industrialization, families and their functions changed. Adults worked outside the home and could no longer provide adequate **education** for the young or care for the sick, the old, and the poor. In the Slovene lands, as elsewhere in Europe, these social functions were first assumed on a voluntary basis by **religious orders**, churches, and well-to-do individuals. Fraternities, such as the Slovenian fraternity of St. Hieronimus (1452–1785) in Udine (Videm), were organized. As early as the late Middle Ages, individual cities established institutions called *špitals* (hospitals) that provided medical care and social welfare. Later the functions of these institutions split. In the late 18th century **Ljubljana** had eight poorhouse-orphanages and three hospitals. **Enlightenment** ideas supported an increasing role for the state in the development of social welfare and **health** care. With increasing industrialization in the 19th century, several such institutions were built in cities. After 1860 cities in the Austro-Hungarian state were also legally required to take care of the poor and the sick. Toward the end of the 19th century the state began to assume some responsibility for injured and sick workers and required partial insurance for workers, but there was no state or public social security system before **World War I**. Workers organized their own private insurance companies and various support activities.

In 1922 the **Kingdom of Serbs, Croats, and Slovenes** passed social welfare legislation that provided uniformly for workers' insurance in cases of disability, old age, and death, but it was not fully enforced until 1937. Social welfare was organized through the Central Institute for Workers Insurance in Zagreb with its regional offices and fraternal insurance companies. In Ljubljana there were three such institutions: the District Office for Workers' Insurance (*Okrožni urad za zavarovanje delavcev*), the Pension Institute for Employees (*Pokojninski zavod za nameščence*), which provided private pension plans, and the Main Fraternal Fund (*Glavna bratovska skladnica*), for example, for miners and steelworkers. The first **Yugoslavia** provided some funds for unemployment assistance, shelters, and apprenticeships, but the funds were far from sufficient and were spent mainly on the elderly in institutional care. In the **Drava *banovina***, the territory of Slovenia, there were more than 60 such institutions, which could take care of about 3,000 people. In the interwar era, health insurance was carried by more people, and newly established centers offered preventive health care for the first time. The **Catholic Church** continued to play an important role in maintaining social welfare and health services, especially for the poor.

After 1945 Yugoslavia built a centralized system of socialized health care and welfare, including a pension system, financed directly by the federal government. Prewar health and social services, provided by voluntary or private organizations, were prohibited. However, because of war devastation and rapid industrialization, social and health care services came under great strain. Not every citizen could be provided legally guaranteed rights to these services. In addition, certain groups of the population (self-employed and especially farmers) were excluded for political reasons. For example, farmers were not covered by the obligatory health and pension insurance systems until 1955 and 1982, respectively, when all active persons secured health and pension insurance, based on payments, proportional to income. With the decentralization of the 1950s, these services became the responsibility of each republic.

Slovenia had a well-developed health system as well as pension system and disability insurance. In the 1950s health care and social security benefits (pensions and disabilities) were administratively split into two sectors, regulated by separate laws and managed by different agencies. The republic Institute for Pension and Disability Insurance (*Zavod za pokojninsko in invalidsko zavarovanje*) organized and managed the pension system, while the Institute for Health Insurance (*Zavod za zdravstveno zavarovanje*) administered the health system. In place was support for families, of which the benefits for parents (maternity/paternity leave and leave for attending to sick children) and child allowances were the most important. Each commune established a health care center (*zdravstveni dom*) and a center for social work (*center za socialno delo*) as well as other types of social service institutions—homes for the aged and specialized schools for the physically handicapped or for mentally retarded children.

Reforms of the 1970s transferred the responsibility for social welfare and health to communes (*občinas*) and the self-managing communities of interest, which assumed the financing and planning of the health and social welfare systems, but the pension and disability insurance remained centralized under the management of the Institute of Pension and Disability Insurance, which managed revenues centrally collected by the Social Accounting Service (*Služba družbenega knjigovodstva*).

The new self-management organization of the health system—with its decentralization and bureaucratization—depleted already strained financial resources for health and social welfare. Thus, many social services in the late 1970s and the 1980s opened the way for the organization of informal and in some cases privately organized professional social and health services (e.g., dentistry), which were illegal but tolerated by the state because the demand could not be satisfied by the public sector. Covert **privatization** was already taking place in the late 1980s in social and health care. From 1960 to 1979 the share of the social product allocated for health and social security rose significantly, but due to the economic crises declined in the 1980s. The pension system was burdened by an increasing number of retirees, especially after the 1980s: In 1980 there was one retiree per 3.6 employed. Within a decade the ratio was 1 to 2.9. After 1990 political and economic changes forced many into retirement, and by 1992 the ratio plummeted to 1 to 1.7. The 1983 Pension and Disability Insurance Act (PDIA) had introduced some measures to alleviate the problem. The length of service needed to qualify for benefits was increased: from 35 to 40 years for men, and from 30 to 35 years for women. The retirement age went up from 55 to 60 for men, and 50 to 55 for women. The pension calculating formula was also changed.

After declaring **independence**, Slovenia took a gradualist approach to reforming the economic and social sectors. Regarding social security, most benefits continued to be available despite Slovenia's serious economic problems (the fall-off in production, a lower GDP, hyperinflation, and high unemployment), but conditions for the benefits and the benefits themselves gradually changed while the new health and pension systems evolved. Social security went through two reforms, the first beginning in 1992. Once socially owned institutions for social security are now managed by state agencies; managers, appointed by the state, are given full authority over the institutions. New legislation allows deinstitutionalization of the public sector and has moved toward privatized services, but the national program also specifies that social services must be accessible to the entire population. The basic goals of the social security reforms were reduction of costs within the public pillar of the pension system, and introduction of the second, privately financed pillar. The high employers' and employees' contributions for social security and health insurance, which amounted to over 50 percent of gross payroll in 1992, were reduced to 38 percent in 1996. Continuing the trend already set by the 1983 Pension and

Disability Insurance Act (PDIA), Slovenia went through two pension reforms in the 1990s, enacted by the 1992 PDIA and the 1999 PDIA, both of which provide for gradual increase in age and working years, and a less favorable base for calculating pensions, as well as narrowing the large gap in conditions for eligibility for retirement between men and women. According to the 1999 PDIA, in order to receive a full pension, women have to be at least 61 years old and have worked for 38 years, while men need to be 63 and have 40 years of work. The base for calculating the pension is set at the highest paid 18 years, instead of the highest five or 10 years as previously.

The legislation introduced a second, voluntary pillar of various collective pension schemes. Individuals or companies that chose to invest in the second pillar were exempted from corporate tax, social security contributions, and personal income tax. The 1999 PDIA also introduced some other measures: narrowing the gap between the maximum and minimum pension, from a ratio of 8:1 to a ratio of 4:1; adjusting old pensions to the lower new ones; and eliminating early retirement. Pension reforms have had multiple effects. They provided a stable environment for social change, and the pension expenditure began to abate after the peak year 2000 of 12.16 percent of GDP. In 2004 the pension expenditure equaled 11.0 percent of GDP, down from 11.85 percent in 2002. In addition, mutual pension funds were established in 2003, and almost 25 percent of all insured chose to participate.

The system of family and child benefits remained unchanged in independent Slovenia. Parents are allowed parental leave with pay for a newborn baby (11 months) or a sick child. However, the eligibility for child allowances (*doklade*) as well as their amount has changed: Child allowances for lower-income beneficiaries are higher, and the average amount per child increases with the number of children. The latter changes are due to demographic factors (a falling birth rate in Slovenia).

Unemployment benefits and housing subsidies are probably the weakest parts of the social security system in Slovenia. Having had full employment after World War II until the late 1980s, Slovenia did not have much experience with unemployment. In the 1990s unemployment benefits were low and only a small percentage of registered unemployed had received them. In 1992 about 55,000 registered unemployed (45 percent) received unemployment compensation or unemployment assistance, whereas in 2002 some help was provided to about 23,000 registered unemployed (23 percent).

Comparing incidence of poverty in 1993 and 1997–1999 for the various groups shows that poverty increased the most among the older unemployed (age 40 and older). The share of GDP spent by Slovenia for social security is comparable to that in the EU countries. *See also* ECONOMY SINCE 1991; FINANCES AND BUDGET; HUMAN DEVELOPMENT INDEX.

SOCIALDEMOKRATSKA STRANKA (SDS). *See* SLOVENE DEMOCRATIC PARTY.

SOCIALISM. *See* ADMINISTRATIVE SOCIALISM; CONTRACTUAL SOCIALISM; MARKET SOCIALISM; SOCIALISTS.

SOCIALIST ALLIANCE OF WORKING PEOPLE / SOCIALISTIČNA ZVEZA DELOVNEGA LJUDSTVA (SAWP/SZDL). In 1953, at its Sixth Congress in **Belgrade**, the **People's Front of Yugoslavia** (PFY) was renamed the Socialist Alliance of Working People (SAWP). The SAWP was the broadest and, other than the **League of Communists of Yugoslavia** (LCY), the only political organization in Yugoslavia until the late 1980s. Besides individual members, it also had collective members in **trade unions** as well as **youth, women's**, and **veterans'** groups and many professional and other specialized organizations. Theoretically, the SAWP allowed its members, individual and collective, regardless of their political persuasion, **religion**, and nationality, to express their ideas and influence the managing of society. In reality, however, it was an adjunct of the LCY. During the political **liberalization of the 1960s**, there was an abortive attempt to reorganize SAWP into a more broadly based national organization. But the attempts failed and the LCY enhanced the centralized role of the SAWP. The SAWP became especially strong with the introduction of the **delegate** system in 1974, when it took over the elections of delegates in every respect and at all levels, from **local communities** to the federation. Each republic had its own SAWP leadership and a network of local SAWP organizations, which tried to adapt their activities to local needs, especially after 1974. *See also* CONTRACTUAL SOCIALISM.

In the mid-1980s, the Slovene leadership of the SAWP under Jože Smole, a journalist, diplomat and politician, began to realize its stated function as a political forum for all people. Smole's first symbolic gesture was a radio and television address to the Slovene people at Christmas in 1986. The SAWP then became involved in changing repressive legislation that limited freedom of speech, but in Slovenia, for the most part, this legislation was ignored by the **courts** despite strong pressures from the federal authorities to prosecute its violators, such as the writers of *Mladina* and *Nova revija*. In the late 1980s, the Slovene SAWP resisted the proposed changes to the Yugoslav **Constitution of 1974**, which would have led to a diminished role for individual republics and strengthened centralistic and unitaristic tendencies. Although they had to remain within Yugoslav's fold, the SAWP nevertheless allowed various political and special interest groups—**alternative movements** of the late 1980s—to function. It also provided financial support for some, e.g., the Council for Defense of **Human Rights**. Under its president, the prominent law professor Ljubo Bavcon, the council with its diverse membership was allowed to function autonomously. This was at the limits of the permissible, and the republic leadership of the SAWP was severely criticized throughout Yugoslavia. The council, the first such institution in communist countries, laid the foundations for the Office of the Human Rights Ombudsman (1995) in Slovenia. In 1989, the SAWP organized the first direct elections since 1974 (requiring a secret ballot) for a Slovene representative to the Yugoslav presidency. With 87 percent of the electorate voting, an establishment communist, Marko Bulc, was rejected in favor of a younger professional, **Janez Drnovšek**.

With the formation of independent political associations in 1988 (they did not officially become parties until 1989), the SAWP, a relic of the old one-party system, disintegrated; its remnants reorganized in January 1990 as the Alliance of Socialists of Slovenia, which later renamed itself the **Socialist Party of Slovenia** (SSS).

SOCIALIST FEDERAL REPUBLIC OF YUGOSLAVIA (SFRY) / SOCIALISTIČNA FEDERATIVNA REPUBLIKA JUGOSLA- VIJA (SFRJ) (1963–1992). The Socialist Federal Republic of Yugoslavia (SFRY) became the official name of **Yugoslavia** with the adoption of the **Constitution of 1963**. From 1946 until 1963 it had been called the **Federal People's Republic of Yugoslavia** (FPRY). Slovenia became the **Socialist Republic of Slovenia** (SRS) in 1963. The federal structure (six republics and two autonomous territories) of Yugoslavia was preserved under the new name and the new constitution. In 1990 all republics of the SFRY held multiparty elections. In those where the **Communist Party** was defeated, among them Slovenia, the official name of the republic was changed. Hence in

1990 the SRS became the **Republic of Slovenia** (RS). In 1991 Slovenia and **Croatia** declared **independence**; the following year Bosnia-Hercegovina and Macedonia separated as well. In April 1992 the SFRY, the second Yugoslavia, officially came to an end, and a third Yugoslavia, the Federal Republic of Yugoslavia (FRY), consisting of Serbia and Montenegro, came into existence.

SOCIALIST PARTY OF SLOVENIA / SOCIALISTIČA STRANKA SLOVENIJE (SSS). The leftist Socialist Party of Slovenia grew out of the **Socialist Alliance of Working People** (SAWP). In the **election** of April 1990 it ran candidates as the Alliance of Socialists of Slovenia, breaking only in the midst of the election campaign from the Socialist Alliance of Working People of Yugoslavia (SAWPY), the all-Yugoslav socialist alliance. With 39,000 members, the SSS was somewhat tainted from having been associated with the SAWP, considered by most as a front organization of the regime. The party nevertheless won 13 seats in parliament, and the writer Ciril Zlobec, a vice president of SAWP, was elected to the republic's presidency. The SSS won no seats in the election of December 1992. Its president at the time was Viktor Žakelj. In March 1994 the SSS merged with the **Democratic Party of Slovenia** (DSS), the **Greens of Slovenia**, and the Liberal Democratic Party to form **Liberal Democracy of Slovenia** (LDS).

The SSS program supported a market **economy** (based predominantly on private property), political pluralism, and the cooperation of labor and capital as the only possible way toward an effective social legal society. It cast aside communism, claiming to have no nostalgia for the past, but retained a leftist political position. The SSS's singular contribution to Slovene developments was its initiation of the **plebiscite for independence** in 1990.

SOCIALIST REALISM. *See* AGITPROP; ARTS; LITERATURE; SOCIAL REALISM.

SOCIALIST REPUBLIC OF SLOVENIA / SOCIALISTIČNA REPUBLIKA SLOVENIJA (SRS) (1963–1990). The Socialist Republic of Slovenia (SRS) became the official name of Slovenia after the adoption of the **Constitution of 1963**. From 1946 until 1963 it was called the **People's Republic of Slovenia** (PRS), a name that embodied the concept of "people's democracy." That concept had been imposed upon Slovenia, as on **Yugoslavia** as a whole, by Joseph Stalin, who conceived of "people's democracies" as a historical stage preceding true socialism. (In postrevolutionary **Russia** the transitional stage was called the "dictatorship of the proletariat." This term, however, was not considered appropriate for the Soviet satellite states, to whom socialism had been brought by the Red Army and where it was being nurtured by a benevolent, mature socialist state, namely the USSR.) Although Slovenia (and Yugoslavia) had long been out from under Soviet dominance, it was not until 1963 that the name change was effected. The new designation confirmed, belatedly, independence from Soviet domination, but it also asserted the conviction that Slovenia had become a "socialist" society.

Slovenia, as the SRS, remained a part of the Yugoslav federation, the **Socialist Federal Republic of Yugoslavia** (SFRY), with rights to secession. The **Constitution of 1974** retained the SRS name. In March 1990, before multiparty **elections** that resulted in defeat for the **Communist Party of Slovenia** (CPS), the name was changed to **Republic of Slovenia** (RS). The following year the RS separated from Yugoslavia and declared its **independence**.

SOCIALISTIČNA STRANKA SLOVENIJE (SSS). See SOCIALIST PARTY OF SLOVENIA.

SOCIALISTIČNA ZVEZA DELOVNEGA LJUDSTVA (SZDL). See SOCIALIST ALLIANCE OF WORKING PEOPLE (SAWP).

SOCIALISTS. Slovene **Marxists** established a party in 1896. It was affiliated with the Austrian Social Democratic Party, which had been founded in 1888–1889 and reorganized on a federal basis in 1899. Association with the Austrian party, mostly because the Slovene Socialists were financially dependent on it, committed the Slovenes to Austro-Marxism. Essentially, that required a commitment to the Austrian state framework, because Marxists believed large states produced socioeconomic conditions favorable to proletarian revolutions. The Slovene party, named the Yugoslav Social Democratic Party (*Jugoslovanska socialnodemokratska stranka*, JSDS), also adopted a federal structure (it was internationalist to do so), in order to attract various South Slav members; however, the party remained essentially Slovene.

Slovene Socialists came from the mining districts of **Idrija** and southern Styria (Trbovlje–Hrastnik–Zagorje coal basin), Southern **Carinthia**, **Trieste**, and **Ljubljana**. In the latter towns they were printers, tailors, cobblers, bakers, and railroad workers, and in Trieste many were employed by the Austrian Lloyd shipping company. The Socialists were strongest in Trieste, a commercial and industrial city, where Italians, Slovenes, and Croats were active in workers' organizations.

The Slovene party headquarters, however, were in Ljubljana, except between 1902 and 1904, when they were in Trieste. A decision in 1914 to return to that port city was precluded by war. The party's leadership, among whom was **Etbin Kristan**, often came from the intelligentsia. The party also attracted Slovene **Masarykites**, intellectuals for whom liberalism lacked appeal because it had no social program.

The Slovene Socialists' national program was that of the Austrian party, resting on a plan for democratic federalism within **Austria**. After the annexation of Bosnia and Hercegovina (1908), they injected a strong Yugoslav component into their program. In 1909 at a Ljubljana conference, Slovene Socialists, focusing on the Yugoslav question as a cultural one, adopted the Tivoli Resolution, calling for the complete national unification of all Yugoslavs, irrespective of name, religion, alphabet, dialect, or language. They favored, in other words, the cultural amalgamation of all Yugoslavs. This was clearly a **Neo-Illyrist** position, whose leading proponent was party head Etbin Kristan. The party's Masarykites did not approve, and among other Slovene political and cultural spokesmen there was much furor over the Socialists' pronouncement. **Ivan Cankar**, a writer and once a Socialist candidate for parliament, broke with Kristan over the Tivoli Resolution.

During **World War I** the Slovene party lacked dynamism until 1917, when new, younger members attempted its rejuvenation. The older, conservative Socialists, however, remained in control, and some joined the first government of the **Kingdom of Serbs, Croats, and Slovenes** in 1919, a development that plunged the party into debate about the ethics of participating in a bourgeois government. (Etbin Kristan was elected to and sat in the constituent parliament.) In 1920 the party split: The left joined the Socialist Workers' Party of Yugoslavia (**Communists**); in 1921 the others united with the Socialist Party of Yugoslavia, with its center in **Belgrade**.

SOCIETIES. Societies that formed to serve the interests of members or for humanitarian purposes can be found in Slovene lands as early as the 13th century. **Medieval** guilds and **religious orders** of the **Catholic Church** established orphanages and maintained hospitals. Based on volunteer work and private donations, they functioned independently of the state. *Druščina sv. Dizma* (Society of St. Dismas, 1688–1801), one of the earliest, was an association of nobles, intellectuals, and **art** promoters; its members were among the founders of both the **Academia Operosorum** and **Academia Philharmonicorum**.

Organizations in the late 18th century included agricultural societies in **Celovec**, Graz, and **Ljubljana**, and also freemasons' lodges. State controls over artisans' associations began in the 1730s and became stricter when revolutionary ideas began to spread in the **Habsburg Empire** during the **Enlightenment**. The **Revolution of 1848** saw the establishment of national political societies in Slovene lands. The first was formed by intellectuals in **Vienna** (1848), while others emerged in regional cities such as **Gorizia**/Gorica, Ljubljana, and **Trieste**. Their common goal was a **United Slovenia**. In 1851, with the introduction of **neoabsolutism** in the **Austrian Empire**, political societies were banned, but they revived after its demise (1861).

In the second half of the 19th century, many and varied national societies were established, including **reading societies**, literary groups such as **Slovenska Matica**, **publishing** societies such as the **Society of St. Hermagoras**, and **music** societies such as Glasbena Matica. An 1867 law was introduced to regulate the establishment and activities of societies, which thereafter had to be registered with the local authorities. Slovene and German **political parties**, cultural organizations, and other social groups were soon established. With the political polarization of Slovenes in the 1870s, the number of cultural, **sports**, or professional societies proliferated as they split and formed along ideological lines. Examples of this are the gymnastic organizations **Orel** and **Sokol**, societies that were conservative and liberal, respectively. At the end of the 19th century, societies that were part of the new **cooperative movement** were an important factor in developing economic life. The number of societies grew: In 1869 there were 58; after **World War I** the number surpassed 3,000. *See also* CLERICALS; LIBERALS.

At the turn of the 20th century, while national political parties in Austria-Hungary were still under state control or prohibited, Slovenes fought for political rights through cultural and emerging professional societies and literary programs, and by the written word. That was true also in the first and second Yugoslavia: in the first, to resist Yugoslav centralism, and in the second, also to oppose **Communist** monopoly on power. Between the establishment of a Yugoslav state in 1918 and the introduction of a royal dictatorship in 1929 (the **Kingdom of Yugoslavia**), many new organizations were founded. Together with the establishment of the **University of Ljubljana** in 1919, these organizations stimulated the creation of new professional societies. Despite the prohibition of most left-leaning societies, the number of societies in the interwar period grew: from around 3,300 in 1922 to almost 12,000 at the eve of **World War II**. After 1929, with the imposition of Yugoslav centralism, nationally oriented organizations were abolished, or at least closely monitored. During World War II the German, Hungarian, and Italian occupiers prohibited political parties and also many societies while attempting to replace them with their own. After 1944 the **Liberation Front** (LF) organized its own professional and cultural societies in **Partisan-controlled territories**.

In 1945 all societies and organizations were dissolved. While cultural, sports, and professional societies were quickly revived, no political or religious societies or associations opposing the **Communist Party of Slovenia** (CPS) were allowed. The **Catholic Church**'s educational and humanitarian organizations were banned, and their functions were assumed by the state either directly through its own institutions or indirectly by secular humanitarian ones, such as the Red Cross (*Rdeči križ*), the Association of Scouts (*Zveza tabornikov*), and the Friends of Youth Society (*Društvo prijateljev mladine*)—all of which remained under strict CP control. Thus, an extremely rich tradition of political and humanitarian societies or nongovernmental organizations (NGOs) of the interwar era was interrupted. Activities of existing cultural, sports, and professional societies were controlled by **Agitprop** until 1952. Subsequently, the **Socialist Alliance of Working People (SAWP)** became the umbrella organization for all societies, which were allowed to function independently as long as their activities were not political or in any way in violation of social taboos. With the development of self-management and **contractual socialism** in the 1970s, a new 1974 law on societies resulted in the establishment of new organizations, each of which had to be registered by the **court**. A society's program and bylaws had to be approved by SAWP before it could be registered.

As all political activity outside the CP was banned, cultural, humanitarian, leisure, professional, and sport societies and associations were important venues for activities outside the home and workplace. Cultural societies, such as the **Society of Slovene Writers**, and student organizations were potential centers of opposition to the CP; they were closely monitored and controlled through regular replacement of leaders and especially censorship of publications. In 1985 there were 10,098 registered societies and associations of various kinds (art, cultural, professional, scientific, sports, technical); the most numerous were volunteer firefighting societies (around 1,500), many of which had a long and rich tradition. The pre–World

War II figure for societies (around 11,700) was not reached until after Slovenia became independent in the early 1990s. *See also* COMMU-NIST PARTY, OPPOSITION TO; LITERATURE; THEATER.

In the 1980s as a civil society began emerging, **alternative movements** formed to promote the **environment**, peace, spirituality, the rights of **homosexuals**, and **human rights**. This had an impact on political life and democratization in Slovenia. After 1988 differentiation within society began: Some groups became a part of the state political scene and formed political parties, such as the **Liberal Democratic Party**; others, such as the Student Cultural Center (*Študentski kulturni center*, ŠKUC) remained nonpolitical. Although some **religious orders** were already providing social services, the church was legally permitted in 1989 to offer educational, humanitarian, and social services, and since then these have greatly expanded. *See also* NEUE SLOWENISCHE KUNST; STUDENT MOVEMENTS.

After Slovene **independence** in 1991, the old law on societies and associations was modernized and a new law, adjusted to **European Union** (EU) standards, was adopted in 2006. The new law regulates the status and financial operation of societies, which are funded from membership dues, nonprofit economic activities (publishing), gifts, and public monies. The latter are available for organizations and societies defined as "societies in the public interest" (*društva v javnem interesu*), which compete for public resources on the basis of their programs. The number of societies has been mushrooming since 1991: Over 1,000 new societies were registered each year between 1996 and 2004 (there were 19,245 in December 2004). Although sports, recreational, and cultural societies have always been active in Slovenia, humanitarian ones and those dealing with human rights, the environment, **minorities**, and international cooperation have also increased since 2000. In Slovenia, several terms for NGOs have been used, such as associations, foundations, institutions, organizations of civil society, societies, and church organizations. Not all those registered in Slovenia qualify as NGOs, since the majority serve private interests. (An NGO must operate in the public interest, be nonprofit, and at least some of its activities have to involve voluntary work.) In 2004 there were 2,129 such organizations. Meanwhile the state retains a monopoly on social services, while NGOs would benefit from a favorable tax code.

SOCIETY OF ST. HERMAGORAS / DRUŽBA SV. MOHORJA (DSM) / MOHORJEVA DRUŽBA. In 1851 the Society of St.

Hermagoras (DSM) was established at the initiative of Bishop **Anton Martin Slomšek** in Celovec/**Klagenfurt** (**Carinthia**). Its purpose was to teach Slovenes to read and write. **Vienna** even supported such activities, hoping to prevent political revolution. By 1918 DSM had 90,000 members and in its first 50 years had published more than 16.3 million books, including textbooks. Although a **Catholic** institution, the DSM published literary works by virtually every Slovene writer, regardless of political or ideological orientation.

After **World War I**, when Slovene ethnic territory was divided among **Yugoslavia**, **Italy**, and **Austria**, the Society's activity slowed and its membership declined. Due to Germanizing pressures in Carinthia, Austria, the Society moved its printing shop to Yugoslavia (to Prevalje in 1919, and to **Celje** in 1927). The **publishing house** and the **society**, whose seat was still in Celovec, became de facto separated. The printery in Slovenia supplied Carinthia with books until 1938, when German occupation of Austria made contacts between Celovec and Celje impossible. In 1940 the DSM in Celovec was outlawed and its property confiscated. A branch of the Society was established in **Gorizia**, Italy, in 1924, as Goriška Mohorjeva Družba (the Gorizia Hermagoras Society) because Italians had barred Slovene books from entering Italy. It published Slovene books until 1941. The DSM in Celje also ceased operating in 1941 when German occupiers confiscated its printing shop and destroyed its books.

After **World War II** DSM's branches in Celovec and Gorizia resumed their activities. Confiscated property was returned to the Celovec DSM, which, besides publishing (a new printing shop was built in 1951), developed strong educational activities. It opened dormitories for Slovene students in Celovec and Vienna, and it established Slovene schools in Celovec: a secondary school, a bilingual kindergarten (1978), and an elementary school (1989). Besides various literary and practical books and textbooks (40 to 50 books published yearly), the Celovec DSM, which has 6,000 members worldwide, publishes the monthly magazine *Družina in dom* (*Family and Home*) and the yearly *Koledar* (*Almanac*). In 1991 the Celovec DSM changed its name to Mohorjeva Družba v Celovcu (Hermagoras Society in Celovec). This institution has not only been a publishing house but also a cultural and political center for Slovenes in Austria. Gorizia's Society resumed publishing Slovene books in 1945. It collaborated with the Celovec DSM in putting out the *Almanac*. Its most important project, begun in 1974, has been *Primorski biografski leksikon* (*The Primorska*

Biographical Lexicon). Although membership of Gorizia's DSM has declined over the years (18,000 members in 1927; 1,400 members in 1990), its activity has always been important for Slovenes in Italy. *See also* MINORITIES, SLOVENES IN AUSTRIA; MINORITIES, SLOVENES IN ITALY.

The DSM in Celje, meanwhile, had to deal with a new postwar regime. In 1946 the Society reclaimed its property, except for the print shop, which was nationalized. Its publishing, however, was restricted to "socialist" books. Renamed Založniško Podjetje Mohorjeva Družba v Celju (Publishing Enterprise Hermagoras Society in Celje), it published the collected works of some Slovene writers. In 1970 Mohorjeva Družba (MD) / Hermagoras Society was again organized as a society (with 60,000 members) and began publishing periodicals and a new series of books. Its membership fell considerably (to 25,000 in 1990). After 1990 the Society was again reorganized and became a part of the Catholic Church establishment under the bishop of **Maribor** (1991). After 1991 the MD in Celje developed rapidly: The number of published books increased fivefold in 10 years. In addition to activities related to publishing, such as workshops to introduce works of world-renowned authors published by the MD, the MD began organizing other cultural activities that became very popular, such as a workshop for graffiti. Having become one of the three largest publishers in Slovenia, the MD renovated its bookstore in Celje and opened new ones in other cities (Ljubljana, Maribor, **Murska Sobota**, and Ajdovščina). Work also began on renovating DSM's original buildings, nationalized after World War II and now returned to the MD. In 2001 the Society celebrated its 150th anniversary, noting with pride the 40 million books published in the Slovene **language** since its establishment in the 19th century. Since 1992 there has been close cooperation among all three DSM societies, in Gorizia (Italy), Klagenfurt (Austria), and Celje (Slovenia).

SOKOL/FALCON. Sokol (Falcon) was a patriotic gymnastic **society** established in 1863 in order to promote the physical well-being of its members and at the same time fight Germanization. It was patterned after the Czech Sokol, and until the beginning of the 20th century it attracted both conservatives and liberals. Although Sokol was nonpolitical, the **Slovene People's Party** (SLS) in 1906 organized a rival gymnastic society, **Orel** (Eagle), which spurred a healthy competition between the two and raised the quality of Slovene gymnastics.

In 1929, when all ethnically defined organizations in **Yugoslavia** were banned, the Slovene Sokol became part of the Yugoslav Sokol organization. The Slovene branch of the Yugoslav National Party (JNS) tried to politicize the Slovene branch of Sokol. A latent conflict errupted between the two organizations and broke into the open in 1936, when dissident Sokols began publishing a bulletin advocating independence from JNS politics. Serious conflicts with the Yugoslav organization and the JNS emerged, causing the Slovene Sokol in 1940 to split into conservative and liberal wings. Sokol was also under attack by the SLS and the **Catholic Church**. During **World War II** Sokol's conservative wing joined the **Slovene Covenant**, while its liberal, dissident wing, which had begun cooperating with the **Communist Party** in 1940, joined the **Liberation Front** (LF). *See also* CLERICALS; JANUARY 6, 1929, DICTATORSHIP.

SPAS, HEALTH. Slovenia has nearly two dozen **health** spas, which contribute to a thriving health **tourism**. Bathing in thermal waters is a featured activity, but the spas also offer recreational activities (golf, tennis, workout rooms), dietary regimens, and various facilities for specific medical complaints. Some are at the seaside (Portorož, Strunjan). Others are in Dolenjska between **Ljubljana** and Zagreb (e.g., Čatež, Dolenjske Toplice, Šmarješke Toplice), and many are being developed in the Mura River basin. The oldest, Dolenjske Toplice, not far from **Novo Mesto**, was known already in the 14th century. **Valvasor**, the nobleman scholar, established a spa there in 1658, but modern spa tourism began in earnest only at the turn of the 20th century when Dolenjske Toplice became a favorite of Viennese society. The best-known Slovene health spas (e.g., Laško, Rogaška Slatina, Radenci) are in Štajerska, where spa tourism has a two-century tradition. Among the oldest spas are Radenci, whose Radenska mineral water was bottled already in 1869 and today is exported abroad, and Rogaška Slatina, whose buildings and sculptured gardens retain a 19th-century elegance and salubrious serenity. Rogaška Slatina, whose springs were known as early as Roman times and were used by 16th-century nobility who "took the waters," is also the center of Slovenia's cut-glass industry. Established in 1860, it produces fine hand-cut and polished lead crystal (exported as Miller-Rogaška, associated with Waterford Crystal).

SPERANS. Edvard Kardelj (1910–1979) used the pen name Sperans when he wrote *The Development of the Slovene National Question* (*Razvoj slovenskega narodnega vprašanja*), a **Marxist** synthesis of

Slovene history published in 1939. Kardelj studied existing secondary "bourgeois" historical literature, submitted it to Karl Marx's theoretical framework (although he rejected Marx's assertion that Slovenes were among the nonhistoric/nonprogressive peoples), and concluded that the Slovene people (a peasant/worker nation) was about to make its mark on history. The book was an ideological tour de force, which served as an inspiration, especially for Slovene leftists, during **World War II**'s resistance movement and revolution. When Communists came to power after the war, **Yugoslavia** became a federation of republics, in which nations were autonomous and nationalities were accorded constitutional rights—all of which Kardelj seemed to have foreseen in the Sperans book.

Sperans's opus, translated and periodically revised, became a guide to where socialist Yugoslavia stood ideologically over the years. In 1957 the first post-Stalin edition appeared, in which Kardelj pronounced the nationality question resolved, for socialism had advanced the Yugoslav nations into a higher stage of development. He acknowledged the existence of troubling remnants of "bourgeois" nationalism, however, but urged concentrating on the advancement of socialism and **Yugoslavism**, for only these two were compatible. The message was intended for all Yugoslav peoples, not only the Slovenes. Slovene historians were critical of Kardelj's revisions of the Sperans work for failing to take into account the findings of postwar historical scholarship. The revisions seemed merely to tinker with **Marxist** language in order to suit **Belgrade**'s evolving political needs.

SPORTS. The earliest record of sporting activitiy in Slovene lands was recorded by **Valvasor** in his late 17th-century work on the Kranjska duchy. He mentions mountaineering, rowing, shooting, and skiing. As in other areas of Europe, however, organized sports would come only in the latter half of the 19th century, spurred on by the physical culture movement of the time in Central Europe. The movement in the 1860s gave impetus for the establishment of **societies** such as the **Sokol**, whose aim was to achieve body building and patriotism through gymnastics. Initially, the Sokol was not political, but after **Orel** was founded by the **Clericals** in 1906, Sokol became largely a liberal society. While the gymnastic societies were expanding, other sporting societies were also forming. Before 1900 the most popular were bicycling and mountain climbing clubs. Soon, too, regional organizations and townwide sports societies were established.

As with everything else in Slovene 20th-century history, sport was shaped by politics. In the years between the two world wars, rival political camps generated rival sporting clubs. During **World War II** Slovene clubs were banned and replaced by the occupier with German ones. After 1945 the new communist regime put its imprint on sport by encouraging the rapid development of competitive sports. Sports in Slovenia were highly subsidized by the federal (60 percent) and local (30 percent) **governments**, and were integrated into the sporting activities of **Yugoslavia** as a whole. (Sports were further financed by membership dues, ticket sales, and the lottery.) In the 1970s and the 1980s over 200 gymnasiums, 30 swimming pools, various stadiums, jogging trails, and lesser facilities, usually adjacent to schools, were built in Slovenia. By 1963 the **University of Ljubljana** had a faculty for physical education.

In independent Slovenia, sports continued to be important, meriting ministerial rank in the national government. The Ministry of Education and Sport sees to the financial needs of sports via the government budget. The Sports Union of Slovenia (*Športna zveza Slovenije*), established in the mid-1950s, remained as the head over the individual sports associations. More than 30 sports and 3,000 sports organizations, with more than 400,000 members, are represented by the Sports Union. Annually about 80,000 of these are registered to compete in sporting events. Meanwhile the others, 21 percent of the population, engage in regular sports activities (at least twice a week). Aside from the sports mentioned, team sports such as basketball, soccer, and volleyball are popular. Slovenia's national teams in these sports rarely excel in international competitions, but in 2002 its soccer team qualified for the World Cup matches.

The Olympic Committee of Slovenia, established in 1991, merged with the Sports Union of Slovenia in 1994. Slovene Olympians are at the pinnacle of sport in the country. In various international Olympics since **independence**, Slovene athletes have fared well in a variety of events: in 1992 in Barcelona, two bronze medals in rowing (coxless pair; four without coxswain); in 1996 in Atlanta, two silver medals (100 meter hurdles; single kayak); in 2000 in Syndey, two gold medals (rowing, double sculls; men's sharpshooting); and in 2004 in Athens, one silver medal (rowing) and three bronze medals (women's judo; athletics 800 meters; sailing). Slovenia's star athlete before independence was Miroslav Cerar, a gymnast who tallied more than 30 medals in international competitions between 1958 and 1970, among them two gold medals (pommel horse) in 1964 and 1968. Perhaps Slovenia's most famous Olympian is Leon Štukelj, who at the Atlanta Olympics in 1998 was featured in opening ceremonies by the International Olympic Committee as the world's oldest living Olympian. Štukelj, who died in 1999 just short of his 101st birthday, was a gymnast who between 1924 and 1936 won six medals (three gold, one silver, and two bronze). Slovenia also competes actively in the Winter Olympics. *See also* SPORTS, WINTER.

SPORTS, WINTER. Although Slovenia has many ice skaters and ski jumpers, skiing—with at least 300,000 recreational skiers—is the country's most popular **sport**. Slovenes have their own terms for skis and skiing (*smuči, smučanje*), indicating that the practice and equipment, used originally for **transportation**, were indigenous. Along with the Scandinavians (the word *ski* has Nordic roots), the Slovenes are among Europe's earliest skiers. **Valvasor** described skiing in the Kranjska duchy in his 17th-century encyclopedic book. Recreational and competitive skiing in Slovenia is a 20th-century phenomenon. Most of Slovenia's 40-plus ski centers have been developed since 1950. The larger resorts, such as Kranjska Gora (and nearby Planica, a ski jumping center) and Pohorje have a full complement of ski services and lodging, and also host international competitions. Kanin, Krvavec, and Vogel—all in northwestern Slovenia—are also popular destinations for recreational skiers. *See also* ALPINE RESORTS.

Slovenia also has a thriving ski manufacturing industry. Elan, which began producing skis in 1945, underwent some restructuring difficulties after Slovenia established **independence** in 1991, and it briefly came under foreign ownership. In 2004 Elan produced more than a half-million skis in Slovenia and 200,000 snowboards in its factory in **Austria**, many exported to 46 markets abroad. It is the sixth largest manufacturer of ski equipment worldwide.

Slovenes have long also been competitive biathlonists, jumpers, and skiers (cross-country and downhill). They were considered national heroes and heroines even before independence, when they skied for **Yugoslavia** (the Yugoslav team was primarily Slovene) in international events, including the Olympics. When Jure Košir (slalom), Katja Koren (slalom), and Alenka Dovžan (downhill) won bronze medals at the Lillehammer Olympics (1994), they became the best-known, most popular persons in the country. Although they failed to medal at the Nagano Olympics (1998), the Slovene jumping team came away from Salt Lake City (2002) with a bronze medal.

STEFAN, JOŽEF (1835–1893). Jožef Stefan (also Štefan), born in **Klagenfurt**, studied at the University of Vienna (1853–1857), where he became full professor of higher mathematics and physics (1863). Stefan was a brilliant experimenter and a well-liked teacher. Several important phyisicts, such as Ludwig Boltzman, studied with him. Among the positions he held at the university were those of director of the Institute for Experimental Physics (1866), dean of the Faculty of Philosophy (1869–1870), and rector magnificus (1876–1877). From 1865 on, he was also a member of the Imperial Academy of Sciences in **Vienna**. In 1883 he presided over the Scientific Commission of the International Electricity Exhibition in Vienna. Two years later he held the same position at the International Conference on Musical Pitch in Vienna.

Stefan's most important work deals with heat radiation. His discoveries led him to the formulation of the Stefan-Boltzmann law of radiation (1879), which was used to calculate the temperature of the sun. Stefan made significant scientific contributions in other areas of physics: in heat conduction, in kinetic theory of heat (he formulated Stefan's number and Stefan's law (1866), and in acoustics. A research institute for basic and applied research in natural **sciences** and technology, the largest research institute in the **Republic of Slovenia** (RS) in **Ljubljana**, is named after him.

STIČNA MONASTERY. Stična, a well-known Cistercian monastery built in 1135, is located in a large village of the same name southeast of **Ljubljana**. The monastery, a beautiful historical and cultural monument, was the most important religious and cultural center, surpassing even Ljubljana, in the area until the late Middle Ages. As early as in the 12th century, theological studies and a famous "manuscript workshop" were established at Stična monastery, where monks produced one of the largest Latin manuscript collections in Europe. In the 15th century the monastery also produced *Stiški rokopisi* (Stična manuscripts)— religious texts in Slovene for the use of non-Slovene priests, consisting of prayers, sermons, and church **folk** songs. The documents, which are of great importance for Slovene literary and linguistic history, are now kept in the **National and University Library**.

In addition to being in charge of 21 parishes and their 255 branches (at the end of the 17th century), Cistercians were very much involved in the everyday life of the local population. Stična monastery had the first, and for over three centuries (the 16th through the 18th) the only, **music** school in Slovenia, which was attended by **Jacobus Gallus**. Besides their religious and cultural work, the monks also benefited the local economy: They cultivated land and introduced the iron plow, better agricultural tools, and new crops and fruits. They are believed to have brought wine growing to the area. They also promoted trade and took care of roads and travelers. Despite serious crises among the Cistercians in the 15th century, the monastery remained active until 1784, when it was dissolved and its **library** mostly dispersed. Revived in 1898, the Cistercians pursued lively liturgical activities and were involved in **education** between the world wars. During **World War II** the monastery offered a home to many exiled priests from the German-occupied parts of Slovenia (Štajerska, Gorenjska). *See also* CATHOLIC CHURCH, HISTORY OF; MEDIEVAL CULTURE AND ART; MEDIEVAL TOWNS AND COMMERCE; RELIGIOUS ORDERS.

STOCK EXCHANGE. Until recently, Slovenes had little experience with stock exchanges. Although one existed in royal **Yugoslavia** (1924 to 1942), trading was suspended during **World War II**. After the war the exchange at first did not operate and was officially abolished in 1953. The liberalization of the Yugoslav **economy** in the late 1980s and two Yugoslav laws—the Securities Act (*Zakon o vrednostnih papirjih*) and the Money Market and Capital Market Act (*Zakon o trgu denarja in trgu kapitala*)—enabled the establishment of the Ljubljana Stock Exchange, Inc., in December 1989. It was the first stock exchange in any socialist country. Three months later, the exchange began its first modest financial operations with 14 stockbrokers and 11 tradable securities. At the outset, trading was primarily limited to short-term government securities and municipal bonds. With **privatization**, which began in 1990, many workers became small shareholders, and individual companies began to list shares on the exchange. The first company to do so was Kolinska, a food processing company (1996). Investors have been mostly Slovenes, as foreign investors have been put off by unfavorable tax laws and complicated regulations.

The macroeconomic environment and slow pace of privatization have not always been favorable to capital market development. One of the most successful years for the Ljubljana Stock Exchange was 2002, when the Slovenian pharmaceutical company Lek was sold to the Swiss company Novartis (a 52 percent owner); this contributed significantly to a big jump in the Slovenian stock market index (*Slovenski borzni indeks*, SBI). Over the last 15 years the Ljubljana Stock Exchange has become the largest owner and manager of domestic capital, with market capitalization (total value of shares) equivalent to 50 percent of GDP. At the end of 2004 there were 254 securities traded, of which 153 were stocks and 101 municipal bonds. The largest volume was in shares (56 percent), followed by bonds (23 percent), and investment companies (15 percent). The most heavily traded shares were those of the most successful Slovene companies such as Gorenje, Intereuropa, Krka, Mercator, and Petrol. In 2004 the SBI 20 rose by 17 percent, while PIX, the investment funds index, went up 38 percent. The Ljubljana Stock Exchange became a full member of the International Federation of Stock Exchanges in 1997 and of the Federation of European Stock Exchanges (FESE) in 2004. *See also* BANKING AND FINANCIAL SECTOR; MANUFACTURING.

STRANKA DEMOKRATIČNE PRENOVE (SDP). *See* UNITED LIST OF SOCIAL DEMOCRATS.

STRANKA MLADIH SLOVENIJE (SMS). *See* PARTY OF YOUNG PEOPLE OF SLOVENIA.

STRITAR, JOSIP (1826–1923). A writer and pedagogue, Josip Stritar studied classical philology in **Vienna**, where he lived and worked most of his life. A tutor of rich students, he traveled extensively and acquainted himself with European **literature**. Being well read, Stritar introduced European contemporary literature to the Young Slovenes and, along with **Fran Levstik**, was an important mentor of the literary movement. Stritar wrote an introduction to the posthumous edition of **Prešeren**'s poems (1866), in which he elucidated the quality of Prešeren's literary work. In letters critical of **Jovan Vesel Koseski**'s poetry, Stritar destroyed Koseski's literary fame. Stritar published a Slovene literary journal, *Zvon* (*The Bell*), in Vienna until 1880. An excellent stylist, he wrote poems, stories, novels, and literature for young people, but only his poems, *Dunajski soneti* (Vienna Sonnets), have an important place in Slovene literature. *See also* REALISM; ROMANTICISM.

STUDENT MOVEMENTS. Although Slovenes did not have their own **university** until 1919, Slovenes studying at other universities were an important factor in political life from 1848 onward. They belonged to the **societies** Slovenija in **Vienna** (1869) and Triglav in Graz (1875), and were strong advocates of a **United Slovenia**. With the development of **political parties**, student organizations formed along political lines. In 1894 **Catholic** students separated from existing societies and established Danica (Morning Star) in Vienna; in 1901 Zarja (Dawn) was established in Graz. Before **World War I** Slovene radical students were active in the secret society **Preporod**. For the most part, Slovene student organizations did not work together except to support the establishment of the first Slovene university in **Ljubljana**. After its founding in 1919, liberal students continued their work in Jadran (established in 1920) and Triglav (established in 1922), while Catholic students continued in Danica and Zarja. The Society of Communist Students (*Društvo študentov komunistov*) was organized in 1920 but soon banned.

Although students in the interwar era collaborated on occasion (e.g., to demonstrate against fascist repression of Slovenes in Italy; to support the founding of the **University of Ljubljana** and the building of the **National University Library**), they were divided politically. Several left-leaning groups that organized were banned during the interwar period (1920–1941). In the 1930s Catholic students belonged to the Akademska Zveza (Academic Union) consisting of three groups: Mladci (The Young Ones), Straža (The Guard), and Zarja (Dawn). In 1939, due to rising fascism and Nazism, student groups of various political orientations unified in a new organization, the National Academic Bloc (*Nacionalni akademski blok*). Although many Catholic students soon left it after **World War II** began in 1941, left-leaning students, including Catholics from Zarja, joined the **Liberation Front** (LF), which had its organization at the university. Anticommunist-oriented Catholic students, particularly Mladci and members of Straža, supported the **Village Guard** and the **Home Guard** and cooperated with the occupiers. *See also* CATHOLIC ACTION.

In 1945 students were part of the unified Student Youth of Slovenia (*Študentska mladina Slovenije*), which mostly organized volunteer work brigades to rebuild the war-torn state and was above all concerned with political education. In 1951 the Student Alliance of Yugoslavia (*Zveza študentov Jugoslavije*, ZŠ) was formed. It dealt not only with narrow student interests but also with broader social and political issues. ZŠ and its newspaper *Tribuna* (established in 1951) were under **Communist Party** control. In 1957 it began publishing *Revija 57* (*Review 57*), which was banned the next year. ZŠ was also involved in several socially critical projects of the 1950s and 1960s, such as *Perspective* and *Oder 57* (*Stage 57*). Under political pressure, issues of *Tribuna* were often confiscated and its editors replaced. In **Maribor**, the student newspaper was *Katedra*. *See also* AGITPROP; RECONSTRUCTION, POST–WORLD WAR II; THEATER.

By the 1960s and 1970s, although leftist in political orientation, students became disillusioned with socialism as the gap widened between reality and the declared goals of the League of Communists of Slovenia (LCS), especially after the economic reform of 1965. The **liberalization of the 1960s** brought to light many acute social and political problems (social differentiation and poverty, inconsistencies in Yugoslav foreign policy, the great power of the LCS). Students demanded equal educational opportunities for all; curriculum reform at the university and in the educational system as a whole; employment at home for the educated, in order to stop the brain drain; and, above all, freedom of speech. Students' demands were supported by the university establishment and its teachers, especially at the School of Humanities (*Filozofska fakulteta*). Although students generally agreed on demands, there were differences among constituent groups as to the means of achieving their goals. The student movement in Slovenia in the late 1960s was predominantly a reaction to domestic political, economic, and social circumstances. As elsewhere in Europe, in **Ljubljana** it began in the spring of 1968. Some 3,000 students protested dormitory rent increases and the notice to vacate dormitories for the summer in order to accommodate seasonal tourists. An Executive Committee of the Student Community of the Ljubljana institutions of higher education was formed, prodding the inert ZŠ to reorganize and become more active, inclusive, and tolerant.

The student movement reached peak activity in the spring of 1971. Often labeled "anarcho-liberals," students from the School of Humanities were its initiators and the intellectual force behind most of the 1971 actions: a protest against unbearable traffic noise near the university buildings; demonstrations in support of French students against French Prime Minister Jacques Chaban-Delmas during his Yugoslav visit; distribution of leaflets calling for a renewed socialist revolution on the eve of the 30th anniversary of the LF; and an eight-day sit-in at the School of Humanities. Students protested police interference at the university and backed students who were investigated and jailed for their critical views. *Tribuna*, whose issues were often banned and confiscated, was the official voice of the movement. Due to many official pressures (police interrogation and arrests of students), the mass movement was reduced to a small committee core, gathered around *Tribuna*. Its leadership soon changed, however, due to a forced merger of the Youth League of Slovenia (ZMS) and the ZŠ into the League of Socialist Youth of Slovenia (*Zveza socialistične mladine Slovenije*, ZSMS) in 1974. Thus the student revolution was reined in by establishment authorities, and *Tribuna*'s critical stance was softened. However, students had acquired two important institutions: Radio Študent in 1969 and the Student Cultural Center (*Študentski kulturni center*, ŠKUC) in 1972. *See also* LEAGUE OF COMMUNIST YOUTH OF YUGOSLAVIA; MARKET SOCIALISM.

In the early 1980s, attempting to shed LCS patronage, the ZSMS supported **alternative movements**. Its media voices *Tribuna, Katedra,* and *Mladina,* and the student institutions Radio Študent and ŠKUC, became important vehicles by which social groups within an emerging civil society disseminated ideas. In the 1980s ŠKUC was instrumental in developing **environmental** awareness, a peace movement, and all forms of **postmodernist** art. After the 12th Congress of ZSMS in 1986, students became very active; they demanded better studying conditions, including support for dormitories and subsidized food. In 1990 students separated from the official youth organization and established the nongovernmental Student Organization of the University of Ljubljana (*Študentska organizacija Univerze v Ljubljani*) and Student Organization of the University of Maribor (*Študentska organizaciija Univerze v Mariboru*). Radio Študent and ŠKUC have continued their activities as independent nongovernmental organizations; *Tribuna* ceased operation in 1998. *See also* ARTS; HOMOSEXUAL RIGHTS MOVEMENT; WOMEN'S RIGHTS MOVEMENTS.

STYRIA. *See* REGIONS OF SLOVENIA.

– Š –

ŠALAMUN, TOMAŽ (1941–). Although born in Zagreb (**Croatia**), Tomaž Šalamun, poet and translator, spent his youth in **Koper** and received his degree in art history at the **University of Ljubljana** (1965). Before he devoted all his energies to poetry, he worked as a conceptual artist and collaborated with conceptualists belonging to the group OHO. For the most part, Šalamun has been a freelancer who has published over 30 poetry collections in Slovenia, many of which have been translated into foreign languages and published in

Europe and in the **United States**. In addition, his poetry has been widely anthologized. Šalamun has spent some time in the United States as a visiting professor at the University of Iowa (1971–1973, 2000–2001), as a visiting Fulbright Fellow at Columbia University, and as a cultural attaché at the Consulate General of the Republic of Slovenia in New York (1996–2000). In 1999 he received several Slovene and international awards for his poetry, among them the **Prešeren** Prize for his life work. He lives in **Ljubljana**.

Šalamun is a major cosmopolitan poet whose stylistically and thematically varied poetry has developed over the years. In his early period he was influenced by **Srečko Kosovel**'s constructivism and the poetry of the American Beat Generation, later by **Edvard Kocbek** and modern European and American poetry. In *Poker* (Poker, 1966), his first collection of poems, he showed his originality and challenged traditional Slovene poetic icons and their formalism with irony, causing upheaval in cultural circles. In his American period, the poetry collections *Amerika* (America, 1972) and *Zvezde* (Stars, 1976) are most characteristic, while the collections *Metoda angela* (Method of an Angel, 1978) and *Ljubljanska pomlad* (Ljubljana Spring, 1986) belong to his later, mature period. *The Four Questions of Melancholy* (1997), edited by Christopher Merrill, has certainly been his most important and voluminous English collection. A master of language, Šalamun has inspired many young Slovene poets born in the 1950s and 1960s. *See also* ARTS; LITERATURE; PERSPEKTIVE.

ŠKOFJA LOKA. One of Slovenia's "old" towns, Škofja Loka, in the Gorenjska **region**, at the confluence of two branches of the Sora River, has 12,300 inhabitants. Its name—the "Bishop's meadow"—says much about its history, for it was given in 973 by Holy Roman Emperor Otto II to the bishop of Brixen as a feudal domain. (Episcopal wealth and power in the Slovene lands was extensive in the premodern period.) Colonists from Bavaria and **Carinthia** were brought in to work the sparsely populated land. By the early 14th century Šofja Loka was a walled town, with five gates and densely clustered houses, some with painted façades. Like **Radovljica**, it was ravaged by the armies of the **Counts of Celje** and the Turks in the mid- to late 15th century. The town remained **Catholic Church** property for 830 years until 1803, when the **Habsburgs** in **Vienna** secularized it. It is noted for its 18th-century Passion play (*Škofjeloški pasijon*)—a Good Friday pageant that was performed in the Slovene **language** and has recently been revived as a theatrical-ethnological statement. *See also* MEDIEVAL TOWNS AND COMMERCE; TURKISH WARS. In the late 18th century Škofja Loka revived somewhat, and town growth began outside the crumbling town walls. Trade with Primorska, including **Trieste**, started up. But the town's expansion was minimal until after **World War II**. Now the spinning mill Gorenjska Predilnica produces **textiles** of natural and synthetic materials; Odeja, with a female management team, makes quilted bedding; and Jelovica specializes in wood products—prefabricated houses, doors, shutters, and windows. All three companies are successful at **manufacturing** goods for export, primarily to Central and Eastern Europe. Recent urban development and industrialization in nearby **Kranj** and **Ljubljana** have also made Škofja Loka a favorable bedroom community for commuters. The town now extends nearly five kilometers along an east–west axis. The bishop's **castle**, perched high above the old town, still dominates the settlement.

ŠTAJERSKA. *See* REGIONS OF SLOVENIA.

ŠUŠTAR, ALOJZIJ (1920–). Born in Grmada near Trebnje, Alojzij Šuštar was a gifted student at Ljubljana's episcopal gymnasium and in 1941 was sent to Rome's Gregorian University to study theology. After being ordained a **Catholic** priest in 1946 and earning doctorates in philosophy and theology, Šuštar moved to Switzerland, where he worked as an assistant pastor in St. Moritz and later as professor of philosophy and religion at the lyceum in Schwyz. After 1965 he was a professor of moral theology at the School of Theology in Chur, of which he became rector. He ended his Swiss career as bishop's vicar and secretary of the Council of European Bishops' Conferences.

In 1977, having lived outside Slovenia for 37 years, Šuštar returned to **Ljubljana** to teach at its theological faculty. In 1980 he was appointed archbishop of Ljubljana and metropolitan of Slovenia and became a central figure not only in the Slovene Catholic Church but also in Slovene society. In addition to being appointed archbishop, he held other important positions: chancellor-general of the School of Theology in Ljubljana, president of the Slovene Bishops' Conference, and vice president of the Council of European Bishops' Conferences. He worked for inclusion of the Catholic Church in Slovene public life and was allowed to broadcast Christmas greetings to Slovenes for the first time in 1986.

Known as a mild and tolerant person, Šuštar played an important role in Slovene **independence** as a mediator and friend of the democratic developments unfolding in the country. (Perhaps his absence during the harsh times of **World War II** and the early years of communism, which had spawned political and ideological animosities, disposed him toward this conciliatory role.) In December 1996, when he celebrated the 50th anniversary of his ordination, Šuštar was also awarded an honorary doctorate from the **University of Maribor**. He was commended for his internationally renowned work as a moral and theological scholar; his membership in the European Academy of Science and Arts was duly noted. Šuštar remained archbishop until spring 1997, when he went into retirement.

ŠUŠTERŠIČ, IVAN (1863–1925). A lawyer and conservative **Catholic** politician, Ivan Šušteršič, along with **Janez Evangelist Krek**, dominated the Slovene People's Party (*Slovenska ljudska stranka*, SLS) from the mid-1890s through **World War I**. A pragmatist, Šušteršič had great organizational skills and ambition, which he displayed at Slovene Catholic congresses and in **Vienna**, where he was the **Clericals'** chief spokesman in parliament. At home he was sometimes known as the uncrowned head of Carniola. He was a strong supporter of the monarchy, and he established opportunistic ties with the Belvedere "court in waiting" of Archduke **Francis Ferdinand**.

Šušteršič and his party supported **trialism**, the creation of a state from the South Slav lands of the empire in order to transform the dual monarchy into a triple one. Šušteršič, however, focused on the Catholic unity of those Yugoslavs and how it might strengthen the **Habsburg** power; he had little use for democracy or for South Slavs who were Orthodox. In 1912 and 1913 during the Balkan Wars, Šušteršič supported Vienna's anti-Serbian policy, even backing Bulgaria in 1913. Meanwhile Krek became more pro-Serb. Developments in the Balkans drove the two party leaders into separate camps during World War I. Šušteršič clung to legitimacy and conservative institutions until the bitter end.

– T –

TAAFFE'S IRON RING (1879–1893). German Liberal nationalists were intent on Germanizing and centralizing **Austria**, and it was believed they longed for union with the new German empire. But Edward Taaffe, Austria's prime minister and former school chum of the Emperor **Francis Joseph**, who chose him for that position, was determined to lock German Liberals out of power. He built a governing coalition of crownland federalists (old nobility), **Clericals**, and Slavs for this purpose. It worked like an iron ring, or barrier, keeping the German Liberals isolated. Slovene politicians, although they were already aligned in two groups, conservative and **liberal**, all belonged to the conservative Hohenwart Parliamentary club. Together, and through the club, they worked with Taaffe's coalition for advances in use of the Slovene **language** in schools and administration in Slovene territories. Their successes were gradual but appreciable, so much so that when a Slovene language gymnasium was proposed in the 1890s for **Celje**, in Styria, German backlash brought down Taaffe's government.

TABOR MOVEMENT (1868–1870). The time between the issuance of the **Compromise of 1867**, which the Slovenes initially opposed, and the Franco-Prussian War, which **Vienna** observed with trepidation because France's loss might be followed by a Prussian advance against **Austria**, was a tense one for Slovenes. Their very existence as a national group appeared threatened. The Young Slovenes, following the Czech example, initiated *tabors*, or open-air meetings, to publicize and rally support for the **United Slovenia** program. For two years, until Vienna banned these public forums, Slovenes assembled in various locations to hear speakers and pass resolutions on national issues. The smallest gathering numbered 5,000 people, the largest as many as 30,000. Many turned out in national costumes, arriving in carriages decorated with national symbols, celebrating the *tabor* event with **music** and **folk** singing. These *tabors* are commemorated as evidence that the Slovene national movement of nearly a century and a half ago had an authentic popular base. *See also* REALISM.

TAVČAR, IVAN (1851–1923). A lawyer by profession, Ivan Tavčar is known both as a writer and a **Liberal** politician, representative of the Slovene middle class. He was mayor of **Ljubljana** from 1911 to 1922. His early, **romantic** literary works were very much surpassed by his later writings, characterized as lyrical **realism**, in which he deals with local history and political as well as everyday life. With his later literary works, he was a forerunner of *Moderna*. Among Tavčar's best-known works are his 12 novels, published as the cycle *Med gorami* (Amid the Mountains). Motifs for his stories, which earned Tavčar a reputation as one of the best Slovene prose writers, were taken from life in his native Poljanska Dolina. Beside his historical novels *Visoška kronika* (The Visoko Chronicle) and *Izza kongresa* (After the Congress), an important work is the satirical utopian novel *4000*, in which he deals with Slovene **clericalism** and its founder **Anton Mahnič**. Another widely known Tavčar work is the beautiful story *Cvetje v jeseni* (Blossoms in the Fall), which has been made into a movie. *See also* LITERATURE.

TEN-DAY WAR (27 JUNE–6 JULY 1991). Even as Slovenia was celebrating its declaration of **independence**, the **Yugoslav People's Army** (JNA) was moving tank units to Brnik, **Ljubljana**'s airport, and toward the 27 border posts that Slovenes had taken over when the **Republic of Slovenia** (RS) announced its separation from **Yugoslavia** on 25 June. By June 28 the JNA was also using air strikes against Brnik, against telecommunications stations and transmitters, and on the 30th was threatening major air attacks on Ljubljana. Slovenia's civil defense procedures were activated and people took to air-raid shelters.

Slovenia's defense was assumed by the republic's territorial defense (TD), or national guard, together with the police, and managed by **Janez Janša**, the RS's minister of defense. Well prepared in **Partisan**-style local defense, the Slovene forces outmatched the JNA and ultimately—though not without some major clashes and loss of life—held onto the RS's frontier posts (13 Slovenes were killed and 112 were wounded; the JNA had 39 dead and 163 wounded). Of the 20,000 federal troops in the area, nearly 2,500 deserted, surrendered, or were captured by the Slovenes. The Yugoslav government soon softened its stand, conceding control of the border posts to the Slovenes, provided revenues reverted to **Belgrade**. Belgrade, JNA's commander, and also leading Serbs then allowed that, if the Slovenes were so intent on independence, force should not be used to keep them part of Yugoslavia. Belgrade had expected that a mere show of force would be enough to stop the Slovenes, and that the outside world would back their effort to prevent a dismemberment of Yugoslavia. They were wrong on both counts and ultimately no match for the well-organized Slovene TD, whose intelligence was also far superior to that of the JNA.

The war alarmed Europe and prompted a flurry of diplomatic activity to end it. Both Slovenia and **Croatia** had declared independence the same day, the latter after a 19 May referendum on separation. When the Serb Borisav Jović had refused on 15 May to turn over the presidency of the **Socialist Federal Republic of Yugoslavia** (SFRY) to the Croat Stipe Mesić (a normal rotation stipulated by the **constitution**), the Croats were convinced that a Greater Serbia plan had been activated, thus justifying their independence vote. The European Community (EC), attempting to mediate the crisis before fighting spread to Croatia, sent delegates to Belgrade to force the change of president and to arrange a cease-fire. The first was accomplished on 30 June, but the truce required another diplomatic intervention, which held only in Slovenia (3 July). A meeting that resulted in the **Brioni Agreement** on 7 July effectively ended the war for Slovenia and essentially sealed its independent status.

TERRITORIAL DEFENSE OF THE REPUBLIC OF SLOVENIA. *See* ARMY, SLOVENE.

TEXTILE AND CLOTHING MANUFACTURING. Slovene textile **manufacturing** began in the first half of the 19th century. Three weaving mills were opened already before the **Revolution of 1848**: in Ajdovščina (1828), in **Ljubljana** (1838), and in Prebold (1839), all of which later developed into important Slovene textile manufacturing centers. With large investments of Czech capital, Slovene textile and clothing manufacturing expanded, especially during the interwar period (1920s and 1930s); this accounted for nearly 40 percent of Yugoslav textile production before **World War II**. During that period **Kranj,** with its many new textile and clothing factories, became one of Slovenia's strongest centers of textile manufacturing. In the 1970s and 1980s the textile industry, together with shoe and furniture manufacturing, remained important pillars of industry.

In the early 1990s the situation changed for textile and clothing manufacturing. In 1991 the industry employed over 50,000 workers and accounted for 4.1 percent of value added in the Slovene gross domestic product. Its products were the second most important Slovene export, accounting for 15 percent of total industrial exports (1992). Some large Slovene textile and clothing manufacturers were Mura in **Murska Sobota**, Merinka in **Maribor**, Beti in **Metlika**, Gorenjska Oblačila and Tekstilindus in **Kranj**, Lisca in Sevnica, and Novotekst in **Novo Mesto**. Due to the loss of former Yugoslav and Soviet Union markets and noncompetitiveness in other foreign markets, textile and clothing production soon exceeded demand. What was needed was higher productivity, and that required new technology, company restructuring, and fewer and better-educated workers. The majority of employees at the time were women with only high school **education**. Restructuring was not popular with owner-workers, but action was imperative and therefore undertaken. Some textile and clothing manufacturers, such as Mura, were bailed out by the **government**, while some others were forced to close. Data show that, after 1995, the production of textiles and clothing increased, while the number of employed fell by over one-half, from 50,000 in 1991 to 21,500 in 2004. Since 2000 the volume of textiles and clothing production has declined steadily. While over 90 percent of total production was still exported in the early 1990s, exports fell below 50 percent by 2004. Although the business results were better in 2004 than in 2003, the industry continues to record substantial net loses, and closures are common. *See also* ECONOMY, 1945–1990; ECONOMY SINCE 1991; INTERNATIONAL TRADE AND FINANCIAL TRANSACTIONS; PRIVATIZATION.

THEATER. The beginnings of Slovene theater go back to the 17th century, but the first Slovene theater text, *Županova Micka*, a comedy, was adapted from a German play in the late 18th century by **Anton Tomaž Linhart**, who was also the first theater producer and director. The forerunner of the modern Slovene theater was the Dramatično Društvo (Drama Society), established in 1867 under the leadership of **Fran Levstik**. Slovene theater began to professionalize after **Ljubljana** acquired the Provincial Theater in 1892 (today the Opera and Ballet House of the Slovene National Theater), which was shared by German and Slovene theater groups. At the turn of the 20th century, Slovene playwrights Fran Govekar and **Ivan Cankar** played an important role in defining national theater, while Ignacij Borštnik (1858–1919), an actor and director, is considered the founder of the Slovene modern theater. In 1911 the German theater acquired its own building, which after **World War I** became the home of the Slovene Drama Theater. In the 1930s guest director Branko Gavella and his successors Bojan Stupica and **Oton Župančič** elevated the theater in all respects to the European standard. In 1919 the National Theater in **Maribor** was opened, but the German occupiers closed it during **World War II**. During the war, besides the Drama and Opera Theaters in Ljubljana, there was also a Slovene **Partisan** Theater, founded in 1944, which performed in **Partisan-controlled territories**. *See also* JESUITS, SOCIETY OF JESUS.

After the war, the theaters were reopened and new professional ones were founded in Ljubljana and in regional centers. After a short-lived socialist realist period (1945–1952), the Slovene National Theater welcomed European psychological **realism**. In the mid-1950s the younger generation of theater professionals, educated at the newly founded Actors' Academy in Ljubljana, rebelled against academism in the theater and created experimental and alternative theaters with semi- and nonprofessional groups. Oder 57 (Stage 57, 1957–1964), which began by introducing theater of the absurd but later focused on the production of Slovene contemporary plays, was the most influential and the strongest group. During its relatively short existence, Oder 57 presented several plays of seven younger contemporary Slovene playwrights, including Peter Božič, Primož Kozak, Dominik Smole, Vitomil Zupan, and Marjan Rožanc, whose *Topla greda* (The Greenhouse), produced in 1964, was banned by the **courts** and the theater was closed. In the 1960s, one of the most productive eras of the Drama Theater in Ljubljana, the theater was liberalized by artistic director Bojan Štih. To expose some plays already produced by Oder 57 to a wider public, the Drama staged *Antigona* by Dominik Smole and *Afera* by Primož Kozak; the plays deal with the individual's search for truth and the struggle against political tyranny. The plays were well accepted by the public but not by the political establishment. Bojan Štih was eventually forced out of the Drama in 1969. The most radical group was a student theater group, Pupilija Ferkerverk, under Dušan Jovanovič's direction (1969).

In the 1970s, although ideological oppression stifled Drama's productions, experimental groups such as Glej (Look) and Pekarna (Bakery) developed and produced **modernist** and **postmodernist** pieces. After 1972 the Slovene Youth Theater (*Slovensko mladinsko gledališče*) produced other plays besides those for children and youth. The performances of *Limite* (Limits) and *Grenki sadeži resnice* (Bitter Fruits of Truth), both written by poet Milan Jesih and directed by Zvone Šedlbauer, showed that Glej was continuing the tradition of Oder 57. These groups enriched the theater and kept it abreast of new international theatrical trends.

In the 1980s many of those active in the experimental theater of the 1970s moved on to Ljubljana's Drama Theater and other professional stages, such as the national theaters in **Celje**, **Maribor**, and **Nova Gorica**, enriching their programs and modernizing their productions. Young theater professionals experimented, mainly with small casts, with plays dealing with social and political problems and socially marginal groups, in a poetic, psychological manner, while integrating other **media** into their productions. The most innovative have been the theater groups Sisters Scipion Nasice (1982–1985), which espoused the principles of **Neue slowenische Kunst (NSK)** and continued as the Red Pilot since 1986, and Ana Monro (since 1981), whose productions were based on Brechtian cabaret theater, **folk** theater, and **puppetry**. In the last two decades of the 20th century, Slovene theater displayed two characteristics. First, in a postmodernist spirit, several parallel theater trends and esthetics coexisted, such as the socially critical and political plays of **Drago Jančar** and Dušan Jovanovič, directed by Zvone Šedlbauer and Ljubiša Ristić, respectively, and also postmodernist and retro-garde movements. Second, the theater became interdisciplinary, incorporating dancing, **literature**, **music**, and visual **arts**. The latter elements were brought in by directors Dragan Živadinov and Vito Taufer in Ljubljana, and Tomaž Pandur in Maribor. Pandur produced huge postmodernist spectacles, including *Šeherezada* (Sheherezade) by playwright Ivo Svetina (1988), *Faust* (1990), and *La Divina Commedia* (1992). Živadinov and Taufer produced a series of retro-gardist events, including *Hinkemann* (1983), *Krst pod Triglavom* (Baptism under Triglav, 1986), and *Petdesetletni projekt Noordung* (The Fifty-Year Project Noordung, 1995), in which close cooperation of various art groups, such as the painting group Irwin, the music band Laibach, and the theater Sisters Scipion Nasice blurred borders between the theater and visual arts.

Besides professional theater, nonprofessional theater groups have thrived in villages and towns since the period of **reading societies**. *See also* SOCIETIES.

TITO (1892–1980). Tito was the underground name of Josip Broz, one of 15 children born to a Croat father and Slovene mother living in Kumrovec **(Croatia)** in the **Habsburg Empire**. His biography bears the classic life-markers of a revolutionary: poverty, which led the young farm boy to towns in the empire and abroad in search of jobs; heightened social consciousness, inspired by reading **realist** and **Marxist** literature, which led to involvement in workers' organizations; and participation in world historical events as a soldier in the Austrian army during **World War I** and as a revolutionary in **Russia** during the October Revolution, which aroused his sense of mission in life. After the war Tito returned home to a country now called the **Kingdom of Serbs, Croats, and Slovenes**, where he at once took up revolutionary work. Serving prison terms, nurturing comradery with other revolutionaries, and training in Moscow during the mid-1930s were all part of Tito's experience before Moscow selected him to head a federated **Communist Party of Yugoslavia** (CPY) in 1937.

During **World War II** Tito organized a resistance movement, the **National Liberation Struggle** (NOB), in **Yugoslavia** in June 1941, and over the next four years he helped to expel foreign occupiers and defeat domestic opponents (primarily Croat Ustaši and Serbian royalists). The effort, described as a resistance and revolution, led to the establishment of a revolutionary government, the **Antifascist Council of National Liberation of Yugoslavia** (AVNOJ), in 1943. Aided by the Western Allies, Tito's forces were winners at the end of the war.

Tito and the CPY, in control of Yugoslavia by 1946, introduced reforms modeled after the Soviet communist system. But what might have been uneventful developments and a pedestrian career for Tito were transformed by a head-on confrontation between the USSR's Joseph Stalin and Tito over control of the "revolution" in Yugoslavia. As a consequence, Yugoslavia was expelled from the Communist Information Bureau (**Cominform**) in 1948 and went its own way, developing a unique kind of socialism that came to be known as **Titoism**. It featured socialist self-management and **nonalignment** in the international area. *See also* KARDELJ, EDVARD.

Tito ruled Yugoslavia until his death in 1980. Under the provisions of the **Constitution of 1974** he had been elected president for life, and two collective leaderships—a rotating presidency and a rotating presidium—were devised to succeed him. From time to time, pressures toward a looser federation (Slovenes and Croats between 1968 and 1972) or greater centralism challenged Titoism, but Tito, "the old man," effectively managed the opposing forces to keep the system balanced. He was Yugoslavia's main integrating force. Abroad, Titoism and Tito, as leader of the third-world countries, achieved an enviable reputation. Jawaharlal Nehru, Gamal Abdul Nasser, and Fidel Castro bowed to his leadership, while the West revered and financially backed him for standing up to the Soviet Union. When he died the *New York Times* called him a "giant among Communists." *See also* LIBERALIZATION OF THE 1960s.

TITOISM. Titoism, a term taken from the name of **Yugoslavia**'s president from 1945 to 1980, refers to that country's brand of socialism, which was developed after Yugoslavia was expelled from the **Cominform** in 1948. Its two main features were **workers' self-management** and **nonalignment**. The first, which went through various stages of elaboration, was introduced in the early 1950s; the second, which brought **Tito**'s influence to the third world, was formalized at the **Belgrade** conference of nonaligned nations in 1961. Justifications for both self-management and nonalignment were made by Yugoslavia's **Marxist** theoreticians, most prominent among them the Slovene **Edvard Kardelj**. Yugoslavia's socialism was characterized as embodying true Marxism. Self-management was meant to inject democracy from the bottom up at home; nonalignment was intent on ending colonialism of both the West and the East, while promoting peace and economic advancement in underdeveloped nations (hence injecting democratic relations among all states in the international arena). Both these pillars of Titoism were undergoing serious erosion by the time of Tito's death in 1980.

Titoism rejected the Western capitalist system but also distanced Yugoslavia from Stalinist socialism (the Soviet model), which was denounced as undemocratic. Some have therefore described Titoism as taking a middle road between East and West, offering a third alternative to development and modernization in the 20th century.

TOMAŽIČ, IVAN JOŽEF (1876–1949). Ivan Tomažič was the Lavantine bishop (i.e., bishop of **Maribor**) from 1933 to 1949. After finishing his priestly studies in Innsbruck in 1906, he held various positions in the Lavantine diocese, including a professorship in church history at the Maribor School of Theology. As bishop, he issued a declaration that the church and the clergy should be above **political parties**, taking a position that was unusual for the 1930s when the **Catholic Church** was an influential political force in Slovenia. **Clericals** rejected him for his stance. Because of his refusal to support any political or military actions during **World War II**, the German occupiers in Maribor treated him like a foreigner. He was denied help in pastoral activities at the cathedral and in administering his diocese, whose members numbered over half a million. After the war Tomažič corresponded with **Boris Kidrič** about problems of the Lavantine diocese and suggested possible directions for future relations between the state and the Catholic Church. Despite these efforts, Tomažič's name was seldom mentioned by Communist authorities: ironically, he did not fit the negative image of the Catholic Church and its role during the war that the Communists wanted to project.

TOURISM. Tourism has long been an important **service** industry of Slovenia's **economy**. From its modest beginnings in the 19th century (the **Alpine resort** of Bled, the seaside resort of Portorož, and the thermal **spa** at Rogaška Slatina), tourism by 1990 had developed into an $850 million enterprise. The first official data on tourism in Slovenia were collected in 1928: The most succesful year before **World War II** was 1939, with approximately 210,000 tourist arrivals and 1,120,000 overnight stays, the majority of which (75 percent) were domestic guests. Before Slovenia's disassociation from **Yugoslavia** in 1991, the most successful tourist year was 1986, with more than 2,800,000 tourist arrivals and 9,200,000 overnight stays. Tourism was among the most adversely affected branches of the economy in 1991, but it was also among the first to begin recovering in 1992; by 1995 the number of tourists approached the level of arrivals and overnight stays of 1990.

Tourism has been a slowly growing industry and represents an important foreign exchange earner with much potential for further development. Tourism revenues amounted to 1,312 million euros ($1,630 million) in 2004 and strongly influenced the country's positive balance of payments. In the 1990s Slovenia developed new and varied tourist offerings (casinos, congress/conference tourism, ecological farms, and various **sports**) and it also became better known as a tourist destination. Tourist development was stimulated in part by the establishment in 1996 of the Slovenia Tourist Board, which put together a long-range development plan and took several steps to promote Slovenia around the world as a tourist country, for which the **government** allocated 5 million euros ($6.2 million) in 2003.

Since 1991 the number of foreign arrivals and overnight stays has been growing. Historically, German tourists were the most numerous, but their share has been slightly declining since 2001. In 2004, for the first time, there were more tourists from **Italy** than from Germany, followed by tourists from **Austria, Croatia**, the Netherlands, and Great Britain. Foreign tourist visits accounted for more than two-thirds of overnight stays in 2004. With over 2.3 million tourist arrivals and over 7.5 million overnight stays (4.2 percent more than in 2003), 2004 has been the record tourist year since Slovenia's independence, although it did not reach the level of tourist activity (recorded arrivals and overnight stays) of 1986. In 2004 a tourist stayed in Slovenia on the average three nights, mostly in hotels, whose capacities were fully occupied close to 50 percent of the time. Since 2002 tourist revenues have exceeded 1 billion euros (1.3 billion in 2004, a 10 percent increase over 2003). In 2004 income from tourism (including hotels and restaurants) accounted for about 9 percent of GDP, and tourism provided work for about 52,000 people, or 8 percent of the entire workforce. While domestic tourism has been on a slow rise since 1991, in recent years Slovenes have begun traveling more abroad. In 2004 Slovenes took 3.98 million private trips (vacations), of which more than half were abroad, where they spent 732 million euros. Although visiting tourist destinations all over the world, Slovenes most often frequented Croatia's Adriatic coast.

Slovenia's varied and beautiful landscape is attractive for tourists, but it is not best suited for mass tourism. In the summer, the peak season, tourism puts a strain on the local **environment** (e.g., the water systems at the seaside and Lake Bled). The Slovene landscape is more suited to tourism for those seeking undisturbed natural settings with opportunities for sports (climbing, fishing, hiking, horseback riding, hunting, skiing, swimming, water sports) and enjoyment of naturally produced foods. According to data from the Statistical Office of the **Republic of Slovenia** (RS), 25 percent of foreign tourists chose Slovenia for its natural beauty and 20 percent because of its peaceful environment. For only 8 percent of tourists was price a deciding factor in coming to Slovenia. The major tourist attractions are thermal **spas**, located mostly in eastern Slovenia. Some, such as Rogaška Slatina, are especially popular destinations for Austrian and German tourists. Besides spas, Slovenia has **Alpine resorts** that offer skiing and hiking, as well as natural beauty. There is also a small (46 kilometers) coastal area with beaches and historic cities, such as **Piran** and **Koper**. Another draw is ecological tourism, with close to 400 farms scattered across Slovenia where active and healthful vacations can be enjoyed. Tourist attractions also include the **Kras/Karst** region, with many beautiful caves (e.g., **Postojna** and Škocjanske) and other unique natural phenomena, such as Cerknica Lake.

Slovenia also offers cultural and historical attractions. There are Roman ruins, **medieval** towns, monasteries, **castles**, and various churches with exceptional artwork, providing opportunities for exploring Central European history. There are more than 60 **museums** (with over 70 museum collections) and art galleries, and nearly every larger town displays its own history, as in the **Kobarid** Museum of World War I. Lively cultural life, organized around festivals, such as the Festival of 20th Century Chamber Music in Radenci, and exhibitions, some with international participation, make Slovenia an interesting destination for specific groups of visitors. **Folk traditions**, still preserved, although in some cases only for tourists, attract many ethnologically curious visitors, especially to **Bela Krajina** and **Prekmurje**. Taking advantage of its geographical, economic, and cultural attributes, Slovenia, in the last two decades, has also made great strides toward developing congress/conference tourism. Conference centers have been developed in **Ljubljana, Maribor**, and other larger cities as well as in tourist locations such as Terme Čatež, Bled, and Portorož. An important share of international congresses in Slovenia take place in **Cankar Center** in Ljubljana. *See also* ARTS; INTERNATIONAL TRADE AND FINANCIAL TRANSACTIONS.

TRADE. *See* INTERNATIONAL TRADE AND FINANCIAL TRANS-ACTIONS; SERVICE INDUSTRY.

TRADE UNIONS. Of the republics of former **Yugoslavia**, Slovenia had the longest tradition of trade unionism. While Slovenia was a part of the **Austrian Empire**, workers associations began to develop in the 1860s, and in 1870 **Austria**'s parliament legally enabled workers to organize by abolishing penal laws against unionization. Briefly there was a flurry of worker activity in the 1870s, even a strike or two, but real trade union building took place only in the 1890s. Unions were organized and sustained primarily by **political parties** and often had ties to workers associations in other parts of Austria. The **Socialists**, the **Christian Socialists** (within the **Clerical** political camp), and even the **Liberals** nurtured workers organizations among the Slovenes in the years before **World War I**. The Socialists began by organizing the miners, the Clericals the tobacco and paper workers, and the Liberals the white- and blue-collar railway workers. The first Slovene conference of trade unions (Socialists) was held in 1901 in **Ljubljana**; its headquarters was established in **Trieste** in 1905, while a secondary center opened in Ljubljana in 1908. The Liberals also established their center for workers in Trieste in 1909; the Clericals' central worker organization, established the same year, was headquartered in Ljubljana. After World War I, when Slovenes became a part of the **Kingdom of Yugoslavia**, prewar trade unions were revived and continued under political sponsorship. On the political left, the emerging communist movement began to exert some influence. The unions gained some organizational experience, but the nature of the regime, particularly after the establishment of the **January 6, 1929, dictatorship**, restricted autonomous activities.

After **World War II** and the establishment of communism, trade unions were no longer independent. They were controlled from **Belgrade** headquarters by the **Communist Party of Yugoslavia** (CPY) and were later considered an integral part of the self-management system. Union membership was virtually obligatory. Trade unions, which were united in the Federation of Trade Unions of Yugoslavia (*Zveza sindikatov Jugoslavije*, ZSJ), acted on behalf of workers within **workers' councils**. They also performed educational functions, ostensibly preparing workers for self-management roles. Before the 1960s, trade unions had little autonomous power; they could not stop work or strike. During the 1960s, under a strong ZSJ head, unions began to assume an active role in formulating economic policy and exerting political clout. By the late 1970s 95 percent (5 million) of all workers in the socialist Yugoslavia were dues-paying union members. *See also* WORKERS' SELF-MANAGEMENT.

In Slovenia in the late 1960s, trade unionists began pressing—although with little success—for greater autonomy for the republic's union component, the Union of Trade Unions of Slovenia (*Zveza sindikatov Slovenije*, ZSS), which linked Slovene unions with, and represented them in, the ZSJ. The ZSS, with headquarters in Ljubljana, operated within the **Socialist Alliance of Working People** (SAWP) and was essentially the only trade union body in Slovenia until the late 1980s, when growing opposition to the old regime was marked by new, freer trade unionist activity and and also strikes. Throughout the 1970s and 1980s, it should be noted, Slovene trade unionists achieved some autonomy and sought to strengthen ties with comparable organizations abroad, particularly in Austria, Germany, and **Italy**. Some of the components of the Slovene **social security** system, even before 1990, contained elements of the systems in place in these Western European countries.

Beginning in 1989 various constitutional changes altered the nature of trade unionism in Slovenia. A Law on Basic Rights of Employment Relationship, passed that year, eliminated the concept of **associated labor** and with it the whole system of self-management. The principle of contractual employment was introduced, strikes were legalized, and regulations regarding collective bargaining and collective agreements were outlined. Workers became free agents, and membership in unions was no longer a necessity. Many chose to remain in the reformed trade union (ZSS) or joined new ones. With laborers' new status, the status of employers also needed redefinition, and this required **privatization** of the means of production (factories, mines, etc.). These changes were undertaken (some are still in progress) in the years between 1989 and 1993, when the Law on the Representativeness of Trade Unions (LRTU) was passed. The LRTU made trade unions legal entities with a right to own property, formalized the acquiring of trade union status, and permitted unions to organize locally or nationally. It also prescribed the procedure by which a trade union might be legally recognized. Larger confederated unions generally registered with the Ministry of Labor, and they were able to acquire seats on the Economic and Social Council of Slovenia (*Ekonomsko socialni svet Slovenije*, ESSS), a governmental policy-making body. As a part of that body, the unions help negotiate labor laws, such as the comprehensive Employment Relationship Act implemented on 1 January 2003. The unions represented workers in negotiating the semiannual tripartite understandings that were the basis of the "social contract" between workers, employers, and the government.

By the spring of 1990, trade union activity was being transformed, and by 1993, with the passage of the LRTU, four large umbrella organizations were recognized. By far the largest, with over 400,000 members, was the Union of Free Trade Unions of Slovenia (*Zveza svobodnih sindikatov Slovenije*, ZSSS), headed by Dušan Semolič. Essentially a reformed and reorganized ZSS with headquarters in Ljubljana, politically it leaned to the left. The second largest union, Freedom, Confederation of New Trade Unions of Slovenia (*Svoboda, Konfederacija novih sindikatov Slovenije*, KNSS), also had headquarters in the capital and was right-leaning politically. It boasted over 100,000, or 10 percent of all trade union members; its head initially was France Tomšič, but he was replaced by Drago Lombar. Two smaller confederated union organizations were also recognized in 1993, both offshoots of the ZSSS. The Confederation of Trade Unions of Pergam Slovenia (*Konfederacija sindikatov Pergam Slovenija*), centered in Ljubljana, represented workers in the pulp/paper and printing industries and was headed by Dušan Rebolj. The Confederation of Trade Unions '90 Slovenia (*Konfederacija sindikatov '90 Slovenija*) represented workers in the coastal areas; it established headquarters in **Koper** and was headed by Boris Mazalin. Each of these four organizations had seats on the ESSS; ZSSS had two, the others one each. They all supported collective bargaining and the use of strikes and accepted the principle of the social contract. They differed primarily over the issue of privatization, specifically how extensive it should be and how it should be attained.

In addition to these large umbrella organizations, there are also many new, small ones, representing professional groups such as journalists, judges, medical workers, dock workers, educators, and so on. Two new ones of note are the Slovene Union of Trade Unions, Alternativa (*Slovenska zveza sindikatov, Alternativa*) and Workers' Union Solidarity (*Zveza delavcev solidarnost*), confirmed in 1999 and 2001, respectively.

Since the late 1980s, when virtually all workers belonged to unions, trade union membership has declined. Of about 800,000 in the workforce, less than half remained members in 2004. Partly this was due to extensive restructuring of the **economy**, particularly in certain industries, such as metallurgy, **mining**, **textile** production, and **leather** and shoe manufacturing. The issue of membership numbers as well as the future of Slovenia's trade unions per se has become part of the larger European labor story. Accession to the **European Union** (EU) in spring 2004 required that Slovene laws be compatible with those of the EU. Laws regarding trade unions and treatment of workers, domestic and foreign, must now submit to the scrutiny of EU commissions.

TRANSPORT. Because of Slovenia's location, transporting people and goods by rail, road, sea, and more recently air has been an important sector of the **economy**. Together with storage and communications, transport has become a major **service industry**. In 2003 it accounted for a significant share of the gross national product (7.5 percent of GNP) and employed 10 percent of the total workforce.

Slovenia's network of railways and roads has a long history. Roads can be traced back to Roman times, whereas Slovenia's first railroad, connecting **Vienna**, **Ljubljana**, and **Trieste**, was completed in 1857. Most of the railway lines (tracks) were laid before **World War II**, although some were added after the war. Among the latter, the line built in 1967 connecting **Koper**, Slovenia's major seaport, with the rest of the railway system is the most important. In 2003 there were 1,229 kilometers of railroad tracks and 297 passenger and freight stations, reaching almost every town in Slovenia. There are good international train connections with **Austria**, **Croatia**, Germany, and **Italy**. Before 1991 the railway system in Slovenia was a part of Yugoslav Railways. Since 1991 it has been operated by the Slovene Railways Holding (Slovenske železnice), a large state-owned company restructured in

2004. Although the railway network had been well developed before Slovenia established its **independence** from **Yugoslavia**, the railway infrastructure was in need of modernization, as were existing lines. Two projects to increase the system's transport capacity were given priority: construction of a direct railway connection with **Hungary**'s railway system, and construction of a second track on the Koper–Divača line. The first project, the railway line Puconci–Hodoš–Zalalővő, Hungary, discontinued in 1968, was restored in 1999, while the other is in its beginning stages. The Koper–Divača line is crucial for connecting the coastal region and the port Koper with the rest of Slovenia and Central Europe. In January 2005 the European Commission allocated 5.47 million euros toward the completion of the 27-kilometer track. Both passenger and freight transport have been increasing since 1995.

Slovenia has approximately 45,000 kilometers of roads (including all driving surfaces, from unpaved to city streets). Of those in 2004, 20,155 kilometers were classified as motorways, major, main, regional, and local roads, mostly hard-surfaced with asphalt or concrete. Before 1991 there were only three short multilane highways, all built after 1972: Ljubljana–**Postojna**–Razdrto (56 kilometers), Ljubljana–**Kranj** (30 kilometers) with the Vrba–Karavanke Tunnel (9 kilometers), and Ljubljana–Višnja Gora (25 kilometers). In 1994, in order to modernize its roads and connect Slovenia with the rest of Europe by modern highways, the Slovene **government** developed a comprehensive highway project (National Motorway Construction Program), co-financed by international financial institutions. Between 1994 and 2005, 358 kilometers of new roads were built—257 kilometers as motorways and international E-roads. Although construction of the road network has been intensive, the existing network is insufficient for the increasing volume of road traffic, and 42 percent of the road network is in bad shape. Between 1995 and 2003 the number of registered motor vehicles increased 42 percent for trucks and 27 percent for personal automobiles. As traffic has increased, so has the number of traffic accidents. In 1995 there were over 6,500 traffic accidents involving death or bodily injury; in 2004 there were more than 12,400, with more than 18,600 injured and 274 deaths. While the number of incidents and injured increased, the number of deaths in the same period decreased about 45 percent. In the past, scheduled public bus transportation between cities was well organized and reached almost every village at least once a day.

However, in the mid-1990s many bus routes were eliminated due to lack of profitability. The number of bus passengers and passenger kilometers dropped dramatically.

Sea transport is based at two major ports along the 46-kilometer Slovene coast: **Piran**, where Splošna Plovba Piran (Piran General Shipping) is engaged in freight transport, shipbuilding, and related services; and Koper, where Pristanišče Koper (Port of Koper) operates one of the major commercial ports on the northern Adriatic coast. Portorož is another port town with berthing capacity, but Portorož Marina is intended primarily for **sports** and **tourism**. The port of Koper, established in 1957, grew from a small facility into a major European freight port, serving Central European countries (Austria, Hungary, Slovakia). In the last 20 years, various storage terminals (for automobiles, coal and ores, grain, and livestock) have been built, as has a parking garage. Since 2000 sea transport has been growing. Over 70 percent of its annual cargo, which exceeded 12 million tons for the first time in 2004, is transit in nature.

Although Slovenes were among the pioneers of world aviation in the late 19th and early 20th centuries (Edvard Rusjan, Stanko Bloudek, and Jurij Kraigher), commercial air transport did not begin in Slovenia until 1933, when the first airport was built near Ljubljana. Today Slovenia, a crossroads of important international flight corridors, has three international airports: Ljubljana and **Maribor** for long-distance passenger and freight flights, and Portorož for smaller aircraft and sports aviation. After the Ljubljana airport and its technical facilities were severely damaged in the 1991 **Ten-Day War**, Slovene air traffic was closed, reopening only in late 1992. Renovated and enlarged, the Ljubljana Airport is managed by Aerodrom Ljubljana, a joint stock company, which has daily or weekly connection with 20 European cities. The national air carrier, Adria Airways, established in 1963, operates regular flights to large cities in Europe and also runs worldwide charter flights. Besides the Slovene carrier, which operates 80 percent of all traffic in and out of the country, several foreign airlines, including Austrian, Yugoslav Aero Transport (JAT), and Lufthansa, fly to and have offices in Slovenia.

Transport and tourism have been Slovenia's fastest growing service industries since 1996. As with tourism, revenues from transport have been rising faster than expenditures and have affected positively the foreign trade balance. *See also* INTERNATIONAL TRADE AND FINANCIAL TRANSACTIONS.

TRIALISM. *See* CLERICALS; FERDINAND, FRANCIS.

TRIESTE/TRST. Located at the northeast corner of the Adriatic 145 kilometers northeast of Venice and 16 kilometers from the Slovene border, Trieste is the capital city of **Italy**'s Trieste province and of the region of Friuli-Venezia Giulia. With a population of about 209,000 in 2004 (10 to 15 percent Slovene), it has a variety of major industries: **banking**, chemicals, electronics, insurance, pharmaceuticals, shipping and shipbuilding (privatized and dominated by the Dutch and Taiwanese since 1998), and **textile** production. Smaller enterprises produce brandy and other liquors, jute cloth and sacks, olive oil, paint and varnish, and paper. It has recently become a center for scientific research. The best known centers are UNIDO, a genetic engineering and biotechnical institute; an institute on theoretical physics; a marine biology laboratory; and an experimental geophysical observatory. Its university had ten faculties and 24,000 students in 2004. (Slovene **language** studies can be undertaken within the Faculty of Philosophy.) The city has long been a **transport** and commercial center, possessing a fine deep-water port and a long waterfront on the Gulf of Trieste. With a **karst** hinterland, Trieste has a temperate climate but is affected by the violent cold northeast wind—the *bora* (*burja*).

Trieste (Tergeste) was a pre-Roman commercial **settlement** that was Romanized after 51 BC, destroyed by Attila the Hun in 453 AD, occupied by the Lombards until 752, and came successively under German invaders, Charlemagne and his successors (until 948), local ecclesiastical and secular authorities, the Venetians (1202), and finally the **Habsburgs**, who held it from 1382 to 1918. It was made a part of Italy only after **World War I**, where it remained in spite of **Yugoslavia**'s claims to it and the surrounding hinterland. A commercial center during the Renaissance, Trieste declined in the 16th century, when voyages of discovery shifted maritime activity to the Atlantic. After 1719 Habsburg subsidies redeveloped it as a free port, and it became **Vienna** and Central Europe's major outlet to the sea. It acquired a stock market in 1735, an insurance company in 1766, and a shipbuilding company in the latter part of the century. *See also* MEDIEVAL TOWNS AND COMMERCE.

In the early 1800s steam power was introduced in **manufacturing** and transportation, and in 1857 the railroad connected it to Vienna via towns in the Slovene lands. The opening of the Suez Canal (1869) was an enormous boon for Trieste. The Austrian Lloyd Triestino, established in 1836, came to dominate Adriatic shipping. Slovene entrepreneurs, bankers, and industrialists (e.g., Martelanc shipbuilding) played an integral part in Trieste's development. The city's population grew from 5,700 in 1719 to 229,510 in 1910 (65 percent Italian, 25 percent Slovene), and the city became cosmopolitan—"Triestine"—although Italian and Slovene nationalist agendas were eroding this identity on the eve of World War I. In 1900, its *fin de siècle* society and culture, too, was cosmopolitan, generated by Italians, Slovenes (e.g., the architect **Maks Fabiani**), a talented group of Triestine **Jews** (e.g., Italo Svevo, pseudonym for Ettore Schmitz), and Austrian Germans. Between the 1920s and 1998 Trieste and its port were subsidized by Italy, for with the breakup of Austria-Hungary, Trieste lost its Central European clients and after **World War II** acquired competitors in Yugoslavia's Rijeka (Fiume) and also **Koper**. In the mid-1970s it was a thriving shopping center for Slovenes. After the breakup of Yugoslavia, there were fewer Slovenes, but more Croats and Hungarians in Trieste's main shopping streets.

Over the centuries Trieste has played an important role in the cultural, economic, and political development of the Slovenes. Beginning with the 16th century, when **humanism** flourished in the northern Adriatic towns, church leaders welcomed Slovene religious reformers like **Primož Trubar**, who spent parts of 1524, 1530, and 1540–1542 there. By 1607 an Italian–Slovene dictionary was produced in the area. In the 1840s, during the Slovene national cultural awakening, Slovene schools and textbooks were in use in Trieste and its environs, and in the 1870s a number of Slovene-language newspapers were being published there. The leading paper *Edinost* (*Unity*), initially a bimonthly, then a weekly, was begun in 1874. It became the national voice of the Slovene **minorities** in Trieste, who remained united—in spite of ideological differences—due to simmering anti-Slovene pressures. Italy, which had become a united state in 1860, annexed Venetia in 1866, and the Papal lands in 1870. Incorporating Trieste and lands along the eastern Adriatic coast was part of the Italian national unification plan.

As Slovene **political parties** were formed, one in particular felt strong association with Trieste. The Yugoslav Social Democratic Party (JSDS), a Slovene **Socialist** party that had organized in 1896, moved its headquarters to Trieste in 1900. Its decision was based on good **Marxist** reasoning that the revolution would come in the most industrialized society and where the proletariat was strongest. At the turn of the century what there was of a Slovene proletariat was mostly in Trieste. In 1911 there were nearly 57,000 Slovenes living in Trieste and its suburbs (almost 30 percent of the population), making Trieste the largest Slovene city ahead of **Ljubljana**, whose total population at the time was less than 42,000. In 1904 a Slovene national home was opened in the city.

After World War I Trieste went to Italy. Denationalization measures against Slovenes began, and in 1920, the year of the postwar **Rapallo Treaty**, the Slovenian national home was burned down and its archives destroyed. When the fascists came to power in 1922, conditions worsened for non-Italians. Many Slovenes **emigrated**, a good portion to Yugoslavia. Some Slovene nationalists who remained in Trieste were radicalized and embarked on terrorist activities (many were caught and executed in 1930), or joined the **Communist Party** and worked with Italian communists to rid Italy of fascism. That goal was achieved during **World War II**, but the outcome for the Slovenes in Trieste was less than hoped for. Although Slovene **Partisans** liberated Trieste in May 1945, they were not allowed by the Western Allies to keep it. After 40 days, they were forced to leave and were replaced by a joint British–American Allied administration of the city that lasted until 1954. That year, which was at the height of the Cold War, the city was turned over to Italy. One result was economic crisis for the city; another was depopulation. The young left for better economic opportunities. Among them were 30,000 Slovenes, many of whom emigrated to Australia. Trieste was left with a population of elderly and declining numbers (from a peak of 260,000 in 1954). *See also* TRIESTE QUESTION.

For Slovenes in Trieste, in spite of post–World War II Allied agreements assuring minority rights (e.g., **London Agreement**, 1954; **Osimo Treaty**, 1975), engaging in political and cultural activities continued to be difficult. To promote their rights, the Slovenes established two community organizations: the Slovene Cultural and Economic Union and the Council of Slovene Organizations. They also organized one political party, "Slovene Community," whose representatives have served on the city (commune) council, as well as in the larger body that represents Trieste province. The right to political representation guaranteed by the Allies, however, has been illusive. A 1993 electoral law has increased the minimum percentage of votes needed for representation in government, thus decreasing Slovene participation. Bilingualism, guaranteed by international agreement, has also declined; the use of Slovene in public bodies (e.g., council, courts, and businesses) is often booed, while public signs using two languages have simply been removed. In 2001, after years of debate, the parliament at last passed the Law on Global Protection of the Slovene Minority in Italy, something the Osimo Treaty had guaranteed a quarter-century earlier. Although Trieste's Italian mayor and city council supported it, it has yet to be fully enabled. Italian–Slovene relations in Trieste improved, yet tensions mounted in early 2005 when Italian television commemorated Italian victims of 1943–1945, killed by Italian Communists and Yugoslav Partisans and buried in pits in the karst area near Trieste.

TRIESTE QUESTION. Until the end of **World War I**, **Trieste** was **Austria**'s principal port on the Adriatic Sea. In 1910, while more than half the population of this cosmopolitan city of 229,510 was Italian, 56,916 Slovenes also lived there, and Trieste's hinterland was predominantly Slovene. During World War I, in return for joining the Entente (London Pact, 1915), **Italy** was promised Austrian territory in the northern Adriatic. At the Paris Peace Conference (1919), the Adriatic question, including the fate of Trieste, was deferred to deliberations at Rapallo, where Italy was awarded the lion's share of the former Austrian territories, which both Italy and the new **Kingdom of Serbs, Croats, and Slovenes** claimed on the basis of national self-determination. According to the **Treaty of Rapallo** (1920), Trieste as well as a large part of Primorska became part of Italy.

After **World War II** the Trieste question was once again on the table. Although Italy had been one of the Axis aggressors, it did not lose Trieste. The Yugoslav **Partisan** forces had entered Trieste in early May 1945, followed within days by the British. After six weeks of joint occupation, the Western Allies issued an ultimatum requiring the Yugoslav forces to leave. At postwar peace conferences in London (1945) and Paris (1946), which took up the matter of Trieste and its hinterland, the Yugoslav position continued to be that Trieste was the natural outlet of the Slovene hinterland and therefore must be part of **Yugoslavia**. But the West was fearful of Soviet influence there, and as the East and West settled into a Cold War, the Allies (with Italy as their new military partner) were unwilling to give up this port to Yugoslavia.

In 1945 the contested territory between the Rapallo line and the old Italian–Austrian border was divided into two zones—the western Zone

A, which included most of **Gorizia** and Trieste provinces, was under American and British military administration, and the eastern Zone B was under Yugoslav military administration. The Partisans had to withdraw from Udine province (Venetian Slovenia and Resia, both a part of Italy since 1866), which immediately came under the Italian administration in 1945. The permanent border between Italy and Yugoslavia was subsequently established by the 1947 Peace Treaty in Paris, which awarded Military Zone A (Trieste and Gorizia provinces) to Italy, and Zone B (Primorska and Istria) to Yugoslavia. As Trieste remained a matter of strong dispute and created political tensions between Italy and Yugoslavia, a buffer entity was established at the suggestion of the big powers—the Free Territory of Trieste (*Svobodno tržaško ozemlje*, STO) under UN protection, which also was divided into two zones: Zone A under the Allied (American–British) administration and Zone B under Yugoslav administration. Refer to map 4.

The Peace Treaty assured equal treatment of the nationalities, with Italian and Slovene as the official languages in both zones. However, in 1949 a decree issued by the Allies made Italian the only official language in Zone A, suggesting a pro-Italian bias on the Allies' part. Similarly, while the treaty required repeal of all fascist measures that discriminated against Slovenes, there was scant willingness on the Allies' part to truly implement the treaty. In 1953, when the Allies announced that they would be replaced by an Italian administration, tensions between Italy and Yugoslavia escalated, sparking many incidents. The following year the border between Italy and Yugoslavia was revised by the **London Agreement** (1954). The STO was abolished, and its territory was consensually divided between Italy and Yugoslavia; virtually all of Zone A with Trieste remained in Italy.

Although Italy did not ratify the London Agreement, Italian–Yugoslav relations were normalized and neighborly after 1954, and the border between the two countries became increasingly more open. Trieste in the 1960s became a major shopping center for its Yugoslav neighbors, Slovenes in particular. In 1975 the **Osimo Treaty** reviewed and basically reaffirmed the London Agreement, which had given Trieste to Italy. *See also* MINORITIES, SLOVENES IN ITALY.

TRIGLAV. Triglav (2,864 meters), in the Julian **Alps**, is the highest mountain in the **Republic of Slovenia** (RS) and a favorite climbing objective among alpinists. The first recorded ascents of Triglav go back to 1778. Triglav National Park, whose beginnings date to 1924, was officially established in 1961. With enlargements in 1981, the park covers 84,807 hectares and encompasses Triglav and much of the Julian Alps **region**. The park's administration, at Bled, sees to the protection of the area's flora and fauna, monitors **environmental** dangers, and tries to limit overdevelopment of **tourist** facilities. However, major **Alpine resorts**, such as Bled, Bohinj, and Kranjska gora, are bordering on the park. Triglav became a national symbol during the Slovene national awakening. Clubs were named after it, and songs written about it. A stylized version of Triglav appears on RS's **flag** and on its coat of arms.

TRUBAR, PRIMOŽ (1508–1586). Sometimes known as the "Slovene Luther," Primož Trubar was the leading figure of the Slovene **Protestant Reformation**. A **humanist** and preacher, his studies took him, among other places, to Salzburg, **Vienna**, and **Trieste**, where Bishop Peter Bonomo, a prominent humanist, was his mentor. Trubar has been associated with various projects, such as bringing religious reform to the Croats and Serbs (using books in the Glagolitic alphabet), and converting the **Turks** who in 1529 were at the gates of Vienna. His most important achievement, for which he is regarded as the father of Slovene **literature**, was issuing the first Slovene printed book, a primer (*Abecedarium*), in 1550. It was followed by a catechism and other religious books, 31 in all, intended as aids to salvation for his Slovene flock. These books, and others written by reformers, were used in the Slovenes' first elementary schools. Most had to be printed in German Protestant lands. Trubar's work was carried on by **Jurij Dalmatin**, who produced the first Slovene translation of the Bible. *See also* BOHORIČ, ADAM; EDUCATION, ELEMENTARY.

TURKISH WARS. Turkish attacks against Slovene lands began in 1469, extending north into **Carinthia** by 1473. Their intensity and frequency were greatest during the reign of Suleiman the Magnificent (1520–1566), when the King of Bohemia and **Hungary** was killed (Battle of Mohács, 1526) and even **Vienna** (1529) came under siege. Slovene peasants experienced the greatest hardship in these times, for their lands were left defenseless and their fields became battlefields. The nobles, later the emperor, who organized anti-Turkish defenses, exacted ever more taxes and dues. The economic pressures precipitated periodic **peasant revolts**. The Uskoks, bands of fighters, were organized by the landed estates to fight Turks but were often used against peasants in revolt. Although the Turkish threat was not eliminated, it was minimized after the 1570s, when the **Habsburgs** greatly increased expenditures on the Military Frontier, established in 1520s just south of the Hereditary Lands. That development afforded the Slovene lands respite from the foreign invaders. It also allowed the Habsburg rulers to fight Protestantism more earnestly at home. *See also* COUNTER REFORMATION; PROTESTANT REFORMATION.

– U –

UNITED LIST OF SOCIAL DEMOCRATS OF SLOVENIA / ZDRUŽENA LISTA SOCIALNIH DEMOKRATOV (ZLSD).
The United List of Social Democrats, a union of former leftist associations, came into being officially in May 1993. The largest of these groups was the Party of Democratic Renewal (*Stranka demokratične prenove*, SDP), a reincarnation of the League of Communists of Slovenia (LCS), which until 1952 had been the **Communist Party of Slovenia**. The new United List name was chosen in spring 1990, just prior to Slovenia's first multiparty **elections**. Many in the old LCS had been distancing themselves from the old system since at least the summer of 1988. In January 1990 they broke decisively when **Milan Kučan**, leading the Slovene LC delegation, walked out of a League of Communists of Yugoslavia (LCY) congress in **Belgrade**. The federal party's newspaper *Borba* captured the meaning of Kučan's walk, writing prophetically: "The League of Communists no longer exists." Within weeks the LCY disintegrated, and Slovene Communists who had rejected unitarism and centralism moved toward support of a pluralistic democracy. In March the LCS, with about 96,000 members, adopted a reformist program and its new name, and it ran candidates in the election of April 1990 with the slogan "For the European Quality of Life."

The former Communists hoped, even expected, that reformism would win the election for them. Slovenes were to a certain extent grateful for the **liberalization**, but the general attitude of voters was that 45 years of Communist rule was enough. **Demos**, by organizing an opposing coalition of parties, assured the Communist defeat. Nevertheless, the SDP, although it got no ministerial posts in the first multiparty **government**, won 25 seats in the three chambers of parliament; one of its candidates (Matjaž Kmecl) was elected to the collective presidency, and **Milan Kučan**, hero of the Belgrade "walkout," was elected president of the republic.

The SDP program was fleshed out in two post-election congresses. The party depicted itself as a co-creator of Slovene sovereignty and defender of workers' rights, regionalism, and access to abortion. In the election of December 1992 it won 14 seats in parliament. It became part of the **Republic of Slovenia**'s (RS) government of December 1992–November 1996, headed by Prime Minister **Janez Drnovšek** of the Liberal Democratic Party (LDS). Four ministers in that government were SDP members.

As the United List (ZL), the Social Democrats ran in all elections after 1996. That year ZLSD won nine seats; in 2000, 11 seats; in 2004, 10 seats. In all cases these were respectable numbers, and between November 2000 and December 2004, this qualified them again to be part of the ruling coalition. Its party president after 1997, **Borut Pahor**, was the president (speaker) of parliament in that coalition, and in summer 2004 Pahor was elected one of the RS's representatives to the European Parliament. *See also* GOVERNMENTS AFTER 1990.

The ZLSD has a broad organizational base, with associations for generational, gender, and occupational groups. In 2005 it had 27,000 members. Since 1996 it has been a member of the Socialist International and has joined the Party of European Socialists. At its national congress in April 2005, the party name was shortened to "Social Democrats."

UNITED NATIONS, RELATIONS WITH. In 1945 the **Federal People's Republic of Yugoslavia** (FPRY) was one of the founding members of the United Nations (UN), and Slovenia was one of the republics within the FPRY. It remained so until 1991 when socialist **Yugoslavia** began to disintegrate. During those socialist years, Yugoslavia pursued a policy of **nonalignment**, which afforded it considerable influence among UN members who came from developing third-world nations. Beginning in the 1980s the Slovene republic's **government** also had its own committees that worked directly with UN agencies dealing with development issues: children, employment, farming and food supply, **health**, and **education**, learning, and culture. One Slovene who was prominent from the early 1950s through the early 1980s on various UN committees and agencies dealing with economic issues was Janez Stanovnik. Another, Ignac Golob, a seasoned diplomat and former UN press secretary, served as Yugoslavia's ambassador to the UN from 1982 to 1986.

After the **Republic of Slovenia** (RS) declared its **independence** (25 June 1991), it quickly sought UN **recognition** for itself. On 22 May 1992 Slovenia was accepted into the organization as its 176th member. The RS has become active in various UN agencies, including the Food and Agriculture Organization (FAO), International Labor Organization (ILO), UN Conference on Trade and Development (UNCTAD), UN Educational, Scientific, and Cultural Organization (UNESCO), UN Children's Fund (UNICEF), UN Industrial Development Organization (UNIDO), and the UN Truce Supervision Organization (UNTSO). It has also committed itself to UN peacekeeping missions in Afghanistan, Bosnia, Cyprus, East Timor, and the Middle East (Golan Heights). *See also* FOREIGN POLICY; FOREIGN RELATIONS; INTERNATIONAL ORGANIZATIONS, MEMBERSHIP IN.

In October 1997, only five years after admission, Slovenia was elected to a two-year term (1998 through 1999) as a nonpermanent member of the UN Security Council. Slovenia's UN ambassador at the time was Danilo Türk, whose term as ambassador ran from September 1992 through January 2000. While Slovenia was a Security Council member, the UN had serious issues before it, including troubles in the Democratic Republic of the Congo, Iraq, and a crisis in Kosovo. When Slovenia's term on the Security Council ended, UN Secretary General Kofi Annan offered Türk the position of Assistant Secretary General for Political Affairs. **Ernest Petrič** replaced Türk, serving as Slovenia's UN ambassador from 2000 until 2002. In 2002 Roman Kirn, a career diplomat, assumed the ambassadorship. Slovenia's current priorities regarding the UN are to pursue peace, stability, and development in Southeastern Europe; and to foster collective security, human rights, and human security, as well as development, environmental, and health goals worldwide.

UNITED SLOVENIA. The very first Slovene political program was entitled *Zedinjena Slovenija*, or United Slovenia. Formulated by Slovene intellectuals living in Graz, **Ljubljana**, and **Vienna**, it was their contribution to the **Revolution of 1848**. Joining together all ethnically Slovene territories, without regard to crownland borders, was the objective. In the new administrative unit, which would remain a part of the **Austrian Empire**, the Slovene **language** would be used in **education** and administration. In 1848 the program was expressly loyal to **Austria**, calling for its separation from the German Confederation, where a German national state was in the making. A United Slovenia was not realized in 1848.

United Slovenia continued to be the Slovenes' political program. Until **World War I** that program was seen—with a few extremist exceptions (**Ivan Cankar** and **Preporod**)—as compatible with a commitment to Austria. Between 1918 and the late 1980s, Slovene politicians generally hoped to realize a United Slovenia within the framework of **Yugoslavia**. However, in Austria and in the first and second Yugoslavias, centralism obstructed its fulfillment, as did the unfavorable borders drawn by the Great Powers after the world wars. Even though not all Slovene territory is included, many would say that the United Slovenia program, born of revolution in 1848, is now fulfilling itself with the emergence of the independent **Republic of Slovenia** (RS) in 1991.

UNITED STATES, RELATIONS WITH. For Slovene **foreign policy** objectives in the 20th century, the United States has been a spoiler. After both world wars, when Slovenes worked for the establishment of a **United Slovenia** (within **Yugoslavia**), the goal proved elusive. The United States and its allies after **World War I** enabled **Italy** (a latecomer to the alliance) to take over a hefty portion of Slovene lands, and even **Austria**, a loser in that conflict, was awarded ethnic Slovene areas after the **Carinthian plebiscite** of 1920. This occurred in spite of Woodrow Wilson's espousal of "national self-determination" principles. After **World War II**, even though both Italy and Austria had been the enemy, the Western Allies were reluctant to award Yugoslavia those lands where Slovenes lived, even though Yugoslav **Partisans** had liberated **Trieste** (Italy) and had also reached southern Carinthia (Austria). The **London Agreement** of 1954 eventually turned some Slovene territories over to Yugoslavia. The Cold War, however, had turned the West against former Allies who also happened to be communist; so again, Slovene aims had to be sacrificed. Eventually the United States would court Yugoslavia because it had broken with the Soviet Union and could be useful in the Cold War, but this brought no changes in U.S. policy toward Slovenia.

By the early 1990s, as communism was collapsing in Eastern Europe, the Slovenes had revived the United Slovenia plan, but this time autonomy within Yugoslavia was no longer acceptable. Independence was the goal because remaining within a Yugoslavia controlled by the Serbs in **Belgrade** would hinder democratization and the introduction of a market **economy**. Again the United States opposed the Slovene plan, for many of the same reasons it objected to independence for the Baltic states and Ukraine. It preferred large states over small ones, sometimes even irrespective of ideological issues. On the eve of Slovenia's declaration of **independence** in mid-June 1991, U.S. President George H. W. Bush's secretary of state, James Baker, rushed to Yugoslavia to lecture particularly the Slovenes and the Croats against breaking from Belgrade. (It was essentially the same talk Ukrainians would get in the "chicken Kiev" speech a few weeks later.) When the Slovenes and the Croats declared independence anyway, the Serbs, on the basis of Baker's intervention, decided they were justified in stopping them. So began the wars in the former Yugoslavia that ended only in late 1995. Some in the United States blamed Slovenia for the country's breakup and its bloody aftermath. Relations between the United States and Slovenia, which was anxious for cordiality, remained cool during much of the 1990s.

For most of the 1990s Slovenia tried hard to gain favor with the United States, the world's superpower. The **European Union** (EU) recognized Slovenia's independence on 15 January 1992, but the United States hesitated. Its recognition came only on 7 April, together with recognition for **Croatia** and Bosnia-Hercegovina, largely because it hoped that acknowledging the latter would avert a war in that country. **United Nations** (UN) recognition soon followed, on 22 May 1992. Meanwhile in Washington, D.C., Slovenia's first ambassador to the United States, **Ernest Petrič**, worked hard, though often fruitlessly, to get Slovenia's interests on the U.S. agenda. Slovenia had much competition for Washington's attention: dozens of new states, most larger, with more money, and stronger ethnic communities in the States to back them. The scramble for attention was frantic, and Petrič was hampered by having only a small staff and temporary quarters. It was during his tenure that Slovenia was bidding for entry into the **North Atlantic Treaty Organization** (NATO), which realistically could be attained only with U.S. support. Under President Bill Clinton, the United States had announced its vision of an expanded NATO in summer 1993, and the following year a transition track, the Partnership for Peace, was established. In general, Slovenia did what it needed to gain U.S. approval. In 1996 it altered its position on working with the Southeast Cooperative Initiative (SECI), which it had resisted because it seemed to be forcing Slovenia back into the Balkans. The United States, which also wanted **Hungary** in SECI, put the squeeze on Slovenia, suggesting compliance on this matter would make NATO accession easier. Slovenia agreed to support SECI, but did not join. Slovenia did not get into NATO in 1997. The number of entrants had to be kept to a minimum, and the United States reconsidered its backing for Slovenia after France began supporting Romania.

Relations between the United States and Slovenia slowly improved after 1997. Slovenia redoubled its efforts toward admission to NATO. The second Clinton administration (1996–2000) was more sympathetic toward Slovenia and supported its candidacy for nonpermanent membership on the UN Security Council, a position it held in 1998 and 1999. Slovenia reciprocated by backing U.S. policies. During the Clinton years, Slovenia became better known in the White House and on Capitol Hill. In 1999 President Clinton made a state visit to Slovenia, and the following year both houses of Congress passed a resolution supporting Slovenia's entry into NATO, a goal that was realized in spring 2004. The administration of U.S. President George W. Bush began on a somewhat awkward note as far as Slovenia was concerned: Bush confused Slovenia with Slovakia, in spite of having met both Slovenia's prime minister and foreign minister when they visited him in Texas earlier. But by spring 2001 Bush made a state visit to Slovenia in order to meet Vladimir Putin, **Russia**'s new leader.

For the United States, Slovenia is important for its geographical location. It constitutes a bridge between Italy and Hungary, and it affords a contact with the former Yugoslav states. Stability in southeastern Europe is of great importance to Washington, and in its view, Slovenia can provide expertise and insight into the region. The United States maintains a staff of 80 in **Ljubljana**, Slovenia's capital, from which it monitors economic and political interests in the region. Slovenia for its part, a post-communist success story both economically and politically, can set an example for other states to the south. Regarding support of U.S. foreign policy, Slovenia remains cautious. Its primary security and economic partnership is with the EU. When the United States embarked upon war in Iraq in 2003, Slovenia declined to participate, though it did offer to train Iraqi police in Jordan. (In 2006 this position was slightly modified by the **government** of 2004, headed by Prime Minister **Janez Janša**.) On the eve of the Iraq war there were anti-U.S. demonstrations in Slovenia, just as there were across Europe. And the Slovene referendum on joining NATO, held in March 2003, tallied only 66 percent approval (as opposed to the 90 percent positive vote for the EU taken the same day).

UNIVERSITY OF LJUBLJANA. Extensive efforts in the 19th and early 20th centuries toward establishing a national university culminated in the founding of the University of Ljubljana in 1919. Five faculties were established: Arts, Law, Theology, Engineering, and Medicine (two-year program). The university began the school year 1919–1920 with 942 students (914 men, 28 women) and 18 professors, appointed by the Ministry of Education in **Belgrade**. Many of the professors came to **Ljubljana** from other European universities to help with the institution's beginnings. The university was located in the remodeled former regional parliament palace in the center of Ljubljana. At its 10th anniversary, the University of Ljubljana was renamed University of Alexander I, after the Yugoslav king.

From a small institution before **World War II**, the university grew into one of the largest in Europe. In 1945–1946, with 2,565 students, the university began expanding by adding new departments and schools, building new structures, and increasing the number of full-time and part-time students. Female students outnumbered male students by the late 1970s. As faculties expanded or were newly established, they dispersed throughout Ljubljana, while only the rector's office remained in the original palace. Ljubljana was declared a university city. Along with university expansion, a student housing complex was built in the city in the 1960s. In 1979 the university was named after **Edvard Kardelj**, a prominent Slovene socialist theoretician, but in 1992 the name was changed back to University of Ljubljana.

The University of Ljubljana has 26 units: three academies (Fine Arts; Music; and Theater, Radio, Film, and Television), 22 schools or *fakultete* (Architecture, Arts and Sciences, Biotechnical, Chemistry and Chemical Engineering, Civil Engineering and Geodesy, Computer and Information Sciences, Economics, Education, Electronics, Law, Mathematics and Physics, Mechanical Engineering, Maritime and Traffic, Medicine, Natural Sciences and Technology, Pharmacy, Public Administration, Social Sciences, Social Work, Sport, Theology, and Veterinary Science), and a University College of Health Care. The individual schools collaborate closely with various research institutes, the University Research and Development Center, and the University Computer Center.

In 1992–1993 the university had 26,655 enrollees; in 2005 the number was 57,064 (undergraduate and graduate students), of whom about 11,200 (25 percent) were part-time. The university currently employs about 3,500 teachers and researchers and a support staff of 900. It offers four- and five-year undergraduate study programs, and graduate studies (specializations, master's and doctoral programs). The 2004 Higher Education Act required **higher education** to be compatible with that in other **European Union (EU)** countries (Bologna declaration). Consequently the Schools of Economics and of Social Sciences began introducing new study programs in the school year 2005–2006. The University of Ljubljana interacts with 23 universities worldwide through exchange of scientific literature, student and teacher exchanges, and cooperation on various research projects. It is a member of the international Association of Universities, the Association of European Universities, and some other international organizations.

UNIVERSITY OF MARIBOR. The beginnings of **higher education** in **Maribor** date to the mid-19th century, when the first bishop of Maribor, **Anton Martin Slomšek**, introduced theological studies there. The first institutions of higher learning, immediate predecessors of the University of Maribor, were the School of Economics and Commerce, established in 1959, and five other two-year colleges, which in 1961 organized as the Association of Higher Educational Institutions of Maribor. The university was formally established in 1975. Located in Maribor, Slovenia's second largest city and the cultural and economic center of northeastern Slovenia, the university pursues educational goals responsive to the needs of the area. In its 36-year existence, its enrollment has grown, as have its fields and quality of studies. In 1991–2005 the number of students more than doubled: from 10,741 in the school year 1990–1991 to 25,621 in 2004–2005. In addition to the Faculty of Arts and the Faculty for Natural Sciences, established in the spring of 2006, the university has 12 faculties: Agriculture, Business and Economics, Chemistry and Chemical Engineering, Civil Engineering, Criminal Justice, Education, Electrical Engineering and Computer Sciences, Law, Mechanical Engineering, Medicine, Organizational Sciences, and the College of Nursing. The largest number of students is enrolled in the School of Organizational Science (approximately 6,000), followed by the School of Education (approximately 5,000). The University has close ties to local industry and cultural institutions of Štajerska and **Prekmurje**.

UNIVERSITY OF PRIMORSKA. Established in 2003, the University of Primorska, Slovenia's third public university, is located in **Koper**, the republic's largest coastal town. The university offers opportunities for **higher education** primarily to people living in the Primorska **region**, along the Italian and Croatian borders. It consists of three schools (Humanistic Studies, Management, and Education and Teacher Training), located in Koper; two colleges (Tourism located in Portorož, and Health Care located in the city of Izola); and two research centers. The university had 5,485 undergraduate students and 900 graduate students in the school year 2005–2006.

URAN, ALOJZ (1945–). Born in Spodnje Gameljne in the Šmartno parish near **Ljubljana**, Alojz Uran studied theology in Ljubljana, where he was ordained a priest in the **Catholic Church** in 1970. His first post was at St. Nicholas's cathedral in Ljubljana as an assistant pastor. In 1974 he went to study in Rome, and in 1978 he obtained a master's degree in catechesis at the Institute of the Salesian University. After returning to Ljubljana, he held different posts in the Slovene Catholic Church, such as the rector of a minor seminary at St. Peter's parish (Ljubljana), dean of the western section of the Ljubljana-Šentvid decanate, and lecturer at the Faculty of Theology. In 1993 Pope John Paul II appointed him auxiliary bishop of Ljubljana. He remained in this position until 2004, when he became archbishop of Ljubljana and metropolitan of Slovenia, replacing **Franc Rode**.

– V –

VALVASOR, JANEZ VAJKARD (1641–1693). Educated by the **Jesuits**, polymath Janez Vajkard Valvasor was a great scholar (historian, ethnologist, topographer). His scientific work was influenced by his extensive travels (1658–1671) through Europe. After returning home, Valvasor settled at the Bogenšperk **castle**, where he worked most of his life. He built a rich **library** and collections of old documents and various interesting objects, the first **museum** collection in the Slovene lands. Valvasor had contacts with European scientists, and was a member of the English Royal Society, where he once lectured on Cerknica Lake (**Kras**/Karst area). He was the author of several books in German. The most important among them was *Die Ehre des Herzogthums Krain* (The Glory of the Duchy of Carniola, 1689), consisting of four illustrated encyclopedic volumes in which Valvasor tried to bring together the entire body of contemporary knowledge of nature and life in the Slovene lands. In 1971 the Association of Museums of Slovenia established an award named after Valvasor; it is bestowed for lifetime work in the preservation of cultural heritage. *See also* SCIENCE.

VARNOSTNO-OBVEŠČEVALNA SLUŽBA (VOS). *See* SECURITY AND INTELLIGENCE SERVICE.

VATICAN. *See* CATHOLIC CHURCH; CATHOLIC CHURCH, HISTORY OF; FOREIGN RELATIONS; RECOGNITION, INTER-NATIONAL; RELIGION.

VEGA, JURIJ (1754–1802). Educated by the **Jesuits**, Jurij Vega was a Slovene engineer and mathematician who taught at the Artillery School of Higher Learning in **Vienna**. Because of reforms he introduced in mathematics, physics, and the ballistics curriculum, he was given the title of baron. Vega wrote several technical books; his best-known work, printed and used worldwide before the computer age, is the *Thesaurus logarithmorum completus*, in which logarithms are calculated precisely to the 10th decimal place. A lunar crater and a star of the first magnitude are named after him. *See also* ENLIGHT-ENMENT; SCIENCE.

VELENJE. With a population of 26,742 and another 7,000 in the surrounding district, Velenje is Slovenia's fifth largest town, and also its newest. In the Štajerska **region**, it is located in the Saleška Valley, north of **Celje**; between 1980 and 1991 it was called Titovo (**Tito**'s) Velenje. Although the **mining** of lignite began there in the late 19th century, Velenje was developed only in the 1950s—an example of socialist Slovenia's push toward rapid industrialization and urbanization. The town soon attracted workers from various parts of **Yugoslavia**; hence only about three-quarters of Velenje's inhabitants today are Slovene. In the 1950s coal mining was accelerated, as was the production of thermoelectric power at the nearby village of Šoštanj, which provides one-third of Slovenia's **energy** needs. Velenje's best-known business is Gorenje, an international corporation with nearly 50 companies at home and abroad. Gorenje makes kitchen appliances, hot water heaters, tools and equipment for industry, and furniture, and it markets environmental protection and waste management **services**. Its products are made for both the domestic and very demanding European market. Gorenje is one of Slovenia's most successful companies, ranking high in number of employees (overwhelmingly women) and first in export of products abroad. It is one of Europe's leading manufacturers of kitchen appliances. In September 2004 Gorenje announced it would build a production facility in Serbia. Other businesses, like Vegrad, a construction company, help make Velenje an important commercial and financial center. *See also* MANUFACTURING; TRADE.

Velenje was designed as a model industrial workers' town. Socialist planners built bright, spacious worker housing (high-rise apartments) and wide streets, interspersed with large, green parks. However, there was a negative side to Velenje's profile—ecological problems brought on by shoddy care of the **environment**. Sulphur dioxide emissions especially have caused serious air and water pollution. In the 1990s a newly established institute of ecological studies began studying pollution problems with an eye toward improving the environment, and in 1999 Velenje opened a **museum** of industry and ecology, featuring a section on coal mining.

VENETI THEORY. Since the mid-1980s the Veneti theory has been vigorously promoted in Slovenia by Matej Bor, a poet, critic, linguist/translator, and member of the **Slovenian Academy of Sciences and Arts**; Jožko Šavli, an economist keenly interested in the cultural history of the area; and Ivan Tomažič, a priest, organizer, and patron of **science**. The theory holds that the Veneti—a people whose presence in Central Europe in 1500–1000 BC has been historically documented and seems to be reflected in countless toponyms of the area—were actually paleo-Slavs and thus ancestors of the Slovenes. The theory is based on the alleged similarity between the language of the Veneti, extant in several hundred inscriptions in an Etruscan-like runic alphabet, and the Slovene **language**. While the Venetic language is considered by mainstream historians and linguists a linguistic mystery, Bor has provided his own translations of the inscriptions, based on similarities with Slovene. According to the theory, the Slovenes, through the Veneti, are early Indo-European settlers of Central Europe. The generally accepted historical view, however, is that the Slovenes arrived later, in the sixth century AD, from the area north of the Carpathians. The Veneti theory is not accepted by leading Slovene historians and linguists. *See also* SETTLEMENT OF THE SLOVENES.

VETERANS. The League of Associations of Veterans of the National Liberation War of Slovenia (*Zveza združenj borcev narodnoosvobodilne vojne Slovenije*, ZZB NOV Slovenije) was established in 1948 as a branch of the Yugoslav Federation of Veterans' Organizations for the purpose of reconstructing Slovenia and protecting its socialist order from foreign aggression. In addition, the organization assisted its members who participated in the **National Liberation Struggle** (NOB) and promoted **Liberation Front** (LF) and **Partisans** traditions. In 1949 the republic committee of the League began publishing the monthly *Borec (The Fighter)*, which has evolved over the years from an organization bulletin into a serious historical journal.

Because of strong Serb centralizing pressures within the federal organization, the Slovene branch separated from it in 1989. Under its new name, League of Associations of Veterans and Participants in the National Liberation War of Slovenia (*Zveza združenj borcev in udeležencev narodnoosvobodilne borbe Slovenije*, ZZBU NOBS), the Slovene group joined the World Veterans Federation in 1993. The ZZBU NOB later reorganized and expanded to include eight other organizations or groups whose members did not participate in Partisan military units or were not LF activists. Among these are the Society of Expellees of Slovenia (*Društvo izgnancev Slovenije*); the Green Ring Society (*Društvo Zeleni prstan*), which maintains the Memorial Path encircling **Ljubljana**; and the Society of History Writers (*Društvo piscev zgodovine*). All of these groups include younger members.

A patriotic organization, the League has a twofold role: assisting its members in need, and perpetuating NOB and Partisan traditions. As aging veterans have died, membership numbers have declined. In 1994 the organization had around 67,000 members. In 2006 its membership was down to 51,000, of which 32,000 were NOB participants (Partisans, expellees, LF activists), while 19,000 were younger supporters of NOB traditions and values. In addition to some national commemorations, ZZBU members are active in regional local branches. The League generally supports left-leaning **political parties**. In addition to *Borec*, ZZBU publishes an organizational biweekly bulletin *Svobodna misel* (*Free Thought*) and maintains an informative website. *See also* COMINFORM CRISIS; COVENANT, NEW SLOVENE.

VIDOVDAN CONSTITUTION (ST. VITUS DAY CONSTITU-TION), 28 JUNE 1921. The Vidovdan Constitution established a parliamentary, constitutional monarchy for the **Kingdom of Serbs, Croats, and Slovenes**, thereby also recognizing a nation with a triple name. The country was divided into 33 local administrative regions (*oblasti*) subordinate directly to **Belgrade**, the capital. Slovene lands had two of these *oblasti*: **Ljubljana** and **Maribor**. Essentially the administration was highly centralized, with ultimate power residing in Belgrade. The king had unrestricted power, calling and dismissing the unicameral parliament and naming government officials and judges, who ruled in his name. Traditional liberties (e.g., press, assembly) were protected by the constitution, yet the rights of liberals and communists were regularly infringed upon.

The constitution was issued on St. Vitus Day, 28 June, a Serbian national holiday. On that day in 1389, Serbs were devastatingly defeated by the **Turks**, initiating centuries of Ottoman domination; and in 1914 on that day, a Bosnian Serb assassinated the symbol of another foreign power, Archduke **Francis Ferdinand**, an act that precipitated **World War I**. The Vidovdan Constitution made the Serbian **Karadjordjević** dynasty the rulers of the new South Slav state, and Serbs tended to dominate various branches of the national administration. Serbs who had been on the winning side in **World War I** were hardly sympathetic to Croats and Slovenes (formerly of Austria-Hungary, a Serbian enemy), who urged federalism. The constitution barely passed the constituent assembly. Among those boycotting the vote were the Communists, the Croat Peasant Party, and the Slovene People's Party. The Vidovdan Constitution was suspended when King Alexander established the **January 6, 1929, dictatorship**. *See also* YUGOSLAVIA, KINGDOM OF.

VIENNA. The capital of **Austria**, a republic since 1918 (except during **World War II** when it was united with Nazi Germany), Vienna was long the political and cultural center of a sprawling multinational **Habsburg** empire. For Slovenes, who lived in Habsburg lands for more than six centuries, Vienna was the seat of their ruler (under either the **Holy Roman Empire** or **Austrian Empire**), and where their parliament convened after 1867. Vienna, too, was the fount of much Slovene culture that was not **folk** based. It drew to it budding intellectuals and educated Slovenes, who particularly after the 19th century studied, organized **societies**, and produced works in **science** and in the **arts**, **literature**, **music**, and **theater**. They were a part of, yet a separate component of, the cultural life of the empire's capital city. *See also* CATHOLIC CHURCH, HISTORY OF; KOPITAR, JERNEJ; PLEČNIK, JOŽE; STEFAN, JOŽEF.

Links with Vienna continued after 1918. As capital of a state contiguous with **Yugoslavia**, and since 1991 with **independent** Slovenia, Vienna's political disposition continued to be important to Slovenes. Culturally, the capital of Austria also acquired new meaning for its neighbor to the south. Since the 1980s, as they began to distance themselves mentally from the Yugoslav cultural milieu, Slovenes sought and rediscovered their cultural roots in what had once been Central Europe's premier capital, Vienna. *See also* MINORITIES, SLOVENES IN AUSTRIA.

VILLAGE GUARD / VAŠKE STRAŽE (1942–1943). In the spring of 1942, during **World War II**, the Village Guard began to form spontaneously as local self-defense units to protect civilians in the countryside from mistreatment by the **Partisans** (e.g., requisition of property, forced mobilization, and murders of real or perceived political opponents). Many Village Guard units were organized with the help of local priests because of the **Catholic Church**'s opposition to communism. At the same time, the Legion of Death, a mobile detachment fighting Partisans in the countryside, was formed by anticommunist Catholic and **liberal** youth.

Since most members of the Village Guard were not experienced soldiers, were poorly armed, and could not protect their villages, they sought **Italy**'s help. The Italians provided arms to both the Village Guard and the Legion of Death, designating them the Volunteer Anticommunist Militia (*Milizia volontaria anticomunista*, MVAC). Because of Partisan terrorism, the strength of the Village Guard in Dolenjska and Notranjska grew to several thousand (6,000 members in 1943). After Italy capitulated in September 1943, many Italians were captured or surrendered with their heavy weapons to the Partisans. With their help, the Partisans took control of most of Dolenjska and Notranjska. Many Village Guardists were captured and most summarily executed; the remainder retreated toward **Ljubljana**. Later they constituted the core of the **Home Guard**.

VITICULTURE. Slovenia's climate and location—where the Pannonian Plain, the Mediterranean, and the eastern **Alps** meet—provide excellent conditions for growing grapes. Since Roman times, wine making has been an important economic activity in the region, and Slovenes have related it to many **folk traditions**. Vineyards were well established by the Middle Ages in all areas where they are found today. Viticulture, however, experienced difficult times brought on by adverse natural, economic, and even political conditions. Especially devastating was *Phylloxera* (plant lice) in the 19th century, destroying many vineyards that have never been renewed. In 2003 there were over 16,000 hectares of vineyards, approximately 15,000 hectares less than in the 19th century. But Slovenes produce much more wine than ever before, due to modern viticultural and wine-producing techniques. Total production of wine in 2004 was 82.9 million liters.

Slovenia has three main wine-producing **regions**: Podravje (Drava basin) in the northeast, Posavje (Sava basin) in the southeast, and

Primorska (the Slovene Littoral) in the southwest. Each region's district is known for its own distinctive wines. Growers cultivate a number of grape varieties and produce some two dozen different white wines and a dozen red ones. Podravje, the largest wine-producing region in Slovenia, produces wines similar to those of Central Europe and is best known for its white wines. Among the many varieties, *laški rizling*, *sauvignon*, and *šipon* are produced in the largest quantities. Posavje is known for its red wines, Dolenjska for its *cviček* (a dry rosé), and **Bela Krajina** for its *metliška črnina* (a dark red wine). The Slovene Littoral, a Mediterranean area with 9,000 hectares of vineyards and the source of one-half of the **Republic of Slovenia**'s (RS) total wine production, has both red and white wines. While white wines (*rebula*, *tokaj*) are predominantly grown in the Vipava valley and in Goriška Brda in the northwest, red wines (*teran*, *refošk*) dominate in the **Kras/Karst** plateau and on the Adriatic coast in southwestern Slovenia. Wine producing, next to farming and animal husbandry, is an important branch of Slovene **agriculture**. Despite its size, however, domestic production satisfies only somewhat over 70 percent of domestic consumption, and thus is supplemented by imports. Slovenia also exports limited quantities of wines to several European countries and to the United States. Slovenia's wine production has good potential for future development, and experts believe that Slovenia could successfully expand its exports of high-quality, bottled wines. The International Wine Fair, held annually in **Ljubljana** since 1955, attracts noted international enologists to judge the quality of wines and fruit juices.

VODNIK, VALENTIN (1758–1819). Valentin Vodnik, a **Catholic** priest, was a Slovene poet and journalist active in the **Zois** Circle. Because of diverse cultural activities, he is considered one of the most important Slovenes in the age of **Enlightenment**. In 1797 he published the first, but short-lived, Slovene journal, *Lublanske novice* (*Ljubljana News*). The first Slovene poems also were written by him, and published in the collection *Pesme za pokušino* (Tryout Poems, 1806). He was an enthusiastic supporter of French rule in the **Illyrian Provinces**, where he was the principal of the **Ljubljana** secondary school. He also wrote school textbooks and popular geography, history, and economics texts. A monument to Vodnik stands in the Ljubljana central food market. *See also* PRESS BEFORE 1990.

– W –

WEDAM-LUKIĆ, DRAGICA (1949–). Born in **Ljubljana**, Dragica Wedam-Lukić, the future president of the Constitutional **Court** of the **Republic of Slovenia** (RS), studied Law at the **University of Ljubljana**. Her bachelor's (1971) and master's (1976) degrees were capped with a Ph.D. in 1982. She taught law, specializing in civil procedure, and advanced from assistant (1982) to associate (1987) to full professor (1993). In addition to civil procedure, Wedam-Lukić is also an expert in international private law and secondarily in **human rights** and medical law. In 1994–1995, she was vice rector of the University of Ljubljana. In spring 1998 Wedam-Lukić became one of nine members of Slovenia's Constitutional Court. She had been nominated for the position by President **Milan Kučan** and elected to it by parliament. From November 2001 to November 2004 she was its president, chosen by her colleagues on the court for a three-year term. She is one of the few women in the RS to attain a major public position.

WOMEN'S RIGHTS MOVEMENTS. Slovene women's public activism began developing in the second half of the 19th century as the number of educated women grew. Female teachers led the fight for equal pay and women's suffrage, and women organized the first strike in **Ljubljana**'s sugar refinery (1871). Women's associations, such as the women's affiliate of the Cyril-Methodius Society (**Trieste**, 1887) and the Association of Slovenian Women Teachers (1898), and a women-oriented press (*Slovenka*, 1897) appeared. Women organized along political lines. The Christian Socialist leader **Janez Evangelist Krek** organized the Catholic Society of Female Workers (1894), which was joined by other women's organizations. In 1901 the Christian Women's Union was established, and after **World War I** it reorganized as the Slovene Women's Union. Influenced by the **Catholic** doctrine of the time, these women's organizations held patriarchal views of society and did not fight for political rights and women's independence; their goal was social rights. Also founded in 1901 was the General Slovenian Women's Society, which at first emphasized educational and cultural activities for women, but after World War I it dealt also with women's social and economic issues.

In the 1920s liberal and socialist-leaning women organized in the Union of Working Women. As the communist faction within the organization was very strong, the Union was banned in 1935. The most radical feminist organization in the interwar era was the Women's Movement (1926–1937), under the leadership of Angela Vode, an internationally known feminist. Although women had no vote and were excluded from political life, they were politically active in the Slovene national movement before World War I and they continued their activities in **Yugoslavia**. In 1925, regardless of their party affiliation, 12 Slovene women's organizations (United Women of Slovenia) held public gatherings across Slovenia, protesting against the extension of the Serbian patriarchal family law to all of postwar Yugoslavia. They demanded inheritance law equality for women and children, and women's right to vote, and they also campaigned for peace.

During **World War II** the Communists initiated the Antifascist Women's League, which became the women's mass organization after World War II—the Antifascist Women's Front (*Antifašistična fronta žensk*, AFŽ). It was disbanded in 1953 because the Communists maintained that, under their rule, there were no separate women's issues and hence no need to have a separate women's organization. Vida Tomšič, a Slovene Communist, provided the ideological basis for socialist women's legislation, which gave women equal legal status in society, but women's problems remained similar to those that women faced in neighboring states. The majority of women worked outside the home while maintaining families, with little help from husbands or society. Due to lack of interest and time, few women were active in self-management and socialist politics. In 1977 women accounted for 30 percent of **Communist Party** members and about 25 percent of one of the chambers of the republic's parliament. They held few important positions in other fields, even though they dominated in some, such as **education**, **health**, and law.

Although women did not constitute an independent political force, women active in the **Socialist Alliance of Working People** (SAWP) fought for and won important milestones in gender equality. Besides gaining suffrage for women (1946), legal equality created favorable conditions for women to fight for equal pay and equal treatment. Paid maternal leave (extended from three months shortly after the war to one year in 1986) and organized preschool education enabled more women to seek employment and to become competitive in the workforce. Although the wage gap between the genders remained significant, it nevertheless decreased. Women's educational attainment rose: In 1945–1946 women accounted for 30 percent of students at the university; by 1985 their share increased to 58 percent. By 1990 about half of all women were employed. The right to abortion was included in the Yugoslav **Constitution of 1974** and remained in the Slovene **Constitution of 1991** despite opposition from some parliamentary parties and the Catholic Church. Despite wide availability of contraceptives, the number of abortions remains high.

The women's movement in Yugoslavia, influenced by West European and North American women's movements, began in the late 1970s. By the mid-1980s Slovenia had several such groups: the women's section of the Sociological Society (1984), Lilith (1985), and later LL (lesbians). Women's groups worked together with other **alternative movements** of the 1980s; for example, Lilith joined forces with the Peace Movement Group to protest obligatory military training for women. After the Chernobyl nuclear accident in 1987, the Working Group for the Women's Movement and Women's Studies, together with the Ecology group and the Peace Movement, organized a large demonstration for a moratorium on building nuclear power plants. SOS, the first telephone line for abused/battered women and children, was set up in 1989. In 1992 the government established the Office of Women's Policies, which, with other nongovernmental organizations, brought the existing but underreported violence against women in the private sphere to national attention. The number of cases of violence against women reported to the Ombudsman of Human Rights has increased since 1995. In 2004 services for battered women, partly financed by the **government**, included SOS Phones and nine shelters with a limited number of beds. Although Slovenia was not the final destination for most women from Eastern Europe, trafficking in women, especially young girls, through and into the country has become a serious problem. According to police estimates, there were 1,000 women trafficked through and 400 trafficked into the country in 2000. Slovenia was slow to address this crime against women, in part perpetuated by organized crime. In 2004 trafficking in persons was made a criminal offense. *See also* HOMOSEXUALS; HUMAN RIGHTS.

Despite women's participation in the "Slovene Spring" (1989–1990), women were generally left out of political leadership. Women members of the Committee for the Protection of Human Rights, the future power structure of Slovenia, were few, and few held leadership positions in the new **political parties**. Demographic policies of the late 1980s and the antiabortion campaign in 1991 gave rise to new women's groups, such as Women for Politics (1990) and the Prenner Club in **Ljubljana**, and Women's Initiative in **Koper**. Some political parties formed women's sections, but women and their problems remained marginalized, as everywhere in post-communist societies. Political participation of women in the National Assembly decreased in the 1990s: In 1992, for example, 12 women were elected to the parliament (90 members), seven in 1996, and 12 in 2000 and 2004. Women's rights in **independent** Slovenia worsened during the 1990s, a fact that energized women to get organized. In Ljubljana, the City of Women Festival was established (1996), and new women's groups were organized within individual political parties, as were independent women's groups. Also, women's studies at the **universities** were expanded, and new legislation compatible with **European Union** (EU) laws was adopted, treating both genders equally. In 2001 the Office of Women Policies was replaced by the Equal Opportunity Office. Political attitudes toward women have been changing, in part due to pressures by the EU to adjust to its standards. More women have entered the business world, and more have assumed leadership roles. In 2004 three of the 16 cabinet ministers were women; in 2005 four of the nine Constitutional **Court** judges, including its president, were women. Two of the three Slovene universities had women provosts in 2005, and both directors of the Medical Research center in Ljubljana (*Klinični center*) were women.

Traditional gender stereotypes still prevail in Slovene society and are manifested in certain forms of discrimination against women. Women are the first to lose jobs; their pay is lower than men's; and child-bearing women have difficulties in finding employment. A 1994 study showed that employed married men spent on average six hours per week on household chores, while employed women spent about 23 hours. A similar study five years later confirmed the 1994 findings. An old Slovene saying still rings true today: "Women support three corners of the house and help their husbands hold up the fourth."

WORKERS' COUNCILS / DELAVSKI SVETI (1950–1990). Workers' councils (WCs), first established in Slovene factories in the spring of 1950, were the highest decision-making bodies and the functional base of **workers' self-management** (WSM). WCs were obligatory institutions in state-owned enterprises, according to the 1950 Basic Law on the Management of State Economic Enterprises and Higher Economic Associations by Workers' Collectives. During the 40 years of their existence, WCs developed from mere consultative bodies into powerful decision-making institutions, not only in economic enterprises but also in other spheres of social life. The WCs' role and functions changed and expanded over the years through legislation: the **Constitutional Law of 1953**, the **Constitution of 1963**, the **Constitution of 1974**, the Law on Elections in Self-Management Organs in Workers' Organizations of 1964 (amended in 1968), and the Law on Associated Labor of 1976.

A WC, elected by secret ballot for a term of two years, had from 30 to 150 members. In organizations of fewer than 30, everyone was a WC member, except those appointed to positions by the WC or performing managerial functions. The WC also elected a managing board (*upravni odbor*) and supervised its implementation of approved policies. While the vocational and educational level of WC members had to reflect the profile of their work organization, data show that WCs had disproportionally high numbers (40 to 50 percent) of League of Communists (LC) members.

With the decentralization of the **economy** after 1953, WCs acquired more responsibilities and decision-making power. Many large enterprises with central WCs were divided into smaller management units, each with its own WC, thus enabling many more workers to take part in decision-making. In the late 1960s, internal bylaws that regulated workers' self-management and their organs, including the election of a manager, were left to the discretion of individual WCs. The Law on Associated Labor of 1976 authorized WCs to make decisions on business policy and to propose and supervise their implementation, to approve short- and long-range development plans, and to decide all important financial matters, including investments and credits.

One of the major problems with the workers' councils was that they usually rubber-stamped decisions already made by management and often failed to voice the real concerns and problems of workers or the work organization. WC members often feared harassment for speaking out. Some were unable to understand complex technical materials distributed before the meetings or were otherwise poorly informed. Some simply did not care. Often, too, social ownership and little reward for hard work did not inspire workers toward efficiency or the development of work organizations. With the abolition of **social property** in 1990, workers' self-management and its institutions lost their reason for existence and were abolished.

WORKERS' SELF-MANAGEMENT (WSM) / DELAVSKO SAMOUPRAVLJANJE (1950–1990). Workers' self-management (WSM) was the basic institution that managed first the national

economy and later the society in general. It was introduced for two reasons. After **Yugoslavia**'s break with the **Cominform**, the party wanted to adopt a modernization plan that would avoid the errors of the Soviet model, and it needed the support of workers for the troubled economy. Under the slogan "Factories to the workers!" the Yugoslav **government**, already in 1949, initiated experimental **workers' councils** (*delavski sveti*) in state-owned economic enterprises. The concept of WSM was basically incompatible with the centrally planned economy. However, despite institutional changes toward decentralization, the economy remained centrally managed because the **Communist Party of Yugoslavia** (CPY) was reluctant to relinquish its power. *See also* ADMINISTRATIVE SOCIALISM.

A first transitional phase in the development of WSM, which ended in 1953, was marked by two important milestones. First, in 1952, a CPY congress formally endorsed WSM as a basic social principle. Renaming the party the League of Communists of Yugoslavia (LCY), it symbolically gave up its role as the direct manager of society and cast itself as the ideological guiding force of the self-management system. Secondly, the **Constitutional Law of 1953** extended decentralization and self-management to the non-economic organizations (culture, **education**, **health** and welfare, and local government). Non-economic organizations were run by *sveti* (councils), made up of elected employees and appointed members from political and government organizations, such as **local communities** and *občinas*. In order to bring decision-making closer to the workers, the managing of large enterprises was decentralized by dividing them up functionally into smaller independent work units with their own workers' councils. WSM was strengthened by the Labor Relations Law (1958), which transferred the power of hiring and firing from the general manager to the workers' council and its committees. Despite the legal authority of workers' councils to run their enterprises and dispose of their income, the federal government still retained almost complete control over income disposition, investments, prices, and foreign trade. In 1958 a workers' strike, the first in Communist Yugoslavia, took place at the coal mines at Trbovlje (Slovenia); workers protested federal price control policies and won. As a result, new legislation was prepared to give workers' management and market forces a greater role in shaping the national economy.

A new phase of WSM began in the early 1960s with the more aggressive introduction of **market socialism**. New legislation increased the autonomy of the enterprises and altered the role of the state in the national economy. In 1964 a Law on the Election of Self-Management Organs in Work Organizations was enacted. Workers were given greater power, and most matters in work organizations became regulated by internal bylaws adopted by the workers' councils. The 1968 constitutional amendments further extended workers' powers. A manager, appointed by the government for four years, also had to be approved by the workers' council. Despite the workers' councils' normative strengths, their autonomy was still restricted. Former state and CPY control were replaced by new ones: **banks**, local governments, and the managers of enterprises. These three, often allied with one another, did not always act in the best long-term interests of the workers or of the national economy. In the late 1960s, the economy continued to experience slower growth, high inflation, and inefficient use of capital and labor. This period also saw the development of self-managing communities of interest (SMCI), in which producers of goods were linked as users with the producers of **services**. These institutions replaced government agencies in planning and financing public services. However, again interfering with the natural development of the economy, the LCY tried, in the name of workers' interests and self-management, to gain control through social reorganization, elements of which were contained in the Constitutional Amendments of 1971, the **Constitution of 1974**, and the Law on Associated Labor of 1976. *See also* CONSTITUTION OF 1963; LIBERALIZATION OF THE 1960s.

The 1970s legislation introduced a period of **contractual socialism**; new social and economic reforms were meant to decentralize decision-making, strengthen WSM, and develop a socialist pluralism. Many new, complicated institutions were introduced, or new names invented for the old ones, among them: associated labor, organizations of associated labor, delegate system, social compacts and self-management agreements, free exchange of labor, courts of associated labor, and social legal defenders of self-management. All employed persons belonged to an organization of associated labor (*združeno delo*), where they were involved in the decision-making process. This required negotiating through a delegate system. Because of the very different interests among negotiating partners at local, republic, and federal levels, WSM became even more time-consuming, expensive, and inefficient. The delegate system was merely a charade and pretense at workers' self-management; the real centers of power were the LCY and the army, which accepted little responsibility for their actions. In the 1980s, with the economy collapsing, the new social system broke down. In 1990 Slovenia held its first multiparty **elections**, and political pluralism and a market economy were established. Workers' self-management, with all its institutions, was abolished.

WORLD TRADE CENTER. In April 1990, Smelt Engineering and the Slovene Chamber of Commerce established Slovenia's World Trade Center (WTC) as a member of the World Trade Center Association. In 1993 the WTC moved its headquarters into the WTC Ljubljana Office Tower and Shopping Mall in **Ljubljana**. The new 15-story structure houses 85 companies from various European, North American, and Asian countries, for whom the center provides technical support and consulting services relating to **international trade**. The WTC has a conference center and a restaurant, and it provides space for the Ljubljana **stock exchange** and for Gea College Business School. The mall has 80 shops, and there is an 800-car underground parking garage.

WORLD WAR I (1914–1918). The First World War began on 28 July 1914, when **Austria** declared war against Serbia in retaliation for the assassination of Archduke **Francis Ferdinand**. Within days Europe's major alliance systems were activated. Austria's chief ally was Germany; the two constituted the nucleus of the Central Powers. Their opponents, who supported Serbia, were **Russia**, France, and Britain—the main Entente forces.

The Slovenes, most of whom lived in the **Habsburg** Empire when the war broke out, fought for their country, as expected. They were sent to the Serbian front, where Austria did badly at first, and to the Russian front, where, as in Serbia, their opponents were fellow Slavs. On these two fronts Slovenes did not always remain loyal to Austria. Early on, many defected to Serbia and fought for the budding "Yugoslav" cause. Similar defections occurred on the eastern front, particularly when Russia's state fell into disarray and eventually revolution (1917). The Italian front, which opened up in mid-1915 after **Italy** was persuaded to join the Entente (London Pact, April, 1915), was a different matter. The Entente had promised Italy land populated by Slovenes and Croats. Hence on the western front, generally along the Soča (Isonzo) River, most Slovenes fought fiercely to keep their homes and land. In the Central Powers' last major offensive against Italy (October 1917), Austria's South Slavs, who did the most fighting here, held losses to one-fourth those of Italy. The chief battleground was at **Kobarid** (Caporetto), now in Slovenia.

During the last two years of the war, Slovene soldiers grew weary and mutinous, as did other participants in the war. In May 1918 Slovene soldiers, waiting to be sent to the Russian front, mutinied at Judenburg. Politically, Slovene representatives in the parliament, which had resumed meeting in May 1917, grew increasingly independence-minded. Even the **Clericals**, whose rightists (e.g., **Ivan Šušteršič**) in the press in 1914 had "greeted the Serbs with cannons," were talking about secession from Austria. Slovene parliamentary spokesmen were prominent in the **National Council of Slovenes, Croats, and Serbs**. With Austria's defeat and collapse in October and November 1918, that council would lead the bulk of Slovenia into a new state, the **Kingdom of Serbs, Croats, and Slovenes**. *See also* MAY DECLARATION; RAPALLO, TREATY OF.

WORLD WAR II (1941–1945). Although World War II began on 1 September 1939 with Germany's invasion of Poland (**Austria** and Czechoslovakia had already been subdued or dismembered), the war in **Yugoslavia** began nearly two years later, on 6 April 1941, with the German bombing of **Belgrade**. The German Reich had attempted to force Yugoslavia's allegiance (as it had with other Balkan states), but the Tripartite Pact (25 March 1941), accepted by Prince Paul (**Karadjordjević**), caused an immediate antigovernment coup. Yugoslavia was therefore attacked and quickly defeated, surrendering in Belgrade on 17 April. The **government** fled into exile, and Yugoslavia's neighbors eagerly exacted territorial spoils. In **Croatia** and the Serbian Protectorate, Axis satellite governments were established. Slovenia completely disappeared. The German Reich claimed the northern and eastern areas (Upper Carniola, Styria, and Posavje); **Hungary** took **Prekmurje**, and **Italy** annexed the rest.

A Slovene Anti-Imperialist Front, renamed the **Liberation Front** (LF; *Osvobodilna fronta*, OF) in late June after Germany's attack on the USSR, was organized on 27 April 1941. Slovene Communists (**Edvard Kardelj** and Franc Leskošek) took the initiative, although the **Communist Party of Yugoslavia** (CPY) was still awaiting directives from Moscow, which at the time was allied with Germany. The LF, headed by Josip Vidmar, an intellectual godfather of the Slovenes, united **Christian Socialists**, the liberal **Sokol** society members, and Slovene Communists in opposition to the Italian and German occupiers. The actual uprising, whose anniversary is celebrated on 22 July, extended to most Slovene lands (except Hungarian-occupied Prekmurje). Slovenes of the Littoral (a part of Italy during the interwar years) became a valuable addition to the **Partisan** resistance. The Partisan LF helped to liberate Slovenia, coordinating operations with **Tito**'s **National Liberation Struggle** (NOB) fighting elsewhere in Yugoslavia.

During the war the **Communist Party of Slovenia** (CPS), which organized and operationally controlled the resistance, began articulating its **Marxist** revolutionary goals. Although the CPS avoided stressing the party's role initially, in early 1943 it persuaded noncommunists in the LF to submit to unity under Communist leadership (**Dolomite Declaration**). Not all in Slovenia joined the LF. The **Village Guard** (*vaške straže*) in 1942 and the **Home Guard** (*domobranci*), who organized after the Italian capitulation in September 1943, mounted armed opposition to the leftist character as well as the excesses of the Partisan resistance. After 1943 the resistance was thus complicated by civil war. The Partisan resistance ultimately won, and many Home Guardists fled to Austria when the Germans retreated in May 1945. Many were sent back by the British, and most of them, treated as traitors, were summarily executed.

On 5 May 1945 the government arm of the LF established a Slovene government, the **Slovene National Liberation Council** (SNOS), at Ajdovščina. (In September 1943 a wartime assembly had already come to represent Slovenes in Partisan-held areas, who subsequently sent delegates to the **Antifascist Council of National Liberation of Yugoslavia** conferences.) On 29 November 1945 a **Federal People's Republic of Yugoslavia** (FPRY) was proclaimed, confirming Slovenia's autonomy within a federation. In July 1946 at the Paris Peace Conference, postwar borders for Yugoslavia were set. The settlement was quite significant for Slovenia, for although it was unable to obtain Carinthian Slovene lands (Austria was considered a victim, not an aggressor in World War II), Slovenia did acquire most territories that had belonged to Italy between the wars, significantly the Littoral and Slovenian Istria. Only Resia (Rezija) and **Gorizia** (Gorica) remained Italian, while the final settlement for the Free Territory of **Trieste** awaited a later decision. *See also* CONCENTRATION CAMPS; MASSACRES, POST-WORLD WAR II.

WRITERS, SOCIETY OF SLOVENE / DRUŠTVO SLOVEN-SKIH PISATELJEV.

The roots of the Society of Slovene Writers go back to the second half of the 19th century and *Društvo slovenskih književnikov*, a Slovene literary society established in 1872 that served as a support group for its members, organized cultural events, and erected commemorative monuments of Slovene cultural figures. The society was disbanded by the Austrian government in 1915. After **World War I** the Society of Slovene Belletrists (*Društvo slovenskih leposlovcev*) was organized anew and later renamed *Društvo slovenskih književnikov*. Its activities in the interwar period were few until 1939, when the society aided Czech writers financially. During the 1940s the number of Slovene writers was depleted. In **World War II** many who were **Partisans** or in **concentration camps** died, while most anticommunist writers **emigrated** from Slovenia immediately after the war.

After World War II the society became a member of the Yugoslav Union of Writers and lost its independence. Until 1952 the organization also included translators. Besides supporting its members and organizing cultural events, the society acted as a political agent. Immediately after the war, it fought against Yugoslav centralism. In the early 1950s the society's members became associated with journals that advocated literary pluralism; in the late 1950s they also expressed politically oppositional views. Since then, the society has been involved in broader social issues relating to the Slovene nation and its culture and **language**, and to freedom of speech and political pluralism. Since 1962 it has also welcomed Slovene writers living in exile. In 1968 the organization changed its name to the Society of Slovene Writers (*Društvo slovenskih pisateljev*). In the 1980s it stepped up its activities and played an important role in promoting Slovenia's **independence**. *See also* COMMUNIST PARTY, OPPOSITION TO; LIBERALIZATION OF THE 1960s; NOVA REVIJA; PERSPEKTIVE.

The society's membership has been growing: 71 members in 1948, 250 in 1987, and 314 in 2005. And it has organized many important cultural events (commemorations, conferences, congresses, educational activities) in Slovenia and abroad. It supports members' literary creativity and publications, and it annually awards four literary prizes: Desetnica for an original literary work by a young writer; the Jenko prize for poetry; the **Stritar** prize for a promising young writer; and the **Župančič** prize for translation. Since 1962, in addition to **publishing** a quarterly literary journal (*Le Livre Slovène*;

Litterae Slovenicae since 1991), the society has also subsidized the publication of Slovene literary works in more than 20 foreign languages worldwide. The society hosts prominent foreign writers visiting Slovenia and, since 1986, sponsors an international literary festival, Vilenica. Slovene writers are active in the Slovene **PEN Center**. *See also* LITERATURE.

WROUGHT IRON. The crafting of wrought iron is an old **art** among the Slovenes. It was developed in the 12th and 13th centuries and advanced in the 15th century with new smelting technology imported from neighboring Friuli. The term *fužina* (forge), used by Slovenes, is of Friulian origin. The new forges depended on water power and charcoal, both of which were plentiful—as was iron ore—in Slovenia's Alpine areas. Iron production was regulated by **mining** codes from the 16th century and promoted, particularly in the 17th and 18th centuries, by feudal landlords. New technology and diminishing ore supplies brought a decline in wrought-iron production after the mid-19th century. The old craft is still practiced, however, in Kropa (in Gorenjska), where iron has been forged for more than 500 years according to traditional methods. Most of the wrought iron that Kropa produces today is decorative.

– Y –

YOUTH ORGANIZATION, COMMUNIST. *See* LEAGUE OF COMMUNIST YOUTH OF YUGOSLAVIA.

YUGOSLAV NATIONAL PARTY / JUGOSLOVANSKA NACIONALNA STRANKA (JNS). *See* CLERICALS; JANUARY 6, 1929, DICTATORSHIP; LIBERALS; SERBS, CROATS, AND SLOVENES, KINGDOM OF; YUGOSLAVIA, KINGDOM OF.

YUGOSLAV PEOPLE'S ARMY. *See* ARMY, YUGOSLAV PEOPLE'S.

YUGOSLAV SOCIAL DEMOCRATIC PARTY (JSDS). *See* SOCIALISTS.

YUGOSLAVIA, KINGDOM OF (1929–1941). A Yugoslav state was created in the wake of **World War I** from remnants of the former Austro-Hungarian Empire and lands that were, or had in the 19th century been, part of the Ottoman Empire. From 1918 until 1929, when King Alexander proclaimed a royal dictatorship, the country, consisting primarily of South Slavs, was known as the **Kingdom of Serbs, Croats, and Slovenes**. Its capital was **Belgrade**, the capital of the former Kingdom of Serbia. Throughout the 1920s the state experienced the daunting problems typically associated with state building, while also grappling with postwar reconstruction. Conflicts over power and policy were commonplace and generally pitted national groups (albeit ostensibly members of one Yugoslav family) against one another.

Throughout the interwar years the peoples of Yugoslavia fundamentally disagreed over how the state should be governed. The Serbs generally supported centralism—rule from Belgrade. The **Vidovdan Constitution** symbolized Serbian centralism and was opposed by many of the state's other constituents. Slovenes (led by the SLS or **Clericals**), Bosnian Muslims, and especially the **Croats** pressed for federalism and autonomy for their respective groups. King Alexander found that nationalistic quarrels made it impossible to govern (even including the Croat Peasant Party in the government did not help), so he suspended the **constitution** and the parliament and proclaimed the **January 6, 1929, dictatorship**. He also renamed the country the Kingdom of Yugoslavia in order to foster Yugoslav political unitarism.

Neither a new constitution (1931) nor a new name improved the situation. Now divided into nine *banovinas* (six with Serb majorities), the country was more polarized than ever. Extremists, particularly on the right, promoted ultranationalism. Non-Serbs regarded Alexander's attempt to create Yugoslav unity as a foil for Great Serbism. In 1934 Croat extremists collaborated in the king's assassination in Marseille; Croat extremism ultimately forced Belgrade into making a deal with Croat moderates in 1939, which granted Croats an autonomous Croat *banovina*, of considerable size. In the end Croat autonomy did not save Yugoslavia. When the Axis powers invaded in April 1941, Croats leapt at the chance to establish their own state, even though it was a client of **Italy** and the German Reich. *See also* LITTLE ENTENTE.

YUGOSLAVIA, RELATIONS WITH. Before 1991 Slovenes were a part of the **Socialist Federal Republic of Yugoslavia** (SFRY), and they had lived together with other South Slavs in a common state since **World War I** ended in 1918. During those years, the country was run from **Belgrade**, the capital, in a centralistic way. In the period before **World War II**, a Serbian dynasty wielded power; during the postwar years, it was the Communist regime. In the mid-1980s, there developed a struggle within the SFRY for control of **Tito**'s Yugoslavia. It began earnestly in 1986 when the Serbian Academy of Arts and Science issued a statement urging Serbs to reassert their dominance of the entire country. Other national groups objected, but the Slovenes stood out in their resistance to Serb hegemony. The *Nova revija* (*New Review*) issue No. 57, published in 1987, was a direct reply to the Serbian Academy. In the ensuing years before Slovenia declared **independence**, the atmosphere between Serbs and Slovenes became increasingly tense. It was punctuated by demonstrations, firey rhetoric in the **media**, the **Ljubljana Four trial** (1988), the defection of the League of Communists of Slovenia (LCS) from the federal League in early 1990, and the **plebiscite for independence** (December 1990). When Slovenia and **Croatia** declared their independence in June 1991, Belgrade, increasingly controlled by Serbs, sent the national army against the Slovenes. Belgrade conceded after the **Ten-Day War**, allowing Slovenia to go its own way.

The next four and a half years were marked by bloody, genocidal wars in what is now the former Yugoslavia. The horrors were perpetrated largely by Serbs against the non-Serb population; Belgrade and the army were run by the Serbs' Slobodan Milošević, who was taken to The Hague in 2001 to be prosecuted for war crimes. The worst of it was borne by Bosnia-Hercegovina, but **Croatia** also suffered greatly. In those years, Slovenia tried hard to distance itself from Yugoslavia and the Balkans; its goal was to be rightfully recognized as a Central European state. Slovenia took in refugees from the south, and fought the fear of being drawn back into the struggle, which never quite subsided until a peace treaty was concluded in Dayton, Ohio, late in 1995.

Resuming relations with the rest of former Yugoslavia was a long, arduous process. First of all, Slovenia wanted nothing to do with the south—that was the past. But Europe disagreed; it wanted Slovenia to act as a liaison with the western Balkan states. Slowly, Slovenia's thinking moved in that direction, particularly because by 1997 **North Atlantic Treaty Orgzanization** (NATO) and **European Union** (EU) membership seemed dependent upon it. Slovenia resumed ties and established economic contacts with Macedonia, Bosnia-Hercegovina, and Croatia (particularly after Croatia's wartime president Franjo Tudjman died in late 1999). But relations were still iffy where Serbia was concerned. Serbia in the late 1990s had begun cracking down on the ethnic Albanians in Kosovo province, constitutionally a part of Serbia. The Slovenes had been early supporters of the Kosovars, going back to the 1980s. The Kosovo situation deteriorated into war in spring 1999, with even NATO striking out militarily against the Serbs. Kosovo, though still technically a province of Serbia, has been administered by the **United Nations** since 1999. Serbia lingered under the control of Slobodan Milošević for another year; in fall 2000 he was ousted by a popular revolution and removed to The Hague in 2001, where he died in 2006.

The SFRY had changed its name to the Federal Republic of Yugoslavia (FRY) in 1992, when it consisted of only two republics, Serbia and Montenegro. The FRY was not permitted to succeed to the SFRY's seat at the United Nations, and it remained outside the UN for eight years. As soon as Serbia was rid of Milošević in late 2000, the United Nations recognized the Federal Republic of Yugoslavia (FRY) as its member. Slovenia and the FRY established diplomatic ties in December 2000. In February 2003, the country was renamed Serbia and Montenegro. Montenegro became independent in June 2006, and Kosovo appears to be moving in that direction as well.

With the former Yugoslav states relatively stabilized, the major task of settling the succession of the former Yugoslavia could be undertaken. A committee to supervise that process had met for the first time in March 1992, and Slovenia was an active participant from the beginning. However, given the turmoil in the area, little headway could be made until there was a regime change in Serbia. A meeting of the five successor states was scheduled for December 2000, and it produced serious results. A Succession Agreement was initialed in **Vienna** in June 2001. The chief arbiter of the settlement was Sir Arthur Watts, who was able to get the states at least to begin the process by agreeing to focus on three aspects of the settlement: dividing the SFRY archives, dividing gold assets, and dividing embassy and consular properties abroad. Slovenia was awarded 16 percent of the SFRY's assets and 14 percent of its embassies, including the Washington, D.C., embassy. The division of the common property was undertaken according to International Monetary Fund (IMF) criteria and a formula prepared by it. The task continues to be complex, given that even the dates of independence for the new states vary. Each of the five governments needed to ratify the agreement—the last to do so was Croatia in March 2004—before the process went into effect. The issue of Slovenia's portion of Yugoslavia's collective debt had been resolved earlier, with Slovenia accepting an obligation for 16 percent of unallocated government debt in 1993. Its portion of commercial bank debt was settled at 18 percent in 1996. Some issues of specific Slovene debt (e.g., Ljubljanska Banka's debts in Croatia and Bosnia-Hercegovina) are still to be resolved and will probably be mediated by an international financial institution. Since 2001 and the exchange of diplomats, Slovene–Serb contacts have broadened on many levels. Most bilateral activity has been in the area of business and finance. Slovenes have opened or reopened Slovene businesses in Serbia, and more than 128 investments have been made in Serbia and Montenegro. Slovenes know the language, are familiar with the culture, and have former business contacts, which give them an edge over outside businesses and **banks**. Slovene and Serbian officials have also met more frequently. In 2005 they agreed to increase bilateral economic interaction and to pursue talks on settling the status of Kosovo. Slovenia has also agreed to instruct Serb personnel on European legislation in preparation for Serbia's bid to join the European Union. Meanwhile Slovenia continues to participate in multilateral organizations, such as the Stability Pact for Southeastern Europe, NATO, the EU, and the **Organization for Security and Cooperation in Europe** (OSCE), that deal locally and on a daily basis with the issues relating to the former Yugoslavia, but particularly Serbia and Montenegro.

YUGOSLAVISM. The "Yugoslav Idea," or Yugoslavism, originated about the time of the French Revolution as a political concept expressing the desire for unification of the South Slavs (Serbs, Croats, Slovenes, and sometimes Bulgarians) in a common sovereign state. It is often associated with **Illyrism**, which is based on the sense that South Slavs have common linguistic and cultural roots and belong to one ethnic family. From the beginning, Yugoslavism acknowledged the diversity of the various Yugoslav nations, each seeking political unity (strength in greater numbers) in order that individual interests (especially cultural) might be fulfilled. A Slovene, for example, might well support the creation of an independent **Yugoslavia** in order that the Slovene nation realizes its own idea. Conceptually, Yugoslavism was democratic.

In the period between the two world wars, Yugoslavism as a concept was redefined by the ruling Serbian dynasty, which interpreted it as requiring national unity and uniformity. **Belgrade** set the criteria. In the post-1945 period, the ruling Communists equated Yugoslavism with internationalism. Slovene, Croat, and other national loyalties were regarded as decadent and bourgeois, while Yugoslav unity was hailed as historically progressive and compatible with **Marxist** internationalism. Belgrade's rulers again set the standard.

– Z –

ZDRUŽENA LISTA SOCIALNIH DEMOKRATOV (ZLSD). *See* UNITED LIST OF SOCIAL DEMOCRATS.

ZELENI SLOVENIJE. *See* GREENS OF SLOVENIA.

ZOIS, ŽIGA (1747–1819). Born in **Trieste** to a well-to-do merchant family, Žiga (Sigismund) Zois was educated in the fashion of the French Encyclopedists in **Italy** and by the **Jesuits** in **Ljubljana**. Although Zois became a large landowner and proprietor of **mines** and smelting furnaces in the Slovene lands, he and his brother Karel were more interested in **science** than in business and trade, and both made important contributions to the field. Highly educated, Zois had contacts with well-known European scientists, owned a rich **library**, and built one of the largest mineral collections in Europe, which formed the base of the National Museum in Ljubljana. Zois did research on *Proteus anguinus*, a unique amphibian endemic to **karst** caves, and other animals. In **Carinthia**, he discovered a colorful silicate mineral, named zoisite after him. Zois was a member of several scientific associations in Europe.

A scientist and inventor, poet, translator, and patron of Slovene cultural figures of the time, including Jurij Japelj, **Jernej Kopitar**, and **Blaž Kumerdej**, Zois was one of the most important personages of the Slovene **Enlightenment** and had a key role in its development in Slovene lands. Zois tried to introduce new poetic forms into Slovene **literature** and encouraged intellectuals to write Slovene books (grammars, dictionaries, and histories). His collaboration with **Anton Tomaž Linhart**, who later joined the Zois circle, was especially productive in **theater** and history. Zois also supported **Valentin Vodnik** in **publishing** the first Slovene newspaper, *Lublanske novice* (*Ljubljana News*). In 1998 the highest awards for research and scientific achievements in the **Republic of Slovenia** (RS) were named after Zois. *See also* PRESS BEFORE 1990.

ZVEZA SINDIKATOV JUGOSLAVIJE (ZSJ). *See* TRADE UNIONS.

ZVEZA ZDRUŽENJ BORCEV IN UDELEŽENCEV NARODO-NOOSVOBODILNE BORBE SLOVENIJE (ZZB NOB SLOVE-NIJE). *See* VETERANS.

ZVEZA ZDRUŽENJ BORCEV NARODONOOSVOBODILNE VOJNE SLOVENIJE (ZZB NOV Slovenije). *See* VETERANS.

– Ž –

ŽEBOT, CIRIL (1914–1989). Ciril Žebot studied law in **Ljubljana** and specialized in economics in Milan and Paris in the late 1930s. He was active in the **Catholic student movement** at the **University of Ljubljana**. Before **World War II** Žebot worked in **Belgrade**, where he had close ties to Slovene politicians in the Yugoslav **government**, such as **Anton Korošec** and **Miha Krek**. During the war, Žebot worked with **Lambert Ehrlich** on plans to establish an **independent** Slovenia after the war. In 1942, after Ehrlich's assassination by the **Security and Intelligence Service** (*Varnostno obveščevalna služba*, VOS), Žebot wrote a short book, *Narod sredi Evrope* (A Nation in the Middle of Europe), in which he unveiled Ehrlich's vision for solving the Slovene national problem. According to Ehrlich and Žebot, **United Slovenia** was to be an independent state and a member of a Central European confederation. The book was printed clandestinely in a limited edition and smuggled to the West.

In 1943, after **Italy**'s capitulation, Žebot settled in the Vatican to escape the Germans, who were pursuing his family. His father, who had been a member of the Yugoslav parliament and deputy mayor of **Maribor**, was interned at Dachau, where he died. After World War II, Žebot **emigrated** to the **United States** (1947), where he taught economics at Duquesne University in Pittsburgh and, after 1958, at Georgetown University in Washington, D.C. In exile, he headed the movement for an independent Slovene state. In the late 1960s he tried to establish contacts with the liberal Communists in Slovenia. In 1968 the Slovene authorities helped him organize a visit to Ljubljana, which caused sharp criticism of the **Stane Kavčič** government. In addition to publishing numerous professional texts, Žebot wrote two books of importance for Slovenia: the two-volume *Slovenija, včeraj, danes in jutri* (Slovenia Yesterday, Today, and Tomorrow, 1967 and 1969), and *Neminljiva Slovenija* (Everlasting Slovenia, 1988), both published by the author and printed by the **Society of St. Hermagoras** in **Klagenfurt**. *See also* CATHOLIC ACTION; LIBERALIZATION OF THE 1960s.

ŽIŽEK, SLAVOJ (1949–). The internationally famous philosopher and Slovene intellectual icon Slavoj Žižek was born in **Ljubljana**. There he studied sociology and philosophy, receiving a B.A. (1971 and Ph.D. (1981) from the **University of Ljubljana**. He then went on to the University of Paris for a doctorate in psychoanalysis (1985). Since 1979 he has been at the University of Ljubljana's Institute for Sociology and Philosophy (after 1992 the Institute for Social Studies). Since 1982 he has also held numerous visiting appointments at universities abroad, mostly in the **United States**. His more than a hundred publications are available in at least 15 languages—many of them originally written in English, a language in which Žižek is fluent. Their topics demonstrate his expertise in **Marxism**, German classical philosophy, psychoanalysis, and the theoretical works of Jacques Lacan, of whom he is a disciple. Žižek, who identifies himself as a traditional Marxist, purports to be not answering questions about contemporary society but rather reframing questions about it. Using psychoanalysis and Lacanian theory, he has been interpreting the current stage of economic development: global capitalism and its cultural, political, and social manifestations.

Žižek writes and lectures in a popular vein, attacking all subjects from the universal to the trivial, and explaining them in terms of his larger contextual framework. Film (Alfred Hitchcock), opera, politics, 9/11, religion, and the **Neue Slowenische Kunst** (NSK) and its Laibach component in 1980s Slovenia are all subjects he has addressed. A loud, rapidly speaking, gesticulating bear of a man, he has attracted huge audiences, particularly abroad, where listeners sit in rapt attention then erupt into cheers of approval when he finishes. He has been called "the Elvis of Popular Culture" and was the subject of a feature-length documentary, *Žižek!*, that premiered in late 2005 at the Toronto film festival and has been drawing crowds of admirers. Books have been written about him, including Matthew Sharpe's *Slavoj Žižek: A Little Piece of the Real*, and Blackwell Publishers has put out *The Žižek Reader* as part of its series on the works of essential philosophers. He is among the more widely read and most influential theorists of the late 20th century.

As a student, Žižek associated with the League of Socialist Youth of Slovenia (ZSMS) and migrated with it into the Liberal Democratic Party (LDS). In 1990, in Slovenia's first multiparty election, Žižek ran for a post on the four-person presidency. He came in fifth.

ŽUPANČIČ, OTON (1878–1949). Oton Župančič, a poet, playwright, and essayist, was one of four main representatives of Slovene **Moderna**. After his studies of history and geography in **Vienna**, he spent several years (1902–1910) traveling in Europe, where he came into contact with contemporary European **literature**. Between the two world wars, besides writing and translating, Župančič devoted much time to **theater**. In the 1920s he wrote a tragedy, *Veronika Deseniška* (Veronika of Desenice), and translated numerous plays by Shakespeare, Molière, and others. During **World War II** he worked with the **Liberation Front** (LF), writing poems for the **Partisan** press. After the war, he became a member of the Slovene assembly and of the **Slovenian Academy of Sciences and Arts** (SAZU).

Župančič's writing span as a poet is long—over 50 years—and varied. His first collection, *Čaša opojnosti* (Intoxicating Cup, 1899), was mostly **impressionistic**, reflecting **folk** motifs and **romanticism**. His second collection, *Čez plan* (Across the Plain, 1904), dedicated to his contemporary, the poet Josip Murn, was influenced by Friedrich Nietzsche and motifs of his native **Bela Krajina**, and it shows a turn toward symbolism. His poetry was also influenced by Walt Whitman and Henri Bergson, as is seen in the collection *Samogovori* (Soliloquies, 1908), which contains his best patriotic poems, including *Duma* (Meditation) and *Z vlakom* (By Train). In his last collection, *Zimzelen pod snegom* (Myrtle under the Snow, 1945), with motifs mostly from the **National Liberation Struggle** (NOB), he returned to romantic poetic forms. Župančič also wrote excellent children's poetry, published in several collections, among which *Pisanice* (Easter Eggs, 1900) and *Ciciban* (1915) are known to every Slovene child.

Appendix 1

Rulers of Slovene Lands

HABSBURG EMPERORS AND EMPRESSES OF THE MODERN PERIOD

Charles VI	1711–1740
Maria Theresa	1740–1780
Joseph II	1765–1790 (co-ruled with Maria Theresa, his mother, 1765–1780)
Leopold II	1790–1792
Francis II (I)	1792–1804; 1804–1835 (Holy Roman Empire numerals before 1804, Austrian after 1804)
Ferdinand I	1835–1848
Francis Joseph	1848–1916
Charles I	1916–1918

KARADJORDJEVIĆ RULERS (KINGS OF YUGOSLAVIA, 1918–1943)

Peter I	1921 (rule began in 1903 as King of Serbia)
Alexander	1921–1934
Peter II	1934–1943 (authority suspended in 1943)

COMMUNIST RULERS OF YUGOSLAVIA

Federal Executive Council Presidents (SFRY Prime Ministers)

Josip Broz Tito	1943–1963 (head of the federal government under various titles)
Petar Stambolić	1963–1967
Mika Špiljak	1967–1969

Mitja Ribičič (Slovene)   1969–1971
Džemal Bijedić   1971–1977
Veselin Djuranović   1977–1982
Milka Planinc   1982–1986
Branko Mikulić   1986–1988 (forced to resign in December)
Ante Marković   1988–1991

Federal Presidency (SFRY Presidents)

Josip Broz Tito

1974, post of president for life by special constitutional provision (after death in May 1980, representatives from the six republics and two autonomous provinces assumed the presidency according to a rotation stipulated by the Constitution of 1974, with presidential terms of one year)

Cvijetan Mijatović (Bosnia-Hercegovina)	1980–1981
Sergej Kraigher (Slovenia)	1981–1982
Petar Stambolić (Serbia)	1982–1983
Mika Špiljak (Croatia)	1983–1984
Veselin Djuranović (Montenegro)	1984–1985
Radovan Vlajković (Vojvodina)	1985–1986
Sinan Hasani (Kosovo)	1986–1987
Lazar Mojsov (Macedonia)	1987–1988
Raif Dizdarević (Bosnia-Hercegovina)	1988–1989
Janez Drnovšek (Slovenia)	1989–1990
Borisav Jović (Serbia)	1990–1991

Stipe Mesić (Croatia)

July 1991 (normal rotation broke down in May, with Serbs refusing to accept a Croat president; Mesić's presidency was forced by European Community pressure, but with war in full swing Mesić was never able to exercise power)

COMMUNIST RULERS OF SLOVENIA (LRS, SRS)

Presidents of the Executive Council (Slovene Prime Ministers)

Josip Vidmar	February 1944–May 1945, noncommunist
Boris Kidrič	May 1945–June 1946
Miha Marinko	June 1946–December 1953
Boris Kraigher	December 1953–June 1962
Viktor Avbelj	June 1962–April 1965
Janko Smole	April 1965–May 1967
Stane Kavčič	May 1967–November 1972
Andrej Marinc	November 1972–May 1978
Anton Vratuša	May 1978–July 1980
Janez Zemljarič	July 1980–May 1984
Dušan Šinigoj	May 1984–May 1990

Presidents of Presidency of Slovenia (Introduced with 1974 Constitution)

Sergej Kraigher	1974–1979
Viktor Avbelj	1979–1984
Franc Popit	1984–1987
Janez Stanovnik	1987–1990

Presidents of SRS Assembly (after 1963)

Ivan Maček	April 1963–May 1967
Sergej Kraigher	May 1967–May 1974
Marijan Brecelj	May 1974–May 1978
Milan Kučan	May 1978–May 1982
Vinko Hafner	May 1982–May 1986
Miran Potrč	May 1986–April 1990

Secretaries, Later Presidents, of the CC-LCS

Miha Marinko	1961–1966
Albert Jakopič	1966–1968
Franc Popit	1968–1982
Andrej Marinc	1982–1986
Milan Kučan	1986–1990

Presidents of SAWP (Socialist Alliance Heads in Slovenia)

Albert Jakopič	1962–1963
Vida Tomšič	1963–1967
Janez Vipotnik	1967–1972
Mitja Ribičič	1972–1982
Franc Šetinc	1982–1986
Jože Smole	1986–1990

RULERS OF INDEPENDENT SLOVENIA

Presidents of Independent Slovenia

Milan Kučan	1992–1997
Milan Kučan	1997–2002
Janez Drnovšek	2002–

Prime Ministers of Independent Slovenia

Lojze Peterle	May 1990–May 1992 (elected before Slovenia became independent on 25 June 1991)
Janez Drnovšek	May 1992–December 1992
Janez Drnovšek	December 1992–November 1996
Janez Drnovšek	November 1996–May 2000
Andrej Bajuk	May 2000–November 2000
Janez Drnovšek	November 2000–December 2002
Anton Rop	December 2002–December 2004
Janez Janša	December 2004–

Appendix 2

Selected Macroeconomic Indicators of Slovenia, 1995–2005

	1995	1997	1999	2001	2003	2004	2005
Gross domestic product, real growth (percent)	4.1	4.6	5.2	2.7	2.7	4.2	3.9
GDP per capita in US$ at current exchange rate	9,431	9,163	10,109	9,925	14,057	16,269	17,008
GDP per capita in US$ at purchasing power parity (PPP)	11,300	12,800	14,500	15,400	16,500	17,900	18,900
Structure of GDP (percent)							
Agriculture, forestry, and fishing	4.6	4.3	3.7	3.0	2.6	2.5	2.3
Manufacturing and construction	38.5	38.2	38.3	35.9	35.6	35.1	34.5
Services	59.2	59.8	60.3	61.1	61.9	62.3	63.2
Employment, productivity, wages							
Rate of unemployment by ILO* method (percent)	7.4	7.4	7.6	6.4	6.7	6.3	6.5
Labor productivity (growth percentage, GDP per capita)	2.5	5.2	3.3	2.2	2.9	3.7	3.1
Wage growth per employee (percent)	5.1	2.4	3.3	3.2	1.8	2.0	2.2
International trade, balance of payments							
Export of goods and services, percent of GDP	55.3	57.4	52.4	57.2	55.8	60.0	64.8
Import of goods and services, percent of GDP	57.2	58.2	56.8	57.8	55.8	61.3	65.3
Foreign exchange reserve, in millions of dollars/euros**	2,703	3,965	4,104	6,514	7,703	7,484	8,832
External debt, percentage of GDP	15.8	22.6	26.9	47.1	53.3	58.4	71.5
National Accounts							
Government deficit (percent of GDP)	0.0	1.1	0.6	1.3	1.4	1.4	1.1
General government debt (percent of GDP)	32.2	32.7	35.2	28.3	29.4	29.5	29.0
Inflation, annual average (percent)	12.6	9.1	6.1	8.4	5.6	3.6	2.5

* International Labor Organization
** Millions of US dollars for 1995–1999; millions of euros for 2001–2005
Data for 1995–1999 are from *Autumn Report*, 1 December 2003. Ljubljana: Institute of Macroeconomic Analysis and Development (*Urad za makroekonomske analize in razvo*). Data for 2001–2005 are from *Slovenia: Spring Report 2006*. Ljubljana: Institute of Macroeconomic Analysis and Development, July 2006.
Reports are available at www.sigov.sl/zmar/apublic/analiza.

Bibliography

CONTENTS

INTRODUCTION

There is a wealth of published material in Slovene on most aspects of Slovene life and fields of Slovene study. Even gaps, such as the dearth of publications on 20th-century history, are being filled with some fine new works. In English, new book-length publications are also now appearing, although perhaps not quickly enough. The reader is urged to seek out some of the articles that have appeared in English-language journals, particularly *Slovene Studies*. In this selected bibliography, we have stressed newer publications, although publications in English have been included regardless of when they were published. All sources in various languages that were used in the preparation for this book have been included.

Bibliographies on Slovenes and Slovenia tend to be field specific. The most comprehensive work in English is Cathie Carmichael's *Slovenia* bibliography, which is very useful although 10 years old. Also useful is Olga Janša-Zorn's *Slovenian Historiography in Foreign Languages*. On geography, the new *National Atlas of Slovenia* is a must, as is the Ivan Gams article "The Republic of Slovenia: Geographical Constants of the New Central-European State," published in *Geojournal*. Of travel and descriptive information available in English, Steve Fallon's *Lonely Planet Slovenia* is very good, regularly updated, and available abroad. Also recommended are Repoša's *Discover Slovenia* and Chvatal and Božek's *Slovenija*.

The best comprehensive and general historical work in English is James Gow and Cathie Carmichael's *Slovenia and the Slovenes: A Small Nation and the New Europe.* An excellent survey of Slovene political and economic life from the mid-19th century through 2000, with a look at cultural heritage from the mid-1500s, the book's coverage is chronological but also offers provocative themes. Three publications on the pre–World War I period that merit notice are: Robert Kann's chapter "The Slovenes" in his two-volume work *The Multinational Empire: Nationalism and National Reform in the Habsburg Monarchy 1848–1914*; Fran Zwitter's "The Slovenes in the Habsburg Monarchy," in *Austrian History Yearbook*; and Carole Rogel's *The Slovenes and Yugoslavism 1890–1914*. The focus of all three works is nationalism of the period.

Joseph Rothschild's chapter "Yugoslavia" in *East Central Europe between the Two World Wars* is a very good, accessible introduction to the interwar period. No balanced or comprehensive descriptions on World War II exist in English. There is Helga Harriman's *Slovenia under Nazi Occupation*, and Sabrina Ramet's *The Three Yugoslavias: State-Building and Legitimation, 1918–2005*, a 2006 publication that includes the results of the latest Slovene research on the war period. Bogdan Novak, in his definitive classical study *Trieste 1941–1954*, covers the Slovene–Italian struggle over Trieste beginning with the outset of the war and covering the postwar years of Allied occupation. Also recommended is Metod Milač's poignant personal memoir *Resistance, Imprisonment, and Forced Labor: A Slovene Student in World War II.*

Dennison Rusinow's *The Yugoslav Experiment, 1948–1974*, although a general work, is a monumental study that lays the groundwork for the impending constitutional, economic, and political crisis in Yugoslavia in the 1980s. So, too, does Sabrina Ramet's *Nationalism and Federalism in Yugoslavia 1962–1991*, where the conflict between Belgrade and Yugoslavia's republics is featured. "The Devil's Finger: The Disintegration of Yugoslavia," in *The Walls Came Tumbling Down*, expertly reviews the causes and chronology of the beginnings of Yugoslavia's disintegration. Viktor Meier continues the story through 1992 in *Yugoslavia: A History of its Demise*. Translated from the German, Meier's book focuses particularly on Slovenia, since so much of the early disintegration involved Yugoslavia's northernmost republic. For a brief survey of Yugoslav history and its effects through 2004, see Carole Rogel's *The Break-Up of Yugoslavia and Its Aftermath.*

Shortly after Slovenia became independent in 1991, two very good publications in English introduced the new country. "Voices from the Slovene Nation, 1990–1992," published by *Nationalities Papers* (Henry R. Huttenbach and Peter Vodopivec, eds.), featured articles by leading Slovenes who were intellectually and politically engaged in current events. *Independent Slovenia: Origins, Movements, Prospects* (Jill Benderly and Evan Kraft, eds.) contains 11 essays by noted scholars who wrote on aspects of the Slovene past and its future potential. The creation of an independent Slovenia is told in *Making of a New Nation: The Formation of Slovenia*, the work of two political scientists, Danica Fink-Hafner and John R. Robbins. Sabrina Ramet and Danica Fink-Hafner, editors of the recent *Democratic Transition in Slovenia*, followed up on how the new state was working from a variety of social and political perspectives. Zlatko Švabič and Charles Bukowski, turning to international and military topics, produced a fine work entitled *Small States in the Post–Cold War World: Slovenia and NATO Enlargement.*

There are only a few comprehensive sources on either economic history or economic developments of independent Slovenia. *The Economic History of Slovenia (1750–1991)* offers a general, brief, yet interesting description of Slovenia's economic development before independence. For economic developments in independent Slovenia up to its accession into the European Union, the most comprehensive source is perhaps the World Bank publication *Slovenia: From Yugoslavia to the European Union.* Reports and analyses on the economy are also readily available in print and electronically in English from various Slovene governmental institutions, such as the Institute for Macroeconomic Analysis and Development. Since 2004, data on the economy and other key indicators from all spheres of life can be obtained from the Statistical Office of the European Communities Eurostat. *The Economist* Intelligence Unit publishes periodic reports on Slovenia, containing overviews of the latest political and economic developments (also available online). A good international and comparative view of Slovenia's developments can be obtained in the *World Competitiveness Yearbook*, published by the Institute for Management (Lausanne, Switzerland) and *World Economic Outlook* by the International Monetary Fund (Washington, D.C.).

Slovenes have been defined by their culture and arts, but no single comprehensive English source is available on arts and architecture. Lev Menaše's beautifully illustrated book *Art Treasures of Slovenia* covers art objects from the prehistoric times through impressionist paintings of the early 20th century. Religious art, which dominated Slovene arts before the 20th century, is introduced briefly but comprehensively in the illustrated *Religious Art in Slovenia*, by Jože Anderlič and Marijan Zadnikar. Early 20th-century art is briefly but interestingly covered in *Modern Art in Eastern Europe*, by Steven Mansbach. There are several English sources on Jože Plečnik, the giant of Slovene and European 20th-century architecture. English sources on Slovene contemporary art, especially since the 1980s, are numerous. Moderna Galerija (Museum of Modern Art) published three volumes, each covering one decade on contemporary visual arts, architecture, design, film, photography, and theater from 1975 to 2005. These books, although in Slovene, have good English summaries and voluminous appendices of photographed art. Among the texts published outside Slovenia, mostly contextualized with wider art trends, Paul Crowther's *The Language of 20th-Century Art: A Conceptual History* covers at length some key Slovene contemporary and innovative artists of the 1980s and 1990s. Two very good and easily accessible sources on art movements in the 1980s and 1990s are the chapter "Neue Slowenische Kunst—Slovenian Art" by Aleš

Erjavec in *Postmodernism and the Post-Socialist Conditions: Politicized Art under Late Socialism*, and an excellent *East Art Map: Contemporary Art and Eastern Europe* by the Irwin group.

On music, for a historical overview, the bilingual Slovene–English proceedings *300 let/Years Academia Philharmonicorum Labacensium 1701–2001* may be consulted. There are also other interesting sources dealing with specific subjects, such as Renaissance music by the noted Jacobus Gallus in his *Moralia— Harmoniae Morales*. Andrej Rijavec's *Twentieth-Century Slovene Composers* may be consulted for contemporary music. Those interested in folk music should consult the bilingual *Glasba in manjšine / Music and Minorities*.

For Slovene literature, the bilingual anthology *Slovene Literature: A Brief Survey of Slovene Literature* (Henry Cooper, ed.), which covers prose and poetry from the 16th through the 20th century, is probably the most representative short historical overview. Slovene literature also can be found in broader anthologies such as *South Slavic Writers since World War II* (Mihailovich, ed.). The bibliography *Key: Slovenia: Contemporary Slovenian Literature in Translation* is a good guide to literary works available in English, published in Slovenia and abroad. Easily accessible information on Slovene literature in English can be found on the regularly updated website www.ijs.si/lit/slov_lit.html-12, authored by Miran Hladnik since 1997. Slovene contemporary literature is also discussed in Andrew Wachtel's *Making a Nation, Breaking a Nation: Literature and Cultural Politics in Yugoslavia*.

For those interested in the Slovene language, *Structure and History of the Slovene Language* by Rado Lenček remains the basic and comprehensive linguistic source. Various Slovene–English and English–Slovene dictionaries are commercially available in print and in electronic form. The most recent, though incomplete, is *The Great Oxford English–Slovene Dictionary, vol. 1 A–K*. A comprehensive grammar *Slovene* by Peter Herrity has been available since 2000. For language learning, Hladnik-Hočevar's *Slovenian for Travelers*, also available electronically with periodical updates, is the most basic and handy practical textbook for foreigners. There is a number of Slovene-language textbooks, but most are not designed for self-study. One exception is Andrea Albretti's *Slovene: Teach Yourself* (2006). Since summer 2006, the *Distance Slovene Course* is available online at no cost.

Social issues are covered in specialized publications and articles. Although brief, Ivan Svetlik's *Social Policy in Slovenia: Between Tradition and Innovation* is a useful general introduction. For a historical perspective on education, one can consult the English Summary in the Ciperle-Vovk book *Šolstvo na Slovenskem skozi stoletja* (*Schooling in Slovenia through the Centuries*); Barica Marentič-Požarnik's contributions "Slovenia: System of Education" to *The International Encyclopedia of Education* and to *White Paper on Education in the Republic of Slovenia*. The latter book is also a good source of basic information on the proposed educational reform that has been underway during the last decade. A more up-to-date source is the Eurydice publication *The Education System in Slovenia*, available online at www.msys.si/eurydice.

Religion in Slovenia is discussed by Slovene scholars in *Religion during and after Communism* (Tomka and Zulehner, eds.). Very informative is France Dolinar's "Normalization of Church/State Relations in Yugoslavia 1945– " in *Slovene Studies* 17 (1995). Since 1998, information on media-related issues have been reported in Media Watch Edition by the Peace Institute, which carries out research and publishes on cultural, political, and social issues, with an emphasis on gender issues, human rights, and minorities. Research reports, published as books in Slovene, and many also in English, are also available for download as ebooks. (See the section on selected websites in this bibliography.)

Archival materials on Slovene economics, history, politics, and belles-lettres are located primarily in Slovenia. It should be noted, however, that since Slovenes have lived for much of their history under foreign rule, archives pertaining to them may also be found in nearby countries: Austria, France (Illyrian Provinces, 1809–1813), Germany (World War II occupation), Hungary, Italy (Venetian Republic and later), Yugoslavia (Royal and Socialist). Materials of the 20th century can also be found in the U.S. National Archives (www.archives.gov) and in Great Britain, particularly as they pertain to World War II and the Allied occupation of Trieste. In Slovenia, there are seven major archives. The most important is the Archive of the Republic of Slovenia (www.arhiv.gov.si). The other six archives are in Ljubljana and major provincial towns: Celje, Koper, Maribor, Nova Gorica, and Ptuj. Information about all these can be found at www.culturalprofiles.net/Slovenia/Directories/Slovenia_Cultural_Profile/-7178.html. This website also provides information and links to smaller archives, such as those pertaining to film, the media (radio and television), as well as to a very important source for early history and genealogy, the Roman Catholic Church's archives housed at the archdiocese of Ljubljana, and the dioceses of Koper and Maribor. The National Manuscript Collection can be found at the National and University Library (NUK). A link to NUK and all Slovene archival databases can be found at the cultural profiles site noted above.

Archival material and information on immigrants and immigration, as expected, are available in Slovenia as well as abroad. Some are located at NUK, others in the Studia Slovenica collection, the private library of John Arnež, who brought his collection from New York City when he returned to Slovenia some years ago (studia.slovenica@guest.arnes.si), and through the Institute for Slovene Emigration Studies (SAZU website is listed later). For Slovenes who emigrated to the United States, the best source is the University of Minnesota's Immigration History Research Center, established in the 1960s: www.ihrc.umn.edu. The Western Reserve Historical Society has a rich collection of materials on Cleveland Slovenes, which includes oral histories: www.wrhs.org/template.asp?id=158.

In the United States there are several library collections with significant Slovene holdings. Both Harvard University (Cambridge, Massachusetts) and

Columbia University (New York) established collections before World War II and hold important 19th- and early 20th-century periodicals as well as later publications. The Library of Congress (www.loc.gov) and the libraries of a number of state universities built or enlarged their holdings after 1945, using Public Law 480 monies that were available for library purchases. Among those state universities are Indiana University, Ohio State University, the University of Kansas, the University of Michigan, the University of Washington, and the University of Illinois, whose excellent website gives a good summary of its holdings: www.library.uiuc.edu/spx/resources/Slovenia.htm. The state universities generally also developed Slavic and East European studies centers during the post–World War II period. In Europe there are two notable centers for information about Slovenes and Slovenia: the School of Slavonic Studies in London (Great Britain) and the European University Institute (Florence, Italy). For British library material, see www.ssees.ac.uk/slovenia.htm. For the European University Institute, see www.iue.it/LIB/.

I. GENERAL

Note: To simplify the multiple citations of sources published by two Slovene scholarly institutions, those institutions are identified in the relevant entries only by the customary acronyms of their Slovene titles as follows:

FDV: Fakulteta za družbene vede, Univerza v Ljubljani / School for Social Sciences, University of Ljubljana.

ZRC SAZU: Znanstveno-raziskovalni center, Slovenska akademija znanosti in umetnosti / Scientific Research Center, Slovene Academy of Sciences and Arts.

A. BIBLIOGRAPHIES AND DICTIONARIES

Bajec, Anton, et al. *Slovar slovenskega knjižnega jezika* (Dictionary of Standard Slovene, condensed book with electronic version). Ljubljana: ZRC SAZU/ Državna založba Slovenije, 1998.

Bezlaj, France. *Etimološki slovar slovenskega jezika* (Etymological Dictionary of the Slovene Language). 4 vols. Ljubljana: ZRC SAZU/Mladinska knjiga, 1977, 1982, 1995, and 2005. Vols. 3 and 4 were completed and edited by Metka Furlan and Marko Snoj.

Blatnik, Andrej, et al. *Key: Slovenia: Contemporary Slovenian Literature in Translation*. Ljubljana: Študentska založba, 2002.

Carmichael, Cathie. *Slovenia*. (Bibliography.) Oxford: Clio Press, 1996.

Contemporary Slovenian Literature in Translation. (Special edition.) Ljubljana: Trubar Foundation, 1998.

Dwyer, Joseph D. *Slovenes in the United States and Canada*. Minneapolis: Immigration Research Center at the University of Minnesota, 1981.

Friedman, Francine. *Yugoslavia: A Comprehensive English-Language Bibliography*. Wilmington, DE: Scholarly Resources, 1993.

Grad, Anton, and Henry Leeming. *Slovensko–angleški slovar / Slovene–English Dictionary*. Ljubljana: Državna založba Slovenije, 1994.

Grad, Anton, et al. *Veliki angleško–slovenski slovar* (The Great English–Slovene Dictionary). Ljubljana: Državna založba Slovenije, 2003.

Hočevar, Toussaint. "The Economic History of Slovenia, 1828–1918: A Bibliography with Subject Index." *Society for Slovene Studies Newsletter*, Documentation Series, 4 (1978): x, 1–49.

Javoršek, Marija. *Slovensko–angleški slovar, Angleško–slovenski slovar* (Slovene–English Dictionary, English–Slovene Dictionary). Celovec: Drava, 1989.

Klasinc, Peter Pavel. "Slovenia: A Guide to East-Central European Archives." *Austrian History Yearbook* 29, 2 (1998): 151–70.

Komac, Daša, and Ružena Škerlj. *English–Slovene and Slovene–English Pocket Dictionary / Angleško–slovenski in slovensko–angleški moderni slovar*. Ljubljana: Cankarjeva založba, 1990.

Koritnik, Andrej, et al. *Key: Slovenia: Contemporary Slovenian Humanities in Translation*. Ljubljana: Študentska založba, 2002.

Krek, Simon, ed. *Veliki angleško–slovenski slovar Oxford* (The Great Oxford English–Slovene Dictionary). Vol. 1, A–K. Ljubljana: Državna založba Slovenije; Oxford: Oxford University Press, 2005.

Lenček, Rado. "American Linguists on Slovene Language: A Comprehensive Annotated Bibliography (1940–1975)." *Society for Slovene Studies Newsletter*, Documentation Series, 1 (1975): ix, 1–49.

Primorski slovenski biografski leksikon (Primorska Slovene Biographical Lexicon). Gorica: Goriška Mohorjeva družba, 1974–1984.

Prispevki za novejšo zgodovino: Trideset let Inštituta za zgodovino delavskega gibanja—Bibliografija (Contributions to Contemporary History: Thirty Years of the Institute for the History of the Workers' Movement—A Bibliography). Ljubljana: Inštitut za novejšo zgodovino, 1989.

Rogel, Carole. *A Reader's Guide to Slovenia*. Arlington, VA: School of Area Studies, Foreign Service Institute, U.S. Department of State, 1992.

———. "Slovenia." In *Nationalism in the Balkans: An Annotated Bibliography*, 105–21. New York: Garland Press, 1984.

Slovenska akademija znanosti in umetnosti ob šestdesetletnici. Biografski zbornik (*Slovenian Academy of Sciences and Arts—60th Anniversary. Biographical notes*). Ljubljana: Slovenska akademija znanosti in umetnosti, 1998.

Slovar slovenskega knjižnega jezika (Dictionary of Standard Slovene). 5 vols. Ljubljana: Slovenska akademija znanosti in umetnosti / Državna založba Slovenije, 1970–1991. Also available electronically.

Slovenski biografski leksikon (Slovene Biographical Lexicon). 15 vols. Ljubljana: Slovenska akademija znanosti in umetnosti, 1925–1991.

Šega, Lidija. *Poslovni moderni veliki slovar: angleško–slovenksi slovar* (The Great Business Modern English–Slovene Dictionary). Ljubljana: Cankarjeva založba, 1997.

B. ENCYCLOPEDIAS AND INTERDISCIPLINARY WORKS

Bajt, Drago. *Slovenski kdo je kdo* (Slovene Who's Who). Ljubljana: Nova revija, 1999.

Benderly, Jill, and Evan Kraft, eds. *Independent Slovenia: Origins, Movements, Prospects.* New York: St. Martin's Press, 1994.

Enciklopedija Slovenije (Encyclopedia of Slovenia). 16 vols. Ljubljana: Mladinska knjiga, 1987–2002.

Grafenauer, Niko, ed. *The Case of Slovenia.* Ljubljana: Nova revija, 1991.

Moritsch, Andreas, ed. *Alpen-Adria—Zur Geschichte einer Region (Alpe-Jadran—K zgodovini neke regije /* Alps-Adriatic—On the History of a Region). Celovec-Ljubljana-Vienna: Mohorjeva založba, 2001.

Prispevki za Slovenski nacionalni program (Contributions to the Slovene National Program). *Nova revija* 6, 57 (1987).

Rupel, Dimitrij. *Slovenske slovesnosti in vsakdanjosti: 1888–1988* (Slovene Things, Solemn and Common: 1888–1988). Maribor: Obzorja, 1990.

Samostojna Slovenija (Independent Slovenia). *Nova revija* 11, 95 (1990).

Slovenci in prihodnost (Slovenes and the Future). *Nova revija* 12, 134–135 (1993).

Toporišič, Jože. *Enciklopedija slovenskega jezika* (Encyclopedia of the Slovene Language). Ljubljana: Cankarjeva založba, 1992.

Voices from the Slovene Nation, 1990–1992. Nationalities Papers 21, 1 (1993).

C. DESCRIPTIONS, GUIDEBOOKS, TRAVEL, AND YEARBOOKS

Avguštin, Cene, et al. *Medieval Towns.* Ljubljana: Ministry of Culture of the Republic of Slovenia, Cultural Heritage Office, 1999.

Capuder, Andrej. *Slovenia without Borders.* Trans. Tom Priestly. Celovec: Mohorjeva družba, 2003.

Chvatal, Matjaž, and Željko Božek. *Slovenija.* (Tourist guide, multilingual.) Ljubljana: Cankarjeva založba, 1992.

Dolenc, Milan. *Lipizzaner: The Story of the Horses in Lipica.* Commemorating the 400th Anniversary of the Lipizzaner. St. Paul, MN: Control Data Arts, 1981.

Fallon, Steve. *Slovenia.* 4th ed. Lonely Planet, 2004.

Guide to Slovene Museums. Ljubljana: Mladinska knjiga, 2001.

A Guide to Triglav National Park. Bled: Triglavski narodni park, 1987.

Kmecl, Matjaž. *Treasure Chest of Slovenia.* Ljubljana: Cankarjeva založba, 1987.

———. *Ljubljana.* Ljubljana: Motovun, 1987.

Repoša, Kazimir, ed. *Discover Slovenia.* Ljubljana: Cankarjeva založba, 1992.

Sattler, Miran. *Ljubljana*. Ljubljana: Cankarjeva založba, 1987.

Shaw, Trevor R. *Foreign Travelers in the Slovene Karst 1537–1900*. Ljubljana: ZRC SAZU, 2001.

Singleton, Fred. "Triglav National Park in the 1980s." *Slovene Studies* 10, 1 (1988): 39–49.

Stopar, Ivan. *Gradovi na Slovenskem* (Castles in Slovenia). Ljubljana: Cankarjeva založba, 1987.

———. *Walks in Old Ljubljana: A Guide to Its Culture and History*. Ljubljana: Marketing 013 ZTP, 1994.

Šumi, Nace. *Slovenija: umetnostni vodnik* (Slovenia: An Art Guide). Ljubljana: Marketing 013 ZTP, 1990.

———. *Na poti baročnih spomenikov Slovenije* (On the Trail of Slovene Baroque Monuments). Ljubljana: Zavod Republike Slovenije za varstvo naravne in kulturne dediščine, 1992.

A Walk through Ljubljana. Ljubljana: Mladinska knjiga, 1989.

Žnidaršič, Joco. *Slovenia: My Country*. Ljubljana: Veduta AZ, 2002.

D. STATISTICAL SOURCES

Slovenija v številkah (Slovenia in Figures). Ljubljana: Zavod Republike Slovenije za statistiko/Statistical Office of the Republic of Slovenia. Annual. Available at www.stat.si.

Statistical Office of the European Communities. Eurostat. http://epp.eurostat. ece.eu.

Statistični letopis / Statistical Yearbook. Ljubljana: Statistični urad Republike Slovenije / Statistical Office of the Republic of Slovenia. Annual. Available at www.stat.si.

Statistični portret Slovenije v EU / Statistical Portrait of Slovenia in the European Union. Ljubljana: Statistični urad Republike Slovenije / Statistical Office of the Republic of Slovenia. Annual since 2004. Partially available at www.stat.si.

Verska, jezikovna in narodna sestava prebivalstva, 1921–2002 (Religious, Linguistic and National Structure of the Population, 1921–2002). Posebna publikacija (Special publication). Ljubljana: Statistični urad Republike Slovenije / Statistical Office of the Republic of Slovenia, 2003. Available at www.stat.si.

World Competitiveness Yearbook. Lausanne, Switzerland: Institute for Management and Development.

World Economic Outlook. Washington, DC: International Monetary Fund.

II. CULTURAL

A. ART AND ARCHITECTURE

Anderlič, Jože, and Marijan Zadnikar. *Religious Art in Slovenia*. Koper: Ognjišče, 1986.

Bibič, Bratko. *The Noise from Metelkova: Ljubljana Spaces and Culture in Transition*. Ljubljana: Peace Institute, 2003.

Burkhardt, François, et al., eds. *Jože Plečnik: Architect 1872–1957*. Cambridge, MA: MIT Press, 1992.

Crowther, Paul. *The Language of 20th-Century Art: A Conceptual History*. New Haven, CT: Yale University Press, 1997.

Čufer, Eda, ed. *NSK Embassy Moscow*. Project Organized by Irwin with Apt-Art International and Ridzhina Gallery. How the East Sees the East. Koper: Loža Gallery, 1992.

East Art Map: Contemporary Art and Eastern Europe. Edited by Irwin. London: Central St. Martin's College of Art and Design, University of the Arts, 2006.

Erjavec, Aleš. "Neue Slowenische Kunst—Slovenian Art." In *Postmodernism and the Postsocialist Conditions: Politicized Art under Late Socialism*, ed. Aleš Erjavec. Berkeley: University of California Press, 2003.

Erjavec, Aleš, and Marina Gržinić. *Ljubljana, Ljubljana: The Eighties in Slovenian Art and Culture*. Ljubljana: Mladinska knjiga, 1991.

Jože Plečnik, 1872–1957: Architecture and the City. Oxford: Urban Design, Oxford Polytechnic, 1983.

Krečič, Peter. *Plečnik: The Complete Works*. New York: Whitney Library of Design, 1993.

Mansbach, Steven A. *Modern Art in Eastern Europe*. Cambridge, MA: Cambridge University Press, 1998. Chapter 4: "The Southern Balkans of the Former Yugoslavia: Slovenia, Croatia, Serbia, and Macedonia."

Menaše, Lev. *Art Treasures of Slovenia*. Belgrade: Jugoslovenska revija, 1981.

Prelovšek, Damjan. *Josef Plečnik, 1872–1957, Architectura Perennis*. Trans. Dorothea Apovnik. Salzburg: Residenz, 1992.

Rihard Jakopič. Ljubljana: Državna založba Slovenije, Moderna Galerija, 1973.

Rush, Michael, ed. *Marjetica Potrč: Urgent Architecture*. Palm Beach, FL: Palm Beach Institute of Contemporary Art, 2004.

Sedej, Ivan. *Ljudska umetnost na Slovenskem* (Folk Art in Slovenia). Ljubljana: Mladinska knjiga, 1985.

Skalar, Peter. *Design in Slovenia 1*. Ljubljana: Društvo oblikovalcev Slovenije, 1995.

Soban, Tamara, et al., eds. *Razširjeni prostori umetnosti: slovenska umetnost 1985–1995* (Extended Art Spaces: Slovene Art 1985–1995). Ljubljana: Moderna galerija, 2004.

Stele, France. *Slovene Impressionists*. St. Paul, MN: Control Data Arts, 1980.

Španjol, Igor, and Igor Zabel, eds. *Do roba in naprej: slovenska umetnost 1975–85* (To the Edge and Beyond: Slovene Art 1975–85) Ljubljana: Moderna galerija, 2003.

———, eds. *Teritoriji, identitite, mreže: slovenska umetnost 1995–2005* (Territories, Identities, Networks: Slovene Art 1995–2005). Ljubljana: Moderna galerija, 2005.

Torres, Ana Maria. *Marjetica Potrč: Urban Negotiations*. Valencia (Spain): Institut Valencia d'Art Modern, 2003.

B. LINGUISTICS, LANGUAGE TEXTBOOKS, LITERARY HISTORY AND THEORY, AND LITERATURE

1. LINGUISTICS

Cooper, Henry, and Rado Lenček, eds. "To Honor Jernej Kopitar: 1780–1980." *Papers in Slavic Philology*, vol. 2. Ann Arbor: University of Michigan, 1982.

Derbyshire, William W. *A Basic Slovene Reference Grammar*. Columbus, OH: Slavica, 1993.

Gadányi, Károly. *The Evolution of Vocabulary in Literary Slovene*. Melbourne: Melbourne Academia Press, 1996.

Greenberg, Marc L. *A Historical Phonology of the Slovene Language*. Historical Phonology of the Slavic Languages, vol. 13. Heidelberg: Universitaetsverlag, 2000. Also available in Slovene: *Zgodovina glasoslovja slovenskega jezika*. Trans. Marta Pirnat-Greenberg. Maribor: Aristej, 2002.

Herrity, Peter. *Slovene: A Comprehensive Grammar*. London: Routledge, 2000.

Lenček, Rado L. "From the Correspondence between Stanislav Škrbec and Jean Baudouin de Courtenay." *Slovene Studies* 5, 2 (1983): 165–88.

———. *Izbrane razprave in eseji* (Selected Articles and Essays). Trans. Rastislav Šušteršič and Marta Pirnat-Greenberg. Ljubljana: Slovenska matica, 1996.

———. *Jean Baudouin de Courtenay on the Dialects Spoken in Venetian Slovenia and Rezija*. Documentation Series, no. 2. New York: Society for Slovene Studies, 1977.

———. "On Dilemmas and Compromises in the Evolution of Modern Slovene." In *Slavic Linguistics and Language Teaching*, ed. Thomas E. Magner, 112–53. Columbus, OH: Slavica, 1976.

———. "The Language Revolution in Slovene Romantic Poetry." *Papers in Slovene Studies* (1978): 15–44.

———. *The Structure and History of the Slovene Language*. Columbus, OH: Slavica, 1982.

———, ed. *The Beginnings of the Scientific Study of Minor Slavic Languages: The Correspondence between Jean Baudouin de Courtenay and Vatroslav Oblak*. Munich: A. Kovač, 1992.

Nećak-Lük, Albina, and Dušan Nećak. "Slovene as a Minority Language: Historical Background and Sociolinguistic Perspectives." *Slovene Studies* 12, 2 (1990): 169–81.

Priestly, Tom M. S. "Five Recent Books on the Slovene Language." *Slovene Studies* 16, 2 (1994): 101–19.

Rupel, Dimitrij. "The Maintenance of National Languages in a Social Setting: Slovene in Yugoslavia." *Slovene Studies* 8, 2 (1986): 43–52.

Steenwijk, Han. *The Slovene Dialect of Resia*. Atlanta, GA: Rhodopi, 1992.

Stone, Gerald. "J. W. Valvasor's *Ehre des Herzogtums Krain* (1689): A Source for the History of the Slovene Language." *Slovene Studies* 12, 1 (1990): 43–54.

Šabec, Nada. *Half pa pu. The Language of Slovene Americans*. Ljubljana: Studia Humanitatis, 1995.

Šabec, Nada, and David Limon. *Across Culture: Slovensko–britansko–ameriško sporazumevanje* (Slovene–British–American Intercultural Communication). Maribor: Založba Obzorja, 2001.

Tollefson, James W. "The Language Planning Process and Language Rights in Yugoslavia." *Language Problems and Language Planning* 4 (1980): 141–56.

———. *The Language Situation and Language Policy in Slovenia*. Washington, DC: University Press of America, 1981.

Toporišič, Jože. "The Language of a Small Nationality in a Multilingual State." In *Sociolinguistic Problems in Czechoslovakia, Hungary, Romania, and Yugoslavia* (William R. Schmalsteig and Thomas F. Magner, eds.). Columbus, OH: Slavica, 1, 3 (1978): 480–86.

———. *Slovenska slovnica* (Slovene Grammar). Revised edition. Maribor: Obzorja, 2000.

———. *Slovenski pravopis* (Slovene Orthography). Ljubljana: ZRC SAZU, 2001.

Toporišič, Jože, et al., eds. *Miklošičev zbornik* (A Miklošič Anthology). Proceedings of International Symposium, June 1991. Ljubljana: Univerza v Ljubljani, 1992.

2. LANGUAGE TEXTBOOKS

Albretti, Andrea. *Colloquial Slovene: The Complete Course for Beginners*. Colloquial Series, multimedia. Reprinted. London: Routledge, 2004.

———. *Phrase finder*. London: HarperCollins, 1996.

———. *Slovene: Teach Yourself: Complete Course*. London: Routledge, 2006.

Černivec, Ljubica. *Slovnične preglednice slovenskega jezika* (Gramatical Tables of the Slovene Language). Ljubljana: Center, 2002.

Derbyshire, William W., and Marta Pirnat-Greenberg. *A Learner's Dictionary of Slovene: With Words in Their Inflected Forms*. Bloomington, IN: Slavica, 2002.

Hladnik, Miran, and Toussaint Hočevar. *Slovene for Travelers / Slovenščina za popotnike: Conversational Phrases, Cultural Information, Travel Tips*. Kranj: Samozaložba (published by the authors), 1994.

———. *Slovenian for Travelers / Slovenščina za popotnike*. www.ff.uni-lj.si/sft/2002 (periodically updated).

Jug-Kranjec, Hermina. *Sloveščina za tujce* (Slovene for Foreigners). 8th revised ed. Ljubljana: Filozofska fakulteta, 1992.

Markovič, Andreja, et al. *Slovenska beseda v živo: Učbenik za začetni tečaj slovenščine kot drugega tujega jezika* (The Slovene Word Alive: A Text-book for Beginners of Slovene as a Foreign Language). Ljubljana: Center za slovenščino kot tuji ali drugi jezik pri Oddelku za slovanske jezike in književnosti Filozofske fakultete Univerze v Ljubljani, 2001.

Pirih, Nataša. *Slovenščina na koncu jezika* (Slovene on the Tip of My Tongue). Ljubljana: Center za slovenščino kot tuji ali drugi jezik pri Oddelku za slovanske jezike in književnosti Filozofske fakultete Univerze v Ljubljani, 2003.

S slovenščino nimam težav (I Have No Difficulties with Slovene). Ljubljana: Center za slovenščino kot tuji ali drugi jezik pri Oddelku za slovanske jezike in knjževnosti Filozofske fakultete Univerze v Ljubljani, 2004.

3. LITERARY HISTORY AND THEORY

Berger, Aleš. *The Key Witnesses: The Younger Slovene Prose at the Turn of the Millennia. Litterae Slovenicae.* Ljubljana: 2003.

Biggins, Michael. "Handke's Slovenia and Šalamun's America: The Literary Uses of Utopia." *Slovene Studies* 13, 2 (1991, published July 1993): 181–90.

Bonazza, Sergio. "Austro-Slavism as the Motive of Kopitar's Work." *Slovene Studies* 5, 2 (1983): 155–64.

Cooper, Henry R., Jr. *France Prešeren.* Boston: Twayne, 1981.

———. "Oton Župančič and Slovene Modernism." *Slovene Studies* 13, 1 (1991): 3–18.

———. "Primož Trubar and Slovene Literature of the Sixteenth Century." *Slovene Studies* 7, 1–2 (1985): 35–50.

———. "Slovene Literature: A Brief Survey. Introduction to Bilingual Anthology of Slovene Literature." *Slovene Studies* 20–21 (1998–1999, published in 2003).

———, ed. *Four Hundred Years of the South Slavic Protestant Reformation (1584–1984).* Conference Proceedings. Published as *Slovene Studies* 6, 1–2 (1984).

Debeljak, Aleš, ed. *The Imagination of Terra Incognita: Slovenian Writing 1945–1995.* Fredonia, NY: White Pine Press, 1997.

Debeljak, Aleš. *Reluctant Modernity: The Institution of Art and Its Historical Forms.* Lanham, MD: Rowman and Littlefield, 1998.

Dimnik, Martin. "Gutenberg, Humanism, the Reformation, and the Emergence of the Slovene Literary Language 1550–1584." *Canadian Slavonic Papers* 26 (June/September 1984): 141–59.

Dolgan, Marjan, ed. *Slovenski literarni programi in manifesti* (Slovene Literary Programs and Manifestos). Ljubljana: Mladinska knjiga, 1990.

Dolinar, Darko, and Marko Juvan, eds. *Writing Literary History: Selective Perspectives from Central Europe.* Frankfurt am Main: Peter Lang, 2006.

Kermauner, Taras. *Drama, gledališče in družba: sociološka analiza literarnih ideologij v slovenski dramatiki* (Drama, Theater, and Society: A Sociological Analysis of Literary Ideologies in Slovene Drama). Ljubljana: Slovenska matica, 1983.

Klančar, Anthony Joseph. "Josip Jurčič, the Slovene Scott." *Slavic Review* 5 (May 1946): 19–33.

Kocijančič Pokorn, Nike. *Beyond the Avant-Garde and Expressionism: Srečko Kosovel's Integrals*. Poetry International, http://Slovenia.poetryinternational.org.

Kos, Janko. *Primerjalna zgodovina slovenske literature* (A Comparative History of Slovene Literature). Ljubljana: Znanstveni inštitut Filozofske fakultete, Partizanska knjiga, 1987.

Lavrin, Janko. "France Prešeren, 1800–1849." *Slavonic and East European Review* 33 (June 1955): 304–26.

Mihailovich, Vasa D., ed. *South Slavic Writers since World War II*. Detroit: Bruccoli Clark Layman, Inc., 1997.

Paternu, Boris. *Od ekspresionizma do postmoderne: študije o slovenskem pesništvu in jeziku* (From Expressionism to the Postmodernism: Studies on Slovene Writing and Language). Ljubljana: Slovenska matica, 1999.

Pirjevec, Marija. *Dvoje izvirov slovenske književnosti* (Two Sources of Slovene Literature). Ljubljana: Slovenska matica, 1997.

Pogačnik, Jože. *Twentieth-Century Slovene Literature. Le Livre Slovène* 1 (1986).

Predan, Vasja. *Kritikovo gledališče* (The Critic's Theater). Ljubljana: Slovenska matica, 1990.

Rupel, Mirko. *Primož Trubar: življenje in delo* (Primož Trubar: Life and Work). Ljubljana: Mladinska knjiga, 1962.

Scherber, Peter. "Regionalism Versus Europeanism as a Leading Concept in the Works of Srečko Kosovel." *Slovene Studies* 13, 2 (1991, published July 1993): 155–65.

Slodnjak, Anton. "Fran Levstik (1831–1887): The First Representative of Realism in Slovene Literature." *Slavonic and East European Review* 35 (December 1956): 24–39.

———. "Ivan Cankar in Slovene and World Literature." *Slavonic and East European Review* 59 (April 1981): 186–96.

Stone, Gerald C. "Matija Čop's Correspondence with English Friends." *Papers in Slovene Studies* (1976): 24–55.

Virk, Tomo. *From Literature to Literature. Litterae Slovenicae* 1 (1991): 202–10.

Wachtel, Andrew Baruch. *Making a Nation, Breaking a Nation: Literature and Cultural Politics in Yugoslavia*. Stanford, CA: Stanford University Press, 1998.

Zadravec, Franc. *Slovenski roman 20. stoletja. Prvi analitični del* (The Slovene Novel of the 20th Century. First Analytical Volume). Ljubljana: Pomurska založba, 1997.

———. *Slovenski roman 20. stoletja. Drugi analitični del in nekaj sintez* (The Slovene Novel of the 20th Century. Second Analytical Volume and Some Syntheses). Ljubljana: Pomurska založba, 2002.

Zawacki, Andrew, ed. *Afterwards: Slovenian Writing, 1945–1999.* Buffalo, NY: White Pine Press, 1999.

Zorn, Aleksander. "The Heady Times of Boundless Literature." *Litterae Slovenicae* 1 (1991): 187–201.

4. LITERATURE

A. NOVELS, PLAYS, AND SHORT STORIES

Bartol, Vladimir. *Alamut.* Trans. Michael Biggins. Seattle: Scala House Press, 2004.

Bergles, Ciril. *Ellis Island.* Trans. Jože Žohar. Ljubljana: Književna mladina Slovenije, 1998.

Blatnik, Andrej. *Skinswaps.* Trans. Tamara Soban. Evanston, IL: Northwestern University Press, 1998.

Cankar, Ivan. *The Bailiff Yerney and His Rights.* Trans. Sidorie Yeras and H. C. Grant. London: John Rodker, 1930.

———. *Dream Visions and Other Selected Stories.* Trans. Anton Družina. Willoughby Hills, OH: Slovenian Research Center, 1982.

———. *My Life and Other Sketches.* Trans. Elza Jereb and Alasdair MacKinnon. Vilenica Collection. Ljubljana: Društvo slovenskih pisateljev / Mladinska knjiga, 1988.

———. *The Ward of Our Lady of Mercy.* Ljubljana: Državna založba Slovenije, 1976.

———. *Yerney's Justice.* Trans. Louis Adamic. New York: Vanguard Press, 1926.

Contemporary Slovene Short Stories. (Drago Jančar, Branko Gradišnik, Uroš Kalčič, Jani Virk, Andrej Blatnik) Essays (Aleksander Zorn, Tomo Virk, Drago Bajt). *Litterae Slovenicae* 29, 1 (1991).

Contemporary Slovenian Drama. Introduction by Blaž Lukan. *Litterae Slovenicae* 35, 1 (1997).

The Day That Tito Died: Contemporary Slovenian Short Stories. London: Forest Books, 1993.

Dolenc, Mate. "The Role of My Boots in the Anlogan Revolution." Trans. John K. Cox. *Slovene Studies* 23, 1–2 (2003): 49–71.

Flisar, Evald. *My Father's Dreams: A Tale of Innocence Abused.* Trans. the author with Alan McConnelly-Duff. Norman, OK: Texture Press, 2003.

———. *Tomorrow.* London: Goldhawk Press, 1992. (A play)

———. *Tristan and Iseult.* London: Goldhawk Press, 1992. (A play)

———. *What about Leonardo?* London: Goldhawk Press, 1992. (A play)

Jančar, Drago. "Aithiopika." *Description of a Struggle: The Vintage Book of Contemporary Eastern European Writing*, ed. Michael March. New York: Vintage Books, 1994.

———. "Augsburg." *Balkan Blues: Writing out of Yugoslavia*, ed. Joanna Labon. Evanston, IL: Northwestern University Press, 1995.

———. *Mocking Desire*. Trans. Michael Biggins. Evanston, IL: Northwestern University Press, 1998.

———. *Northern Lights*. Trans. Michael Biggins. Evanston, IL: Northwestern University Press, 2000.

———. "The Slovene Exile." *Nationalities Papers* 21, 1 (1993): 91–105.

———. *Stakeout at Godot's*. Trans. Ann Čeh and Peter Perhonis. Washington, DC: SCENA Press, 1997.

———."Terra Incognita." *Cross Culture: A Yearbook of Central European Culture* 6 (1987): 331–39.

Kavčič, Vladimir. *The Golden Bird: Folk Tales from Slovenia*. Trans. Jan Dekker and Lena Lenček. Cleveland, NY: World, 1969.

The Key Witnesses: The Younger Slovene Prose at the Turn of the Millennia. Selection and introduction by Mitja Čander. *Litterae Slovenicae* 41, 1 (2003).

Kosmač, Ciril. *A Day in Spring*. Trans. Fanny S. Copeland. Ljubljana: Vilenica Collection, Društvo slovenskih pisateljev / Mladinska knjiga, 1988.

Lainšček, Feri. *Instead of Whom Does the Flower Bloom*. Introductory essay by Matej Bogataj. Trans. Tamara M. Soban. *Litterae Slovenicae* 50, 2 (2002).

Levstik, Vladimir. *An Adder's Nest*. Trans. Fanny S. Copeland. London: John Rodker, 1931.

Matajc, Vanesa, ed. *Fragments from Slovene Literature: An Anthology of Slovene Literature*. *Litterae Slovenicae* 53, 1, (2005).

Naši na tujih tleh: Antologija književnosti Slovencev v Ameriki (Ours [Slovenes] on Foreign Soil: Anthology of Slovene Literature in North America). Ljubljana: Cankarjeva založba, 1982.

Pahor, Boris. *Pilgrim among the Shadows*. Trans. Michael Biggins. New York: Harcourt Brace, 1995.

Petan, Žarko. *Aphorisms*. Essay by Andrijan Lah. English, French, German, and Italian translations. *Litterae Slovenicae* 36, 1, (1998).

Potrč, Ivan. *The Land and the Flesh*. Trans. Harry Leeming. Ljubljana: Vilenica Collection, Društvo slovenskih pisateljev / Mladinska knjiga, 1988.

Prežihov, Voranc. *The Self-Sown*. Trans. Irma Ožbalt. New Orleans: Prometej, 1982.

———. *Three Short Stories*. Trans. Irma Ožbalt. *Slovene Studies* 8, 2 (1986): 77–86.

The Slovenian Essays of the Nineties. Selection by Matevž Kos. *Litterae Slovenicae* 38, 2 (2000).

Smole, Dominik. *Antigone*. Trans. Harry Leeming. Vilenica Collection. Ljubljana: Društvo slovenskih pisateljev / Mladinska knjiga, 1988.

Tales Growing Up into Secrets: An Anthology of Contemporary Slovene Youth Prose. Litterae Slovenicae 52, 1 (2004).

Zupan, Vitomil. *A Minuet for Guitar.* Trans. Harry Leeming. Vilenica Collection. Ljubljana: Društvo slovenskih pisateljev / Mladinska knjiga, 1988.

B. POETRY

Balantič, France. *Pot brez konca / Path without End / Weg ohne Ende.* Trans. Klaus Detlev-Olof and Tom Priestly. Celovec/Ljubljana/Vienna: Mohorjeva družba, 2005.

Berger, Aleš. *Ten Slovene Poets of the Nineties.* Ljubljana: Slovene Writers' Association, 2002.

Bergles, Ciril. *Ellis Island.* Trans. Jože Žohar. Ljubljana: Aleph 15, Književna mladina Slovenije, 1988.

Bister, Feliks J., and Herbert Kuhner, eds. *Koroška slovenska poezija* (Carinthian Slovenian Poetry). Klagenfurt: Mohorjeva-Hermagoras; and Columbus, OH: Slavica, 1984.

Cummins, Walter, ed. *Shifting Borders: East European Poetry in the 1980s.* Rutherford, NJ: Fairleigh Dickinson University Press, 1993.

Debeljak, Aleš. *Anxious Moments.* New York: White Pine Press, 1994.

———. *The Chronicle of Melancholy.* Chattanooga: Poetry International Chapbooks, 1989.

———. *The City and the Child.* Trans. Christopher Merril. Fredonia, NY: White Pine Press, 1999.

———. *Dictionary of Silence.* Trans. Sonja Kravanja. Santa Fe, NM: Lumen Books, 2000.

———, ed. *Prisoners of Freedom: Contemporary Slovenian Poetry.* Santa Fe, NM: Pedernal, 1994.

"Edvard Kocbek: Five Poems." Trans. Tom Ložar. *Slovene Studies* 8, 2 (1986): 73–76.

Edvard Kocbek. Trans. Michael Biggins *Litterae Slovenicae* 33, 2 (1995).

Glušič, Helga. "The Prose and Poetry of Edvard Kocbek (1904–1981)." *Slovene Studies* 8, 2 (1986): 65–71.

"Gregor Strniša: Three Poems." Trans. Michael Biggins. *Slovene Studies* 12, 1 (1990): 99–101.

Jackson, Richard, ed. *Double Vision: Four Slovene Poets.* Chattanooga: Aleph and Poetry Miscellany Books, 1993.

Kocbek , Edvard. *Na vratih zvečer / At the Door at Evening.* Trans. Tom Ložar. Dorion, Quebec: Muses' Co.; and Ljubljana: Aleph, 1990.

———. *Nothing Is Lost: Selected Poems.* Trans. Michael Scammel and Veno Taufer. Princeton, NJ: Princeton University Press, 2004.

Kosovel, Srečko. *Integrals.* Introduction and trans. Wilhelm Heiliger. Santa Barbara, CA: Mudborn Press, 1983.

Kovič, Kajetan. *Poems. Litterae Slovenicae* 35, 2 (1997).

Kuntner, Tone. *My House.* Trans. Mara Mericka. Sydney: Slovenian Australian Literary and Arts Circle, 1987.

Kušar, Meta, Maja Vidmar, and Erika Vouk. *Glas v telesu: tri slovenske pesnice / La voix dans le corps: trois poétesses slovènes / The Voice in the Body: Three Slovenian Women Poets. Litterae Slovenicae* 43, 9 (2006).

Lavrin, Janko, and Anton Slodnjak, eds. *Parnassus of a Small Nation.* 2nd ed. Ljubljana: Državna založba Slovenije, 1965.

Matthews, W. K., and Anton Slodnjak, eds. *France Prešeren, 1800–1849: Poems.* 2nd ed. London: John Calder, 1969.

Novak, Boris A. *Coronation.* Chattanooga: Poetry Miscellany Chapbooks, 1991.

————. *Gardener of Silence.* Ljubljana: Mladinska knjiga International, 1990.

————. *The Master of Insomnia / Le maître de l'insomnie.* Introductory essay by Aleš Debeljak. Trans. Michael Biggins. *Litterae Slovenicae* 41, 2 (2003).

————. *Vertigo.* Chattanooga: Poetry Miscellany Chapbooks, 1992.

"Oton Župančič, Duma." Trans. and notes Henry R. Cooper. *Slovene Studies* 8, 2 (1986): 87–94.

Prešeren, France. "The Baptism on the Savica." Trans. and notes Henry Cooper Jr. *Slovene Studies* 7, 1–2 (1986): 87–94.

————. *Pesmi/Poems.* Ed. France Pibernik and Franc Drole. Trans. Tom M. S. Priestly and Henry Cooper Jr. Celovec: Mohorjeva družba; Ljubljana: Mestna občina Kranj, 1999.

Scammell, Michael. "Slovenia and Its Poet [Edvard Kocbek]." *New York Review of Books,* 24 October 1991.

Srečko Kosovel. *Integrals.* Trans. Philip Burt and others. Essay by Nike Kocijančič Pokorn. *Litterae Slovenicae* 36, 1 (1998).

Šalamun, Tomaž. *A Ballad for Metka Krašovec.* Trans. Michael Biggins. Prague: Twisted Spoon Press, 2001.

————. *The Four Questions of Melancholy: New and Selected Poems.* Ed. Christopher Merrill. Fredonia, NY: White Pine Press, 1997.

————. *Poker.* Trans. Joshua Beckman and the author. Berkeley, CA: Ugly Duckling Press, 2003.

————. *Selected Poems.* Trans. Charles Simić. New York: Ecco Press, 1988.

————. *The Shepherd, the Hunter.* Trans. Sonja Kravanja. Santa Fe, NM: Pedernal, 1992.

————. *Snow.* Iowa City: Toothpaste Press, 1974.

————. *Turbines: Twenty-one Poems.* Iowa City: Windhover Press, University of Iowa, 1973.

Taufer, Veno. *New Music.* Chattanooga: Poetry Miscellany, 1991.

————. *Poems.* Introductory essay by Matevž Kos. Trans. Irena Zorko Novak. *Litterae Slovenicae* 37, 1 (1999).

————. *Tongues of the Waterlings*. Chattanooga: Poetry Miscellany, 1992.

Ten Slovenian Poets of the Nineties. *Litterae Slovenicae* 40, 1 (2002).

Zajc, Dane. *Scorpions*. Essay by Ilma Rakusa. English trans. Sonja Kravanja and Lili Potpara. French trans. Zdenka Štimac. *Litterae Slovenicae* 38, 1 (2000).

Župančič, Oton. *A Selection of Poems*. Trans. Janko Lavrin. Ljubljana: Državna založba Slovenije, 1967.

C. FILM

Brenk, France. *Slovenski film: dokumenti in razmišljanja* (Slovene Film: Documents and Musings). Ljubljana: Partizanska knjiga, 1980.

Nemanič, Ivan. *Filmsko gradivo slovenskega filmskega arhiva pri Arhivu Republike Slovenije: dokumentarni, igrani in animirani film* (Film Materials in the Slovene Film Archive at the Archives of the Republic of Slovenia: Documentaries, Performed and Animated Film). Ljubljana: Arhiv R Slovenije, 1998.

Rezec-Stibilj, Tereza, and Lojz Tršan. *Filmsko gradivo slovenskega filmskega arhiva pri Arhivu Republike Slovenije* (Film Materials in the Slovene Film Archive at the Archives of the Republic of Slovenia). Ljubljana: Arhiv R Slovenije, 2000.

Štefančič, Marcel. "Neznosna unikatnost slovenskega filma" (Unbearable Uniqueness of the Slovene Film). *Mladina*, 30 April 2005.

Šuvaković, Miško. *Anatomija angelov: razprave o umetnosti in teoriji v Sloveniji po letu 1960* (The Anatomy of Angels: Discussions about Art and Theory in Slovenia after 1960). Trans. Vlasta Vičič. Ljubljana: Publicistični center, 2001.

Traven, Janko. *Pregled razvoja kinematografije pri Slovencih, do 1918* (A Survey of the Development of Slovene Cinematography, to 1918). Ljubljana: Slovenski gledališki in filmski muzej, 1992.

V kraljestvu filma: fotozgodovina slovenskega filma, filmografija: 1905–1945 (In the Kingdom of Film: A Photohistory of Slovene Film, Filmography: 1905–1945). Ljubljana: Slovenski gledališki in filmski muzej, 1988.

Vrdlovec, Zdenko. *40 udarcev: slovenska publicistika o slovenskem in jugoslovanskem filmu v obdobju 1949–1988* (Forty Blows: Slovene Publishing on Slovene and Yugoslav Film in the Period 1949–1988). Ljubljana: Slovenski gledališki in filmski muzej, 1988.

D. MUSIC

Bizjak, Milko, and Edo Škulj. *Pipe Organs in Slovenia*. Ljubljana: Državna založba Slovenije, 1985.

Budkovič, Cvetko. *Razvoj glasbenega šolstva na Slovenskem I: od začetka 19. stoletja do nastanka konservatorija* (The Development of Music Education in Slovenia I: From the Beginning of the Nineteenth Century to the Establishment of the Conservatory). Ljubljana: Znanstveni inštitut Filozofske fakultete, 1992.

Cutter, Paul F. "Notes on Secular Music of Jacobus Gallus." *Papers in Slovene Studies* (1976): 179–205.

Cvetko, Dragotin. "The Renaissance in Slovene Music." *Slavic and East European Review* 36 (December 1957): 27–36.

———. *Slovenska glasba v evropskem prostoru* (Slovene Music in European Space). Ljubljana: Slovenska matica, 1991.

Evropski glasbeni klasicizem in njegov odmev na Slovenskem / Musikklassizismus und sein Widerhall in Slowenien. Ed. Dragotin Cvetko and Danilo Pokorn. Proceedings of International Symposium. Ljubljana: Slovenska akademija znanosti in umetnosti, 1988.

Gallus, Jacobus. *Moralia—Harmoniae Morales.* Ed. Tomaž Faganel. Three CDs and a book in four languages. Ljubljana: ZRC SAZU; Freiburg: Freiburger Music Forum, 2000.

Klemenčič, Ivan. *Slovenska filharmonija in njene predhodnice* (The Slovene Philharmonic and Its Predecessors). Ljubljana: Slovenska filharmonija, 1988.

———, ed. *300 let/Years Academia Philharmonicorum Labancesium 1701–2001.* Bilingual proceedings of the international conference, Ljubljana, 25–27 October 2001. Ljubljana: ZRC SAZU, 2004.

Kumer, Zmaga, et al. *Slovenske ljudske pesmi* (Slovene Folk Songs). Vols. 1 and 2. Ljubljana: Slovenska matica, 1970 and 1981.

Kuret, Primož, ed. *Umetnik in družba: slovenska glasbena misel po prvi vojni* (The Artist and Society: Slovene Musical Thought after the First War). Ljubljana: Državna založba Slovenije, 1988.

Pettan, Svanibor, et al., eds. *Glasba in manjšine / Music and Minorities.* Proceedings of the Internatioinal Council of Traditional Music conference, Ljubljana, 25–30 June 2000. Ljubjana: ZRC SAZU, 2001.

Rijavec, Andrej. *Twentieth-Century Slovene Composers / Slowenische Komponisten des 20. Jahrhunderts.* Ljubljana: Društvo slovenskih skladeteljev; Köln: Musikverlag H. Gerig, 1975.

Sivec, Ivan. *Brata Avsenik: evropski glasbeni fenomen iz Begunj na Gorenjskem* (The Avsenik Brothers: European Music Phenomenon). Mengeš: ICO, 1999.

Snoj, Jurij, and Gregor Pompe. *Pisna podoba glasbe na Slovenskem / Music in Slovenia through the Aspects of Notation.* Ljubljana: ZRC SAZU, 2003.

III. ECONOMIC

Alpe-Adria. Panel proceedings and commentary. Published in *Slovene Studies* 10, 1 (1988).

Arnež, John A. *Slovenian Lands and Their Economies, 1848–1973*. New York: Studia Slovenica, 1983.

Bombelles, Joseph, T. *Yugoslav Agricultural Production and Productivity, Prewar Years and 1948–1965*. New York: Riverside Research Institute, 1970.

Comisso, Ellen Turkish. *Workers' Control under Plan and Market: Implications of Yugoslav Self-Management*. New Haven, CT: Yale University Press, 1979.

Cvikel, Milan, et al. *Costs and Benefits of Independence: Slovenia*. Washington, DC: World Bank, 1993.

Dimovski, Vlado, et al. *Slovenska industrija v pogojih notranjega trga EU. Sintezno poročilo* (Slovene Industry under Conditions of the EU Internal Market. Synthesis Report). Ljubljana: Center za mednarodno konkurenčnost, 2000.

Ferfila, Bogomil. *The Economics and Politics of the Socialist Debacle: The Yugoslav Case*. Lanham, MD: University Press of America, 1991.

———. "Yugoslavia: Confederation or Disintegration." *Problems of Communism* 40 (July–August 1991): 18–30.

Ferfila, Bogomil, and Paul Phillips. *Slovenia*. Lanham, MD: University Press of America, 2000.

Gillingham, John. *European Integration, 1950–2003*. Cambridge: Cambridge University Press, 2003.

Hočevar, Toussaint. "Economic Determinants in the Development of the Slovene National System." *Papers in Slovene Studies* (1975): 27–78.

———. *Slovenia's Role in Yugoslav Economy*. Columbus, OH: Slovenian Research Center, 1964.

Jagrič, Timotej, and Rasto Ovin. "Method of Analyzing Business Cycles in a Transition Economy: The Case of Slovenia." *Developing Economies* 42, 1 (2004): 42–62.

Jagrič, Timotej, et al. "The Performance of Slovenian Mutual Funds." *Slovene Studies* 26, 1–2 (2004): 81–92.

Jaklič, Marko. "Symbolic Interactionism Approach to Study Socio-Economic Development in Slovenia." *East European Quarterly* 38, 1 (2004): 109–27.

Javornik, Jana, and Valerija Korošec, eds. *Poročilo o človekovem razvoju. Slovenija 2002–2003. Človek, razvoj in zdravje* (Report on Human Development in Slovenia 2002–2003. People, Development, and Health). Ljubljana: Urad za makroekonomske analize in razvoj (UMAR), 2003.

Kladnik, Drago, and Marjan Ravbar. "The Importance of the Division of the Countryside in Stimulating Regional Development." *Acta Geografica Slovenica* 42, 1 (2003): 9–51.

Kosi, Danilo. "Sonaravno kmetijstvo v Sloveniji" (Ecological Agriculture in Slovenia). *Geografski vestnik* 76, 2 (2004): 43–52.

Kračun, Davorin. *Economics of Transition: Stabilization and Economic Performance*. Maribor: Univerza v Mariboru, 2000.

Labor Market Policies in Slovenia. OECD and Centre for Co-operation with Economies in Transition, 1997.

Lokar, Aleš, et al. *In Honor of the Memory of Toussaint Hočevar*. Festschrift published in *Slovene Studies* 11, 1–2 (1989). (Articles listed individually in the first edition of this book.)

Mazek, Warren F., ed. *Slovene Economy in the Eighties*. Documentation Series, no. 5. New York: Society for Slovene Studies, 1981.

Mencinger, Jože. *The Yugoslav Economy: Systemic Changes, 1945–1986*. Carl Beck Papers, no. 707. Pittsburgh: University of Pittsburgh, Center for Russian and East European Studies, July 1989.

Milenkovitch, Deborah D. *Plan and Market in Yugoslav Economic Thought*. New Haven, CT: Yale University Press, 1971.

Mrak, Mojmir, et al., eds. *Slovenia: From Yugoslavia to the European Union*. Washington, DC: International Bank for Reconstruction and Development / World Bank, 2004.

Oražem, Peter F., and Milan Vodopivec. *Winners and Losers in Transition: Returns to Education, Experience, and Gender in Slovenia*. Policy Research Working Paper. Washington, DC: World Bank, August 1994.

Petrin, Tea. *Industrial Policy Supporting Economic Transition in Central-Eastern Europe: Lessons from Slovenia*. Berkeley: University of California, Institute of International Studies, 1995.

Phillips, Paul Arthur, and Bogomil Ferfila. *The Rise and Fall of the Third Way: Yugoslavia 1945–1991*. Halifax, Nova Scotia: Fernwood, 1992.

Pleskovič, Boris, and Jeffrey D. Sachs. "Political Independence and Economic Reform in Slovenia." In *Transition in Eastern Europe*, vol. 1, Country Studies, ed. Oliver Jean Blanchard, Kenneth A. Froot, and Jeffrey D. Sachs, 191–220. Chicago: University of Chicago Press, 1994.

Reuvid, Jonathan. *Doing Business with Slovenia*. London: Kogan Page, 2004.

Sirc, Ljubo. *The Yugoslav Economy under Self-Management*. New York: St. Martin's Press, 1979.

Slovenia: Country Profile. Annual. London: Economist Intelligence Unit. www.eiu.com.

Slovenia: Country Report. Quarterly. London: Economist Intelligence Unit. www.eiu.com.

Turk, Jeffrey D. "The Failure of Economics and Slovenia's Remarkable Development." *Slovene Studies* 27, 1–2 (2005): 51–73.

Tyson, Laura D'Andrea. *The Yugoslav Economic System and Its Performance in the 1970s*. Berkeley: University of California Institute of International Studies, 1980.

Vahčič, Aleš, and Tea Petrin. "Restructuring the Slovene Economy through Development of Entrepreneurship, and the Role of the Financial System." *Slovene Studies* 12, 1 (1990): 67–73.

Vendarmin, Mojca, ed. *Slovenia: Spring Report 2005*. Analysis, Research, and Development Series. Ljubljana: Urad za makroekonomske analize in razvoj (UMAR), 2005.

Vodopivec, Milan. *The Slovenian Labor Market in Transition: Issues and Lessons Learned.* Washington, DC: World Bank, 1993.

Žebot, Cyril A. "Private Sector in the Economy in the Socialist Republic of Slovenia." In *Cooperative Movements in Eastern Europe,* ed. Aloysius Balawyder, 111–47. Montclair, NJ: Allanheld Osmun, 1980.

IV. HISTORICAL

A. GENERAL

Arnež, John A. *Slovenia in European Affairs: Reflections on Slovenian Political History.* New York: Studia Slovenica, 1958.

Blaznik, Pavle, et al., eds. *Gospodarska in družbena zgodovina Slovencev: Zgodovina agrarnih panog* (Economic and Social History of the Slovenes: History of Agricultural Branches). Ljubljana: Slovenska akademija znanosti in umetnosti; Državna založba Slovenije, 1980.

Borak, Neven, and Jasna Fisher, eds. *Od programa Zedinjena Slovenija do mednarodnega priznanja Republike Slovenije 1848–1992* (From the Program for United Slovenia to International Recognition of the Republic of Slovenia 1848–1992). Ljubljana: Mladinska knjiga, 2005.

Čepič, Zdenko, et al., eds. *Zgodovina Slovencev* (History of the Slovenes). Ljubljana: Cankarjeva založba, 1979.

Djokić, Dejan. *Yugoslavism: Histories of a Failed Idea, 1918–1992.* Madison: University of Wisconsin Press, 2003.

Fischer, Jasna, et al. *The Economic History of Slovenia (1750–1991).* Vrhnika: Razum, 1990.

Gow, James, and Cathie Carmichael. *Slovenia and the Slovenes: A Small State and the New Europe.* Bloomington: Indiana University Press, 2000.

Janša-Zorn, Olga, et al. *Slovenian Historiography in Foreign Languages, Published from 1918–1993.* Ljubljana: ZRC SAZU, 1995.

Jelavich, Barbara. *History of the Balkans.* 2 vols. New York: Cambridge University Press, 1983.

———. *Modern Austria: Empire and Republic, 1815–1986.* New York: Cambridge University Press, 1987.

Lampe, John R. *Yugoslavia as History: Twice There Was a Country.* 2nd ed. Cambridge: Cambridge University Press. 2000.

Mal, Josip. *Zgodovina slovenskega naroda; najnovejša doba* (History of the Slovene Nation; the Most Recent Period). Celje: Mohorjeva družba, 1919; reprint, 1993.

Moritsch, Andreas, and Theodor Domej, eds. *Problemfelder der Geschichte und Geschichtsschreibung der Kaerntner Slovenen / Problemska polja zgodovine in zgodovinopisja koroških Slovencev.* Klagenfurt/Celovec: Verlag Hermagoras, 1995.

Nećak, Dušan, ed. *Avstrija. Jugoslavija. Slovenija. Slovenska narodna identiteta skozi čas* (Austria. Yugoslavia. Slovenia. Slovene National Identity through Time). Ljubljana: Faculty of Philosophy, University of Ljubljana, 1997.

Pavlowitch, Stevan K. *The Improbable Survivor: Yugoslavia and Its Problems 1918–1988*. Columbus: Ohio State University Press, 1988.

Perovšek, Jurij. *Na Poti v Moderno: Poglavja iz zgodovine evropskega in slovenskega liberalizma 19. in 20. stoletja* (On the Road to the Modern: Chapters from the History of European and Slovene Liberalism in the 19th and 20th Centuries). Ljubljana: Institute for Contemporary History, 2005.

Petrovich, Michael Boro. "The Rise of Modern Slovenian Historiography." *Journal of Central European Affairs* 22 (January 1963): 440–67.

Pirjevec, Jože. *Jugoslavia 1918–1992: Nastanek, razvoj ter razpad Karadjordjevićeve in Titove Jugoslavije* (The Establishment, Development, and Disintegration of Karadjordjević and Tito's Yugoslavia). Koper: Lipa, 1995.

———. "Slovene Nationalism in Trieste, 1848–1982." *Nationalities Papers* 11 (Fall 1983): 152–61.

Pleterski, Janko. *Narodi, Jugoslavija, revolucija* (Nations, Yugoslavia, Revolution). Ljubljana: ČZDO Komunist, 1986.

Priestly, Tom. "Denial of Ethnic Identity: The Political Manipulation of Beliefs about Language in Slovene Minority Areas of Austria and Hungary." *Slavic Review* 55, 2 (1997): 364–98.

Prunk, Janko. *A Brief History of Slovenia*. Ljubljana: Mihelač, 1994.

———. *Slovenski narodni programi: Narodni programi v slovenski politični misli od 1848–1945* (Slovene National Programs: National Programs in Slovene Political Thought from 1848–1945). Ljubljana: Društvo 2000, 1986.

———. *Slovenski narodni vzpon: Narodna politika, 1768–1992* (Slovene National Ascent: National Politics, 1768–1992). Ljubljana: Državna založba Slovenije, 1992.

Ramet, Sabrina P. *The Three Yugoslavias. State-building and Legitimation, 1918–2005*. Bloomington and Washington, DC: Indiana University Press and Woodrow Wilson Center Press, 2006.

Singleton, Fred. *Twentieth-Century Yugoslavia*. New York: Columbia University Press, 1976.

———. *A Short History of the Yugoslav Peoples*. New York: Cambridge University Press, 1985.

Slovenci in država: Zbornik prispevkov z znanstvenega posveta na SAZU, od 9. do 11. novembra 1994 (Slovenes and the State: A Collection of Contributions to a Scholarly Conference at the Slovene Academy of Sciences and Arts November 9–11, 1994). Ljubljana: SAZU, 1995.

Stiplovšek, Miroslav. *Prispevki za zgodovino sindikalnega gibanja na Slovenskem: od začetkov strokovnega gibanja do enotnih sindikatov Slovenije, 1868–1945* (Contributions to the History of the Trade Unions Movement in Slovenia: From the Beginnings of Professional Movement to the Unified Trade Unions of Slovenia, 1868–1945). Maribor: Obzorja, 1989.

Švajncer, Janez. *Vojna in vojaška zgodovina Slovencev* (War and Military History of the Slovenes). Ljubljana: Prešernova družba, 1992.

Vidic, Marko, et al., eds. *Ilustrirana zgodovina Slovencev* (Ilustrated History of Slovenes). Ljubljana: Mladinska knjiga, 1999.

Vilfan, Sergij, ed. *Slovenian Historiography in Foreign Languages* (Published from 1918–1993). Ljubljana: Skušek, 1995.

Vodopivec, Peter. "Slovenes and Yugoslavia 1918–1991." *East European Politics and Societies* 6, 3 (1992): 220–41.

———. *Od Pohlinove slovnice do samostojne države: slovenska zgodovina od konca 18. stoletja do konca 20. stoletja* (From Pohlin's Grammar to an Independent State: Slovene History from the End of the 18th Century to the End of the 20th Century). Ljubljana: Modrijan, 2006.

Žebot, Ciril A. *Neminljiva Slovenija* (Everlasting Slovenia). Published by the author; distributed by Družba sv. Mohorja v Celovcu, Klagenfurt, Austria, 1988.

———. *Slovenija včeraj, danes, jutri* (Slovenia Yesterday, Today, Tomorrow). 2 vols. Published by the author; distributed by Družba sv. Mohorja v Celovcu, Klagenfurt, Austria, 1967 and 1969.

B. EARLY HISTORY (TO 1918)

Bister, Feliks. *Anton Korošec, državnozborski poslanec na Dunaju: Življenje in delo 1872–1918* (Anton Korošec, Parliamentary Representative in Vienna: Life and Work 1872–1918). Ljubljana: Slovenska matica, 1992.

Čuješ, Rudolf P. *Slovenia: Land of Cooperators.* Willowdale, Ontario: Slovenian Research Centre, 1985.

Dolgan, Marjan, ed. *Družbena in kulturna podoba slovenske reformacije* (A Social and Cultural Picture of the Slovene Reformation). Ljubljana: Slovenska akademija znanosti in umetnosti, 1986.

Felicijan, Joseph. *The Genesis of the Contractual Theory and the Installation of the Dukes of Carinthia.* Klagenfurt: Družba sv. Mohorja v Celovcu, 1968.

Gantar Godina, Irena. *Neoslavizem in Slovenci* (Neoslavism and the Slovenes). Ljubljana: Znanstveni inštitut Filozofske fakultete, 1994.

———. *T. G. Masaryk in masarykovstvo na Slovenskem, 1895–1914* (T. G. Masaryk and Masarykism among the Slovenes, 1895–1914). Ljubljana: Slovenska matica, 1987.

Gelt, Draga. *The Slovenians from the Earliest Times: Illustrated Study of Slovenia.* Victoria, Australia: Coordinating Committee of Slovenian Organizations, 1985.

Gestrin, Ferdo, and Vasilij Melik. *Slovenska zgodovina od konca osemnajstega stoletja do 1918* (Slovene History from the End of the 18th Century to 1918). Ljubljana: Državna založba Slovenije, 1966.

Grafenauer, Bogo. *Boj za staro pravdo v 15. in 16. stoletju na Slovenskem* (The Fight for Old Rights in the Fifteenth and Sixteenth Centuries in Slovenia). Ljubljana: Državna založba Slovenije, 1974.

————. *Slovensko narodno vprašanje in slovenski zgodovinski položaj* (The Slovene National Question and Slovene Historical Situation). Ljubljana: Slovenska matica, 1987.

Jelavich, Barbara, and Charles Jelavich. *The Establishment of the Balkan National States, 1804–1920*. Seattle: University of Washington Press, 1977.

Jelavich, Charles. *South Slavic Texbooks and Yugoslav Union before 1914*. Columbus: Ohio State University Press, 1990.

Kann, Robert. "The Slovenes." In *The Multinational Empire: Nationalism and National Reform in the Habsburg Monarchy 1848–1914*, 294–304. New York: Columbia University Press, 1950.

Kardelj, Edvard. *Razvoj slovenskega narodnega vprašanja* (Development of the Slovene National Question). Ljubljana: Državna založba Slovenije, 1957, 1970, 1977, and 1980. (A 1939 edition was published under the pseudonym Sperans.)

Koren, Anton. "140 let Mohorjeve družbe" (One Hundred and Forty Years of Hermagoras Society). *Koledar Mohorjeve družbe* (Hermagoras Society Almanac), 8–37. Klagenfurt: Mohorjeva družba v Celovcu, 1992.

Kos, Franc. *Izbrano delo. Poglavja iz zgodovine Slovencev do leta 900* (Selected Works. Chapters from the History of Slovenes to the year 900). Ed. Bogo Grafenauer. Ljubljana: Slovenska matica, 1982.

Kos, Milko. *Srednjeveška zgodovina Slovencev: Izbrane razprave* (Medieval History of the Slovenes: Selected Papers). Ed. Bogo Grafenauer. Ljubljana: Slovenska matica, 1985.

————. *Zgodovina Slovencev do petnajstega stoletja* (History of the Slovenes to the Fifteenth Century). Ljubljana: Slovenska matica, 1955.

Kuhar, Aloysius L. *The Conversion of the Slovenes and the German-Slav Ethnic Boundary in the Eastern Alps*. New York: Studia Slovenica, 1959.

————. *Slovene Medieval History: Selected Studies*. New York: Studia Slovenica, 1962.

Linhart, Anton. *Poskus zgodovine Kranjske in ostalih dežel južnih Slovanov Avstrije* (An Attempt at a History of Carniola and the Other Southern Slavic Lands of Austria). 2 vols. Ljubljana: Slovenska matica 1981. Translation from German and reprint of the 1788 (vol. 1) and the 1791 (vol. 2) editions of the first Slovene history.

Lončar, Dragotin. *The Slovenes: A Social History. From the Earliest Times to 1910*. Trans. Anthony Klančar. Cleveland, OH: American Jugoslav, 1939.

Melik, Vasilij. *Volitve na Slovenskem, 1861–1918* (Elections in the Slovene Lands, 1861–1918). Ljubljana: Slovenska matica, 1965.

Moritsch, Andreas, and Vincenz Rajšp, eds. *Matija Majar-Ziljski*. Klagenfurt/Celovec: Verlag Hermagoras, 1995.

Novak, Bogdan C. "The Controversy about the Kosezi in Slovene Historiography." *Slovene Studies* 4, 1–2 (1979): 125–54.

————. "At the Roots of Slovene National Individuality," *Papers in Slovene Studies* (1975): 79–125.

Otorepec, Božo. *Srednjeveški pečati in grbi mest in trgov na Slovenskem* (Medieval Seals and Coats of Arms of Slovene Towns and Market Towns). Ljubljana: Slovenska matica / Slovenska akademija znanosti in umetnosti, 1988.

Pleterski, Janko. *Prva odločitev Slovencev za Jugoslavijo: Politika na domačih tleh med vojno 1914–1918* (The First Decision of Slovenes for Yugoslavia: Domestic Politics during the War 1914–1918). Ljubljana: Slovenska matica, 1971.

Prijatelj, Ivan. *Slovenska kulturnopolitična in slovstvena zgodovina, 1848–1895* (Slovene Cultural and Literary History, 1848–1895). 5 vols. Ljubljana: Državna založba Slovenije, 1955–1966.

Rogel, Carole. *The Slovenes and Yugoslavism 1890–1914*. East European Monographs, vol. 24. Boulder, CO: East European Quarterly; New York: Columbia University Press, 1977.

———. "The Slovenes in the Revolutionary Period," In *The Consortium on Revolutionary Europe, 1750–1850*. Proceedings, 1 (1980): 265–74.

Rotar, Janez. *Trubar in južni Slovani* (Trubar and the South Slavs). Ljubljana: Državna založba Slovenije, 1988.

Seton-Watson, Robert William. *The Southern Slav Question and the Habsburg Monarchy*. London: Constable, 1911; reprint, New York: Howard Fertig, 1969.

Simoniti, Primož. *Humanizem na Slovenskem in slovenski humanisti do srede XVI. stoletja* (Humanism in the Slovene Lands and Slovene Humanists up to the Mid-Sixteenth Century). Ljubljana: Slovenska matica, 1979.

Šavli, Jožko, et al. *Veneti: First Builders of European Community*. Vienna: Editiones Veneti; co-published by Anton Škerbinc, Boswell (B.C., Canada), 1996.

Turk, Ernest. *Dobrovoljci proti Avstro-Ogrski med prvo svetovno vojno 1914–1918* (Volunteers against Austria-Hungary during the First World War 1914–1918). Ljubljana: Borec, 1978.

Voje, Ignacij. "The Influence of the Ottoman Empire on Slovenian Countries in the Fifteenth and Sixteenth Centuries: Problems and State of Historiography." In *Ottoman Rule in Middle Europe and Balkans in the Sixteenth and Seventeenth Centuries*. Proceedings of the Ninth International Conference of the Czechoslovak-Yugoslav Historical Committee, 108–41. Prague: Oriental Institute, 1978.

Zwitter, Fran. *Les problèmes nationaux dans la monarchie des Habsburg* (Nationality Problems in the Habsburg Monarchy). Belgrade, 1960. Also published as *Nacionalni problemi v habsburški monarhiji*. Ljubljana: Slovenska matica, 1962.

———. *O slovenskem narodnem vprašanju* (On the Slovene National Question). Ljubljana: Slovenska matica, 1992.

———. "The Slovenes in the Habsburg Monarchy." *Austrian History Yearbook* 3, part 2 (1967): 159–88. Houston: Rice University Press.

C. THE YUGOSLAV EXPERIENCE (1919–1990)

Drnovšek, Marjan, et al., eds. *Slovenska kronika XX stoletja: 1941–1995* (Slovene Chronicle of the Twentieth Century: 1941–1995). Ljubljana: Nova revija, 1996.

———. *Slovenska kronika XX. stoletja: 1900–1941* (Slovene Chronicle of the Twentieth Century: 1900–1941). Ljubljana: Nova revija, 1995.

Huttenbach, Henry R., and Peter Vodopivec, eds. "Voices from the Slovene Nation." Special issue, *Nationalities Papers* 31, 1 (1993).

Sluga, Glenda. *The Problem of Trieste and the Italo-Yugoslav Border: Difference, Identity, and Sovereignty in Twentieth-Century Europe.* Albany: State University of New York Press, 2001.

1. ROYAL YUGOSLAVIA

Adamic, Louis. *The Native's Return: An American Immigrant Visits Yugoslavia and Discovers His Old Country.* 1934; reprint, Westport, CT: Greenwood Press, 1975.

———. *My Native Land: Yugoslavia 1933–1943.* New York: Harper Brothers, 1943.

Dolenc, Ervin. *Slovenska kulturna politika v Kraljevini SHS 1918–1929* (Slovene Cultural Politics in the Kingdom of Serbs, Croats, and Slovenes 1918–1929). Ljubljana: Cankarjeva založba, 1996.

———. "Comparative Analysis of Cultural Development Statistics: The Case of the First Yugoslavia." *East European Quarterly* 39, 4 (2006): 465–89.

Dragoš, Srečo. *Katolicizem na Slovenskem: Socialni koncepti do druge svetovne vojne* (Catholicism in Slovenia: Social Concepts up to the Second World War). Ljubljana: Krtina, 1998.

Ehrlich, Lambert. *Pariška mirovna konferenca in Slovenci 1919/20* (Paris Peace Conference and Slovenes 1919/20). Ljubljana: Inšitut za zgodovino Cerkve pri Teološki fakulteti Univerze, 2002.

Hametz, Maura. "The Nefarious Former Authorities: Name Change in Trieste, 1918–22." *Austrian History Yearbook* 35 (2004): 233–52.

Mikuž, Metod. *Oris zgodovine Slovencev v stari Jugoslaviji, 1917–1941* (An Outline of the History of the Slovenes in Old Yugoslavia, 1917–1941). Ljubljana: Mladinska knjiga, 1965.

Nećak, Dušan, et al., eds. *Slovensko–avstrijski odnosi v 20. stoletju / Slowenisch–Oesterreichische Beziehungen im 20. Jahrhundert* (Slovene–Austrian Relations in the Twentieth Century). Ljubljana: Faculty of Philosophy, University of Ljubljana, 2004.

Perovšek, Jurij. *Liberalizem in Vprašanje Slovenstva: Nacionalna politika liberalnega tabora v letih 1918–1929* (Liberalism and the Question of Slovenism: The National Politics of the Liberal Camp 1918–1929). Ljubljana: Modrijan, 1996.

Rahten, Andrej. *Slovenska ljudska stranka v beograjski skupščini. Jugoslovanski klub v parlamentarnem življenju kraljevine SHS 1919–1929* (Slovene People's Party in the Belgrade Assembly. Yugoslav Club in the Parliamentary Life of the Kingdom SHS 1919–1929). Ljubljana: ZRC SAZU, 2002.

Repe, Božo, and Dušan Nećak. *Prelom 1914–1918: Svet in Slovenci v prvi svetovni vojni* (The Break 1914–1918: The World and the Slovenes in the First World War). Ljubljana: Sophia, 2005.

Rothschild, Joseph. "Yugoslavia." In *East Central Europe between the Two World Wars*, 201–80. Seattle: University of Washington Press, 1974.

Vidovič-Miklavčič, Anka. *Mladina med nacionalizmom in katolicizmom* (Youth between Nationalism and Catholicism). Ljubljana: Krt, Študentska organizacija Univerze v Ljubljani, 1994.

Vode, Angela. *Zbrana dela Angele Vode* (Collected Works of Angela Vode). 3 vols. Ljubljana: Krtina, 1998–2000.

Zečević, Momčilo. *Slovenska ljudska stranka in jugoslovansko zedinjenje 1917–1921* (Slovene People's Party and Yugoslav Unification 1917–1921). Maribor: Obzorja, 1977.

2. WORLD WAR II (1941–1945)

Arnež, Janez. *SLS, 1941–1945* (SLS [Slovenian People's Party], 1941–1945). Ljubljana: Studia Slovenica, 2001.

Bajt, Aleksander. *Bermanov dosje* (Berman's File). Ljubljana: Mladinska knjiga, 1999.

Barker, Thomas Mack. *Social Revolutionaries and Secret Agents: The Carinthian Slovene Partisans and Britain's Special Operations Executive.* Boulder, CO: East European Monographs, distributed by Columbia University Press, 1990.

Bela knjiga slovenskega protikomunističnega upora 1941–1945 (White Paper on the Slovene Anti-Communist Uprising 1941–1945). Cleveland, OH: Ameriška domovina, 1985.

Blumenwitz, Dieter. *Okupacija in revolucija v Sloveniji, 1941–1946* (Occupation and Revolution in Slovenia 1941–1945). Celovec: Mohorjeva družba, 2005.

Corsellis, John, and Marcus Ferrar. *Slovenia 1945: Memories of Death and Survival.* London: J.B. Tauris, 2005.

Griesser-Pečar, Tamara. *Razdvojeni narod: Slovenija 1941–1945. Okupacija, kolaboracija, državljanska vojna, revolucija* (A Divided Nation: Slovenia 1941–1945. Occupation, Collaboration, Civil War, Revolution). Mladinska knjiga, 2004. Translation of *Das zerrissene Volk: Slowenien 1941–1946. Okkupation, Kollaboration, Bürgerkrieg, Revolution.* Studien zu Politik und Verwaltung, vol. 86. Wien-Köln-Graz: Böhlau Verlag, 2003.

Harriman, Helga H. *Slovenia under Nazi Occupation, 1941–1945.* New York: Studia Slovenica, 1977.

———. "Slovenia as an Outpost of the Third Reich." *East European Quarterly* 5 (1971): 222–31.

Hribar, Spomenka. *Dolomitska izjava (Dolomite Declaration).* Ljubljana: Nova revija, 1991.

Karapandžić, Borivoje M. *The Bloodiest Yugoslav Spring: 1945; Tito's Katyns and Gulags.* Hearthstone Book. New York: Carlton Press, 1980.

———. *Kočevje, Tito's Bloodiest Crime.* Cleveland, OH: n.p. 1965 (printed by Iskra in München).

Kos, Stanko (Nikolaj Jeločnik). *Stalinistična revolucija na Slovenskem 1941–1945* (The Stalinist Revolution in Slovenia 1941–1945). Vol. 1, Rome, 1986; vol. 2, Buenos Aires, 1991.

Kranjc, Gregor. "Two Solitudes Revisited: A Historiographical Survey of Collaboration in Slovenia during World War II," *Slovene Studies* 24, 1–2 (2002): 3–26.

Krek, Miha. "The Slovenes: German Policy of Extermination." *Central European Observer* 19 (24 July 1942): 231–32.

Lindsay, Franklin. *Beacons in the Night: With the OSS and Tito's Partisans in Wartime Yugoslavia.* Stanford, CA: Stanford University Press, 1993.

Milač, Metod M. *Resistance, Imprisonment, and Forced Labor: A Slovene Student in World War II.* New York: Peter Lang, 2002. Also available in Slovene: *Kdo solze naše posuši: Doživetja slovenskega dijaka med drugo svetovno vojno.* Celje: Mohorjeva družba, 2003.

Mikuž, Metod. *Pregled zgodovine narodnoosvobodilne borbe v Sloveniji* (A Survey of the National Liberation War in Slovenia). 5 vols. Ljubljana: Cankarjeva založba, 1960–1973.

Mlakar, Boris. *Slovensko Domobranstvo 1943–1945. Ustanovitev, organizacija, idejno ozadje* (Slovene Home Guardism, Establishment, Organization, Ideological Background). Ljubljana: Slovenska matica, 2003.

Schmidt, Amy. "WWII Yugoslav Materials in the National Archives." *Slovene Studies,* 16, 2 (1994): 13–30.

Sirc, Ljubo. *Between Hitler and Tito: Nazi Occupation and Communist Oppression.* London: A. Deutsch, 1989.

Slovenski upor 1941: Osvobodilna fronta slovenskega naroda pred pol stoletja (The Slovene Uprising 1941: The Liberation Front of the Slovene Nation Half a Century Ago). Ljubljana: Slovenska akademija znanosti in umetnosti, 1991.

Tolstoy, Nikolai. *The Minister and the Massacres.* London: Century Hutchinson, 1986.

Ude, Lojze. *Moje mnenje o položaju: Članki in pisma 1941–1944* (My Opinion on the Situation: Articles and Letters 1941–1944). Ed. Boris Mlakar. Ljubljana: Slovenska matica, 1994.

Vodušek-Starić, Jera. *Prevzem oblasti 1944–1946* (The Takeover of Power 1944–1946). Ljubljana: Cankarjeva založba, 1992.

———. *Slovenski špijoni in SOE 1938–1942* (Slovene Spies and SOE 1938–1942). Published by the author, Ljubljana, 2002.

Vovko, Andrej. "The Foundation of the Yugoslav Emergency Council in New York." *Slovene Studies* 10, 2 (1988): 191–97.

Žrtve vojne in revolucije (Victims of War and Revolution). Ljubljana: Institute of Contemporary History, in collaboration with the State Assembly of the Republic of Slovenia, 2005.

3. SOCIALIST YUGOSLAVIA (1945–1990)

Adamic, Louis. *The Eagle and the Roots*. Westport, CT: Greenwood Press, 1970.

Banac, Ivo. *The National Question in Yugoslavia: Origins, History, and Politics*. Ithaca, NY: Cornell University Press, 1984.

———. *With Stalin against Tito: Cominformist Splits in Yugoslav Communism*. Ithaca, NY: Cornell University Press, 1988.

Bebler, Anton. *The Yugoslav Crisis and the "Yugoslav People's Army."* Zurich: Forschungsstelle für Sicherheitspolitik und Konfliktanalyse, Eidgenossische Technische Hochschule, 1992.

Bohanec, Franček, and Brane Grabeljšek, eds. *Študentske pomladi* (Student Springtimes). Ljubljana: Partizanska knjiga, 1986.

Davis, James C. "Slovenian Laborer and His Experience of Industrialization, 1888–1976." *East European Quarterly* 10 (1976): 3–20.

Doder, Duško. *The Yugoslavs*. New York: Random House, 1978.

Ferenc, Tone. *Ljudska oblast na Slovenskem* (People's Rule in Slovenia). Ljubljana: Mladika, 1991.

Gabrič, Aleš. *Slovenska Agitpropovska kulturna politika, 1945–1952* (Slovene Agitprop Cultural Policy, 1945–1952). *Borec* 43, 7, 8, 9 (1991).

———. *Socialistična kulturna revolucija. Slovenska kulturna politika 1953–1962* (The Socialist Cultural Revolution: Slovene Cultural Politics 1953–1962). Ljubljana: Cankarjeva založba, 1995.

Griesser-Pečar, Tamara. *Cerkev na zatožni klopi: sodni procesi, administrativne kazni, posegi "ljudske oblasti" v Sloveniji od 1943 do 1960* (Church in the Dock: Judicial Processes, Administrative Punishments, Interventions of "Peoples Rule" in Slovenia from 1943 to1960). Ljubljana: Družina, 2005.

———. *Stanislav Lenič: Življenjepis iz zapora* (Stanislav Lenič: A Biography from Jail). Celovec-Ljubljana-Dunaj: Mohorjeva založba, 1997.

Griesser-Pečar, Tamara, and France Martin Dolinar. *Rožmanov process* (The Rožman Trial). Ljubljana: Družina, 1996.

Horvat, Marjan, et al., eds. *V imenu ljudstva: Proces pred vojaškim sodiščem v Ljubljani, junij-julij 1988* (In the Name of the People: The Trial before the Court Martial in Ljubljana, June–July 1988). Ljubljana: Repro Studio, 1988.

Hribar, Spomenka. *Krivda in Greh* (Guilt and Sin). Maribor: ZAT, 1990.

Kavčič, Stane. *Dnevnik in spomini: 1972–1987* (Diary and Memoirs: 1972–1987). Ljubljana: Časopis za kritiko znanosti, 1988.

Kocbek, Edvard. *Dnevnik 1945* (Diary 1945). Ljubljana: Cankarjeva založba, 1991.

————. *Dnevnik 1946* (Diary 1946) Ljubljana: Cankarjeva založba, 1991.

Pleterski, Janko. *Senca Ajdovskega gradca* (The Shadow of Ajdovski gradec). Ljubljana: Tiskarna Pleško, 1993.

Plut-Pregelj, Leopoldina, ed. *The Repluralization of Slovenia in the 1980s: New Revelations from Archival Records.* Donald W. Treadgold Papers. Seattle: University of Washington, 2000.

Prunk, Janko. *Nova slovenska samozavest: Pogovori s slovenskimi političnimi prvaki* (New Slovene Self-Confidence: Talks with Slovene Political Leaders). Ljubljana: Lumi, Panatal, 1991.

Ramet, Sabrina P. *Nationalism and Federalism in Yugoslavia 1962–1991.* Bloomington: Indiana University Press, 1992.

————. *Balkan Babel: The Disintegration of Yugoslavia from the Death of Tito to the Fall of Milošević.* 4th ed. Boulder, CO: Westview Press, 2002.

Repe, Božo. *Liberalizem v Sloveniji* (Liberalism in Slovenia). *Borec* 44, 9 and 10 (1992).

————. *Slovenci v osemdesetih letih* (Slovenes in the Eighties). Ljubljana: Zveza zgodovinskih društev Slovenije, 2001.

————. *Rdeča zemlja: tokovi in obrazi iz obdobja socializma* (The Red Land: Currents and Faces from the Era of Socialism). Ljubljana: Sophia, 2003.

Rogel, Carole R. "Slovenia's Independence: A Reversal of History." *Problems of Communism* 40 (July/August 1991): 31–40.

Rupel, Dimitrij. "The Heresy of Edvard Kocbek." *Slovene Studies* 10, 1 (1988): 51–60.

————. *Slovenska pot do samostojnosti in priznanja* (The Slovenian Path to Independence and Recognition). Ljubljana: Kres, 1992.

————. *Slovenstvo kot politično prepričanje* (Slovenism as a Political Conviction). Ljubljana: Kres, 1992

Rusinow, Dennison I. *Slovenia: Modernization without Urbanization?* Southeast Europe series, 20. Hanover, NH: American University Field Staff, 1973.

————. *The Yugoslav Experiment, 1948–1974.* London: C. Hurst for the Royal Institute of International Affairs, 1977.

Stavrou, Nicholas A. *Edvard Kardelj, 1910– : The Historical Roots of Non-Alignment.* Washington, DC: University Press of America, 1980.

Stokes, Gale. "The Devil's Finger: The Disintegration of Yugoslavia." In *The Walls Came Tumbling Down: The Collapse of Communism in Eastern Europe.* New York: Oxford University Press, 1993.

Temna stran meseca: Kratka zgodovina totalitarizma v Sloveniji 1945–1990: zbornik člankov in dokumentov (The Dark Side of the Moon: A Short History of Totalitarianism in Slovenia 1945–1990: Anthology of Essays and Documents). Ed. Drago Jančar. Ljubljana: Nova revija, 1998.

Tomc, Gregor. *Druga Slovenija: Zgodovina mladinskih gibanj na Slovenskem* (The Other Slovenia: A History of Youth Movements in Slovenia). Krt, no. 54. Ljubljana: Študentska organizacija Univerze v Ljubljani, 1989.

Trifunovska, Snežana, ed. *Yugoslavia through Documents: From Its Creation to Its Dissolution*. Boston: Martinus Nijhoff, 1994.

Ude, Lojze. *Slovenci in jugoslovanska skupnost* (The Slovenes and the Yugoslav Community). Maribor: Obzorja, 1972.

Vode, Angela. *Skriti spomin*. Uredila in spremno besedo napisala Alenka Puhar (The Hidden Memory. Editing and foreword by Alenka Puhar). Ljubljana: Nova revija, 2004.

Vodopivec, Peter, ed. *Usoda slovenskih demokratičnih izobražencev: Angela Vode in Boris Furlan žrtve Nagodetovega procesa* (The Fate of Slovene Democratic Intellectuals: Angela Vode and Boris Furlan Victims of the Nagode Trial). Ljubljana: Slovenska matica, 2001.

Željeznov, Dušan. *Rupnikov proces* (The Rupnik Trial). Ljubljana: Cankarjeva založba, 1980.

Žitnik, Janja. *Louis Adamič in sodobniki, 1948–1951* (Louis Adamič and His Contemporaries, 1948–1951). Ljubljana: Slovenska akademija znanosti in umetnosti, 1992.

———. *Pero in politika: Zadnja leta Louisa Adamiča* (Pen and Politics: The Last Years of Louis Adamič). Ljubljana: Slovenska matica, 1993.

D. INDEPENDENT SLOVENIA (1991–)

Bennett, Christopher. *Yugoslavia's Bloody Collapse: Causes, Course, and Consequence*. New York: New York University Press, 1995.

Bukowski, Charles. "Slovene Foreign Policy toward Serbia: Reclaiming the Past." *Slovene Studies*, 28 (2006): 3–30.

Caplan, Richard. *Europe and the Recognition of New States in Yugoslavia*. Cambridge: Cambridge University Press, 2005.

Cohen, Leonard. *Broken Bonds: The Disintegration of Yugoslavia and Balkan Politics in Transition*. 3rd ed. Boulder, CO: Westview Press, 1997.

Cox, John. *Slovenia: Evolving Loyalties. Postcommunist States and Nations*. New York: Routledge, 2005.

Drnovšek, Janez. *Moja Resnica* (My Truth). Ljubljana: Mladinska knjiga, 1996.

Janša, Janez. *The Making of the Slovene State 1988–1992: The Collapse of Yugoslavia*. Ljubljana: Mladinska knjiga, 1994. Translation of *Premiki: Nastajanje in obramba slovenske države 1988–1992*. Ljubljana: Mladinska knjiga, 1992.

Meier, Viktor. *Yugoslavia: A History of Its Demise*. Trans. Sabrina Ramet from the German *Wie Jugoslawien verspielt wurde* (1995). New York: Routledge, 1999.

Patterson, Patrick Hyder. "On the Edge of Reason: The Boundaries of Balkanism in Slovenian, Austrian, and Italian Discourse." *Slavic Review* 62, 1 (2003): 110–41.

Požun, Brian. *Shedding the Balkan Skin: Slovenia's Quiet Emergence in the New Europe*. *Central European Review* ebook, 2000. Available at www.ce -review.org.

Ramet, Sabrina P. "Democratization in Slovenia—The Second Stage." In *Politics, Power, and the Struggle for Democracy in South-East Europe*, ed. Karen Dawisha and Bruce Parrot. Cambridge: Cambridge University Press, 1997.

———. *Thinking about Yugoslavia*. New York: Cambridge University Press, 2005.

———. "The United States and Slovenia, 1990–1992." *Acta Histriae* 11, 1 (2003): 53–72.

———. "Views from Inside: Memoirs Concerning the Yugoslav Breakup and War." *Slavic Review* 61, 3 (2002): 558–80.

Repe, Božo. "Historical Consequences of the Disintegration of Yugoslavia for Slovene Society." *Österrechische Osthefte* 43, 1–2 (2001): 5–26.

———. *Jutri je nov dan: Slovenci in razpad Jugoslavije* (Tomorrow Is a New Day: The Slovenes and the Disintegration of Yugoslavia). Ljubljana: Modrijan, 2002.

———. "Slovenes and Their National Position in the 20th Century." *Slovak Foreign Policy Affairs* 4, 1 (2003): 57–62.

Rizman, Rudi. *Uncertain Path: Democratic Transition and Consolidation in Slovenia*. College Station: Texas A&M University Press, 2006.

Rogel, Carole. *The Breakup of Yugoslavia and Its Aftermath*. Westport, CT: Greenwood Press, 2004.

Silber, Laura, and Allan Little. *Yugoslavia: Death of a Nation*. 2nd ed. New York: Penguin Books, 1997. Also available as a six-hour documentary made for television through TV Books / Penguin USA, 1996.

Stokes, Gale. "The Devil's Finger: The Disintegration of Yugoslavia." *The Walls Came Tumbling Down: The Collapse of Communism in Eastern Europe*. New York: Oxford University Press, 1993.

Stokes, Gale, et al. "Instant History: Understanding the Wars of Yugoslav Succession." *Slavic Review* 55, 1 (1996): 136–60.

Zimmermann, Warren. *Origins of a Catastrophe: Yugoslavia and Its Destroyers—America's Last Ambassador Tells What Happened and Why*. New York: Times Books, 1996.

V. JURIDICAL

The Constitution of the Socialist Federal Republic of Yugoslavia. Ljubljana: Dopisna delavska univerza, 1974.

Hayden, Robert M. *The Beginning of the End of Federal Yugoslavia: The Slovenian Amendment Crisis of 1989*. Carl Beck papers, no. 1001. Pittsburgh:

University of Pittsburgh, Center for Russian and East European Studies, 1992.

————. *Social Courts in Theory and Practice: Yugoslav Workers' Courts in Comparative Perspective.* Philadelphia: University of Pennsylvania Press, 1990.

Inter-University Associates. "Republic of Slovenia." Updated to 2003. In *Constitutions of the Countries of the World*, ed. Gisbert H. Glanz and Patricie H. Ward, vol. 16. Dobbs Ferry, NY: Oceana, 1971– .

Jambrek, Peter. *Ustavna demokracija: graditev slovenske demokracije, države in ustave* (Constitutional Democracy: The Building of Slovene Democracy, State, and Constitution). Ljubljana: Državna založba Slovenije, 1992.

Ustava republike Slovenije in ustavni zakon za izvedbo ustave republike Slovenije (The Constitution of the Republic of Slovenia and the Constitutional Law for the Implementation of the Constitution of the Republic of Slovenia). Celje: Mavrica, 1991.

VI. POLITICAL

Allcock, John B., et al., eds. *Yugoslavia in Transition: Choices and Constraints: Essays in Honour of Fred Singleton.* New York: Berg, distributed by St. Martin's Press, 1992.

Almond, Mark. *Blundering in the Balkans: The European Community and the Yugoslav Crisis.* Oxford: School of European Studies, 1991.

Antić-Gaber, Milica. "Women in the Slovene Parliament: Working towards Critical Mass." In *Women in East European Politics*, 19–32. Washington, DC: Woodrow Wilson International Center for Scholars, 2005.

Balkovec, Bojan. "Political Parties in Slovenia." *Nationalities Papers* 21, 1 (1993): 189–92.

Bučar, France. *The Reality and the Myth.* Trans. Rudolf P. Čuješ, of *Resničnost in utvara.* Maribor: Obzorja, 1986. Antigonish, Canada: St. Francis Xavier University Press, 1989.

Bukowski, Charles. "Slovenia's Transition to Democracy: Theory and Practice." *East European Quarterly* 38, 1 (1999): 69–96.

Burg, Steven L. *Conflict Cohesion in Socialist Yugoslavia: Political Decision Making Since 1966.* Princeton: Princeton University Press, 1993.

Cviic, Christopher. *Remaking the Balkans.* New York: Council on Foreign Relations Press, 1991.

Čelik, Pavle. *Izza barikad* (From Behind the Barricades). Ljubljana: Slovenske novice, 1992.

————. *Policija, demonstracije, oblast* (Police, Demonstrations, Power). Ljubljana: ČZP Enotnost, 1994.

Fink-Hafner, Danica. *Politčne stranke* (Political Parties). Ljubljana: FDV, Univerza v Ljubljani, 2001.

Fink-Hafner, Danica, and Tomaž Boh. *Parlamentarne volitve 2000* (Parliamentary Elections 2000). Ljubljana: FDV, Univerza v Ljubljani, 2002.

Fink-Hafner, Danica, and Terry Cox, eds. *Into Europe: Perspectives from Britain and Slovenia.* Ljubljana: FDV, Univerza v Ljubljani, 1996.

Fink-Hafner, Danica, and Damjan Lajh. *Managing Europe from Home: The Europeanisation of the Slovenian Core Executive.* Ljubljana: Faculty of Social Sciences, University of Ljubljana, 2003.

Fink-Hafner, Danica, and John R. Robbins. *Making of a New Nation: The Formation of Slovenia.* Brookfield, VT: Dartmouth, 1997.

Gáthy, Vera, ed. *State and Civil Society: Relationship in Flux.* Budapest: Hungarian Academy of Sciences, 1989.

Gow, James. *Legitimacy and the Military: The Yugoslav Crisis.* New York: St. Martin's Press, 1992.

Grizold, Anton, ed. *Razpotja nacionalne varnosti: obramboslovne raziskave v Sloveniji* (Crossroads of National Security: Defense Science Research in Slovenia). Ljubljana: FDV, Univerza v Ljubljani, 1992.

Hall, Brian. *The Impossible Country: A Journey through the Last Days of Yugoslavia.* Boston: D. R. Godine, 1993.

Harris, Erika. *Nationalism and Democratization: Politics of Slovakia and Slovenia.* Burlington, VT: Ashgate, 2002.

Hribar, Tine. *Slovenska državnost* (Slovene Statehood). Ljubljana: Cankarjeva založba, 1989.

Hubad, Jože. *Dolga slovenska pot v svobodno Evropo* (The Long Slovene Journey into a Free Europe). Ljubljana: Litera, 2005.

Jambrek, Peter. *Oblast in opozicija v Sloveniji* (Power and Opposition in Slovenia). Maribor: Obzorja, 1989.

Jazbec, Milan, ed. *Diplomacija in Slovenci* (Diplomacy and Slovenes). Celovec: Drava, 1998.

Kardelj, Edvard. *Democracy and Socialism.* London: Summerfield Press, 1978.

Klemenčič, Matjaž. "Slovenia at the Crossroads of the Nineties: From the First Multiparty Elections and the Declaration of Independence to Membership in the Council of Europe." *Slovene Studies* 14, 1 (1992, published March 1994): 9–34.

Kocijančič, Janez. *The Yugoslav Youth Movement 1919–1966.* Belgrade: Mladost, 1969.

Magaš, Branka. *The Destruction of Yugoslavia: Tracing the Break-up 1980–92.* London: Verso, 1993.

Mastnak, Tomaž. "Civil Society in Slovenia: From Opposition to Power." *Studies in Comparative Communism* 23 (1990): 305–17. Also published in *The Tragedy of Yugoslavia.* Ed. Jim Seroka and Vukašin Pavlović, 49–66. Armonk, NY: M. E. Sharpe, 1992.

———. "Even the Future Is Not What It Used to Be." *Across Frontiers* 3, 3 (1987): 13–15.

————. "Modernization of Repression." In *State and Civil Society: Relationship in Flux*, ed. Vera Gáthy. Budapest: Hungarian Academy of Sciences, 1989.

————. "The Night of Long Knives." *Across Frontiers* 4, 4 (1989): 4–7.

Mastnak, Tomaž, and Lynne Jones. "Yugoslavia: The Awakening." *New York Review of Books*, 28 June 1990, 42–47; 19 July 1990, 37–42.

Perko, Drago, and Milan Orožen Adamič. *Slovenske občine* (Slovene Municipalities). Ljubljana: Mladinska knjiga, 1998.

Ramet, Sabrina P., and Danica Fink-Hafner, eds. *Democratic Transition in Slovenia*. College Station: Texas A&M University Press, 2006.

Rupel, Dimitrij. *Čas politike* (A Time of Politics). Ljubljana: Državna založba Slovenije, 1994.

————. *Skrivnost države: spomini na domače in zunanje zadeve 1989–1992* (The Mystery of the State: Remembrances of Domestic and Foreign Affairs 1989–1992). Ljubljana: Delo-Novice, 1992.

Smole, Jože. *Pred usodnimi odločitvami* (Facing Fateful Decisions). Ljubljana: Delavska enotnost, 1992.

Švabič, Zlatko, and Charles Bukowski. *Small States in the Post–Cold War World: Slovenia and NATO Enlargement*. London: Praeger, 2002.

Thompson, Mark. *A Paper House: The Ending of Yugoslavia*. New York: Pantheon Books, 1992.

Tomc, Gregor. "Alternative Politics: Example of the Initiative for Civil Service." In *State and Civil Society: Relationship in Flux*, ed. Vera Gáthy. Budapest: Hungarian Academy of Sciences, 1989.

————. "Punk and Protest in Slovenia." *Across Frontiers* 3, 1–2 (1986): 26–28.

Woodward, Susan L. *Balkan Tragedy: Chaos and Dissolution after the Cold War*. Washington, DC: Brookings Institution, 1995.

Zimmerman, William. *Open Borders, Non-Alignment, and the Political Evolution of Yugoslavia*. Princeton: Princeton University Press, 1987.

VII. SCIENTIFIC

A. GENERAL

Lah, Tamara, and Radko Osredkar, eds. *Science in Slovenia: Overview with Highlights*. 2nd, revised ed. Ljubljana: Ministry of Science and Technology of the Republic of Slovenia, 1992.

"Pregl, Fritz." In *Nobel Laureates in Chemistry 1901–1992*, ed. Laylin K. James, 146–50. Washington, DC: American Chemical Society and the Chemical Heritage Foundation, 1993.

Sitar, Sandi. *Sto slovenskih znanstvenikov, zdravnikov in tehnikov* (One Hundred Slovene Scientists, Physicians, and Technicians). Ljubljana: Prešernova družba, 1987.

"Stefan, Josef." In *Dictionary of Scientific Biography*, ed. Charles Coulston Gillispie, vol. 13, 10–11. New York: Scribner's, 1976.

B. DEMOGRAPHY, ECOLOGY, GEOGRAPHY

Alexander, Paul Brittain. *Land Utilization in the Karst Region of Zgornja Pivka, Slovenia.* New York: Studia Slovenica, 1967.

Atlas Slovenije (Atlas of Slovenia). Ljubljana: Mladinska knjiga in Geodetski zavod RS Slovenije, 1986.

Coley, J. A. *The Development of the Triglav National Park, Slovenia.* Bradford Studies on Yugoslavia, no. 8. Bradford, UK: Postgraduate School of Yugoslav Studies, University of Bradford, 1985.

Friedl, Jerneja, et al., eds. *National Atlas of Slovenia.* Ljubljana: Rokus, 2001.

Gams, Ivan. *Kras v Sloveniji—v prostoru in času* (Karst in Slovenia—in Space and Time), 2nd ed. Ljubljana: ZRC SAZU, 2003.

———. "The Republic of Slovenia: Geographical Constants of the New Central-European State." *Geojournal* 24 (August 1991): 331–40.

Geografija Slovenije (Geography of Slovenia). Ljubljana: Slovenska matica, 1998.

Josipovič, Damir, and Peter Repulsk. "Demographic Characteristic of the Romany in Prekmurje." *Acta Geographica Slovenica* 43, 1 (2003): 127–47.

Kladnik, Drago, and Marjan Ravbar. *Členitev slovenskega podeželja* (Classification of Slovene Rural Areas). *Geografija* 8. Ljubljana: ZRC SAZU, 2003.

Kranjc, Maja. *Škocjanske jame* (Škocijanske Caves)—*A Contribution to Bibliography.* Ljubljana: ZRC SAZU, 1996.

Kromm, David E. "Perception of Air Pollution Hazard in Ljubljana, Yugoslavia." In *Environmental Deterioration in the Soviet Union and Eastern Europe,* ed. Ivan Volgyes. Praeger Special Studies in International Politics and Government. New York: Praeger, 1974.

Okolje v Sloveniji 1996 (Environment in Slovenia, 1996). Ljubljana: Ministrstvo za okolje in prostor. Uprava RS za varstvo okolja, 1998.

Okolje v Sloveniji, 2002. Povzetek (Environment in Slovenia, 2002. Summary). Ljubljana: Vlada Republike Slovenije, February 2003.

Orožen Adamič, Milan. *Slovenia—A Geographical Overview.* Ljubljana: ZRC SAZU, 2004.

Perko, Drago, and Milan Orožen Adamič, eds. *Slovenija: Pokrajine in ljudje* (Slovenia: Lands and People). Ljubljana: Mladinska knjiga, 1998.

Urbanc, Mimi. *Kulturne pokrajine v Sloveniji* (Cultural Regions in Slovenia). *Geografija* 5. Ljubljana: ZRC SAZU, 2002.

Velikonja, Joseph. "Slovene Identity in Contemporary Europe." *Papers in Slovene Studies* (1975): 1–26.

VIII. SOCIAL

Kolarič, Zinka, et al. *Zasebne neprofitne-volonterske organizacije v mednarodni perspektivi* (Private Nonprofit-Voluntary Organizations in International Perspective). Ljubljana: FDV, 2002.

Marega, Milena, and Mateja Šepec. *Vloga in financiranje nevladnih organizacij* (The Role and Financing of Nongovernemental Organizations). Zbornik strokovnih prispevkov. Ljubljana: REC—Regionalni center za okolje za Srednjo in Vzhodno Evropo, 1998.

Milosavljević, Marko. "The Slovenian Media Landscape." *European Journalism Centre*. www.ejc.nl/jr/emland/slovenia.html.

A. ARCHEOLOGY, ANTHROPOLOGY, AND ETHNOLOGY

Bogataj, Janez. *Handicrafts of Slovenia: Encounters with Contemporary Slovene Craftsmen*. Ljubljana: Rokus, 2002.

Baš, Angelos, ed. *Slovensko ljudsko izročilo* (Slovene Folk Tradition). Ljubljana: Cankarjeva založba, 1980.

Berk, Edi, et al.. *Traditional Arts and Crafts in Slovenia*. UNESCO. Ljubljana: DOMUS, 1993.

Cvetko, Igor, ed. *Med godci in glasbili na Slovenskem / Among Musicians and Instruments in Slovenia*. Ljubljana: Slovenski etnografski muzej; ZRC SAZU, 1991.

Golež, Metka, ed. *Ljudske balade med izročilom in sodobnostjo / Ballads between Tradition and Modern Times*. Ljubljana: ZRC SAZU, 1998.

Horvat, Jana, ed. *Sermin—prazgodovinska in zgodnjerimska naselbina v severovzhodni Istri / Sermin—Prehistoric and an Early Roman Settlement in northeast Istria*. Ljubljana: ZRC SAZU, 1997.

Kuret, Niko. *Praznično leto Slovencev* (Slovene Holidays through the Year). 4 vols. Celje: Mohorjeva družba, 1965–1971.

Lazar, Irena. *Rimsko steklo Slovenije / Roman Glass of Slovenia*. Ljubljana: ZRC SAZU, 2003.

Minnich, Robert Gary. *Homesteaders and Citizens: A Collective Identity Formation on the Austro–Italian–Slovene Frontier*. Bergen Studies in Social Anthropology 52. Bergen: Norse, 1998.

Portis-Winner, Irene. *Semiotics of Peasants in Transition: Slovene Villagers and Their Ethnic Relatives in America*. Durham, NC: Duke University Press, 2002.

Turk, Ivan. *Viktorjev Spodmol in Mala Triglavca / Viktor's Spodmol and Mala Triglavca*. Ljubljana: ZRC SAZU, 2004.

———, ed. *Mousterianska koščena piščal in druge najdbe iz Divjih bab I v Sloveniji / Mousterian Bone Flute and Other Finds from Divje babe I—Cave Site in Slovenia*. Ljubljana: ZRC SAZU, 1997.

Velušček, Anton. *Hočevarica. Eneolitsko kolišče na ljubljanskem barju* (Hočevarica—An Eneolithic Pile Dwelling in the Ljubljansko Barje). Ljubljana: ZRC SAZU, 2004.

Winner, Irene P. "The Question of the Zadruga in Slovenia: Myth and Reality in Žerovnica." *Anthropology Quarterly* 50 (1977): 125–34.

———. *A Slovenian Village: Žerovnica*. 1971. Revised paperback edition. Boston: Schenkman, 1983.

B. EDUCATION

Ciperle, Jože, and Andrej Vovko. *Šolstvo na Slovenskem skozi stoletja* (Schooling in Slovenia through the Centuries). Ljubljana: Slovenski šolski muzej, 1987.

The Education System in Slovenia. Eurydice, 1999. www.mszs.si/eurydice/pub.

Moritsch, Andreas. "History Teaching in Austria and Carinthia: A Slovene Perspective." *Nationalities Papers* 7 (Fall 1979): 147–54.

Plut-Pregelj, Leopoldina. "Illyrian Provinces: The South Slavs and the French Revolution. A Closer Look at Education." In *The Consortium on Revolutionary Europe, 1750–1850: Proceedings*, ed. Donald D. Horward and John C. Horgan, 600–609. Tallahassee, FL: Institute on Napoleon and the French Revolution, Florida State University, 1990.

———. "Slovenia's Education in the Process of Change: Legal Aspects." *Slovene Studies* 13, 1 (1991, published July 1993): 129–41.

———. *Educational Reform in the First Decade of Slovenian Political Pluralism.* East European Studies, Meeting Reports, 229. www.wilsoncenter.org.

Požarnik, Barica. "Slovenia: System of Education." In *The International Encyclopedia of Education*, ed. Torsten Husen and T. Neville Postlethwaite, 2nd ed., vol. 9, 5490–97. Oxford: Pergamon Press, 1994.

Schmidt, Vlado. *Zgodovina šolstva in pedagogike na Slovenskem* (The History of Slovene Schooling and Pedagogy). Ljubljana: Delavska enotnost, 1988.

Slovenia: Review of National Policies for Education. Report. Paris: Organization for Economic Cooperation and Development, 1999.

The White Paper on Education of Slovenia. Ljubljana: Ministrstvo RS za šolstvo in šport, 1996.

C. HEALTH AND SOCIAL WELFARE

Albreht, Tit. *Health Reforms in Slovenia—Twelve Years after—Time to Reevaluate.* Ljubljana: Institute of Public Health of the Republic of Slovenia, 2004.

Česen, Marjan, et al. "The Process of Health Legislation Reform in the Republic of Slovenia." *European Journal of Health Law* 7 (2000): 73–84.

Dyck, R. G. "Health Care Planning in Slovenia." *Papers in Slovene Studies* (1977): 105–23.

Markota, Mladen, et al. "Slovenian Experience on Health Care Reform." *CMJonline* 40, 2 (1999).

Svetlik, Ivan, ed. *Social Policy in Slovenia: Between Tradition and Innovation.* Brookfield, VT: Avebury, 1992.

D. EMIGRATION AND SLOVENES ABROAD

Adamic, Louis. *Laughing in the Jungle.* New York: Harper and Brothers, 1931.

———. *From Many Lands.* New York: Harper and Brothers, 1940.

Arnež, John A. *Slovenci v New Yorku* (Slovenians in New York). New York: Studia Slovenica, 1966.

———. *The Slovenian Community in Bridgeport, Connecticut*. New York: Studia Slovenica, 1971.

Barker, Thomas Mack. "The Carinthian Slovene Question in the Light of Recent German Austrian Scholarship." *Nationalities Papers* 7 (Fall 1979): 125–27.

———. "The Ethnic Evolution of Austria's Carinthian Slovenes in Recent Years." *Canadian Review of Studies in Nationalities* 16 (1989): 189–96.

Barker, Thomas, and Andreas Moritsch. *The Slovene Minority of Carinthia*. New York: Columbia University Press, 1984.

Bennet, Linda A. *Personal Choice in Ethnic Identity Maintenance: Serbs, Croats, and Slovenes*. Palo Alto, CA: Ragusan Press, 1978.

Birsa-Škofič, Irena. "The Development of a Slovene Press in Australia: A Short History of *Vestnik* 1955–1987." *Slovene Studies* 10, 1 (1988): 81–86.

Cattaruzza, Marina. "Slovenes and Italians in Trieste, 1850–1914." In *Ethnic Identity in Urban Europe*, ed. Max Engmann and Francis Carter, 189–217. Strasbourg: European Science; New York: New York University Press, 1992.

Ceglar, Dean. *Vodnik po arhivskem gradivu Inštituta za slovensko izseljenstvo* (A Guide to Archival Sources at the Institute for Slovene Emigration). Ljubljana: ZRC SAZU, 2000.

Christian, Henry A. "Louis Adamic and the American Dream." *Journal of General Education* 27 (Fall 1975): 113–23.

———. "Two Homelands to One World: Louis Adamic's Search for Unity." *Papers in Slovene Studies* (1975): 133–44.

Cukjati, Katica. "Perspectives on Slovene Migration to Argentina." *Slovene Studies* 8, 2 (1986): 31–35.

Čebulj-Sajko, Breda. *Med srečo in svobodo: Avstralski Slovenci o sebi* (Between Happiness and Freedom: Australian Slovenes about Themselves). Ljubljana, 1992.

———. *Razpot izseljencev: Razdvojena identiteta avstralskih Slovencev* (The Crossroads of Emigrants: Divided Identity of Australian Slovenes). Ljubljana: ZRC SAZU, 2000.

———. "The Religious Life of Slovenes in Australia." *Slovene Studies* 14, 2 (1992): 185–203.

Čeferin, Aleksandra. *Slovenian Language in Australia: 25 Years of Slovenian Language in Victorian Schools*. Victoria: Institute for Slovenian Studies of Victoria, 2003.

Čuješ, Rudolf Paul. "Minorities: Methodological Questions in Relation to Slovenes in Carinthia." *Nationalities Papers* 7 (Fall 1979): 138–46.

Davis, James C. "The Slovenes in Northeastern Italy: An Introduction." *Nationalities Papers* 11 (1983): 148–50.

Devetak, Silvo. *The Equality of Nations and Nationalities in Yugoslavia: Successes and Dilemmas*. Vienna: W. Braumuller, 1988.

Drnovšek, Marjan. *Pot slovenskih izseljencev na tuje; od Ljubljane do Ellis Islanda, otoka solza v New Yorku 1880–1924* (The Journey of Slovene Emigrants to Foreign Lands; from Ljubljana to Ellis Island, Island of Tears in New York 1880–1924). Ljubljana: Mladika, 1991.

Dwyer, Joseph D. "The Slovene American Press: A History." In *The Ethnic Press in the United States*, ed. Sally M. Miller, 369–78. Westport, CT: Greenwood Press, 1987.

Ferenc, Tone, et al. *Slovenci v zamejstvu* (Slovenes in the Near Abroad). Ljubljana: Državna založba Slovenije, 1974.

Fräss-Ehrfeld, Claudia. "The Role of the United States of America and the Carinthian Question, 1918–1920." *Slovene Studies* 8, 1 (1986): 7–13.

Friš, Darko. *Ameriški Slovenci in katoliška cerkev 1871–1924* (American Slovenes and the Catholic Church 1871–1924). Klagenfurt: Mohorjeva družba, 1995.

Gantar Godina, Irena, ed. *Soočenje mita in realnosti ob prihodu izseljencev v novo okolje* (The Confrontation between Myth and Reality on the Arrival of the Emigrants to a New Land). Ljubljana: Inštitut za izseljenstvo, 1995.

———, ed. *Intelektualci v diaspori / Intellectuals in the Diaspora*. Ljubljana: ZRC SAZU, 1999.

Genorio, Rado. *Slovenci v Kanadi* (Slovenes in Canada). Ljubljana: Inštitut za geografijo, 1989.

Gobetz, Edward, ed. *Ohio's Lincoln: Frank J. Lausche*. Willoughby Hills, OH: Slovenian Research Center of America, 1985.

Gobetz, Edward, et al., eds. *Slovenian Heritage*. Vol. 1. Willoughby Hills, OH: Slovenian Research Center of America, 1980.

Grill, Vatro. *Med dvema svetovoma* (Between Two Worlds). Ljubljana: Mladinska knjiga, 1979.

Hočevar, Toussaint. "Geographical Distribution, Age Structure, and Comparative Language Maintenance of Persons of Slovene Language in the United States." *Society for Slovene Studies Newsletter*, Documentation Series, 3 (1978): iv, 1–21.

Horak, Stephan, ed. "The Slovenes of Northeastern Italy." *Nationalities Papers* 11, 2 (1983).

Jezernik, Maksimilijan. *Frederick Baraga: A Portrait of the First Bishop of Marquette Based on the Archives of the Congregatio de Propaganda de Fide*. New York: Studia Slovenica, 1968.

Klemenčič, Matjaž. "American Slovenes and the Leftist Movements in the United States in the First Half of the Twentieth Century." *Journal of American Ethnic History* 15, 3 (1996): 20–43.

———. *Ameriški Slovenci in NOB v Jugoslaviji* (American Slovenes and NOB in Yugoslavia). Maribor: Obzorja, 1987.

———. *Jurij Trunk med Koroško in ZDA ter zgodovina slovenskih neselbin v Leadvillu, Kolorado, in v San Francisco, Kalifornija* (Jurij Trunk between

Carinthia and the USA and the History of the Slovene Settlements in Lead-ville, Colorado, and San Francisco, California). Klagenfurt: Mohorjeva založba, 1999.

——. "Research on Slovene Immigration to the United States: Past Achievements and Future Direction." *Slovene Studies* 8, 2 (1986): 9–14.

——. *Slovenes of Cleveland*. Novo mesto: Dolenjska založba, 1995.

Klemenčič, Matjaž, and Samo Kristen. "Zapisniki United Americans for Slovenia. Delovanje slovenskih izseljencev v ZDA za neodvisno Slovenijo" (Minutes of the United Americans for Slovenia. The Activity of Slovene Immigrants to the USA for Independent Slovenia). *Razprave in gradivo / Treaties and Documents* 34, 9–127. Ljubljana: Inštitut za narodnostna vprašanja, 1999.

Klemenčič, Matjaž, and Jernej Zupančič. "The Effects of the Dissolution of Yugoslavia on the Minority Rights of Hungarian and Italian Minorities in the Post-Yugoslav States." *Nationalities papers* 32, 4 (2004): 853–96.

Kocjančič, Cvetka. *Gospodar golega ozemlja* (The Lord of Barren Land). Novo Mesto: Dolenjska založba, 1996.

Kromer, Claudia. *Die Vereinigte Staaten von America und die Frage Kärntens 1918–1920* (United States of America and the Carinthian Question). Klagenfurt: Geschichtensverein für Kärnten, 1970.

Kuzmič, Mihael. *Slovenski izseljenci iz Prekmurja v Bethlehemu v ZDA 1893–1924* (Slovene Emigrants from Prekmurje in Bethlehem [PA] USA 1893–1924). Ljubljana: ZRC SAZU, 2001.

Linška, Janko, et al., eds. *Koroški Slovenci v Avstriji včeraj in danes* (Carinthian Slovenes in Austria Yesterday and Today). Ljubljana: ČZDO Komunist; Klagenfurt: Drava, 1984.

Lokar, Aleš. "Modernization and Ethnic Problems in Carinthia." *Slovene Studies* 14, 1 (1994): 35–50.

Lokar, Aleš, and Marko Oblak. "The Slovene Minority in Italy from an Economic Perspective." *Slovene Studies* 8, 1 (1986): 27–43.

Lukan, Walter, and Andreas Moritsch, eds. *Geschichte der Kärnten Slowenen von 1918 bis zur Gegenwart* (History of Carinthian Slovenes from 1918 to the Present). Klagenfurt: Hermagoras, 1988.

Molek, Ivan. *Slovene Immigrant History 1900–1950: Autobiographical Sketches*. Dover, DE: Molek, 1979.

Novak, Bogdan. "American Policy toward the Slovenes in Trieste, 1941–1947." *Papers in Slovene Studies* (1977): 1–25.

——. *Trieste 1941–1954: The Ethnic, Political, and Ideological Struggle*. Chicago: University of Chicago Press, 1970.

Praček-Krasna, Ana. *Med dvema domovinama* (Between Two Homelands). Ljubljana: Lipa, 1978.

Priestly, Tom. "The Contributions of Discourse Analysis to Research on the Slovene Minority Situation in Carinthia." Review Essay. *Slovene Studies* 23, 1–2 (2001): 73–92.

————. "Cultural Consciousness and Political Nationalism: Language Choice among Slovenes in Carinthia, Austria." *Canadian Review of Studies in Nationalism* 6 (1989): 79–97.

————, ed. *Problems of European Minorities: The Slovene Case.* Special Third World Congress for Soviet and East European Studies, Washington, DC, 1985. *Slovene Studies* 8, 1 (1986).

Skrbiš, Zlatko. *Long-distance Nationalism: Diasporas, Homelands, and Identities.* Brookfield, VT: Ashgate, 1999.

Susel, Rudolf M. "Slovenes." In *Harvard Encyclopedia of American Ethnic Groups*, ed. Stephan Thernstorm, 932–942. Cambridge, MA: Belknap Press, 1980.

Susič, Emidij. "The Case of the Slovene Minority in Italy." *Slovene Studies* 12, 1 (1992): 37–46.

Susič, Emidij, and Danilo Sedmak. *Tiha asimilacija; psihološki vidiki nacionalnega odtujevanja* (Silent Assimilation: Psychological Aspects of National Alienation). Trieste: Tržaški tisk, 1983.

Ude, Lojze. *Koroško vprašanje* (The Carinthian Question). Ljubljana: Državna založba Slovenije, 1977.

Winner, Irene P. "Ethnicity among Urban Slovene Villagers in Cleveland, Ohio." *Papers in Slovene Studies* (1977): 51–63.

Zbornik avstralskih Slovencev 1985 / Anthology of Australian Slovenes 1985. Slovensko-avstralski literarno-umetniški krožek / Slovene-Australian Literary and Art Circle. Ljubljana: Tisk UD, 1985.

Zupančič, Jernej. *Slovenci v Avstriji* (Slovenes in Austria). Ljubljana: Institute of Geography, 1999.

Žigon, Zvone. *Iz spomina v prihodnost: Slovenska politična emigracija v Argentini* (From Memories to the Future: The Slovene Political Emigration to Argentina). Ljubljana: ZRC SAZU, 2001.

————. *Otroci dveh domovin: Slovenstvo v Južni Ameriki* (Children of Two Homelands: Slovenism in South America). Ljubljana: ZRC SAZU, 1998.

Žitnik, Janja. *Louis Adamič in sodobniki: 1948–1951* (Louis Adamič and His Contemporaries: 1948–1951). Ljubljana: ZRC SAZU, 1992.

Žitnik, Janja, and Helga Glušič, eds. *Slovenska izseljenska književnost: 1. Evropa, Avstralija, Azija; 2. Severna Amerika; 3. Južna Amerika* (Slovene Emigrant Literature: 1. Europe, Australia, Asia; 2. North America; 3. South America). Ljubljana: ZRC SAZU, 1999.

E. GENDER AND MINORITY ISSUES

Auersperger, Alenka. *Iskalci grala: Poskus oživljanja nemške manjšine v Sloveniji* (The Seekers of the Grail: An attempt to Revive the German Minority in Slovenia). Ljubljana: Modrijan, 2004.

Dedič, Jasminka, et al. *The Erased: Organized Innocence and the Politics of Exclusion.* Ljubljana: Peace Institute, 2003.

Jalušič, Vlasta, and Milica Antič Gaber. *Women–Politics–Equal Opportunities.* Ljubljana: Peace Institute, 2001.

Jogan, Maca. "Redomestication of Women and Democratization in Postsocialist Slovenia." In *Family, Women, and Employment in Central-Eastern Europe,* ed. Barbara Łobodzińska, 219–29. Westport, CT: Greenwood Press, 1995.

————. "The Stubborness of Sexism in the Second Part of the Twentieth Century in Slovenia." In *Political Faces of Slovenia,* ed. Niko Toš and Karl Mueller. Vienna: Echoraum, 2005.

Pajnik, Mojca, et al. *Immigrants, Who Are You?* Ljubljana: Peace Institute, 2001.

Ramet, Sabrina, ed. *Gender Politics in the Western Balkans: Women and Society in Yugoslavia and Yugoslavia's Successor States.* University Park: Pennsylvania State University Press, 1999.

Švab, Alenka, and Roman Kuhar. *The Unbearable Comfort of Privacy: The Everyday Life of Gays and Lesbians.* Ljubljana: Peace Institute, 2005.

F. RELIGION AND THE CATHOLIC CHURCH

Benedik, Metod. *Cerkev na Slovenskem v 20. stoletju* (The Church in Slovenia in the Twentieth Century). Ljubljana: Družina, 2002.

Benedik, Metod, et al., eds. *Zgodovina cerkve na Slovenskem* (History of the [Catholic] Church in Slovenia). Celje: Mohorjeva družba, 1991.

Dolinar, France. "Normalization of Church/State Relations in Yugoslavia 1945–." *Slovene Studies* 17, 1–2 (1995): 25–36.

Dolinar, France, et al., eds. *Cerkev, kultura in politika* (Church, Culture, and Politics). Ljubljana: Slovenska matica, 1993.

Drnovšek, Marjan. "The Catholic Church and Mass Emigration of Slovenes to the United States before 1924." *Slovene Studies* 14, 2 (1992): 169–84.

Gergolj, Stanko. "Modes of Religious Education in Slovenia." In *Religion during and after Communism,* ed. Miklós Tomka and Paul M. Zulehner, 82–88. London: SCM Press, 2000.

Hvala, Ivan, ed. *Država in cerkev: laična država kot jamstvo* (State and Church: The Lay State as a Guarantor). Ljubljana: FDV, 2002.

Izberi življenje. Gradivo za dekanijske pastoralne svete (Choose Life: The Sources for Decanry Pastoral Councils). Ljubljana: Družina, 2004.

Kerševan, Marko. "The Change in the Religious Situation in the Eyes of Non-Believers." In *Religion during and after Communism,* ed. Miklós Tomka and Paul M. Zulehner, 74–81. London: SCM Press, 2000.

Lesjak, Gregor. "Nova religijska in duhovna gibanja v Sloveniji" (New Religious and Spiritual Movements in Slovenia). *Teorija in praksa* 38, 6 (2001): 1108–24.

Makarovič, Jan. *Od črne boginje do sina božjega* (From the Black Goddess to the Son of God). Ljubljana: FDV, Univerza v Ljubljani, 1998.

Pirc, Joško. *Aleš Ušeničnik in znamenja časov: katoliško gibanje na Slovenskem od konca 19. stoletja do srede 20. stoletja* (Aleš Ušeničnik and Hallmarks of Time: The Catholic Movement in Slovenia from the End of the Nineteenth Century to the Mid-Twentieth Century). Ljubljana: Družina, 1986.

Potočnik, Vinko. "Priests and Religious Orders." In *Religion during and after Communism*, ed. Miklós Tomka and Paul M. Zulehner, 89–96. London: SCM Press, 2000.

Šturm, Lovro, ed. *Država in cerkev* (State and Church). Ljubljana: Nova revija, 2000.

Tomka, Miklós and Paul M. Zulehner, eds. *Religion during and after Communism*. London: SCM Press, 2000.

Žigon, Zvone. *Ljudje odprtih src: Slovenski misijonarji o sebi* (People with Open Hearts: Slovene Missionaries about Themselves). Ljubljana: Slovene Academy of Sciences and Arts, 2005.

G. SOCIOLOGY, PHILOSOPHY, AND INTELLECTUAL LIFE

Barber-Keršovan, Alenka. *Vom 'Punk-Fruehling' zum 'Slowenischen Fruehling': Der Beitrag des slowenischen Punk zur Demontage des sozialistischen Wertesystems* (From "Punk-Spring" to "Slovene Spring": How Slovene Punk Contributed to the Dismantling of the Socialist Value System). Hamburg: Reinhold Kraemer, 2005.

Barbič, Ana. *Izzivi in priložnosti podeželja* (Challenges and Opportunities of the Countryside). Ljubljana: FDV, Univerza v Ljubljani, 2005.

Boh, Ivan. "The Philosophical Contributions of Anton Erber (1695–1746)." *Slovene Studies* 13, 1 (1991): 57–69.

Buila, Theodore. "Program Issues in Improving the Quality of Slovene Rural Life." *Papers in Slovene Studies* (1977): 83–104.

Davis, James C. *Rise from Want: A Peasant Family in the Machine Age*. Philadelphia: University of Pennsylvania Press, 1986.

Debeljak, Aleš. *Twilight of the Idols: Recollections of a Lost Yugoslavia*. Trans. Michael Biggins. Fredonia, NY: White Pine Press, 1994.

Jerman, Frane. "The History of Philosophy in Slovenia: A Brief Sketch." *Slovene Studies* 13, 1 (1991): 53–56.

Milčinski, Lev. *Samomor in Slovenci* (Suicide and the Slovenes). 2nd ed. Ljubljana: Cankarjeva založba, 1985.

Potrč, Matjaž. "The Sensory Basis in the Content of Veber." *Slovene Studies* 13, 1 (1991): 71–90.

Rupel, Dimitrij. *Slovenski intelektualci: od vojaške do civilne družbe* (Slovene Intellectuals: From Military to Civil Society). Ljubljana: Mladinska knjiga, 1989.

Svetina, Janez. *Slovenci in prihodnost* (Slovenes and the Future). Radovljica: Didakta, 1992.

Urbančič, Ivan. *Zgodovina filozofije na Slovenskem* (A History of Philosophy in Slovenia). Ljubljana: RSS, 1970.

Vidmar, Josip. *Kulturni problem slovenstva* (The Cultural Problem of Slovene-
dom). Reissued with commentary by Aleš Debeljak. Ljubljana: Cankarjeva
založba, 1995.
Žižek, Slavoj. *Jezik, ideologija in Slovenci* (Language, Ideology, and the Slovenes). Ljubljana: Delavska enotnost, 1987.

IX. SELECTED WEBSITES

Note: Most of the Slovene websites listed in this section have an English-
language version.

Mat'Kurja, a general Slovenia website: www.matkurja.com/si/.
Government of the Republic of Slovenia (RS): www.sigov.si/.
Statistical Office of RS: www.stat.si/.
Institut for Macroeconomic Analisys of RS: www.sigov.si/zmar/.
Slovenian Academy for Sciences and Arts (SAZU): www.sazu.si.
Scientific Research Center of SAZU: http://odmev.zrc-sazu.si/zrc/.
National and University Library, Ljubljana: www.nuk.uni-lj.si/vstop.cgi.
Roman Catholic Church: www.rkc.si.
Ljubljana Life Magazine: www.geocities.com/ljubljanalife/.
Slovenia Times: www.sloveniatimes.com.
Finance: www.finance-on.net/.
Peace Institute, Ljubljana: www.mirovni-institut.si.
Media Watch: www.mediawatch.mirovni-institut.si/bilten/obiltenu/.
Eurostat, Statistical Office of the European Union: http://epp.eurostat.ec.europa
.eu/portal/page.
Society for Slovene Studies: www.arts.ualberta.ca/~ljubljan/.
Slovenia: Country Reports on Human Rights Practices. Bureau of Democracy,
Human Rights, and Labor. U.S. Department of State: www.state.gov/g/drl/
rls/hrrpt.

X. LEARNED JOURNALS AND MAGAZINES

Dve domovini / Two Homelands. Ljubljana: Institute for Slovene Emigration
Research, Center for Scientific Research of the Slovene Academy of Sciences and Arts (ZRC SAZU), 1990– .
Slovene Studies. Journal of the Society for Slovene Studies, 1977– . Successor to
Papers in Slovene Studies (1975–1978). Volume 16, 1 (1996–1997), contains
a cumulative index with abstracts for 1975 through 1993. See Society website
for recent journal contents: www.arts.ualberta.ca~ljublan/.
Slovenski jezik / Slovene Linguistic Studies. Ljubljana: Inštitut za slovenski
jezik; Lawrence: University of Kansas, 1997– .

About the Authors

Leopoldina Plut-Pregelj, born in 1946 in Ljubljana, Slovenia, received her B.A. in education and sociology (1971), M.A. in education (1978), and Ph.D. in education (1984) from the University of Ljubljana, where she taught in the Department of Pedagogy from 1975 to 1982. IREX and Fulbright scholarships enabled her to study in the United States from August 1977 to May 1978. In 1982 she moved to the United States and has been working on various research projects, most concerning education. She is an assistant professor of didactics at the Department of Pedagogy, Faculty of Philosophy at the University of Ljubljana, and a research associate at College of Education, University of Maryland. Her main interests are history of education, curriculum studies, and educational policies. She has published three books and over 70 articles in Slovenia and in the United States. She lives in Washington, D.C.

Carole Rogel was born in 1939 in Cleveland, Ohio. She received a B.A. (1960) from Western Reserve University, and from Columbia University an M.A. (1961), a Certificate from its Institute on East Central Europe (1962), and a Ph.D. (1966). From 1964 until 1990 she taught in the History Department at Ohio State University. Her research interest has been 19th- and 20th-century Slovene and Yugoslav history. In addition to numerous articles, she has published *The Slovenes and Yugoslavism 1890–1914* (1977), *The Breakup of Yugoslavia and the War in Bosnia* (1998), and *The Breakup of Yugoslavia and Its Aftermath* (2004). An Emerita since 1990, she has lectured and written extensively on recent developments in Slovenia and the former Yugoslavia. From 1984 to 1989 she was president of the Society for Slovene Studies, an international academic organization that sponsors conferences and publishes *Slovene Studies*, an annual journal. She lives in Columbus, Ohio.